REGIONAL TRENDS 2001

ISBN 0 11 621464 3
ISSN 0261-1783

CORRECTIONS

Please note that there is an amendment to a figure shown in some of the Regional Profiles in Chapter 1.

Page 11   The third paragraph should read:

The Infant Mortality rate for 1998–2000 for the West Midlands was higher than the UK rate (respectively 6.8 and **5.8** deaths of infants under one year old per 1,000 live births); within the region it ranged between 3.7 for County of Herefordshire UA and 8.5 for Stoke-on-Trent UA. *(Table 14.2)*

Page 13   The third paragraph should read:

The Infant Mortality rate for 1998–2000 for the East of England was lower than the UK average (respectively 4.7 and **5.8** deaths of infants under one year old per 1,000 live births); within the region it ranged between 4.2 for Cambridgeshire, Essex and Hertfordshire and 8.2 for Luton UA. *(Table 14.2)*

Page 15   The third paragraph should read:

The Infant Mortality rate for 1998–2000 for London **was the same as the UK rate** (5.8 deaths of infants under one year old per 1,000 live births). *(Table 14.2)*

Page 17   The third paragraph should read:

The Infant Mortality rate for 1998–2000 for the South East was lower than the UK rate (respectively 4.5 and **5.8** deaths of infants under one year old per 1,000 live births); within the region it ranged between 2.6 for Bracknell Forest UA and 7.0 for Portsmouth UA. *(Table 14.2)*

Page 19   The third paragraph should read:

The Infant Mortality rate for 1998–2000 for the South West was lower than the UK rate (respectively 4.7 and **5.8** deaths of infants under one year old per 1,000 live births); within the region it ranged between 3.5 for South Gloucestershire UA and 5.8 for North Somerset UA. *(Table 14.2)*

Page 21   The third paragraph should read:

The Infant Mortality rate for 1998–2000 for Wales was the same as the UK rate (**5.8** deaths of those under one year old per 1,000 live births); by local authority area, it ranged between 3.5 for Flintshire and 7.8 for Conwy. *(Table 14.2)*

London: The Stationery Office

Regional Trends

No 36

2001 edition

Editors: Jon McGinty

Tricia Williams

London: The Stationery Office

Contact points
For enquiries about this publication, contact
Darren Stillwell
Tel: 020 7533 5804
E-mail: regional.publications@ons.gov.uk

To order this publication, call The Stationery Office
on **0870 600 5522**. Also see the back cover.

For general enquiries, contact the National Statistics
Public Enquiry Service on **0845 601 3034**
(minicom: 01633 812399)
E-mail: info@statistics.gov.uk
Fax: 01633 652747
Letters: Room DG/18, 1 Drummond Gate,
London SW1V 2QQ

You can also find National Statistics on the Internet
go to **www.statistics.gov.uk**

A National Statistics publication
National Statistics are produced to high professional
standards set out in the National Statistics Code of
Practice. They undergo regular quality assurance reviews
to ensure that they meet customer needs. They are
produced free from any political interference.

About the Office for National Statistics
The Office for National Statistics (ONS) is the
government agency responsible for compiling,
analysing and disseminating many of the United
Kingdom's economic, social and demographic
statistics, including the retail prices index, trade
figures and labour market data, as well as the
periodic census of the population and health
statistics. The Director of ONS is also the National
Statistician and the Registrar General for England
and Wales, and the agency administers the statutory
registration of births, marriages and deaths there.

Contents

Contents

Housing

6

Health and Care

7

Contents

Regional trends 36, © Crown copyright 2001

Environment 11

Regional Accounts 12

Industry and Agriculture 13

Contents

Introduction

Regional Trends seeks to contribute to decision making at national, local and European level, and to inform debate about the current state of the nation. It brings together data from a wide range of sources, both from within government and outside, to paint a comprehensive picture of the regions and countries of the United Kingdom.

In recent years there has been increased interest in regional diversity across the United Kingdom. While it is true that differences in income, housing costs, health and employment exist, in other aspects of life the regions may be similar.

One often-quoted difference is that income is higher in the south-east and lower in the north. Over the period 1997–2000, average gross weekly income for households in London was more than one and a half times that of households in the North East. London and the South East also have the highest proportion of people with a personal taxable income of £50,000 or more. However, this does not give a full picture as weekly household expenditure and housing costs for those living in the south are higher than the national average and house prices continue to rise at a faster rate. The increase in house prices in the South East between 1999 and 2000 was almost 19 per cent compared with increases of 3 and 4 per cent in the North East and North West respectively.

While these overall regional averages give a broad picture, they also mask considerable variability within regions. For example, although average weekly earnings for full-time employees in London in 2000 were the highest in the UK at £530 compared with the UK average of £409, within the region, average weekly earnings varied considerably. Some 10 per cent of men in London earned more than £1,010 but 10 per cent also earned less than £259.

One area where there is strong north-south difference is in people's health. In particular, death rates from circulatory diseases are much lower in the southern parts of the United Kingdom. The contrast is particularly striking for females: in 1999, the age-standardised mortality rates from ischaemic heart disease for females in the South East, South West, London and Eastern NHS regions were all lower than 170 deaths per 100,000 population, whereas in Scotland, Northern Ireland and the North West the rates were over 210.

There are also differences in people's behaviour; for example, the proportion of men who drank more than 8 units of alcohol per day and women who drank more than 6 units per day in the week before the interview were higher in the North West than in the East of England, London, the South East and the South West. However, people in Northern Ireland are least likely to drink. Almost half of men and over three-fifths of women in Northern Ireland had not had an alcoholic drink in the week prior to interview, far higher than in any other region.

Comprehensive and up-to-date statistics about regions and sub-regional areas are increasingly in demand. In response to this, we have produced the *Region in Figures* series to complement *Regional Trends*. The set of nine publications presents a wide range of sub-regional data at lower administrative levels for each Government Office Region in England and will be as valuable as the information in *Regional Trends* is to regional decision making. Further development of sub-regional data, which will also affect regional data, will be influenced by the Neighbourhood Statistics programme which is being led by the Office for National Statistics. The aim of this programme is to develop and make available new statistics for small areas to meet the needs of the National Strategy Action Plan 'A New Commitment to Neighbourhood Renewal'. As these statistics become available over a number of years they will grow to cover an increasing range of subjects, such as crime, education and health. More information about the service can be found on the Neighbourhood Statistics web pages at www.statistics.gov.uk/neighbourhood.

Overview

Regional Trends provides a unique description of the regions of the United Kingdom. In 17 chapters it covers a wide range of demographic, social and economic statistics, taking a look at most aspects of life. The chapters fall broadly into four sections: regional profiles (Chapter 1), the European Union (Chapter 2), the main topic areas (Chapters 3 to 13) and sub-regional statistics (Chapters 14 to 17). To make comparison between regions and countries easy, information is provided in clear tables, maps and charts.

Regional statistics are essential for a wide range of people including: policy-makers and planners in both the public and private sectors; marketing professionals; researchers; students and teachers; journalists; and everyone with a general interest in regional information. *Regional Trends 36* brings together data from diverse sources and, for some topics, is the only publication where data for the whole of the United Kingdom are available in one place. Wherever data for the four countries of the United Kingdom are sufficiently comparable, figures have been aggregated to give a national average or total.

Coverage and definitions

Due to variations in coverage and definitions, some care may be needed when comparing data from more than one source. Readers should consult the Notes and Definitions section towards the back of the book as well as reading the footnotes relevant to each table, map and chart for help in analysing trends or comparing different sources.

Availability of electronic data

The contents of *Regional Trends 36* are available free of charge on the National Statistics website (www.statistics.gov.uk). Information can be accessed either through StatBase, the Government's online statistics service, or via a PDF version with downloadable Excel files (in the Bookshelf section under the Compendia and Reference theme).

Further information

Regional and sub-regional statistics can be found in a range of other National Statistics publications, statistical bulletins and regular press releases. Much of the information included in the Population and Migration and the Labour Market chapters of *Regional Trends 36* can be accessed free of charge via Nomis®, the on-line database run by Durham University under contract to the Office for National Statistics (www.nomisweb.co.uk). Nomis® contains government statistics down to the smallest available geographic area, which may not be published elsewhere. Additional sub-regional data (particularly on a range of benefits from the Department for Work and Pensions, but also on other subjects) can also be accessed from the Neighbourhood Statistics web pages (http://www.statistics.gov.uk/neighbourhood). In addition, sub-regional data for the Government Office Regions in England can be found in the series *Region in Figures*; data for Wales are published in the *Digest of Welsh Statistics* and the *Digest of Welsh Local Area Statistics*; data for Scotland are published in the *Scottish Abstract of Statistics* and the *Scottish Economic Report*; data for Northern Ireland are published in the *Northern Ireland Annual Abstract of Statistics*. Details of these publications and others can be found by using the StatBase 'text search' facility on the National Statistics website (www.statistics.gov.uk).

Contributors

The Editors wish to thank all their colleagues in the ONS, the rest of the Government Statistical Service and all contributors in other organisations without whose help this publication would not be possible.

Acknowledgements

The editors would like to thank the following people for their help in producing this book:

Production Manager:	Darren Stillwell
Production team:	Mike Harris
	Neyire Hassan
	Richard Seymour
Authors:	Nicola Amaranayake
	Ben Bradford
	Victoria Busuttil
	Alex Clifton-Fearnside
	Sunita Dedi
	David Harper
	Nigel King
	Christine Lillistone
	Anne-Marie Manners
	Nina Mill
	Nosa Okunbor
	Conor Shipsey
	Mike Short
	Dave Vincent
Charts:	DTP, Titchfield
Maps:	Alistair Dent
	Pam Owen
Data:	SARD Data Collection Team

Information

Regional boundaries

The United Kingdom comprises Great Britain and Northern Ireland; Great Britain consists of England, Wales and Scotland. The Isle of Man and the Channel Islands are not part of the United Kingdom. The Isles of Scilly are included as part of Cornwall throughout.

The statistical regions of the United Kingdom comprise the Government Office Regions (GORs) for England, Wales, Scotland and Northern Ireland. The local government administrative structure provides the framework for breaking down the regions into subregional areas. Maps of the statistical regions of the United Kingdom and the sub-regions in each of the four countries are given in Chapter 1 and Chapters 14 to 17. Apart from the GORs which are used as far as is possible throughout, there are a number of other regional classifications used in *Regional Trends 36*. Maps of these non-standard regions are given on pages 239 and 240 of the Notes and Definitions.

Nomenclature for Territorial Units (NUTS)

Some data are presented using the European Nomenclature for Territorial Units (NUTS) area classification, primarily economic data in chapters 12 and 13. Further information on the NUTS classification is contained in the Notes and Definitions section. Maps showing the NUTS areas for the four constituent countries are given in the sub-regional chapters on pages 214, 224, 233 and 236.

Sub-regional geography

The sub-regional information presented in Chapters 14 to 17 reflect the complete implementation of the local government reorganisation that happened between 1 April 1995 and 1 April 1998. Data for England in Chapter 14 are presented first by region. Within each region, Unitary Authorities (UAs) are listed first in alphabetical order. Counties are listed next, again in alphabetical order. Within each county the Local Authority Districts (LADs) are then listed alphabetically. Figures for former counties are shown at the end of the region. Chapter 15 on Wales and Chapter 16 on Scotland present data for the UAs and the New Councils respectively which replaced the former two-tier systems on 1 April 1996. Chapter 17 on Northern Ireland gives figures based on the boundaries from the last review of Local Government District boundaries in 1992. The map on page 179 shows the boundaries of the Counties/UAs as at 1 April 1998.

Full details of the local government reorganisation and the NUTS area classification are given in the *Gazetteer of old and new geographies of the United Kingdom* available from ONS Direct Tel: 01633 812078, price £20 for the printed version and £50 plus VAT for a CD-ROM.

1 Regional Profiles[1]

Statistical Regions of the United Kingdom

SCOTLAND

NORTHERN IRELAND

NORTH EAST

NORTH WEST

YORKSHIRE AND THE HUMBER

ENGLAND

——— Government Office Region boundary

EAST MIDLANDS

WEST MIDLANDS

WALES

EAST

LONDON

SOUTH WEST

SOUTH EAST

[1] For the purposes of statistical analyses, the United Kingdom has been divided into 12 'statistical regions'.

1.1 Key statistics for the North East

	North East	United Kingdom		North East	United Kingdom
Population, 1999 (thousands)	2,581.3	59,500.9	Gross domestic product, 1999 (£ million)	25,875	771,849
Percentage aged under 16	20.1	20.4	Gross domestic product per head index, 1999 (UK=100)	77.3	100.0
Percentage pension age and over[1]	18.7	18.1	Total business sites, 2000 (thousands)	74.2	2,488.4
Standardised mortality rate (UK=100), 1999	110	100	Average dwelling price, 2000 (£)[3]	62,945	110,221
Infant mortality ratio,[2] 1998–2000	5.7	5.8			
Percentage of pupils achieving 5 or more grades A* to C			Motor cars currently licensed,[4] 2000 (thousands)	867	24,406
at GCSE level,1999/00	43.2	50.3	Fatal and serious accidents on roads,[4] 1999		
			(rates per 100,000 population)	43	63
Economic activity rate,[6]			Recorded crime rate, 1999–00		
Spring 2000 (percentages)	74.3	78.7	(notifiable offences per 100,000 population)[3]	9,896	10,111
Employment rate,[6] Spring 2000 (percentages)	67.4	74.3			
ILO unemployment rate, Spring 2000 (percentages)	9.2	5.6	Average gross weekly household income, 1997–2000[5] (£)	363	455
Average gross weekly earnings: males in full-time					
employment, April 2000 (£)	398.90	451.60	Average weekly household expenditure, 1997–2000[5] (£)	285	348
Average gross weekly earnings: females in full-time			Households in receipt of Income Support/Family Credit,[4]		
employment, April 2000 (£)	306.00	336.70	1999–00 (percentages)	21	16

1 Males aged 65 and over, females aged 60 and over.
2 Deaths of infants under 1 year of age per 1,000 live births.
3 Figure for the United Kingdom relates to England and Wales.
4 Figure for the United Kingdom relates to Great Britain.
5 Combined years 1997–98, 1998-99 and 1999–00.
6 For people of working age. Men aged 16–64 and women aged 16–59.

1.2 Population density: by local authority, 1999

Population density, 1999
(persons per sq km)

2,500 or over

1,000 - 2,499

500 - 999

250 - 499

100 - 249

99 or under

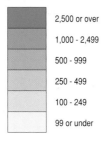

1 Wansbeck
2 Newcastle-upon-Tyne
3 Chester-le-Street
4 Hartlepool UA
5 Stockton-on-Tees UA
6 Middlesbrough UA

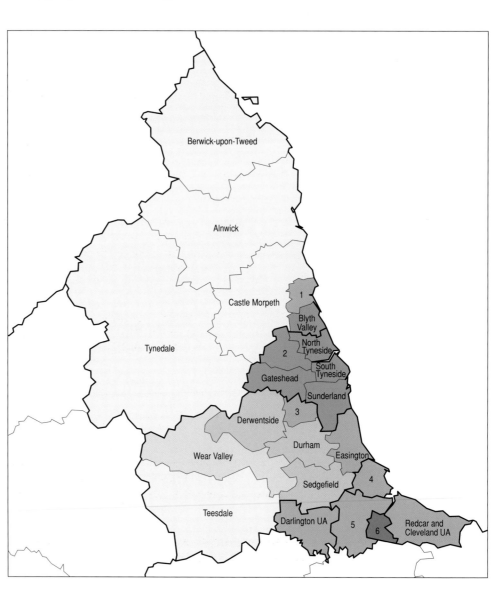

North East

Population	In 1999, the North East had a population of 2.6 million people. Within the North East the population density was highest in Middlesbrough UA at over 2,600 people per sq km and lowest in the local authority districts of Berwick-upon-Tweed and Tynedale at 27 people per sq km each.

(Tables 3.1 and 14.1)

Mortality	Overall for the North East the Standardised Mortality Ratio was 10 per cent higher than the UK as a whole in 1999, at 110 (UK=100); within the region this ranged from 93 in Castle Morpeth to 124 in Blyth Valley.

(Table 14.1)

The Infant Mortality rate for 1998–2000 for the North East was lower than the UK rate for 1998–2000 (respectively 5.7 and 5.8 deaths of infants under one year old per 1,000 live births); within the region it ranged between 4.5 for Redcar and Cleveland UA and 6.5 for Darlington UA.

(Table 14.2)

Education	In 1999/00, all areas in the North East, with the exception of Northumberland, had a lower proportion of pupils achieving 5 or more GCSE grade A* to C results than the UK average. With the exception of Darlington UA, Stockton-on-Tees UA and Northumberland, a higher proportion of pupils than the UK average achieved no graded results.

(Table 14.3)

The proportion of people of working age qualified to GCE A level or equivalent or higher in the North East in Spring 2001 was 43.2 per cent, lower than the UK average of 47.6 per cent.

(Table 4.12)

Labour Market	The employment rate for people of working age in Spring 2000, at 67.4 per cent, was among the lowest in the UK. Within the North East the employment rate varied between 56.1 per cent in Middlesbrough to 72.1 per cent in Northumberland in 1999–2000.

(Table 5.1 and 14.5)

In April 2000, average gross weekly earnings for people in the North East, at £365.80, was lower than the UK average of £409.20. Within the region average gross weekly earnings varied considerably; in Redcar & Cleveland UA, 10 per cent of men earned more than £694.80 but 10 per cent also earned less than £243.50.

(Tables 5.17 and 14.5)

Economy	In the North East, manufacturing industry accounted for some 27.3 per cent of GDP in 1998, compared to 20.3 percent for the UK as a whole. Agriculture, forestry and fishing accounted for 0.7 per cent of GDP in 1998, compared to 1.3 per cent for the UK.

(Table 12.5)

Of the 74,000 business sites in 2000, over 33 per cent were in distribution, hotels and catering and repairs industries, the highest rate in the UK; this compares with a UK average of 28.9 per cent.

(Table 13.3)

Over 76 per cent of export trade in 2000 was to the EU, the highest rate in the UK, and well above the UK average of 58.6 per cent. Trade from the EU accounted for over 45 per cent of imports, slightly lower than the overall UK average of 48.6 per cent.

(Table 13.7)

Environment	Over a sixth of the total area in the North East is designated as an Area of Outstanding Natural Beauty and 6 per cent is Green Belt land.

(Table 11.13)

1.3 Key statistics for the North West

	North West	United Kingdom		North West	United Kingdom
Population, 1999 (thousands)	6,880.5	59,500.9	Gross domestic product, 1999 (£ million)	77,562	771,849
Percentage aged under 16	20.8	20.4	Gross domestic product per head index, 1999 (UK=100)	86.9	100.0
Percentage pension age and over[1]	18.2	18.1	Total business sites, 2000 (thousands)	250.7	2,488.4
Standardised mortality ratio (UK=100), 1999	108	100	Average dwelling price, 2000 (£)[3]	70,837	110,221
Infant mortality rate,[2] 1998–2000	6.3	5.8			
Percentage of pupils achieving 5 or more grades A* to C			Motor cars currently licensed,[4] 2000 (thousands)	2,751	24,406
at GCSE level,1999/00	47.5	50.3	Fatal and serious accidents on roads,[4] 1999		
			(rates per 100,000 population)	55	63
Economic activity rate,[6]			Recorded crime rate, 1999–00		
Spring 2000 (percentages)	76.8	78.7	(notifiable offences per 100,000 population)[3]	10,686	10,111
Employment rate,[6] Spring 2000 (percentages)	72.7	74.3			
ILO unemployment rate, Spring 2000 (percentages)	5.4	5.6	Average gross weekly household income, 1997–2000[5] (£)	421	455
Average gross weekly earnings: males in full-time					
employment, April 2000 (£)	428.60	451.60	Average weekly household expenditure, 1997–2000[5] (£)	335	348
Average gross weekly earnings: females in full-time			Households in receipt of Income Support/Family Credit,[4]		
employment, April 2000 (£)	312.80	336.70	1999–00 (percentages)	18	16

1 Males aged 65 and over, females aged 60 and over.
2 Deaths of infants under 1 year of age per 1,000 live births.
3 Figure for the United Kingdom relates to England and Wales.
4 Figure for the United Kingdom relates to Great Britain.
5 Combined years 1997–98, 1998-99 and 1999–00.
6 For people of working age. Men aged 16–64 and women aged 16–59.

1.4 Population density: by local authority, 1999

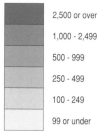

Population density, 1999
(persons per sq km)

- 2,500 or over
- 1,000 - 2,499
- 500 - 999
- 250 - 499
- 100 - 249
- 99 or under

1 Barrow-in-Furness
2 Blackpool UA
3 Preston
4 Hyndburn
5 South Ribble
6 Blackburn with Darwen UA
7 Rossendale
8 Sefton
9 Bury
10 Rochdale
11 Salford
12 Manchester
13 Tameside
14 Trafford
15 Liverpool
16 Knowsley
17 St Helens
18 Warrington UA
19 Halton UA
20 Stockport
21 Ellesmere Port and Neston
22 Congleton

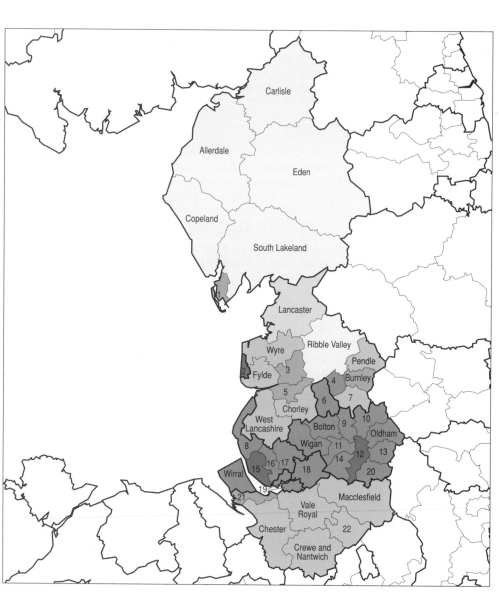

North West

<table>
<tr><td>Population</td><td>In 1999, the North West had a population of 6.9 million people. Within the North West the population density was highest in Blackpool UA at just over 4,200 people per sq km and lowest in the local authority district of Eden at 23 people per sq km.

(Tables 3.1 and 14.1)</td></tr>
<tr><td>Mortality</td><td>Overall for the North West the Standardised Mortality Ratio was 8 per cent higher than the UK as a whole in 1999, at 108 (UK=100); within the region this ranged from 86 in South Lakeland to 127 in Manchester.

(Table 14.1)

The Infant Mortality rate for 1998–2000 for the North West was higher than the UK rate (respectively 6.3 and 5.8 deaths of infants under one year old per 1,000 live births); within the region it ranged between 4.6 for Cheshire and 8.4 for Blackburn with Darwen UA.

(Table 14.2)</td></tr>
<tr><td>Education</td><td>In 1999/00, the proportion of pupils achieving 5 or more GCSE grade A* to C results in the North West was lower than the UK average. The proportion of pupils with no graded results was the same as the UK average.

(Table 14.3)

The proportion of people of working age qualified to GCE A level or equivalent or higher in the North West was 47.6 per cent in Spring 2001, the same as the UK average.

(Table 4.12)</td></tr>
<tr><td>Labour Market</td><td>The employment rate for people of working age in Spring 2000, at 72.7 per cent, was among the lowest in the UK. Within the North West the employment rate varied between 62.9 per cent in Halton UA to 78.5 per cent in Warrington UA in 1999–2000.

(Tables 5.1 and 14.5)

In 2000, average gross weekly earnings for people in the North West, at £385.70, was lower than the UK average of £409.20. Within the region average gross weekly earnings varied considerably; in Halton UA, 10 per cent of men earned more than £709.20 but 10 per cent also earned less than £235.60.

(Tables 5.17 and 14.5)</td></tr>
<tr><td>Economy</td><td>In the North West, manufacturing industry accounted for some 25.1 per cent of GDP in 1998, compared to 20.3 percent for the UK as a whole. Agriculture, forestry and fishing accounted for 0.9 per cent of GDP in 1998, compared to 1.3 per cent for the UK.

(Table 12.5)

Of the 251,000 business sites in 2000, nearly 33 per cent were in distribution, hotels and catering and repairs industries, higher than the overall UK average of 28.9 per cent.

(Table 13.3)

Nearly 63 per cent of export trade in 2000 was to the EU, higher than the UK average of 58.6 per cent. Trade from the EU accounted for nearly 41 per cent of imports, below the overall UK average of 48.6 per cent.

(Table 13.7)</td></tr>
<tr><td>Environment</td><td>Over a sixth of the total area in the North West is Green Belt land and under a ninth is designated as an Area of Outstanding Natural Beauty.

(Table 11.13)</td></tr>
</table>

1.5 Key statistics for Yorkshire and the Humber

	Yorkshire and the Humber	United Kingdom		Yorkshire and the Humber	United Kingdom
Population, 1999 (thousands)	5,047.0	59,500.9	Gross domestic product, 1999 (£ million)	57,554	771,849
Percentage aged under 16	20.5	20.4	Gross domestic product per head index, 1999 (UK=100)	87.9	100.0
Percentage pension age and over[1]	18.3	18.1	Total business sites, 2000 (thousands)	184.9	2,488.4
Standardised mortality ratio (UK=100), 1999	100	100	Average dwelling price, 2000 (£)[3]	70,007	110,221
Infant mortality rate,[2] 1998–2000	6.8	5.8			
Percentage of pupils achieving 5 or more grades A* to C			Motor cars currently licensed,[4] 2000 (thousands)	1,908	24,406
at GCSE level,1999/00	43.6	50.3	Fatal and serious accidents on roads,[4] 1999		
			(rates per 100,000 population)	64	63
Economic activity rate,[6]			Recorded crime rate, 1999–00		
Spring 2000 (percentages)	78.2	78.7	(notifiable offences per 100,000 population)[3]	11,242	10,111
Employment rate,[6] Spring 2000 (percentages)	73.5	74.3			
ILO unemployment rate, Spring 2000 (percentages)	6.1	5.6	Average gross weekly household income, 1997–2000[5] (£)	401	455
Average gross weekly earnings: males in full-time					
employment, April 2000 (£)	409.90	451.60	Average weekly household expenditure, 1997–2000[5] (£)	330	348
Average gross weekly earnings: females in full-time			Households in receipt of Income Support/Family Credit,[4]		
employment, April 2000 (£)	308.80	336.70	1999–00 (percentages)	16	16

1 Males aged 65 and over, females aged 60 and over.
2 Deaths of infants under 1 year of age per 1,000 live births.
3 Figure for the United Kingdom relates to England and Wales.
4 Figure for the United Kingdom relates to Great Britain.
5 Combined years 1997–98, 1998-99 and 1999–00.
6 For people of working age. Men aged 16–64 and women aged 16–59.

1.6 Population density: by local authority, 1999

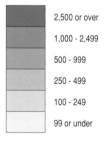

Population density, 1999
(persons per sq km)

- 2,500 or over
- 1,000 - 2,499
- 500 - 999
- 250 - 499
- 100 - 249
- 99 or under

1 City of Kingston upon Hull UA
2 North Lincolnshire UA
3 North East Lincolnshire UA

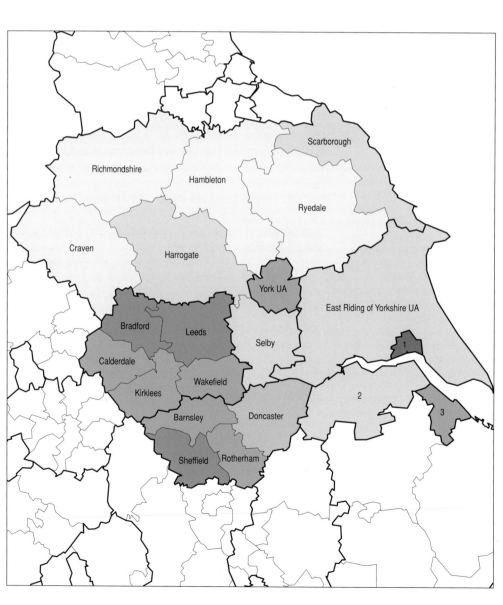

Yorkshire and the Humber

Population

In 1999, Yorkshire and the Humber had a population of 5.0 million people. Within Yorkshire and the Humber the population density was highest in City of Kingston upon Hull UA at 3,632 people per sq km and lowest in the local authority district of Ryedale in North Yorkshire at 32 people per sq km.

(Tables 3.1 and 14.1)

Mortality

Overall for Yorkshire and the Humber the Standardised Mortality Ratio was the same as the UK as a whole in 1999; within the region this ranged from 81 in Ryedale to 111 in Doncaster (UK = 100).

(Table 14.1)

The Infant Mortality rate for 1998–2000 for Yorkshire and the Humber was higher than the UK rate (respectively 6.8 and 5.8 deaths of infants under one year old per 1,000 live births); within the region it ranged between 4.8 for North Yorkshire and 7.5 for West Yorkshire.

(Table 14.2)

Education

In 1999/00, with the exception of East Riding of Yorkshire UA, York UA and North Yorkshire, all areas in the region had a lower proportion of pupils achieving 5 or more GCSE grade A* to C results than the UK average. A higher proportion of pupils than the UK average achieved no graded results.

(Table 14.3)

The proportion of people of working age qualified to GCE A level or equivalent or higher in Yorkshire and the Humber was 45.3 per cent in Spring 2001, lower than the UK average of 47.6 per cent.

(Table 4.12)

Labour Market

The employment rate for people of working age in Spring 2000, at 73.5 per cent, was among the highest in the UK. Within Yorkshire and the Humber the employment rate varied between 68.0 per cent in North East Lincolnshire to 78.0 per cent in East Riding of Yorkshire UA in 1999–2000.

(Tables 5.1 and 14.5)

In 2000, average gross weekly earnings for people in Yorkshire and the Humber, at £373.70, were lower than the UK average of £409.20. Within the region average gross weekly earnings varied considerably; in York UA, 10 per cent of men earned more than £728.30 but 10 per cent also earned less than £219.60.

(Tables 5.17 and 14.5)

Economy

In Yorkshire and the Humber, manufacturing industry accounted for some 26.1 per cent of GDP in 1998, compared to 20.3 per cent for the UK as a whole. Agriculture, forestry and fishing accounted for 1.6 per cent of GDP in 1998, compared to 1.3 per cent for the UK.

(Table 12.5)

Of the 185,000 business sites in 2000, over 32 per cent were in distribution, hotels and catering and repairs industries, higher than the overall UK average of 28.9 per cent.

(Table 13.3)

Over 63 per cent of export trade in 2000 was to the EU, higher than the UK average of 58.6 per cent. Trade from the EU accounted for 48.5 per cent of imports, about the same as the overall UK average of 48.6 per cent.

(Table 13.7)

Environment

Over a sixth of the total area in Yorkshire and the Humber is Green Belt land and six per cent is designated as an Area of Outstanding Natural Beauty.

(Table 11.13)

1.7 Key statistics for the East Midlands

	East Midlands	United Kingdom		East Midlands	United Kingdom
Population, 1999 (thousands)	4,191.2	59,500.9	Gross domestic product, 1999 (£ million)	50,906	771,849
Percentage aged under 16	20.1	20.4	Gross domestic product per head index, 1999 (UK=100)	93.6	100.0
Percentage pension age and over[1]	18.4	18.1	Total business sites, 2000 (thousands)	165.8	2,488.4
Standardised mortality ratio (UK=100), 1999	99	100	Average dwelling price, 2000 (£)[3]	78,780	110,221
Infant mortality rate,[2] 1998–2000	5.7	5.8			
Percentage of pupils achieving 5 or more grades A* to C at GCSE level,1999/00	47.8	50.3	Motor cars currently licensed,[4] 2000 (thousands)	1,813	24,406
			Fatal and serious accidents on roads,[4] 1999 (rates per 100,000 population)	74	63
Economic activity rate,[6] Spring 2000 (percentages)	81.1	78.7	Recorded crime rate, 1999–00 (notifiable offences per 100,000 population)[3]	10,182	10,111
Employment rate,[6] Spring 2000 (percentages)	76.8	74.3			
ILO unemployment rate, Spring 2000 (percentages)	5.2	5.6	Average gross weekly household income, 1997–2000[5] (£)	439	455
Average gross weekly earnings: males in full-time employment, April 2000 (£)	407.00	451.60	Average weekly household expenditure, 1997–2000[5] (£)	339	348
Average gross weekly earnings: females in full-time employment, April 2000 (£)	301.10	336.70	Households in receipt of Income Support/Family Credit,[4] 1999–00 (percentages)	14	16

1 Males aged 65 and over, females aged 60 and over.
2 Deaths of infants under 1 year of age per 1,000 live births.
3 Figure for the United Kingdom relates to England and Wales.
4 Figure for the United Kingdom relates to Great Britain.
5 Combined years 1997–98, 1998-99 and 1999–00.
6 For people of working age. Men aged 16–64 and women aged 16–59.

1.8 Population density: by local authority, 1999

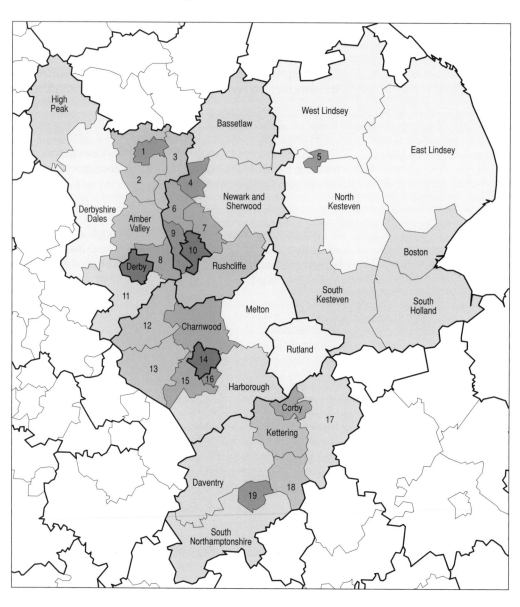

Population density, 1999 (persons per sq km)
- 2,500 or over
- 1,000 - 2,499
- 500 - 999
- 250 - 499
- 100 - 249
- 99 or under

1 Chesterfield
2 North East Derbyshire
3 Bolsover
4 Mansfield
5 Lincoln
6 Ashfield
7 Gedling
8 Erewash
9 Broxtowe
10 Nottingham UA
11 South Derbyshire
12 North West Leicestershire
13 Hinckley and Bosworth
14 Leicester UA
15 Blaby
16 Oadby and Wigston
17 East Northamptonshire
18 Wellingborough
19 Northampton

East Midlands

Population

In 1999, the East Midlands had a population of 4.2 million people. Within the East Midlands the population density was highest in Leicester UA at 3,985 people per sq km and lowest in the local authority district of West Lindsey in Lincolnshire at 67 people per sq km.

(Tables 3.1 and 14.1)

Mortality

Overall for the East Midlands the Standardised Mortality Ratio was the same as the UK as a whole in 1999, at 99 (UK=100); within the region this ranged from 81 in Rutland UA to 118 in Corby.

(Table 14.1)

The Infant Mortality rate for 1998–2000 for the East Midlands was lower than the UK rate for 1998–2000 (respectively 5.7 and 5.8 deaths of infants under one year old per 1,000 live births); within the region it ranged between 4.1 for Rutland UA and 8.3 for Leicester UA.

(Table 14.2)

Education

In 1999/00, all areas in the region, with the exception of Rutland UA, Derbyshire and Lincolnshire had a lower proportion of pupils achieving 5 or more GCSE grade A* to C results than the UK average. A higher proportion of pupils than the UK average achieved no graded results.

(Table 14.3)

The proportion of people of working age qualified to GCE A level or equivalent or higher in the East Midlands was 44.0 per cent in Spring 2001, lower than the UK average of 47.6 per cent.

(Table 4.12)

Labour Market

The employment rate for people of working age in Spring 2000, at 76.8 per cent, was among the highest in the UK. Within the East Midlands the employment rate varied between 61.9 per cent in Nottingham UA to 82.1 per cent in Leicestershire in 1999–2000.

(Tables 5.1 and 14.5)

In 2000, average gross weekly earnings for people in the East Midlands, at £371.40, were lower than the UK average of £409.20. Within the region average gross weekly earnings varied considerably; in Derby UA, 10 per cent of men earned more than £761.20 but 10 per cent also earned less than £217.60.

(Tables 5.17 and 14.5)

Economy

In the East Midlands, manufacturing industry accounted for some 28.8 per cent of GDP in 1998, compared to 20.3 per cent for the UK as a whole. Agriculture, forestry and fishing accounted for 2.0 per cent of GDP in 1998, compared to 1.3 per cent for the UK.

(Table 12.5)

Of the 166,000 business sites in 2000, over 30 per cent were in distribution, hotels and catering and repairs industries, slightly higher than the overall UK average of 28.9 per cent.

(Table 13.3)

Over 51 per cent of export trade in 2000 was to the EU, lower than the UK average of 58.6 per cent. Trade from the EU accounted for nearly 48 per cent of imports, slightly below the overall UK average of 48.6 per cent.

(Table 13.7)

Environment

Five per cent of the total area in the East Midlands is Green Belt land and three per cent is designated as an Area of Outstanding Natural Beauty.

(Table 11.13)

1.9 Key statistics for the West Midlands

	West Midlands	United Kingdom		West Midlands	United Kingdom
Population, 1999 (thousands)	5,335.6	59,500.9	Gross domestic product, 1999 (£ million)	63,495	771,849
Percentage aged under 16	20.9	20.4	Gross domestic product per head index, 1999 (UK=100)	91.7	100.0
Percentage pension age and over[1]	18.2	18.1	Total business sites, 2000 (thousands)	205.8	2,488.4
Standardised mortality ratio (UK=100), 1999	102	100	Average dwelling price, 2000 (£)[3]	87,719	110,221
Infant mortality rate,[2] 1998–2000	6.8	5.8			
Percentage of pupils achieving 5 or more grades A* to C			Motor cars currently licensed,[4] 2000 (thousands)	2,392	24,406
at GCSE level,1999/00	46.5	50.3	Fatal and serious accidents on roads,[4] 1999		
			(rates per 100,000 population)	61	63
Economic activity rate,[6]			Recorded crime rate, 1999–00		
Spring 2000 (percentages)	78.0	78.7	(notifiable offences per 100,000 population)[3]	11,010	10,111
Employment rate,[6] Spring 2000 (percentages)	73.1	74.3			
ILO unemployment rate, Spring 2000 (percentages)	6.3	5.6	Average gross weekly household income, 1997–2000[5] (£)	445	455
Average gross weekly earnings: males in full-time					
employment, April 2000 (£)	425.30	451.60	Average weekly household expenditure, 1997–2000[5] (£)	336	348
Average gross weekly earnings: females in full-time			Households in receipt of Income Support/Family Credit,[4]		
employment, April 2000 (£)	311.20	336.70	1999–00 (percentages)	17	16

1 Males aged 65 and over, females aged 60 and over.
2 Deaths of infants under 1 year of age per 1,000 live births.
3 Figure for the United Kingdom relates to England and Wales.
4 Figure for the United Kingdom relates to Great Britain.
5 Combined years 1997–98, 1998-99 and 1999–00.
6 For people of working age. Men aged 16–64 and women aged 16–59.

1.10 Population density: by local authority, 1999

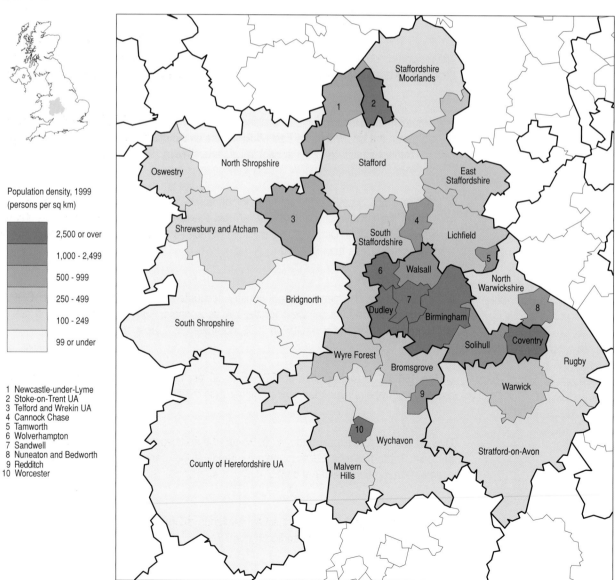

Population density, 1999
(persons per sq km)

- 2,500 or over
- 1,000 - 2,499
- 500 - 999
- 250 - 499
- 100 - 249
- 99 or under

1 Newcastle-under-Lyme
2 Stoke-on-Trent UA
3 Telford and Wrekin UA
4 Cannock Chase
5 Tamworth
6 Wolverhampton
7 Sandwell
8 Nuneaton and Bedworth
9 Redditch
10 Worcester

West Midlands

Population

In 1999, the West Midlands had a population of 5.3 million people. Within the West Midlands the population density was highest in Birmingham at over 3,800 people per sq km and lowest in the local authority district of South Shropshire in Shropshire at 41 people per sq km.

(Tables 3.1 and 14.1)

Mortality

Overall for the West Midlands the Standardised Mortality Ratio was 2 per cent higher than the UK as a whole in 1999, at 102 (UK=100); within the region this ranged from 82 in South Shropshire to 122 in Cannock Chase.

(Table 14.1)

The Infant Mortality rate for 1998–2000 for the West Midlands was higher than the UK rate (respectively 6.8 and 5.7 deaths of infants under one year old per 1,000 live births); within the region it ranged between 3.7 for County of Herefordshire UA and 8.5 for Stoke-on-Trent UA.

(Table 14.2)

Education

In 1999/00, all the areas in the West Midlands, with the exception of County of Herefordshire UA, Shropshire and Warwickshire, had a lower proportion of pupils achieving 5 or more GCSE grade A* to C results than the UK average. A higher proportion of pupils than the UK average achieved no graded results.

(Table 14.3)

Labour Market

The proportion of people of working age qualified to GCE A level or equivalent or higher in the West Midlands was 42.3 per cent in Spring 2001, lower than the UK average of 47.6 per cent.

(Table 4.12)

The employment rate for people of working age in Spring 2000, at 73.1 per cent, was among the highest in the UK. Within the West Midlands the employment rate varied between 68.6 per cent in Stoke-on-Trent UA to 79.5 per cent in Worcestershire in 1999–2000.

(Tables 5.1 and 14.5)

In 2000, average gross weekly earnings for people in the region, at £385.90, was lower than the UK average of £409.20. Within the region average gross weekly earnings varied considerably; in Warwickshire, 10 per cent of men earned more than £741.20 but 10 per cent also earned less than £226.50.

(Tables 5.17 and 14.5)

Economy

In the West Midlands, manufacturing industry accounted for some 28.9 per cent of GDP in 1998, compared to 20.3 per cent for the UK as a whole. Agriculture, forestry and fishing accounted for 1.5 per cent of GDP in 1998, compared to 1.3 per cent for the UK.

(Table 12.5)

Of the 206,000 business sites in 2000, over 30 per cent were in distribution, hotels and catering and repairs industries, slightly higher than the overall UK average of 28.9 per cent.

(Table 13.3)

Over 58 per cent of export trade in 2000 was to the EU, slightly lower than the UK average of 58.6 per cent. Trade from the EU accounted for over 61 per cent of imports, the highest rate in the UK and well above the overall average of 48.6 per cent.

(Table 13.7)

Environment

Over a fifth of the total area in the West Midlands is Green Belt land and a tenth is designated as an Area of Outstanding Natural Beauty.

(Table 11.13)

1.11 Key statistics for the East of England

	East	United Kingdom		East	United Kingdom
Population, 1999 (thousands)	5,418.9	59,500.9	Gross domestic product, 1999 (£ million)	81,793	771,849
Percentage aged under 16	20.2	20.4	Gross domestic product per head index, 1999 (UK=100)	116.4	100.0
Percentage pension age and over[1]	18.5	18.1	Total business sites, 2000 (thousands)	240.6	2,488.4
Standardised mortality ratio (UK=100), 1999	93	100	Average dwelling price, 2000 (£)[3]	114,392	110,221
Infant mortality rate,[2] 1998–2000	4.7	5.8			
Percentage of pupils achieving 5 or more grades A* to C			Motor cars currently licensed,[4] 2000 (thousands)	2,542	24,406
at GCSE level,1999/00	53.0	50.3	Fatal and serious accidents on roads,[4] 1999		
			(rates per 100,000 population)	70	63
Economic activity rate,[6]			Recorded crime rate, 1999–00		
Spring 2000 (percentages)	81.2	78.7	(notifiable offences per 100,000 population)[3]	7,391	10,111
Employment rate,[6] Spring 2000 (percentages)	78.3	74.3			
ILO unemployment rate, Spring 2000 (percentages)	3.6	5.6	Average gross weekly household income, 1997–2000[5] (£)	484	455
Average gross weekly earnings: males in full-time					
employment, April 2000 (£)	455.50	451.60	Average weekly household expenditure, 1997–2000[5] (£)	358	348
Average gross weekly earnings: females in full-time			Households in receipt of Income Support/Family Credit,[4]		
employment, April 2000 (£)	333.80	336.70	1999–00 (percentages)	11	16

1 Males aged 65 and over, females aged 60 and over.
2 Deaths of infants under 1 year of age per 1,000 live births.
3 Figure for the United Kingdom relates to England and Wales.
4 Figure for the United Kingdom relates to Great Britain.
5 Combined years 1997–98, 1998-99 and 1999–00.
6 For people of working age. Men aged 16–64 and women aged 16–59.

1.12 Population density: by local authority, 1999

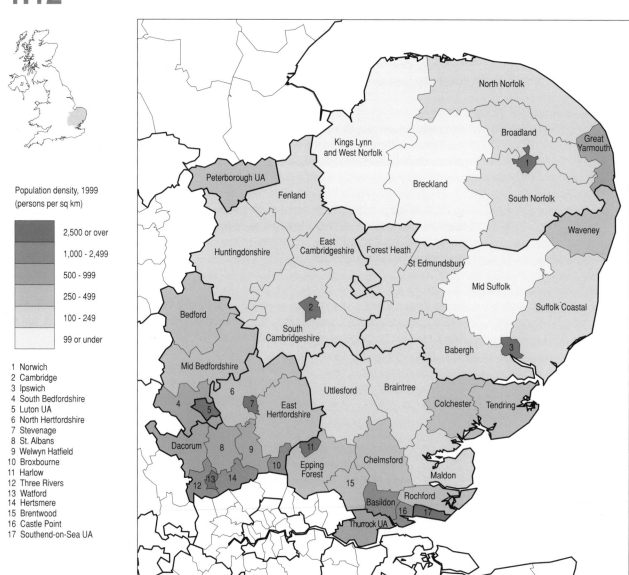

Population density, 1999
(persons per sq km)

- 2,500 or over
- 1,000 - 2,499
- 500 - 999
- 250 - 499
- 100 - 249
- 99 or under

1 Norwich
2 Cambridge
3 Ipswich
4 South Bedfordshire
5 Luton UA
6 North Hertfordshire
7 Stevenage
8 St. Albans
9 Welwyn Hatfield
10 Broxbourne
11 Harlow
12 Three Rivers
13 Watford
14 Hertsmere
15 Brentwood
16 Castle Point
17 Southend-on-Sea UA

East of England

Mortality	In 1999, the East of England had a population of 5.4 million people. Within the East of England the population density was highest in Luton UA at 4,264 people per sq km and lowest in the local authority district of Breckland in Norfolk at 92 people per sq km.

(Tables 3.1 and 14.1)

Overall for the East of England the Standardised Mortality Ratio was 7 per cent lower than the UK as a whole in 1999, at 93 (UK=100); within the region this ranged from 78 in Cambridge to 115 in Watford.

(Table 14.1)

The Infant Mortality rate for 1998–2000 for the East of England was lower than the UK average (respectively 4.7 and 5.7 deaths of infants under one year old per 1,000 live births); within the region it ranged between 4.2 for Cambridgeshire, Essex and Hertfordshire and 8.2 for Luton UA.

(Table 14.2)

Education In 1999/00, the proportion of pupils achieving 5 or more GCSE grade A* to C results was higher in the East of England than the UK average. With the exception of Peterborough UA, Southend-on-Sea UA and Thurrock UA, a lower proportion of pupils achieved no graded results.

(Table 14.3)

The proportion of people of working age qualified to GCE A level or equivalent or higher in the East of England was 46.7 per cent in Spring 2001, lower than the UK average of 47.6 per cent.

(Table 4.12)

Labour Market The employment rate for people of working age in Spring 2000, at 78.3 per cent, was among the highest in the UK. Within the East of England the employment rate varied between 71.8 per cent in Luton UA to 81.1 per cent in Cambridgeshire in 1999–2000.

(Tables 5.1 and 14.5)

In 2000, average gross weekly earnings for people in the East of England, at £412.70, was higher than the UK average of £409.20. Within the region average gross weekly earnings varied considerably; in Hertfordshire, 10 per cent of men earned more than £854.60 but 10 per cent also earned less than £241.50.

(Tables 5.17 and 14.5)

Economy In the East of England, manufacturing industry accounted for some 17 per cent of GDP in 1998, compared to 20.3 per cent for the UK as a whole. Agriculture, forestry and fishing accounted for 1.7 per cent of GDP in 1998, compared to 1.3 per cent for the UK.

(Table 12.5)

Of the 241,000 business sites in 2000, over 27 per cent were in financial intermediation, real estate, renting and business activities, slightly higher than the overall UK average of 26.0 per cent.

(Table 13.3)

Over 54 per cent of export trade in 2000 was to the EU, lower than the UK average of 58.6 per cent. Trade from the EU accounted for 59 per cent of imports, higher than the overall UK average of 48.6 per cent.

(Table 13.7)

Environment Almost an eighth of the total area in the East of England is Green Belt land and 6 per cent is designated as an Area of Outstanding Natural Beauty.

(Table 11.13)

1.13 Key statistics for London

	London	United Kingdom		London	United Kingdom
Population, 1999 (thousands)	7,285.0	59,500.9	Gross domestic product, 1999 (£ million)	122,816	771,849
Percentage aged under 16	20.5	20.4	Gross domestic product per head index, 1999 (UK=100)	130.0	100.0
Percentage pension age and over[1]	14.6	18.1	Total business sites, 2000 (thousands)	380.7	2,488.4
Standardised mortality ratio (UK=100), 1999	95	100	Average dwelling price, 2000 (£)[3]	177,949	110,221
Infant mortality rate,[2] 1998–2000	5.8	5.8			
Percentage of pupils achieving 5 or more grades A* to C			Motor cars currently licensed,[4] 2000 (thousands)	2,414	24,406
at GCSE level,1999/00	48.1	50.3	Fatal and serious accidents on roads,[4] 1999		
			(rates per 100,000 population)	76	63
Economic activity rate,[6]			Recorded crime rate, 1999–00		
Spring 2000 (percentages)	76.5	78.7	(notifiable offences per 100,000 population)[3]	13,784	10,111
Employment rate,[6] Spring 2000 (percentages)	71.1	74.3			
ILO unemployment rate, Spring 2000 (percentages)	7.1	5.6	Average gross weekly household income, 1997–2000[5] (£)	571	455
Average gross weekly earnings: males in full-time					
employment, April 2000 (£)	593.00	451.60	Average weekly household expenditure, 1997–2000[5] (£)	404	348
Average gross weekly earnings: females in full-time			Households in receipt of Income Support/Family Credit,[4]		
employment, April 2000 (£)	434.30	336.70	1999–00 (percentages)	18	16

1 Males aged 65 and over, females aged 60 and over.
2 Deaths of infants under 1 year of age per 1,000 live births.
3 Figure for the United Kingdom relates to England and Wales.
4 Figure for the United Kingdom relates to Great Britain.
5 Combined years 1997–98, 1998-99 and 1999–00.
6 For people of working age. Men aged 16–64 and women aged 16–59.

1.14 Population density: by local authority, 1999

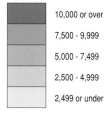

Population density, 1999
(persons per sq km)

- 10,000 or over
- 7,500 - 9,999
- 5,000 - 7,499
- 2,500 - 4,999
- 2,499 or under

1 Waltham Forest
2 Camden
3 Islington
4 Hackney
5 Tower Hamlets
6 Newham
7 Barking and Dagenham
8 Hammersmith and Fulham
9 Kensington and Chelsea
10 Westminster
11 City of London
12 Richmond upon Thames
13 Wandsworth
14 Lambeth
15 Southwark
16 Lewisham
17 Kingston upon Thames

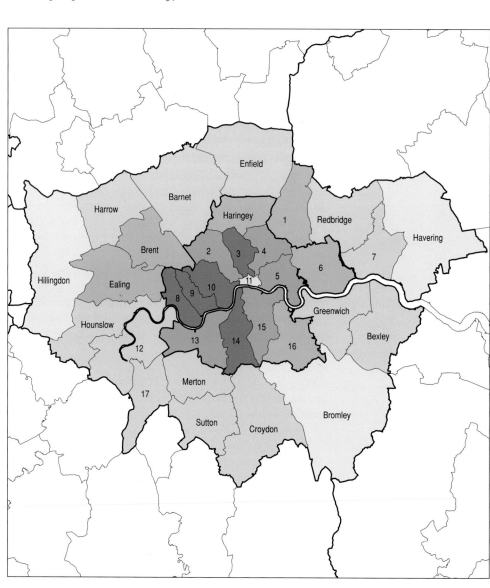

London

Population
In 1999, London had a population of 7.3 million people. Within London the population density was highest in Kensington and Chelsea at 14,930 people per sq km and lowest in Havering at 1,957 people per sq km.

(Tables 3.1 and 14.1)

Mortality
Overall for London the Standardised Mortality Ratio was 5 per cent lower than the UK as a whole in 1999, at 95 (UK=100); within the region this ranged from 60 in the City of London to 116 in Newham.

(Table 14.1)

The Infant Mortality rate for 1998-2000 for London was similar to the UK rate (respectively 5.8 and 5.7 deaths of infants under one year old per 1,000 live births).

(Table 14.2)

Education
In 1999/00, the proportion of pupils achieving 5 or more GCSE grade A* to C results in London was lower than the UK average, but both Inner and Outer London had a lower proportion of pupils than the UK average with no graded results.

(Table 14.3)

The proportion of people of working age qualified to GCE A level or equivalent or higher in London in Spring 2001 was 49.9 per cent, higher than the UK average of 47.6 per cent.

(Table 4.12)

Labour Market
The employment rate for people of working age in Spring 2000, at 71.1 per cent, was among the lowest in the UK.

(Table 5.1)

In 2000, average gross weekly earnings for people in London, at £529.80, was higher than the UK average of £409.20. Within the region average gross weekly earnings varied considerably; 10 per cent of men earned more than £1009.80 but 10 per cent also earned less than £258.8.

(Tables 5.17 and 14.5)

Economy
In London, manufacturing industry accounted for some 10.9 percent of GDP in 1998, compared to 20.3 per cent for the UK as a whole. Agriculture, forestry and fishing accounted for virtually none of the region's GDP in 1998, compared to 1.3 per cent for the UK.

(Table 12.5)

Of the 381,000 business sites in 2000, 40 per cent were in financial intermediation, real estate, renting and business activities, the highest rate in the UK; this compares with the UK average of 26.0 per cent.

(Table 13.3)

Some 43 per cent of export trade in 2000 was to the EU, the lowest rate in the UK and well below the average of 58.6 per cent. Trade from the EU accounted for over 40 per cent of imports, lower than the overall UK average of 48.6 per cent.

(Table 13.7)

Environment
Over a fifth of the total area in London is Green Belt land.

(Table 11.13)

1.15 Key statistics for the South East

	South East	United Kingdom		South East	United Kingdom
Population, 1999 (thousands)	8,077.6	59,500.9	Gross domestic product, 1999 (£ million)	121,956	771,849
Percentage aged under 16	20.0	20.4	Gross domestic product per head index, 1999 (UK=100)	116.4	100.0
Percentage pension age and over[1]	18.5	18.1	Total business sites, 2000 (thousands)	373.6	2,488.4
Standardised mortality ratio (UK=100), 1999	92	100	Average dwelling price, 2000 (£)[3]	147,271	110,221
Infant mortality rate,[2] 1998–2000	4.5	5.8			
Percentage of pupils achieving 5 or more grades A* to C			Motor cars currently licensed,[4] 2000 (thousands)	3,904	24,406
at GCSE level,1999/00	54.8	50.3	Fatal and serious accidents on roads,[4] 1999		
			(rates per 100,000 population)	64	63
Economic activity rate,[6]			Recorded crime rate, 1999–00		
Spring 2000 (percentages)	83.4	78.7	(notifiable offences per 100,000 population)[3]	8,212	10,111
Employment rate,[6] Spring 2000 (percentages)	80.6	74.3			
ILO unemployment rate, Spring 2000 (percentages)	3.4	5.6	Average gross weekly household income, 1997–2000[5] (£)	538	455
Average gross weekly earnings: males in full-time					
employment, April 2000 (£)	482.10	451.60	Average weekly household expenditure, 1997–2000[5] (£)	393	348
Average gross weekly earnings: females in full-time			Households in receipt of Income Support/Family Credit,[4]		
employment, April 2000 (£)	353.10	336.70	1999–00 (percentages)	10	16

1 Males aged 65 and over, females aged 60 and over.
2 Deaths of infants under 1 year of age per 1,000 live births.
3 Figure for the United Kingdom relates to England and Wales.
4 Figure for the United Kingdom relates to Great Britain.
5 Combined years 1997–98, 1998-99 and 1999–00.
6 For people of working age. Men aged 16–64 and women aged 16–59.

1.16 Population density: by local authority, 1999

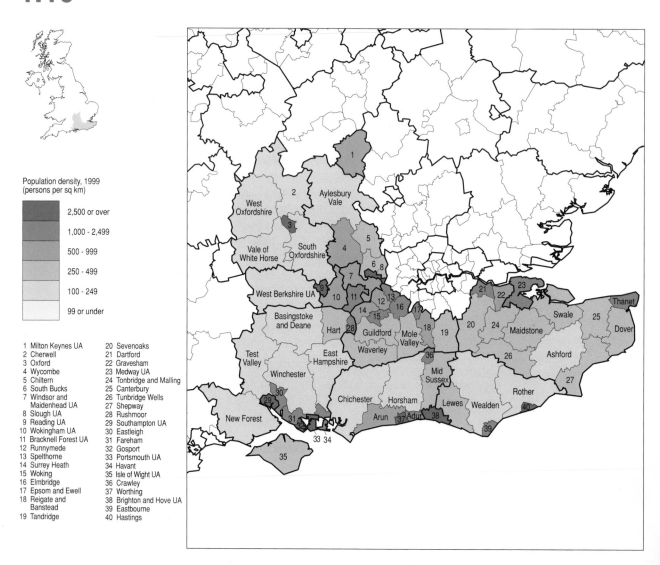

Population density, 1999
(persons per sq km)

2,500 or over
1,000 - 2,499
500 - 999
250 - 499
100 - 249
99 or under

1 Milton Keynes UA
2 Cherwell
3 Oxford
4 Wycombe
5 Chiltern
6 South Bucks
7 Windsor and Maidenhead UA
8 Slough UA
9 Reading UA
10 Wokingham UA
11 Bracknell Forest UA
12 Runnymede
13 Spelthorne
14 Surrey Heath
15 Woking
16 Elmbridge
17 Epsom and Ewell
18 Reigate and Banstead
19 Tandridge
20 Sevenoaks
21 Dartford
22 Gravesham
23 Medway UA
24 Tonbridge and Malling
25 Canterbury
26 Tunbridge Wells
27 Shepway
28 Rushmoor
29 Southampton UA
30 Eastleigh
31 Fareham
32 Gosport
33 Portsmouth UA
34 Havant
35 Isle of Wight UA
36 Crawley
37 Worthing
38 Brighton and Hove UA
39 Eastbourne
40 Hastings

South East

Population

In 1999, the South East had a population of 8.0 million people. Within the South East the population density was highest in Portsmouth UA at 4,720 people per sq km and lowest in the local authority districts of West Oxfordshire and Chichester at 138 people per sq km each.

(Tables 3.1 and 14.1)

Mortality

Overall for the South East the Standardised Mortality Ratio was 8 per cent lower than the UK as a whole in 1999, at 92 (UK=100); within the region this ranged from 77 in Guildford to 110 in Dartford.

(Table 14.1)

The Infant Mortality rate for 1998–2000 for the South East was lower than the UK rate (respectively 4.5 and 5.7 deaths of infants under one year old per 1,000 live births); within the region it ranged between 2.6 for Bracknell Forest UA and 7.0 for Portsmouth UA.

(Table 14.2)

Education

In 1999/00, the proportion of pupils achieving 5 or more GCSE grade A* to C results in the South East was higher than the UK average and a lower proportion of pupils than the UK average achieved no graded results.

(Table 14.3)

The proportion of people of working age qualified to GCE A level or equivalent or higher in the South East was 50.0 per cent in Spring 2001, higher than the UK average of 47.6 per cent.

(Table 4.12)

Labour Market

The employment rate for people of working age in Spring 2000, at 80.6 per cent, was the highest in the UK. Within the South East the employment rate varied between 87.5 per cent in West Berkshire UA to 71.0 per cent in Isle of Wight UA in 1999–2000.

(Tables 5.1 and 14.5)

In 2000, average gross weekly earnings for people in the South East, at £434.20, was higher than the UK average of £409.20. Within the region average gross weekly earnings varied considerably; in Brighton and Hove UA, 10 per cent of men earned more than £1,180.90 but 10 per cent also earned less than £236.30.

(Tables 5.17 and 14.5)

Economy

In the South East, manufacturing industry accounted for some 15.2 per cent of GDP in 1998, compared to 20.3 per cent for the UK as a whole. Agriculture, forestry and fishing accounted for 0.8 per cent of GDP in 1998, compared to 1.3 per cent for the UK.

(Table 12.5)

Of the 374,000 business sites in 2000, just over 32 per cent were in financial intermediation, real estate, renting and business activities, higher than the overall UK average of 26.0 per cent.

(Table 13.3)

Fifty-six per cent of export trade in 2000 was to the EU, slightly lower than the UK average of 58.6 per cent. Trade from the EU accounted for over 58 per cent of imports, higher than the overall average of 48.6 per cent.

(Table 13.7)

Environment

Almost a third of the total area in the South East and London combined is designated as an Area of Outstanding Natural Beauty and around a fifth (excluding London) is Green Belt land.

(Table 11.13)

1.17 Key statistics for the South West

	South West	United Kingdom		South West	United Kingdom
Population, 1999 (thousands)	4,935.7	59,500.9	Gross domestic product, 1999 (£ million)	58,151	771,849
Percentage aged under 16	19.3	20.4	Gross domestic product per head index, 1999 (UK=100)	90.8	100.0
Percentage pension age and over[1]	21.0	18.1	Total business sites, 2000 (thousands)	228.3	2,488.4
Standardised mortality ratio (UK=100), 1999	90	100	Average dwelling price, 2000 (£)[3]	110,132	110,221
Infant mortality rate,[2] 1998–2000	4.7	5.8			
Percentage of pupils achieving 5 or more grades A* to C			Motor cars currently licensed,[4] 2000 (thousands)	2,382	24,406
at GCSE level,1999/00	54.0	50.3	Fatal and serious accidents on roads,[4] 1999		
			(rates per 100,000 population)	52	63
Economic activity rate,[6]			Recorded crime rate, 1999–00		
Spring 2000 (percentages)	82.0	78.7	(notifiable offences per 100,000 population)[3]	8,146	10,111
Employment rate,[6] Spring 2000 (percentages)	78.6	74.3			
ILO unemployment rate, Spring 2000 (percentages)	4.2	5.6	Average gross weekly household income, 1997–2000[5] (£)	427	455
Average gross weekly earnings: males in full-time					
employment, April 2000 (£)	418.20	451.60	Average weekly household expenditure, 1997–2000[5] (£)	332	348
Average gross weekly earnings: females in full-time			Households in receipt of Income Support/Family Credit,[4]		
employment, April 2000 (£)	309.80	336.70	1999–00 (percentages)	14	16

1 Males aged 65 and over, females aged 60 and over.
2 Deaths of infants under 1 year of age per 1,000 live births.
3 Figure for the United Kingdom relates to England and Wales.
4 Figure for the United Kingdom relates to Great Britain.
5 Combined years 1997–98, 1998-99 and 1999–00.
6 For people of working age. Men aged 16–64 and women aged 16–59.

1.18 Population density: by local authority, 1999

Population density, 1999
(persons per sq km)

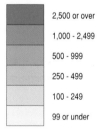

- 2,500 or over
- 1,000 - 2,499
- 500 - 999
- 250 - 499
- 100 - 249
- 99 or under

1 Forest of Dean
2 Tewkesbury
3 Gloucester
4 Cheltenham
5 South Gloucestershire UA
6 Swindon UA
7 City of Bristol UA
8 North Somerset UA
9 Bath and North East Somerset UA
10 West Wiltshire
11 Sedgemoor
12 Poole UA
13 Bournemouth UA
14 Christchurch
15 Exeter
16 Restormel
17 Plymouth UA
18 Torbay UA
19 Weymouth and Portland
20 Penwith

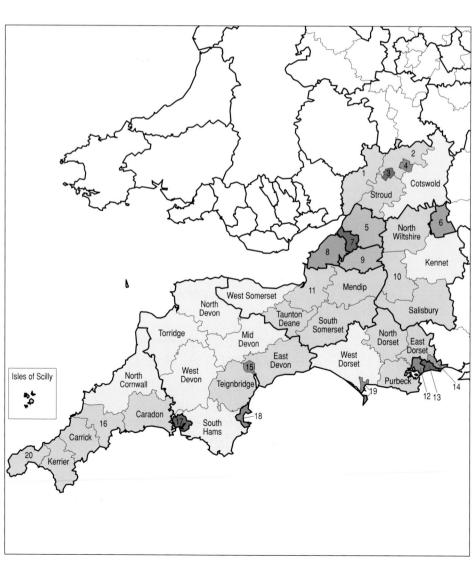

South West

Population	In 1999, the South West had a population of 4.9 million people. Within the South West the population density was highest in City of Bristol UA at 3,684 people per sq km and lowest in the local authority district of West Devon at only 41 people per sq km.

(Tables 3.1 and 14.1)

Mortality	Overall for the South West the Standardised Mortality Ratio was 10 per cent lower than the UK as a whole in 1999, at 90 (UK=100); within the region this ranged from 75 in East Dorset to 102 in Swindon UA.

(Table 14.1)

The Infant Mortality rate for 1998–2000 for the South West was lower than the UK rate (respectively 4.7 and 5.7 deaths of infants under one year old per 1,000 live births); within the region it ranged between 3.5 for South Gloucestershire UA and 5.8 for North Somerset UA.

(Table 14.2)

Education	In 1999/00, the proportion of pupils achieving 5 or more GCSE grade A* to C results was higher in the South West than the UK average. A lower proportion of pupils than the UK average achieved no graded results.

(Table 14.3)

The proportion of people of working age qualified to GCE A level or equivalent or higher in the South West was 48.9 per cent in Spring 2001, higher than the UK average of 47.6 per cent.

(Table 4.12)

Labour Market	The employment rate for people of working age in Spring 2000, at 78.6 per cent, was the second highest in the UK. Within the South West the employment rate varied between to 71.8 per cent in Plymouth UA to 85.0 per cent in Swindon UA in 1999–2000.

(Tables 5.1 and 14.5)

In 2000, average gross weekly earnings for people in the region, at £379.10, was lower than the UK average of £409.20. Within the region average gross weekly earnings varied considerably; in Gloucestershire, 10 per cent of men earned more than £717.70 but 10 per cent also earned less than £243.70.

(Tables 5.17 and 14.5)

Economy	In the South West, manufacturing industry accounted for some 19.6 per cent of GDP in 1998, compared to 20.3 per cent for the UK as a whole. Agriculture, forestry and fishing accounted for 2.5 per cent of GDP in 1998, compared to 1.3 per cent for the UK.

(Table 12.5)

Of the 228,000 business sites in 2000, nearly 29 per cent were in distribution, hotels and catering and repairs industries, about the same as the overall UK average of 28.9 per cent.

(Table 13.3)

Nearly 71 per cent of export trade in 2000 was to the EU, higher than the UK average of 58.6 per cent. Trade from the EU accounted for over 35 per cent of imports, lower than the overall average of 48.6 per cent.

(Table 13.7)

Environment	Almost a third of the total area in the South West is designated as an Area of Outstanding Natural Beauty and four per cent is Green Belt land.

(Table 11.13)

1.19 Key statistics for Wales

	Wales	United Kingdom		Wales	United Kingdom
Population, 1999 (thousands)	2,937.0	59,500.9	Gross domestic product, 1999 (£ million)	30,689	771,849
Percentage aged under 16	20.3	20.4	Gross domestic product per head index, 1999 (UK=100)	80.5	100.0
Percentage pension age and over[1]	19.9	18.1	Total business sites, 2000 (thousands)	112.9	2,488.4
Standardised mortality ratio (UK=100), 1999	104	100	Average dwelling price, 2000 (£)[3]	67,598	110,221
Infant mortality rate,[2] 1998–2000	5.8	5.8			
Percentage of pupils achieving 5 or more grades A* to C			Motor cars currently licensed,[4] 2000 (thousands)	1,171	24,406
at GCSE level,1999/00	49.1	50.3	Fatal and serious accidents on roads,[4] 1999		
			(rates per 100,000 population)	50	63
Economic activity rate,[5]			Recorded crime rate, 1999–00		
Spring 2000 (percentages)	74.0	78.7	(notifiable offences per 100,000 population)[3]	8,710	10,111
Employment rate,[5] Spring 2000 (percentages)	69.4	74.3			
ILO unemployment rate, Spring 2000 (percentages)	6.2	5.6	Average gross weekly household income, 1997–2000 (£)	364	455
Average gross weekly earnings: males in full-time					
employment, April 2000 (£)	400.50	451.60	Average weekly household expenditure, 1997–2000 (£)	316	348
Average gross weekly earnings: females in full-time			Households in receipt of Income Support/Family Credit,[4]		
employment, April 2000 (£)	313.70	336.70	1999–00 (percentages)	17	16

1 Males aged 65 and over, females aged 60 and over.
2 Deaths of infants under 1 year of age per 1,000 live births.
3 Figure for the United Kingdom relates to England and Wales.
4 Figure for the United Kingdom relates to Great Britain.
5 For people of working age. Men aged 16–64 and women aged 16–59.

1.20 Population density: by local authority, 1999

Population density, 1999
(persons per sq km)

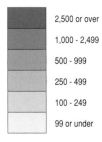

2,500 or over

1,000 - 2,499

500 - 999

250 - 499

100 - 249

99 or under

1 Swansea UA
2 Neath Port Talbot UA
3 Bridgend UA
4 Rhondda, Cynon, Taff UA
5 Merthyr Tydfil UA
6 Caerphilly UA
7 Blaenau Gwent UA
8 Torfaen UA
9 The Vale of Glamorgan UA
10 Newport UA

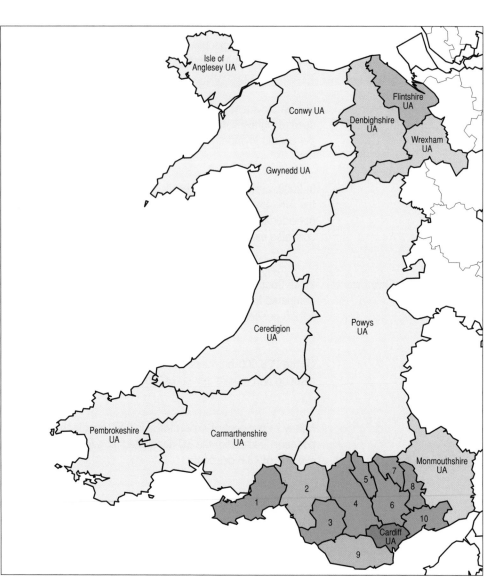

Wales

Population
In 1999, Wales had a population of just over 2.9 million people. Within Wales the population density was highest in the unitary authority area of Cardiff at 2,317 people per sq km and lowest in Powys at 24 people per sq km.

(Tables 3.1 and 15.1)

Mortality
Overall for Wales, the Standardised Mortality Ratio was 4 per cent higher than for the UK as a whole, at 104 in 1999 (UK=100); by local authority within Wales the SMR ranged from 88 in Powys to 125 in Merthyr Tydfil.

(Table 15.1)

The Infant Mortality rate for 1998–2000 for Wales was almost the same as the UK rate (respectively, 5.8 and 5.8 deaths of those under one year old per 1,000 live births); by local authority area, it ranged between 3.5 for Flintshire and 7.8 for Conwy.

(Table 15.2)

Education
In 1999/00, over half of the areas in Wales had higher proportions of pupils achieving 5 or more A* to C graded results than the UK average; and all areas except Gwynedd, Conwy, Flintshire, Ceredigion, Pembrokeshire and Torfaen had higher proportions of pupils with no graded results.

(Table15.3)

The proportion of people of working age qualified to GCE A level or equivalent or higher in Wales was 43.3 per cent in Spring 2001, lower than the UK average of 47.6 per cent.

(Table 4.12)

Labour Market
The employment rate for people of working age in Spring 2000, at 69.4 per cent, was among the lowest in the UK. Within Wales the employment rate varied between 59.0 per cent in Merthyr Tydfil and Neath Port Talbot to 80.8 per cent in Powys in 1999–2000.

(Tables 5.1 and 15.5)

In 2000, average weekly earnings for people in Wales, at £368.0, were lower than the UK average of £409.20. Only the North East of England and Northern Ireland had lower average earnings.

(Tables 5.17 and 14.5)

Economy
In Wales, manufacturing industry accounted for some 27.0 per cent of GDP in 1998, compared to 20.3 per cent for the UK as a whole. Agriculture, forestry and fishing accounted for 1.8 per cent of GDP in 1998, compared to 1.3 per cent for the UK.

(Table 12.5)

Of the 113,000 business sites in Wales in 2000, over 30 per cent were in distribution, hotels and catering and repairs industries, slightly higher than the overall UK average of 28.9 per cent.

(Table 13.3)

Over 71 per cent of export trade in 2000 was to the EU, higher than the UK average of 58.6 per cent. Trade from the EU accounted for over 33 per cent of imports, the lowest rate in the UK and well below the overall UK average of 48.6 per cent.

(Table 13.7)

Environment
A fifth of the total area of Wales is within a National Park.

(Table 11.13)

1.21 Key statistics for Scotland

	Scotland	United Kingdom		Scotland	United Kingdom
Population, 1999 (thousands)	5,119.2	59,500.9	Gross domestic product, 1999 (£ million)	64,050	771,849
Percentage aged under 16	19.7	20.4	Gross domestic product per head index, 1999 (UK=100)	96.5	100.0
Percentage pension age and over[1]	18.0	18.1	Total business sites, 2000 (thousands)	194.8	2,488.4
Standardised mortality rate (UK=100), 1999	118	100			
Infant mortality ratio,[2] 1998–2000	5.4	5.8	Motor cars currently licensed,[3] 2000 (thousands)	1,872	24,406
Percentage of pupils achieving 5 or more grades A* to C			Fatal and serious accidents on roads,[3] 1999		
at GCSE level,1999/00	58.3	50.3	(rates per 100,000 population)	68	63
Economic activity rate,[5]			Recorded crime rate, 2000		
Spring 2000 (percentages)	77.9	78.7	(notifiable offences per 100,000 population)	8,274	..
Employment rate,[5] Spring 2000 (percentages)	71.9	74.3			
ILO unemployment rate, Spring 2000 (percentages)	7.7	5.6	Average gross weekly household income, 1997–2000[4] (£)	403	455
Average gross weekly earnings: males in full-time					
employment, April 2000 (£)	423.00	451.60	Average weekly household expenditure, 1997–2000[4] (£)	317	348
Average gross weekly earnings: females in full-time			Households in receipt of Income Support/Family Credit,[3]		
employment, April 2000 (£)	316.10	336.70	1999–00 (percentages)	18	16

1 Males aged 65 and over, females aged 60 and over.
2 Deaths of infants under 1 year of age per 1,000 live births.
3 Figure for the United Kingdom relates to Great Britain.
4 Combined years 1997–98, 1998–99 and 1999–00
5 For people of working age. Men aged 16–64 and women aged 16–59.

1.22 Population density: by local authority, 1999

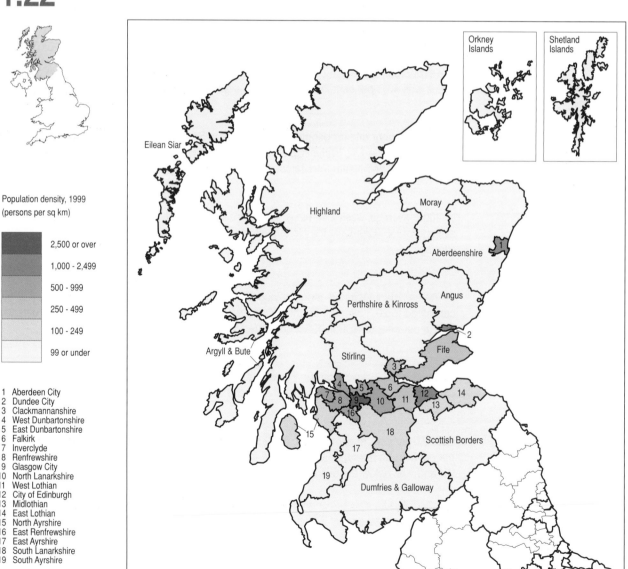

Population density, 1999
(persons per sq km)

- 2,500 or over
- 1,000 - 2,499
- 500 - 999
- 250 - 499
- 100 - 249
- 99 or under

1 Aberdeen City
2 Dundee City
3 Clackmannanshire
4 West Dunbartonshire
5 East Dunbartonshire
6 Falkirk
7 Inverclyde
8 Renfrewshire
9 Glasgow City
10 North Lanarkshire
11 West Lothian
12 City of Edinburgh
13 Midlothian
14 East Lothian
15 North Ayrshire
16 East Renfrewshire
17 East Ayrshire
18 South Lanarkshire
19 South Ayrshire

Scotland

Population	In 1999, Scotland had a population of 5.1 million people. Within Scotland the population density was highest in Glasgow City at 3,493 people per sq km and lowest in the Highland council area at only 8 people per sq km.

(Tables 3.1 and 16.1)

Mortality	Overall for Scotland, the Standardised Mortality Ratio was 18 per cent higher than the UK as a whole in 1999, at 118 (UK=100); by council areas within Scotland this ranged from 94 in East Renfrewshire to 144 in Glasgow City.

(Table 16.1)

The Infant Mortality rate for 1998–2000 for Scotland was lower than the UK rate (respectively 5.4 and 5.8 deaths of infants under one year old per 1,000 live births); by council area it ranged between 1.3 for the Shetland Islands and 9.2 for South Ayrshire.

(Table 16.2)

Education	In 1999/00, all areas in Scotland, with the exception of Dundee City and Glasgow City, had a higher proportion of pupils achieving 5 or more Standard grade 1–3 results (equivalent to 5 or more GCSE grade A* to C results) than the UK average. The proportion of pupils with no graded results was the same as the UK average.

(Table 16.3)

The proportion of people of working age qualified to GCE A level or equivalent or higher in Scotland was 56.8 per cent in Spring 2001, higher than the UK average of 47.6 per cent.

(Table 4.12)

Labour Market	The employment rate for people of working age in Spring 2000, at 71.9 per cent, was among the lowest in the UK. Within Scotland the employment rate varied between 54.9 per cent in Glasgow City to 87.0 per cent in Orkney Islands in 1999–2000.

(Tables 5.1 and 16.5)

In 2000, average gross weekly earnings for people in Scotland, at £379.80, were lower than the UK average of £409.20.

(Tables 5.17)

Economy	In Scotland, manufacturing industry accounted for some 21.0 per cent of GDP in 1998, compared to 20.3 per cent for the UK as a whole. Agriculture, forestry and fishing accounted for 2.0 per cent of GDP in 1998, compared to 1.3 per cent for the UK.

(Table 12.5)

Of the 195,000 business sites in 2000, nearly 31 per cent were in distribution, hotels and catering and repairs industries, slightly higher than the overall UK average of 28.9 per cent.

(Table 13.3)

Nearly 69 per cent of export trade in 2000 was to the EU, higher than the UK average of 58.6 per cent. Trade from the EU accounted for nearly 34 per cent of imports, well below the overall UK average of 48.6 per cent.

(Table 13.7)

Environment	Over an eighth of the total area in Scotland is designated as a National Scenic Area and 2 per cent is Green Belt land.

(Table 11.13)

1.23 Key statistics for Northern Ireland

	Northern Ireland	United Kingdom		Northern Ireland	United Kingdom
Population, 1999 (thousands)	1,691.8	59,500.9	Gross domestic product, 1999 (£ million)	17,003	771,849
Percentage aged under 16	24.3	20.4			
Percentage pension age and over[1]	15.2	18.1	Gross domestic product per head index, 1999 (UK=100)	77.5	100.0
Standardised mortality ratio (UK=100), 1999	100	100			
Infant mortality rate,[2] 1998–2000	6.4	5.8	Total business sites, 2000 (thousands)	76.0	2,488.4
Percentage of pupils achieving 5 or more grades A* to C			Motor cars currently licensed, 1999 (thousands)	608	..
at GCSE level,1999/00	56.9	50.3			
			Motor cars currently licensed, 1999 (thousands)	608	..
Economic activity rate,[5]			Fatal and serious accidents on roads,[4] 1999		
Spring 2000 (percentages)	69.9	78.7	(rates per 100,000 population)	72	63
Employment rate,[5] Spring 2000 (percentages)	64.9	74.3			
ILO unemployment rate, Spring 2000 (percentages)	7.2	5.6	Average gross weekly household income, 1997–2000[3] (£)	357	455
Average gross weekly earnings: males in full-time					
employment, April 2000 (£)	393.30	451.60	Average weekly household expenditure, 1997–2000[3] (£)	312	348
Average gross weekly earnings: females in full-time					
employment, April 2000 (£)	307.30	336.70			

1 Males aged 65 and over, females aged 60 and over.
2 Deaths of infants under 1 year of age per 1,000 live births.
3 Combined years 1997–98, 1998–99 and 1999–00.
4 Figure for the United Kingdom relates to Great Britain.
5 For people of working age. Men aged 16–64 and women aged 16–59.

1.24 Population density: by local authority, 1999

Population density, 1999
(persons per sq km)

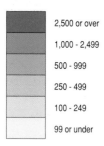

2,500 or over

1,000 - 2,499

500 - 999

250 - 499

100 - 249

99 or under

1 Newtownabbey
2 Carrickfergus
3 Belfast
4 North Down
5 Castlereagh

Northern Ireland

Population

In 1999, Northern Ireland had a population of 1.7 million people. Within Northern Ireland the population density was highest in the district council area of Belfast at 2,594 people per sq km and lowest in Moyle at only 31 people per sq km.

(Tables 3.1 and 17.1)

Mortality

Overall for Northern Ireland, the Standard Mortality Ratio was the same as the UK as a whole in 1999; by district council area this ranged from 85 in Cookstown to 112 in Dungannon (UK = 100).

(Table 17.1)

The Infant Mortality rate for 1999 for Northern Ireland was higher than the UK rate for 1998–2000 (respectively 6.4 and 5.8 deaths of infants under one year old per 1,000 live births). Within Northern Ireland it ranged between 4.5 for the Northern Health and Social Services Board area and 8.3 for the Eastern area.

(Table 17.2)

Education

In 1999/00, all Education Boards in Northern Ireland had a higher proportion of pupils achieving 5 or more GCSE grade A* to C results than the UK average, and a lower proportion of pupils than the UK average with no graded results.

(Table17.3)

The proportion of people of working age qualified to GCE A level or equivalent or higher in Northern Ireland was 43.2 per cent in Spring 2001, lower than the UK average of 47.6 per cent.

(Table 4.12)

Labour Market

The employment rate for people of working age in Spring 2000, at 64.9 per cent, was the lowest in the UK. Within Northern Ireland the employment rate varied between 52.6 per cent in Strabane to 75.4 per cent in Ballymoney in 1999–2000.

(Table 5.1 and 17.4)

In 2000, average gross weekly earnings for people in Northern Ireland were the lowest in the UK; £360.40 compared with the UK average of £409.20.

(Table 5.17)

Economy

Manufacturing industry accounted for some 19.0 per cent of Northern Ireland's GDP in 1998, compared to 20.3 per cent for the UK as a whole. Agriculture, forestry and fishing accounted for 4.0 per cent of Northern Ireland's GDP in 1998, compared to 1.3 per cent for the UK.

(Table 12.5)

Of the 76,000 business sites in 2000, nearly 26 per cent were in distribution, hotels and catering and repairs industries, the lowest rate in the UK; this compares with the UK average of 28.9 per cent.

(Table 13.3)

In 2000, 58.5 per cent of export trade was to the EU, about the same as the UK average of 58.6 per cent. Trade from the EU accounted for nearly 36 per cent of imports, lower than the overall average UK of 48.6 per cent.

(Table 13.7)

Environment

A fifth of the total area in Northern Ireland is designated as an Area of Outstanding Natural Beauty and just under a sixth is Green Belt land.

(Table 11.13)

2 European Union

Population

The most densely populated region in the European Union in 1998 was Brussels, with over 5,900 persons per square kilometre; London was second with a density of over 4,500.

(Table 2.1)

All regions of the United Kingdom had a higher proportion of their population aged under 15 than the EU average in 1998. The highest rate of all, at 23.1 per cent, was in Northern Ireland, just above the rate in the Republic of Ireland.

(Table 2.1)

Dependency

Dependency rates – those economically inactive as a percentage of economically active people – in the United Kingdom were lower than the EU average in 1999 except in the North East and Northern Ireland. The South East had one of the lowest rates of all, only Denmark was lower.

(Table 2.2)

Transport

Rates of car ownership in Scotland were among the lowest in the European Union countries in 1998; only in the Irish Republic, Denmark, and Greece were rates lower. Luxembourg had the highest rate.

(Table 2.2)

Labour market

At 1.6 per cent, the United Kingdom had the lowest percentage of workers employed in agriculture of all EU countries in 1999. At regional level, Brussels had the lowest percentage, 0.2, just below London, 0.3.

(Table 2.3)

Only in Luxembourg in 1999 was there a higher percentage of the workforce employed in the services sector than in the United Kingdom as a whole.

(Table 2.3)

Gross domestic product

Within the UK, only in London, the South East and the East of England was GDP per head higher than the overall EU average in 1998.

(Table 2.3, Map 2.5)

The lowest GDP per head in the United Kingdom in 1998 was in Northern Ireland, which was 23 per cent below the EU average.

(Table 2.3)

Agriculture

The United Kingdom, at 67.5 per cent, had the highest percentage of land used for agricultural purposes in the European Union in 1998.

(Table 2.4)

Ireland had the lowest proportion of agricultural land used for arable purposes within the European Union, at 24.6 per cent.

(Table 2.4)

Wales had by far the highest density of sheep and lambs in the European Union in 1998, at over 5,400 per 1,000 hectares of utilised agricultural land.

(Table 2.4)

NUTS level 1 areas in the European Union[1]

NETHERLANDS
1 Noord-Nederland
2 Oost-Nederland
3 Zuid-Nederland
4 West-Nederland

BELGIUM
5 Vlaams Gewest
6 Région Wallonne
7 Bruxelles-Brussels

8 LUXEMBOURG

GERMANY
9 Saarland
10 Rheinland-Pfalz
11 Baden-Württemberg
12 Mecklenburg-Vorpommern
13 Hamburg
14 Schleswig-Holstein

☐ non-EU countries

Açores
(Portugal)

Madeira
(Portugal)

Cueta y Melilla
(Spain-Sur)

Canarias
(Spain)

1 NUTS (Nomenclature of Units for Territorial Statistics) is a hierachical classfication of areas that provides a breakdown of the EU's economic territory. See Notes and Definitions.

2.1 Population and vital statistics, 1998

| | Area (sq km) | Popu- lation (thousands) | Persons per sq km | Percentage of population | | Births (per 1,000 population)[1] | Deaths (per 1,000 population)[2,3] | Infant mortality (per 1,000 births)[4] |
				Aged under 15	Aged 65 and over			
EUR 15	**3,191,120**	**374,348**	**117**	*17.1*	*15.9*	**10.8**	**9.8**	..
Austria	**83,859**	**8,075**	**96**	*17.2*	*15.4*	**10.1**	**9.7**	**4.9**
Ostösterreich	23,554	3,410	145	*16.0*	*16.4*	9.5	11.0	5.5
Südösterreich	25,921	1,769	68	*16.9*	*16.2*	9.4	9.6	3.7
Westösterreich	34,384	2,897	84	*18.7*	*13.7*	11.1	8.3	5.0
Belgium	**30,518**	**10,192**	**334**	*17.7*	*16.5*	**11.2**	**10.2**	**5.2**
Bruxelles-Brussels	161	953	5,913	*17.6*	*17.2*	13.5	10.9	5.2
Vlaams Gewest	13,512	5,912	438	*17.3*	*16.2*	10.6	9.6	5.1
Région Wallonne	16,844	3,327	198	*18.6*	*16.7*	11.5	11.1	5.3
Denmark	**43,094**	**5,295**	**123**	*18.0*	*14.9*	**12.5**	**11.0**	**4.7**
Finland	**304,529**	**5,147**	**17**	*18.7*	*14.6*	**11.1**	**9.6**	**4.2**
Manner-Suomi	303,003	5,122	17	*18.7*	*14.6*	11.1	9.6	4.2
Åland	1,527	25	17	*18.7*	*16.4*	12.2	9.3	..
France	**543,965**	**58,728**	**107**	*19.0*	*15.5*	**12.4**	**9.0**	**4.1**
Ile de France	12,012	11,088	910	*20.1*	*11.4*	14.6	6.8	4.5
Bassin Parisien	145,645	10,526	72	*19.5*	*15.7*	12.1	9.5	4.1
Nord-Pas-de-Calais	12,414	4,009	322	*21.7*	*13.5*	13.7	9.1	4.3
Est	48,030	5,151	107	*19.4*	*14.6*	12.2	8.7	3.6
Ouest	85,099	7,728	91	*18.3*	*17.3*	11.7	9.9	4.1
Sud-Ouest	103,599	6,155	59	*16.4*	*19.1*	10.4	10.7	3.5
Centre-Est	69,711	6,997	99	*19.0*	*15.1*	12.1	8.6	3.6
Méditerranée	67,455	7,073	104	*18.0*	*18.2*	11.4	10.0	3.8
Germany	**357,022**	**82,057**	**230**	*16.0*	*15.8*	**9.6**	**10.4**	**4.7**
Baden-Württemberg	35,752	10,397	291	*16.9*	*15.1*	10.7	9.3	4.2
Bayern	70,548	12,066	171	*16.5*	*15.7*	10.5	10.0	4.3
Berlin	890	3,426	3,835	*14.4*	*13.7*	8.7	10.4	4.4
Brandenburg	29,476	2,573	88	*15.4*	*14.0*	6.6	10.2	4.0
Bremen	404	674	1,660	*13.9*	*17.7*	9.5	11.7	4.7
Hamburg	755	1,705	2,253	*13.5*	*16.8*	9.5	11.3	4.2
Hessen	21,115	6,032	286	*15.6*	*15.9*	10.0	10.1	4.8
Mecklenburg-Vorpommern	23,171	1,808	78	*16.0*	*13.3*	6.8	9.8	5.1
Niedersachsen	47,614	7,845	165	*16.6*	*16.2*	10.5	10.6	4.9
Nordrhein-Westfalen	34,080	17,974	527	*16.3*	*16.2*	10.1	10.5	5.1
Rheinland-Pfalz	19,847	4,018	203	*16.5*	*16.6*	9.8	10.6	4.3
Saarland	2,570	1,081	419	*15.2*	*17.3*	8.5	11.6	4.6
Sachsen	18,413	4,522	245	*14.1*	*17.2*	6.7	11.6	4.5
Sachsen-Anhalt	20,447	2,702	132	*14.7*	*16.0*	6.5	11.6	5.3
Schleswig-Holstein	15,769	2,756	175	*15.9*	*16.0*	10.0	10.9	4.6
Thüringen	16,172	2,478	153	*14.8*	*15.5*	6.7	11.0	6.3
Greece	**131,625**	**10,511**	**80**	*15.8*	*16.5*	**9.6**	**9.8**	**6.7**
Voreia Ellada	56,457	3,400	60	*16.0*	*16.0*	9.8	9.7	6.9
Kentriki Ellada	53,902	2,644	49	*15.0*	*18.5*	7.7	9.7	7.0
Attiki	3,808	3,451	906	*15.6*	*15.1*	10.5	9.8	6.9
Nisia Aigaiou, Kriti	17,458	1,016	58	*17.4*	*16.6*	10.6	9.9	4.9
Ireland	**70,273**	**3,694**	**53**	*22.7*	*11.4*	**14.5**	**8.5**	**6.2**

2.1 (continued)

	Area (sq km)	Popu-lation (thousands)	Persons per sq km	Percentage of population		Births (per 1,000 population)[1]	Deaths (per 1,000 population)[2,3]	Infant mortality (per 1,000 births)[4]
				Aged under 15	Aged 65 and over			
Italy	**301,316**	**57,563**	**191**	*14.6*	*17.4*	**9.4**	**9.8**	**5.4**
Nord Ovest	34,081	6,053	177	*11.4*	*20.9*	7.7	12.0	6.0
Lombardia	23,872	8,989	377	*12.9*	*16.9*	9.0	9.6	3.5
Nord Est	39,816	6,578	166	*13.1*	*17.9*	9.2	9.9	3.6
Emilia-Romagna	22,124	3,947	179	*10.9*	*21.7*	7.6	11.7	5.9
Centro	41,142	5,810	141	*11.9*	*21.3*	7.8	11.3	5.1
Lazio	17,227	5,243	305	*14.2*	*16.4*	9.0	9.3	5.2
Abruzzo-Molise	15,232	1,606	105	*15.1*	*19.1*	8.9	10.3	5.4
Campania	13,595	5,797	426	*19.9*	*12.9*	12.4	8.1	6.4
Sud	44,430	6,771	152	*17.9*	*15.0*	10.6	8.3	6.7
Sicilia	25,707	5,108	199	*18.5*	*15.3*	11.3	9.2	7.8
Sardegna	24,090	1,661	69	*15.3*	*14.5*	8.3	8.2	4.2
Luxembourg	**2,586**	**424**	**165**	*18.7*	*14.3*	**12.6**	**9.0**	**5.0**
Netherlands[5]	**33,882**	**15,654**	**464**	*18.4*	*13.5*	**12.7**	**8.8**	**5.2**
Noord-Nederland	8,353	1,641	197	*18.1*	*14.5*	12.1	9.5	5.8
Oost-Nederland	9,749	3,252	335	*19.4*	*13.1*	13.2	8.4	5.5
West-Nederland	8,680	7,304	844	*18.2*	*13.7*	12.9	8.9	5.1
Zuid-Nederland	7,101	3,457	488	*18.0*	*13.0*	12.1	8.4	4.9
Portugal	**91,906**	**9,957**	**108**	*17.0*	*15.1*	**11.4**	**10.6**	**6.0**
Continente	88,797	9,454	107	*16.8*	*15.2*	11.3	10.7	5.9
Açores	2,330	244	105	*23.2*	*12.0*	14.1	11.1	4.9
Madeira	779	259	334	*20.4*	*12.2*	11.8	10.0	10.4
Spain	**504,790**	**39,348**	**78**	*15.6*	*16.1*	**9.2**	**9.3**	**4.9**
Noroeste	45,297	4,308	95	*13.1*	*19.0*	6.6	12.1	4.8
Noreste	70,366	4,022	57	*13.0*	*17.8*	8.1	9.5	5.3
Madrid	7,995	5,025	629	*15.1*	*14.6*	9.8	7.6	4.2
Centro	215,025	5,283	25	*15.3*	*19.4*	8.1	9.8	4.4
Este	60,249	10,723	178	*15.0*	*16.2*	9.5	9.5	4.1
Sur	98,616	8,403	85	*18.9*	*13.5*	10.8	8.4	5.9
Canarias	7,242	1,583	220	*18.0*	*11.3*	10.7	7.3	5.0
Sweden	**410,934**	**8,839**	**22**	*18.8*	*17.2*	**10.1**	**10.5**	**3.0**
United Kingdom[6]	**243,820**	**58,862**	**243**	*19.2*	*15.7*	**12.3**	**10.6**	**5.7**
North East	8,612	2,602	301	*19.1*	*16.1*	11.3	11.8	5.0
North West	14,165	6,885	486	*19.7*	*15.7*	12.0	11.5	6.3
Yorkshire and the Humber	15,566	4,805	324	*19.3*	*15.9*	12.0	11.0	6.9
East Midlands	15,627	4,182	267	*19.0*	*16.0*	11.6	10.7	5.6
West Midlands	13,004	5,341	410	*19.7*	*15.7*	12.5	10.5	6.5
East	19,120	5,356	281	*19.0*	*16.0*	12.2	10.1	5.0
London	1,584	7,155	4,538	*19.6*	*12.9*	14.8	8.6	6.0
South East	19,111	8,137	419	*18.9*	*16.2*	12.0	10.2	4.4
South West	23,971	4,888	204	*18.1*	*18.5*	11.2	10.1	4.8
Wales	20,768	2,705	141	*19.1*	*17.4*	11.8	11.6	5.6
Scotland	78,132	5,121	66	*18.6*	*15.3*	11.6	11.6	5.6
Northern Ireland	14,160	1,684	119	*23.1*	*13.0*	14.5	8.9	5.7

1 1997 for EUR 15, France, Italy and United Kingdom.
2 Deaths are by date of occurrences and not date of registration.
3 1997 for EUR 15, France and Italy.
4 1997 for France.
5 Including 'central persons register'.
6 Government Office Regions for the United Kingdom equal NUTS 1 regions for the European Union. See Notes and Definitions.

Source: Eurostat

2.2 Social statistics

	Dependency rate[1] 1999	Proportion of 16–18 year olds in education or training (percentages) 1995/96[2]	Causes of death 1994[3] (rate per 100,000 population)				Transport	
			Circulatory system	Cancer (all neoplasms)	All accidents	Motor vehicle accidents	Length of motorways (km) per 1,000 sq km 1998[4]	Private cars per 1,000 population 1998[5]
EUR 15	**131**	..	..	..	..	..	14	429
Austria	**110**	*82*	**544**	**244**	**40**	**15**	19	481
Ostösterreich	107	..	660	271	44	15	18	462
Südösterreich	119	..	516	250	37	15	21	518
Westösterreich	109	..	426	210	36	15	19	481
Belgium	**147**	*97*	**399**	**270**	**42**	**18**	55	440
Bruxelles-Brussels	163	..	409	302	44	12	68	485
Vlaams Gewest	136	..	386	263	38	17	61	448
Région Wallonne	164	..	419	273	48	23	50	413
Denmark	**90**	*83*	**514**	**276**	**47**	**11**	20	343
Finland	**107**	*90*	**449**	**197**	**51**	**9**	2	392
Manner-Suomi	..	*90*	449	197	51	9	2	392
Åland	..	*81*	450	307	36	8	0	517
France	**139**	*91*	**301**	**247**	**53**	**15**	17	490
Ile de France	116	..	210	201	39	9	49	452
Bassin Parisien	141	..	312	260	59	18	18	501
Nord-Pas-de-Calais	182	..	304	258	46	10	48	426
Est	132	..	307	243	51	15	20	504
Ouest	138	..	318	263	57	15	9	492
Sud-Ouest	145	..	381	269	63	18	11	517
Centre-Est	132	..	291	238	56	14	21	505
Méditerranée	166	..	340	266	60	17	18	521
Germany	**114**	*92*	**543**	**263**	**33**	**12**	32	508
Baden-Württemberg	108	*91*	444	236	30	10	29	532
Bayern	101	*91*	508	248	33	14	31	542
Berlin	111	*92*	576	253	24	8	66	349
Brandenburg	105	*91*	583	245	54	25	26	498
Bremen	129	*107*	571	327	35	8	119	429
Hamburg	105	*97*	502	302	45	8	107	419
Hessen	114	*93*	479	270	37	10	45	548
Mecklenburg-Vorpommern	111	*89*	504	223	60	24	11	467
Niedersachsen	123	*91*	542	267	35	14	28	529
Nordrhein-Westfalen	128	*95*	553	281	21	8	64	500
Rheinland-Pfalz	119	*87*	558	267	23	12	42	541
Saarland	132	*94*	626	283	24	8	92	549
Sachsen	110	*93*	702	281	56	15	24	479
Sachsen-Anhalt	118	*88*	648	277	47	18	12	467
Schleswig-Holstein	114	*92*	580	273	32	10	30	522
Thüringen	103	*88*	650	237	34	15	17	488
Greece	**147**	*69*	**460**	**202**	**36**	**19**	2	252
Voreia Ellada	148	..	465	208	33	18	1	195
Kentriki Ellada	153	..	483	191	35	19	3	128
Attiki	147	..	428	209	40	21	18	416
Nisia Aigaiou, Kriti	132	..	496	189	34	17	0	208
Ireland	**129**	*83*	**402**	**212**	**28**	**11**	1	323

2.2 (continued)

	Dependency rate[1] 1999	Proportion of 16–18 year olds in education or training (percentages) 1995/96[2]	Causes of death 1994[3] (rate per 100,000 population)				Transport	
			Circulatory system	Cancer (all neoplasms)	All accidents	Motor vehicle accidents	Length of motorways (km) per 1,000 sq km 1998[4]	Private cars per 1,000 population 1998[5]
Italy	**163**	..	**422**	**264**	**38**	**14**	**21**	**535**
Nord Ovest	143	..	532	326	50	15	36	555
Lombardia	128	..	385	307	38	16	23	555
Nord Est	131	..	416	298	43	18	22	543
Emilia-Romagna	122	..	483	341	45	21	28	584
Centro	146	..	501	313	45	16	16	561
Lazio	162	..	373	250	39	14	28	591
Abruzzo-Molise	181	..	470	236	43	12	24	499
Campania	238	..	368	185	24	9	33	521
Sud	227	..	359	179	31	12	14	443
Sicilia	251	..	431	194	29	9	22	498
Sardegna	190	..	339	209	41	14	0	478
Luxembourg	**138**	..	**417**	**255**	**49**	**20**	**44**	**594**
Netherlands[5]	**101**	**91**	**336**	**237**	**22**	**8**	**66**	**392**
Noord-Nederland	110	..	369	257	25	10	37	377
Oost-Nederland	102	..	333	229	23	10	60	391
West-Nederland	99	..	340	244	22	6	86	377
Zuid-Nederland	99	..	315	222	21	10	83	420
Portugal	**102**	**70**	**430**	**193**	**38**	**22**	**14**	..
Continente	100	73	430	194	38	22	14	485
Açores	151	..	509	208	30	13	0	..
Madeira	120	21	355	157	39	19	0	..
Spain	**165**	**74**	**342**	**212**	**32**	**15**	**16**	**408**
Noroeste	179	79	408	250	40	22	18	380
Noreste	151	86	326	231	32	16	16	377
Madrid	143	82	252	182	27	10	61	506
Centro	184	73	408	235	33	16	10	346
Este	145	70	352	222	35	16	31	454
Sur	204	69	331	183	26	15	17	346
Canarias	155	71	264	170	31	8	26	468
Sweden	**110**	**96**	**515**	**229**	**33**	**6**	**4**	**509**
United Kingdom[6]	**108**	**71**	..	**280**	**21**	..	**14**	**393**
North East	137	..	553	312	20	7	7	..
North West	120	..	548	296	22	8	41	354
Yorkshire and the Humber	114	64	514	279	20	8	20	359
East Midlands	103	69	495	273	21	9	12	407
West Midlands	109	76	486	278	22	8	29	429
East	97	..	451	263	20	9	13	..
London	104	..	..	252	19	..	45	..
South East	93	..	480	278	18	7	34	444
South West	99	68	540	303	20	8	12	455
Wales	130	64	547	301	23	8	6	385
Scotland	114	82	..	296	31	..	4	347
Northern Ireland	134	77	439	220	23	..	8	..

1 Dependency rates are calculated as the number of non-active persons (total population less labour force) expressed as a percentage of those economically active. 1998 for EUR 15 and Greece.
2 Participation rates are calculated by dividing the number of pupils enrolled in a region by the resident population in that region. As some young people may be resident in one region and in education in another, this inter-regional movement may influence the results. Data for Belgium and Portugal are for 1994/95. The UK data exclude Open University, independent and special schools in Wales, and Youth Training with employers, all of which are not available by region and age. For all countries, age is taken at 1 January except for the UK where it is taken at 31 August (the start of the academic year).
3 Unadjusted death rates using 1994 population estimates. 1990 for Belgium. 1992 for United Kingdom. 1993 for Denmark, Germany, Greece, Spain, France, Ireland, Italy, Luxembourg and Austria.
4 1994 for EUR 15 and Italy. 1996 for Greece, Ireland, Sweden and United Kingdom. 1997 for Denmark and the Netherlands.
5 1995 for EUR 15. 1997 for Italy and the Netherlands.
6 Government Office Regions for the United Kingdom equal NUTS 1 regions for the European Union. See Notes and Definitions.

Source: Eurostat

2.3 Economic statistics

	Persons in employ-ment,[1] 1999[2] (thousands)	Employment,[1] 1999[2] percentage in			Unem-ployment rate[1] (percent-ages) 1999	Long-term unemployed[1] as a percentage of all unem-ployed, 1999[3]	Gross domestic product per head (PPS)[4] EUR 15=100 1998	Estimates[5,6] of the percentage of GDP in 1996 derived from		
		Agriculture	Industry	Services				Agriculture	Industry	Services
EUR 15	**152,494**	*4.7*	*29.6*	*65.5*	*9.4*	*49.1*	100	..	..	..
Austria	**3,678**	*6.2*	*29.8*	*64.0*	*4.0*	*37.1*	112	*1.5*	*31.6*	*66.9*
Ostösterreich	1,572	5.3	26.6	68.1	4.5	59.0	123	1.2	27.5	71.3
Südösterreich	778	8.3	32.8	58.9	4.3	29.4	91	2.4	35.0	62.5
Westösterreich	1,327	6.1	31.7	62.2	3.4	8.1	111	1.4	35.4	63.2
Belgium	**3,987**	*2.4*	*25.8*	*71.8*	*8.8*	*59.3*	111	*1.4*	*27.3*	*71.3*
Bruxelles-Brussels	338	0.2	13.4	86.4	14.0	62.0	169	0.0	13.2	86.8
Vlaams Gewest	2,450	2.5	28.0	69.5	5.6	51.1	115	1.6	31.5	66.9
Région Wallonne	1,199	2.8	24.7	72.5	13.3	65.1	88	1.7	25.8	72.5
Denmark	**2,708**	*3.3*	*26.8*	*69.5*	*5.6*	*18.6*	119	*4.1*	*27.6*	*68.3*
Finland	**2,333**	*6.4*	*27.6*	*65.7*	*11.5*	*23.6*	102	*5.5*	*33.0*	*61.5*
Manner-Suomi	2,321	6.3	27.7	65.6	11.5	23.6	101	5.5	33.1	61.4
Åland	12	9.1	11.6	78.5	2.1	14.8	122	8.8	13.1	78.0
France	**22,755**	*4.3*	*26.3*	*69.4*	*11.4*	*41.3*	99	*2.4*	*27.4*	*70.1*
Ile de France	4,903	0.5	19.7	79.8	10.3	41.3	152	0.2	23.0	76.8
Bassin Parisien	3,936	5.9	30.4	63.7	11.5	42.2	89	4.1	33.2	62.6
Nord-Pas-de-Calais	1,342	1.7	29.4	68.9	15.8	44.9	79	1.4	30.1	68.5
Est	2,075	3.0	35.3	61.7	8.4	36.2	91	2.4	34.0	63.6
Ouest	3,117	7.6	29.2	63.2	9.7	41.0	84	4.8	27.7	67.5
Sud-Ouest	2,365	7.7	23.1	69.2	11.5	42.7	88	4.7	24.6	70.7
Centre-Est	2,722	4.4	29.5	66.1	10.3	37.9	97	2.0	33.2	64.7
Méditerranée	2,295	4.0	19.3	76.7	16.5	42.1	85	2.8	20.2	77.0
Germany	**36,089**	*2.9*	*33.8*	*63.3*	*8.9*	*50.6*	108	*1.1*	*34.9*	*64.0*
Baden-Württemberg	4,807	2.5	41.4	56.1	5.1	53.9	122	1.1	41.3	57.7
Bayern	5,787	4.1	35.6	60.3	5.0	47.6	123	1.0	35.3	63.7
Berlin	1,459	0.8	23.4	75.8	13.7	46.5	102	0.2	32.2	67.6
Brandenburg	1,145	5.4	32.2	62.3	16.0	39.8	71	2.2	39.3	58.6
Bremen	274	1.3	26.4	72.3	11.4	61.7	144	0.2	31.2	68.5
Hamburg	788	0.5	22.4	77.1	7.9	57.7	186	0.3	20.9	78.8
Hessen	2,684	1.7	31.7	66.7	6.7	56.2	131	0.5	26.8	72.7
Mecklenburg-Vorpommern	757	6.8	26.9	66.3	17.5	39.6	71	2.9	29.8	67.3
Niedersachsen	3,370	4.0	32.5	63.5	8.2	58.8	99	2.9	34.1	63.0
Nordrhein-Westfalen	7,511	1.8	34.3	63.9	8.2	61.2	110	0.7	36.6	62.7
Rheinland-Pfalz	1,759	2.5	36.3	61.3	6.4	52.3	98	1.4	38.4	60.2
Saarland	436	0.9	34.8	64.3	8.5	64.3	99	0.3	36.0	63.7
Sachsen	1,927	3.0	34.8	62.3	16.2	42.9	71	1.2	36.9	61.9
Sachsen-Anhalt	1,074	4.2	31.9	63.9	19.9	42.5	68	2.1	37.0	60.9
Schleswig-Holstein	1,223	3.2	24.8	71.9	7.4	52.9	102	2.2	29.4	68.4
Thüringen	1,090	3.8	34.0	62.1	14.3	37.7	70	1.9	36.1	62.0
Greece	**3,967**	*17.8*	*23.0*	*59.2*	*11.7*	*55.3*	66	*14.9*	*25.0*	*60.0*
Voreia Ellada	1,265	26.0	23.8	50.2	12.4	51.5	63	22.1	28.8	49.2
Kentriki Ellada	805	32.5	20.7	46.8	11.0	60.5	59	24.6	27.2	48.2
Attiki	1,493	1.0	25.3	73.7	12.5	57.8	74	2.2	24.9	72.9
Nisia Aigaiou, Kriti	404	24.6	16.6	58.7	7.9	44.0	68	23.5	14.1	62.3
Ireland	**1,593**	*8.5*	*28.3*	*62.5*	*5.9*	*56.0*	108	*7.2*	*40.4*	*52.4*

2.3 (continued)

	Persons in employ-ment,[1] 1999[2] (thousands)	Employment,[1] 1999[2] percentage in			Unem-ployment rate[1] (percent-ages) 1999	Long-term unemployed[1] as a percentage of all unem-ployed, 1999[3]	Gross domestic product per head (PPS)[4] EUR 15=100 1998	Estimates[5,6] of the percentage of GDP in 1996 derived from		
		Agriculture	Industry	Services				Agriculture	Industry	Services
Italy	**20,618**	*5.4*	*32.4*	*62.2*	*11.7*	*60.8*	101	*3.5*	*28.9*	*67.6*
Nord Ovest	2,363	*3.8*	*35.2*	*61.0*	8.0	*61.9*	114	*2.7*	*31.9*	*65.4*
Lombardia	3,830	*2.1*	*41.1*	*56.8*	4.9	*43.7*	135	*1.8*	*37.4*	*60.8*
Nord Est	2,756	*5.3*	*39.0*	*55.7*	4.7	*30.1*	120	*3.8*	*32.4*	*63.8*
Emilia-Romagna	1,723	*6.7*	*36.4*	*56.9*	4.8	*27.0*	129	*4.1*	*32.7*	*63.1*
Centro	2,260	*3.8*	*35.8*	*60.4*	7.2	*47.7*	106	*3.0*	*30.8*	*66.1*
Lazio	1,868	*2.9*	*19.0*	*78.1*	13.2	*68.3*	113	*1.7*	*17.7*	*80.6*
Abruzzo-Molise	541	*7.7*	*33.2*	*59.1*	11.6	*65.4*	82	*5.3*	*28.5*	*66.2*
Campania	1,561	*7.5*	*24.5*	*68.0*	23.7	*73.0*	64	*3.8*	*20.1*	*76.1*
Sud	1,883	*12.0*	*24.9*	*63.1*	21.9	*62.6*	64	*7.4*	*20.2*	*72.4*
Sicilia	1,318	*9.1*	*19.3*	*71.6*	24.8	*66.4*	65	*6.2*	*19.1*	*74.7*
Sardegna	515	*8.1*	*22.7*	*69.2*	21.9	*57.9*	76	*5.4*	*22.5*	*72.1*
Luxembourg	**176**	*1.9*	*21.9*	*75.8*	*2.4*	*32.2*	176	*1.3*	*23.9*	*74.8*
Netherlands	**7,605**	*..*	*..*	*..*	*3.3*	*41.5*	113	*3.2*	*26.8*	*70.0*
Noord-Nederland	751	*..*	*..*	*..*	5.3	*47.0*	105	*3.9*	*38.6*	*57.5*
Oost-Nederland	1,578	*..*	*..*	*..*	3.0	*39.1*	96	*3.9*	*27.0*	*69.1*
West-Nederland	3,579	*..*	*..*	*..*	3.1	*42.1*	125	*2.7*	*20.1*	*77.2*
Zuid-Nederland	1,698	*..*	*..*	*..*	3.1	*38.1*	107	*3.7*	*32.5*	*63.8*
Portugal	**4,830**	*12.6*	*35.3*	*52.1*	*4.7*	*39.9*	75	*4.1*	*33.9*	*62.0*
Continente	4,619	*12.5*	*35.6*	*52.0*	4.8	*39.9*	76	*4.0*	*34.5*	*61.4*
Açores	96	*18.4*	*26.0*	*55.7*	3.7	*34.9*	52	*11.8*	*19.7*	*68.4*
Madeira	115	*15.0*	*31.2*	*53.8*	3.4	*44.7*	58	*3.8*	*18.2*	*78.0*
Spain	**13,773**	*7.4*	*30.6*	*62.0*	*16.1*	*45.0*	81	*4.5*	*29.0*	*66.5*
Noroeste	1,423	*15.6*	*30.3*	*54.1*	17.0	*53.3*	68	*7.1*	*30.4*	*62.5*
Noreste	1,502	*5.4*	*37.2*	*57.5*	12.0	*47.7*	96	*4.0*	*37.3*	*58.8*
Madrid	1,933	*1.0*	*25.8*	*73.2*	13.3	*48.5*	110	*0.2*	*24.6*	*75.1*
Centro	1,715	*12.0*	*30.3*	*57.7*	17.6	*40.6*	67	*9.9*	*30.7*	*59.4*
Este	4,124	*4.0*	*35.4*	*60.6*	11.8	*45.9*	92	*2.1*	*32.0*	*65.9*
Sur	2,493	*11.7*	*25.3*	*63.0*	25.1	*42.5*	59	*8.6*	*22.8*	*68.6*
Canarias	584	*6.6*	*19.8*	*73.7*	14.4	*36.6*	77	*3.5*	*16.2*	*80.3*
Sweden	**4,054**	*3.0*	*25.0*	*72.0*	*7.6*	*29.1*	102	*2.2*	*30.0*	*66.9*
United Kingdom[7]	**27,107**	*1.6*	*26.0*	*72.3*	*6.1*	*30.3*	102	*1.8*	*29.8*	*68.4*
North East	1,035	*1.1*	*28.4*	*70.2*	9.9	*35.5*	79	*0.7*	*37.3*	*62.0*
North West	3,018	*1.2*	*28.2*	*70.5*	6.8	*30.9*	90	*1.5*	*35.7*	*62.8*
Yorkshire and the Humber	2,258	*1.2*	*28.5*	*70.3*	7.2	*28.1*	90	*2.2*	*36.2*	*61.6*
East Midlands	1,992	*2.0*	*31.6*	*66.3*	5.1	*26.7*	95	*2.6*	*38.6*	*58.8*
West Midlands	2,438	*1.4*	*33.0*	*65.4*	6.5	*28.9*	93	*2.1*	*39.0*	*58.9*
East	2,616	*1.6*	*26.4*	*72.0*	3.9	*26.6*	104	*2.6*	*28.6*	*68.8*
London	3,284	*0.3*	*16.0*	*83.6*	7.8	*34.2*	153	*0.1*	*17.1*	*82.8*
South East	3,946	*1.3*	*22.9*	*75.7*	3.2	*28.3*	113	*1.0*	*24.9*	*74.1*
South West	2,354	*2.4*	*25.6*	*72.0*	4.2	*24.6*	94	*3.7*	*30.3*	*66.1*
Wales	1,216	*2.7*	*29.5*	*67.6*	6.9	*24.5*	80	*2.3*	*38.7*	*59.0*
Scotland	2,273	*2.0*	*25.3*	*72.5*	7.6	*31.1*	98	*2.8*	*34.0*	*63.2*
Northern Ireland	676	*5.0*	*26.5*	*68.5*	9.4	*41.2*	77	*4.7*	*30.7*	*64.5*

1 See Notes and Definitions.
2 1998 for EUR15 and Greece.
3 1997 for EUR15 and Ireland.
4 Purchasing Power Standard. See Notes and Definitions.
5 Estimates for GDP by sector are based on the Gross Value Added (GVA) figures for each area.
6 Estimates for Government Office Regions are provided by the Office for National Statistics.
7 Government Office Regions for the United Kingdom equal NUTS 1 regions for the European Union. See Notes and Definitions.

Source: Eurostat; Office for National Statistics

2.4 Agricultural statistics, 1998

	Agricultural land as a percentage of total land area[1]	Arable land as a percentage of agricultural land[1]	Average yield[2]		Livestock per 1,000 ha of utilised agricultural land			Economic value of farms (SGM)[4,5] EUR 15=100
			Wheat 100kg/ha	Barley 100kg/ha	All cattle	All sheep and lambs	All pigs[3]	
EUR 15	*41.2*	*56.9*	60	46	620	743	937	100
Austria	*40.7*	*40.6*	51	46	637	106	1,117	70
Ostösterreich	*49.3*	*73.9*	49	45	460	54	1,049	88
Südösterreich	*32.3*	*25.6*	48	42	671	136	1,511	51
Westösterreich	*41.1*	*22.2*	59	51	761	130	939	68
Belgium	*45.6*	*61.6*	80	70	2,146	84	5,429	280
Bruxelles-Brussels	*4.3*	*..*	..	..	..	..	..	..
Vlaams Gewest	*47.0*	*67.5*	82	67	2,445	114	11,386	282
Région Wallonne	*44.8*	*56.6*	80	71	1,895	57	414	276
Denmark	*62.8*	*93.6*	72	52	727	40	4,431	340
Finland	*6.5*	*98.8*	29	24	502	44	703	102
Manner-Suomi	*..*	*..*	..	..	..	..	..	..
Åland	*..*	*..*	..	..	..	..	..	..
France	*54.6*	*60.7*	76	65	669	320	516	206
Ile de France	*49.2*	*95.6*	88	73	63	..	..	512
Bassin Parisien	*64.9*	*70.5*	82	70	582	..	..	282
Nord-Pas-de-Calais	*71.1*	*76.1*	84	74	858	..	878	292
Est	*47.0*	*52.7*	72	63	799	..	..	183
Ouest	*69.5*	*76.2*	70	59	973	..	1,802	212
Sud-Ouest	*49.1*	*54.5*	60	49	633	..	..	147
Centre-Est	*46.6*	*35.0*	68	58	775	..	228	133
Méditerranée	*33.6*	*23.2*	40	39	129	..	..	190
Germany	*48.7*	*68.4*	72	57	860	165	1,513	184
Baden-Württemberg	*41.9*	*57.0*	72	59	858	219	1,602	102
Bayern	*47.8*	*63.0*	69	56	1,195	128	1,132	120
Berlin	*2.6*	*69.6*	..	..	435	217	522	224
Brandenburg	*46.0*	*77.2*	61	45	502	118	598	511
Bremen	*22.3*	*18.9*	85	70	1,422	33	222	..
Hamburg	*17.7*	*44.8*	79	67	649	119	246	..
Hessen	*36.6*	*63.9*	73	57	735	246	1,220	117
Mecklenburg-Vorpommern	*59.2*	*78.8*	74	63	434	68	448	871
Niedersachsen	*56.5*	*66.5*	76	56	1,070	114	2,799	253
Nordrhein-Westfalen	*45.4*	*70.4*	74	58	1,027	180	4,030	204
Rheinland-Pfalz	*36.4*	*55.5*	69	53	631	209	579	148
Saarland	*30.5*	*52.1*	66	52	789	233	327	137
Sachsen	*49.6*	*79.1*	66	57	658	160	694	521
Sachsen-Anhalt	*57.7*	*85.6*	72	59	341	121	695	856
Schleswig-Holstein	*66.2*	*57.2*	83	73	1,286	351	1,292	292
Thüringen	*49.8*	*77.5*	68	57	536	317	872	590
Greece	*38.7*	*44.3*	22	23	113	1,727	177	40
Voreia Ellada	*42.1*	*65.3*	21	25	177	1,272	154	48
Kentriki Ellada	*35.8*	*30.7*	25	24	58	1,959	235	37
Attiki	*23.1*	*16.1*	13	32	99	1,407	176	36
Nisia Aigaiou, Kriti	*40.2*	*13.8*	14	14	47	2,679	97	29
Ireland	*62.8*	*24.6*	80	56	1,607	1,274	408	107

2.4   (continued)

	Agricultural land as a percentage of total land area[1]	Arable land as a percentage of agricultural land[1]	Average yield[2]		Livestock per 1,000 ha of utilised agricultural land			Economic value of farms (SGM)[4,5] EUR 15=100
			Wheat 100kg/ha	Barley 100kg/ha	All cattle	All sheep and lambs	All pigs[3]	
Italy	*51.2*	*54.0*	36	38	462	706	539	49
Nord Ovest	*39.6*	*48.8*	53	48	743	93	641	68
Lombardia	*48.0*	*70.9*	59	57	1,713	96	2,865	117
Nord Est	*40.1*	*51.8*	64	54	778	53	506	55
Emilia-Romagna	*55.5*	*76.2*	61	52	578	92	1,286	91
Centro	*45.9*	*69.4*	40	42	152	541	359	56
Lazio	*48.3*	*51.2*	33	32	367	1,412	148	37
Abruzzo-Molise	*52.0*	*53.8*	31	35	213	637	254	32
Campania	*49.9*	*52.6*	31	33	394	501	220	41
Sud	*60.2*	*50.5*	27	24	160	408	120	35
Sicilia	*61.4*	*47.9*	26	25	290	820	43	33
Sardegna	*69.0*	*28.3*	21	21	177	3,030	146	44
Luxembourg	*49.6*	*48.2*	61	52	1,584	55	635	198
Netherlands	*47.2*	*48.2*	93	57	2,184	711	6,857	518
Noord-Nederland	*48.1*	*45.4*	89	58	1,746	801	1,116	554
Oost-Nederland	*50.7*	*40.2*	93	56	3,036	491	9,229	412
West-Nederland	*40.4*	*51.5*	98	60	1,366	1,130	1,858	625
Zuid-Nederland	*52.0*	*59.8*	86	50	2,601	374	17,990	514
Portugal	*42.9*	*57.2*	12	9	321	893	594	36
Continente	*43.0*	*58.6*	12	9	279	919	599	37
Açores	*51.8*	*11.6*	..	..	1,615	33	339	32
Madeira	*9.7*	*46.3*	10	..	792	1,451	2,243	14
Spain	*51.0*	*56.7*	28	31	232	940	838	56
Noroeste	*29.7*	*31.8*	23	21	1,385	406	793	26
Noreste	*52.0*	*58.2*	29	31	188	1,280	1,060	71
Madrid	*46.3*	*55.5*	27	26	227	527	167	51
Centro	*57.8*	*63.7*	30	31	152	1,010	487	60
Este	*37.3*	*40.4*	36	34	348	956	3,070	50
Sur	*56.6*	*52.9*	24	18	115	728	635	69
Canarias	*15.5*	*39.2*	20	15	130	223	603	67
Sweden	*7.0*	*88.4*	57	38	552	134	726	152
United Kingdom[6]	*67.5*	*39.7*	76	53	681	1,885	458	343
North East	..	*37.2*	65	52	604	3,196	204	..
North West	..	*24.1*	62	45	1,274	3,371	346	..
Yorkshire and the Humber	*68.3*	*60.2*	77	58	588	1,823	1,742	413
East Midlands	*75.9*	*74.9*	78	56	485	998	507	547
West Midlands	*69.8*	*55.6*	71	56	942	2,352	435	293
East	..	*87.7*	82	59	187	248	1,151	..
London	..	*..*	..	..	..	..	..	..
South East	..	*65.4*	73	55	519	1,180	507	..
South West	*71.3*	*45.2*	67	49	1,155	1,824	470	260
Wales	*68.4*	*15.1*	64	46	884	5,429	63	173
Scotland	*67.1*	*18.7*	74	49	384	1,297	115	241
Northern Ireland	*74.4*	*20.4*	69	44	1,600	1,773	571	130

1 Estimated data for the Netherlands. 1997 for Portugal.
2 1995 for EUR15 and the Netherlands. 1996 for Greece. 1997 for Portugal.
3 1997 for France.
4 The economic value of farms is measured in Standard Gross Margins (SGMs). Data relate to 1995. See Notes and Definitions.
5 Vlaams Gewest includes Brussels. Berlin includes Bremen and Hamburg.
6 Government Office Regions for the United Kingdom equal NUTS 1 regions for the European Union. See Notes and Definitions.

Source: Eurostat

2.5 Gross domestic product per head:[1] by NUTS level 1 areas, 1998

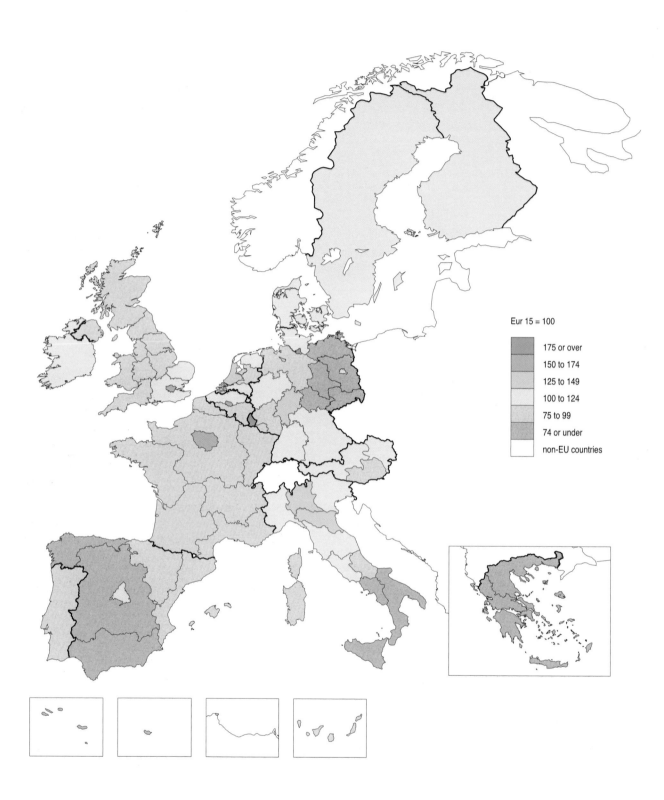

Eur 15 = 100

175 or over
150 to 174
125 to 149
100 to 124
75 to 99
74 or under
non-EU countries

1 Purchasing Power Standard. See Notes and Definitions.

Source: Eurostat

3 Population and Migration

Population

The population of the United Kingdom rose by around 1.7 million people between 1991 and 1999 to 59.5 million. Population growth over this period was higher among males than females, at 3.7 per cent and 2.2 per cent respectively.

(Table 3.1)

Age

Around 37 per cent of the population in Northern Ireland were aged less than 25 years old in 1999, a higher proportion than in any other region in the United Kingdom.

(Table 3.2)

Population density

Portsmouth UA in the South East had the highest population density of any Unitary Authority in the United Kingdom (excluding the London Boroughs) in 1999. The Highlands and Eilean Siar Council Areas in Scotland had the lowest.

(Map 3.3)

In 1999, the region of the United Kingdom with the highest proportion of pensioners was the South West, at just over one in five of the population.

(Map 3.5)

Social characteristics

London had the highest proportions of people of working age in professional occupations in Spring 2000. The North East had the highest percentage in unskilled occupations.

(Table 3.6)

Over a quarter of people in London were from an ethnic minority in 2000/2001, compared with one in fourteen people in Great Britain as a whole.

(Table 3.7)

Population change

Milton Keynes Unitary Authority had the greatest increase in population of any Unitary Authority or county between 1981 and 1999: the population rose by 64 per cent. Bracknell Forest UA, which had the second largest increase, grew by 32 per cent over the same period.

(Map 3.8)

Milton Keynes Unitary Authority in the South East has the highest projected population growth between 1999 and 2011, at 14 per cent. The population of Inverclyde in Scotland is projected to decline the most over this period with a fall of 12 per cent.

(Map 3.9)

London and Northern Ireland had higher crude live birth rates and lower death rates in 1999 than any other English region or country of the United Kingdom.

(Table 3.10)

The number of births between mid-1998 and mid-1999 was higher than the number of deaths over the same period in all regions and countries, except in the North East, the South West, Wales and Scotland.

(Table 3.11)

Conceptions

The North East had the highest conception rate for women aged under 18. Over 63 per cent of these pregnancies led to a maternity compared with 47 per cent in London.

(Table 3.12)

Births

In 1999, birth rates in London and the South East were highest for women aged 30 to 34. In all other regions except the East of England, the birth rates were higher for women aged between 25 and 29 than for any other age group shown. In the East of England, the birth rates for these two age groups were the same.

(Table 3.13)

Deaths

For those aged between 55 and 74, death rates in 1999 were highest in the North East, the North West and Scotland. Scotland also had the highest death rates across the older age bands.

(Table 3.14)

Migration

More international migrants come to London than to any other region in 1999. London also had a higher net outflow of people to the rest of the United Kingdom.

(Table 3.15)

The highest volumes of inter-regional movement occurred between London and the South East and London and the East of England.

(Table 3.16)

Marriage and cohabitation

The number of marriages in the United Kingdom decreased by a quarter between 1976 and 1999, with the greatest decline taking place in the North East.

(Table 3.17)

Unmarried people aged between 16 and 59 were less likely to cohabit in Northern Ireland than anywhere else in the United Kingdom during 1996–99.

(Chart 3.18)

Households

The South East and South West are projected to have 21 per cent more households in 2021 than in 1999. This compares with an increase of 7 per cent projected for the North East over the same period.

(Table 3.19)

Scotland had the highest proportion of one person households in the United Kingdom in Spring 2000, and the lowest proportion of married couples with dependent children.

(Table 3.20)

3.1 Resident population:[1] by gender

Thousands and percentages

	Population (thousands)				Total population growth (percentages)		
	1971	1981	1991	1999	1971–1981	1981–1991	1991–1999
Males							
United Kingdom	27,167.3	27,411.6	28,247.8	29,298.9	0.9	3.1	3.7
North East	1,304.0	1,283.1	1,267.5	1,264.2	-1.6	-1.2	-0.3
North West	3,422.4	3,357.6	3,348.7	3,382.9	-1.9	-0.3	1.0
Yorkshire and the Humber	2,384.9	2,395.0	2,441.7	2,492.9	0.4	2.0	2.1
East Midlands	1,797.8	1,894.8	1,989.6	2,075.9	5.4	5.0	4.3
West Midlands	2,542.4	2,555.6	2,596.3	2,642.0	0.5	1.6	1.8
East	2,194.6	2,385.5	2,536.9	2,675.9	8.7	6.3	5.5
London	3,611.4	3,277.6	3,352.0	3,616.3	-9.2	2.3	7.9
South East	3,321.1	3,528.6	3,759.8	3,975.2	6.2	6.6	5.7
South West	1,989.9	2,117.2	2,295.6	2,417.7	6.4	8.4	5.3
England	22,568.5	22,795.0	23,588.1	24,542.9	1.0	3.5	4.0
Wales	1,328.5	1,365.1	1,407.0	1,441.7	2.8	3.1	2.5
Scotland	2,515.7	2,494.9	2,469.5	2,485.6	-0.8	-1.0	0.7
Northern Ireland	754.6	756.6	783.2	828.6	0.3	3.5	5.8
Females							
United Kingdom	28,760.7	28,945.9	29,566.0	30,202.0	0.6	2.1	2.2
North East	1,374.5	1,353.1	1,335.0	1,317.1	-1.6	-1.3	-1.3
North West	3,685.4	3,582.7	3,536.7	3,497.6	-2.8	-1.3	-1.1
Yorkshire and the Humber	2,517.4	2,523.5	2,541.1	2,554.1	0.2	0.7	0.5
East Midlands	1,854.1	1,958.0	2,045.8	2,115.4	5.6	4.5	3.4
West Midlands	2,603.6	2,631.1	2,669.1	2,693.6	1.1	1.4	0.9
East	2,259.7	2,468.5	2,613.0	2,743.0	9.2	5.9	5.0
London	3,918.0	3,528.0	3,538.0	3,668.8	-10.0	0.3	3.7
South East	3,508.6	3,716.8	3,919.1	4,102.4	5.9	5.4	4.7
South West	2,121.9	2,264.1	2,422.1	2,517.9	6.7	7.0	4.0
England	23,843.2	24,025.8	24,619.9	25,210.0	0.8	2.5	2.4
Wales	1,411.8	1,448.4	1,484.5	1,495.3	2.6	2.5	0.7
Scotland	2,719.9	2,685.3	2,637.5	2,633.6	-1.3	-1.8	-0.1
Northern Ireland	785.8	786.3	824.1	863.2	0.1	4.8	4.7
All persons							
United Kingdom	55,928.0	56,357.5	57,813.8	59,500.9	0.8	2.6	2.9
North East	2,678.5	2,636.2	2,602.5	2,581.3	-1.6	-1.3	-0.8
North West	7,107.8	6,940.3	6,885.4	6,880.5	-2.4	-0.8	-0.1
Yorkshire and the Humber	4,902.3	4,918.4	4,982.8	5,047.0	0.3	1.3	1.3
East Midlands	3,651.9	3,852.8	4,035.4	4,191.2	5.5	4.7	3.9
West Midlands	5,146.0	5,186.6	5,265.5	5,335.6	0.8	1.5	1.3
East	4,454.3	4,854.1	5,149.8	5,418.9	9.0	6.1	5.2
London	7,529.4	6,805.6	6,889.9	7,285.0	-9.6	1.2	5.7
South East	6,829.7	7,245.4	7,678.9	8,077.6	6.1	6.0	5.2
South West	4,111.8	4,381.4	4,717.8	4,935.7	6.6	7.7	4.6
England	46,411.7	46,820.8	48,208.1	49,752.9	0.9	3.0	3.2
Wales	2,740.3	2,813.5	2,891.5	2,937.0	2.7	2.8	1.6
Scotland	5,235.6	5,180.2	5,107.0	5,119.2	-1.1	-1.4	0.2
Northern Ireland	1,540.4	1,543.0	1,607.3	1,691.8	0.2	4.2	5.3

1 See Notes and Definitions.

Source: Office for National Statistics; General Register Office for Scotland; Northern Ireland Statistics and Research Agency

3.2   Resident population:[1] by age and gender, 1999

Thousands and percentages

	0–4	5–15	16–19	20–24	25–44	45–59	60–64	65–79	80 and over	All ages
Males (thousands)										
United Kingdom	1,858.0	4,352.7	1,517.9	1,803.3	9,067.7	5,453.7	1,400.5	3,124.9	720.3	29,298.9
North East	75.5	190.4	70.0	78.7	374.7	239.5	63.8	144.2	27.4	1,264.2
North West	211.6	522.8	178.5	199.5	1,026.1	639.4	166.9	361.0	77.2	3,382.9
Yorkshire and the Humber	155.8	374.1	132.0	159.0	757.2	465.2	121.2	268.4	59.9	2,492.9
East Midlands	127.5	306.5	108.3	122.1	624.2	402.6	101.5	231.6	51.6	2,075.9
West Midlands	169.5	401.2	138.7	156.5	790.6	503.8	131.2	288.7	61.8	2,642.0
East	170.3	389.3	131.4	144.1	829.2	513.2	129.8	297.4	71.2	2,675.9
London	256.3	507.2	172.3	285.2	1,293.0	580.8	143.7	303.1	74.6	3,616.3
South East	249.3	583.0	202.5	219.1	1,236.1	761.9	188.3	425.6	109.4	3,975.2
South West	141.6	346.0	122.5	132.6	706.6	468.5	122.4	298.4	79.2	2,417.7
England	1,557.4	3,620.5	1,256.2	1,496.6	7,637.7	4,575.0	1,168.8	2,618.3	612.4	24,542.9
Wales	87.8	218.0	77.6	85.9	409.0	278.8	74.3	171.6	39.0	1,441.7
Scotland	151.1	365.1	132.6	162.4	774.2	462.4	122.6	262.4	53.1	2,485.6
Northern Ireland	61.7	149.1	51.5	58.5	246.8	137.4	34.8	72.7	16.0	828.6
Females (thousands)										
United Kingdom	1,766.6	4,136.6	1,438.1	1,713.2	8,742.5	5,497.0	1,460.2	3,859.3	1,588.6	30,202.0
North East	72.0	181.1	66.4	73.0	371.5	240.9	67.9	179.6	64.7	1,317.1
North West	201.9	495.2	172.5	188.3	991.5	637.1	174.0	454.3	182.8	3,497.6
Yorkshire and the Humber	148.5	357.0	125.3	144.9	718.8	463.1	127.3	332.3	136.8	2,554.1
East Midlands	120.3	289.7	102.0	114.3	604.5	398.1	103.2	274.6	108.6	2,115.4
West Midlands	160.5	381.0	131.9	146.1	757.4	497.8	133.5	349.3	136.0	2,693.6
East	161.9	372.4	124.5	135.4	801.5	514.4	133.0	354.6	145.3	2,743.0
London	243.4	483.8	161.0	286.7	1,211.3	597.5	148.3	369.7	167.2	3,668.8
South East	237.6	550.4	189.6	213.3	1,188.8	766.5	194.6	525.5	236.2	4,102.4
South West	134.6	328.1	112.9	123.3	679.9	478.8	127.6	366.8	166.0	2,517.9
England	1,480.7	3,438.7	1,186.0	1,425.5	7,325.2	4,594.3	1,209.4	3,206.6	1,343.6	25,210.0
Wales	83.5	207.5	75.0	77.3	396.5	281.7	76.9	210.9	86.0	1,495.3
Scotland	143.7	348.4	128.0	155.4	772.7	479.8	136.2	346.0	123.3	2,633.6
Northern Ireland	58.7	142.0	49.0	55.0	248.1	141.3	37.7	95.8	35.6	863.2
All persons (percentages)										
United Kingdom	*6.1*	*14.3*	*5.0*	*5.9*	*29.9*	*18.4*	*4.8*	*11.7*	*3.9*	*100.0*
North East	*5.7*	*14.4*	*5.3*	*5.9*	*28.9*	*18.6*	*5.1*	*12.5*	*3.6*	*100.0*
North West	*6.0*	*14.8*	*5.1*	*5.6*	*29.3*	*18.6*	*5.0*	*11.8*	*3.8*	*100.0*
Yorkshire and the Humber	*6.0*	*14.5*	*5.1*	*6.0*	*29.2*	*18.4*	*4.9*	*11.9*	*3.9*	*100.0*
East Midlands	*5.9*	*14.2*	*5.0*	*5.6*	*29.3*	*19.1*	*4.9*	*12.1*	*3.8*	*100.0*
West Midlands	*6.2*	*14.7*	*5.1*	*5.7*	*29.0*	*18.8*	*5.0*	*12.0*	*3.7*	*100.0*
East	*6.1*	*14.1*	*4.7*	*5.2*	*30.1*	*19.0*	*4.8*	*12.0*	*4.0*	*100.0*
London	*6.9*	*13.6*	*4.6*	*7.9*	*34.4*	*16.2*	*4.0*	*9.2*	*3.3*	*100.0*
South East	*6.0*	*14.0*	*4.9*	*5.4*	*30.0*	*18.9*	*4.7*	*11.8*	*4.3*	*100.0*
South West	*5.6*	*13.7*	*4.8*	*5.2*	*28.1*	*19.2*	*5.1*	*13.5*	*5.0*	*100.0*
England	*6.1*	*14.2*	*4.9*	*5.9*	*30.1*	*18.4*	*4.8*	*11.7*	*3.9*	*100.0*
Wales	*5.8*	*14.5*	*5.2*	*5.6*	*27.4*	*19.1*	*5.1*	*13.0*	*4.3*	*100.0*
Scotland	*5.8*	*13.9*	*5.1*	*6.2*	*30.2*	*18.4*	*5.1*	*11.9*	*3.4*	*100.0*
Northern Ireland	*7.1*	*17.2*	*5.9*	*6.7*	*29.3*	*16.5*	*4.3*	*10.0*	*3.1*	*100.0*

1 See Notes and Definitions.

Source: Office for National Statistics; General Register Office for Scotland; Northern Ireland Statistics and Research Agency

3.3 Population density,[1] 1999

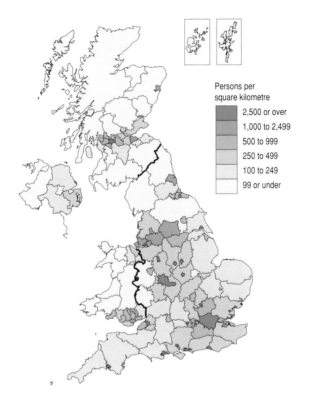

Persons per
square kilometre

- 2,500 or over
- 1,000 to 2,499
- 500 to 999
- 250 to 499
- 100 to 249
- 99 or under

1 See Notes and Definitions.

Source: Office for National Statistics; General Register Office for Scotland; Northern Ireland Statistics and Research Agency

3.4 Population under 16,[1] 1999

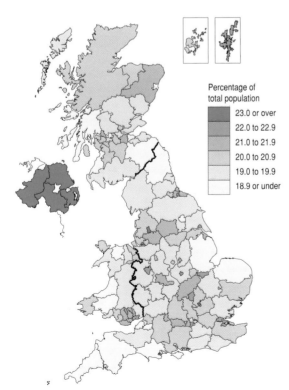

Percentage of
total population

- 23.0 or over
- 22.0 to 22.9
- 21.0 to 21.9
- 20.0 to 20.9
- 19.0 to 19.9
- 18.9 or under

1 See Notes and Definitions.

*Source: Office for National Statistics; General Register Office for
Scotland; Northern Ireland Statistics and Research Agency*

3.5 Population of retirement age,[1] 1999

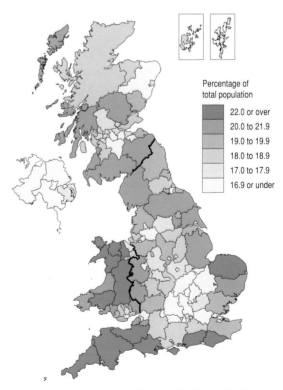

Percentage of
total population

- 22.0 or over
- 20.0 to 21.9
- 19.0 to 19.9
- 18.0 to 18.9
- 17.0 to 17.9
- 16.9 or under

1 Males aged 65 and over, females aged 60 and over. See Notes and Definitions.

*Source: Office for National Statistics; General Register Office for
Scotland; Northern Ireland Statistics and Research Agency*

3.6 Social class[1] of working age[2] population, Spring 2000

Percentages and thousands

	Social class							Total working age population (=100%) (thousands)
	Professional occupations (I)	Managerial and technical (II)	Skilled occupations non-manual (IIIN)	Skilled occupations manual (IIIM)	Partly skilled occupations (IV)	Unskilled occupations (V)	Other[3]	
United Kingdom	6.6	31.1	22.8	19.5	14.6	4.4	1.0	36,312
North East	4.6	26.3	25.0	21.5	15.8	6.0	..	1,573
North West	6.0	30.2	23.1	21.1	14.6	4.4	0.6	4,180
Yorkshire and the Humber	5.3	28.8	23.0	21.0	16.1	4.9	0.9	3,078
East Midlands	5.8	28.9	20.9	21.7	16.9	4.9	0.9	2,569
West Midlands	6.0	26.9	22.3	22.6	17.1	4.4	0.6	3,239
East	6.4	32.4	22.8	18.8	14.2	4.4	1.0	3,301
London	9.0	38.6	23.5	14.6	10.1	3.3	0.9	4,619
South East	7.9	34.1	23.5	16.8	12.8	3.8	1.1	4,907
South West	6.1	29.5	22.8	19.3	15.7	4.6	2.0	2,921
England	6.7	31.5	23.0	19.2	14.4	4.3	1.0	30,386
Wales	6.1	28.8	20.8	21.2	17.2	5.1	..	1,750
Scotland	6.4	29.2	22.3	20.8	15.3	5.1	0.9	3,160
Northern Ireland	5.6	27.7	23.9	23.9	14.0	3.6	..	1,017

1 Based on occupation. See Notes and Definitions.
2 Men aged 16–64 and women aged 16–59.
3 Includes members of the armed forces, those who did not state their social class, and those whose previous occupation was more than eight years ago, or who have never had a job.

Source: Labour Force Survey, Office for National Statistics; Department of Economic Development, Northern Ireland

3.7 Resident population:[1] by ethnic group,[2] 2000/2001[3]

Percentages and thousands

	Ethnic minority population					White population (thousands)	Total population (thousands)	Ethnic minority population as a percentage of total population
	Percentage in each group				Total (=100%) (thousands)			
	Black	Indian	Pakistani/ Bangladeshi	Mixed/ other				
Great Britain	32	24	23	21	4,039	53,004	57,057	7
North East	15	22	40	23	41	2,505	2,546	2
North West	20	22	42	16	282	6,500	6,783	4
Yorkshire and the Humber	20	13	53	14	290	4,700	4,990	6
East Midlands	25	51	12	12	204	3,951	4,156	5
West Midlands	23	36	32	9	525	4,755	5,281	10
East	29	27	20	23	216	5,155	5,372	4
London	40	21	15	24	1,982	5,177	7,165	28
South East	23	24	19	34	282	7,682	7,966	4
South West	36	21	13	31	91	4,767	4,859	2
England	32	25	23	21	3,912	45,193	49,117	8
Wales	28	18	18	37	50	2,853	2,903	2
Scotland	13	19	40	28	77	4,958	5,037	2

1 Population in private households, students in halls of residence and those in NHS accommodation. See Notes and Definitions.
2 For some ethnic origins in some regions, sample sizes are too small to provide a reliable estimate.
3 Four quarter average, Spring 2000 to Winter 2000/01.

Source: Labour Force Survey, Office for National Statistics

3.8 Population change, mid 1981-1999[1]

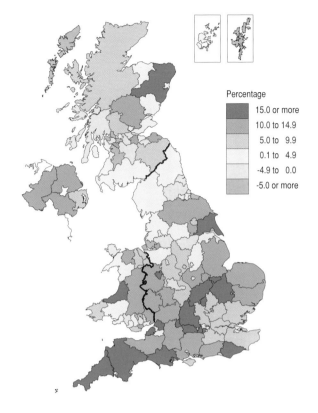

Percentage

- 15.0 or more
- 10.0 to 14.9
- 5.0 to 9.9
- 0.1 to 4.9
- -4.9 to 0.0
- -5.0 or more

1 See Notes and Definitions.

Source: Office for National Statistics; General Register Office for Scotland; Northern Ireland Statistics and Research Agency

3.9 Projected population change,[1] 1999-2011

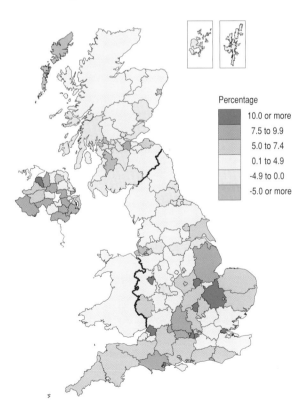

Percentage

- 10.0 or more
- 7.5 to 9.9
- 5.0 to 7.4
- 0.1 to 4.9
- -4.9 to 0.0
- -5.0 or more

1 1996-based subnational projections for England; 1998-based projections for Scotland and Wales; 1999 mid-year estimates for Northern Ireland.
See Notes and Definitions.

Source: Office for National Statistics; National Assembly for Wales; General Register Office for Scotland; Northern Ireland Statistics and Research Agency

3.10 Live births, deaths and natural change in population

Thousands and rates

	Thousands				Rates per 1,000 population			
	1981	1986	1991	1999	1981	1986	1991	1999
Live births[1]								
United Kingdom	730.8	755.0	792.5	700.2	13.0	13.3	13.7	11.8
North East	34.2	34.7	34.9	27.7	13.0	13.3	13.4	10.7
North West	90.4	93.4	97.5	79.1	13.0	13.6	14.2	11.5
Yorkshire and the Humber	62.6	65.3	68.6	58.2	12.7	13.3	13.8	11.5
East Midlands	49.2	50.3	54.0	47.0	12.8	12.8	13.4	11.2
West Midlands	67.5	70.4	74.2	63.5	13.0	13.5	14.1	11.9
East	62.6	64.4	68.4	62.7	12.9	12.8	13.3	11.6
London	92.4	97.7	105.8	105.5	13.6	14.4	15.4	14.5
South East	89.0	92.9	99.8	93.6	12.3	12.4	13.0	11.6
South West	50.4	54.5	57.6	52.1	11.5	12.0	12.2	10.6
England	598.2	623.6	660.8	589.5	12.8	13.2	13.7	11.8
Wales	35.8	37.0	38.1	32.1	12.7	13.1	13.2	10.9
Scotland	69.1	65.8	67.0	55.1	13.3	12.8	13.1	10.8
Northern Ireland	27.3	28.2	26.3	23.0	17.8	18.0	16.3	13.6
Deaths[2]								
United Kingdom	658.0	660.7	646.2	629.5	11.7	11.6	11.2	10.6
North East	32.1	32.0	31.8	29.4	12.2	12.3	12.2	11.4
North West	86.6	85.5	82.7	77.9	12.5	12.5	12.0	11.3
Yorkshire and the Humber	59.1	58.9	57.3	53.9	12.0	12.0	11.5	10.7
East Midlands	42.8	43.5	43.9	44.3	11.1	11.1	10.9	10.6
West Midlands	56.4	57.7	57.0	56.5	10.9	11.1	10.8	10.6
East	50.7	52.4	53.3	54.7	10.4	10.5	10.3	10.1
London	77.6	73.9	68.9	61.7	11.4	10.9	10.0	8.5
South East	81.3	84.2	83.0	82.6	11.2	11.2	10.8	10.2
South West	54.4	56.4	56.2	56.1	12.4	12.4	11.9	11.4
England	541.0	544.5	534.0	517.1	11.6	11.5	11.1	10.4
Wales	35.0	34.7	34.1	34.9	12.4	12.3	11.8	11.9
Scotland	63.8	63.5	61.0	60.3	12.3	12.4	12.0	11.8
Northern Ireland	16.3	16.1	15.1	15.7	10.6	10.3	9.4	9.3
Natural change								
United Kingdom	72.8	94.2	146.3	70.7	1.3	1.7	2.5	1.2
North East	2.1	2.7	3.1	-1.6	0.8	1.0	1.2	-0.7
North West	3.8	7.9	14.8	1.1	0.5	1.2	2.2	0.2
Yorkshire and the Humber	3.5	6.4	11.3	4.3	0.7	1.3	2.3	0.8
East Midlands	6.4	6.8	10.1	2.8	1.7	1.7	2.5	0.6
West Midlands	11.1	12.7	17.2	7.0	2.1	2.4	3.3	1.3
East	11.9	12.0	15.1	7.9	2.5	2.4	3.0	1.5
London	14.8	23.8	36.9	43.8	2.2	3.5	5.4	6.0
South East	7.7	8.8	16.8	11.0	1.1	1.2	2.2	1.4
South West	-4.0	-1.9	1.4	-4.0	-0.9	-0.4	0.3	-0.8
England	57.2	79.1	126.8	72.3	1.2	1.7	2.6	1.4
Wales	0.8	2.3	4.0	-2.8	0.3	0.8	1.4	-1.0
Scotland	5.3	2.3	6.0	-5.1	1.0	0.5	1.1	-1.0
Northern Ireland	10.9	11.9	10.9	7.3	6.5	7.2	6.6	4.3

1 Based on the usual area of residence of the mother. See Notes and Definitions for details of the inclusion or exclusion of births to non-resident mothers in the individual
  countries and regions of England. The United Kingdom figures have been calculated on all births registered in the United Kingdom, including births to mothers usually resident
  outside the United Kingdom. Data relate to year of occurrence in England and Wales, and year of registration in Scotland and Northern Ireland.
2 Based on the usual area of residence of the deceased. See Notes and Definitions for details of the inclusion or exclusion of deaths of non-resident persons in the individual
  countries and regions of England. The figures for the United Kingdom have been calculated on all deaths registered in the United Kingdom in 1999, including deaths of persons
  usually resident outside the United Kingdom.

Source: Office for National Statistics; General Register Office for Scotland; Northern Ireland Statistics and Research Agency

3.11 Components of population change, mid-1998 to mid-1999[1]

Thousands

	Resident population mid-1998	Births	Deaths	Net natural change	Net migration and other changes	Total change	Resident population mid-1999
United Kingdom	59,236.5	710.8	634.8	76.0	188.4	264.4	59,500.9
North East	2,589.6	28.1	29.9	-1.7	-6.5	-8.3	2,581.3
North West	6,890.8	80.7	80.0	0.8	-11.0	-10.3	6,880.5
Yorkshire and the Humber	5,042.9	59.2	55.4	3.8	0.3	4.1	5,047.0
East Midlands	4,169.3	48.3	44.9	3.4	18.5	21.9	4,191.2
West Midlands	5,332.5	64.5	56.8	7.7	-4.6	3.1	5,335.6
East	5,377.0	63.5	55.6	8.0	33.9	41.9	5,418.9
London	7,187.2	105.4	62.6	42.8	55.0	97.8	7,285.0
South East	8,003.8	95.1	82.8	12.2	61.5	73.7	8,077.6
South West	4,901.3	53.1	56.2	-3.1	37.4	34.3	4,935.7
England	49,494.6	597.8	524.1	73.8	184.6	258.3	49,752.9
Wales	2,933.3	32.9	34.9	-2.0	5.7	3.7	2,937.0
Scotland	5,120.0	56.6	60.3	-3.7	2.9	-0.8	5,119.2
Northern Ireland	1,688.6	23.4	15.5	7.9	-4.7	3.2	1,691.8

1 See Notes and Definitions.

Source: Office for National Statistics; General Register Office for Scotland; Northern Ireland Statistics and Research Agency

3.12 Conceptions[1] to women aged under 18:[2] by outcome

	1994				1999			
	Percentage of conceptions:				Percentage of conceptions:			
	Leading to maternities	Leading to abortions	Total (thousands)	Rate per 1,000 population[3]	Leading to maternities	Leading to abortions	Total (thousands)	Rate per 1,000 population[3]
England and Wales	60.2	39.8	36,091	42.0	56.9	43.1	42,005	45.0
North East	69.1	30.9	2,411	53.6	63.1	36.9	2,666	55.0
North West	64.7	35.3	5,599	47.5	60.1	39.9	6,288	48.6
Yorkshire and the Humber	65.8	34.2	4,180	50.0	60.9	39.1	4,616	50.9
East Midlands	60.3	39.7	2,913	42.0	59.8	40.2	3,215	43.2
West Midlands	60.4	39.6	4,252	47.0	59.3	40.7	4,835	49.2
East	57.4	42.6	2,780	31.2	54.0	46.0	3,420	36.4
London	50.3	49.7	4,850	46.0	46.6	53.4	5,960	51.1
South East	56.2	43.8	4,114	31.4	54.4	45.6	5,056	35.8
South West	55.9	44.1	2,695	34.2	53.9	46.1	3,169	37.1
England	59.8	40.2	33,794	41.7	56.5	43.5	39,225	44.7
Wales	66.6	33.4	2,297	46.5	63.8	36.2	2,780	50.8

1 Conception statistics are derived from numbers of registered births and registered abortions. They do not include spontaneous miscarriages and illegal abortions. See Notes and Definitions.
2 Based on place of usual residence. Information about usual residence of women undergoing abortions is known to be not wholly accurate. Some women living outside London and other big cities may have given a temporary address in the city as their usual place of residence.
3 The rates for girls aged less than 18 are based on the population of girls aged 15 to 17.

Source: Office for National Statistics

3.13 Age specific birth rates[1]

	Less than 20	20–24	25–29	30–34	35–39	40 and over	All ages	TFR[3]
	Live births per 1,000 women in age groups[2]							
1981								
United Kingdom	28	107	130	70	22	5	62	1.81
North East	34	114	128	60	18	4	62	1.79
North West	35	114	130	65	21	5	63	1.85
Yorkshire and the Humber	31	117	128	59	18	6	62	1.80
East Midlands	30	113	127	63	19	4	61	1.79
West Midlands	32	108	133	69	20	7	62	1.84
East	22	110	138	70	20	4	61	1.82
London	29	83	114	80	31	6	62	1.71
South East	20	97	138	73	23	4	59	1.77
South West	24	103	131	63	18	3	57	1.71
England	28	104	129	69	22	5	61	1.78
Wales	30	121	127	67	21	6	63	1.86
Scotland	31	112	131	66	21	4	63	1.84
Northern Ireland	27	135	172	117	52	13	86	2.59
1991								
United Kingdom	33	89	120	87	32	5	64	1.82
North East	44	102	119	72	23	4	63	1.82
North West	42	101	124	84	29	5	67	1.93
Yorkshire and the Humber	41	99	122	78	26	4	64	1.85
East Midlands	34	95	126	81	26	4	63	1.83
West Midlands	39	102	126	84	31	5	67	1.93
East	24	86	129	91	31	5	62	1.83
London	29	69	97	96	47	10	64	1.74
South East	23	78	122	95	35	5	61	1.80
South West	25	84	125	86	30	5	60	1.77
England	33	89	119	87	32	5	64	1.81
Wales	39	103	127	77	27	5	64	1.88
Scotland	33	82	117	78	27	4	60	1.69
Northern Ireland	29	97	146	105	46	10	75	2.16
1999								
United Kingdom	31	72	99	89	40	8	57	1.69
North East	39	81	98	73	29	5	53	1.62
North West	35	84	100	83	34	6	57	1.71
Yorkshire and the Humber	37	84	109	80	32	6	57	1.74
East Midlands	32	76	102	84	34	6	56	1.67
West Midlands	34	89	108	84	36	7	59	1.79
East	25	74	93	93	42	8	57	1.67
London	28	57	96	102	53	13	62	1.75
South East	24	64	92	97	47	9	57	1.67
South West	25	69	100	90	39	8	55	1.65
England	30	73	99	90	40	8	58	1.69
Wales	37	85	106	81	32	7	57	1.74
Scotland	30	61	90	81	34	6	51	1.51
Northern Ireland	29	71	112	105	46	9	63	1.85

1 Based on the usual area of residence of the mother. See Notes and Definitions for details of the inclusion or exclusion of births to non-resident mothers in the individual countries and regions of England. The United Kingdom figures have been calculated on all births registered in the United Kingdom, i.e. including births to mothers usually resident outside the United Kingdom. Data relate to year of occurrence in England and Wales, and year of registration in Scotland and Northern Ireland.
2 The rates for women aged less than 20, 40 and over and all ages are based upon the population of women aged 15–19, 40–44 and 15–44 respectively. See Notes and Definitions.
3 The Total Fertility Rate (TFR) is the average number of children which would be born to a women if the current pattern of fertility persisted throughout her child-bearing years. Previously known as Total Period Fertility. See Notes and Definitions.

Source: Office for National Statistics; General Register Office for Scotland; Northern Ireland Statistics and Research Agency

3.14 Age specific death rates: by gender, 1999[1]

Rates and Standardised Mortality Ratios

	Under 1[3]	1–4	5–15	16–24	25–34	35–44	45–54	55–64	65–74	75–84	85 and over	SMR[2] (UK = 100)
Males												
United Kingdom	6.5	0.3	0.2	0.8	1.0	1.6	4.1	11.2	32.1	80.7	188.7	100
North East	6.3	0.3	0.2	0.7	1.0	1.6	4.4	13.8	35.8	87.4	196.7	110
North West	7.7	0.3	0.2	0.8	1.2	1.8	4.7	12.8	36.0	86.4	190.8	109
Yorkshire and the Humber	6.8	0.4	0.2	0.8	1.1	1.5	4.1	11.4	33.0	82.5	181.2	101
East Midlands	6.2	0.3	0.2	0.7	1.0	1.4	3.8	10.6	32.4	79.7	194.8	99
West Midlands	8.5	0.2	0.1	0.7	0.9	1.7	4.3	11.0	32.5	83.0	197.8	102
East	5.2	0.3	0.1	0.6	0.7	1.2	3.3	9.0	28.2	76.4	190.0	91
London	6.4	0.3	0.1	0.5	0.9	1.5	4.1	11.3	31.5	78.2	166.7	96
South East	5.4	0.2	0.1	0.7	0.8	1.3	3.3	9.0	27.3	74.6	188.4	90
South West	4.6	0.3	0.1	0.7	0.9	1.3	3.3	9.0	27.4	72.2	181.6	88
England	6.4	0.3	0.2	0.7	0.9	1.5	3.9	10.7	31.2	79.3	186.3	97
Wales	7.2	0.4	0.2	0.9	1.2	1.6	4.0	12.0	34.4	83.3	188.5	104
Scotland	5.6	0.2	0.2	1.1	1.4	2.1	5.5	14.6	38.3	90.9	211.1	119
Northern Ireland	6.8	0.4	0.2	1.0	0.9	1.6	4.2	11.5	34.4	85.7	209.8	107
Females												
United Kingdom	5.1	0.2	0.1	0.3	0.4	1.0	2.7	6.9	19.7	54.0	156.1	100
North East	4.7	0.3	0.2	0.3	0.4	1.0	3.0	7.9	23.6	60.3	158.9	110
North West	5.5	0.3	0.2	0.3	0.5	1.2	3.1	7.9	22.4	58.0	159.0	107
Yorkshire and the Humber	5.5	0.3	0.1	0.4	0.4	1.0	2.5	6.7	20.0	54.8	150.8	99
East Midlands	6.1	0.2	0.1	0.3	0.5	1.0	2.7	6.5	18.9	53.1	157.2	99
West Midlands	5.3	0.3	0.1	0.3	0.5	1.0	2.8	6.9	19.9	54.8	157.4	101
East	4.0	0.2	0.1	0.3	0.3	0.9	2.3	5.8	17.0	51.0	159.0	95
London	5.6	0.2	0.1	0.2	0.5	1.0	2.5	6.6	19.3	51.5	138.4	93
South East	4.1	0.2	0.1	0.3	0.4	0.9	2.3	5.9	17.0	49.7	154.6	93
South West	4.6	0.2	0.1	0.3	0.4	0.8	2.1	5.8	16.1	48.0	151.1	91
England	5.0	0.2	0.1	0.3	0.4	1.0	2.6	6.6	19.1	52.9	153.4	98
Wales	5.7	0.3	0.1	0.3	0.5	1.2	2.7	7.2	20.8	56.1	158.2	103
Scotland	4.3	0.2	0.1	0.4	0.5	1.2	3.3	8.7	23.8	61.7	181.6	117
Northern Ireland	5.9	0.2	0.2	0.4	0.4	1.0	2.7	7.2	19.2	59.3	168.7	106
All persons												
United Kingdom	5.8	0.3	0.1	0.5	0.7	1.3	3.4	9.0	25.5	64.4	164.9	100
North East	5.5	0.3	0.2	0.5	0.7	1.3	3.7	10.8	29.2	70.8	168.2	110
North West	6.6	0.3	0.2	0.6	0.9	1.5	3.9	10.3	28.6	68.8	167.0	108
Yorkshire and the Humber	6.2	0.3	0.2	0.6	0.8	1.2	3.3	9.0	26.0	65.6	158.7	100
East Midlands	6.1	0.3	0.1	0.5	0.7	1.2	3.2	8.5	25.2	63.9	167.4	99
West Midlands	6.9	0.3	0.1	0.5	0.7	1.3	3.5	8.9	25.8	65.7	168.1	102
East	4.6	0.2	0.1	0.5	0.5	1.0	2.8	7.4	22.3	61.2	167.9	93
London	6.0	0.3	0.1	0.4	0.7	1.3	3.3	8.9	25.0	61.9	146.0	95
South East	4.8	0.2	0.1	0.5	0.6	1.1	2.8	7.4	21.8	59.4	163.9	92
South West	4.6	0.3	0.1	0.5	0.7	1.1	2.7	7.4	21.4	57.6	159.6	90
England	5.7	0.3	0.1	0.5	0.7	1.2	3.2	8.6	24.7	63.2	162.3	98
Wales	6.4	0.3	0.1	0.6	0.9	1.4	3.4	9.5	27.1	66.7	166.2	104
Scotland	5.0	0.2	0.2	0.8	0.9	1.6	4.4	11.5	30.3	72.6	189.4	118
Northern Ireland	6.4	0.3	0.2	0.7	0.7	1.3	3.4	9.3	25.9	69.3	179.4	100

1 Based on the usual area of residence of the deceased. See Notes and Definitions for details of the inclusion or exclusion of deaths of non-resident persons in the individual countries and regions of England. The UK figures have been calculated on all deaths registered in the UK in 1999, i.e. including deaths of persons usually resident outside the UK.
2 Standardised Mortality Ratio (SMR) is the ratio of observed deaths to those expected by applying a standard death rate to the regional population. See Notes and Definitions.
3 Deaths of infants less than 1 year of age per 1,000 live births.

Source: Office for National Statistics; General Register Office for Scotland; Northern Ireland Statistics and Research Agency

3.15 Migration

Thousands

	Inter-regional migration[1]				International migration[2,3]			
	1991	1996	1998	1999	1991	1996	1998	1999
Inflow								
United Kingdom					337	331	402	450
North East	40	39	39	39	7	3	7	7
North West	96	105	104	105	18	19	27	30
Yorkshire and the Humber	85	91	93	95	22	15	16	19
East Midlands	90	102	108	111	14	15	15	13
West Midlands	83	91	93	94	16	27	18	15
East	122	139	143	148	29	27	29	29
London	149	168	174	163	111	122	167	197
South East	198	228	226	229	54	48	64	74
South West	121	139	139	143	21	19	20	21
England	96	111	111	112	293	296	363	405
Wales	51	55	56	58	9	8	8	9
Scotland	56	47	53	51	31	25	30	33
Northern Ireland	12	11	12	12	4	3	2	3
Outflow								
United Kingdom					264	238	224	269
North East	41	45	44	44	4	4	4	5
North West	105	114	116	115	21	20	16	24
Yorkshire and the Humber	85	98	98	97	15	10	11	14
East Midlands	81	94	97	96	8	10	9	16
West Midlands	88	101	101	102	20	19	11	17
East	113	121	125	126	23	14	19	21
London	202	213	218	228	77	63	75	92
South East	185	199	209	209	40	53	32	43
South West	99	110	111	111	21	15	16	15
England	112	105	111	112	227	207	192	246
Wales	47	53	54	53	7	7	5	4
Scotland	47	54	54	55	25	21	21	13
Northern Ireland	9	12	12	12	5	4	7	5
Net								
United Kingdom					73	93	178	182
North East	-1	-6	-5	-5	3	-1	3	2
North West	-9	-9	-12	-9	-3	-1	11	5
Yorkshire and the Humber	0	-7	-5	-2	8	5	5	4
East Midlands	8	8	11	15	6	5	6	-3
West Midlands	-5	-10	-7	-8	-3	8	7	-2
East	9	18	18	23	6	13	10	8
London	-53	-45	-44	-65	34	60	93	106
South East	13	29	17	20	14	-4	32	31
South West	22	29	28	33	1	4	4	6
England	-16	6	0	0	66	89	171	159
Wales	4	2	2	5	2	1	3	5
Scotland	9	-7	-1	-4	6	4	9	20
Northern Ireland	3	0	-1	-1	-1	-1	-5	-2

1 Based on patients re-registering with NHS doctors in other parts of the United Kingdom. See Notes and Definitions. Figures have been adjusted for minor changes caused by database realignment during Health Authority reorganisation

2 Subject to relatively large sampling errors where estimates are based on small numbers of contacts. See Notes and Definitions.

3 The figures in this table combine migration data from three sources to provide Total International Migration. See Notes and Definitions.

Source: National Health Service Central Register and International Passenger Survey, Office for National Statistics; General Register Office for Scotland; Northern Ireland Statistics and Research Agency

3.16 Inter-regional movements,[1] 1999

Thousands

Region of destination	Region of origin												
	United Kingdom	North East	North West	Yorkshire and the Humber	East Midlands	West Midlands	East	London	South East	South West	Wales	Scotland	Northern Ireland
United Kingdom	.	44	115	97	96	102	126	228	209	111	53	55	12
North East	39	.	6	8	3	2	3	4	4	2	1	4	1
North West	105	7	.	18	10	13	7	11	12	8	9	8	2
Yorkshire and the Humber	95	10	19	.	16	8	8	8	11	6	3	5	1
East Midlands	111	4	11	18	.	16	17	11	18	8	3	4	1
West Midlands	94	3	13	8	14	.	8	10	14	13	8	3	1
East	148	3	8	8	14	8	.	59	29	10	3	5	1
London	163	5	13	10	10	11	29	.	54	16	5	8	2
South East	229	5	14	11	14	14	30	88	.	34	8	8	1
South West	143	2	10	7	9	17	14	22	47	.	10	5	1
Wales	58	1	12	3	3	10	4	6	9	9	.	2	-
Scotland	51	4	8	5	3	3	5	7	8	4	2	.	2
Northern Ireland	12	-	2	1	1	1	1	2	1	1	-	2	.

1 Based on patients re-registering with NHS doctors in other parts of the United Kingdom. See Notes and Definitions. Figures have been adjusted for minor changes caused by database realignment during Health Authority organisation.

Source: Office for National Statistics; General Register Office for Scotland; Northern Ireland Statistics and Research Agency

3.17 Marriages[1,2]

Thousands

	1976	1986	1999
United Kingdom	406.0	393.9	301.1
North East	20.1	17.6	11.5
North West	50.3	46.3	31.6
Yorkshire and the Humber	36.3	35.2	23.9
East Midlands	26.7	27.4	20.6
West Midlands	36.6	35.2	25.3
East	32.2	34.7	27.4
London	58.4	47.5	38.9
South East	48.5	52.0	43.3
South West	30.1	32.5	27.0
England	339.0	328.4	249.5
Wales	19.5	19.5	14.0
Scotland	37.5	35.8	29.9
Northern Ireland	9.9	10.2	7.6

1 Marriages solemnised outside the United Kingdom are not included.
2 Region of occurrence of marriage.

Source: Office for National Statistics; General Register Office for Scotland; Northern Ireland Statistics and Research Agency

3.18 Cohabitation among non-married people aged 16–59, 1996–99[1]

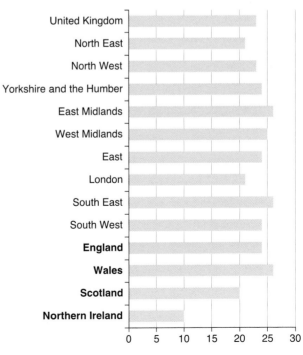

1 Combined data from the 1996–97 and 1998–99 surveys.

Source: General Household Survey, Office for National Statistics; Continuous Household Survey, Northern Ireland Statistics and Research Agency

3.19 Household numbers and projections[1]

Millions

	Household numbers			Household projections				
	1981	1991	1999	2001[1]	2006[1]	2011[1]	2016[1]	2021[1]
Great Britain	19.16	21.27	24.12	23.22	24.05	24.93	..	..
North East	0.98	1.05	1.09	1.10	1.12	1.14	1.15	1.17
North West	2.55	2.72	2.85	2.88	2.93	3.00	3.06	3.11
Yorkshire and the Humber	1.83	1.99	2.11	2.14	2.20	2.26	2.32	2.37
East Midlands	1.41	1.60	1.73	1.76	1.83	1.90	1.97	2.03
West Midlands	1.86	2.04	2.17	2.19	2.24	2.30	2.35	2.40
East	1.76	2.04	2.25	2.28	2.39	2.49	2.60	2.70
London	2.64	2.84	3.12	3.13	3.25	3.38	3.52	3.65
South East	2.64	3.04	3.35	3.40	3.57	3.74	3.91	4.06
South West	1.64	1.90	2.08	2.12	2.21	2.32	2.42	2.52
England	17.31	19.21	20.74	20.99	21.73	22.52	23.31	24.00
Wales	1.02	1.13	1.19	1.20	1.24	1.27	1.31	1.34
Scotland	1.85	2.05	2.19	2.22	2.32	2.41	..	..

1 1996-based projections. See Notes and Definitions.

Source: Department of Transport, Local Government and the Regions; National Assembly for Wales; Scottish Executive

3.20 Households: by type, Spring 2000

Percentages and thousands

	Types of households (percentages)								Total house-holds (=100%) (thou-sands)
			Married couple			Lone parent			
	One person	Two or more un-related adults	With dependent children	With non-dependent children only	With no children	With dependent children	With non-dependent children only	Two or more families[1]	
United Kingdom	28.5	3.1	23.3	6.6	28.5	6.3	3.0	0.8	24,554
North East	29.0	2.2	23.5	6.2	27.5	7.9	3.2	..	1,083
North West	27.6	2.2	23.6	7.2	28.3	7.6	3.1	0.6	2,820
Yorkshire and the Humber	29.1	2.8	22.7	6.4	29.2	6.3	2.9	0.8	2,116
East Midlands	26.7	2.7	23.3	6.9	31.8	5.0	2.9	0.7	1,745
West Midlands	27.3	2.8	23.8	7.1	28.7	6.1	3.2	1.0	2,172
East	26.9	2.4	23.7	6.5	32.0	5.1	2.7	0.6	2,257
London	30.9	6.5	22.5	5.2	22.0	8.1	3.2	1.7	2,925
South East	26.7	2.7	24.7	6.3	31.5	4.8	2.7	0.7	3,302
South West	28.5	2.6	23.5	5.9	31.6	4.7	2.5	0.8	2,051
England	28.1	3.1	23.5	6.4	29.0	6.2	2.9	0.9	20,471
Wales	29.7	2.4	22.6	6.7	27.6	7.7	2.7	..	1,233
Scotland	32.4	3.1	20.7	7.3	26.4	6.4	3.2	0.5	2,228
Northern Ireland	26.1	2.3	26.6	9.6	21.6	8.2	4.4	..	623

1 For some regions, sample sizes are too small to provide reliable estimates.

Source: Labour Force Survey Household Datasets, Office for National Statistics; Department of Economic Development, Northern Ireland

4 Education and Training

Teachers

Primary school pupil – teacher ratios in 2000/01 ranged from 19.0 in Scotland to 23.5 in the East Midlands

(Table 4.1)

Nearly half of new female entrants to teaching in the United Kingdom in 1998/99 were aged under 25 compared with less than a third of new male entrants.

(Table 4.4)

Under fives

In January 2001, 99 per cent of three and four year olds in the East Midlands and the South West regions enrolled in education compared with 88 per cent in London, the highest and lowest proportions in England respectively.

(Table 4.2)

Class sizes

Around 36 per cent of primary school Key Stage 2 classes in the North West and the South West contained 31 or more pupils in 2000/2001, compared with just over 10 per cent in Northern Ireland.

(Table 4.3)

Examination results

In 1999/00, just over two-fifths of pupils in the North East and Yorkshire and the Humber achieved 5 or more GCSE grades A* to C. In Scotland nearly three-fifths of pupils achieved the equivalent at Standard Grade.

(Table 4.5)

The proportion of pupils who achieved no graded GCSE's or Standard Grades in 1999/00 was lowest in Northern Ireland at 3.6 per cent and highest in Wales at 7.7 per cent.

(Table 4.5)

In 1999/00 almost two-fifths of pupils in Northern Ireland achieved 2 or more A levels compared with just over a fifth in the North East, the highest and lowest proportions in the United Kingdom respectively.

(Table 4.5)

Key Stages

72 per cent of pupils in Northern Ireland reached or exceeded the expected standards in Key Stage 3 Mathematics in Summer 2000, compared with 61 per cent in London.

(Table 4.7)

Post-compulsory education

In 1998/99, Wales had the largest proportion of 16-year-olds in full-time education or on a government-supported training scheme, 92.5 per cent, compared with 81.2 per cent in the North East.

(Table 4.8)

Further education

Around a quarter of further education students from the North East were studying courses leading to Level 1 NVQ/GNVQ qualifications in 2000/01, compared with around 17 per cent of students from the South East, East of England and South West regions.

(Table 4.9)

Higher education

Higher education students whose home was in the East of England were the least likely to be studying within their own region in 2000/01, while those from Scotland were the most likely.

(Table 4.10)

| Graduates | Of those graduating in 2000, 6.5 per cent of first degree graduates who had studied in Wales were believed to be unemployed 6 months after graduating, compared to 4.0 per cent of those who had studied in the East of England. |

(Table 4.11)

| Qualifications | In Spring 2001 a quarter of people of working age in London were qualified to degree level or equivalent, compared with around one in seven in the United Kingdom overall. |

(Table 4.12)

| National Learning Targets | In Spring 2001, 37 per cent of adults living in London had an NVQ level 4 qualification (degree level), exceeding the National Learning Target for England by 9 percentage points. |

(Table 4.13)

| Training | Among female employees of working age, those in the West Midlands were the most likely to have received job-related training in Spring 2001. |

(Table 4.14)

In Spring 2001, male employees of working age in the East of England were the most likely to have received on-the-job training.

(Table 4.14)

In the East of England, South East and South West regions more than three quarters of leavers from Work-Based Training for Young People were in employment six months later, higher than any other region in England, Wales and Northern Ireland.

(Table 4.15)

4.1 Pupils and teachers: by type of school, 2000/01[1]

Thousands and numbers

	Public sector schools				Non-maintained schools[3]	All special schools	All schools
	Nursery schools	Primary schools[2]	Secondary schools	Pupil Referral Units			
Pupils[4] (thousands)							
United Kingdom	74.3	5,135.7	3,913.9	..	610.3	112.2	9,856.2
North East	2.5	222.5	181.7	0.5	15.8	6.1	429.1
North West	4.7	635.4	462.0	1.4	55.9	15.4	1,174.9
Yorkshire and the Humber	2.2	458.0	339.4	1.1	33.1	8.2	841.9
East Midlands	1.6	364.4	289.9	0.5	34.9	5.9	697.2
West Midlands	3.7	483.1	369.8	0.9	44.7	12.6	914.9
East	2.3	444.4	372.8	0.8	61.0	8.9	890.3
London	5.5	612.5	407.3	2.1	123.5	12.4	1,163.4
South East	2.6	638.6	494.2	1.3	142.1	17.0	1,295.8
South West	1.3	393.1	314.7	0.6	60.5	7.7	777.9
England	26.5	4,251.9	3,231.8	9.3	571.6	94.4	8,185.6
Wales	1.6	274.3	210.4	0.4	9.4	3.8	499.8
Scotland	41.9	425.2	317.7	.	28.0	9.4	822.2
Northern Ireland	4.2	184.4	153.9	.	1.3	4.7	348.6
Teachers[4] (thousands)							
United Kingdom	3.1	230.0	236.7	..	62.4	18.2	552.6
North East	0.1	9.8	10.7	0.1	1.4	0.9	23.0
North West	0.3	27.7	27.8	0.2	5.2	2.4	63.7
Yorkshire and the Humber	0.1	19.8	19.6	0.2	3.0	1.3	44.1
East Midlands	0.1	15.5	16.7	0.1	3.5	1.0	36.9
West Midlands	0.2	21.0	21.7	0.3	4.5	1.8	49.4
East	0.1	19.5	21.4	0.3	6.6	1.3	49.2
London	0.3	27.2	24.6	0.5	11.9	2.1	66.6
South East	0.2	27.9	28.5	0.3	15.9	2.6	75.4
South West	0.1	17.1	18.0	0.1	6.7	1.2	43.3
England	1.5	185.5	189.0	2.1	58.8	14.7	451.5
Wales	0.1	12.8	12.7	..	1.0	0.6	27.1
Scotland	1.3	22.4	24.5	.	2.5	2.3	53.1
Northern Ireland	0.2	9.3	10.5	.	0.1	0.7	20.9
Pupils per teacher[4] (numbers)							
United Kingdom	23.9	22.3	16.5	..	9.8	6.2	17.9
North East	19.9	22.6	17.0	4.4	11.4	6.9	18.7
North West	18.1	22.9	16.6	6.8	10.7	6.3	18.4
Yorkshire and the Humber	16.8	23.1	17.3	5.5	10.9	6.2	19.1
East Midlands	16.7	23.5	17.3	4.1	10.0	6.1	18.9
West Midlands	21.3	23.1	17.1	3.4	9.9	6.9	18.5
East	17.0	22.8	17.4	2.8	9.3	6.9	18.1
London	16.4	22.5	16.6	4.7	10.4	5.9	17.5
South East	15.9	22.9	17.4	3.9	8.9	6.5	17.2
South West	17.4	23.0	17.5	4.6	9.0	6.3	18.0
England	17.6	22.9	17.1	4.4	9.7	6.4	18.1
Wales[5]	17.2	21.5	16.6	..	9.6	6.8	18.4
Scotland	31.3	19.0	13.0	.	11.0	4.1	15.5
Northern Ireland	23.7	19.9	14.6	.	10.0	6.4	16.7

1 See Notes and Definitions. Provisional. Data for Northern Ireland and nursery schools in Scotland refer to 1999/00.
2 For Northern Ireland, figures include pupils and teachers in the preparatory departments of grammar schools.
3 Excluding special schools.
4 Full-time equivalents.
5 Pupils per teacher data for all schools excludes Pupil Referral Units as information on teachers is not collected for Wales.

Source: Department for Education and Skills; National Assembly for Wales; Scottish Executive; Northern Ireland Department of Education

4.2 Three and four year olds[1,2,3] by type of early years education provider[4]

Thousands and percentages

| | January 2000 | | | | | | January 2001[5] | | | | | |
| | | Participation rates[6] (percentages) | | | | | | Participation rates[6] (percentages) | | | | |
	Three and four year olds in early years education (thousands)	Maintained nursery and primary schools	Independent and special schools	All schools	Private and voluntary providers[7]	All providers	Three and four year olds in early years education (thousands)	Maintained nursery & primary schools	Independent and special schools	All schools	Private and voluntary providers[7]	All providers
United Kingdom	1,310.1	59	4	63	27	90	1,330.4	59	4	63	28	91
North East	57.5	84	2	86	9	95	58.2	85	2	86	12	98
North West	158.4	67	3	71	24	95	162.2	67	3	70	27	98
Yorkshire and the Humber	116.0	71	3	73	20	94	118.2	70	3	73	23	97
East Midlands	95.2	59	3	63	32	95	97.4	60	4	64	35	99
West Midlands	121.8	66	4	70	22	91	123.5	66	4	70	23	93
East	121.8	49	5	54	37	91	124.5	50	5	55	39	93
London	170.9	62	7	69	18	87	175.1	62	7	69	19	88
South East	184.6	39	8	47	47	94	186.7	39	8	47	48	96
South West	111.4	44	5	49	51	100	110.4	44	5	49	50	99
England	1,137.7	58	5	63	30	93	1,156.1	58	5	63	32	95
Wales	55.4	79	1	80	..	..	55.4	79	1	80	..	..
Scotland	89.2	56	-	56	18	74	89.2	56	-	56	18	74
Northern Ireland	27.8	50	1	50	7	57	29.7	52	1	53	8	61

1 Headcounts of children aged three and four at 31 December in the previous calendar year.
2 Numbers of three and four year olds in schools may include some two year olds.
3 Any child attending more than one provider in England may have been counted twice.
4 These figures must be interpreted carefully in the light of differing types of education providers between the countries.
5 Provisional. Data for Wales and Scotland relate to January 2000.
6 Number of three and four year olds attending provider expressed as a percentage of the three and four year old population.
7 Includes some Local Authority providers (other than schools) registered to receive nursery education grants.

Source: Department for Education and Skills; National Assembly for Wales; Scottish Executive; Northern Ireland Department of Education

4.3 Class sizes for all classes,[1] 2000/01

Numbers and percentages

| | Primary schools | | | | | | Secondary schools | |
| | Key Stage 1[2] | | Key Stage 2[2] | | All Primary schools | | | |
	Average number in class	Percentage of classes with 31 or more pupils	Average number in class	Percentage of classes with 31 or more pupils	Average number in class	Percentage of classes with 31 or more pupils	Average number in class	Percentage of classes with 31 or more pupils
Great Britain	25.0	3.7	27.5	28.0	26.5	17.3	22.1	..
North East	24.5	1.8	27.2	25.6	25.9	15.2	22.2	7.4
North West	25.0	3.4	28.3	36.7	26.8	21.7	22.1	8.9
Yorkshire and the Humber	25.1	3.9	28.0	30.4	26.8	19.5	22.3	8.6
East Midlands	24.8	2.8	28.3	34.3	26.8	20.6	22.2	8.4
West Midlands	25.1	3.6	27.8	29.0	26.5	17.6	22.1	9.2
East	25.2	3.3	27.8	28.5	26.5	16.6	21.9	7.7
London	26.8	3.8	27.7	18.2	27.2	12.2	22.2	6.4
South East	25.8	4.0	28.2	30.8	27.0	18.8	22.0	7.7
South West	25.4	3.0	28.3	35.8	26.8	20.4	22.3	10.4
England	25.4	3.4	28.0	29.9	26.8	18.1	22.1	8.3
Wales	24.1	4.7	26.7	23.6	25.4	14.9	21.3	..
Scotland	22.4	5.1	23.9	14.8	24.3	11.1	..	..
Northern Ireland[3]	23.1	2.6	24.6	10.4	23.7	5.8	..	..

1 Maintained schools only. Figures relate to all classes – not just those taught by one teacher. Primary figures for Scotland include composite classes covering more than one year group. In Northern Ireland a class is defined as a group of pupils normally under the control of one teacher. See Notes and Definitions.
2 In Scotland primary P1-P3 is interpreted to be Key Stage 1 and P4-P7, Key Stage 2. See Notes and Definitions.
3 Pupils in composite classes which overlap Key Stage 1 and Key Stage 2 are included in the 'All Primary Schools' total, but are excluded from all other categories.

Source: Department for Education and Skills; National Assembly for Wales; Scottish Executive; Northern Ireland Department of Education

4.4 New entrants to teaching:[1] by age and gender, March 1999[2,3]

Percentages and numbers

	Percentages							Total (=100%) (thousands)
	Under 25	25–29	30–34	35–39	40–49	50–59	60 and over	
Males								
United Kingdom	32	35	15	9	8	1	-	5.4
North East	33	33	17	13	8	-	-	0.2
North West	35	35	15	8	7	2	-	0.6
Yorkshire and Humber	33	30	18	10	8	-	-	0.4
East Midlands	36	33	14	11	8	-	-	0.4
West Midlands	36	32	14	7	9	-	-	0.6
East	34	36	13	7	9	2	-	0.6
London	23	41	18	11	8	1	-	0.8
South East	37	35	14	7	7	1	-	0.8
South West	31	33	15	10	13	3	-	0.4
England	32	35	15	9	8	1	-	4.7
Wales	40	33	13	7	7	-	-	0.3
England and Wales	33	35	15	9	8	1	-	5.0
Scotland[2]	20	29	18	18	12	2	-	0.2
Northern Ireland[3]	14	51	14	7	10	3	-	0.2
Females								
United Kingdom	47	28	8	7	8	1	-	16.6
North East	51	22	8	11	6	-	-	0.7
North West	51	26	9	7	6	1	-	1.7
Yorkshire and Humber	50	27	10	7	6	-	-	1.2
East Midlands	55	25	7	7	7	-	-	1.2
West Midlands	51	26	8	8	6	1	-	1.6
East	51	25	7	8	9	1	-	1.6
London	41	34	10	7	7	1	-	2.7
South East	50	26	7	7	9	-	-	2.5
South West	47	28	9	7	8	1	-	1.2
England	49	27	8	7	7	1	-	14.3
Wales	56	27	6	6	4	-	-	0.8
England and Wales	49	27	8	7	7	1	-	15.1
Scotland[2]	33	26	9	9	19	3	-	0.9
Northern Ireland[3]	18	54	10	6	9	2	-	0.6
All persons								
United Kingdom	44	30	10	8	8	1	-	22.0
North East	47	24	11	11	6	1	-	1.0
North West	47	28	11	8	6	-	-	2.3
Yorkshire and Humber	46	28	12	7	7	1	-	1.6
East Midlands	50	26	8	8	7	-	-	1.5
West Midlands	47	28	9	8	7	-	-	2.1
East	47	27	8	7	9	1	-	2.2
London	37	35	12	8	7	1	-	3.5
South East	47	28	9	8	8	1	-	3.3
South West	43	29	10	7	9	1	-	1.6
England	45	29	10	8	7	1	-	19.0
Wales	51	29	8	7	5	-	-	1.1
England and Wales	45	29	10	8	7	1	-	20.1
Scotland[2]	31	27	11	10	18	3	-	1.1
Northern Ireland[3]	17	53	11	7	9	2	-	0.8

1 Some teachers in England and Wales classed as new entrants by the Database of Teacher Records may have experience outside the scope of the Teachers Pension Scheme.
2 Data for Scotland comes from the Teacher Flow (TF) survey, and relates to the period Easter 1998 to Easter 1999. See Notes and Definitions.
3 Figures for Northern Ireland comprise newly appointed permanent teachers at September 1999 in nursery, primary, secondary, grammar and special schools.

Source: Department for Education and Skills; Scottish Executive; Northern Ireland Department of Education

4.5 Examination achievements:[1] by gender, 1999/00

| | Pupils in their last year of compulsory education[1] | | | | | Pupils/students in education[5] achieving 2 or more A levels/ | |
| | Percentage achieving GCSE[2] or SCE Standard Grade/National Qualifications(NQ)[3] | | | | Total (=100%) (thousands) | 3 or more SCE/NQ[3] Highers (percentages) | Average A/AS level point scores |
	5 or more grades A*–C	1–4 grades A*–C	Grades D–G only[4]	No graded GCSEs/SCEs			
Males							
United Kingdom[6]	44.9	25.0	23.6	6.6	357.7	26.7	18.0
North East	38.7	24.0	29.5	7.7	16.1	19.4	17.3
North West	42.5	25.2	25.6	6.7	43.5	24.4	18.8
Yorkshire and the Humber	38.8	23.8	29.8	7.6	31.0	22.2	18.5
East Midlands	42.7	23.8	26.9	6.5	25.5	25.8	18.0
West Midlands	40.9	25.0	27.4	6.6	33.3	24.4	17.9
East	47.7	24.5	22.4	5.4	32.2	30.7	18.0
London	42.5	27.3	23.5	6.7	37.7	25.9	17.1
South East	49.6	23.3	20.9	6.2	47.3	32.4	18.2
South West	48.4	24.1	22.0	5.5	28.9	29.2	18.4
England	44.0	24.6	24.9	6.5	295.5	26.7	18.1
Wales	43.4	24.3	23.3	8.9	18.1	23.3	16.4
Scotland	53.1	28.3	12.4	6.2	31.2	27.4	.
Northern Ireland	48.7	24.8	21.2	5.3	12.8	30.5	..
Females							
United Kingdom[6]	55.8	23.9	15.6	4.6	346.0	34.0	18.7
North East	47.7	24.7	21.8	5.8	15.8	24.8	17.2
North West	52.7	24.8	17.8	4.8	42.4	30.9	19.6
Yorkshire and the Humber	48.6	24.1	21.4	5.9	30.0	28.6	19.4
East Midlands	53.1	24.1	17.9	4.9	24.2	31.9	18.2
West Midlands	52.3	25.2	17.8	4.7	31.9	31.3	18.3
East	58.5	23.3	14.4	3.8	30.9	37.1	19.0
London	53.7	26.7	14.9	4.6	37.1	34.5	17.5
South East	60.3	22.0	13.5	4.2	44.8	39.0	19.4
South West	59.8	22.4	14.2	3.5	27.8	36.6	19.5
England	54.6	24.1	16.6	4.6	284.8	33.5	18.8
Wales	54.9	23.0	15.7	6.4	17.5	31.2	17.4
Scotland	63.6	23.2	8.2	5.0	31.1	35.4	.
Northern Ireland	65.4	21.0	11.7	1.9	12.6	45.2	..
All pupils/students							
United Kingdom[6]	50.3	24.4	19.7	5.6	703.1	30.2	18.4
North East	43.2	24.4	25.7	6.7	31.9	22.0	17.2
North West	47.5	25.0	21.7	5.8	85.9	27.6	19.2
Yorkshire and the Humber	43.6	24.0	25.6	6.8	61.0	25.3	19.0
East Midlands	47.8	24.0	22.6	5.7	49.7	28.8	18.1
West Midlands	46.5	25.1	22.7	5.7	65.2	27.8	18.1
East	53.0	23.9	18.5	4.6	63.2	33.9	18.5
London	48.1	27.0	19.2	5.7	74.9	30.1	17.3
South East	54.8	22.7	17.3	5.2	92.1	35.6	18.9
South West	54.0	23.3	18.2	4.5	56.6	32.8	19.0
England	49.2	24.4	20.8	5.6	580.4	30.0	18.5
Wales	49.1	23.7	19.5	7.7	35.6	27.2	16.9
Scotland	58.3	25.8	10.3	5.6	62.3	31.4	.
Northern Ireland	56.9	22.9	16.5	3.6	25.4	37.7	..

1 See Notes and Definitions.
2 England figures include GNVQ equivalents.
3 From 1999/00 new National Qualifications (NQ) were introduced in Scotland.
4 No grades above D and at least one in the D–G range. Figures for Wales, England and the English regions include pupils with one GCSE short course only.
5 Pupils in schools and students in further education institutions aged 17–19 at the end of the academic year in England, Wales and Northern Ireland as a percentage of the 18 year old population. Pupils in Scotland generally sit Highers one year earlier and the figures tend to relate to the results of pupils in Year S5/S6 as a percentage of the 17 year old population.
6 England and Wales only for 'Average A/AS level point scores'.

Source: Department for Education and Skills; National Assembly for Wales; Scottish Executive; Northern Ireland Department of Education

4.6 Pupils[1] achieving GCSE grades A*-C:[2] by selected subjects and gender, 1999/00[3]

Percentages

	English	Mathe-matics	Science Any science[4]	Science Single award[5]	Science Double award	Any modern langu-age[6]	French	Geo-graphy	History	Craft Design Techno-logy	All core sub-jects[7]
Males											
United Kingdom	47.4	45.9	46.3	2.1	33.0	32.5	22.3	23.3	18.7	29.7	26.1
North East	41.0	40.2	40.3	1.1	31.7	24.3	17.0	19.5	15.1	29.8	19.6
North West	44.9	44.2	43.7	1.0	35.1	30.1	20.6	21.2	17.4	29.5	23.6
Yorkshire and the Humber	40.3	40.8	40.9	0.7	34.4	27.4	17.7	20.7	16.4	30.5	20.9
East Midlands	44.2	43.9	44.6	1.2	38.7	31.0	22.0	22.0	16.8	31.7	23.9
West Midlands	43.1	42.9	41.6	0.8	33.8	28.8	19.5	22.1	17.3	29.3	22.2
East	48.8	49.5	48.6	1.2	41.6	33.6	22.7	25.1	21.0	32.9	26.9
London	45.3	44.2	41.9	1.7	32.5	33.2	20.9	19.2	17.8	24.0	23.8
South East	50.7	50.8	50.3	2.0	37.8	37.6	26.9	25.8	21.9	30.8	30.3
South West	49.0	49.6	50.6	1.0	41.8	34.2	24.2	27.5	20.1	36.4	28.0
England	45.8	45.6	45.1	1.3	36.5	31.8	21.7	22.8	18.5	30.3	24.9
Wales	44.7	41.9	46.2	2.0	34.7	19.8	15.4	26.8	19.5	22.8	33.1
Scotland	64.0	51.4	59.4	7.3	.	44.6	29.4	26.1	19.1	31.6	34.8
Northern Ireland	48.7	44.4	42.0	8.2	32.5	37.2	27.0	24.5	20.2	21.3	24.8
Females											
United Kingdom	64.0	48.1	49.9	2.5	37.5	49.0	34.2	20.7	22.4	35.9	36.2
North East	56.0	41.3	41.8	1.8	33.6	38.6	27.7	17.7	18.4	41.0	28.1
North West	60.6	46.4	46.7	1.4	39.5	45.7	32.1	17.9	20.1	38.5	33.5
Yorkshire and the Humber	56.6	42.1	42.9	1.1	37.3	43.8	28.6	17.8	19.4	42.4	30.5
East Midlands	61.1	45.5	46.6	2.0	41.4	46.8	33.5	19.4	20.3	43.4	33.3
West Midlands	60.6	44.5	45.5	1.2	39.5	45.3	30.8	19.7	20.6	39.9	32.0
East	66.0	50.9	51.6	2.0	45.1	50.3	35.0	22.1	24.2	45.8	37.3
London	61.0	46.7	47.3	2.5	40.5	48.1	30.8	18.4	22.1	34.2	33.7
South East	67.5	52.9	53.9	2.2	44.7	53.8	37.7	23.6	24.5	39.5	40.9
South West	66.5	51.3	53.8	1.7	45.4	52.5	38.4	25.5	23.4	48.9	39.6
England	62.3	47.4	48.3	1.8	41.2	47.9	33.1	20.4	21.7	41.0	34.9
Wales	63.4	44.8	49.5	2.7	39.0	33.9	27.3	22.2	24.6	17.3	39.9
Scotland	78.1	54.8	64.1	5.7	.	63.7	44.3	21.2	26.3	11.7	46.0
Northern Ireland	68.8	52.4	50.7	11.0	42.3	57.6	43.8	26.5	25.7	5.5	35.8
All pupils											
United Kingdom	55.6	47.0	48.1	2.3	35.2	40.6	28.1	22.0	20.5	32.8	31.1
North East	48.4	40.8	41.0	1.4	32.7	31.4	22.3	18.6	16.7	35.4	23.8
North West	52.7	45.3	45.2	1.2	37.3	37.8	26.3	19.6	18.7	33.9	28.5
Yorkshire and the Humber	48.3	41.4	41.9	0.9	35.8	35.5	23.1	19.3	17.9	36.4	25.6
East Midlands	52.4	44.7	45.6	1.6	40.0	38.7	27.6	20.7	18.5	37.4	28.4
West Midlands	51.7	43.7	43.5	1.0	36.6	36.9	25.0	20.9	18.9	34.5	27.0
East	57.2	50.2	50.1	1.6	43.3	41.8	28.7	23.6	22.6	39.2	32.0
London	53.1	45.4	44.6	2.1	36.5	40.6	25.8	18.8	19.9	29.0	28.7
South East	58.8	51.8	52.0	2.1	41.1	45.5	32.2	24.7	23.2	35.0	35.5
South West	57.6	50.4	52.2	1.4	43.5	43.1	31.1	26.5	21.7	42.5	33.7
England	53.9	46.5	46.7	1.5	38.8	39.7	27.3	21.6	20.1	35.6	29.8
Wales	53.9	43.3	47.8	2.3	36.8	26.8	21.3	24.6	22.0	20.1	36.4
Scotland	71.0	53.1	61.7	6.5	.	54.1	36.8	23.4	22.7	21.7	40.4
Northern Ireland	58.7	48.4	46.3	9.6	37.3	47.3	35.3	25.5	22.9	13.5	30.3

1 Pupils in their last year of compulsory education.
2 SCE Standard Grade awards at levels 1–3 in Scotland. From 1999/00 new National Qualifications (NQ) were introduced in Scotland.
3 See Notes and Definitions.
4 Includes double award, single award and individual science subjects. In Scotland, 'Any science' includes Biology, Chemistry, Physics or General Science Standard Grade.
  See Notes and Definitions.
5 General Science in Scotland.
6 Including French.
7 The core subjects of the National Curriculum applicable in England are English, mathematics and a science. Figures in this column for England also include a modern language.
  The core subjects applicable in Wales are mathematics, a science, and either English or Welsh (as a first language). In 1999/2000, 8.3 per cent of pupils achieved GCSE grade
  A* to C in Welsh as a first language. The National Curriculum does not apply in Scotland.

Source: Department for Education and Skills; National Assembly for Wales; Scottish Executive; Northern Ireland Department of Education

4.7 Pupils reaching or exceeding expected standards:[1] by Key Stage Teacher Assessment, Summer 2000

Percentages

	Key Stage 1[2]			Key Stage 2[3]			Key Stage 3[4]		
	English	Mathematics	Science	English	Mathematics	Science	English	Mathematics	Science
England[5]	84	88	88	70	72	79	64	66	62
North East	84	88	88	68	71	79	60	62	57
North West	84	88	88	72	73	80	64	65	60
Yorkshire and the Humber	83	87	87	67	70	77	60	63	58
East Midlands	85	89	89	68	71	78	65	67	63
West Midlands	83	87	86	69	70	78	63	64	60
East	85	88	89	71	73	79	67	71	67
London	80	86	85	67	70	76	60	61	55
South East	85	89	89	72	74	81	68	71	67
South West	85	88	89	71	73	80	67	70	67
Wales	82	88	87	70	71	78	63	64	62
Northern Ireland[6]	95	95	.	71	75	.	73	72	71

1 See Notes and Definitions.
2 Percentage of pupils achieving level 2 or above at Key Stage 1
3 Percentage of pupils achieving level 4 or above at Key Stage 2.
4 Percentage of pupils achieving level 5 or above at Key Stage 3.
5 Includes non-LEA maintained schools. These are not included in the regions figures.
6 In Northern Ireland Key Stage 1, pupils are assessed at the age of 8. Pupils are not assessed in Science at Key Stages 1 and 2.

Source: Department for Education and Skills; National Assembly for Wales; Northern Ireland Department of Education

4.8 16 and 17 year olds participating in post-compulsory education[1] and government-supported training: 1998/99

Percentages[2]

	16 year olds					17 year olds				
	At school[1]	In further education[1,3] Full-time	Part-time	Government-supported training (GST)	All in full-time education and GST[4]	At school[1]	In further education[1,3] Full-time	Part-time	Government-supported training (GST)	All in full-time education and GST[4]
Region of study										
United Kingdom	38.0	32.4	7.2	..	..	28.7	27.7	9.0	..	..
North East	25.9	35.3	7.8	13.9	81.2	19.8	29.0	9.4	15.8	72.5
North West	24.5	40.5	8.4	12.3	82.0	19.8	33.5	9.9	14.7	73.7
Yorkshire and the Humber	29.6	33.9	9.7	13.1	83.3	23.8	27.6	11.6	14.7	73.9
East Midlands	37.2	29.4	7.4	10.6	82.2	29.8	24.9	9.2	13.3	74.1
West Midlands	31.1	36.4	7.9	9.8	82.5	24.7	30.3	10.0	11.6	73.7
East	40.9	33.2	5.0	6.4	83.0	32.6	27.9	7.1	8.2	72.7
London	39.4	34.6	4.2	4.5	81.9	29.8	31.7	5.8	5.9	72.3
South East	39.3	34.9	4.5	5.9	82.9	31.7	29.8	6.1	8.2	73.8
South West	39.2	33.8	5.8	8.2	84.4	31.1	28.7	7.9	12.0	76.4
England	34.5	35.0	6.5	8.9	82.6	27.4	29.6	8.4	11.1	73.7
Wales	37.7	31.0	7.6	16.1	92.5	28.4	26.3	9.4	15.7	79.8
Scotland[5]	67.4	11.2	11.0	9.4	88.0	37.6	10.9	13.4	14.9	63.4
Northern Ireland[6]	46.5	27.9	13.3	..	..	37.0	25.9	13.7	..	..

1 See Notes and Definitions.
2 As a percentage of the estimated 16 and 17 year old population respectively.
3 Including sixth form colleges in England and a small element of further education in higher education institutions in England and Scotland.
4 Figures for England exclude overlap between full-time education and government-supported training.
5 The estimates of 16 year olds at school exclude those pupils who leave school in the winter term at the minimum statutory school-leaving age.
6 Participation in part-time further education should not be aggregated with full-time further education or schools activity due to the unquantifiable overlap of these activities.

Source: Department for Education and Skills; National Assembly for Wales; Scottish Executive; Northern Ireland Department of Education

4.9 Home students in further education[1] in England: by level of course of study,[2] 2000/01

Percentages and thousands

	Courses leading to NVQ/GNVQ or equivalent academic qualifications (percentages)					Total FE students[1] studying in England (=100%) (thousands)
	Level 1 and Entry	Level 2	Level 3	Level 4, 5 and higher education	Other courses	
Region of study[3]						
North East	27.1	30.5	28.1	6.9	7.4	148.9
North West	19.7	26.4	30.5	6.6	16.9	390.0
Yorkshire and the Humber	23.3	27.1	30.7	5.1	13.8	242.8
East Midlands	23.7	29.5	30.7	4.7	11.4	198.2
West Midlands	23.3	25.7	29.7	6.8	14.5	267.3
East	17.6	24.6	34.2	7.1	16.5	202.7
London	19.1	25.0	30.0	5.3	20.6	290.1
South East	17.3	22.9	32.8	6.3	20.7	347.3
South West	17.7	25.0	34.9	6.6	15.8	197.3
England	20.5	25.9	31.3	6.1	16.1	2,284.8
Other[4]	11.3	22.0	31.8	15.4	19.5	4.7

1 Further education (FE) institutions only. See Notes and Definitions.
2 Highest level of qualification aimed for by students.
3 English domiciled students only.
4 Those studying within England domiciled in Wales, Scotland, Northern Ireland, Channel Islands and the Isle of Man.

Source: Department for Education and Skills

4.10 Home domiciled higher education students:[1] by region of study and domicile, 2000/01[2]

Percentages and thousands

	Region of study												All students (=100%) (thousands)
	North East	North West	York-shire and the Humber	East Mid-lands	West Mid-lands	East	London	South East	South West	Wales	Scot-land	Nor-thern Ireland	
Region of domicile													
United Kingdom[3]	4.5	9.2	12.0	6.8	8.2	5.6	15.2	10.5	6.7	5.3	13.0	2.9	1,684.5
North East	72.0	4.0	10.9	2.8	1.7	1.1	1.8	1.4	0.8	0.5	3.1	0.1	63.6
North West	3.8	58.1	17.9	3.7	5.0	1.3	2.4	2.1	1.5	1.9	2.3	-	136.9
Yorkshire and the Humber	5.6	9.8	66.4	4.9	3.1	1.5	2.4	1.9	1.3	1.2	1.8	-	146.2
East Midlands	2.5	4.9	18.0	48.1	8.7	4.0	4.2	4.2	2.6	1.6	1.2	-	98.5
West Midlands	1.2	5.5	7.7	7.7	58.6	1.9	3.7	4.0	4.5	4.2	1.0	-	129.6
East	1.7	2.5	6.9	9.0	4.9	42.7	15.5	9.4	4.3	1.8	1.3	-	127.7
London	0.8	1.9	2.8	2.6	2.7	5.2	69.9	9.3	2.8	0.9	1.1	-	230.4
South East	1.4	2.2	4.5	5.2	4.4	4.3	16.6	48.8	8.4	2.8	1.4	-	210.3
South West	1.1	2.2	4.0	3.7	5.2	2.6	7.1	13.3	52.4	7.2	1.2	-	115.3
England	5.5	11.1	14.5	8.4	10.1	6.9	18.7	12.9	8.0	2.4	1.5	-	1,337.5
Wales	0.6	4.4	4.9	2.4	3.9	1.1	3.0	3.7	5.7	69.5	0.8	-	81.1
Scotland	0.8	0.8	0.8	0.4	0.3	0.4	0.7	0.6	0.3	0.3	94.7	-	203.7
Northern Ireland	1.4	2.2	3.0	1.0	0.9	0.8	1.7	1.2	0.5	0.8	9.0	77.5	62.2

1 Including higher education students in further education institutions for England, Wales, Scotland and Northern Ireland. Excluding Open University students. These data are not comparable with figures prior to those shown in *Regional Trends 35*. See Notes and Definitions.
2 Data for higher education students in further education institutions in Wales relates to 1999/00.
3 Including students from the Channel Islands and Isle of Man and students whose region of domicile was unknown or unclassified.

Source: Department for Education and Skills; Higher Education Statistics Agency; National Assembly for Wales; Scottish Executive; Department of Higher and Further Education, Training and Employment, Northern Ireland

4.11 Destination of 2000 full-time first degree graduates[1]

Percentages and thousands

	UK employment		Overseas employment[2]	Total employment	Continuing education or training	Believed unemployed	Other destinations[3]	All first degree graduates[4] (thousands)
	Permanent	Temporary						
Region of study								
United Kingdom	44.1	19.5	2.6	66.2	20.3	5.3	8.2	225.4
North East	42.5	20.1	2.6	65.2	20.6	5.8	8.4	11.5
North West	41.6	22.8	2.3	66.7	19.4	6.3	7.6	25.4
Yorkshire and the Humber	48.9	17.6	3.1	69.7	17.4	5.1	7.7	24.5
East Midlands	48.8	19.8	2.2	70.8	17.6	4.1	7.6	17.0
West Midlands	44.6	19.1	2.2	65.8	21.2	5.6	7.4	18.3
East	42.4	18.7	2.3	63.4	24.8	4.0	7.8	12.0
London	44.1	18.8	1.5	64.4	20.1	6.2	9.3	31.7
South East	45.9	19.2	2.6	67.7	19.5	4.4	8.3	26.9
South West	48.4	17.9	3.0	69.3	16.7	5.3	8.6	16.3
England	45.4	19.4	2.4	67.1	19.4	5.3	8.1	183.7
Wales	36.5	22.2	2.8	61.4	24.5	6.5	7.5	13.9
Scotland	41.3	20.4	3.4	65.1	21.8	4.8	8.3	22.3
Northern Ireland	33.8	13.7	5.5	53.0	31.7	5.0	10.2	5.5

1 Home and EU students graduating from higher education institutions in 2000. As a percentage of known destinations. As from 1999/00 the target population excludes non-EU overseas domiciled students.
2 Home students only.
3 Includes overseas graduates leaving the United Kingdom and graduates not available for employment.
4 Includes known and unknown destinations.

Source: Department for Education and Skills, and the Higher Education Statistics Agency

4.12 Population of working age:[1] by highest qualification,[2] Spring 2001

Percentages and thousands

	Degree or equivalent	Higher education qualifications[3]	GCE A Level or equivalent[4]	GCSE grades A*–C or equivalent	Other qualifications	No qualifications	Total[5] (=100%) (thousands)
United Kingdom	15.2	8.3	24.0	22.3	13.7	16.4	36,554
North East	10.4	7.9	24.9	23.8	13.9	19.1	1,573
North West	12.9	8.9	25.8	24.1	11.4	16.9	4,185
Yorkshire and the Humber	12.2	8.2	25.0	21.3	14.7	18.6	3,087
East Midlands	12.6	7.5	23.9	23.4	14.0	18.6	2,587
West Midlands	11.9	8.2	22.2	23.3	14.6	19.8	3,246
East	14.4	7.7	24.7	24.8	14.5	14.0	3,324
London	25.0	6.0	18.9	17.5	18.0	14.7	4,707
South East	17.8	8.1	24.1	23.9	13.8	12.2	4,956
South West	15.5	9.2	24.2	25.8	13.4	11.9	2,945
England	15.6	7.9	23.5	22.9	14.4	15.7	30,609
Wales	12.3	9.2	21.8	24.1	11.8	20.8	1,758
Scotland	14.1	12.5	30.2	15.9	10.5	16.8	3,164
Northern Ireland	12.8	6.2	24.2	21.7	8.4	26.7	1,023

1 Males aged 16–64 and females aged 16–59.
2 See Notes and Definitions.
3 Below degree level.
4 Includes recognised trade apprenticeship.
5 Population in private households, students in halls of residence and those in NHS accommodation. Includes those who did not state their qualifications, but percentages are based on figures excluding them.

Source: Department for Education and Skills, from the Labour Force Survey (Office for National Statistics)

4.13 Progress towards achieving the National Learning Targets for England for 2002, Spring 2001[1,2]

Percentages

Target	85 per cent of 19 year olds with an NVQ level 2 qualification or equivalent			60 per cent of 21 year olds with an NVQ level 3 qualification or equivalent			50 per cent of adults[3] with an NVQ level 3 qualification or equivalent			28 per cent of adults[3] with an NVQ level 4 qualification		
	Males	Females	All	Males	Females	All	Males	Females	All	Males	Females	All
Region of residence												
North East	74	77	75	50	51	51	48	38	43	23	23	23
North West	72	80	76	50	52	51	52	42	48	26	26	26
Yorkshire and the Humber	73	73	73	54	55	55	50	40	45	23	26	24
East Midlands	70	79	75	52	52	52	47	39	44	23	24	23
West Midlands	70	76	73	45	50	48	46	39	43	23	25	24
East	74	82	78	55	50	52	49	39	45	25	24	25
London	72	79	75	57	59	58	55	52	54	37	38	37
South East	77	78	78	58	61	60	53	43	48	30	28	29
South West	79	79	79	59	58	59	51	43	47	28	27	28
England	74	78	76	54	55	54	51	42	47	27	28	27

1 See Notes and Definitions for details of the targets.
2 The questions on qualifications in the Labour Force Survey were changed substantially in Spring 1996. Figures are therefore not directly comparable with those for earlier years.
3 Males aged 18–64 and females aged 18–59, who are in employment or actively seeking employment.

Source: Department for Education and Skills from Labour Force Survey (Office for National Statistics)

4.14 Employees of working age[1] receiving job-related training:[2] by gender, Spring 2001

Percentages[3]

	Males				Females			
	On-the-job training only	Off-the-job training only	Both on and off-the-job training	Any job-related training	On-the-job training only	Off-the-job training only	Both on and off-the-job training	Any job-related training
United Kingdom	4.7	6.8	2.9	14.4	5.5	9.5	3.6	18.5
North East	4.3	6.7	3.3	14.3	6.0	7.6	3.5	17.1
North West	4.8	7.1	3.8	15.7	5.6	9.6	3.7	18.9
Yorkshire and the Humber	5.2	6.3	2.9	14.4	6.6	9.1	3.7	19.4
East Midlands	5.0	4.7	2.9	12.6	5.9	7.9	2.7	16.4
West Midlands	4.8	6.0	2.6	13.4	5.6	10.3	4.4	20.3
East	5.4	6.7	2.7	14.7	5.4	8.4	3.8	17.6
London	4.8	8.3	2.7	15.8	5.6	10.8	3.3	19.8
South East	4.6	7.4	2.5	14.5	5.8	9.7	3.6	19.1
South West	4.5	8.0	3.5	16.0	4.4	10.6	3.2	18.3
England	4.8	6.9	2.9	14.7	5.6	9.5	3.6	18.7
Wales	3.8	6.6	3.2	13.7	4.7	9.8	4.3	18.8
Scotland	4.3	6.1	2.7	13.0	5.0	9.1	3.5	17.7
Northern Ireland	3.8	5.7	..	11.8	3.3	9.2	..	14.3

1 Males aged 16–64 and females aged 16–59.
2 Job-related education or training received in the four weeks before interview. In some cases sample sizes are too small to provide reliable estimates.
3 As a percentage of all employees of working age.

Source: Department for Education and Skills from Labour Force Survey (Office for National Statistics)

4.15 Work-based learning and training,[1] 1999–00

Percentages and thousands

| | Work-based Learning for Adults | | | | | | Work-based Training for Young People[2] | | | | | |
| | Status six months after leaving[3] (percentages) | | | | | | Status six months after leaving[3] (percentages) | | | | | |
	In employ-ment	In further educ-ation or training	Unemp-loyed	Other	Gained full qualifi-cation[4] (percent-ages)	All leavers[5] (thou-sands)	In employ-ment	In further educ-ation or training	Unemp-loyed	Other	Gained full qualifi-cation[4] (percent-ages)	All leavers[5] (thou-sands)
England and Wales	41	5	48	7	40	107.3	70	11	12	6	52	250.5
North East	35	5	54	6	43	8.4	63	14	17	6	51	19.9
North West	42	5	48	5	42	16.7	69	11	13	6	53	46.1
Yorkshire and the Humber	36	5	52	7	37	11.6	67	12	14	7	48	28.6
East Midlands	38	5	50	7	38	6.6	73	11	11	6	53	21.3
West Midlands	41	6	46	6	39	12.2	71	11	11	6	51	26.5
East	46	4	43	7	45	6.5	78	8	8	6	56	19.5
London	39	5	48	7	38	23.8	63	15	14	7	48	21.4
South East	46	4	42	7	38	8.4	77	8	8	7	54	26.5
South West	45	5	42	7	41	7.7	76	10	7	7	55	20.2
England	40	5	48	7	40	101.8	71	11	12	6	52	229.8
Wales	42	5	47	6	47	5.5	60	15	17	7	46	20.7
Northern Ireland[1]	60	7	25	8	91	1.2	63	9	19	9	88	7.7

1 Schemes in Northern Ireland differ from those in England and Wales. See Notes and Definitions.
2 Work Based Training for Young People data in England and Wales consist of Advanced Modern Apprenticeships, Foundation Modern Apprenticeships and Other Training for Young People.
3 Status on completion of courses in Northern Ireland.
4 In Northern Ireland, full qualifications gained by completers expressed as a percentage of completers.
5 All those who left the programme during 1999–00, except in Northern Ireland where the figure covers completers of courses only and does not include early leavers.

Source: Department for Education and Skills; Department of Higher and Further Education and Training and Employment, Northern Ireland

5 Labour Market

Employment rates
The South East had the highest employment rate in 2000 at 81 per cent, compared with 65 per cent in Northern Ireland.

(Table 5.1)

Men had a higher employment rate than women in the United Kingdom in 2000, at 79 per cent and 69 per cent respectively.

(Table 5.1)

Labour force
Nearly 4 per cent of the labour force in the South West in Spring 2000 were females aged 60 and over or males aged 65 and over compared with around 2 per cent in the North East.

(Table 5.2)

Around 83 per cent of people of working age in the South East were economically active in Spring 2000 compared with 70 per cent in Northern Ireland, the highest and lowest proportions.

(Table 5.7)

Employment status
The proportion of employees who were working part-time in Spring 2000 was highest in the South West at 18 per cent.

(Table 5.3)

Employee jobs
In December 1999 just over three in ten employee jobs in London were in financial and business services compared with just over 1 in 10 in the North East and Wales.

(Table 5.4)

The proportion of employee jobs in manufacturing was highest in the East Midlands in December 1999.

(Table 5.4)

Jobs
The highest number of self-employment jobs for both males and females in 2000 were in the South East and London.

(Table 5.5)

In Northern Ireland in Spring 2000, 28 per cent of self-employed people worked in agriculture and fishing, compared with 3 per cent in the East of England.

(Table 5.6)

The region with the lowest proportion of female part-time workers was London, at 35 per cent.

(Chart 5.8)

The proportion of men who said that the reason why they were working part-time was because they could not find a full-time job was highest in the North East at nearly 35 per cent, over three times the proportion in the South East.

(Table 5.9)

People in employment in the South West in Spring 2000 were more likely to have a second job than people in employment in other regions.

(Table 5.11)

Hours of work
The highest average hours worked were by managers and administrators in the East Midlands, West Midlands and South West, at 47 hours a week.

(Table 5.12)

Labour Disputes
In 2000, the number of working days lost due to labour disputes in Scotland was 136 days for every one thousand employees, compared with only 1 day in the South West.

(Table 5.13)

Sickness absence	Sickness absence from work in Spring 2000 was highest in Scotland and the West Midlands and lowest in North East.
	(Chart 5.14)
Trade Unions	In Autumn 2000, Trade union membership among manual employees ranged from 41 per cent in the North East to 22 per cent in the South East and East of England and from 44 per in Wales to 24 per cent in London for non-manual employees.
	(Table 5.15)
Earnings	In April 2000, average weekly earnings for full-time employees in England varied from £593 in London to £399 in the North East for men and from £434 in London to £301 in the East Midlands for women.
	(Table 5.17)
Unemployment	In Spring 2000, the North East had the highest ILO unemployment rate at 9.2 per cent, compared with 3.4 per cent in the South East, the lowest rate in the United Kingdom.
	(Table 5.18)
	In 2000, the seasonally adjusted claimant count rate in the South East was 1.8 per cent, lower than in any other region.
	(Table 5.19)
	The ILO unemployment rate for 16–24 year olds in the North East over the period 2000/2001 was 18.7 per cent, more than double the rate for the South East.
	(Table 5.20)
Claimant count	In March 2001, the highest proportion of those claiming unemployment-related benefits in the United Kingdom were aged between 20–29 years old; among this age group, the populations with the highest number of claimants were in the North West and Yorkshire and the Humber.
	(Table 5.21)
	In March 2001, claimant count rates in North Ayrshire, West Dunbartonshire and Strabane were among the highest in the United Kingdom.
	(Map 5.22)
Redundancies	In Spring 2000, redundancy rates in the North East and Scotland were around three-fifths higher than in the South East.
	(Table 5.25)
New deal	In 2000, the highest number of new starts on the New Deal for young people aged 18–24 in Great Britain were in London and North West.
	(Table 5.27)

GLOSSARY OF TERMS

Employees (Labour Force Survey)	A household-based measure of persons aged 16 and over who regard themselves as paid employees. In this publication, people are counted only once in their main job.
Employee jobs (New Earnings Survey)	A measure of employees in employment, obtained from surveys of employers, of jobs held by civilians who are paid by an employer who runs a PAYE tax scheme. Those people with two or more jobs represented for each of those jobs in the same survey.
(Employer Survey)	A measure, obtained from surveys of employees, of jobs held by civilians. People with two or more jobs are counted in each job.
Self-employed	A household-based measure (from the Labour Force Survey (LFS)) of persons aged 16 and over who regard themselves as self-employed in their main job.
People on government-supported training and employment programmes (Labour Force Survey)	A household-based measure of persons aged 16 or over participating in Work-based learning for Adults and Young People, Work Trial and Project Work as well as other similar programmes organised by a Training Enterprise Council (England and Wales), Local Enterprise Company (Scotland) or the Training and Employment Agency (Northern Ireland). Because of the nature of many of these programmes, the LFS has difficulty in identifying scheme participants.
Labour force in employment (Labour Force Survey)	A household-based measure of employees, self-employed persons, participants in government-supported training and employment programmes, and persons doing unpaid work for a family business.
Workforce jobs	A measure of employee jobs (obtained from employer surveys), self-employment jobs (obtained from the Labour Force Survey), all HM Forces, and government-supported trainees (obtained from the Employment Service).
ILO unemployed	An International Labour Organisation (ILO) recommended measure, used in household surveys such as the LFS, which counts as unemployed those aged 16 or over who are without a job, are available to start work in the next two weeks and who have been seeking a job in the last four weeks, or were waiting to start a job already obtained in the next two weeks.
Claimant count	A count derived from administrative sources, of those people who are claiming unemployment-related benefits at Employment Service local offices (formerly Unemployment Benefit Offices).
Economically active/labour force	The **labour force in employment** *plus* the **ILO unemployed**.
ILO unemployment rate	The percentage of the **economically active** who are **ILO unemployed**.
Claimant count rate	The number of people claiming unemployment-related benefit as a percentage of **workforce jobs** plus the **claimant count**.
Economically inactive	Persons who are neither part of the labour force in employment nor ILO unemployed. For example, all people under 16, those retired or looking after a home, or those permanently unable to work.
Population of working age	Males aged 16 to 64 years and females aged 16 to 59 years.
Economic activity rate	The percentage of the population in a given age group which is in the labour force.

Some of these items are covered in more detail in the Notes and Definitions section.

5.1 Labour force and employment rates[1]

Thousands and percentages

	Labour force (thousands)					Employment rates[2] (percentages)				
	1996	1997	1998	1999	2000	1996	1997	1998	1999	2000
Males										
United Kingdom	15,776	15,818	15,813	15,937	16,034	76.4	77.5	78.1	78.4	79.1
North East	665	657	653	634	658	70.4	70.3	71.6	68.3	71.6
North West	1,781	1,773	1,737	1,788	1,822	73.3	74.4	73.3	75.4	78.2
Yorkshire and the Humber	1,337	1,328	1,337	1,349	1,356	75.3	74.6	76.0	76.7	77.4
East Midlands	1,147	1,142	1,146	1,147	1,165	79.2	79.5	81.4	80.4	81.3
West Midlands	1,453	1,452	1,459	1,447	1,426	76.3	78.9	79.7	78.4	77.9
East	1,484	1,481	1,510	1,513	1,511	82.5	81.5	84.0	84.0	83.9
London	1,938	1,973	1,949	2,005	1,989	72.6	75.9	75.0	76.9	76.5
South East	2,212	2,226	2,251	2,267	2,281	82.4	83.5	84.6	85.9	85.9
South West	1,279	1,308	1,307	1,323	1,331	79.3	82.0	82.7	82.6	83.1
England	13,295	13,340	13,350	13,474	13,539	77.1	78.3	79.0	79.4	80.1
Wales	726	727	705	725	730	72.0	72.2	71.2	72.1	73.7
Scotland	1,351	1,344	1,341	1,329	1,356	73.8	74.2	74.9	74.0	75.3
Northern Ireland	404	407	417	409	408	70.0	72.0	73.4	71.8	71.4
Females										
United Kingdom	12,098	12,208	12,284	12,422	12,534	66.5	67.2	67.6	68.3	68.9
North East	502	510	489	502	510	61.2	63.0	61.3	61.2	62.8
North West	1,372	1,349	1,355	1,371	1,389	65.1	64.9	64.8	66.0	66.6
Yorkshire and the Humber	1,032	1,015	1,030	1,030	1,052	67.1	65.9	67.4	67.7	69.1
East Midlands	878	895	892	901	918	68.8	70.7	70.5	71.0	71.9
West Midlands	1,070	1,064	1,087	1,110	1,101	65.1	65.8	67.3	68.3	67.8
East	1,114	1,129	1,162	1,164	1,171	68.8	69.7	70.8	71.5	72.1
London	1,502	1,528	1,518	1,547	1,545	63.1	64.4	63.9	65.4	65.2
South East	1,715	1,734	1,751	1,770	1,810	71.8	71.9	72.7	73.0	74.7
South West	996	1,024	1,040	1,058	1,066	70.0	71.8	72.1	73.2	73.7
England	10,180	10,251	10,324	10,454	10,561	67.0	67.7	68.1	68.9	69.6
Wales	549	563	553	559	565	62.8	63.8	63.5	64.3	64.7
Scotland	1,070	1,085	1,098	1,091	1,106	65.7	66.1	67.7	67.4	68.2
Northern Ireland	298	310	309	318	303	58.6	60.7	60.3	61.1	58.0
All persons										
United Kingdom	27,873	28,026	28,097	28,359	28,568	71.6	72.6	73.1	73.6	74.3
North East	1,167	1,167	1,142	1,137	1,168	66.0	66.8	66.7	64.9	67.4
North West	3,153	3,123	3,092	3,160	3,212	69.4	69.9	69.3	70.9	72.7
Yorkshire and the Humber	2,368	2,343	2,367	2,379	2,408	71.4	70.5	71.9	72.5	73.5
East Midlands	2,025	2,037	2,039	2,047	2,082	74.3	75.3	76.2	75.9	76.8
West Midlands	2,523	2,516	2,546	2,558	2,527	71.0	72.7	73.8	73.6	73.1
East	2,598	2,610	2,672	2,677	2,682	76.0	75.9	77.7	78.1	78.3
London	3,440	3,502	3,467	3,552	3,534	68.0	70.3	69.7	71.4	71.1
South East	3,927	3,960	4,002	4,037	4,091	77.3	77.9	78.9	79.7	80.6
South West	2,275	2,332	2,347	2,381	2,396	74.9	77.1	77.7	78.1	78.6
England	23,475	23,591	23,674	23,928	24,100	72.3	73.3	73.8	74.4	75.1
Wales	1,275	1,290	1,259	1,285	1,295	67.7	68.2	67.5	68.4	69.4
Scotland	2,421	2,428	2,439	2,420	2,461	69.9	70.3	71.4	70.8	71.9
Northern Ireland	702	717	726	726	711	64.4	66.5	67.0	66.6	64.9

1 At Spring of each year. Based on the population of working age in private households, students halls of residence and NHS accommodation. See Notes and Definitions.
2 Total in employment as a percentage of all persons of working age in each region.

Source: Labour Force Survey, Office for National Statistics

5.2 Labour force:[1] by age, Spring 2000

Percentages and thousands

	Percentage aged					All ages (=100%) (thousands)
	16–24	25–34	35–44	45-59/ 45–64[2]	60 and over/ 65 and over[3]	
United Kingdom	15.1	25.2	25.7	31.2	2.9	29,412
North East	15.9	24.4	27.3	30.2	2.1	1,193
North West	15.5	25.6	26.0	30.6	2.3	3,288
Yorkshire and the Humber	15.5	24.8	26.0	31.2	2.5	2,471
East Midlands	14.6	24.6	25.2	33.0	2.6	2,139
West Midlands	15.0	24.4	25.6	32.1	2.8	2,600
East	14.2	25.1	24.7	32.5	3.5	2,779
London	15.2	28.1	26.7	27.0	2.9	3,641
South East	14.4	24.4	24.9	32.8	3.5	4,238
South West	14.5	23.7	24.8	33.5	3.6	2,484
England	14.9	25.2	25.6	31.4	2.9	24,832
Wales	15.8	24.2	25.4	32.3	2.3	1,326
Scotland	16.1	25.0	26.6	29.9	2.4	2,522
Northern Ireland	16.7	27.6	25.1	27.9	2.7	731

1 See Notes and Definitions.
2 Males aged 45–64 and females aged 45–59.
3 Males aged 65 and over and females aged 60 and over.

Source: Labour Force Survey, Office for National Statistics

5.3 Employment status and rates, Spring 2000

Percentages and thousands

	In employment				ILO unem- ployed	Econom- ically active	Econom- ically inactive	All aged 16 and over[2] (=100%) (thousands)	Employment rates[3]		
	Employees		Self- employed	Total[1]					Males	Females	All persons
	Full- time	Part- time									
United Kingdom	49.9	15.6	8.1	74.3	5.6	78.7	21.3	36,312	79.1	68.9	74.3
North East	45.3	15.6	5.8	67.4	9.2	74.3	25.7	1,573	71.6	62.8	67.4
North West	49.9	15.3	7.0	72.7	5.4	76.8	23.2	4,180	78.2	66.6	72.7
Yorkshire and the Humber	48.9	16.6	7.2	73.5	6.1	78.2	21.8	3,078	77.4	69.1	73.5
East Midlands	51.7	16.7	7.8	76.8	5.2	81.1	18.9	2,569	81.3	71.9	76.8
West Midlands	50.4	15.1	6.9	73.1	6.3	78.0	22.0	3,239	77.9	67.8	73.1
East	52.2	16.5	9.2	78.3	3.6	81.2	18.8	3,301	83.9	72.1	78.3
London	48.8	12.4	9.2	71.1	7.1	76.5	23.5	4,619	76.5	65.2	71.1
South East	54.0	16.5	9.5	80.6	3.4	83.4	16.6	4,907	85.9	74.7	80.6
South West	49.9	18.1	9.8	78.6	4.2	82.0	18.0	2,921	83.1	73.7	78.6
England	50.5	15.7	8.3	75.1	5.3	79.3	20.7	30,386	80.1	69.6	75.1
Wales	45.0	15.5	8.1	69.4	6.2	74.0	26.0	1,750	73.7	64.7	69.4
Scotland	49.0	16.0	6.1	71.9	7.7	77.9	22.1	3,160	75.3	68.2	71.9
Northern Ireland	43.2	12.0	8.2	64.9	7.2	69.9	30.1	1,017	71.4	58.0	64.9

1 Total also includes those on government-supported employment and training schemes and unpaid family workers.
2 Based on the population of working age in private households, student halls of residence and NHS accommodation. See Notes and Definitions.
3 Total in employment as a percentage of all persons of working age in each region.

Source: Labour Force Survey, Office for National Statistics

5.4 Employee jobs: by industry[1] and gender, December 1999

Percentages and thousands

	Agriculture, hunting, forestry and fishing	Mining, quarrying, (inc oil and gas extraction)	Manufacturing	Electricity, gas, water	Construction	Distribution, hotels and catering, repairs
Males						
Great Britain	1.5	0.5	22.3	0.7	7.7	21.6
North East	1.0	0.6	27.5	1.0	10.2	19.2
North West	0.9	0.1	26.0	0.8	7.6	21.7
Yorkshire and the Humber	1.5	0.6	27.7	0.7	8.8	20.7
East Midlands	2.0	0.7	31.2	0.7	8.0	20.7
West Midlands	1.3	0.2	32.0	0.8	7.0	20.8
East	2.3	0.3	21.9	0.8	7.9	22.2
London	-	0.2	9.8	0.3	5.7	22.6
South East	1.5	0.2	17.4	0.6	7.1	23.6
South West	2.5	0.6	23.2	0.9	7.7	22.3
England	1.3	0.3	22.2	0.7	7.4	21.9
Wales	2.5	0.6	28.9	0.8	8.2	19.4
Scotland	2.7	1.9	20.3	1.1	10.6	19.7
Females						
Great Britain	0.6	-	9.0	0.2	1.3	26.8
North East	0.2	-	9.2	0.3	1.2	27.4
North West	0.4	-	10.1	0.2	1.2	27.9
Yorkshire and the Humber	0.5	-	10.5	0.3	1.5	26.8
East Midlands	0.9	-	14.9	0.3	1.4	26.2
West Midlands	0.6	-	12.6	0.4	1.3	26.6
East	1.2	-	8.5	0.3	1.6	27.5
London	-	-	5.1	0.1	1.0	23.6
South East	1.0	-	6.8	0.2	1.3	27.3
South West	0.8	-	8.5	0.3	1.2	29.5
England	0.6	-	8.9	0.2	1.3	26.8
Wales	0.5	-	10.2	0.3	1.1	27.1
Scotland	0.7	0.3	9.0	0.3	1.5	26.9
All persons						
Great Britain	1.1	0.3	15.7	0.5	4.5	24.2
North East	0.6	0.4	18.1	0.6	5.6	23.4
North West	0.6	-	18.0	0.5	4.4	24.8
Yorkshire and the Humber	1.0	0.3	19.2	0.5	5.2	23.7
East Midlands	1.5	0.4	23.3	0.5	4.8	23.3
West Midlands	0.9	0.1	22.6	0.6	4.3	23.6
East	1.7	0.2	15.3	0.5	4.8	24.8
London	-	0.1	7.5	0.2	3.4	23.1
South East	1.2	0.1	12.2	0.4	4.2	25.4
South West	1.7	0.4	15.8	0.6	4.4	25.9
England	1.0	0.2	15.7	0.5	4.4	24.3
Wales	1.5	0.3	19.4	0.6	4.6	23.3
Scotland	1.7	1.1	14.7	0.7	6.1	23.2

5.4 *(Continued)*

Percentages and thousands

	Transport, storage and communi- cation	Financial and business services	Public adminis- tration and defence	Education, social work and health services	Other	Whole economy (=100%) (thousands)
Males						
Great Britain	8.5	19.5	5.1	8.0	4.6	12,524
North East	7.1	12.3	7.1	9.5	4.5	477
North West	8.1	16.8	5.7	8.2	4.1	1,413
Yorkshire and the Humber	8.2	13.9	4.9	9.1	4.0	1,037
East Midlands	7.9	13.9	4.1	7.3	3.6	879
West Midlands	7.6	14.7	4.2	7.7	3.6	1,181
East	10.0	19.3	3.8	7.4	4.0	1,097
London	10.3	33.0	5.0	6.9	6.2	2,025
South East	9.1	24.1	4.4	7.7	4.3	1,823
South West	7.4	16.5	5.7	8.5	4.6	987
England	8.7	20.3	4.9	7.8	4.5	10,919
Wales	6.2	11.2	6.8	10.4	5.1	523
Scotland	8.0	15.1	6.6	8.6	5.5	1,082
Females						
Great Britain	3.5	18.6	5.6	29.0	5.3	12,232
North East	2.4	11.0	8.5	33.2	6.3	496
North West	3.2	15.2	6.0	31.0	4.7	1,423
Yorkshire and the Humber	2.7	15.2	5.0	32.8	4.7	1,014
East Midlands	2.9	13.3	5.1	30.1	4.8	829
West Midlands	2.9	16.1	4.6	30.1	4.9	1,107
East	4.2	18.6	4.3	28.8	5.0	1,056
London	4.9	30.2	6.5	21.7	6.8	1,935
South East	.5	21.4	4.6	27.8	5.1	1,778
South West	2.7	16.0	5.5	30.9	4.6	1,006
England	3.7	19.1	5.5	28.6	5.3	10,644
Wales	2.4	12.5	6.8	33.7	5.4	547
Scotland	3.0	15.9	6.7	29.8	5.9	1,041
All persons						
Great Britain	6.1	19.0	5.4	18.4	5.0	24,755
North East	4.7	11.7	7.8	21.6	5.4	973
North West	5.6	16.0	5.9	19.6	4.4	2,836
Yorkshire and the Humber	5.5	14.5	5.0	20.8	4.3	2,051
East Midlands	5.5	13.6	4.6	18.4	4.2	1,708
West Midlands	5.3	15.4	4.4	18.5	4.2	2,287
East	7.2	19.0	4.0	17.9	4.5	2,153
London	7.7	31.6	5.8	14.1	6.5	3,960
South East	6.8	22.8	4.5	17.6	4.7	3,601
South West	5.0	16.2	5.6	19.8	4.6	1,993
England	6.2	19.7	5.2	18.1	4.9	21,563
Wales	4.2	11.8	6.8	22.3	5.3	1,070
Scotland	5.6	15.5	6.6	19.0	5.7	2,122

1 Based on SIC 1992. See Notes and Definitions.

Source: Annual Business Inquiry, Office for National Statistics

5.5 Employee jobs and self-employment jobs:[1] by gender

Thousands

| | Employee jobs[2] | | | | | | Self-employment jobs[3] | | | | | |
| | Males | | | Females | | | Males | | | Females | | |
	1998	1999	2000	1998	1999	2000	1998	1999	2000	1998	1999	2000
United Kingdom	12,654	12,795	12,818	12,250	12,466	12,543	2,525	2,487	2,446	980	947	950
North East	472	473	474	485	480	487	73	81	65	22	24	28
North West	1,372	1,437	1,421	1,359	1,386	1,417	251	268	233	85	83	84
Yorkshire and the Humber	1,048	1,049	1,023	995	1,004	1,021	191	188	188	77	61	63
East Midlands	896	860	857	813	855	830	168	169	162	63	68	61
West Midlands	1,191	1,162	1,172	1,074	1,096	1,105	211	195	190	68	73	70
East	1,104	1,100	1,102	1,055	1,060	1,057	263	261	255	104	103	103
London	1,946	2,010	2,045	1,863	1,888	1,936	361	345	351	147	132	150
South East	1,735	1,785	1,816	1,724	1,756	1,765	392	377	385	181	174	166
South West	992	1,000	994	996	998	1,003	256	249	250	110	106	109
England	10,756	10,876	10,904	10,364	10,523	10,621	2,166	2,133	2,079	857	824	834
Wales	534	538	518	514	540	552	111	118	118	42	38	43
Scotland	1,058	1,067	1,082	1,063	1,087	1,052	175	167	171	67	69	58
Northern Ireland	306	314	314	309	316	318	73	69	78	14	16	15

1 At September each year. See Notes and Definitions.
2 All employee jobs data has been revised due to the introduction of the Annual Business Inquiry, which has replaced the Annual Employment Survey as the annual benchmark inquiry for STES.
3 With or without employees.

Source: Short-term Employment and Labour Force Surveys, Office for National Statistics

5.6 Self-employment:[1] by broad industry group,[2] Spring 2000

Percentages and thousands

| | | Industry | | | | | Total self-employed[4] (=100%) (thousands) |
	Agriculture and fishing	Manufacturing	Construction	All industry[3]	Services	
United Kingdom	5.9	7.1	19.8	27.2	66.8	3,139
North East	..	..	12.4	21.1	76.7	98
North West	4.3	7.1	18.7	25.8	69.9	309
Yorkshire and the Humber	..	7.7	20.2	28.2	69.2	236
East Midlands	5.6	9.2	22.4	31.8	62.6	215
West Midlands	4.3	9.2	20.5	29.7	66.0	241
East	3.3	7.8	26.5	34.4	62.3	322
London	..	6.6	15.4	21.9	77.3	457
South East	4.3	7.0	21.3	28.5	67.2	497
South West	8.8	6.2	19.5	26.0	65.3	315
England	4.0	7.4	20.0	27.6	68.5	2,690
Wales	19.3	..	19.7	26.3	54.5	151
Scotland	12.1	4.8	17.4	24.0	63.9	208
Northern Ireland	28.2	..	21.3	26.1	45.7	90

1 Main job only.
2 Based on SIC 1992. In some cases, sample sizes are too small to provide a reliable estimate.
3 Includes SIC 1992 groups C and E: Quarrying, Energy and Water.
4 Total includes those who did not state their industry and those whose workplace was outside the United Kingdom, but percentages are based on figures which exclude them.

Source: Labour Force Survey, Office for National Statistics

5.7 Economic activity rates:[1] by gender

Percentages

	Males			Females			All persons		
	1998	1999	2000	1998	1999	2000	1998	1999	2000
United Kingdom	83.9	84.1	84.3	71.5	72.1	72.5	78.0	78.4	78.7
North East	79.4	77.1	80.0	65.2	67.0	68.0	72.6	72.3	74.3
North West	79.4	81.5	82.9	68.5	69.2	70.1	74.2	75.7	76.8
Yorkshire and the Humber	82.8	83.2	83.3	71.4	71.3	72.5	77.4	77.6	78.2
East Midlands	85.8	85.3	86.2	74.0	74.3	75.3	80.2	80.1	81.1
West Midlands	85.7	84.7	83.3	71.3	72.7	72.1	78.9	79.1	78.0
East	88.3	87.9	87.3	74.8	74.5	74.5	81.9	81.5	81.2
London	82.3	84.0	82.9	69.1	70.0	69.6	75.9	77.3	76.5
South East	88.8	88.9	88.9	75.7	76.1	77.4	82.6	82.8	83.4
South West	86.6	87.0	86.8	75.7	76.6	76.7	81.4	82.1	82.0
England	84.6	84.9	84.9	72.0	72.6	73.1	78.6	79.1	79.3
Wales	77.2	79.1	79.3	67.2	67.7	68.1	72.5	73.7	74.0
Scotland	82.1	81.3	82.9	72.0	71.5	72.5	77.2	76.6	77.9
Northern Ireland	80.8	78.5	77.9	63.4	64.8	61.5	72.3	71.9	69.9

1 At Spring of each year. Based on the population of working age in private households, student halls of residence and NHS accomodation. See Notes and Definitions.

Source: Labour Force Survey, Office for National Statistics

5.8 Part-time[1] working: by gender, Spring 2000

1 Part-time workers as a percentage of all in employment. Based on respondents' own definition of part-time.

Source: Labour Force Survey, Office for National Statistics

5.9 Reasons given for working part-time,[1] Spring 2000

Percentages and thousands

	Males				Females			
	Did not want a full-time job	Could not find a full-time job	Student or at school	All part-time workers[2,3] (=100%) (thousands)	Did not want a full-time job	Could not find a full-time job	Student or at school	All part-time workers[2,3] (=100%) (thousands)
United Kingdom	41.6	19.4	35.7	1,350	80.2	7.2	11.3	5,468
North East	32.3	34.8	31.1	49	80.1	10.9	7.5	226
North West	35.6	23.7	36.6	146	79.2	8.2	11.4	588
Yorkshire and the Humber	35.7	26.1	33.9	111	80.8	7.5	10.6	486
East Midlands	44.9	14.2	36.7	89	81.9	7.6	9.5	420
West Midlands	44.5	17.7	33.3	102	82.7	6.0	10.0	483
East	49.2	12.6	35.1	122	83.8	4.5	10.7	552
London	40.6	23.6	33.3	201	75.1	7.5	15.6	524
South East	47.7	9.1	40.9	210	82.0	4.5	12.2	819
South West	45.0	15.7	35.7	136	82.4	5.9	10.4	521
England	42.5	18.4	35.8	1,166	81.0	6.6	11.2	4,620
Wales	38.7	23.4	35.4	53	75.9	10.2	11.8	257
Scotland	34.5	24.0	37.7	107	74.5	11.9	11.7	473
Northern Ireland[4]	..	..	..	24	80.9	8.6	9.6	118

1 Based on respondents' own definition of part-time.
2 Employees and the self-employed only.
3 Includes people who said they worked part-time because they were ill or disabled. Hence percentages shown do not add to 100 per cent.
4 Some sample sizes are too small to provide reliable estimates.

Source: Labour Force Survey, Office for National Statistics

5.10 Employees with flexible working patterns:[1,2] by gender, Spring 2000

1 Includes those on flexi-time, annualised hours, term-time working, job sharing, nine day fortnight, four and a half day week and zero hours contract (not contracted to work a set number of hours but paid for the actual number of hours worked).
2 See Notes and Definitions.

Source: Labour Force Survey, Office for National Statistics and Department of Economic Development, Northern Ireland

5.11 People in employment with a second job: by gender, Spring 2000

Thousands and percentages

	People with a second job (thousands)			As a percentage of all in employment		
	Males	Females	All persons	Males	Females	All persons
United Kingdom	513	696	1,209	3.3	5.6	4.4
North East	13	28	41	2.1	5.8	3.8
North West	50	68	118	2.9	4.9	3.8
Yorkshire and the Humber	45	54	99	3.5	5.2	4.3
East Midlands	32	52	84	2.8	5.7	4.1
West Midlands	46	67	113	3.4	6.1	4.6
East	47	68	115	3.2	5.7	4.3
London	66	70	135	3.5	4.6	4.0
South East	76	101	178	3.4	5.5	4.3
South West	66	90	155	5.0	8.3	6.5
England	441	597	1,039	3.4	5.7	4.4
Wales	17	38	55	2.5	6.8	4.4
Scotland	36	50	86	2.9	4.7	3.7
Northern Ireland	19	10	29	4.9	3.5	4.3

Source: Labour Force Survey, Office for National Statistics

5.12 Average usual weekly hours[1] of work of full-time employees: by occupational group, Spring 2000

Hours

	Managers & admin- istrators	Professional, associate professional & technical	Clerical & secretarial	Craft & related	Personal & protective services	Sales	Plant & machine operatives	Other[2]	All occu- pations[3]
United Kingdom	46.1	44.1	39.4	44.3	42.2	41.9	45.2	43.6	43.6
North East	43.5	43.6	39.4	45.2	43.1	39.9	44.3	44.1	43.1
North West	44.4	43.6	38.8	43.1	41.0	40.7	44.7	43.5	42.7
Yorkshire and the Humber	45.6	43.9	39.0	44.6	40.7	41.5	45.1	42.2	43.2
East Midlands	47.1	44.4	39.4	44.5	42.3	42.2	46.8	42.4	44.1
West Midlands	46.8	43.3	39.7	44.2	43.0	42.1	43.8	43.3	43.4
East	46.5	45.0	39.8	45.0	42.8	42.4	45.7	45.1	44.3
London	46.2	44.4	39.5	45.2	42.7	42.0	45.6	44.3	43.9
South East	46.7	44.4	39.5	44.5	42.6	42.4	45.3	44.0	44.0
South West	47.4	44.1	39.6	44.5	42.5	42.2	45.1	43.4	43.9
England	46.2	44.2	39.5	44.4	42.3	41.9	45.2	43.7	43.7
Wales	45.0	43.7	39.0	42.9	41.4	42.8	44.5	41.6	42.8
Scotland	45.8	43.6	39.1	44.2	41.9	42.2	45.5	44.3	43.4
Northern Ireland	44.7	42.8	39.4	42.0	41.5	40.4	45.4	40.9	42.2

1 Includes paid and unpaid overtime and excludes meal breaks. The table also excludes those who did not state the number of hours they worked.
2 See Notes and Definitions.
3 Includes those whose workplace is outside the United Kingdom, and those who did not specify their occupation.

Source: Labour Force Survey, Office for National Statistics

5.13 Working days lost due to labour disputes[1]

				Days lost per 1,000 employees
	1997	1998	1999	2000
United Kingdom	10	11	10	20
North East	36	9	3	6
North West	7	9	4	20
Yorkshire and the Humber	7	1	11	4
East Midlands	3	1	1	5
West Midlands	7	7	1	20
East	5	11	2	6
London	12	12	15	7
South East	2	1	4	4
South West	-	1	2	1
England	7	6	6	8
Wales	3	2	4	6
Scotland	25	23	21	136
Northern Ireland	23	6	10	33

1 Regional rates are based on data for stoppages that exclude widespread disputes that cannot be allocated to a specific region. These are included in the United Kingdom strike rate only. See Notes and Definitions.

Source: Office for National Statistics

5.14 Employees absent due to sickness,[1] Spring 2000

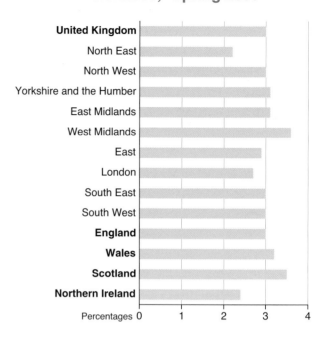

Percentages

1 Percentages of employees absent from work due to illness or injury for at least one day in the week before interview.

Source: Labour Force Survey, Office for National Statistics

5.15 Trade union membership[1], Autumn 2000

	Manual			Non-manual			Percentages
	Males	Females	All manual employees	Males	Females	All non-manual employees	All employees[2]
United Kingdom	33	21	29	28	32	30	30
North East	44	34	41	35	40	38	39
North West	37	23	33	36	38	37	35
Yorkshire and the Humber	34	24	30	31	35	33	32
East Midlands	31	23	28	29	32	31	30
West Midlands	33	24	30	29	32	31	30
East	27	13	22	21	27	24	23
London	28	22	26	19	28	24	24
South East	27	13	22	23	25	24	23
South West	30	15	24	27	28	28	26
England	32	20	28	26	31	29	28
Wales	40	26	35	43	44	44	40
Scotland	36	28	33	33	39	36	35
Northern Ireland	36	25	32	38	42	40	37

1 As a percentage of all employees in each region, excluding the armed forces and those who did not say whether they belonged to a trade union.
2 Includes some people who did not state whether they were a manual or non-manual employee.

Source: Labour Force Survey, Office for National Statistics

5.16 Average weekly earnings:[1] by industry[2] and gender, April 2000

£ per week

	Whole economy			Agriculture, forestry, fishing & hunting		Manufacturing	
	Males	Females	All persons	Males	Females	Males	Females
United Kingdom	451.6	336.7	409.2	295.4	246.7	433.9	301.8
North East	398.9	306.0	365.8	..	..	408.7	282.2
North West	428.6	312.8	385.7	256.9	..	436.6	296.9
Yorkshire and the Humber	409.9	308.8	373.7	311.5	..	411.3	267.8
East Midlands	407.0	301.1	371.4	302.4	..	409.5	262.5
West Midlands	425.3	311.2	385.9	..	..	409.2	274.6
East	455.5	333.8	412.7	315.3	..	471.6	326.8
London	593.0	434.3	529.8	..	..	549.2	435.9
South East	482.1	353.1	434.2	314.7	..	480.1	343.3
South West	418.2	309.8	379.1	271.2	..	420.9	304.5
England	459.2	341.5	416.3	298.1	241.0	439.2	308.4
Wales	400.5	313.7	368.0	..	..	402.7	276.1
Scotland	423.0	316.1	379.8	305.9	..	422.8	270.5
Northern Ireland	393.3	307.3	360.4	228.3	..	363.4	248.2

	Mining, quarrying & electricity, gas, water		Construction		Distribution, hotels & catering, repairs		Transport, storage & communication	
	Males	Females	Males	Females	Males	Females	Males	Females
United Kingdom	536.5	382.1	420.1	316.5	387.1	268.7	434.3	350.3
North East	555.1	..	371.7	..	318.8	236.1	360.7	..
North West	485.0	..	402.1	..	361.6	252.6	402.4	306.4
Yorkshire and the Humber	476.8	..	403.4	..	370.5	241.8	372.6	294.3
East Midlands	439.5	..	..	..	371.8	259.0	377.3	304.2
West Midlands	514.0	..	434.4	..	376.0	245.7	381.1	309.9
East	..	..	440.2	281.5	399.6	271.9	454.7	330.1
London	..	..	535.4	..	440.3	328.7	554.8	451.8
South East	..	406.2	446.3	..	444.8	307.7	451.3	368.5
South West	510.5	..	373.6	..	350.4	232.4	388.5	311.0
England	538.9	392.2	427.4	319.9	394.3	275.0	441.3	356.5
Wales	..	..	368.4	..	356.0	243.3	370.8	306.8
Scotland	589.9	349.5	411.9	..	346.6	234.8	393.2	322.1
Northern Ireland	390.5	..	340.5	241.3	318.5	214.5	382.5	273.4

	Financial & business services		Public administration & defence		Education, social work & health services		Other	
	Males	Females	Males	Females	Males	Females	Males	Females
United Kingdom	557.2	368.2	449.3	337.5	458.6	361.5	435.1	325.4
North East	419.9	304.1	401.0	316.4	414.9	338.6	..	..
North West	496.6	307.2	426.2	331.3	450.4	348.5	..	289.3
Yorkshire and the Humber	444.5	317.2	420.8	328.2	447.3	350.6	..	260.1
East Midlands	455.8	300.6	419.1	321.3	440.7	347.0	341.5	..
West Midlands	504.5	324.0	453.2	329.9	459.5	350.5	..	..
East	507.1	349.1	438.6	331.6	462.6	367.8	382.1	..
London	749.3	500.7	546.5	413.7	532.7	423.7	568.0	443.2
South East	565.1	373.4	450.0	362.7	465.2	368.3	..	304.8
South West	503.3	319.8	434.9	296.9	440.4	344.9	373.5	284.0
England	570.5	376.3	453.0	344.2	462.8	363.7	445.6	331.9
Wales	411.4	303.9	416.8	319.9	450.5	350.1	..	..
Scotland	483.6	322.8	428.0	327.0	429.3	341.8	..	282.7
Northern Ireland	440.3	283.3	468.4	294.9	466.2	380.9	359.0	274.1

1 Average gross weekly earnings; data relate to full-time employees on adult rates whose pay for the survey pay-period was not affected by absence. See Notes and Definitions.
2 Classification is based on SIC 1992.

Source: New Earnings Survey, Office for National Statistics and Department of Enterprise, Trade and Investment, Northern Ireland

5.17 Average weekly earnings and hours: by gender, April 2000[1]

		Average gross weekly earnings								Percentage of employees who received overtime pay	Average weekly hours	
		of which				Percentage earning under:						
	Total (£)	Overtime pay (£)	PBR pay[2] (£)	Shift etc premium pay (£)	£200	£300	£400	£500		Total including overtime (hours)	Overtime (hours)
All full-time male employees												
United Kingdom	451.6	27.5	15.1	6.8	6.6	29.5	53.0	70.8	32.0	41.2	2.6	
North East	398.9	31.6	14.1	10.6	8.7	35.1	58.0	77.2	37.1	41.2	2.8	
North West	428.6	27.7	14.8	8.3	7.3	32.2	56.4	74.5	32.3	41.1	2.6	
Yorkshire and the Humber	409.9	32.3	16.4	7.8	7.5	33.5	59.1	77.5	34.9	41.8	3.1	
East Midlands	407.0	28.7	13.0	6.3	7.8	33.4	60.4	77.6	34.2	41.8	2.9	
West Midlands	425.3	27.4	15.8	6.5	6.6	31.4	57.4	75.3	32.7	41.2	2.6	
East	455.5	30.0	16.9	6.3	5.8	27.4	52.4	69.7	34.2	41.8	2.8	
London	593.0	22.4	18.0	5.3	3.6	16.8	34.9	52.2	24.1	40.1	1.8	
South East	482.1	24.9	18.0	5.0	4.9	24.7	47.7	65.8	29.1	41.0	2.2	
South West	418.2	26.0	11.2	6.5	7.3	32.7	56.2	74.5	33.4	41.0	2.3	
England	459.2	27.2	15.8	6.6	6.2	28.4	52.0	69.9	31.5	41.1	2.5	
Wales	400.5	27.6	11.8	9.9	8.4	35.2	59.7	78.0	34.0	41.3	2.6	
Scotland	423.0	29.0	12.8	7.3	7.6	33.0	56.6	74.2	34.4	41.3	2.8	
Northern Ireland	393.3	31.8	9.3	6.4	12.3	40.7	61.1	76.0	35.0	41.4	3.1	
Full-time manual male employees												
United Kingdom	342.7	46.1	12.0	11.5	9.6	43.1	72.9	89.2	50.7	44.3	4.6	
North East	346.1	47.0	17.4	15.5	10.6	44.6	69.5	87.5	52.1	43.4	4.4	
North West	337.9	43.0	12.6	13.0	10.0	44.5	73.6	89.6	49.1	43.7	4.4	
Yorkshire and the Humber	340.9	53.5	14.9	12.4	10.1	44.7	74.2	90.2	53.2	44.7	5.2	
East Midlands	327.7	44.8	12.5	10.1	10.3	46.3	77.4	92.5	50.8	44.6	4.8	
West Midlands	335.8	44.6	12.4	10.6	9.0	43.7	75.7	91.6	50.2	43.9	4.6	
East	351.3	50.8	10.9	10.8	8.0	38.3	71.5	87.7	55.8	45.1	5.1	
London	386.6	48.7	9.5	11.5	7.1	31.6	60.8	79.9	46.8	44.9	4.5	
South East	355.5	46.6	9.4	8.9	7.3	38.1	69.5	87.9	49.9	44.6	4.5	
South West	328.5	41.7	8.0	11.1	9.9	46.8	76.3	92.3	52.8	43.9	4.2	
England	345.4	46.7	11.8	11.4	9.1	42.0	72.2	88.9	51.1	44.3	4.7	
Wales	335.5	41.3	10.5	15.3	11.2	46.8	73.1	90.6	48.9	43.6	4.2	
Scotland	335.4	45.8	15.0	11.0	10.6	45.9	75.3	90.2	50.6	44.2	4.8	
Northern Ireland	306.2	40.6	11.1	9.5	16.6	57.7	81.9	92.2	46.1	43.7	4.6	
Full-time non-manual male employees												
United Kingdom	532.5	13.7	17.5	3.4	4.4	19.3	38.3	57.1	18.1	38.8	1.0	
North East	457.3	14.6	10.4	5.3	6.7	24.6	45.4	65.8	20.6	38.8	1.0	
North West	504.3	14.9	16.6	4.3	5.0	21.9	42.1	61.8	18.3	38.9	1.1	
Yorkshire and the Humber	475.5	12.2	17.8	3.4	5.0	22.9	44.7	65.5	17.6	39.0	1.0	
East Midlands	480.9	13.8	13.5	2.8	5.5	21.5	44.5	63.7	18.8	39.3	1.1	
West Midlands	504.8	12.0	18.8	2.8	4.5	20.4	41.2	60.8	17.1	38.8	0.9	
East	532.8	14.5	21.3	3.0	4.2	19.4	38.2	56.4	18.1	39.3	1.1	
London	669.8	12.6	21.2	3.0	2.3	11.3	25.3	42.0	15.7	38.3	0.8	
South East	553.7	12.7	22.8	2.7	3.5	17.0	35.4	53.4	17.3	38.9	0.9	
South West	488.0	13.9	13.7	2.9	5.2	21.7	40.6	60.6	18.3	38.8	0.9	
England	540.7	13.3	18.6	3.2	4.2	18.7	37.5	56.3	17.5	38.8	1.0	
Wales	462.8	14.5	13.1	4.8	5.6	23.9	46.9	66.0	19.8	39.0	1.1	
Scotland	496.4	14.9	11.0	4.3	5.1	22.2	41.0	60.7	20.8	38.7	1.1	
Northern Ireland	478.1	23.1	6.9	3.4	8.2	24.2	40.8	60.3	24.2	39.2	1.6	

5.17 (Continued)

	Average gross weekly earnings								Percentage of employees who received overtime pay	Average weekly hours	
		of which									
	Total (£)	Overtime pay (£)	PBR pay[2] (£)	Shift etc premium pay (£)	Percentage earning under:					Total including overtime (hours)	Overtime (hours)
					£200	£300	£400	£500			
All full-time female employees											
United Kingdom	336.7	7.1	6.2	3.3	17.3	52.0	73.2	86.9	16.3	37.4	0.7
North East	306.0	6.5	4.2	3.6	22.5	59.5	78.8	90.7	17.0	37.3	0.7
North West	312.8	7.1	6.1	3.3	19.4	58.1	78.0	90.4	16.9	37.4	0.7
Yorkshire and the Humber	308.8	7.0	5.6	3.2	23.5	59.4	78.2	89.7	17.5	37.3	0.7
East Midlands	301.1	7.3	5.8	3.5	23.5	60.8	79.7	91.1	17.9	37.6	0.8
West Midlands	311.2	6.1	6.8	2.7	19.4	58.5	78.7	90.4	15.6	37.4	0.7
East	333.8	6.9	6.0	2.9	16.3	53.0	74.9	87.7	17.3	37.6	0.7
London	434.3	7.4	9.2	2.3	7.2	28.7	53.8	72.9	13.2	37.2	0.6
South East	353.1	8.0	7.4	2.8	11.8	46.3	71.2	85.5	17.4	37.6	0.8
South West	309.8	7.1	5.2	3.0	20.8	59.0	79.2	90.8	18.1	37.5	0.7
England	341.5	7.1	6.7	2.9	16.7	50.9	72.5	86.2	16.5	37.4	0.7
Wales	313.7	6.3	6.4	4.4	21.4	57.0	77.0	89.7	15.7	37.5	0.7
Scotland	316.1	6.9	3.5	5.2	19.0	57.0	76.4	90.9	16.1	36.9	0.7
Northern Ireland	307.3	6.3	2.1	5.2	23.5	57.7	75.0	89.5	14.0	37.3	0.7
Full-time manual female employees											
United Kingdom	227.2	13.6	6.5	6.5	44.8	84.7	96.4	98.9	29.3	39.8	1.7
North East	215.4	11.0	3.5	7.2	51.8	87.1	97.1	99.3	23.4	39.3	1.3
North West	222.8	13.9	7.8	5.6	45.9	86.4	96.7	99.2	28.5	39.8	1.9
Yorkshire and the Humber	213.0	13.4	7.4	7.2	53.9	88.0	98.0	99.1	31.8	39.5	1.7
East Midlands	216.1	14.6	8.1	5.8	49.8	88.6	96.8	99.3	30.6	39.9	1.9
West Midlands	228.9	13.5	8.1	4.9	42.5	85.1	96.9	99.3	29.2	39.7	1.7
East	228.7	15.0	6.4	6.0	43.3	87.0	96.4	98.9	31.6	40.1	1.9
London	261.0	13.7	5.0	6.1	32.6	71.6	90.9	96.0	24.9	39.9	1.6
South East	247.2	16.2	5.5	7.9	30.6	78.5	96.0	98.3	33.8	40.5	2.0
South West	226.0	14.1	5.3	6.5	46.6	83.7	96.2	99.2	33.1	39.9	1.9
England	230.1	14.2	6.5	6.3	43.2	83.6	96.0	98.7	30.0	39.9	1.8
Wales	214.2	13.5	4.7	6.8	53.5	89.3	97.0	99.6	31.7	39.3	1.6
Scotland	217.3	10.6	5.7	8.2	50.4	87.8	97.6	99.7	24.3	39.2	1.4
Northern Ireland	207.1	9.7	10.3	4.9	51.0	93.9	100.0	100.0	24.2	39.0	1.5
Full-time non-manual female employees											
United Kingdom	356.6	5.9	6.1	2.7	12.3	46.0	69.0	84.8	14.0	36.9	0.5
North East	324.9	5.5	4.4	2.9	16.4	53.8	75.0	88.9	15.7	36.9	0.5
North West	329.4	5.9	5.7	2.8	14.4	52.9	74.5	88.8	14.8	36.9	0.5
Yorkshire and the Humber	328.6	5.6	5.2	2.4	17.2	53.5	74.1	87.8	14.5	36.9	0.5
East Midlands	326.1	5.1	5.1	2.8	15.8	52.6	74.7	88.7	14.1	36.9	0.4
West Midlands	329.3	4.5	6.5	2.2	14.4	52.7	74.7	88.5	12.6	36.9	0.4
East	351.5	5.5	6.0	2.3	11.8	47.3	71.3	85.8	14.8	37.1	0.5
London	452.9	6.7	9.6	1.8	4.5	24.0	49.8	70.5	11.9	36.9	0.5
South East	370.6	6.6	7.7	2.0	8.7	41.1	67.1	83.4	14.7	37.1	0.6
South West	326.0	5.8	5.1	2.3	15.8	54.1	75.9	89.2	15.1	37.1	0.5
England	361.6	5.9	6.7	2.3	11.9	45.0	68.3	83.9	14.0	37.0	0.5
Wales	332.5	4.9	6.7	3.9	15.3	50.9	73.2	87.8	12.7	37.1	0.5
Scotland	335.3	6.2	3.0	4.6	12.9	51.0	72.2	89.2	14.5	36.4	0.6
Northern Ireland	327.8	5.6	0.9	5.2	17.9	50.3	69.9	87.4	11.9	36.9	0.5

1 Data relate to full-time employees on adult rates whose pay for the survey pay-period was not affected by absence. See Notes and Definitions.
2 PBR pay is payments-by-results, bonuses, commission and all other incentive payments plus profit-related payments.

Source: New Earnings Survey, Office for National Statistics and Department of Enterprise, Trade and Investment, Northern Ireland

5.18 ILO unemployment rates[1]

Percentages

	| Spring quarter of each year				
	1996	1997	1998	1999	2000
United Kingdom	8.3	7.2	6.3	6.1	5.6
North East	11.0	10.0	8.2	10.2	9.2
North West	8.5	6.9	6.7	6.3	5.4
Yorkshire and the Humber	8.2	8.2	7.1	6.6	6.1
East Midlands	7.6	6.3	4.9	5.2	5.2
West Midlands	9.5	6.9	6.4	6.9	6.3
East	6.2	5.9	5.1	4.2	3.6
London	11.5	9.3	8.2	7.7	7.1
South East	6.2	5.3	4.4	3.7	3.4
South West	6.5	5.3	4.6	4.9	4.2
England	8.2	7.0	6.1	5.9	5.3
Wales	8.5	8.5	6.8	7.2	6.2
Scotland	8.8	8.6	7.5	7.6	7.7
Northern Ireland	9.8	7.6	7.4	7.4	7.2

1 For those of working age. Not seasonally adjusted. See Notes and Definitions.

Source: Labour Force Survey, Office for National Statistics

5.19 Claimant count rates[1]

Percentages

	| Seasonally adjusted annual averages				
	1996	1997	1998	1999	2000
United Kingdom	7.0	5.3	4.5	4.2	3.6
North East	10.0	8.1	7.2	7.0	6.3
North West	7.5	5.9	5.1	4.6	4.1
Yorkshire and the Humber	7.6	6.1	5.4	5.0	4.4
East Midlands	6.5	4.7	4.0	3.7	3.5
West Midlands	6.9	5.3	4.6	4.5	4.0
East	5.7	4.0	3.2	2.9	2.5
London	8.2	6.2	5.0	4.5	3.8
South East	4.9	3.3	2.6	2.3	1.8
South West	5.9	4.2	3.4	3.1	2.5
England	6.8	5.1	4.3	3.9	3.4
Wales	7.7	6.2	5.4	5.0	4.4
Scotland	7.3	6.2	5.5	5.1	4.6
Northern Ireland	10.7	8.1	7.3	6.4	5.3

1 See Notes and Definitions.

Source: Office for National Statistics

5.20 ILO unemployment rates: by age, 2000–2001[1]

Percentages and thousands

	| Percentage of the economically active[2] who were ILO unemployed and aged:				All ILO unemployed of working age (thousands)
	16–24	25–34	35–49	Males 50–64, females 50–59	
United Kingdom	12.4	4.8	3.8	4.0	1,569
North East	18.7	7.4	6.0	6.3	101
North West	12.5	5.3	3.3	4.1	175
Yorkshire and the Humber	14.1	6.0	4.1	3.5	148
East Midlands	11.9	4.0	3.4	3.6	102
West Midlands	13.8	5.8	4.0	4.6	156
East	8.4	3.2	2.5	2.9	100
London	15.6	5.4	5.4	6.0	254
South East	8.1	2.7	2.4	2.5	137
South West	9.5	3.5	3.0	3.3	101
England	12.1	4.6	3.6	3.9	1,274
Wales	15.4	5.5	4.4	3.7	84
Scotland	13.9	6.5	4.4	5.1	166
Northern Ireland	9.9	6.2	5.3	5.5	46

1 Average of four quarters ending Winter 2000/2001. See Notes and Definitions.
2 Those of working age who were economically active.

Source: Labour Force Survey, Office for National Statistics

5.21 Claimant count:[1] by age and gender, March 2001

Percentages and thousands

	Less than 20	20–29	30–39	40–49	50–59	60 and over	Total (=100%) (thousands)
			Percentage aged:				
Males							
United Kingdom	8.8	30.2	27.0	17.9	14.7	1.3	793.1
North East	10.5	30.6	24.9	17.9	15.1	1.0	54.4
North West	10.2	32.2	26.5	16.7	13.3	0.9	104.2
Yorkshire and the Humber	9.8	31.9	25.7	17.0	14.4	1.2	80.8
East Midlands	9.2	31.1	25.4	17.3	15.4	1.7	52.3
West Midlands	8.9	30.6	26.6	17.6	14.8	1.6	80.8
East	8.0	28.3	26.4	18.3	17.0	1.9	44.6
London	5.6	27.9	33.3	19.6	12.7	1.0	114.9
South East	7.2	27.8	26.7	19.3	17.2	1.8	54.1
South West	8.5	29.8	25.4	17.7	17.0	1.6	42.7
England	8.6	30.1	27.4	17.9	14.7	1.3	628.8
Wales	11.0	32.6	24.6	16.6	14.3	0.9	44.0
Scotland	10.0	30.1	25.7	18.0	15.0	1.2	89.5
Northern Ireland	8.1	29.6	26.3	19.6	15.4	0.9	30.8
Females							
United Kingdom	16.4	29.1	18.4	18.2	17.9	-	242.2
North East	22.5	28.8	16.0	17.2	15.5	-	13.6
North West	20.1	29.3	17.5	17.0	16.0	-	28.5
Yorkshire and the Humber	19.0	30.0	17.2	17.1	16.7	-	23.2
East Midlands	15.8	28.2	17.5	18.6	19.9	-	17.4
West Midlands	16.8	29.6	17.3	17.6	18.7	-	24.5
East	14.7	26.4	18.4	19.0	21.5	-	15.5
London	10.4	30.8	23.7	19.2	15.9	-	39.9
South East	13.3	27.4	19.2	19.4	20.8	-	17.1
South West	14.4	28.6	17.6	18.5	20.9	-	14.8
England	15.9	29.2	18.8	18.2	17.9	-	194.5
Wales	19.0	29.9	15.9	17.3	17.9	-	12.9
Scotland	19.1	27.2	17.4	18.7	17.6	-	25.7
Northern Ireland	16.9	31.5	16.7	17.3	17.7	-	9.1
All persons							
United Kingdom	10.6	30.0	25.0	18.0	15.5	1.0	1,041.1
North East	12.9	30.2	23.1	17.7	15.2	0.8	68.3
North West	12.4	31.6	24.6	16.8	13.9	0.7	133.2
Yorkshire and the Humber	11.9	31.4	23.8	17.0	14.9	1.0	104.3
East Midlands	10.8	30.4	23.4	17.6	16.5	1.2	70.0
West Midlands	10.7	30.4	24.4	17.6	15.7	1.2	105.7
East	9.7	27.9	24.3	18.5	18.2	1.4	60.5
London	6.8	28.6	30.8	19.5	13.5	0.7	156.4
South East	8.7	27.7	24.9	19.3	18.1	1.3	71.6
South West	10.0	29.5	23.4	17.9	18.0	1.2	58.0
England	10.3	29.9	25.3	18.0	15.5	1.0	827.9
Wales	12.8	32.0	22.6	16.8	15.1	0.7	57.0
Scotland	12.0	29.5	23.8	18.2	15.6	0.9	115.3
Northern Ireland	10.1	30.0	24.1	19.1	15.9	0.7	39.9

1 Not seasonally adjusted. See Notes and Definitions.

Source: Office for National Statistics

5.22 Claimant count rate:[1] by sub-region,[2] March 2001

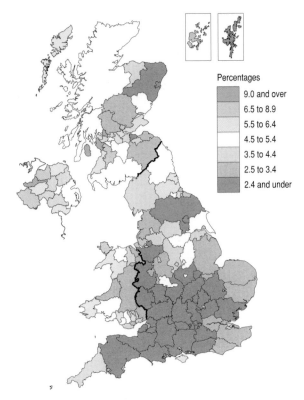

Percentages

- 9.0 and over
- 6.5 to 8.9
- 5.5 to 6.4
- 4.5 to 5.4
- 3.5 to 4.4
- 2.5 to 3.4
- 2.4 and under

1 The claimant count rate is the number of people claiming unemployment-related benefit as a proportion of claimant count and workforce jobs in each area.
  Not seasonally adjusted. See Notes and Definitions.
2 Travel-to-work areas for Northern Ireland.

Source: Office for National Statistics

5.23 ILO unemployment rates:[1] by duration and gender, 1999–2000[2]

Percentages and thousands

	Males					Females				
	6 months or less	6 months and up to 12 months	1 year and up to 2 years	2 years and over	Total ILO unemployed (thousands)	6 months or less	6 months and up to 12 months	1 year and up to 2 years	2 years and over	Total ILO unemployed (thousands)
United Kingdom	3.1	0.9	0.8	1.2	981	3.3	0.7	0.5	0.4	647
North East	4.9	1.7	1.4	2.2	68	3.8	1.2	..	..	36
North West	3.2	0.9	0.7	1.5	116	3.1	0.8	0.5	..	70
Yorkshire and the Humber	3.9	1.1	0.9	1.2	96	3.5	0.8	..	..	57
East Midlands	2.8	0.8	0.7	1.0	62	3.3	..	..	..	43
West Midlands	3.6	0.9	0.8	1.2	96	3.6	1.0	0.6	..	63
East	2.4	0.5	0.5	0.5	62	2.3	..	..	..	42
London	3.7	1.2	1.3	1.4	154	4.2	1.1	0.6	0.7	108
South East	2.1	0.4	0.3	0.5	77	2.6	0.4	..	..	65
South West	2.4	0.8	..	0.7	59	2.9	..	..	..	44
England	3.1	0.9	0.7	1.0	790	3.2	0.7	0.4	0.4	528
Wales	3.3	1.2	1.2	1.7	54	3.4	..	..	..	32
Scotland	3.8	1.1	1.0	1.8	107	3.7	1.0	0.8	0.6	71
Northern Ireland	2.7	..	..	2.5	30	2.9	..	..	..	17

1 For those aged 16 and over. Not seasonally adjusted. See Notes and Definitions.
2 Average of four quarters ending Autumn 2000. See Notes and Definitions.

Source: Labour Force Survey, Office for National Statistics

5.24 ILO unemployment rates: by highest qualification,[1] Spring 2000

Percentages and thousands

	Degree or equivalent	Higher education qualifications[2]	GCE A Level or equivalent[3]	GCSE grades A*–C or equivalent	Other qualifications	No qualifications	Total ILO unemployed (=100%) (thousands)
United Kingdom	2.3	2.6	4.5	6.4	7.7	11.1	1,602
North East	..	..	7.8	9.0	12.0	18.0	108
North West	2.4	..	3.9	6.4	7.5	10.6	172
Yorkshire and the Humber	..	..	4.9	6.2	8.8	12.0	146
East Midlands	..	..	4.7	6.1	6.4	8.9	109
West Midlands	..	..	4.3	7.7	7.7	12.2	158
East	..	..	2.7	3.8	5.4	6.7	97
London	2.8	..	5.5	10.0	10.4	14.9	252
South East	1.7	..	3.0	3.5	6.0	5.6	138
South West	..	..	3.3	4.3	5.4	8.5	100
England	2.2	2.4	4.1	6.0	7.7	10.4	1,282
Wales	..	..	4.3	7.3	6.6	13.7	80
Scotland	2.8	4.1	7.0	10.5	8.8	15.0	190
Northern Ireland	..	..	5.6	7.7	..	11.8	51

1 See Notes and Definitions.
2 Below degree level.
3 Includes recognised trade apprenticeships.

Source: Labour Force Survey, Office for National Statistics

5.25 Redundancies,[1] Spring 2000[2]

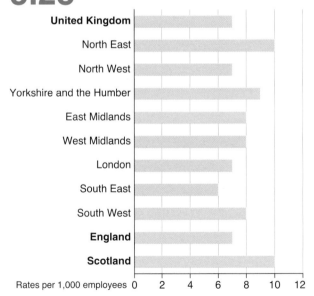

Rates per 1,000 employees

1 See Notes and Definitions. For the East of England, Wales and Northern Ireland the sample sizes are too small to provide reliable estimates, but are included in the United Kingdom total.
2 Due to a change in definition, the figures shown are not comparable with those shown in previous editions of *Regional Trends*. See Notes and Definitions.

Source: Labour Force Survey, Office for National Statistics

5.26 Vacancies[1] at jobcentres

Thousands

	1996	1997	1998	1999[2]	2000
United Kingdom	224.9	283.3	295.9	314.3	358.3
North East	8.1	10.1	11.0	16.0	19.7
North West	26.6	34.3	40.9	37.1	41.1
Yorkshire and the Humber	16.7	20.9	22.6	24.1	32.6
East Midlands	14.8	20.3	20.6	21.2	22.4
West Midlands	18.8	23.1	30.1	35.7	35.8
East	17.7	23.5	24.0	24.0	24.5
London	28.8	35.0	28.2	32.0	36.4
South East	28.2	34.4	34.8	37.5	43.5
South West	19.2	25.4	26.1	27.8	34.5
England	178.0	227.2	238.1	255.4	290.4
Wales	14.5	18.0	17.9	17.0	19.0
Scotland	25.5	31.4	31.0	32.9	39.9
Northern Ireland	7.0	6.8	8.9	..	..

1 Vacancies remaining unfilled at jobcentres. Seasonally adjusted annual averages.
2 The publication of the vacancy figures for Northern Ireland has been suspended since March 1999 as a result of a difficulty caused by the introduction of a new computer system for processing vacancies to Training and Employment Agency Offices. For the purposes of the seasonally adjusted United Kingdom figures it has been assumed provisionally that the Northern Ireland figures have remained constant since February 1999.

Source: Employment Service

5.27 Number of starts on the New Deal 18 to 24:[1] by gender

Thousands

	Males		Females		All persons	
	1999	2000	1999	2000	1999	2000
Great Britain[2]	135.0	124.1	54.7	51.5	189.7	175.9
North East	10.4	10.0	3.8	3.7	14.2	13.8
North West	19.2	18.3	7.0	6.9	26.2	25.2
Yorkshire and the Humber	15.2	13.7	6.0	5.8	21.2	19.5
East Midlands	8.3	7.9	3.4	3.3	11.7	11.2
West Midlands	13.9	13.1	6.0	5.9	19.9	19.0
East	7.1	6.0	3.1	2.7	10.2	8.7
London	18.2	17.8	9.4	8.9	27.6	26.9
South East	8.5	7.4	3.2	2.9	11.7	10.3
South West	7.8	6.9	3.3	2.8	11.1	9.7
England	108.6	101.1	45.2	42.9	153.8	144.3
Wales	8.5	8.1	3.0	3.0	11.5	11.1
Scotland	16.0	14.7	6.0	5.4	22.0	20.2

1 See Notes and Definitions.
2 Includes clients for whom the region is recorded as 'unknown'.

Source: Employment Service

5.28 Reasons for economic inactivity, Spring 2000

Percentages and thousands

	Does not want a job					Wants a job but not seeking in last four weeks						Wants a job and seeking work but not able to start[2]	All inactive (=100%) (thousands)
	Looking after family or home	Long term sick or disabled	Student	Other	All	Long term sick or disabled	Looking after family or home	Student	Discouraged worker[1]	Other	All		
United Kingdom	21.7	18.1	16.2	13.6	69.6	9.9	8.4	3.4	0.8	4.9	27.4	3.0	7,744
North East	20.7	22.7	12.6	13.0	69.0	10.7	8.6	3.8	..	4.9	28.4	..	405
North West	20.9	22.5	14.9	12.6	70.9	11.3	7.1	3.5	..	4.1	26.7	2.4	968
Yorkshire and the Humber	20.8	18.0	14.5	13.8	67.1	11.2	9.4	3.3	..	4.4	29.0	3.9	670
East Midlands	25.5	16.2	16.1	14.1	71.9	9.7	6.6	3.1	..	4.9	25.4	2.7	487
West Midlands	21.8	19.1	16.4	12.8	70.1	10.0	8.3	3.4	..	5.0	27.4	2.6	712
East	22.8	14.1	17.2	16.2	70.2	8.1	9.6	2.8	..	4.7	26.7	3.1	619
London	22.8	12.5	21.7	11.7	68.8	9.0	8.2	3.4	..	6.6	27.9	3.3	1,085
South East	24.8	10.2	14.6	18.7	68.2	8.8	9.1	3.1	..	5.9	27.9	3.9	815
South West	20.6	13.7	15.2	18.2	67.6	10.0	9.9	4.4	..	4.6	29.8	2.7	524
England	22.3	16.3	16.4	14.4	69.3	9.8	8.5	3.4	0.9	5.1	27.7	3.1	6,285
Wales	19.4	26.3	12.7	11.2	69.5	11.5	7.8	4.5	..	3.9	28.2	2.3	455
Scotland	16.6	26.5	13.7	11.1	67.9	11.5	8.0	3.9	..	4.6	28.9	7.4	698
Northern Ireland	24.0	23.7	24.5	7.9	80.1	6.0	8.2	..	..	..	18.6	..	306

1 People who believed no jobs were available.
2 Not available for work in the next two weeks. Includes those who did not state whether or not they were available.

Source: Labour Force Survey, Office for National Statistics

6 Housing

Dwelling stock

Dwelling stock

During the period 1991 to 2000, the stock of dwellings grew by more than 9 per cent in the East of England. This rate of growth was nearly double that of London.

(Table 6.1)

New homes

Although private developers remained the main providers of new dwellings across the UK in 2000, there were almost 13,000 fewer completions than in 1991.

(Table 6.2)

Council house sales and transfers

Between 1979 and March 2000, local authorities in the South East had sold or transferred almost 60 per cent of their housing stock since 1979 compared to less than 30 per cent in Yorkshire and the Humber.

(Table 6.3)

Tenure of dwelling

At 58 per cent, owner-occupation was lowest in London compared with any other area.

(Table 6.4)

Renting from a local authority or New Town was highest in Scotland and the North East, and lowest in the South East and South West.

(Table 6.4)

Type of dwelling

Over two-fifths of households in the North East lived in a semi-detached house, in comparison with one in five households in London in 1999-00.

(Table 6.5)

Over three in ten households in London lived in a purpose built flat or maisonette.

(Table 6.5)

One in twenty households in London lived in a detached house, compared with a third of those in Northern Ireland.

(Table 6.5)

Household mobility

Over three in ten households in Wales and Northern Ireland had lived at their current address for 20 years or more.

(Table 6.6)

Household satisfaction with accommodation and area

The percentage of householders living in London who were very satisfied with the area in which they lived was lower than in any other region.

(Table 6.7)

Owner-occupier housing costs

In 1999-00, average weekly mortgage payments for owner-occupiers ranged from £35 in Northern Ireland to £82 in London. Average weekly total housing costs for all owner-occupiers were also lowest in Northern Ireland and Wales, and highest in London.

(Table 6.8)

Dwelling prices

The average sale price of dwellings in the South East rose by almost 19 per cent between the last quarters of 1999 and 2000; over the same period, prices in the North East rose by less than 3 per cent.

(Table 6.9)

Mortgages

The average percentage of price advanced towards home purchase for first time buyers was lowest in the South West in 2000 at 76 per cent, compared to 83 per cent in the North East.

(Table 6.10)

Weekly rents

Private sector renters' average weekly rent in London in 1999-00 was more than double that in the North East.

(Table 6.11)

Council tax

Almost three-quarters of dwellings in the North East were in Council Tax Bands A-B compared with one in six in London.

(Table 6.12)

Homelessness

In 1999–00, the breakdown of a relationship with partner was cited by four in ten households accepted as homeless in the East Midlands as the reason for their homelessness, compared with just over one in ten of those in London.

(Table 6.14)

6.1 Stock of dwellings[1]

Thousands and percentages

	Thousands				Percentage increase 1991–2000[2]
	1991	1994	1997	2000	
United Kingdom	23,550	24,117	24,681	25,229	7.1
North East	1,073	1,092	1,110	1,128	5.1
North West	2,791	2,844	2,904	2,955	5.9
Yorkshire and the Humber	2,021	2,060	2,105	2,143	6.0
East Midlands	1,634	1,680	1,729	1,776	8.7
West Midlands	2,079	2,123	2,167	2,207	6.2
East	2,094	2,158	2,224	2,285	9.1
London	2,912	2,966	3,014	3,053	4.8
South East	3,099	3,177	3,258	3,333	7.6
South West	1,968	2,019	2,072	2,127	8.1
England	19,671	20,120	20,582	21,008	6.8
Wales	1,184	1,214	1,243	1,267	7.0
Scotland	2,124	2,193	2,248	2,305	8.5
Northern Ireland	571	590	608	649	13.3

1 At 1 April each year, except for Scotland and Northern Ireland where the figure is at 31 December. The figure shown for the United Kingdom is the sum of the component countries for these periods.

Source: Department for Transport, Local Government and the Regions; National Assembly for Wales; Scottish Executive; Department for Social Development, Northern Ireland

6.2 New dwellings[1] completed: by sector

Thousands

	Private enterprise[2]		Registered Social Landlords		Local authorities, new towns and government departments[3]	
	1990–91	1999–00	1990–91	1999–00	1990–91	1999–00
United Kingdom	160.9	161.3	20.2	22.9	16.1	0.3
North East	5.8	6.6	0.9	0.8	0.1	0.0
North West	15.4	15.9	2.8	2.8	0.8	-
Yorkshire and the Humber	9.9	12.3	1.7	1.2	0.6	0.0
East Midlands	13.0	15.2	1.0	1.2	0.8	0.0
West Midlands	13.4	13.2	2.1	2.2	1.1	0.0
East	19.4	17.1	0.6	1.8	2.8	-
London	13.2	9.3	2.3	2.9	1.7	-
South East	24.4	20.4	2.1	3.0	3.4	0.0
South West	18.0	14.3	1.1	1.5	1.5	0.0
England[4]	132.5	124.3	14.6	17.3	13.0	0.1
Wales[4]	7.7	7.6	2.5	1.0	0.4	-
Scotland	15.5	18.7	2.3	5.1	1.7	0.1
Northern Ireland[5]	5.2	10.4	0.8	0.9	1.0	0.1

1 Permanent dwellings only i.e. those with a life expectancy of 60 years or more. See Notes and Definitions.
2 Includes private landlords (persons or companies) and owner-occupiers.
3 Northern Ireland Housing Executive in Northern Ireland.
4 Data for Private enterprise and Local authorities are on a calendar year basis. Data for Registered Social Landlords are on a financial year basis.
5 Data are on a calendar year basis.

Source: Department for Transport, Local Government and the Regions; National Assembly for Wales; Scottish Executive; Department for Social Development, Northern Ireland

6.3 Sales and transfers of local authority dwellings[1]

Thousands and percentages

	April 1979 to March 2000				1999–00				Total sales and transfers April 1979 to March 2000	
	Right-to-buy sales[2]	Large scale voluntary transfers[3]	Other sales and transfers	Total sales and transfers	Right-to-buy sales[2]	Large scale voluntary transfers[3]	Other sales and transfers	Total sales and transfers	Stock at 1 April 2000	as a percentage of notional stock at 1 April 1979[4]
United Kingdom	1,831	468	379	2,679	71	95	7	175	3,894	41
North East	120	4	5	129	4	3	-	8	276	32
North West	162	60	41	263	5	30	1	36	445	37
Yorkshire and the Humber	148	8	15	171	5	0	-	5	419	29
East Midlands	131	14	16	161	5	9	-	14	265	38
West Midlands	171	64	25	259	7	18	-	25	354	42
East	158	46	42	246	7	7	-	13	277	47
London	225	45	70	340	11	9	-	21	553	38
South East	182	135	51	368	6	10	-	16	252	59
South West	124	73	19	216	4	10	-	14	170	56
England	1,421	447	284	2,153	54	95	2	152	3,012	42
Wales	109	0	7	116	4	0	-	4	193	38
Scotland	301	21	2	324	13	-	-	14	565	36
Northern Ireland[5,6,7]	.	.	.	86	.	.	.	5	124	41

1 Includes shared ownership deals and dwellings transferred to housing associations and private developers. Excludes New Towns. Figures for Scotland exclude sales by Scottish Homes.
2 Right-to-buy sales were introduced in Great Britain in October 1980. Figures for United Kingdom therefore relate to Great Britain.
3 Figure for United Kingdom relates to Great Britain. For Scotland includes large scale voluntary transfers and trickle transfers to housing associations. For England, includes Estate Renewal Challenge Fund transfers.
4 Calculated as sales in the period April 1979 to March 2000 expressed as a percentage of stock at 1 April 2000 plus sales in the period April 1979 to March 2000.
5 The Northern Ireland Housing Executive (NIHE) is responsible for public sector housing in Northern Ireland. Under the Housing (NI) Order 1992 NIHE operates a voluntary house sales scheme which is comparable to the Right-to-buy schemes in Great Britain.
6 Figures relate to sales only (excluding SPED cases) and do not include transfers.
7 NIHE housing stock is at December 1999.

Source: Department for Transport, Local Government and the Regions; National Assembly for Wales; Scottish Executive; Department for Social Development, Northern Ireland

6.4 Tenure of dwellings[1]

Percentages

	Owner-occupied			Rented from local authority or New Town[2]			Rented from private owners or with job or business			Rented from registered social landlord		
	1991	1996	2000[3]	1991	1996	2000[3]	1991	1996	2000[3]	1991	1996	2000[3]
Great Britain	67	68	69	21	18	15	9	10	10	3	5	6
North East	60	62	65	31	27	25	6	6	6	3	4	5
North West	67	67	68	21	18	15	8	8	9	4	5	7
Yorkshire and the Humber	66	65	66	24	21	20	8	11	11	2	4	4
East Midlands	71	71	73	19	17	15	8	9	9	2	3	4
West Midlands	68	68	70	23	20	16	7	7	7	3	4	7
East	72	73	74	17	14	12	8	9	9	3	4	5
London	59	57	58	24	21	18	12	15	15	5	7	8
South East	75	76	75	12	9	7	9	9	11	3	6	7
South West	74	74	74	14	11	8	11	11	12	2	4	6
England	68	69	69	20	17	14	9	10	10	3	5	6
Wales	71	71	72	19	17	15	8	8	9	2	4	4
Scotland	52	59	62	38	30	25	7	7	7	3	4	6
Northern Ireland[4]	66	69	73	29	24	19	4	4	5	2	2	3

1 As at 31 March each year, except for Wales, as at 1 April each year, and Scotland and Northern Ireland, as at 31 December each year. The figure shown for Great Britain is the sum of these components for these periods. See Notes and Definitions.
2 Including Scottish Homes, formerly the Scottish Special Housing Association and Northern Ireland Housing Executive.
3 Data for Scotland and Northern Ireland are as at 31 December 1999, and are provisional for Scotland.
4 Changes in the method of data collection mean that the 1999 figures for Northern Ireland are not comparable with either the 1999 data for Great Britain or the Northern Ireland figures before 1995. The figures are based on occupied housing stock and do not include 'split hereditaments' where the domestic portion is less than the commercial portion i.e flats above shops. From 1995 they relate solely to properties liable for a rates charge.

Source: Department for Transport, Local Government and the Regions; National Assembly for Wales; Scottish Executive; Department for Social Development, Northern Ireland

6.5 Households: by type of dwelling, 1999–00[1]

Percentages

	Detached house	Semi-detached house	Terraced house	Purpose-built flat or maisonette	Other[2]
United Kingdom	23	32	28	12	5
North East	11	44	32	10	4
North West	17	39	32	9	2
Yorkshire and the Humber	19	38	32	9	3
East Midlands	29	40	21	7	3
West Midlands	21	40	25	10	3
East	32	33	22	10	3
London	5	21	29	31	15
South East	29	32	23	11	5
South West	28	28	28	8	7
England	21	34	27	13	5
Wales	28	33	32	6	1
Scotland	21	23	16	35	4
Northern Ireland	33	23	36	7	1

1 Data for Wales and Scotland are for 1998–99.
2 Includes converted flats which are particularly common in London.

Source: Department for Transport, Local Government and the Regions; General Household Survey, Office for National Statistics; Continuous Household Survey, Northern Ireland Statistics and Research Agency

6.6 Households: by length of time at current address, 1999–00[1]

Percentages

	Less than 12 months	12 months, less than 5 years	5 years, less than 10 years	10 years, less than 20 years	20 years or more
United Kingdom	11	25	16	23	25
North East	11	25	16	23	26
North West	10	24	16	23	27
Yorkshire and the Humber	13	25	17	21	25
East Midlands	12	26	16	22	24
West Midlands	10	24	15	23	28
East	12	28	16	23	22
London	14	28	16	19	23
South East	12	27	16	24	21
South West	12	27	15	24	22
England	12	26	16	22	24
Wales	9	25	15	21	31
Scotland	9	28	20	23	20
Northern Ireland	6	19	19	25	31

1 Data for Wales and Scotland are for 1998–99.

Source: Department for Transport, Local Government and the Regions; General Household Survey, Office for National Statistics; Continuous Household Survey, Northern Ireland Statistics and Research Agency

6.7 Householders' satisfaction with their accommodation and area, 1999–00

Percentages

	Accommodation		Area[1]	
	Very satisfied	Fairly satisfied	Very satisfied	Fairly satisfied
North East	59	34	47	39
North West	58	33	48	37
Yorkshire and the Humber	62	29	50	34
East Midlands	62	30	56	33
West Midlands	61	30	49	37
East	60	32	54	35
London	49	37	40	41
South East	61	31	56	33
South West	62	30	61	30
England	59	32	51	36
Scotland	58	36	52	40

1 Area data for Scotland are for 1996. See Notes and Definitons.

Source: Survey of English Housing, Department for Transport, Local Government and the Regions; Scottish House Condition Survey, Scottish Homes; Scottish Household Survey, Scottish Executive

6.8 Selected housing costs[1] of owner-occupiers, 1999–00

£ per week

	Mortgage payments	Endow-ment policies	Structural insur-ance	Service payments	All owner-occupiers[2]
Great Britain	56	20	5	5	46
North East	43	16	5	2	36
North West	46	17	5	1	38
Yorkshire and the Humber	45	17	5	3	39
East Midlands	45	16	4	5	38
West Midlands	50	17	4	5	41
East	60	21	5	9	48
London	82	25	6	11	72
South East	72	25	5	10	59
South West	54	20	4	8	41
England	58	20	5	6	48
Wales	41	15	4	2	29
Scotland	48	18	4	3	44
Northern Ireland	35	22	2	1	30

1 Those who did not make any payments within each category are excluded, this table is therefore not directly comparable with data published in previous editions of *Regional Trends* which included all owner occupiers. See Notes and Definitions.
2 Relates to both householders with a mortgage and those who own their house outright.

Source: Family Resources Survey, Department for Work and Pensions; Family Expenditure Survey, Northern Ireland Statistics and Research Agency

6.9 Average dwelling prices,[1] 2000

£ and percentages

	Average sale price (£)				All dwellings		
	Detached houses	Semi-detached houses	Terraced houses	Flats/maisonettes	Average price (£) 1999	Average price (£) 2000	Percentage increase 1999–2000
England and Wales	167,027	91,826	81,148	113,069	98,408	110,221	12.0
North East	111,374	57,417	43,255	47,401	61,249	62,945	2.8
North West	130,791	66,623	42,232	67,414	68,137	70,837	4.0
Yorkshire and the Humber	114,648	60,984	44,510	67,242	65,437	70,007	7.0
East Midlands	118,923	61,879	49,729	53,464	72,665	78,780	8.4
West Midlands	150,514	73,653	58,313	60,453	79,618	87,719	10.2
East	177,897	102,839	84,540	70,990	99,296	114,392	15.2
London	446,615	212,068	194,967	171,771	158,179	177,949	12.5
South East	250,531	132,132	104,242	87,581	124,115	147,271	18.7
South West	168,963	96,218	80,035	75,163	95,058	110,132	15.9
England	171,103	113,908	93,465	83,241	99,923	112,388	12.5
Wales	102,985	53,339	60,025	46,353	64,958	67,598	4.1

1 Excludes those bought at non-market prices. Averages are taken from the last quarter of each year. See Notes and Definitions.

Source: HM Land Registry

6.10 Mortgage advances, and income and age of borrowers,[1] 2000

	First-time buyers				Previous owner-occupiers			
	Number of loans (thousands)	Average percentage of price advanced	Average recorded income[2] (£ per annum)	Average age of borrowers (years)	Number of loans (thousands)	Average percentage of price advanced	Average recorded income[2] (£ per annum)	Average age of borrowers (years)
United Kingdom	481	79.7	26,259	33	602	64.3	35,197	40
North East	21	82.9	21,434	33	21	71.1	28,685	39
North West	51	82.7	23,130	32	57	69.4	31,555	40
Yorkshire and the Humber	43	82.7	21,593	32	47	69.5	29,861	40
East Midlands	40	82.2	22,974	33	52	68.4	30,193	39
West Midlands	41	81.2	23,217	34	53	66.0	32,306	40
East	47	79.4	28,150	34	63	62.8	36,446	40
London	58	77.9	37,642	33	54	61.3	51,275	40
South East	59	77.3	32,027	34	106	60.5	41,270	41
South West	38	76.2	25,854	34	68	62.3	32,463	42
England	398	79.4	27,146	33	520	63.7	35,948	40
Wales	26	82.8	21,766	33	30	69.8	29,846	41
Scotland	40	82.2	22,355	34	40	73.0	31,615	40
Northern Ireland	17	80.1	21,711	33	12	61.7	27,813	40

1 See Notes and Definitions.
2 The income of borrowers is the total recorded income taken into account when the mortgage is granted.

Source: Department for Transport, Local Government and the Regions

6.11 Average weekly rents:[1] by tenure, 1999–00[2]

£ per week

	Private sector	Local authorities	Registered Social Landlords
Great Britain	86	42.50	51.40
North East	56	36.80	44.50
North West	75	40.60	45.50
Yorkshire and the Humber	68	35.10	48.10
East Midlands	62	38.10	48.40
West Midlands	70	39.80	47.60
East	80	45.60	54.10
London	141	58.00	61.40
South East	99	50.30	59.90
South West	78	43.70	52.20
England	90	43.80	53.10
Wales	70	39.10	44.90
Scotland	71	36.40	38.97
Northern Ireland	..	37.60	40.40

1 See Notes and Definitions.
2 Local authority rents are as at April 1999 and are the rents for the forthcoming financial year 1999–00. Registered Social Landlord rents are as at March 2000 and are the retrospective rents for the previous financial year 1999–00.

Source: Department of Social Security; Department for Transport, Local Government and the Regions; National Assembly for Wales; Scottish Executive; Scottish Homes; Northern Ireland Housing Executive; Housing Corporation, Northern Ireland

6.12 Dwellings in council tax bands, 1999–00

Percentages

	Council Tax Bands			
	A–B	C–D	E–F	G–H
North East	73	21	5	1
North West	63	27	8	2
Yorkshire and the Humber	66	24	8	2
East Midlands	62	28	9	2
West Midlands	58	30	10	2
East	36	44	16	4
London	17	52	23	8
South East	25	46	21	7
South West	42	39	16	3
England	46	36	14	4
Wales[1]	45	35	17	3
Scotland[2]	52	27	17	4
Northern Ireland[3]	..	..	..	..

1 Figures for Wales are estimates as at December 2000 for the average number of chargeable dwellings during 2001-02, before reductions and discounts.
2 Data for Scotland are percentage of total number of dwellings. Council Tax bands in Scotland differ from those in England. See Notes and Definitons.
3 Council Tax does not apply in Northern Ireland.

Source: Department for Transport, Local Government and the Regions; National Assembly for Wales; Scottish Executive; Department for Social Development, Northern Ireland

6.13 County Court mortgage possession orders[1]

Thousands

	1991			1998			1999			2000		
	Actions entered	Sus-pended orders	Orders made	Actions entered	Sus-pended orders	Orders made	Actions entered	Sus-pended orders	Orders made	Actions entered	Sus-pended orders	Orders made
England and Wales	186.6	69.1	73.9	84.8	40.8	25.3	81.6	36.6	23.5	73.0	31.7	20.4
North East	6.0	2.9	1.9	4.3	2.3	1.2	4.2	2.3	1.1	4.0	1.9	1.1
North West	22.3	8.6	7.5	14.2	6.4	3.7	13.9	6.0	3.7	12.4	5.7	3.7
Yorkshire and the Humber	14.1	5.1	5.7	8.2	4.3	3.1	8.1	4.1	3.0	7.8	3.7	2.4
East Midlands	13.5	4.5	5.2	6.4	3.1	1.7	6.8	2.8	1.8	5.7	2.4	1.6
West Midlands	17.7	6.5	6.9	8.1	3.8	2.4	9.5	4.1	2.3	9.8	3.7	2.3
East	18.6	6.0	8.4	8.5	3.9	2.6	7.3	3.5	2.2	6.2	2.5	1.6
London	35.3	13.1	14.4	11.4	5.3	3.5	10.0	4.5	3.4	8.1	3.1	2.1
South East	32.2	13.2	13.2	11.2	5.8	3.4	9.4	4.4	2.7	8.6	3.9	2.6
South West	16.7	5.8	6.5	7.3	3.0	2.1	7.0	2.8	2.0	5.2	2.3	1.3
England	176.4	65.6	69.9	79.6	37.9	23.7	76.1	34.9	22.2	67.7	29.1	18.7
Wales	10.2	3.5	4.0	5.4	2.8	1.7	5.5	2.2	1.5	5.3	2.6	1.6
Northern Ireland[2]	3.1	..	..	1.6	0.2	0.5	1.9	0.3	0.7	1.7	0.2	0.6

1 Local authority and private. See Notes and Definitions.
2 Mortgage possession actions are heard in Chancery Division of Northern Ireland High Court.

Source: The Court Service; Northern Ireland Court Service

6.14 Households accepted as homeless: by reason,[1] 1999–00

Percentages and numbers

	Reasons for homelessness							
	No longer willing or able to remain with			Break-down of relation-ship with partner	Rent arrears or other reason for loss of rented or tied accomm-odation		Other reasons[2]	Total (=100%) (numbers)
	Parents	Relatives or friends	Parents, relatives or friends		Mortgage arrears			
England and Wales	16	12	29	24	4	25	19	******
North East	19	8	27	37	5	19	12	4,850
North West	12	8	20	28	5	16	31	12,820
Yorkshire and the Humber	13	14	27	31	5	21	16	8,370
East Midlands	12	8	20	39	5	20	15	7,120
West Midlands	15	11	25	33	5	19	17	13,210
East	19	9	28	24	6	31	10	8,720
London	18	20	38	12	2	24	25	28,440
South East	21	11	32	18	4	34	12	12,810
South West	15	9	24	23	5	37	11	9,790
England	16	12	29	24	4	25	19	106,130
Wales	16	7	23	31	7	30	9	3,652
Scotland[3]	..	..	33	36	4	16	12	17,000
Northern Ireland	..	..	26	14	2	11	48	5,192

1 See Notes and Definitions.
2 A large proportion of the Northern Ireland total is classified as 'Other reasons' due to differences in the definitions used.
3 In Scotland, the basis of these figures is households assessed by the local authorities as unintentionally homeless, or potentially homeless, and in priority need, as defined in section 24 of the Housing (Scotland) Act 1987. The figures relate to 1998–99.

Source: Department of Transport, Local Government and the Regions; National Assembly for Wales; Scottish Executive; Department for Social Development, Northern Ireland

7 Health and Care

Population	More than two-fifths of people in the South West NHS region were aged 45 and over in 1999, compared with a third in Northern Ireland.
	(Table 7.1)
Death rates	In 1999, Wales and Scotland had the highest death rates in the UK, at 11.9 and 11.8 per 1,000 population respectively; London's rate of 8.5 deaths per 1,000 population was the lowest.
	(Table 7.1)
Infant mortality	Infant mortality was lowest in the East and South West in 1999, at 4.6 deaths per 1,000 live births.
	(Table 7.2)
Causes of death	Allowing for the age structure of the population, 490 deaths per 100,000 population were caused by circulatory diseases in Scotland in 1999, compared with around 360 per 100,000 population in the Eastern, London, South East and South West NHS regions.
	(Table 7.3)
	Northern Ireland had the highest death rate from respiratory disease in 1999, at 218 deaths per 100,000 population, compared with 133 per 100,000 in the South West.
	(Table 7.3)
Self-reported health	In the South West, 45 per cent of women aged 65 and over reported having 'good' general health in 1998–99, compared with 25 per cent in Wales and 27 per cent in Yorkshire and the Humber.
	(Table 7.4)
Coronary heart disease	In 1994–1998, treated coronary heart disease was most prevalent in the Northern and Yorkshire and North West NHS regions and in Wales, for both males and females.
	(Table 7.5)
Cervical screening	Within the English Health regions, the percentage of women recalled early ranged from 4.8 to 7.1 per cent in 1999–2000
	(Table 7.7)
Breast cancer screening	At 31 March 2000, the proportion of women aged between 50 and 64 who had been screened for breast cancer in the previous five years was similar in most regions of the United Kingdom, at around 70 per cent; however the figure was 58 per cent in London.
	(Table 7.7)
Cancer	The incidence of lung cancer in 1997 was above the UK average in the northern parts of England and in Scotland, but below average in the southern parts of England and in Northern Ireland. For breast and prostate cancers, above average incidence occurred in the southern parts of England.
	(Chart 7.8)
Tuberculosis	Thirty-nine cases of tuberculosis per 100,000 population were recorded in London in 2000, more than three times the rate for the United Kingdom as a whole and 11 times more than in Northern Ireland.
	(Table 7.9)
HIV	Of the 20,000 people in the United Kingdom who were known in 1999 to be infected with the HIV virus, more than half were residents of London, and only 95 were in Northern Ireland.
	(Table 7.10)

Smoking	Nearly two-fifths of males aged 16 and over in Northern Ireland used to be regular smokers but had given up by 1998–99, compared with around a quarter of males of the same age in London, Scotland and Wales.
	(Table 7.12)
Alcohol consumption	61 per cent of females in Northern Ireland had not had an alcoholic drink in the week before interview in 1998–99, compared with less than two-fifths in the North West, South West and South East of England.
	(Table 7.13)
Drug use	Thirty per cent of 16–29 year olds in London reported having used Cannabis in the 12 months before interview in 1998, compared with 16 per cent in Wales, and 15 percent in Scotland in 2000.
	(Chart 7.14)
Waiting lists	Within the English Health regions, the South East had the highest proportion of patients waiting 12 months or longer, at 6.7 per cent, compared with less than one per cent in the Northern and Yorkshire region.
	(Table 7.15)
Prescriptions	On average 14 prescription items were dispensed per person in Wales in 1999–00; higher than in England and Scotland in 1999 and Northern Ireland in 1998–99.
	(Table 7.17)
GPs	Some 40 per cent of GPs in London were women at 30 September 2000, compared with 28 per cent in Wales and 29 per cent in the West Midlands.
	(Table 7.19)
Dentists	Only 40 per cent of people in London were registered with a dentist at 30 September 2000, a lower proportion than in any other region. *(Table 7.19)*
Residential care	Around a third of the places in residential care homes in Wales, Scotland and Northern Ireland were provided by local authorities at 31 March 2000, compared with less than a fifth in England.
	(Table 7.20)
	In Yorkshire and the Humber, 23 per cent of places in residential care homes at 31 March 2000 were for people with mental health problems, more than in any other UK region.
	(Table 7.20)
Children looked after	10 children per 1,000 aged under 18 were being looked after by local authorities in Scotland at 31 March 2000, compared with rates of between 4 per 1,000 and 6 per 1,000 in every other country and region of the United Kingdom. The Scottish figures, however, include those being looked after under a supervision requirement made by the Scottish Children's Hearings System.
	(Table 7.21)
Child protection	At 31 March 2000, 36 children per 10,000 in both Wales and the North East were on a child protection register, compared with 21 per 10,000 in the South East and a rate of 23 in the South West.
	(Table 7.22)
	Neglect was the reason for nearly half of all placements on child protection registers in London, and it was the most common reason in every region of the United Kingdom.
	(Table 7.22)

7.1 Population and vital statistics: by NHS Regional Office area, 1999

	Population aged (mid-year estimates) (percentages and thousands)						Vital statistics (rates)				
	0–4	5–15	16–44	45–74	75 and over	All ages	Live births[1,2]	Still births[2,3]	Deaths[4]	Perinatal mortality[5]	Infant mortality[6]
United Kingdom	6.1	14.3	40.8	31.5	7.3	59,500.9	57.2	5.3	10.6	8.2	5.8
Northern and Yorkshire	5.9	14.4	40.1	32.3	7.3	6,335.7	55.5	5.3	10.9	8.3	6.0
North West	6.0	14.9	40.2	31.7	7.2	6,595.3	56.8	5.4	11.3	8.6	6.6
Trent	5.9	14.2	40.0	32.4	7.5	5,147.9	55.2	4.8	10.8	8.1	6.1
West Midlands	6.2	14.7	39.8	32.2	7.2	5,335.6	59.4	6.1	10.6	9.9	6.9
Eastern	6.1	14.1	40.0	32.3	7.6	5,418.9	57.4	4.9	10.1	7.1	4.6
London	6.9	13.6	46.8	26.7	6.1	7,285.0	62.2	5.9	8.5	8.9	6.0
South East	6.0	14.1	40.3	31.8	7.8	8,698.7	57.2	4.5	10.2	6.9	4.9
South West	5.6	13.7	38.0	33.6	9.1	4,935.7	55.1	5.3	11.4	7.8	4.6
England	6.1	14.2	40.9	31.4	7.4	49,752.9	57.6	5.3	10.4	8.2	5.7
Wales	5.8	14.5	38.2	33.4	8.1	2,937.0	56.6	4.8	11.9	7.8	6.4
Scotland	5.8	13.9	41.5	32.1	6.7	5,119.2	50.8	5.3	11.8	7.6	5.0
Northern Ireland	7.1	17.2	41.9	28.0	5.8	1,691.8	13.6	4.8	9.3	10.0	6.4

1 Per 1,000 women aged 15–44.
2 See Notes and Definitions for the Population chapter.
3 Per 1,000 live and still births. A still birth relates to a baby born dead after 24 completed weeks gestation or more.
4 Per 1,000 population.
5 Still births and deaths of infants under 1 week of age per 1,000 live and still births.
6 Deaths of infants under 1 year of age per 1,000 live births.

Source: Office for National Statistics; General Register Office for Scotland; Northern Ireland Statistics and Research Agency

7.2 Still births, perinatal mortality and infant mortality[1]

Rates

	Still births[2,3]		Still births[2,3]		Perinatal mortality[3,4]		Perinatal mortality[3,4]		Infant mortality[5]		
	1981	1993	1993	1999	1981	1993	1993	1999	1981	1993	1999
United Kingdom	6.6	4.4	5.7	5.3	12.0	7.6	9.0	8.2	11.2	6.3	5.8
North East	7.5	4.6	5.9	5.1	12.6	7.9	9.2	8.3	10.4	6.7	5.5
North West	7.0	4.5	5.8	5.4	12.7	7.7	9.0	8.7	11.3	6.5	6.6
Yorkshire and the Humber	7.8	4.6	5.9	5.2	13.5	8.0	9.4	8.3	12.1	7.3	6.2
East Midlands	6.2	3.9	5.4	4.6	11.4	7.2	8.7	7.9	11.0	6.6	6.1
West Midlands	7.0	4.4	6.0	6.2	12.9	8.4	9.9	9.9	11.7	7.1	6.9
East	5.5	3.9	5.2	4.9	10.0	6.8	8.1	7.1	9.7	5.4	4.6
London	6.3	4.9	6.1	5.9	10.3	8.2	9.5	8.9	10.7	6.4	6.0
South East	5.8	4.0	5.4	4.5	10.5	7.0	8.3	6.9	10.3	5.3	4.8
South West	6.3	4.0	5.0	5.3	10.8	6.9	7.9	7.8	10.4	5.8	4.6
England	6.5	4.3	5.7	5.3	11.7	7.6	8.9	8.2	10.9	6.3	5.7
Wales	7.3	4.5	5.8	4.8	14.1	7.0	8.3	7.8	12.6	5.5	6.4
Scotland	6.3	4.8	6.4	5.2	11.6	8.0	9.6	7.6	11.3	6.5	5.0
Northern Ireland	8.8	4.1	5.2	5.7	15.3	7.7	8.8	10.0	13.2	7.1	6.4

1 See Notes and Definitions for the Population chapter.
2 Rate per 1,000 live and still births.
3 On 1 October 1992 the legal definition of a still birth was altered from a baby born dead after 28 completed weeks gestation or more to one born dead after 24 weeks gestation or more. Figures for 1993 are given on both the old and new definitions for continuity/comparison.
4 Still births and deaths of infants under 1 week of age per 1,000 live and still births.
5 Deaths of infants under 1 year of age per 1,000 live births.

Source: Office for National Statistics; General Register Office for Scotland; Northern Ireland Statistics and Research Agency

7.3 Age-standardised mortality rates:[1] by cause,[2] gender and NHS Regional Office area, 1999

Rates per 100,000 population

	All circulatory diseases			All respiratory diseases			All injuries and poisonings				
	Total	Ischaemic heart disease	Cerebro-vascular disease	Total	Bronchitis and allied conditions	Cancer[3]	Total	Road traffic accidents	Suicides and open verdicts	All other causes	All causes[4]
Males											
United Kingdom	380	231	74	149	54	255	42	9	16	129	956
Northern and Yorkshire	392	245	80	158	58	276	41	8	16	127	995
North West	419	258	83	170	66	280	48	8	18	133	1,049
Trent	385	243	71	154	58	256	42	11	16	128	965
West Midlands	395	240	77	151	55	253	40	8	16	135	975
Eastern	342	202	64	134	44	231	37	9	13	116	860
London	350	207	64	164	60	243	36	6	13	127	922
South East	335	194	66	135	47	233	36	9	14	115	854
South West	333	203	66	116	43	235	37	8	15	115	835
England	368	223	71	147	53	251	39	8	15	124	929
Wales	406	252	75	157	63	255	52	11	19	127	997
Scotland	462	284	99	152	59	298	60	9	27	167	1,140
Northern Ireland	418	268	85	183	60	247	52	12	16	119	1,019
Females											
United Kingdom	412	190	127	188	46	241	24	3	5	185	1,049
Northern and Yorkshire	430	206	132	196	55	249	20	3	5	188	1,082
North West	447	216	136	210	58	261	24	3	5	187	1,129
Trent	405	197	123	184	43	232	23	4	5	196	1,041
West Midlands	428	194	133	187	44	233	25	4	5	189	1,062
Eastern	376	166	119	177	36	225	23	4	3	188	989
London	360	167	98	200	45	233	21	2	6	169	983
South East	373	157	121	176	35	229	19	3	4	179	976
South West	371	168	118	147	32	221	22	3	5	179	940
England	398	183	123	185	44	236	22	3	5	184	1,024
Wales	437	200	128	191	52	247	29	3	4	180	1,084
Scotland	517	244	169	199	63	281	36	3	8	202	1,235
Northern Ireland	469	225	147	249	43	236	26	4	3	137	1,117
All persons											
United Kingdom	399	213	101	170	51	250	33	6	11	157	1,010
Northern and Yorkshire	414	227	107	179	57	264	30	5	10	158	1,045
North West	435	238	110	191	62	271	36	5	11	161	1,094
Trent	400	223	97	172	52	247	33	7	10	163	1,014
West Midlands	415	220	106	172	50	245	33	6	10	163	1,028
Eastern	364	187	92	158	41	231	30	6	8	153	936
London	358	189	81	184	53	240	29	4	9	149	960
South East	357	178	94	157	42	234	27	6	9	148	924
South West	356	188	93	133	38	230	29	5	10	148	897
England	386	205	98	168	49	245	31	6	10	155	985
Wales	425	228	102	176	58	253	40	7	12	154	1,049
Scotland	490	264	135	176	61	290	48	6	17	185	1,189
Northern Ireland	445	247	117	218	52	242	39	8	9	129	1,072

1 Based on deaths registered in 1999. Rates standardised to the mid-1991 United Kingdom population for males and females separately. See Notes and Definitions.
2 Deaths at ages under 28 days occurring in England and Wales are not assigned an underlying cause.
3 Malignant neoplasms only.
4 Including deaths at ages under 28 days.

Source: Office for National Statistics; General Register Office for Scotland; Northern Ireland Statistics and Research Agency

7.4 Proportion of population reporting 'good' state of general health: by gender and age, 1998–99

Percentages

	Males				Females			
	16–44	45–64	65 and over	All aged 16 and over	16–44	45–64	65 and over	All aged 16 and over
United Kingdom	73	57	42	62	68	54	38	57
North East	68	51	40	57	68	38	32	50
North West	68	57	42	59	68	55	39	57
Yorkshire and the Humber	75	50	40	61	68	48	27	54
East Midlands	72	55	36	59	71	53	39	59
West Midlands	67	56	40	57	65	58	32	56
East	75	60	41	63	67	57	43	59
London	72	59	52	65	69	50	41	59
South East	78	63	42	66	71	62	40	61
South West	74	62	46	63	69	63	45	60
England	73	58	43	62	69	55	38	58
Wales	77	57	35	61	66	44	25	49
Scotland	77	56	49	65	66	54	41	58
Northern Ireland	72	51	34	58	67	47	31	53

Source: General Household Survey, Office for National Statistics; Continuous Household Survey, Northern Ireland Statistics and Research Agency

7.5 Treated Medical Conditions:[1] by NHS Regional Office area, 1994–1998

Rates per 1,000 patients[2]

	Males					Females				
	Coronary heart disease	Hyper-tension	Depress-ion	Insulin treated diabetes	Non-insulin treated diabetes	Coronary heart disease	Hyper-tension	Depress-ion	Insulin treated diabetes	Non-insulin treated diabetes
England and Wales	35.8	56.2	24.9	5.1	9.9	21.3	66.5	61.3	4.6	7.2
Northern and Yorkshire	42.2	53.0	29.6	4.9	9.0	28.0	64.4	70.6	4.9	6.6
North West	41.0	59.1	30.4	5.2	10.3	25.7	67.2	70.3	4.6	7.4
Trent	35.9	56.6	24.7	5.1	9.5	21.8	67.0	61.2	4.6	7.2
West Midlands	33.2	56.5	21.6	5.0	10.1	19.3	67.2	58.6	4.5	8.0
Anglia and Oxford	31.9	53.1	23.7	5.2	9.5	18.4	65.4	61.1	5.2	7.3
North Thames	30.1	53.5	18.8	4.7	11.3	16.1	61.2	46.5	3.7	7.6
South Thames	29.4	55.0	20.6	4.8	8.8	16.3	65.5	49.7	4.0	6.0
South and West	32.9	54.9	24.1	5.1	9.9	17.2	66.1	60.5	4.3	6.9
England	35.5	55.6	24.9	5.0	9.8	21.1	65.8	61.4	4.5	7.1
Wales	41.8	67.3	24.0	6.6	11.1	24.2	77.4	58.6	5.5	7.8

1 Data are recorded in general practice. See Notes and Definitions.
2 All ages. Age-standardised to the European Standard Population.

Source: General Practice Research Database, Office for National Statistics, from data supplied by the Medicines Control Agency

7.6 Prevalence of treated asthma:[1] by NHS Regional Office area, gender and age, 1994–1998

Rates per 1,000 patients

	Males						Females					
	0–4	5–15	16–44	45–64	65 and over	All ages[2]	0–4	5–15	16–44	45–64	65 and over	All ages[2]
England and Wales	100.5	130.6	53.0	35.7	78.7	70.7	66.0	103.0	64.5	65.3	73.6	72.7
Northern and Yorkshire	103.3	130.5	47.6	47.5	75.9	68.3	63.5	94.0	62.5	66.9	69.2	70.0
North West	100.6	131.1	52.2	52.7	84.2	72.4	63.7	104.9	62.3	69.5	78.6	73.4
Trent	92.5	129.5	54.3	47.6	79.5	70.4	59.2	108.4	65.7	64.0	70.2	73.0
West Midlands	98.1	130.2	48.0	43.7	77.5	67.2	61.0	104.7	59.6	63.9	73.9	70.0
Anglia and Oxford	117.7	139.4	61.0	48.2	79.2	76.8	82.2	117.1	78.1	67.6	74.8	82.3
North Thames	101.1	125.8	47.7	42.3	73.8	66.0	70.9	94.1	53.6	60.8	67.7	65.9
South Thames	90.7	116.6	51.0	41.3	66.3	64.2	66.9	89.6	60.7	60.6	67.5	67.7
South and West	97.7	130.4	59.0	48.4	82.5	73.6	63.6	103.0	69.8	64.2	77.8	75.3
England	100.3	130.0	52.8	34.9	78.5	70.4	65.5	103.0	64.4	65.2	73.5	72.6
Wales	104.3	141.3	57.6	57.6	82.8	77.2	77.2	103.3	67.7	65.9	75.7	75.4

1 Data are recorded in general practice. See Notes and Definitions.
2 Age-standardised to the European Standard population.

Source: General Practice Research Database, Office for National Statistics from data supplied by the Medicines Control Agency

7.7 Cervical and breast cancer – screening and age-standardised death rates: by NHS Regional Office area

	Cervical screening programme at 31 March 2000						Breast screening programme at 31 March 2000				Age-adjusted death rates,[7] 1999	
	Percentage of target population screened: women aged[1]					Per-centage recalled early[4,5]	Percentage of target population[6] screened: women aged					
	25–34[2,3]	35–44	45–54	55–64[3]	All aged 25–64[2,3]		50–54	55–59	60–64	All aged 50–64	Cervical cancer	Breast cancer
United Kingdom	..	..	..	..	83.4	..	61.5	76.1	74.4	69.8	5.4	55.2
Northern and Yorkshire	84.6	88.3	87.2	80.6	85.6	5.1	60.6	77.2	75.3	70.1	6.5	51.6
North West	83.1	86.1	84.9	78.0	83.5	6.6	59.8	75.5	73.4	68.7	7.2	56.1
Trent	86.2	89.2	87.8	81.9	86.6	5.0	61.5	78.5	77.0	71.4	5.5	54.4
West Midlands	82.5	87.2	86.6	80.8	84.5	6.4	62.6	79.0	76.7	72.0	5.0	57.6
Eastern	83.3	87.6	87.1	81.4	85.1	5.6	60.4	77.5	76.6	70.3	4.1	55.2
London	73.4	79.3	80.7	76.0	76.8	7.1	49.2	64.9	63.5	58.2	5.2	54.6
South East	83.0	88.0	87.8	82.6	85.5	4.8	61.7	78.3	77.8	71.4	4.3	56.9
South West	83.5	87.8	86.7	80.9	85.1	6.3	63.3	79.9	78.8	73.1	4.5	52.7
England	81.5	86.3	86.0	80.3	83.7	5.9	59.8	76.3	74.8	69.3	5.3	54.9
Wales	76.4	86.5	85.9	78.6	81.3	6.7	61.5	77.0	75.2	70.5	6.1	58.3
Scotland	80.2	91.5	92.0	86.7	86.7	..	74.0	72.7	69.2	72.1	6.0	56.0
Northern Ireland	..	..	..	..	69.0	..	80.0	79.3	77.0	78.9	6.1	48.8

1 For England the target population relates to women aged 25–64, for Wales to women 20–64 and for Scotland to women 20–60 years screened in the previous 5 years (five and a half years in Scotland). Medically ineligible women (women who for example, as a result of surgery, do not require screening) in the target population are excluded from the figures, except in Northern Ireland.
2 For Wales the age groups are 20–34 and 20–64 respectively.
3 For Scotland the age groups are 20–34, 55–60 and 20–60 respectively.
4 Percentages recalled early relate to the year 1999–2000.
5 Women whose screening test results are borderline or show mild dyskaryosis are recalled for a repeat smear in approximately 6 months instead of the routine 5 years. If the condition persists they are referred to a gynaecologist.
6 Percentage of the target population – women aged 50–64 years – screened in the previous 3 years. Medically ineligible women (women who for example, as a result of surgery, do not require screening) in the target population are excluded from the figures, except in Scotland. See Notes and Definitions.
7 Deaths per 100,000 women aged 20 and over. Standardised to mid–1991 UK population. See Notes and Definitions.

Source: Office for National Statistics; Department of Health; National Assembly for Wales; General Register Office for Scotland; Information and Statistics Division, NHS in Scotland; Northern Ireland Statistics and Research Agency; Department of Health, Social Services and Public Safety, Northern Ireland

7.8 Cancer - comparative incidence ratios[1] for select sites: by gender and NHS Regional Office area, 1997

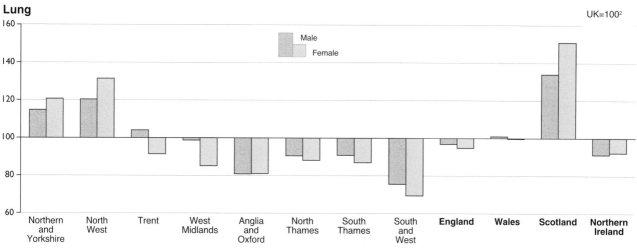

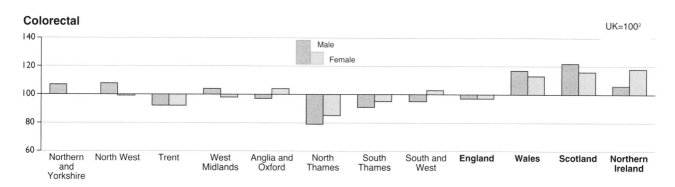

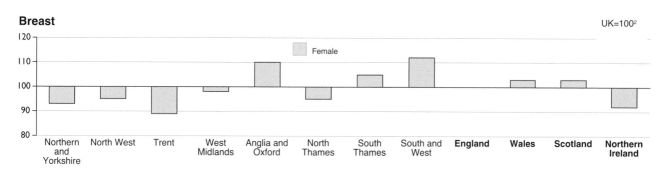

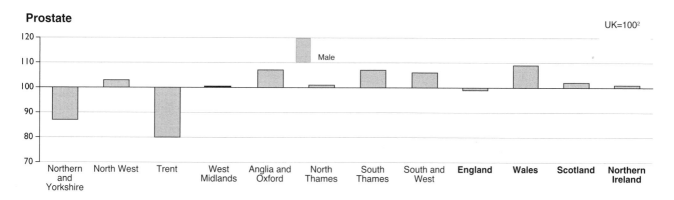

1 Comparative incidence ratio: the directly age-standardised incidence rate for each country and region as a percentage of the UK rate.
2 The UK age-standardised rates are given in the Notes and Definitions.

Source: Office for National Statistics; Information and Statistics Division, Scottish Health Service; Northern Ireland Cancer Registry

7.9 Notification rates of tuberculosis: by NHS Regional Office area

Rates per 100,000 population

	1990	1991	1992	1993	1994	1995	1996	1997	1998	1999	2000
United Kingdom	10.2	10.5	11.1	11.3	10.7	10.5	10.6	10.8	11.2	11.3	11.8
Northern and Yorkshire	9.9	11.1	10.1	11.0	8.9	9.8	9.5	9.7	10.1	9.6	9.4
North West	11.4	10.1	11.7	12.1	10.0	9.6	8.8	9.4	10.3	10.5	9.9
Trent	9.3	9.3	8.6	10.5	9.2	10.2	10.6	9.4	9.6	9.7	10.6
West Midlands	13.9	15.5	16.5	14.9	13.8	12.3	12.3	11.5	12.6	13.3	13.6
Eastern	5.1	4.9	5.6	5.2	4.7	5.1	4.9	4.3	5.0	4.2	4.7
London	23.4	26.0	29.0	28.3	29.8	29.1	31.0	33.9	34.0	34.2	38.9
South East	4.9	4.9	4.7	5.6	5.5	5.7	5.4	5.6	5.8	5.7	6.4
South West	3.7	3.5	4.2	4.4	4.2	4.2	4.2	4.3	4.3	4.2	4.6
England	10.4	10.9	11.6	11.8	11.1	11.1	11.2	11.5	12.0	11.9	12.8
Wales	6.7	5.7	6.9	6.8	6.2	6.2	5.5	6.7	5.9	7.0	6.6
Scotland	11.0	10.7	10.9	10.8	10.6	9.3	9.9	8.5	8.9	9.7	7.9
Northern Ireland	8.2	6.0	5.2	5.5	5.6	5.5	4.5	4.5	3.6	3.6	3.4

Source: Public Health Laboratory Service, Communicable Disease Surveillance Centre; Scottish Centre for Infection and Environmental Health; Department of Health, Social Services and Public Safety, Northern Ireland

7.10 Diagnosed HIV-infected patients: by probable route of HIV infection and NHS Regional Office area of residence when last seen for care in 1999[1]

Numbers

	Homo/ bisexual	Injecting drug use	Heterosexual	Blood/blood products	Mother to infant	Other/ not known	Total
United Kingdom[2]	10,911	1,335	5,699	525	616	951	20,037
Northern and Yorkshire	371	29	184	51	10	19	664
North West	909	78	248	73	22	35	1,365
Trent	293	66	178	32	12	10	591
West Midlands	420	22	205	26	6	20	699
Eastern	327	64	209	35	18	30	683
London	6,417	478	3,593	137	464	716	11,805
South East	1,075	110	486	90	40	57	1,858
South West	436	50	177	12	14	34	723
England[2]	10,252	897	5,280	456	586	921	18,392
Wales	179	17	77	32	3	6	314
Scotland	422	415	313	35	27	24	1,236
Northern Ireland	58	6	29	2	0	0	95

1 Patients living in the UK who were seen for statutory medical HIV-related care at services in 1999 (includes 212 children born to HIV infected mothers in 1999 whose HIV infection status had not been confirmed: two resident in Northern and Yorkshire, four in North West, three in Trent, three in West Midlands, four in Eastern, 172 in London, 14 in South East, one in South West, one in Wales and eight in Scotland).
2 Includes four patients whose region of residence was not known.

Source: Public Health Laboratory Service, Communicable Disease Surveillance Centre; Institute of Child Health; Scottish Centre for Infection and Environmental Health

7.11 Contributions of selected foods to nutritional intakes (household food), 1998–1999[1]

| | Percentage of fat and energy derived from: | | | | | | | | | | Total intake[2] per person per day | | Per-centage of food energy derived from fat[2] |
| | Liquid and processed milk and cream | | Meat and meat products | | All fats | | Fresh and processed fruit and vegetables | | Cereals including bread | | | | |
	Fat	Energy	Fat	Energy	Fat	Energy	Fat	Energy	Fat	Energy	Fat (grams)	Energy (Kcal)	
United Kingdom	11.1	10.4	22.3	14.6	28.1	10.9	8.3	15.4	17.4	35.4	73	1,714	39
North East	10.5	9.8	24.0	15.7	25.7	10.0	8.6	15.4	18.6	36.4	73	1,704	39
North West	12.5	11.4	23.8	15.6	26.5	10.4	7.6	14.6	17.2	35.1	70	1,635	39
Yorkshire and the Humber	11.3	10.5	22.9	15.1	28.8	11.4	7.2	14.2	17.3	35.6	73	1,694	38
East Midlands	11.3	10.6	22.1	14.2	29.2	11.3	8.2	15.2	16.7	35.1	74	1,744	39
West Midlands	11.3	10.5	21.0	13.5	29.5	11.4	8.4	15.4	16.8	35.1	73	1,732	38
East	10.1	9.8	22.6	14.5	26.1	10.0	9.5	16.5	18.1	35.8	70	1,671	37
London	10.3	9.6	20.2	13.2	33.1	12.8	8.3	15.8	15.7	36.0	73	1,724	39
South East	10.6	10.2	21.6	14.1	27.2	10.7	8.7	15.7	17.9	35.2	75	1,751	39
South West	10.4	10.1	21.7	14.2	26.8	10.5	9.0	16.3	18.1	35.2	76	1,778	39
England	10.9	10.3	22.1	14.4	28.2	11.0	8.4	15.5	17.4	35.4	73	1,715	39
Wales	11.0	10.2	23.4	15.5	29.8	11.7	7.6	15.2	16.8	34.3	76	1,763	39
Scotland	11.6	10.5	23.8	15.9	25.0	9.9	8.2	14.4	18.3	35.7	73	1,684	40
Northern Ireland	13.3	12.1	22.4	14.3	31.7	12.3	6.9	15.5	16.6	35.0	72	1,681	39

1 See Notes and Definitions.
2 Total intake from all household food, excluding household consumption of soft and alcoholic drinks and confectionery.

Source: National Food Survey, Department for Environment, Food and Rural Affairs

7.12 Cigarette smoking among people aged 16 and over: by gender, 1998–99

Percentages

| | Males | | | | | Females | | | | |
	Smoked less than 10[1]	10, less than 20[1]	20 or more[1]	Ex-regular smoker	Never or only occasionally smoked	Smoked less than 10[1]	10, less than 20[1]	20 or more[1]	Ex-regular smoker	Never or only occasionally smoked
United Kingdom	7	11	11	31	41	8	11	7	21	53
North East	5	8	13	28	46	7	12	10	20	50
North West	5	13	11	31	41	8	13	10	21	47
Yorkshire and the Humber	6	12	11	32	39	8	13	6	20	52
East Midlands	5	11	9	35	39	9	10	7	20	55
West Midlands	7	13	11	31	38	8	11	6	20	55
East	8	8	9	32	43	7	11	5	24	53
London	11	11	11	24	43	10	10	7	17	56
South East	6	11	9	33	41	7	8	6	24	55
South West	6	11	8	34	42	9	8	7	21	55
England	7	11	10	31	41	8	11	7	21	53
Wales	7	13	9	27	45	8	12	7	20	54
Scotland	6	12	15	26	41	6	12	10	20	52
Northern Ireland	3	10	15	37	35	6	12	11	22	49

1 Per day.

Source: General Household Survey, Office for National Statistics; Continuous Household Survey, Northern Ireland Statistics and Research Agency

7.13 Alcohol consumption[1] among people aged 16 and over: by gender, 1998–99

Percentages

	Males				Females			
	Drank nothing last week	Drank up to 4 units last week[2]	Drank more than 4 and up to 8 units[2]	Drank more than 8 units last week[2]	Drank nothing last week	Drank up to 3 units last week[2]	Drank more than 3 and up to 6 units[2]	Drank more than 6 units last week[2]
United Kingdom	26	36	17	21	41	38	13	8
North East	23	32	22	23	43	35	14	8
North West	23	33	18	27	38	37	15	11
Yorkshire and the Humber	27	34	15	24	44	36	13	7
East Midlands	24	35	21	20	40	40	12	7
West Midlands	26	36	17	21	42	38	11	9
East	23	44	19	14	42	42	10	6
London	33	36	13	18	49	34	11	6
South East	21	44	17	18	34	46	13	7
South West	24	41	17	18	38	42	12	8
England	25	38	17	20	41	39	12	8
Wales	32	29	17	22	46	33	12	9
Scotland	29	32	16	24	40	32	15	12
Northern Ireland	47	18	13	22	61	18	10	10

1 Comparative consumption levels are different for males and females. See Notes and Definitions.
2 On the heaviest drinking day last week.

Source: General Household Survey, Office for National Statistics; Continuous Household Survey, Northern Ireland Statistics and Research Agency

7.14 Drug use among 16–29 year olds,[1] 1998[2,3]

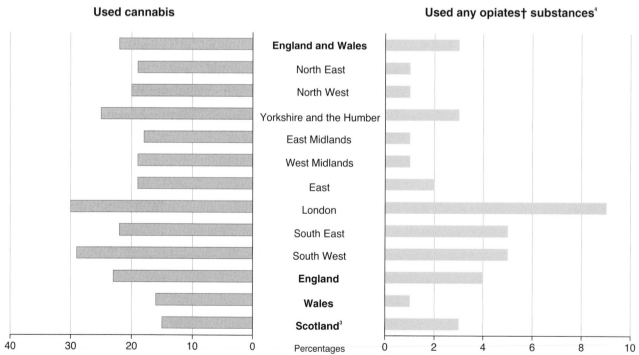

Used cannabis   **Used any opiates† substances[4]**

England and Wales
North East
North West
Yorkshire and the Humber
East Midlands
West Midlands
East
London
South East
South West
England
Wales
Scotland[3]

1 See Notes and Definitions.
2 Interviews were conducted between January and April, asking about drug use in the previous 12 months.
3 Data for Scotland relate to 2000.
4 Heroin, methadone, cocaine or crack.

Source: British Crime Survey, Home Office, Scottish Crime Survey, Scottish Executive

7.15 NHS hospital waiting lists: by patients' region of residence[1] and NHS Regional Office area, at 31 March 2001

| | NHS hospital waiting lists[2] | | | | | | |
| | Percentage waiting: | | | | Total waiting (=100%) (thousands) | Mean waiting time (months)[3] | Median waiting time (months)[3] |
	Less than 6 months	6 months but less than 12	Less than 12 months	12 months or longer			
Northern and Yorkshire	78.8	20.5	99.4	0.6	118.7	3.8	2.8
North West	78.0	18.3	96.3	3.7	156.2	4.0	2.7
Trent	80.2	18.4	98.6	1.4	99.1	3.7	2.7
West Midlands	80.2	17.4	97.5	2.5	84.1	3.7	2.7
Eastern	73.9	20.9	94.7	5.3	116.9	4.4	3.0
London	71.6	22.4	94.0	6.0	135.1	4.6	3.2
South East	70.7	22.6	93.3	6.7	189.5	4.7	3.4
South West	76.3	19.0	95.3	4.7	95.6	4.2	2.9
England	75.6	20.2	95.8	4.2	995.1	4.2	2.9
Wales	66.0	20.2	86.2	13.8	65.6	..	..
Scotland	83.7	15.0	98.7	1.3	82.0	3.2	2.1
Northern Ireland	58.6	19.6	78.2	21.8	52.0	..	..

1 In Scotland, waiting lists are based on NHS lists for each Trust, irrespective of the patient's residence.
2 The figures relate to people on the waiting lists on 31 March 2001 who were waiting for admission as either an in-patient or a day case and the length of time they had waited to date. Figures for Northern Ireland included all patients waiting for treatment at Northern Ireland Trusts including private patients and patients from outside Northern Ireland. Patients undergoing a series of repeat admissions and those who were temporarily suspended from the waiting list for medical or social reasons are excluded. There are differences between countries in the ways that waiting times are calculated, so comparisons between countries should be made with caution.
3 Average time patients had been waiting at 31 March 2001. The mean and median are different types of 'average'. See Notes and Definitions. Figures for Northern Ireland are available only in quarterly time bands.

Source: Department of Health; National Assembly for Wales; Information and Statistics Division, NHS in Scotland; Department of Health, Social Services and Public Safety, Northern Ireland

7.16 NHS hospital activity:[1] by NHS Regional Office area, 1999–00

| | In-patients (all specialties) | | | | Average length of stay in hospital for non-psychiatric specialties (mean)(days) | Day cases (thousands) | Total accident & emergency attend-ances (thousands) | Consultant out-patient attendances | |
	Average daily available beds[2] per 1,000 population	Cases[3] treated per available bed[2]	Cases[3] treated per 1,000 population	Finished consultant episodes/ discharges and deaths[3] (thousands)				Total (thousands)	Of which new[4] (percentages)
United Kingdom	4.1	42.6	175	10,422	..	..	17,928	52,032	28.0
Northern and Yorkshire	4.2	44.5	187	1,186	5.9	496	1,940	5,589	27.1
North West	4.1	49.3	203	1,339	5.9	665	2,234	6,418	26.7
Trent	3.8	48.4	184	947	5.5	368	1,329	4,474	29.0
West Midlands	3.6	48.1	174	927	5.9	379	1,740	4,609	27.7
Eastern	3.3	46.0	153	829	6.0	313	1,173	4,032	28.6
London	4.0	41.9	168	1,221	6.7	508	2,584	7,977	27.5
South East	3.1	46.1	144	1,253	5.9	461	2,155	6,210	29.5
South West	3.9	46.7	182	900	6.2	403	1,473	3,733	30.9
England	3.7	46.2	173	8,604	6.0	3,593	14,629	43,041	28.2
Wales	5.0	35.0	176	516	6.7	..	1,026	2,706	25.6
Scotland	6.8	27.9	190	969	7.5	434	1,602	4,849	27.6
Northern Ireland	5.1	38.4	196	332	5.7	119	671	1,435	28.6

1 See Notes and Definitions.
2 Excluding cots for healthy new-born babies except in Northern Ireland.
3 Finished consultant episodes in England and discharges and deaths in Wales. Data for Scotland relate to discharges and deaths and transfers to other specialties and hospitals. Data for Northern Ireland relate to discharges and deaths and transfers to another hospital. Healthy new-born babies are included for Northern Ireland but excluded for the other countries.
4 In Northern Ireland, data refer to GP referrals, not first attendances.

Source: Department of Health; National Assembly for Wales; Information and Statistics Division, NHS in Scotland; Department of Health, Social Services and Public Safety, Northern Ireland

7.17 Prescriptions dispensed: by NHS Regional Office area, 1999[1]

	Prescription items dispensed (millions)[2]	Percentage of prescription items exempt from charge[3,4]	Percentage of prescription items[3,5] that were for		Number of prescription items per person	Average net ingredient cost[6]	
			Children	People aged 60 or over		£ per person	£ per pres-cription item
Northern and Yorkshire	74.8	86.4	8.9	52.4	11.8	111.0	9.4
North West	83.7	86.7	8.7	51.5	12.7	121.6	9.6
Trent	59.2	85.3	8.1	54.3	11.5	109.1	9.5
West Midlands	58.5	86.0	10.3	51.0	11.0	106.4	9.7
Anglia and Oxford	52.6	81.9	9.0	52.1	9.6	99.2	10.4
North Thames	65.9	84.8	11.2	47.1	9.2	97.8	10.6
South Thames	65.5	84.1	9.0	53.8	9.4	102.6	10.9
South and West	69.5	84.4	7.5	57.2	10.3	103.7	10.0
England	529.8	85.1	9.1	52.3	10.6	106.4	10.0
Wales[1]	41.2	87.9	8.6	51.6	14.0	132.0	9.4
Scotland	60.4	89.7	..	..	11.7	122.8	10.5
Northern Ireland[1]	22.2	94.7	..	..	13.0	129.4	10.0

1 For Wales, data relate to 1999–00. For Northern Ireland, data relate to 1998–99.
2 Figures relate to NHS prescription items dispensed by community pharmacies, appliance contractors (appliance suppliers in Scotland and Northern Ireland), and dispensing doctors, and prescriptions submitted by prescribing doctors for items personally administered, known as stock orders in Scotland and Northern Ireland.
3 For England, figures relate to items dispensed by community pharmacists and appliance contractors only. Items dispensed by dispensing doctors and personal administration are not analysed into exempt, non-exempt or other categories and are therefore excluded. Personally administered items are free of charge.
4 Figures for the English regions, England and Wales exclude prescriptions for which prepayment certificates have been purchased. For Scotland and Northern Ireland they are included. Due to this, and the issues mentioned in footnote 3, comparisons across the four countries should not be made.
5 Items for children includes those for young adults aged 16 to 18 who are in full-time education. Data for Wales are calculated from a 5 per cent sample of prescriptions. Age specfic data are not available in Scotland or Northern Ireland.
6 Net ingredient cost is the cost of medicines before any discounts and does not include any dispensing costs or fees. This is known as Gross Ingredient Cost in Scotland or Northern Ireland.

Source: Department of Health; National Assembly for Wales; Information and Statistics Division, NHS in Scotland; Central Services Agency, Northern Ireland

7.18 NHS Hospital and Community Health Service staff: by type of staff[1] and NHS Regional Office area, 30 September 2000

Percentages and thousands

	Direct care staff				Management and support staff			
	Medical and dental	Nursing, midwifery and health visiting[2]	Scientific, therapeutic and technical	All direct care staff	Adminis-tration and estates	Other	All management and support staff[3]	Total staff[1] (=100%) (thousands)
Northern and Yorkshire	7.4	47.0	13.0	67.3	20.9	11.8	32.7	109.3
North West	7.7	47.8	13.6	69.1	21.3	9.6	30.9	115.6
Trent	7.4	46.9	13.4	67.6	21.5	10.9	32.4	83.7
West Midlands	7.3	46.8	13.2	67.3	21.7	10.9	32.7	85.3
Eastern	7.7	48.8	13.4	69.9	21.5	8.6	30.1	69.8
London	10.0	44.2	14.7	68.9	23.8	7.2	31.1	127.1
South East	7.6	46.5	13.0	67.1	22.0	10.9	32.9	118.0
South West	7.3	47.5	14.1	68.8	20.3	10.8	31.2	75.9
England[4]	7.7	46.3	13.8	67.8	22.3	9.9	32.2	801.5
Wales	7.0	46.8	13.0	66.8	20.9	12.3	33.2	55.7
Scotland	7.6	47.8	15.5	71.0	18.2	10.8	29.0	107.2
Northern Ireland	6.7	39.5	11.6	57.8	24.2	18.0	42.2	37.9

1 Directly employed whole-time equivalents. See Notes and Definitions.
2 Nursing, midwifery and health visiting staff includes learners and healthcare assistants.
3 The Northern Ireland figure includes management and support for Social Services.
4 The England totals include staff in special health authorities and other statutory authorities which are not assigned to a specific region.

Source: Department of Health; National Assembly for Wales; Information and Statistics Division, NHS in Scotland; Department of Health, Social Services and Public Safety, Northern Ireland

7.19 General practitioners, dentists and opticians:[1] by NHS Regional Office area, 30 September 2000

Numbers and percentages

	General medical services					General dental services[1,2]			
	Number of practices	Number of general medical practitioners (GPs)[1]	Percentage who were female GPs	Average list size per GP	Number of practice staff[3] (whole-time equivalents)	Percentage who were direct care practice staff3,[4]	Number of dentists	Persons registered with a dentist as a percentage of the population[5]	Average regis- trations per dentist	Number of opticians[6]
United Kingdom	10,815	34,287	33	1,792	73,363	19.8	21,864	..	..	..
Northern and Yorkshire	1,041	3,604	31	1,774	8,199	19.0	2,103	52	1,580	1,091
North West	1,348	3,613	32	1,880	8,417	16.6	2,278	52	1,509	1,099
Trent	866	2,796	30	1,871	6,729	22.0	1,587	52	1,692	1,010
West Midlands	1,041	2,895	29	1,899	6,654	20.3	1,656	46	1,492	951
Eastern	828	2,971	31	1,853	6,648	24.7	1,975	49	1,340	1,249
London	1,691	3,951	40	2,030	9,275	19.0	3,141	40	931	1,565
South East	1,297	4,803	34	1,845	10,331	19.3	3,363	44	1,126	2,216
South West	766	3,071	31	1,637	6,331	22.0	1,946	48	1,224	910
England	8,878	27,704	33	1,853	62,583	20.1	18,049	48	1,311	7,824
Wales	522	1,775	28	1,695	3,983	20.5	1,006	50	1,449	602
Scotland	1,050	3,750	37	1,426	6,796	16.4	2,018	52	1,305	1,329
Northern Ireland	365	1,058	33	1,673	..	..	681	52	1,291	370

1 See Notes and Definitions.
2 Dentists are assigned to the region where they carry out their main work.
3 Other than GPs. Figure for the United Kingdom relates to Great Britain as figures for Northern Ireland are not held centrally.
4 Figures relate to practice nurses, physiotherapists, chiropodists, counsellors, dispensers and complementary therapists.
5 Registrations with dentists practising in each region.
6 Optometrists and ophthalmic medical practitioners contracted to perform NHS sight tests at 31 December 2000 (31 March 2000 for optometrists in Scotland). As some practitioners have contracts in more than one region, the sum of the regions does not equal the England total. Similarly, as some practitioners have contracts in more than one country, it is not possible to calculate a United Kingdom figure.

Source: Department of Health; National Assembly for Wales; Information and Statistics Division, NHS in Scotland; Central Services Agency, Northern Ireland

7.20 Places available in residential care homes:[1] by type of care home, at 31 March 2000

Percentages and thousands

	Percentage of places available in			Percentage of places available in homes for				Total number of places available (=100%) (thousands)
	Local authority homes[2]	Registered homes		Older people	People with physical, sensory or learning disabilities	People with mental health problems	Other people[5]	
		Voluntary homes[3]	Other[4]					
United Kingdom	18	20	62	70	18	11	2	396
North East	20	11	69	73	15	12	1	21
North West	16	18	66	77	13	9	1	50
Yorkshire and the Humber	20	13	67	60	16	23	1	36
East Midlands	17	12	71	73	16	10	1	31
West Midlands	20	17	63	72	21	7	1	32
East	17	21	62	74	18	8	1	35
London	21	38	41	62	20	17	2	30
South East	11	21	68	65	22	12	1	64
South West	10	20	70	71	18	9	2	46
England	16	19	65	70	18	12	1	346
Wales	29	11	60	75	10	3	12	20
Scotland	32	44	25	66	23	6	5	24
Northern Ireland	36	25	39	69	17	9	5	7

1 The figures for places available in Scotland exclude children's homes. All data include residential places in homes registered as both residential and nursing. See Notes and Definitions.
2 For England, figures relate to local authority staffed homes. For Wales, figures relate to local authority staffed homes for adults and children. For Northern Ireland, figures relate to places available in statutory homes operated by the Health and Social Services Trusts.
3 For England, figures include dual registered voluntary homes. For Wales, figures include all voluntary homes for adults and children, regardless of size.
4 The figures for England include independent small homes (fewer than 4 places) and private homes. The figures for Wales include all private homes for adults and children, regardless of size. The figures for Scotland relate to private homes only. The figures for Northern Ireland relate to all private homes regardless of size and dual registered homes.
5 The figures for Wales include places in small homes, children's homes and homes for people with substance misuse problems.

Source: Department of Health; National Assembly for Wales; Scottish Executive; Department of Health, Social Services and Public Safety, Northern Ireland

7.21 Children looked after by local authorities, year ending 31 March 2000[1]

	Total children looked after per 1,000 resident population[2]			Manner of accommodation (percentages)			Number of children looked after (=100%)
	Children admitted	Ceased to be looked after	Looked after	Foster homes	Community homes[3]	Other[4]	
North East	2.8	2.7	5.7	64.4	13.1	22.5	3,352
North West	2.6	2.4	6.1	61.8	12.7	25.5	9,873
Yorkshire and the Humber	2.4	2.3	5.7	62.4	13.4	24.2	6,630
East Midlands	2.0	2.0	4.3	67.6	9.6	22.8	4,098
West Midlands	2.3	2.1	5.2	64.8	10.8	24.4	6,440
East	2.2	2.0	4.2	67.7	8.8	23.5	5,115
London	3.2	2.8	6.3	65.3	13.7	21.0	10,395
South East	2.0	1.9	4.1	64.7	8.7	26.5	7,442
South West	2.4	2.3	4.5	73.7	6.7	19.5	4,782
England	2.4	2.3	5.1	65.3	11.2	23.5	58,127
Wales[1]	2.8	2.3	4.9	76.0	6.1	17.9	3,313
Scotland	4.2	..	10.0	27.0	14.0	59.0	11,309
Northern Ireland	2.2	1.9	5.2	66.5	11.8	21.7	2,422

1 Data for Wales relate to year ending 31 March 1999.
2 Rates are based on mid-1999 estimates of population aged under 18.
3 Scottish figures relate to residential care homes for children.
4 Includes children looked after at home and, for Scotland, children looked after through being under a supervision requirement made by the Scottish Children's Hearings System.

Source: Department of Health; National Assembly for Wales; Scottish Executive Education Department; Department of Health, Social Services and Public Safety, Northern Ireland

7.22 Children and young people on child protection registers: by age and category, at 31 March 2000

	Percentage aged					Number of children on registers[2] (=100%)	Rate per 10,000 children aged under 18[3]	Percentage of children in each category of abuse					
	Under 1	1–4	5–9[1]	10–15[1]	16 and over			Neglect	Physical injury	Sexual abuse	Emotional abuse	Multiple categories	Other[4]
North East	9	31	29	28	2	2,106	36	33	22	10	15	16	4
North West	10	32	30	26	1	4,049	25	36	20	11	14	15	4
Yorkshire and the Humber	10	31	31	26	2	3,388	29	35	21	14	14	11	4
East Midlands	11	31	30	26	2	3,135	33	28	21	18	17	15	1
West Midlands	9	30	29	27	3	3,598	29	37	19	14	22	8	-
East	9	29	32	28	2	2,885	24	36	20	12	20	12	0
London	8	29	31	29	2	4,809	29	47	16	10	20	8	-
South East	9	30	30	28	2	3,833	21	38	18	10	22	11	-
South West	10	30	28	30	2	2,487	23	30	21	18	18	12	1
England	9	30	30	28	2	30,300	27	36	20	13	18	12	1
Wales	10	31	30	26	3	2,416	36	34	25	11	20	11	.
Northern Ireland	6	27	41	22	4	1,483	32	37	20	16	16	12	.

1 Agebands for Northern Ireland are 5 to 11 and 12 to 15.
2 Includes a number of unborn children not included elsewhere in this table.
3 Figure for Northern Ireland calculated using the mid-1999 population estimate.
4 For England and Wales data relate to children or young people on the child protection registers who have not been allocated a specific category.

Source: Department of Health; National Assembly for Wales; Department of Health, Social Services and Public Safety, Northern Ireland

8 Income and Lifestyles

Household income

During the period 1997–2000, households in London had the highest average gross weekly income at around £570, while those in Northern Ireland had the lowest at under £360 per week.

(Table 8.1)

During the period 1997–2000, the proportion of households with a weekly income of less than £100 ranged from around a tenth in the East of England, the South East, South West and the East Midlands to almost a fifth of households in the North East.

(Table 8.2)

Income distribution

In 1999–00, individuals living in the North East, Yorkshire and the Humber and Wales were over-represented at the lower end of the distribution. These regions had 27 per cent, 24 per cent and 23 per cent of individuals in the bottom quintile respectively. In contrast, 14 per cent of individuals in the South East and 16 per cent of individuals in the East of England lived in households with incomes in the bottom quintile.

(Table 8.3)

Savings

In 1999–00, almost a quarter of households in the North East did not have a current account.

(Table 8.4)

Income tax

In 1998–99, the percentage of individuals with an income liable to assessment for tax in excess of £50,000 ranged from 1.5 per cent in the North East and in Wales, to 5.8 per cent in London.

(Table 8.5)

During 1998–99, the average total income for individuals in Wales was lower than in any other region of the UK, for both men and women, and consequently the average income tax payable was also lowest in Wales, at £2,843 for men and £1,550 for women, in comparison with the highest level of £6,274 for men and £3,041 in London.

(Chart 8.6)

Receipt of benefit

In many of the large cities in the UK over a quarter of the population of working age were claiming key social security benefits in November 2000.

(Map 8.7)

In 1999–00, the North East had the highest percentage of households in receipt of any benefit, at 79 per cent, while London had the lowest percentage of households in receipt of any benefits, at 65 per cent.

(Table 8.8)

Expenditure

Households in London spent 16 per cent more than the UK average of £350 per week over the period 1997–2000. The region with the lowest average expenditure was the North East, where households spent 18 per cent less than the national average.

(Chart 8.9)

Over the period 1997–2000, households in Northern Ireland spent, on average, 10 per cent of their total weekly expenditure on housing, a lower proportion than in any other UK region.

(Table 8.11)

In 1998–1999, Londoners spent more eating out than any people in other region, £9.63 per person per week, compared with an average for Great Britain of £6.91 per person per week.

(Table 8.12)

Children in Scotland spent on average £12.70 per head per week during 1997–2000, the highest amount in Great Britain; children in the South East spent 30 per cent less than this, an average of £8.90 per child per week.

(Chart 8.10)

Consumption

In 1998–1999, the greatest quantity of meat and meat products were consumed by households in Wales, while households in the South West consumed the most vegetables and vegetable products, households in Northern Ireland consumed the most liquid and processed milk and cream, and Londoners consumed the largest amount of fruit.

(Table 8.13)

Consumer goods

During the period 1997–2000, almost two-fifths of households in London had a mobile phone, about two and a half times the proportion of households in Northern Ireland.

(Table 8.14)

In 1999–00, households within the UK with internet access ranged from a quarter of households in London and the South East to a ninth of households in Northern Ireland.

(Chart 8.15)

Leisure

On average, men in the UK watched around 26 hours of television a week in 2000. This ranged from almost 22 hours in the East of England and the South, South East and Channel Islands up to 28 hours in Scotland.

(Table 8.16)

In 1999–00, the East of England issued the largest number of library books per child, with 12 books issued per child: a third more than the UK average. Wales and Yorkshire and the Humber issued the smallest number, averaging under seven issues per child.   *(Table 8.17)*

In 1999-00, there was one library for around 8,000 residents in Scotland compared with one library per 18,000 residents in London.

(Table 8.17)

Tourism

During the period 1997–2000, households in London spent 26 per cent more money than the UK average on holidays while households in the North East and Northern Ireland spent 29 per cent less than the UK average.

(Chart 8.18)

In 1999, overseas visitors to the UK (excluding transit passengers and residents of the Channel Islands) spent £12.3 billion and stayed 212 million nights. Over half of the spending and two-fifths of those nights were in London.

(Table 8.19)

National Lottery

Average household expenditure on the National Lottery during the period 1997-2000 ranged from £3.70 per week in the South West up to £4.50 in the West Midlands.

(Chart 8.20)

By the end of 2000, nearly 80,000 National Lottery grants had been allocated in the United Kingdom to a value of £8.6 billion. Of the English regions, London received the greatest total value of grants at £1.3 billion. Scotland received £0.8 billion, Wales received £0.5 billion and Northern Ireland received £0.3 billion.

(Table 8.21)

8.1 Household income: by source, 1997–2000[1]

Percentages and £

	Percentage of average gross weekly household income						Average gross weekly household income[3] (=100%) (£)
	Wages and salaries	Self-employ-ment	Invest-ment	Annuities and pensions[2]	Social security benefits[3]	Other income	
United Kingdom	67	8	4	7	12	1	455
North East	62	6	4	8	19	1	363
North West	67	8	3	7	15	1	421
Yorkshire and the Humber	65	8	4	7	15	1	401
East Midlands	69	7	4	7	12	1	439
West Midlands	66	9	5	6	13	1	445
East	68	9	5	7	10	1	484
London	69	11	5	5	9	1	571
South East	69	8	5	7	9	1	538
South West	61	10	6	9	13	2	427
England	67	9	5	7	12	1	469
Wales	61	7	4	8	19	2	364
Scotland	68	6	3	7	15	1	403
Northern Ireland	62	9	2	5	21	1	357

1 Combined data from the 1997–98, 1998–99 and 1999–2000 surveys. See Notes and Definitions.
2 Other than social security benefits.
3 Excluding Housing Benefit and Council Tax Benefit (rates rebate in Northern Ireland).

Source: Family Expenditure Survey, Office for National Statistics and Northern Ireland Statistics and Research Agency

8.2 Distribution of household income, 1997–2000[1]

Percentages and £

	Percentage of households in each weekly income group								Average gross weekly income[2] (£)	
	Under £100	£100 but under £150	£150 but under £250	£250 but under £350	£350 but under £450	£450 but under £600	£600 but under £750	£750 or over	Per house-hold	Per person
United Kingdom	11	10	16	13	11	14	9	16	455	194
North East	18	11	19	13	10	10	7	10	363	162
North West	12	10	17	13	11	14	10	13	421	176
Yorkshire and the Humber	12	11	18	13	11	13	9	12	401	168
East Midlands	9	10	14	14	12	15	10	15	439	184
West Midlands	12	10	16	12	11	15	8	16	445	180
East	9	9	16	13	10	14	11	18	484	209
London	11	8	13	11	11	12	9	24	571	246
South East	9	9	13	12	10	14	10	23	538	236
South West	10	11	16	14	12	15	8	14	427	186
England	11	10	15	12	11	14	9	17	469	200
Wales	12	13	18	14	12	14	7	10	364	152
Scotland	13	11	17	13	11	13	9	13	403	177
Northern Ireland	13	15	21	12	10	12	8	9	357	134

1 Combined data from the 1997–98, 1998–99 and 1999–00 surveys. See Notes and Definitions.
2 Excluding Housing Benefit and Council Tax Benefit (rates rebate in Northern Ireland).

Source: Family Expenditure Survey, Office for National Statistics and Northern Ireland Statistics and Research Agency

8.3 Income distribution of individuals,[1] 1999–00

Percentages

	Quintile groups of individuals ranked by net equivalised household income[2]				
	1	2	3	4	5
Great Britain	20	20	20	20	20
North East	27	23	22	16	12
North West	22	22	20	20	15
Yorkshire and the Humber	24	22	21	18	15
East Midlands	20	19	21	22	17
West Midlands	21	22	21	20	16
East	16	18	20	22	24
London	20	18	16	18	28
South East	14	16	18	22	31
South West	19	22	22	22	16
England	20	20	20	20	21
Wales	23	23	22	18	13
Scotland	22	19	20	20	18

1 See Notes and Definitions.
2 Income before housing costs.

Source: Households Below Average Income, Department for Work and Pensions

8.4 Households[1] with different types of saving, 1999–00

Percentages[2]

	Accounts					Other savings					
	Current[3]	Post Office	TESSA	ISA	Other bank/ building society[4]	Gilts or unit trusts	Stocks and shares	National Savings	Save As You Earn	Premium Bonds	PEPs
Great Britain	86	8	14	11	61	7	26	5	2	26	14
North East	76	4	10	8	47	4	17	2	1	16	8
North West	85	8	15	11	56	6	26	5	2	24	13
Yorkshire and the Humber	85	8	13	10	59	5	24	4	2	23	11
East Midlands	86	8	16	11	65	5	25	5	2	27	13
West Midlands	83	6	14	10	65	6	23	5	1	23	13
East	90	10	17	10	69	7	31	6	2	33	15
London	84	7	13	10	57	7	27	4	2	25	14
South East	91	11	18	13	72	10	36	7	2	36	19
South West	91	11	17	14	65	9	29	8	2	33	16
England	86	8	15	11	62	7	27	5	2	27	14
Wales	84	7	13	10	53	5	19	5	1	21	12
Scotland	78	5	11	7	53	6	22	4	1	16	11

1 Households in which at least one member has an account. See Notes and Definitions.
2 As a percentage of all households.
3 A current account may be either a bank account or a building society account.
4 All bank/building society accounts excluding current accounts, TESSAs and ISAs plus other accounts yielding interest.

Source: Family Resources Survey, Department for Work and Pensions

8.5 Distribution of income liable to assessment for tax, 1998–99[1]

Percentages and thousands

	£4,195–£4,999	£5,000–£7,499	£7,500–£9,999	£10,000–£14,999	£15,000–£19,999	£20,000–£29,999	£30,000–£49,999	£50,000 and over	Individuals with incomes of £4,195 or more (=100%) (thousands)
			Percentage of individuals in each income range						
United Kingdom[2]	5.2	16.9	13.9	22.3	15.6	15.6	7.2	3.2	28,611
North East	6.5	19.4	13.3	24.3	14.1	16.0	4.9	1.5	1,121
North West	5.4	18.1	14.3	24.5	15.5	14.3	5.6	2.2	3,168
Yorkshire and the Humber	5.9	17.6	15.8	23.0	15.0	15.0	5.7	2.0	2,296
East Midlands	4.8	17.7	15.5	23.2	16.2	14.1	6.2	2.3	2,083
West Midlands	6.0	16.3	15.2	23.5	16.2	14.4	6.3	2.2	2,528
East	4.8	15.7	12.7	21.8	15.3	16.9	8.7	4.0	2,739
London	3.5	14.7	11.5	19.1	16.5	18.9	10.0	5.8	3,468
South East	4.4	15.5	12.2	20.0	16.4	16.6	9.7	5.3	4,139
South West	7.3	17.8	14.4	22.7	15.1	13.6	6.6	2.6	2,505
England	5.2	16.6	13.7	22.1	15.8	15.7	7.5	3.5	24,047
Wales	6.2	19.6	17.3	22.8	14.0	13.4	5.1	1.5	1,246
Scotland	4.5	17.4	14.0	24.3	15.5	15.6	6.5	2.3	2,459
Northern Ireland	6.9	18.0	16.5	23.7	14.1	14.4	4.5	1.8	677

1 See Notes and Definitions.
2 Figures for United Kingdom include members of HM Forces and others who are liable to some UK tax but reside overseas on a long-term basis. In addition, the United Kingdom total includes a very small number of individuals who could not be allocated to a region.

Source: Survey of Personal Incomes, Board of Inland Revenue

8.6 Average total income[1] and average income tax payable:[2] by gender, 1998–99[3]

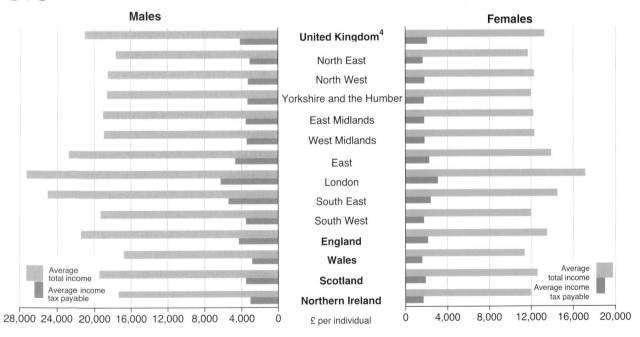

1 Figures are based on individuals with total income above the single person's allowance (£4,195 in 1998–99).
2 Figures relate to taxpayers only.
3 See Notes and Definitions.
4 Figures for United Kingdom include members of HM Forces and others who are liable to some UK tax but reside overseas on a long-term basis.

Source: Survey of Personal Incomes, Board of Inland Revenue

8.7 Percentage of the population of working age claiming a key social security benefit:[1] by local authority, November 2000

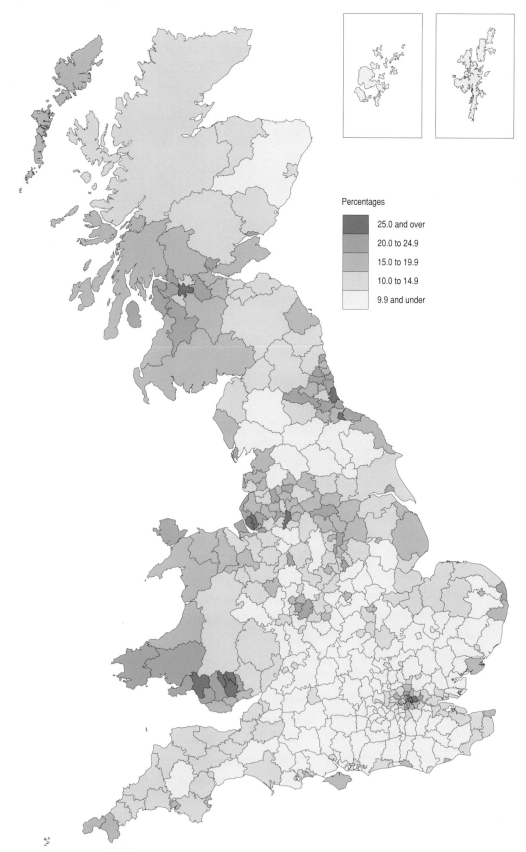

Percentages

25.0 and over
20.0 to 24.9
15.0 to 19.9
10.0 to 14.9
9.9 and under

1 Key benefits are Jobseeker's Allowance (JSA), Incapacity Benefit (IB), Severe Disablement Allowance, Disability Living Allowance, Income Support and National Insurance credits only (through JSA or IB).

Source: Department for Work and Pensions

8.8 Households in receipt of benefit:[1] by type of benefit, 1999–00

Percentages[2]

	Family Credit/WFTC[3] or Income Support	Housing Benefit	Council Tax Benefit	Jobseeker's Allowance	Retirement Pension	Incapacity or Disablement Benefits[4]	Child Benefit	Any benefit
Great Britain	16	18	22	4	30	16	29	70
North East	21	27	35	6	30	25	28	79
North West	18	17	24	4	31	19	31	74
Yorkshire and the Humber	16	20	26	5	29	16	30	72
East Midlands	14	14	19	3	29	15	28	68
West Midlands	17	17	22	4	31	17	29	71
East	11	13	18	3	31	12	27	67
London	18	23	26	4	25	11	30	65
South East	10	11	13	2	30	10	29	66
South West	14	14	19	3	34	14	27	70
England	15	17	22	4	30	15	29	69
Wales	17	18	24	5	33	25	29	76
Scotland	18	24	29	5	29	20	27	72

1 Households in which at least one member is in receipt of benefit. See Notes and Definitions.
2 As a percentage of all households.
3 In October 1999 Family Credit was replaced by Working Families Tax Credit.
4 Incapacity Benefit, Disability Living Allowance (Care and Mobility components), Severe Disablement Allowance, Disability Working Allowance, Industrial Injuries Disablement Benefit, War Disablement Pension and Attendance Allowance. In October 1999 Disability Working Allowance was replaced by Disabled Person's Tax Credits.

Source: Family Resources Survey, Department for Work and Pensions

8.9 Total expenditure[1] in relation to the UK average, 1997–2000[2]

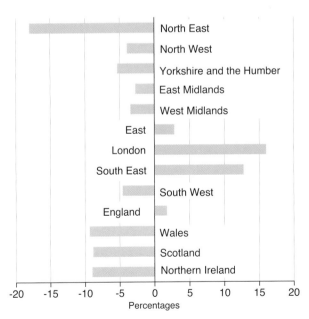

1 Combined data from the 1997–98, 1998–99 and 1999–00 surveys. See Notes and Definitions.

Source: Family Expenditure Survey, Office for National Statistics

8.10 Children's spending,[1] 1997–2000[2]

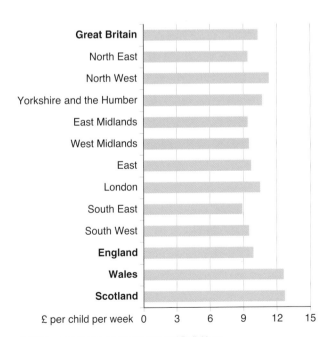

1 Children aged 7 to 15. See Notes and Definitions.
2 Combined data from the 1997–98, 1998–99 and 1999–00 surveys.

Source: Family Expenditure Survey, Office for National Statistics

8.11 Household expenditure:[1] by commodity and service, 1997–2000

£ per week and percentages

	Housing	Fuel, light and power	Food	Alcohol and tobacco	Clothing and footwear	House-hold goods and services	Motoring and fares	Leisure goods and services	Miscellan-eous and personal goods and services	Average house-hold expend-iture	Average expend-iture per person
£ per week											
United Kingdom	55.20	11.90	58.50	20.50	21.00	47.60	59.20	59.70	14.50	348.20	148.30
North East	43.50	12.00	50.10	20.60	19.70	39.20	42.30	47.10	10.90	285.40	126.80
North West	49.00	12.40	56.00	23.50	22.50	42.30	57.30	57.90	13.80	334.60	140.00
Yorkshire and the Humber	48.70	11.70	54.70	22.20	20.20	44.70	56.10	57.80	13.30	329.60	138.30
East Midlands	51.50	11.90	58.00	20.50	18.30	47.30	60.00	57.80	13.50	338.70	141.50
West Midlands	50.30	12.40	57.30	19.80	19.80	46.60	58.00	58.60	13.30	336.20	136.20
East	57.60	11.30	60.10	17.30	21.00	49.70	65.40	59.60	15.80	357.90	154.10
London	74.50	10.90	65.90	21.00	24.50	54.60	62.80	72.00	17.70	403.90	173.80
South East	67.70	11.30	61.40	18.90	21.40	56.00	71.20	67.60	17.10	392.50	172.50
South West	54.80	11.20	55.40	18.00	17.30	47.10	58.00	55.80	14.70	332.20	144.60
England	57.50	11.60	58.60	20.20	20.90	48.70	60.80	61.10	15.00	354.30	151.20
Wales	44.70	12.60	55.20	20.60	20.50	43.70	48.20	56.60	13.60	315.60	131.70
Scotland	46.70	12.90	57.70	23.00	21.00	41.00	51.80	51.70	11.50	317.30	139.70
Northern Ireland	30.70	15.10	64.40	21.40	25.90	43.90	50.90	46.50	13.20	312.10	117.30
As a percentage of average weekly household expenditure											
United Kingdom	16	3	17	6	6	14	17	17	4	100	
North East	15	4	18	7	7	14	15	17	4	100	
North West	15	4	17	7	7	13	17	17	4	100	
Yorkshire and the Humber	15	4	17	7	6	14	17	18	4	100	
East Midlands	15	4	17	6	5	14	18	17	4	100	
West Midlands	15	4	17	6	6	14	17	17	4	100	
East	16	3	17	5	6	14	18	17	4	100	
London	18	3	16	5	6	14	16	18	4	100	
South East	17	3	16	5	5	14	18	17	4	100	
South West	16	3	17	5	5	14	17	17	4	100	
England	16	3	17	6	6	14	17	17	4	100	
Wales	14	4	17	7	6	14	15	18	4	100	
Scotland	15	4	18	7	7	13	16	16	4	100	
Northern Ireland	10	5	21	7	8	14	16	15	4	100	

1 See Notes and Definitions. Combined data from the 1997–98, 1998–99 and 1999–00 surveys.

Source: Family Expenditure Survey, Office for National Statistics and Northern Ireland Statistics and Research Agency

8.12 Expenditure on selected foods bought for household consumption and expenditure on eating out, 1998–1999[1]

£ per person per week

	Liquid and processed milk and cream	Cheese	Uncooked carcass meat and poultry	Other meat and meat products	Fish	Veg-etables and Veg-etable products[2]	Fresh and other fruit	Bread	Cereals other than bread	Drinks and confect-ionery	Total house-hold food and drink	Eating out[3]
United Kingdom[4]	1.34	0.52	1.86	1.98	0.78	2.30	1.32	0.72	1.97	2.12	16.86	6.91
North East	1.21	0.41	1.66	2.06	0.77	2.06	1.00	0.71	2.00	1.91	15.57	7.90
North West	1.36	0.44	1.90	1.98	0.71	2.07	1.14	0.72	1.81	1.83	15.73	6.54
Yorkshire and the Humber	1.31	0.41	1.76	1.86	0.80	2.01	1.11	0.70	1.86	1.76	15.37	5.70
East Midlands	1.33	0.52	1.66	1.83	0.71	2.15	1.11	0.71	1.81	1.99	15.61	6.23
West Midlands	1.32	0.50	1.72	1.80	0.74	2.29	1.14	0.68	1.82	1.87	15.84	6.11
East	1.31	0.52	1.93	2.01	0.86	2.37	1.51	0.67	2.00	2.06	17.20	6.97
London	1.31	0.53	1.96	1.86	0.93	2.73	1.68	0.71	2.11	2.09	17.99	9.63
South East	1.42	0.65	1.98	2.12	0.89	2.56	1.60	0.72	2.17	2.60	18.88	7.37
South West	1.42	0.63	1.89	1.90	0.71	2.47	1.48	0.76	2.04	2.20	17.58	6.04
England	1.34	0.52	1.85	1.95	0.80	2.33	1.35	0.71	1.97	2.07	16.85	7.01
Wales	1.27	0.47	1.79	2.17	0.78	2.20	1.24	0.72	1.83	2.22	16.69	6.18
Scotland	1.24	0.53	1.91	2.25	0.72	2.14	1.20	0.79	2.08	2.78	17.59	6.36
Northern Ireland	1.51	0.34	2.01	1.91	0.50	2.00	0.97	0.80	1.87	1.42	14.99	..

1 See Notes and Definitions.
2 Including tomatoes, fresh potatoes and potato products.
3 Individual expenditure on all food and drink consumed outside the home and not obtained from household stocks, whether consumed by the purchaser or others or both. Expenditure which is to be reclaimed as business expenses is not included.
4 Figure relating to eating out is for Great Britain only.

Source: National Food Survey, Department for Environment, Food and Rural Affairs

8.13 Household consumption of selected foods, 1991–1992 and 1998–1999[1]

Kilograms per person per week[2]

	Liquid and processed milk and cream		Meat and meat products		Fish		Vegetables and vegetable products[3]		Fresh and other fruit		Cereals including bread	
	1991–1992	1998–1999	1991–1992	1998–1999	1991–1992	1998–1999	1991–1992	1998–1999	1991–1992	1998–1999	1991–1992	1998–1999
Great Britain	2.15	2.06	0.97	0.92	0.14	0.14	2.24	2.01	0.92	1.04	1.46	1.47
North East	2.08	1.93	1.02	0.99	0.15	0.15	2.44	1.97	0.83	0.91	1.56	1.53
North West	2.11	2.09	0.98	0.95	0.14	0.14	2.23	1.84	0.81	0.94	1.42	1.41
Yorkshire and the Humber	2.13	2.04	0.97	0.94	0.16	0.15	2.21	1.88	0.85	0.98	1.46	1.46
East Midlands	2.35	2.13	0.91	0.89	0.13	0.14	2.26	2.06	0.95	0.97	1.42	1.50
West Midlands	2.02	2.09	0.99	0.87	0.13	0.15	2.33	2.04	0.70	0.99	1.52	1.48
East	2.13	1.91	0.97	0.89	0.15	0.15	2.21	1.98	1.06	1.19	1.44	1.44
London	2.02	1.90	0.99	0.86	0.16	0.17	2.15	2.08	1.15	1.26	1.41	1.48
South East	2.20	2.05	0.90	0.91	0.13	0.15	2.15	2.02	1.10	1.23	1.41	1.48
South West	2.25	2.07	0.96	0.94	0.12	0.14	2.45	2.18	0.98	1.24	1.46	1.50
England	2.13	2.03	0.97	0.92	0.14	0.15	2.26	2.00	0.95	1.10	1.45	1.47
Wales	2.29	2.08	1.02	1.02	0.14	0.15	2.41	2.14	0.74	0.99	1.52	1.45
Scotland	2.20	1.98	0.92	0.97	0.13	0.13	2.02	1.17	0.82	0.94	1.52	1.47
Northern Ireland	..	2.36	..	0.87	..	0.09	..	2.15	..	0.76	..	1.48

1 See Notes and Definitions.
2 Except equivalent litres of milk and cream.
3 Including tomatoes, fresh potatoes and potato products.

Source: National Food Survey, Department for Environment, Food and Rural Affairs

8.14 Households with selected durable goods, 1997–2000[1]

Percentages

	Micro-wave oven	Washing machine	Dish-washer	Fridge-freezer or deep freezer	Tumble dryer	Video recorder	Compact-disc player	Satellite receiver	Mobile phone
United Kingdom	78	91	22	91	51	85	68	28	31
North East	83	93	15	90	48	83	63	28	23
North West	80	91	19	91	52	87	68	33	27
Yorkshire and the Humber	82	94	19	90	52	85	66	28	27
East Midlands	80	94	22	92	55	87	69	29	32
West Midlands	78	89	21	91	53	85	67	31	33
East	78	91	25	94	51	85	69	28	35
London	70	87	23	90	44	83	69	30	39
South East	78	90	30	92	53	86	72	26	37
South West	77	90	26	90	50	83	68	22	29
England	78	91	23	91	51	85	69	28	32
Wales	82	92	17	91	50	83	61	31	27
Scotland	80	94	19	88	54	84	67	27	24
Northern Ireland[2]	76	93	25	85	40	82	56	26	15

1 Combined data from the 1997–98, 1998–99 and 1999–00 surveys. See Notes and Definitions.
2 Northern Ireland data are from the 1998–99 and 1999–00 surveys.

Source: Family Expenditure Survey, Office for National Statistics

8.15 Households with internet access, 1998–99 and 1999–00

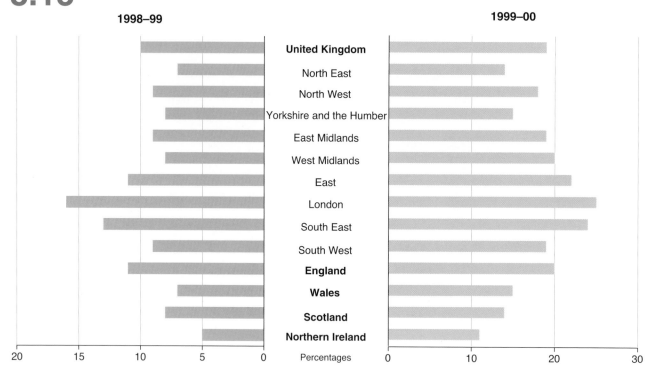

Source: Family Expenditure Survey, Office for National Statistics

8.16 Average weekly television viewing:[1] by audience

Hours[2]

	Men[3]			Women[3]			Children[3]		
	1995	1997	2000	1995	1997	2000	1995	1997	2000
ITV viewing regions									
United Kingdom[4]	24.9	25.0	25.7	28.3	28.2	28.7	18.1	17.7	18.3
North East	24.0	25.7	26.9	27.9	28.3	28.6	16.7	17.7	18.9
North West	25.5	25.1	26.0	28.7	29.8	30.6	18.3	17.4	18.8
Yorkshire	25.3	25.3	25.5	28.6	28.6	28.9	17.9	18.5	17.6
Midlands	22.9	23.5	25.1	27.4	27.1	26.9	17.6	16.1	16.2
East of England	21.3	21.7	21.7	24.9	25.0	26.3	17.8	16.3	17.2
London	22.5	23.1	23.9	24.6	25.0	25.4	16.1	16.2	17.6
South, South East and Channel Islands	23.0	23.2	22.0	26.6	25.6	26.1	16.2	17.2	17.1
South West	24.6	24.5	25.2	25.8	26.4	28.3	18.0	16.0	17.6
Wales and West	23.2	23.3	24.5	27.4	26.9	26.9	17.0	16.5	17.3
Border	24.0	24.8	27.0	28.2	29.5	29.3	17.5	19.2	21.0
Scotland	26.7	27.3	27.9	29.1	30.0	31.0	18.0	17.9	17.5
Ulster	25.9	25.9	24.8	29.6	28.6	29.6	19.0	18.1	20.5

1 Including timeshift, i.e. viewing of broadcast material recorded at home and played back within seven days of recording.
2 Per person in UK private households containing a television set in working order.
3 Men and women are defined as individuals aged 16 and over and children are defined as individuals aged 4 to 15 years old.
4 Figures for the regions exclude viewing of other regions' broadcasts, whereas figures for the United Kingdom include all viewing, and are therefore higher.

Source: Broadcasters' Audience Research Board; RSMB Television Research Limited

8.17 Library resources and use, 1999–00

	Library books issued per head of population to		Number of visits to libraries per head of population	Expenditure (£ millions)	Expenditure per head of population (£)	Stock of books (thousands)	Stock of books per head of population	Resident population per library
	Adults	Children[1]						
United Kingdom	6.8	8.9	5.6	848.1	14.25	121,329	2.04	12,850
North East	7.7	7.5	5.6	38.4	14.86	5,319	2.06	11,223
North West	7.2	8.2	5.5	97.8	14.21	14,346	2.09	14,275
Yorkshire and the Humber	5.9	6.9	4.6	60.0	11.88	9,097	1.80	12,340
East Midlands	6.7	8.9	4.8	53.3	12.71	7,484	1.79	12,255
West Midlands	6.2	7.8	4.5	69.2	12.97	10,348	1.94	15,927
East	8.1	12.0	6.1	73.4	13.54	9,530	1.76	14,260
London	5.9	9.7	6.8	152.0	20.86	17,524	2.41	18,122
South East	7.1	9.9	5.9	104.3	12.91	14,253	1.76	15,127
South West	7.6	9.6	5.9	56.9	11.53	8,744	1.77	12,753
England	6.9	9.1	5.6	705.1	14.17	96,644	1.94	14,211
Wales	7.0	6.9	4.5	35.4	12.05	7,275	2.48	8,538
Scotland	7.2	8.3	6.0	87.9	17.17	13,465	2.63	8,152
Northern Ireland	4.7	7.7	4.0	19.7	11.70	3,945	2.34	10,754

1 Children are aged 14 and under.

Source: Library and Information Statistics Unit, Loughborough University

8.18 Expenditure on holidays in relation to the UK average, 1997–2000[1]

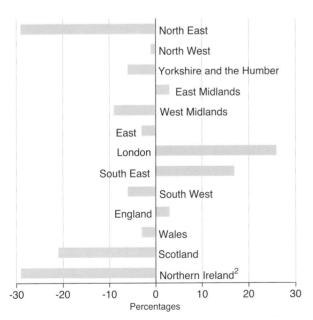

Percentages (x-axis from -30 to 30)

Regions: North East, North West, Yorkshire and the Humber, East Midlands, West Midlands, East, London, South East, South West, England, Wales, Scotland, Northern Ireland[2]

1 Combined data from the 1997–98, 1998–99 and 1999–00 surveys. See Notes and Definitions.
2 Northern Ireland data from the 1998–99 and 1999–00 surveys.

Source: Family Expenditure Survey, Office for National Statistics

8.19 Overseas visitors:[1] by UK region of visit, 1999

Thousands and £ million

	Number of nights	Spending
United Kingdom[2]	211,735	12,370
North East	4,676	181
North West	10,767	544
Yorkshire and the Humber	6,584	239
East Midlands	6,717	246
West Midlands	9,953	459
East	13,708	546
London	85,755	6,708
South East	30,913	1,394
South West	16,671	694
England[3]	186,178	11,030
Wales	7,204	269
Scotland	15,920	817
Northern Ireland	1,623	109

1 Spending by residents of the Channel Islands and transit passengers is excluded from this table.
2 Includes nights and spending in the Channel Islands, Isle of Man, unknown areas, and nights spent travelling.
3 Includes nights and spending in England not assigned to a specific region.

Source: International Passenger Survey, Office for National Statistics

8.20 Participation in the National Lottery,[1] 1997–2000[2]

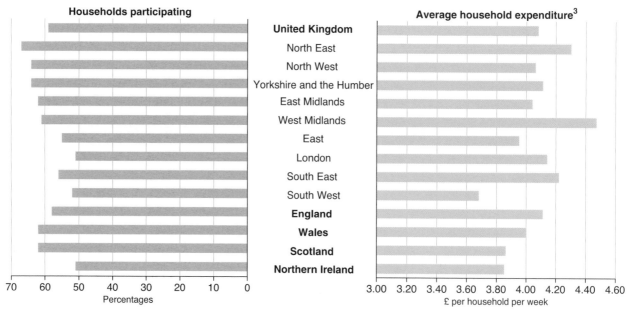

Households participating

Average household expenditure[3]

United Kingdom
North East
North West
Yorkshire and the Humber
East Midlands
West Midlands
East
London
South East
South West
England
Wales
Scotland
Northern Ireland

70 60 50 40 30 20 10 0
Percentages

3.00 3.20 3.40 3.60 3.80 4.00 4.20 4.40 4.60
£ per household per week

1 In the two-week diary keeping period following interview; including scratchcards.
2 Combined data from the1997–98, 1998–99 and 1999–00 surveys. See Notes and Definitions.
3 Average weekly expenditure of participating households.

Source: Family Expenditure Survey, Office for National Statistics; Northern Ireland Statistics and Research Agency

8.21 The National Lottery grants: totals from 1997 to 2000

Numbers and £ million

	Number of grants awarded from the start of National Lottery to:				Total value of grants (£ million):			
	end 1997	end 1998	end 1999	end 2000	end 1997	end 1998	end 1999	end 2000
United Kingdom[1]	26,310	35,640	55,821	79,745	5,161.4	6,223.8	7,655.8	8,615.0
North East	1,249	1,840	2,878	4,223	198.0	230.3	339.9	382.9
North West	2,120	2,613	4,009	6,282	380.8	521.0	702.0	802.9
Yorkshire and the Humber	1,837	2,230	3,524	5,426	289.1	349.6	408.6	476.2
East Midlands	1,385	1,744	3,863	5,431	155.2	199.6	251.4	292.9
West Midlands	2,094	2,475	3,946	6,193	244.2	326.6	410.7	474.2
East	1,414	1,771	3,009	4,510	233.1	295.7	348.4	400.1
London	2,563	3,124	4,730	7,377	957.1	1,123.2	1,240.9	1,347.4
South East	2,399	2,930	4,382	6,574	273.3	392.5	474.7	552.3
South West	2,909	3,840	5,572	7,445	252.5	325.4	392.6	454.7
England[2]	18,494	23,345	37,218	55,206	4,154.8	4,979.5	6,066.0	6,776.1
Wales	2,323	3,515	4,933	6,489	251.2	301.6	393.0	459.2
Scotland	3,989	6,795	10,135	12,588	493.9	618.1	743.9	828.2
Northern Ireland	1,153	1,575	2,463	3,150	147.8	191.1	257.8	283.9

1 Includes grants made UK-wide or to institutions of national significance. Further grants have been made overseas. See Notes and Definitions.
2 Includes grants not allocated to a specific English region. See Notes and Definitions.

Source: Department for Culture, Media and Sport

9 Crime and Justice

Crime Rates

In 1999–00, London had the highest recorded crime rate in England and Wales, at just under 14,000 crimes per 100,000 people. The East of England had the lowest recorded crime rate, at just over 7,000 crimes per 100,000 people.

(Table 9.1)

London had the highest recorded rates of theft and handling stolen goods, over 30 per cent higher than the average for England and Wales in 1999–00. Yorkshire and the Humber region had the highest rate for burglary, over half as high again as the average for England and Wales.

(Table 9.1)

The rate of vehicle theft in 1999–00 was highest in the North West, more than double the rates in the East of England and the South West.

(Table 9.1)

Victims

Adults surveyed in the North West were more likely than adults in other regions to have been the victims of personal violence in 1999.

(Table 9.2)

Adults in London were most likely to have been the victims of robbery: some 14 per 1,000 in London had been victims of robbery at least once in 1999, compared with less than 1 per 1,000 in Wales.

(Table 9.2)

Excluding police force areas affected by boundary changes, South Wales had the biggest decrease in recorded crime between 1999 and 2000 at 17 per cent; Suffolk and Staffordshire had amongst the biggest increases, at 11 per cent and 13 per cent respectively.

(Map 9.3)

The proportion of households surveyed in England and Wales suffering vehicle theft in 1999 was almost 3 times higher than the proportion of households suffering burglary. Households surveyed in the East of England were least likely to be the victims of burglary. Households surveyed in Scotland were least likely to be victims of vehicle theft.

(Table 9.4)

Clear Ups

The UK region with the highest clear-up rate for recorded crime was Scotland, with a clear-up rate of 44 per cent. The clear-up rate for recorded crimes in England and Wales in 1999–00 was highest in Wales, at 40 per cent, compared to 16 per cent in London. The clear-up rate for England and Wales was 25 per cent.

(Table 9.5)

Firearms

In 1999–00 Wales had the lowest number of recorded offences in which firearms were reported to have been used. During the same period, London had more than twice as many operations where firearms were issued to the police than any other region.

(Table 9.6)

Drug Seizures

In 1999, Northern Ireland had the lowest number of drug seizures for class A, B and C drugs of any region of the United Kingdom. Class B drugs (including Cannabis) accounted for around three-quarters of all seizures in the UK.

(Table 9.7)

A fifth of cannabis seizures in the United Kingdom were in London.

(Table 9.7)

Police

Scotland had the highest rate of police as a proportion of the population as a whole with one member of the police service for every 350 people; the East of England had the lowest proportion of serving police officers, with one member of the police service for every 550 people.

(Table 9.8)

Cautions

Of the young offenders aged 10 to 17 found guilty or cautioned for offences in the North East, around half were cautioned; this compared with a proportion of two-thirds in the South East in 1999. The cautioning rate for young offenders in England and Wales was 58 per cent.

(Table 9.9)

Offenders

The North East had one of the highest rates of young males found guilty or cautioned for an offence in England and Wales in 1999, at around 6,000 per 100,000 of the population, compared with a rate of around 4,000 per 100,000 of the population for England and Wales.

(Table 9.10)

In the North East in 1999, 12 per cent of males aged 21 or over found guilty of offences received an absolute or conditional discharge; the highest rate of any UK region. For females, Scotland had the highest rate at 19 per cent. A fine was the most likely form of sentence for males and females across every UK region.

(Table 9.11)

Prisoners

Of the total number of women aged 21 and over who were sentenced to immediate imprisonment in 1999, London had the highest proportion of females sentenced for four years or more, at one in ten, compared to an average of one in twenty five female prisoners sentenced for four years or more in Great Britain.

(Table 9.12)

In April 2001, Northern Ireland had the lowest prison population in the United Kingdom (excluding female area and high security prisons), accounting for around 900 prisoners. Scotland and Yorkshire and Humber had the highest populations accounting for around 6,200 and 6,300 prisoners respectively.

(Table 9.13)

9.1 Recorded crimes:[1] by offence group, 1999–00

Rates per 100,000 population

	Violence against the person	Sexual offences	Burglary	Robbery	Theft and handling stolen goods	Theft of vehicles	Theft from vehicles	Fraud and forgery	Criminal damage	Drug offences	Other	Total
England and Wales	1,108	72	1,729	161	4,241	715	1,276	639	1,804	232	125	10,111
North East	849	64	1,976	95	4,182	711	1,157	351	2,004	249	126	9,896
North West	1,097	66	2,041	187	4,276	1,041	1,282	470	2,182	234	134	10,686
Yorkshire and the Humber	784	69	2,656	107	4,791	844	1,502	449	2,038	246	104	11,242
East Midlands	1,050	71	1,910	97	4,306	587	1,353	604	1,821	171	151	10,182
West Midlands	1,241	72	2,063	213	4,364	871	1,361	719	1,964	208	167	11,010
East	708	57	1,173	53	3,280	456	1,036	424	1,437	168	90	7,391
London	2,047	120	1,685	473	5,604	819	1,465	1,383	1,977	346	149	13,784
South East	835	62	1,239	58	3,682	514	1,154	523	1,507	198	109	8,212
South West	768	55	1,400	75	3,749	458	1,258	544	1,276	197	83	8,146
England	1,097	73	1,757	168	4,293	712	1,293	652	1,800	229	124	10,194
Wales	1,293	60	1,253	31	3,366	764	1,004	405	1,872	290	139	8,710
Scotland[3]	370	72	952	86	3,588	513	838	513	1,626	615	451	8,274
Northern Ireland[3]	1,264	70	937	104	2,180	639	338	476	1,910	86	62	7,088

1 See Notes and Definitions.
2 Figures may not reflect published Home Office estimates due to rounding.
3 Figures for Scotland are for 2000. Figures for Northern Ireland are for 2000–01. They are not comparable with those for England and Wales, nor with each other, because of the differences in the legal systems, recording practices and classifications.

Source: Home Office; Scottish Executive; Royal Ulster Constabulary

9.2 Violent offences committed against the person, 1999

Percentage of individuals victimised at least once

	Common assault[1]	Wounding	Robbery	All violent incidents
England and Wales	3.0	0.9	0.5	4.2
North East	3.0	0.5	0.2	3.6
North West	3.4	1.2	0.6	5.0
Yorkshire and the Humber	3.3	1.1	0.4	4.6
East Midlands	3.5	0.6	0.1	4.0
West Midlands	2.5	1.1	0.7	4.3
East	3.0	1.2	0.5	4.2
London	2.3	0.7	1.4	4.4
South East	3.0	0.6	0.3	3.8
South West	2.8	0.9	0.5	4.2
England	3.0	0.9	0.6	4.3
Wales	2.9	1.1	-	3.5
Scotland	3.7	.	0.4	4.1
Northern Ireland[2]	2.7	1.1	0.5	4.4

1 'Assault' for Scotland includes both serious assaults and petty assaults.
2 Data for Northern Ireland relate to 1997.

Source: British Crime Survey, Home Office; Scottish Crime Survey, Scottish Executive; Northern Ireland Crime Survey, Northern Ireland Office

9.3 Percentage change in recorded crimes between the twelve months ending September 2000 and the previous twelve months: by Police Force area

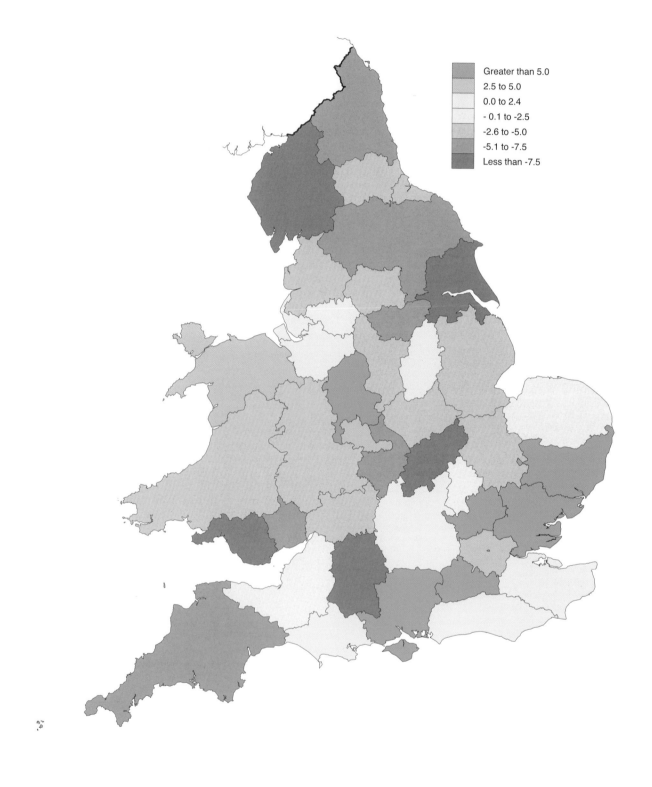

Greater than 5.0
2.5 to 5.0
0.0 to 2.4
- 0.1 to -2.5
-2.6 to -5.0
-5.1 to -7.5
Less than -7.5

1 The figures for Essex, Hertfordshire, Metropolitan Police and Surrey include the effects of boundary changes implemented on 1 April 2000.
The estimated percentage changes prior to boundary changes are 3, 3, 5 and 3 percent respectively.

Source: Home Office

9.4 Offences committed against households,[1] 1999

Rates per 10,000 households[2] and percentages

| | Offences per 10,000 households[2] | | | | Percentage of households[2] victimised at least once | | | |
	Vandalism	Burglary[3]	Vehicle thefts[4]	All household offences[5]	Vandalism	Burglary[3]	Vehicle thefts[4]	All household offences[5]
England and Wales	1,300	585	1,741	4,287	7.8	4.3	12.6	24.6
North East	953	512	1,579	3,388	6.9	3.8	11.8	22.4
North West	1,518	761	2,096	5,196	8.6	6.1	15.2	28.3
Yorkshire and the Humber	1,349	993	2,047	5,447	8.2	7.2	14.9	29.4
East Midlands	1,116	628	1,431	3,870	6.6	4.6	10.0	23.1
West Midlands	1,101	659	1,887	3,841	6.5	4.0	13.3	21.8
East	1,246	296	1,328	3,433	8.4	2.2	10.1	21.0
London	1,227	602	2,025	4,064	8.2	4.4	14.9	24.8
South East	1,587	496	1,562	4,513	8.8	3.6	11.3	24.9
South West	1,318	461	1,619	4,320	7.5	3.1	11.5	24.0
England	1,312	602	1,737	4,316	7.9	4.4	12.6	24.7
Wales	1,127	328	1,799	3,836	6.6	2.9	12.6	23.4
Scotland	999	385	850	2,817	6.0	3.2	7.3	22.5
Northern Ireland[6]	863	301	1,163	2,112	6.9	2.4	8.4	15.4

1 See Notes and Definitions.
2 The vehicle theft risks are based on vehicle-owning households only.
3 The term used in Scotland is housebreaking. The figures include attempts at burglary/housebreaking.
4 Comprises theft of vehicles, thefts from vehicles and associated attempts.
5 Comprises the three individual categories plus thefts of bicycles and other household thefts.
6 Data for Northern Ireland relate to 1997.

Source: British Crime Survey, Home Office; Scottish Crime Survey, Scottish Executive; Northern Ireland Crime Survey, Northern Ireland Office

9.5 Recorded crimes cleared up by the police:[1] by offence group, 1999–00[2]

Percentages

	Violence against the person	Sexual offences	Burglary	Robbery	Theft and handling stolen goods	Fraud and forgery	Criminal damage[3]	Drugs	Other[3]	Total[3]
England and Wales	65	59	13	18	18	30	15	97	74	25
North East	81	70	12	29	23	51	16	99	92	29
North West	74	70	11	18	20	43	14	99	83	26
Yorkshire and the Humber	80	70	13	26	19	43	13	98	85	24
East Midlands	74	62	13	27	19	39	17	96	82	27
West Midlands	73	57	13	19	18	30	16	97	72	26
East	80	65	14	28	20	41	18	99	76	29
London	31	32	10	12	11	10	10	91	43	16
South East	75	65	13	29	18	31	17	98	74	27
South West	78	74	14	22	19	43	20	98	80	28
England	63	57	12	18	17	29	15	96	73	24
Wales	92	90	21	48	27	56	22	100	95	40
Scotland[4,5]	81	77	24	38	33	82	24	100	97	44
Northern Ireland[4]	64	75	16	19	22	44	15	90	66	30

1 See Notes and Definitions.
2 Some offences cleared up may have been initially recorded in an earlier year.
3 The Northern Ireland figure excludes Offences against the State.
4 Figures for Scotland and Northern Ireland are not comparable with those for England and Wales, nor with each other, because of the differences in the legal systems, recording practices and classifications.
5 Figures for Scotland relate to the calendar year 2000.

Source: Home Office; Scottish Executive; Royal Ulster Constabulary

9.6 Firearms

Numbers

	Offences recorded[1] by the police in which firearms were reported[2] to have been used					Operations in which firearms were issued to the police[3,4,5]				
	1995	1996	1997	1998–99[6]	1999–00[6]	1995–96	1996–97	1997–98	1998–99[6]	1999–00[6]
United Kingdom	15,730	16,177	14,424	15,784	18,719	8,671	12,649	12,134	11,184	11,056
North East	723	681	486	727	783	1,050	2,517	1,029	832	655
North West	2,308	2,426	1,751	2,308	2,619	922	1,578	1,462	1,611	1,390
Yorkshire and the Humber	2,270	2,175	1,968	2,079	2,206	1,026	1,128	1,506	1,183	1,304
East Midlands	1,014	1,187	1,140	1,407	1,619	346	470	671	659	867
West Midlands	1,510	1,570	1,251	1,092	1,375	420	730	751	935	840
East	771	730	607	761	996	871	1,172	1,327	1,327	1,239
London	2,248	2,605	2,930	3,005	4,123	2,203	2,747	2,885	2,889	2,987
South East	1,367	1,232	1,123	1,276	1,579	883	1,064	1,284	562	626
South West	588	608	560	628	934	511	575	403	294	305
England	12,799	13,214	11,816	13,283	16,234	8,232	11,981	11,318	10,292	10,213
Wales	635	662	594	591	712	244	398	524	636	702
Scotland	1,721	1,650	1,187	985	1,033	195	270	292	256	141
Northern Ireland	575	651	827	925	740	.	.	.	.	.

1 See Notes and Definitions.
2 'Alleged' in Scotland.
3 In England and Wales, police shots were fired in 5 operations in both 1995–96 and 1996–97, 3 in 1997–98, 5 in 1998–99. In Scotland, police shots were fired in 4 operations in 1995–96, 9 in 1996–97, 1 in 1997–98, 8 in 1998–99.
4 In Northern Ireland, police officers are armed at all times.
5 Figures for the United Kingdom relate to Great Britain only.
6 The collection of recorded crime data in England and Wales changed to a financial year basis from 1 April 1998, which coincided with a change in the counting rules for recorded crime. Due to this, the data shown for 1998–99 and 1999–00 are not comparable with those shown for previous years. See Notes and Definitions.

Source: Home Office; Scottish Executive Justice Department; Royal Ulster Constabulary

9.7 Seizures of controlled drugs:[1] by type of drug, 1999

Number of seizures

	Class A drugs						Class B drugs			
	Heroin	Cocaine	Crack	LSD	Ecstasy type	All class A drugs[2]	Cannabis	Ampheta-mines	All class B drugs[2]	All class C drugs[2,3]
United Kingdom[4]	15,108	5,619	2,436	465	6,438	30,032	97,356	13,194	107,117	2,503
North East	753	183	30	15	401	1,400	4,677	1,019	5,492	205
North West	1,659	362	150	30	476	2,706	8,583	1,349	9,604	120
Yorkshire and the Humber	2,292	176	205	36	509	3,225	5,934	1,228	6,868	228
East Midlands	603	64	62	13	364	1,092	4,525	927	5,141	138
West Midlands	1,044	95	128	17	344	1,657	5,561	760	6,129	42
East	767	355	64	26	315	1,522	6,064	684	6,498	81
London	2,491	2,421	1,427	97	1,096	7,223	19,255	1,645	20,519	305
South East	1,073	436	148	34	669	2,346	9,484	1,382	10,374	128
South West	1,108	201	136	54	632	2,180	7,482	1,160	8,278	141
England	11,790	4,293	2,350	322	4,806	23,351	71,565	10,154	78,903	1,388
Wales	434	62	15	46	356	999	6,105	1,181	6,914	163
Scotland	2,405	291	34	50	684	3,445	12,755	1,543	13,784	888
Northern Ireland	92	24	5	15	375	486	1,729	113	1,782	23
National Crime Squad[4]	40	42	0	3	37	102	90	35	102	2
British Transport Police[4]	184	38	26	12	55	329	1,280	66	1,330	5
Customs and Excise[4]	158	869	6	17	125	1,315	3,828	102	4,298	34

1 See Notes and Definitions.
2 Since a seizure may involve drugs other than those listed, figures for individual drugs cannot be added together to produce totals.
3 Class C drugs include benzodiazepines (including temazepam) and anabolic steroids.
4 Figures for the National Crime Squad, the British Transport Police and the Customs and Excise cannot be split by region or country, but are included in the UK totals.

Source: Home Office

9.8 Police manpower: by type, March 2000[1]

	Police officers on ordinary duty[2]				Special constables and civilian staff (rates per 1,000 officers on ordinary duty)		
		Percentage of which		Population per officer[3]	Special con- stables[4]	Civilian staff[5]	Traffic wardens (numbers)
	Number	Ethnic minorities	Women officers				
United Kingdom[6]	147,736	1.9	16.0	403	114	411	3,331
North East	6,749	0.9	16.3	382	91	386	105
North West	17,153	1.7	17.2	401	107	408	326
Yorkshire and the Humber	11,200	1.9	16.1	451	103	439	249
East Midlands	8,206	2.8	14.6	511	163	459	211
West Midlands	12,151	3.4	19.8	439	156	411	236
East	9,364	1.7	16.9	554	192	479	251
London	26,216	3.9	15.6	297	31	415	817
South East	14,971	1.3	17.2	521	137	465	237
South West	9,313	0.8	15.9	530	215	484	268
England	115,324	2.3	16.6	431	117	435	2,700
Wales	6,632	0.9	14.8	443	126	370	156
Scotland[7]	14,699	0.5	16.0	348	91	321	317
Northern Ireland[7]	11,081	..	11.0	153	104	302	159

1 Full-time equivalents as at 31 March 2000 for England and Wales and for Scotland. Actual numbers (whether full or part-time) as at 31 March 2000 for Northern Ireland.
2 Includes full-time reserves in Northern Ireland.
3 Based on mid-1999 population estimates.
4 Part-time reserves in Northern Ireland.
5 Excludes traffic wardens.
6 Great Britain for ethnic minorities.
7 For civilian staff and traffic wardens, part-time staff are counted as half full-time.

Source: Home Office; Scottish Executive; Royal Ulster Constabulary

9.9 Persons given a police caution:[1] by type of offence and age, 1999

Percentages and thousands

	Violence against the person	Sexual offences	Burglary	Robbery	Theft and handling stolen goods	Fraud and forgery	Criminal damage	Other indictable offences	Total indictable offences	Summary offences[2]	Indictable offences	Summary offences[2]
Persons aged 10-17												
England and Wales	59	55	44	20	66	61	42	24	58	56	120.0	61.2
North East	56	58	36	15	57	55	34	22	51	53	9.7	6.0
North West	54	46	44	13	66	64	34	21	57	56	18.4	10.3
Yorkshire and the Humber	56	47	37	14	61	56	37	14	52	54	12.5	6.4
East Midlands	52	53	40	15	60	48	40	23	52	52	8.4	4.5
West Midlands	63	56	39	24	64	68	26	18	56	61	13.2	6.3
East	59	73	48	17	66	57	42	23	60	54	9.0	4.5
London	63	52	47	25	72	66	24	33	64	52	17.9	7.7
South East	64	61	49	16	67	57	54	31	62	58	15.0	6.9
South West	66	69	58	27	72	63	66	36	67	62	7.6	3.8
England	59	56	44	20	66	61	39	24	58	59	111.8	56.6
Wales	55	37	47	20	65	59	60	24	58	53	8.2	4.6
Persons aged 18 and over												
England and Wales	30	19	7	2	25	22	11	7	26	13	383.1	465.9
North East	26	21	6	2	25	30	8	8	27	22	23.7	31.1
North West	24	17	5	0	21	19	6	4	22	18	59.6	72.0
Yorkshire and the Humber	26	15	4	0	18	16	11	3	18	11	41.8	47.7
East Midlands	24	17	7	1	24	17	17	6	22	11	26.6	38.1
West Midlands	37	17	8	2	27	23	5	8	27	15	39.1	44.8
East	33	22	8	3	26	19	9	6	27	10	27.4	39.3
London	41	19	10	4	34	29	3	13	35	8	69.2	83.9
South East	34	22	8	2	25	23	19	8	27	16	41.9	40.6
South West	28	20	7	2	24	24	23	8	28	12	28.6	35.8
England	31	19	7	2	25	22	10	7	26	13	357.9	433.3
Wales	17	19	6	0	24	20	26	6	25	13	25.2	32.6

1 Persons committing an offence who on admission of guilt were given a formal oral caution by the police as a proportion of those found guilty or cautioned. See Notes and Definitions.
2 Excludes motoring offences for which written warnings were issued.

Source: Home Office

9.10 Persons found guilty or cautioned:[1] by type of offence and age, 1999

Rates per 100,000 population in the relevant age group

	Persons aged 10–17						Persons aged 18 and over					
	Violence against the person plus common assault[2]	Sexual off-ences	Burglary, robbery and theft[3]	Drugs off-ences	Other indict-able off-ences[4]	All indictable offences plus common assault[2]	Violence against the person plus common assault[2]	Sexual off-ences	Burglary, robbery and theft[3]	Drugs off-ences	Other indict-able off-ences[4]	All indictable offences plus common assault[2]
Males												
England and Wales	683	39	1,121	430	408	3,744	324	23	677	383	333	1,741
North East	923	62	3,562	551	513	5,611	371	29	917	412	373	2,101
North West	752	36	1,229	547	487	4,224	337	25	815	417	417	2,012
Yorkshire and the Humber	716	47	1,248	356	434	3,984	330	24	824	364	419	1,961
East Midlands	740	54	1,073	208	353	3,438	357	25	648	241	297	1,567
West Midlands	844	57	1,159	360	482	3,997	366	27	684	328	398	1,803
East	571	32	880	324	284	2,930	275	20	496	278	228	1,297
London	626	30	1,106	786	423	4,019	325	20	738	634	373	2,091
South East	572	27	1,002	330	344	3,220	274	20	506	292	242	1,335
South West	527	28	774	278	256	2,589	289	22	579	309	216	1,416
England	680	39	1,110	429	396	3,706	320	23	676	376	329	1,723
Wales	732	37	1,299	449	589	4,347	399	32	689	512	410	2,042
Females												
England and Wales	233	1	373	41	81	1,124	50	0	183	48	67	348
North East	374	0	1,302	55	141	1,873	63	1	277	55	86	482
North West	251	4	351	38	90	1,101	55	0	234	50	87	426
Yorkshire and the Humber	263	3	397	47	80	1,207	52	0	204	58	85	399
East Midlands	257	0	319	21	70	1,007	59	0	172	35	61	327
West Midlands	314	0	350	33	92	1,160	63	0	161	33	66	323
East	189	1	330	39	69	974	44	0	133	39	45	261
London	139	0	417	53	75	1,125	42	1	224	59	82	408
South East	197	1	349	33	61	1,011	36	0	128	38	44	246
South West	203	0	290	35	60	898	39	0	145	48	43	277
England	231	1	370	39	79	1,110	49	0	183	46	66	344
Wales	270	1	433	68	118	1,343	72	1	189	78	80	421
All persons												
England and Wales	464	20	1,495	241	249	2,469	183	12	423	211	196	1,025
North East	656	32	2,462	310	332	3,792	212	14	586	227	224	1,264
North West	507	20	1,580	298	293	2,699	192	12	515	228	247	1,194
Yorkshire and the Humber	495	25	1,645	205	262	2,633	188	12	506	207	248	1,161
East Midlands	506	28	1,392	117	216	2,259	205	12	405	135	176	934
West Midlands	586	29	1,509	201	293	2,619	211	13	417	177	229	1,047
East	385	17	1,210	185	179	1,976	157	10	310	156	134	767
London	389	16	1,523	429	254	2,611	180	10	475	339	224	1,229
South East	390	14	1,351	186	207	2,148	152	10	311	161	140	774
South West	370	15	1,065	160	161	1,770	160	11	355	174	127	826
England	462	21	1,480	239	242	2,444	181	11	422	206	194	1,015
Wales	506	19	1,731	263	359	2,879	230	16	431	288	240	1,206

1 See Notes and Definitions.
2 Following the introduction of a charging standard on 31 August 1994, some people who would have been charged with an indictable offence are now charged with common
  assault, a summary offence. Common assaults have therefore been included for comparability with figures in previous editions of *Regional Trends*.
3 Includes handling stolen goods.
4 Includes criminal damage and fraud and forgery.

Source: Home Office

9.11 Persons aged 21 and over found guilty of offences:[1] by gender and type of sentence, 1999

	Result as a percentage of number of persons sentenced						All sentenced	
	Absolute or conditional discharge	Fine	All community penalties	Fully suspended sentence[2]	Immediate custodial sentence[3]	Otherwise dealt with	(=100%) (numbers)	Rates[4]
Males								
England and Wales	7	75	8	-	8	2	951,514	54
North East	12	69	9	-	8	2	46,512	51
North West	8	75	8	-	8	1	153,982	63
Yorkshire and the Humber	7	71	10	-	8	3	102,702	57
East Midlands	6	74	9	-	8	2	76,285	51
West Midlands	6	79	8	-	7	1	103,735	55
East	5	78	8	-	7	2	83,295	45
London	5	78	7	-	9	1	139,193	51
South East	7	75	9	-	7	2	106,634	39
South West	8	74	9	-	7	2	77,860	44
England	7	75	8	-	8	2	890,198	54
Wales	7	77	8	-	7	1	61,316	59
Scotland[5]	8	72	7	.	12	1	80,265	45
Northern Ireland[6]	5	72	2	8	7	6	19,416	35
Females								
England and Wales	10	77	8	-	3	1	190,700	10
North East	15	72	9	1	3	1	10,315	10
North West	10	76	9	-	4	1	32,729	13
Yorkshire and the Humber	11	74	9	-	4	3	20,841	11
East Midlands	9	77	8	1	3	2	15,104	10
West Midlands	8	82	7	-	3	1	17,667	9
East	8	80	7	-	3	1	15,931	8
London	7	80	7	1	5	1	29,166	10
South East	10	76	9	-	3	1	18,656	6
South West	11	77	8	-	2	1	15,901	8
England	10	77	8	-	3	1	176,310	9
Wales	10	80	6	1	2	1	14,390	13
Scotland[5]	19	65	10	.	5	1	12,618	6
Northern Ireland[6]	11	70	1	6	2	11	2,586	4

1 See Notes and Definitions. The coverage of the table is all offences, including motoring offences. A defendant is recorded only once for each set of court proceedings, against the principal offence.
2 Fully suspended sentences are not available to courts in Scotland.
3 Includes custodial sentences imposed following a sentence deferred for good behaviour in Scotland.
4 Rates per 1,000 population aged 21 and over.
5 To improve comparability, this table excludes breaches of probation and community service orders normally included in Scottish figures.
6 Northern Ireland figures relate to 1998.

Source: Home Office; Scottish Executive; Northern Ireland Office

9.12 Persons aged 21 and over sentenced to immediate imprisonment: by gender and length of sentence imposed for principal[1] offence, 1999

Percentages and numbers

	Males				Females			
	Length of sentence (percentages)			Total sentenced to immediate imprisonment (=100%) (numbers)	Length of sentence (percentages)			Total sentenced to immediate imprisonment (=100%) (numbers)
	One year or less	Over one year but less than four years	Four years and over		One year or less	Over one year but less than four years	Four years and over	
Great Britain	76	17	7	83,546	85	11	4	6,800
North East	74	20	6	3,652	90	9	1	258
North West	75	18	7	12,434	86	11	3	1,314
Yorkshire and the Humber	73	20	7	8,448	86	12	2	704
East Midlands	77	18	6	6,217	87	10	3	430
West Midlands	74	20	7	7,194	86	11	2	445
East	79	15	6	5,930	86	11	3	427
London	74	17	9	12,580	78	12	10	1,347
South East	73	19	8	7,466	77	15	8	545
South West	77	18	5	5,338	86	12	2	379
England	75	18	7	69,265	84	12	5	5,849
Wales	75	19	5	4,262	84	13	2	283
Scotland[2]	87	9	4	10,019	94	4	2	668
Northern Ireland[3]	21	44	35	333	82	9	9	11

1 Figures for Scotland are for the length of sentence in total given for all offences and not just for the principal offence. Figures on sentence lengths for principal offences only are not available for Scotland.
2 To improve comparability, this table excludes breaches of probation and community service orders normally included in Scottish figures.
3 Data for Northern Ireland relate to 1998. They are not comparable with those for Great Britain as they relate to Crown Court only.

Source: Home Office; Scottish Executive; Northern Ireland Office

9.13 Prison population in the United Kingdom: by prison service region,[1] April 2001

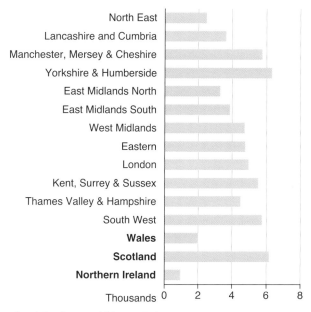

1 People in prison establishments in the region excluding female area and high security prisons.

Source: Home Office; Scottish Executive; Northern Ireland Office

9.14 Feelings of insecurity:[1] by gender, 2000

Percentages

| | Percentage feeling 'very' unsafe at night when: | | | |
| | Alone at home | | Walking alone[2] | |
	Males	Females	Males	Females
England and Wales	1	3	4	18
North East	-	2	4	15
North West	-	4	3	20
Yorkshire and the Humber	1	3	4	20
East Midlands	-	3	4	20
West Midlands	1	3	5	19
East	-	1	3	16
London	1	3	5	20
South East	1	2	3	15
South West	1	2	3	17
England	1	3	4	18
Wales	1	3	4	15
Scotland[3]	-	2	4	15
Northern Ireland[4]	3	12	11	34

1 People aged 16 and over.
2 For Northern Ireland the question relates to fear of 'walking in the dark' (i.e. alone or with others); the figures also include those people who never go out.
3 Data for Scotland relate to 1999.
4 Data for Northern Ireland relate to 1998. See Notes and Definitions.

Source: British Crime Survey, Home Office; Scottish Crime Survey, Scottish Executive; Northern Ireland Crime Survey, Northern Ireland Office

10 Transport

Cars

In 1999, the percentage of households who did not own a car ranged from 21 per cent in the East of England to 38 per cent in the North East.

(Table 10.2)

During 1998-2000, a third of cars in Scotland were less than 3 years old, compared with just under a quarter of cars in the South West.

(Table 10.3)

The South East had the highest proportion of women with a full driving licence over the period 1998-2000: almost 50 per cent more than the proportion of women in the North East.

(Chart 10.4)

Travel

In Great Britain, people in the South East make, on average, the most trips per person per year, while people within Wales make the least.

(Table 10.5)

People within the North East made the greatest number of trips a year on foot during 1998–2000, over a quarter more than people in the East of England.

(Table 10.5)

During 1998-2000, people in the East of England travelled the furthest distance per person per year, 50 per cent further than Londoners.

(Table 10.6)

People in the East Midlands made on average the most trips per year on a bicycle during the period 1998–2000: 29 trips per person. In contrast, people in London made the least number: just 11 journeys per person.

(Chart 10.7)

Over the period 1992–1994 to 1998–2000, the greatest improvement in bus service accessibility was seen in the South East, with an increase of 19 percentage points in households being within 13 minutes of a bus stop having at least an hourly service.

(Chart 10.8)

Across Great Britain, women make proportionally fewer commuting trips than men: in 1998-2000, for instance, a fifth of all men's trips in the East Midlands were commuting trips compared with a seventh of women's trips.

(Table 10.9)

In Autumn 2000, travel by car, van or minibus were the most popular methods for travelling to work for all regions. There was still great variation, however, ranging from over four-fifths of all trips made to work in Northern Ireland to over two-fifths of the trips to work made by Londoners.

(Table 10.10)

During 1998–2000, under two-fifths of all trips made to and from school in the South East and East of England were by car, nearly double the proportion in the North East, Yorkshire and the Humber, and Scotland

(Table 10.11)

Expenditure on travel and roads

Average weekly motoring expenditure per car or van ranged from £36.80 in the North East to £55.30 in the South East during the period 1997–2000.

(Table 10.12)

In 1998–99, around 8 per cent of all expenditure on local roads in the North East was on road safety, compared with under 4 per cent of expenditure in the West Midlands, East Midlands, Wales and Yorkshire and the Humber.

(Table 10.13)

Traffic

The average daily motor vehicle flow on motorways in Great Britain in 1999 varied from 35,200 vehicles per day in Scotland to 93,900 vehicles per day in London.

(Table 10.14)

Traffic increases between 1990 and 1999 on major roads in Great Britain ranged from 6 per cent in London to 26 per cent in the North East.

(Chart 10.15)

Accidents

The distribution of accidents on non built-up 'A' roads in the UK ranged from 3.2 per cent in London to 49.8 per cent in Wales in 1999.

(Table 10.16)

In 1999, the fatal or serious accident rate per 100 million vehicle kilometres on major roads in Great Britain ranged from 2.9 accidents in the South West to 11.7 accidents in London.

(Table 10.17)

In 1999, the rate of fatal and serious accidents on all roads fell in all regions compared with the 1981-1985 average. The greatest decline was in the South West, where there was a 62 per cent decrease in fatal and serious accidents.

(Table 10.17)

Motorcyclists made up around 16 per cent of all road casualties in London in 1999, compared with less than 3 per cent in Northern Ireland.

(Table 10.18)

Airports

In 2000, almost 80 per cent of all air passengers using UK airports were on international flights.

(Table 10.19)

In 2000, Heathrow Airport handled almost three-fifths of all UK air freight.

(Table 10.19)

Seaports

A half of all sea freight was handled by East coast ports in 1999.

(Table 10.20)

Regional Trends 36, © Crown copyright 2001

10.1 Motor cars currently licensed and new registrations[1]

Thousands and percentages

	Currently licensed[2]				Percentage company cars	New registrations		
	1994	1996	1998	2000[3]	2000	1996	1998	2000[3]
United Kingdom[4]	21,708	22,784	23,878	24,406	10	2,077	2,366	2,335
North East	745	783	824	867	6	74	78	82
North West	2,375	2,501	2,647	2,751	13	235	265	284
Yorkshire and the Humber	1,633	1,707	1,808	1,908	10	138	157	179
East Midlands	1,532	1,609	1,698	1,813	10	140	173	168
West Midlands	2,070	2,183	2,290	2,392	17	275	288	264
East	2,168	2,295	2,429	2,542	8	200	232	225
London	2,310	2,362	2,369	2,414	10	277	270	221
South East	3,295	3,469	3,709	3,904	10	292	361	373
South West	1,976	2,109	2,230	2,382	10	130	138	186
England	18,104	19,018	20,006	20,973	11	1,762	1,961	1,982
Wales	1,012	1,067	1,129	1,171	5	73	83	87
Scotland	1,575	1,674	1,775	1,872	9	154	175	186
Northern Ireland	515	540	585	608	9	55	71	72

1 Figures for United Kingdom include motor vehicles where the country of the registered keeper is unknown. Total includes vehicles under disposal and counties unknown.
2 At 31 December.
3 Northern Ireland figures are for 1999.
4 Figures for 2000 are GB figures.

Source: Annual Vehicle Census/Vehicle Information Database, Department for Transport, Local Government and the Regions; Department of the Environment, Northern Ireland

10.2 Households with a regular use of a car[1], 1999

Percentages

	Percentage of households with regular use of			
	No car	One car only	Two cars	Three or more cars
Great Britain	28	44	22	5
North East	38	43	15	3
North West	30	44	22	4
Yorkshire and the Humber	31	43	21	5
East Midlands	26	45	24	5
West Midlands	28	43	24	5
East	21	47	26	6
London	36	45	16	3
South East	23	43	28	6
South West	23	46	24	7
England	28	44	23	5
Wales	27	46	23	4
Scotland	34	44	19	4

1 Includes cars and light vans normally available to the household.

Source: General Household Survey and Family Expenditure Survey, Office for National Statistics; National Travel Survey, Department of Transport, Local Government and the Regions; Continuous Household Survey, Northern Ireland Statistics and Research Agency

10.3 Age of household cars, 1992–1994 and 1998–2000

Percentages

	1992–1994			1998–2000		
	Age of car[1]					
	Less than 3 years old	3–6 years old	More than 6 years old	Less than 3 years old	3–6 years old	More than 6 years old
Great Britain	26	29	44	28	23	49
North East	32	29	39	29	22	49
North West	28	29	43	29	23	49
Yorkshire and the Humber	28	34	38	26	26	48
East Midlands	31	30	39	25	22	53
West Midlands	25	27	47	31	22	47
East	25	30	46	29	22	49
London	20	29	52	25	21	53
South East	29	30	41	27	25	48
South West	21	27	52	24	20	55
England	26	29	45	27	23	50
Wales	23	26	51	26	24	50
Scotland	31	33	36	33	28	40

1 Age of main or only car or light van normally available to the household. See Notes and Definitions.

Source: National Travel Survey, Department for Transport, Local Government and the Regions

10.4 Full car driving licence holders:[1] by gender, 1992–1994 and 1998–2000

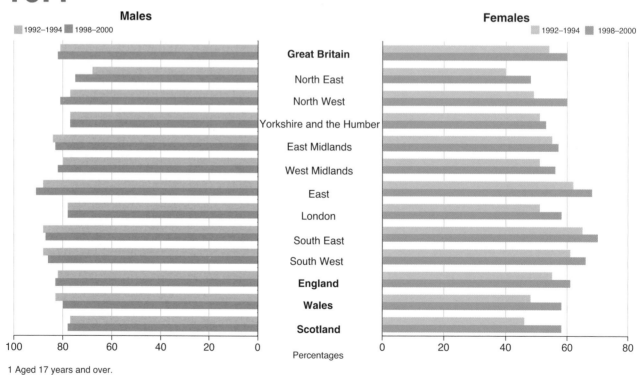

1 Aged 17 years and over.

Source: National Travel Survey, Department for Transport, Local Government and the Regions; Department of the Environment, Northern Ireland

10.5 Trips per person[1] per year: by mode of transport, 1998–2000

Number

	Walk	Pedal cycle[2]	Car driver	Cars and passenger	Other private[2]	Local bus	Rail[2]	Taxi/ minicab[2]	Other public[2]	All modes
Great Britain	271	16	411	228	11	58	19	12	3	1,030
North East	312	..	365	223	..	92	..	15	..	1,035
North West	244	12	413	230	10	66	9	18	..	1,006
Yorkshire and the Humber	307	19	394	214	8	67	8	13	..	1,032
East Midlands	249	29	416	221	12	54	..	10	..	998
West Midlands	278	13	417	233	8	70	..	9	..	1,039
East	246	21	476	254	11	22	19	7	..	1,058
London	300	11	305	186	10	94	82	15	..	1,007
South East	251	20	478	262	13	31	17	10	..	1,084
South West	255	19	422	239	15	39	..	..	..	1,001
England	269	17	412	230	11	57	20	11	3	1,031
Wales	256	..	401	224	15	37	..	13	..	957
Scotland	302	14	407	210	11	78	13	18	..	1,058

1 Within Great Britain only. Figures relate to region of residence of the traveller and include trips undertaken outside of this region. They include trips of less than one mile; these were excluded from the table in *Regional Trends 32* and earlier editions.
2 For some regions, sample sizes are too small to provide reliable estimates.

Source: National Travel Survey, Department for Transport, Local Government and the Regions

10.6 Distance travelled per person[1] per year: by mode of transport, 1998–2000

Miles

	Walk	Pedal cycle[2]	Cars and other private road vehicles	Bus	Rail[2]	Taxi and other	All public transport	All modes of transport
Great Britain	186	38	5,738	246	428	206	880	6,843
North East	195	..	5,024	389	..	153	742	5,994
North West	172	27	5,079	254	238	216	708	5,985
Yorkshire and the Humber	192	43	5,456	304	363	195	861	6,553
East Midlands	178	57	5,751	249	..	190	805	6,791
West Midlands	172	31	5,447	274	..	247	687	6,336
East	170	46	7,062	98	676	133	907	8,184
London	226	38	3,767	322	947	168	1,437	5,467
South East	188	46	7,070	139	512	190	841	8,144
South West	173	48	6,778	164	..	183	592	7,592
England	186	41	5,750	232	445	188	865	6,842
Wales	163	..	5,665	166	..	146	437	6,278
Scotland	205	31	5,669	426	454	424	1,304	7,210

1 Within Great Britain only. Figures relate to region of residence of the traveller and include trips undertaken outside of this region. They include trips of less than one mile; these were excluded from the table in *Regional Trends 32* and earlier editions. See Notes and Definitions.
2 For some regions, sample sizes are too small to provide reliable estimates.

Source: National Travel Survey, Department for Transport, Local Government and the Regions

10.7 Trips per person per year and distance travelled: by bicycle,[1] 1992–1994 and 1998–2000

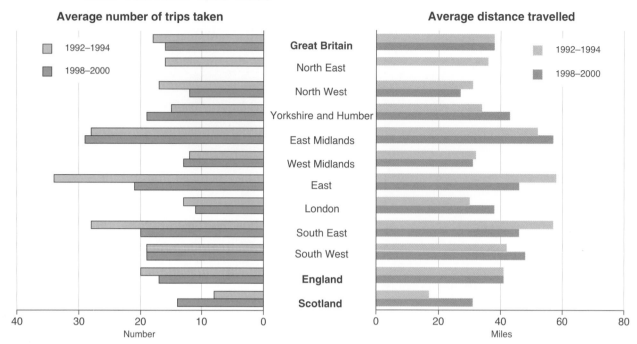

Average number of trips taken   **Average distance travelled**

1992–1994
1998–2000

Great Britain
North East
North West
Yorkshire and Humber
East Midlands
West Midlands
East
London
South East
South West
England
Scotland

Number   Miles

1 Within Great Britain only. By region of residence but includes trips undertaken outside of this region. Includes trips of less than one mile. See Notes and Definitions.

Source: National Travel Survey, Department for Transport, Local Government and the Regions

10.8 Bus accessibility,[1] 1992–1994 and 1998–2000

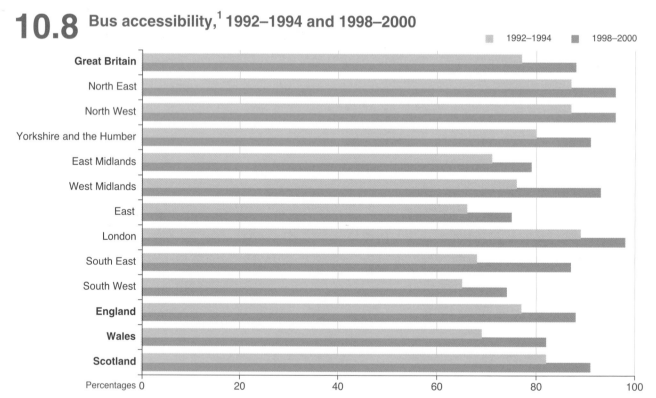

1992–1994   1998–2000

Great Britain
North East
North West
Yorkshire and the Humber
East Midlands
West Midlands
East
London
South East
South West
England
Wales
Scotland

Percentages

1 Percentage of households within 13 minutes of a bus stop with a service at least once an hour.

Source: National Travel Survey, Department for Transport, Local Government and the Regions.

10.9 Trips per person[1] per year: by purpose and gender, 1998–2000

Percentages and numbers

	Commuting	Business	Education	Shopping	Other personal business	Leisure	Average number of journeys (=100%)
Males							
Great Britain	18	5	7	19	20	31	1,041
North East	18	3	9	20	16	34	1,058
North West	18	4	8	19	21	30	1,012
Yorkshire and the Humber	18	4	7	20	19	32	1,041
East Midlands	21	4	7	19	19	30	1,019
West Midlands	19	4	8	19	20	31	1,061
East	19	7	6	18	21	29	1,065
London	17	6	7	18	21	29	1,015
South East	17	6	6	17	22	30	1,094
South West	19	6	5	19	19	32	1,026
England	18	5	7	19	20	31	1,045
Wales	18	5	5	19	19	35	964
Scotland	19	4	6	19	19	32	1,045
Females							
Great Britain	13	2	7	23	25	31	1,020
North East	14	1	7	25	20	32	1,014
North West	14	2	7	23	25	29	1,001
Yorkshire and the Humber	13	1	6	25	23	32	1,024
East Midlands	14	2	6	22	25	30	979
West Midlands	13	1	8	23	23	30	1,017
East	13	1	6	22	28	30	1,051
London	13	2	8	22	27	29	999
South East	13	2	6	23	27	29	1,074
South West	13	2	5	23	23	33	977
England	13	2	7	23	25	30	1,019
Wales	12	1	7	24	22	34	950
Scotland	13	2	7	25	21	33	1,069
All persons							
Great Britain	16	3	7	21	22	31	1,030
North East	16	2	8	23	18	33	1,035
North West	16	3	7	21	23	30	1,006
Yorkshire and the Humber	15	3	7	23	21	32	1,032
East Midlands	18	3	7	20	22	30	998
West Midlands	16	3	8	21	22	30	1,039
East	16	4	6	20	24	30	1,058
London	15	4	7	20	24	29	1,007
South East	15	4	6	20	25	30	1,084
South West	16	4	5	21	21	33	1,001
England	16	4	7	21	23	30	1,031
Wales	15	3	6	21	21	34	957
Scotland	16	3	7	22	20	32	1,058

1 Within Great Britain only. Figures relate to region of residence of the traveller and include trips undertaken outside of their region. They include trips of less than one mile; these were excluded from the table in *Regional Trends 32* and earlier editions. See Notes and Definitions.

Source: National Travel Survey, Department for Transport, Local Government and the Regions

10.10 Main method of travel to work, Autumn 2000[1]

Percentages

	Car, van, minibus, works van	Motorbike, moped, scooter[2]	Bicycle[2]	Bus, coach, private bus	Rail[2]	Other rail[2,3]	Foot	Other[2,4]
United Kingdom	70.0	1.1	3.2	7.6	3.7	2.4	11.1	0.8
North East	70.5	..	2.3	11.7	..	1.6	11.6	1.0
North West	75.4	0.8	2.7	7.8	1.6	0.5	10.2	0.9
Yorkshire and the Humber	69.5	1.3	3.6	10.9	1.7	..	11.8	0.7
East Midlands	74.6	1.1	4.4	6.7	0.8	..	11.8	..
West Midlands	75.8	1.1	2.7	8.1	1.2	..	10.4	0.6
East	72.6	1.3	5.0	3.6	6.0	1.1	10.0	0.6
London	43.8	1.4	2.6	11.8	12.1	17.1	10.1	1.1
South East	73.7	1.0	3.7	4.3	5.5	0.5	10.6	0.8
South West	75.1	1.7	4.4	4.2	1.0	..	12.5	0.9
England	69.5	1.2	3.5	7.3	4.0	2.8	10.9	0.8
Wales	78.7	..	1.7	5.4	1.4	..	11.9	..
Scotland	67.0	0.5	1.7	12.6	2.9	..	13.5	1.4
Northern Ireland	81.2	..	..	4.7	..	..	10.3	..

1 See Notes and Definitions to the Labour Market chapter. Analyses exclude those on government schemes, those who work from home or in the same grounds or building as their home, and those who work in different places using their home as a base.
2 For some regions, sample sizes are too small to provide reliable estimates.
3 Underground, light railway and tram.
4 Includes taxi as main method.

Source: Labour Force Survey, Office for National Statistics; Department of Enterprise, Trade and Investment, Northern Ireland

10.11 Trips to and from school:[1] by main mode of transport, 1998–2000

Percentages and miles

	Walk	Car	Bus[2]	Other	Average length (miles) Age 5–10	Average length (miles) Age 11–16
Great Britain	49	27	19	4	1.5	3.1
North East	59	20	20	-	0.8	2.4
North West	46	29	23	-	1.4	2.7
Yorkshire and the Humber	60	20	17	-	0.8	3.3
East Midlands	48	30	19	-	1.6	3.0
West Midlands	61	23	15	-	1.4	2.0
East	44	36	13	-	1.8	3.9
London	49	25	19	-	1.4	3.1
South East	43	37	16	-	1.9	3.1
South West	41	29	24	-	1.7	4.7
England	50	28	18	4	1.5	3.1
Wales	39	29	30	-	1.7	3.1
Scotland	53	20	26	-	1.2	2.8

1 By region of residence. See Notes and Definitions.
2 Including school bus.

Source: National Travel Survey, Department for Transport, Local Government and the Regions

10.12 Household expenditure on transport, 1997–2000[1]

Average weekly household expenditure (£)

	Motoring					Fares and other travel costs				
	Cars, vans & motorcycles purchase and repairs	Spares & access-ories	Motor vehicle insurance & taxation	Petrol, diesel & other motor oils	Other motoring costs	Rail & tube fares	Bus & coach fares	Other travel costs[2]	Total expenditure per household	Motoring expenditure per car/van
United Kingdom	22.20	1.90	6.90	13.40	1.90	1.70	1.40	5.60	348.20	48.50
North East	14.80	1.30	5.40	10.60	1.10	0.90	1.80	3.30	285.40	36.80
North West	23.70	2.20	6.80	13.20	1.60	0.80	1.50	4.00	334.60	50.00
Yorkshire and the Humber	22.50	2.10	6.50	12.30	1.60	0.80	1.70	4.60	329.60	47.20
East Midlands	24.00	1.90	6.90	14.10	2.00	0.70	1.10	5.10	338.70	50.60
West Midlands	21.90	2.30	7.40	14.50	1.90	0.70	1.40	3.80	336.20	49.10
East	25.00	1.70	7.60	14.90	2.20	2.90	0.80	5.50	357.90	50.50
London	19.20	1.60	6.70	10.40	2.00	4.30	1.80	11.80	403.90	45.40
South East	26.40	2.40	8.00	15.70	2.30	3.00	1.00	6.50	392.50	55.30
South West	22.10	2.10	6.90	14.40	2.10	0.60	1.10	3.90	332.20	48.80
England	22.70	2.00	7.10	13.50	1.90	1.90	1.30	5.80	354.30	49.30
Wales	16.50	2.20	6.00	13.00	1.50	0.70	1.20	3.60	315.60	41.10
Scotland	21.00	1.20	5.40	11.70	1.40	1.10	2.00	4.50	317.30	44.70
Northern Ireland	18.30	2.10	8.30	14.70	1.20	0.30	1.40	4.40	316.90	47.90

1 Combined data from the 1997–1998, 1998–1999 and 1999–2000 surveys. See Notes and Definitions.
2 Other travel costs include taxis, air and other travel, and bicycles and boats: purchase and repair.

Source: Family Expenditure Survey, Office for National Statistics

10.13 Public expenditure on roads, 1998–99

Millions (£)

	Motorways and trunk roads[1]				Local roads[2]				
	New construction/ improvement and structural maintenance	Public lighting and routine maintenance[3]	Total	Expenditure per 1,000 kilometres	New construction/ improvement and structural maintenance[4]	Public lighting and routine maintenance[3,5]	Revenue expenditure on road safety[6]	Total	Expenditure per 1,000 kilometres
North East	22.3	5.3	27.6	53.0	66.2	56.5	10.4	133.1	8.6
North West	157.6	24.2	181.8	211.7	154.3	162.4	15.6	332.4	10.0
Yorkshire and the Humber	36.2	15.7	51.9	46.9	134.0	117.5	10.1	261.6	9.1
East Midlands	48.2	5.9	54.1	42.5	93.8	93.2	7.2	194.3	6.9
West Midlands	96.9	16.1	113.0	134.7	135.1	94.3	7.8	237.3	7.9
East	91.8	19.6	111.4	85.7	100.3	128.0	10.0	238.3	6.6
London	144.2	16.7	160.9	238.6	180.1	151.5	24.6	356.1	13.5
South East	146.9	34.4	181.3	186.5	245.2	173.3	18.0	436.6	9.2
South West	84.1	10.9	95.0	102.0	104.0	115.4	13.3	232.7	5.5
England	828.2	148.8	977.0	115.2	1,213.0	1,092.1	117.1	2,422.2	8.4
Wales	67.1	5.2	72.3	42.3	105.6	93.1	7.7	206.4	6.5
Scotland[7]	109.3	67.1	176.4	50.7	100.5	264.1	27.3	391.9	7.9
Northern Ireland[8]	..	..	..	..	66.0	34.0	..	100.0	4.1

1 Expenditure on motorway and trunk roads excludes expenditure under DBFO schemes.
2 Local Authority expenditure excludes car parks.
3 Includes expenditure on gritting and snow clearing.
4 In Northern Ireland, includes revenue expenditure on certain road safety items.
5 In Northern Ireland, includes revenue expenditure on highway structures.
6 In Scotland, includes traffic management surveys and school crossing patrols.
7 The total figure for local roads includes construction and improvement capital figures which are on a cash basis, and revenue figures which are on an accruals basis.
8 In Northern Ireland, figures for motorways and trunk roads are included in local roads totals.

Source: Department of Transport, Local Government and the Regions; Department for Regional Development, Northern Ireland; Scottish Executive; National Assembly for Wales

10.14 Average daily motor vehicle flows:[1] by road class, 1999

Thousand vehicles per day

	Major roads			Minor roads		
	Motorway	Non built-up	Built-up	Non built-up	Built-up	All roads
Great Britain	68.2	11.0	15.1	0.8	2.1	3.4
North East	47.5	14.8	13.4	0.7	2.2	3.3
North West	65.7	11.0	15.6	0.8	1.9	4.0
Yorkshire and the Humber	60.3	12.1	15.4	0.9	2.0	3.5
East Midlands	85.3	12.8	14.0	0.9	1.7	3.4
West Midlands	77.2	11.5	16.5	0.9	2.5	3.9
East	79.9	17.7	13.9	1.1	2.2	3.9
London	93.9	57.0	24.7	-	2.2	6.0
South East	84.3	17.6	15.5	1.4	2.5	5.1
South West	58.6	10.2	13.4	0.6	1.9	2.5
England	72.9	14.0	16.2	0.9	2.1	3.8
Wales	55.2	7.9	9.2	0.6	1.8	2.1
Scotland	35.2	4.5	10.8	0.6	2.1	2.2

1 Average daily flow is the annual traffic divided by road length divided by 365. See Notes and Definitions.

Source: National Road Traffic Survey, Department for Transport, Local Government and the Regions

10.15 Traffic increase on major roads[1] between 1990 and 1999

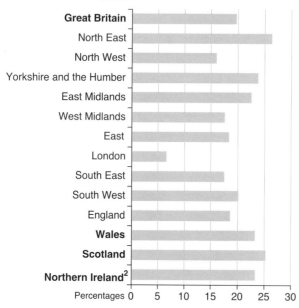

1 See Notes and Definitions.
2 Traffic increase between 1991 and 1998.

Source: Department for Transport, Local Government and the Regions; Department of the Environment, Northern Ireland.

10.16 Road traffic and distribution of accidents on major roads, 1999

	Motor vehicle traffic on major roads (percentages)			All major roads (=100%) (billion vehicle kilo-metres)	All roads (billion vehicle kilo-metres)	Distribution of accidents (percentages)			Total accidents	
									On major roads (=100%) (num-bers)	On all roads (num-bers)[1]
	Motorway	Built-up 'A'	Non built-up 'A'			Motor-way	Built-up 'A'	Non built-up 'A'		
Great Britain	28.0	26.8	45.2	298.3	467	7.8	63.0	29.2	116,592	235,048
North East	10.5	21.9	67.5	11.4	19.4	3.3	53.2	43.6	3,539	8,223
North West	41.5	31.8	26.7	33.7	50.4	11.9	69.6	18.5	15,468	30,993
Yorkshire and the Humber	30.1	30.5	39.3	23.9	38.5	7.8	65.2	27.0	9,369	21,152
East Midlands	23.8	20.2	56.0	24.8	36.2	7.2	48.7	44.1	8,226	16,552
West Midlands	37.4	27.0	35.6	27.8	44.5	9.8	62.3	27.9	9,713	21,099
East	23.9	16.8	59.3	33.9	53.1	10.8	44.3	45.0	10,105	21,788
London	11.7	68.8	19.5	20.5	30.0	2.0	94.8	3.2	24,007	38,368
South East	37.2	19.7	43.1	54.3	82.1	12.6	48.8	38.6	16,329	33,047
South West	25.3	22.7	52.0	27.3	44.4	7.0	48.9	44.1	8,397	18,629
England	29.6	27.0	43.3	257.7	398.6	8.0	64.8	27.2	105,153	209,851
Wales	17.5	23.4	59.1	15.4	25.5	5.3	44.9	49.8	4,413	9,893
Scotland	18.4	25.6	56.0	25.0	42.9	6.0	47.2	46.8	7,026	15,304

1 Includes B,C and unclassified roads. See Notes and Definitions.

Source: Department for Transport, Local Government and the Regions

10.17 Fatal and serious road accidents[1]

Numbers and rates

	Fatal and serious accidents on all roads						Fatal and serious accidents on major roads[2]			
	Numbers			Rates per 100,000 population			Numbers		Rates per 100 million vehicle kms	
	1981–1985 average[3]	1991	1999	1981–1985 average[3]	1991	1999	1991	1999	1991	1999
Great Britain	67,843	47,931	36,405	124	85	63	24,344	18,606	9.4	4.0
North East	2,255	1,769	1,111	86	68	43	734	451	5.9	3.7
North West	6,178	4,914	3,778	90	71	55	2,506	1,889	9.6	3.7
Yorkshire and the Humber	5,713	4,352	3,207	117	87	64	2,084	1,435	10.1	3.7
East Midlands	5,333	3,451	3,095	138	86	74	1,796	1,629	9.3	4.5
West Midlands	6,526	4,447	3,244	126	84	61	2,055	1,558	8.5	3.5
East	6,885	4,802	3,816	140	93	70	2,264	1,787	6.5	3.4
London	7,588	7,279	5,515	112	105	76	4,399	3,501	23.7	11.7
South East	10,169	5,843	5,135	139	76	64	2,882	2,609	6.9	3.2
South West	6,697	3,793	2,570	158	80	52	1,833	1,269	7.1	2.9
England	57,348	40,650	31,471	123	84	63	20,553	16,128	9.2	4.0
Wales	3,083	2,112	1,469	107	73	50	1,139	754	8.9	3.0
Scotland	7,412	5,169	3,465	144	101	68	2,652	1,724	12.1	4.0
Northern Ireland	..	1,381	1,214	..	85	72	643	..	9.5	..

1 See Notes and Definitions.
2 Motorways, A(M) roads and A roads.
3 Used as a basis for the government targets for reducing road casualties in Great Britain, and fatal and serious road casualties in Northern Ireland, by a third by the year 2000.

Source: Department for Transport, Local Government and the Regions; Royal Ulster Constabulary

10.18 Road casualties:[1] by age and type of road user, 1999

Percentages and numbers

	Percentage of all road casualties								All road casualties (=100%) (numbers)	Per-centage change over 1981–85 average[4]
	Who were aged:[2]			Type of road user:						
	0–15	16–59	60 and over	Pedes-trians	Pedal cyclists	Motor cyclists	Car occupants[3]	Other road users		
United Kingdom	13.1	75.0	9.7	13.2	6.9	8.0	64.8	7.1	333,759	1.1
North East	15.3	74.5	10.2	14.7	6.4	4.2	66.2	8.5	11,536	3.9
North West	15.0	75.2	9.5	13.5	6.1	5.0	67.8	7.5	44,750	23.3
Yorkshire and the Humber	14.6	74.7	9.9	13.4	6.8	6.2	65.6	7.9	29,759	14.8
East Midlands	12.9	75.0	9.2	10.8	6.8	8.0	66.8	7.6	23,597	2.2
West Midlands	14.6	74.6	9.6	13.7	6.6	6.0	66.6	7.1	29,037	4.8
East	11.0	74.7	9.7	9.4	7.7	8.4	68.7	5.7	30,186	-0.3
London	10.7	75.8	8.3	19.6	9.1	15.9	47.9	7.6	45,978	-15.1
South East	11.5	74.5	10.1	10.0	8.1	9.1	66.9	5.9	45,070	-1.0
South West	12.7	75.1	11.7	11.0	7.9	8.8	66.5	5.7	25,213	-4.3
England	12.9	75.0	9.7	13.1	7.4	8.6	63.9	7.0	285,126	1.7
Wales	14.9	74.0	10.8	12.3	4.6	5.5	71.0	6.6	14,347	-0.4
Scotland	15.3	73.6	10.8	17.9	4.9	4.9	63.6	8.7	20,837	-23.2
Northern Ireland	13.0	79.1	8.0	8.4	2.0	2.7	78.4	8.5	13,449	63.9

1 See Notes and Definitions.
2 Excludes age not reported.
3 Includes occupants of taxis and minibuses.
4 Used as a basis for the government targets for reducing road casualties in Great Britain, and fatal and serious road casualties in Northern Ireland, by a third by the year 2000.

Source: Department of Transport, Local Government and the Regions; Royal Ulster Constabulary

10.19 Activity at major airports,[1] 2000

	Air passengers (thousands)[2]				Freight handled[3] (thousands tonnes)
		International			
	Domestic[3]	Scheduled	Non-scheduled	Total	
All UK Airports[4]	37,306	105,559	37,136	180,001	2,326
Newcastle	973	685	1,490	3,147	1
Manchester	2,867	6,273	9,212	18,352	117
Leeds/Bradford	455	508	612	1,575	1
East Midlands	341	438	1,448	2,227	179
Birmingham	1,212	3,425	2,856	7,493	10
Luton	1,720	3,095	1,354	6,170	36
Stansted	1,417	9,142	1,301	11,860	168
Heathrow	7,404	56,721	154	64,279	1,307
Gatwick	2,912	18,050	10,986	31,949	319
Bristol	413	574	1,138	2,126	-
Cardiff	95	311	1,095	1,500	1
Aberdeen	1,666	336	479	2,481	5
Edinburgh	3,995	1,108	394	5,498	18
Glasgow	3,568	1,256	2,099	6,924	9
Belfast City	1,282	6	3	1,290	1
Belfast International	2,226	105	797	3,128	31
Other UK airports	4,760	3,524	1,717	10,002	125

1 Airports handling one million passengers or more in 2000. Passengers are recorded at both airport of departure and arrival. Includes British Government/armed forces on official business and travel to/from oil rigs.
2 Arrivals and departures.
3 Domestic traffic is counted at airports on arrival and departure.
4 Including airports handling fewer than one million passengers.

Source: Civil Aviation Authority

10.20 Activity at major seaports,[1] 1999

Millions and million tonnes

	International sea passenger movements (millions)	Freight handled (million tonnes)
All UK ports	31.9	565.6
All East coast ports	3.1	282.3
Sullom Voe	0.0	37.7
Forth	0.0	45.4
Tees and Hartlepool	-	49.3
Hull	1.0	10.1
Grimsby and Immingham	-	49.8
Felixstowe	0.1	31.5
Harwich	1.3	4.1
All Thames and Kent ports	19.2	87.9
London	-	52.2
Ramsgate	-	1.2
Dover	18.5	19.4
All South coast ports	5.2	47.6
Portsmouth	3.5	4.3
Southampton	0.2	33.3
All West coast ports	4.4	126.5
Milford Haven	0.5	32.2
Holyhead	2.5	3.4
Liverpool	0.4	28.9
All Northern Ireland ports	0.0	21.3

1 Individual ports handling one million passengers or more in 1999 and/or 25 million tonnes of freight. See Notes and Definitions.

Source: Department for Transport, Local Government and the Regions

11 Environment

Rainfall
: In 1999, the UK had 16 per cent more rain than the 1961–1990 average. This ranged from 4 per cent more rain in the South West and Southern regions to 20 per cent more rain in the Severn Trent region.

(Table 11.1)

Atmospheric pollution
: In 1996, estimated annual mean background sulphur dioxide concentrations were highest around Belfast. Concentrations were lowest in Scotland.

(Map 11.2)

In 1999, estimated annual mean background nitrogen dioxide concentrations were highest around London and the major cities in England. Concentrations were lowest in Scotland.

(Map 11.3)

Water consumption
: In 1999–00, water consumption in metered households in England and Wales ranged from 122 litres per head per day in the South West to 156 litres in the Thames region. For unmetered households consumption ranged from 138 litres in the North West to 166 litres in the Thames region.

(Table 11.4)

Water abstraction
: In 1998, estimated abstractions from groundwater for the purpose of public water supply ranged from 161 megalitres per day in the North West to 1,571 megalitres per day in the Thames region.

(Table 11.5)

Water quality
: Water quality has improved across all regions within England, Wales and Northern Ireland between 1988–90 and 1997–99.

(Table 11.6)

In 2000, all of the bathing waters in Northern Ireland and the Anglian and Thames regions complied with the EC Bathing Water Directive coliform standards.

(Table 11.7)

The North West had 5,780 water pollution incidents in 1999, 25 per cent of which were industrial incidents. Northern Ireland had the least number of incidents – 1,507 – almost 30 per cent of which were agricultural incidents.

(Table 11.8)

Prosecution for pollution
: There were 690 prosecutions for pollution incidents in England and Wales in 2000, 31 per cent of which were in the North West and North East regions.

(Table 11.9)

In 2000, three-fifths of all prosecutions for pollution incidents in England and Wales were for waste. This ranged from three-quarters of all prosecutions in the North East, to a third of all prosecutions in the South West.

(Table 11.9)

Scheduled monuments
: In 2001, the South West region had 6,790 listed monuments compared with 150 listed monuments in London.

(Chart 11.10)

Land | Over 60 per cent of East Anglia broad habitat cover was arable and horticulture in 1990, compared with only 15 per cent in the North West.

(Table 11.11)

In 1990, half of all land covered by broad habitats in the South West and North West was grassland.

(Table 11.11)

A fifth of Wales and Yorkshire and the Humber is within a National Park, nearly a third of the South East and South West are in an Area of Outstanding Natural Beauty and over a fifth of London and the West Midlands is Green Belt land.

(Table 11.13)

Three-fifths of all Designated Heritage Coasts are in the South West.

(Table 11.13)

Waste and recycling | Households in the North West produced proportionally the most waste per week in 1999–00 – over 24 kilograms.

(Map 11.15)

In 1999–00, households within England and Wales recycled 122 kilogrammes of waste on average per household (or 2.7 million tonnes in total). The South East recycled the most waste per household: 185 kilogrammes, four and a half times the amount recycled by households in the North East.

(Table 11.16)

Over a third of all waste recycled was paper and card and a quarter was compost. Households in the South East recycled the most paper and card (57 kilogrammes per household per year) which was three and a half times more than households in the North East.

(Table 11.16)

In 1999–00, of all the regions in England and Wales, the West Midlands was least inclined to use landfill as a waste disposal option: 58 per cent of all waste went to landfill compared with 94 per cent of all waste in Wales. The West Midlands also made the greatest use of incineration with energy recovery: 31 per cent of all waste.

(Table 11.17)

The South East made greatest use of recycling as a method for waste disposal in 1999–00: a sixth of all waste disposed was recycled.

(Table 11.17)

Noise | The number of noise offences relating to motor vehicles halved between 1985 and 1999 in England and fell by over two-thirds in Wales. Wales had the fewest number of such offences while the South East region had the most.

(Table 11.18)

11.1 Average annual rainfall[1]

Percentages and millimetres

	Annual rainfall as a percentage of the 1961–1990 rainfall average											1961–1990 rainfall average (=100%)
	1989	1990	1991	1992	1993	1994	1995	1996	1997	1998	1999[2]	(millimetres)
United Kingdom	97	112	94	113	107	113	98	87	98	121	116	1,080
North West	89	105	93	103	97	113	85	80	92	119	108	1,201
Northumbria	71	101	94	99	113	103	96	85	98	122	109	853
Severn Trent	96	91	86	112	111	114	90	82	98	117	120	754
Yorkshire	81	95	82	102	109	108	84	85	94	116	107	821
Anglian	91	79	79	118	122	108	91	79	97	120	112	596
Thames	94	80	88	116	112	108	100	78	91	118	110	688
Southern	86	90	90	103	117	122	98	83	101	112	104	778
Wessex	97	88	91	101	115	123	111	93	105	120	114	839
South West	96	100	93	96	118	126	100	96	102	122	104	1,173
England	89	91	87	106	111	113	93	83	96	117	110	823
Wales[3]	98	101	94	107	105	121	92	88	97	120	113	1,355
Scotland	104	134	102	121	104	112	104	88	99	121	119	1,436
Northern Ireland	91	117	96	109	109	110	101	102	99	120	117	1,059

1 The regions of England shown in this table correspond to the original nine English regions of the National Rivers Authority (NRA); the NRA became part of the Environment Agency upon its creation in April 1996. See Notes and Definitions.
2 1999 rainfall is provisional.
3 The figures in this table relate to the country of Wales, not the Environment Agency Welsh Region.

Source: Meteorological Office; Centre for Ecology and Hydrology, Wallingford

11.2 Sulphur dioxide concentration across the UK, 1996[1]

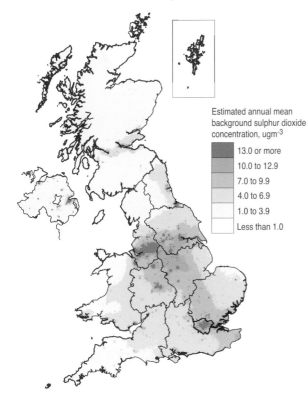

Estimated annual mean background sulphur dioxide concentration, ugm⁻³

- 13.0 or more
- 10.0 to 12.9
- 7.0 to 9.9
- 4.0 to 6.9
- 1.0 to 3.9
- Less than 1.0

1 In units of micrograms per cubic metre.

Source: Department for Environment, Food & Rural Affairs

11.3 Nitrogen dioxide concentration across the UK, 1999[1]

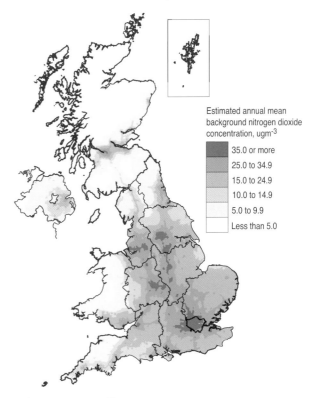

Estimated annual mean background nitrogen dioxide concentration, ugm⁻³

- 35.0 or more
- 25.0 to 34.9
- 15.0 to 24.9
- 10.0 to 14.9
- 5.0 to 9.9
- Less than 5.0

1 In units of micrograms per cubic metre.

Source: Department for Environment, Food & Rural Affairs

11.4 Estimated household water consumption[1]

Litres per head per day and percentages

	Unmetered households			Metered households			Percentage of billed households that are metered		
	1997–98	1998–99	1999–00	1997–98	1998–99	1999–00	1997–98	1998–99	1999–00
Water and sewerage companies									
England and Wales[2]	150	148	151	137	136	137	11	14	17
North West	141	138	138	134	132	131	7	8	10
Northumbrian	144	147	148	119	132	138	3	3	5
Yorkshire[3]	137	135	139	125	121	128	12	16	18
Severn Trent	137	138	140	130	131	132	13	15	17
Anglian[4]	153	149	150	141	134	133	30	37	42
Thames	161	156	166	155	154	156	8	12	16
Southern	161	158	160	138	138	139	14	16	18
Wessex	141	138	139	124	124	129	14	18	23
South West	155	156	161	123	129	122	14	18	23
Welsh	146	144	144	132	132	127	5	6	7

1 Excluding underground supply pipe leakage.
2 Figures for England and Wales are industry averages; these include both the ten major water and sewerage companies and 14 smaller water companies.
3 The entries for Yorkshire Water include the weighted averages for Yorkshire Water and York Waterworks that now operate under a single licence.
4 The entries for Anglian Water include the weighted averages for Anglian Water and Hartlepool Water that now operate under a single licence.

Source: OFWAT

11.5 Estimated abstractions from groundwaters: by purpose, 1998[1]

Megalitres per day

	Public water supply	Spray irrigation	Agriculture (excluding spraying)	Electricity supply	Other industry	Mineral washing	Fish farming, etc	Private water supply[2]	Other[3]	Total
Environment Agency Regions[4,5]										
England and Wales	5,042	137	100	25	669	187	313	86	94	6,653
North East	349	20	9	10	88	1	2	12	39	530
North West	161	0	5	0	106	28	3	0	1	304
Midlands[4]	890	20	8	8	139	0	4	4	0	1,072
Anglian	724	61	23	0	95	90	3	32	2	1,032
Thames	1,571	21	7	1	105	47	45	24	0	1,821
Southern	1,003	11	7	2	87	18	133	5	12	1,279
South West	256	2	35	1	24	2	121	7	39	489
England[5]	4,954	135	94	23	643	187	311	85	94	6,526
Wales[5]	88	1	6	3	26	0	2	2	0	127

1 Some regions report licensed and actual abstractions for financial rather than calendar years. As figures represent an average for the whole year expressed in daily amounts, differences between amounts reported for financial and calendar years are small.
2 Private abstractions for domestic use by individual households.
3 'Other' includes some private domestic water supply wells and boreholes, public water supply transfer licenses and frost protection use.
4 Other industry for the Midlands region included figures on Mineral washing.
5 The boundaries of the Environment Agency Regions are based on river catchment areas and not county borders. In particular, the figures shown for Wales are for the Environment Agency Welsh Region, the boundary of which does not coincide with the boundary of Wales. Figures for England are derived by adding up figures for the English regions. See map on page 239 and Notes and Definitions.

Source: Environment Agency

11.6 Rivers and canals: by chemical quality,[1] 1988–90 and 1997–99

Percentages and kilometres

	1988–90[2]				1997–99			
	Very good/good	Fairly good/fair	Poor/bad	Total length surveyed (=100%) (kms)	Very good/good	Fairly good/fair	Poor/bad	Total length surveyed (=100%) (kms)
England and Wales[3]	48	37	15	34,160	63	29	8	40,530
North East	71	21	8	1,150	85	11	4	2,090
North West	42	32	27	3,040	60	29	11	5,430
Yorkshire and the Humber	52	24	24	3,200	56	31	13	4,060
East Midlands	20	60	20	3,090	50	44	6	3,550
West Midlands	40	42	18	3,480	56	34	10	3,930
East	21	61	18	3,490	28	56	16	3,580
London	13	58	29	380	26	43	31	420
South East	40	45	15	4,310	58	34	9	4,470
South West	62	31	7	6,340	78	19	3	6,560
England	43	41	17	28,480	59	32	9	34,090
Wales	87	11	2	3,510	93	5	1	4,510
Scotland[4]	97	..	3	49,050	90	7	3	50,250
Northern Ireland	44	51	5	1,680	56	39	4	2,430

1 Based on the chemical quality grade of the General Quality Assessment (GQA) scheme for England, Wales and Northern Ireland. The chemical quality classification for Scotland is different and changed in 1996. See Notes and Definitions.
2 Data for Northern Ireland are taken from the 1989–91 survey.
3 The total river length for England and Wales is that published by the Environment Agency and based on the full set of GQA results. It is greater than the sum of totals for the English regions (or England) and Wales. This is because to derive the regional figures a different method was used to calculate river lengths and some river lengths were excluded.
4 For 1988–1990 it is not possible to split 'Very good/good' and 'Fairly good/fair'.

Source: Environment Agency; Scottish Environment Protection Agency; Environment and Heritage Service, Northern Ireland

11.7 Bathing water – compliance with EC Bathing Water Directive[1] coliform standards:[2] by coastal region

Numbers and percentages

	Identified bathing waters (numbers)					Percentage complying during the bathing season[3]				
	1996	1997	1998	1999	2000	1996	1997	1998	1999	2000
Environment Agency Regions[4]										
United Kingdom	472	486	496	535	545	90	88	89	91	94
North East[5]	56	56	56	55	56	88	91	84	95	91
North West[6]	34	34	34	34	34	59	50	62	68	82
Midlands	.	.	.	.	.	.	.	.	.	.
Anglian	35	35	36	36	37	97	100	100	94	100
Thames	3	3	3	3	3	67	100	100	100	100
Southern	69	75	77	79	79	90	89	97	94	97
South West	180	180	183	184	187	93	91	91	91	96
England	377	383	389	391	396	89	88	90	90	95
Wales	56	64	68	70	75	93	94	94	99	99
Scotland	23	23	23	58	58	91	78	52	88	84
Northern Ireland	16	16	16	16	16	100	88	94	100	100

1 76/160/EEC.
2 At least 95 per cent of samples must have counts not exceeding the mandatory limit values for total and faecal coliforms.
3 The bathing season is from mid-May to end-September in England and Wales, but is shorter in Scotland and Northern Ireland. Bathing waters which are closed for a season are excluded for that year.
4 In England and Wales. The boundaries of the Environment Agency Regions are based on river catchment areas and not county borders. In particular, the figures shown for Wales are for the Environment Agency Welsh Region, the boundary of which does not coincide with the boundary of Wales. See map on page 239 and Notes and Definitions.
5 Figures for 1996 to 1998 include Alnmouth, which was undesignated in 1999.
6 In 1997 West Kirby was reclassified from the Welsh region to the North West region. West Kirby data are presented in the North West region for all years for consistency.

Source: Environment Agency; Scottish Environment Protection Agency; Environment and Heritage Service, Northern Ireland

11.8 Water pollution incidents: by source, 1999[1]

Numbers

	Industrial		Sewage and water related		Agricultural		Other		Total		Number of prose-cutions[3]
	All	Major[2]	All	Major[2]	All	Major[2]	All	Major[2]	All	Major[2]	
Environment Agency Regions[4]											
United Kingdom	7,477	146	4,490	108	5,015	86	17,752	71	34,734	411	428
North East	413	5	653	4	247	2	1,207	9	2,520	20	16
North West	1,453	4	356	3	756	6	3,215	4	5,780	17	31
Midlands	1,149	2	651	3	601	4	2,428	1	4,829	10	27
Anglian	463	0	371	1	340	1	1,982	0	3,156	2	44
Thames	441	0	325	3	167	3	2,064	2	2,997	8	21
Southern	583	2	269	2	430	1	1,744	5	3,026	10	32
South West	971	0	603	0	1,167	6	2,561	2	5,302	8	27
England	5,473	13	3,228	16	3,708	23	15,201	23	27,610	75	198
Wales[4]	1,035	6	302	2	546	6	1,429	2	3,312	16	32
Scotland[1]	623	120	613	81	323	38	747	43	2,306	282	26
Northern Ireland	347	7	347	9	438	19	375	3	1,507	38	68

1 Data relate to substantiated reports of pollution only. Figures for Scotland relate to the financial year 1999–00.

2 Major incidents are those corresponding to Category 1 in the Environment Agency's pollution incidents classification scheme. For Scotland the term 'serious incidents' is used and compares broadly with all of Category 1 and most of Category 2 used by the Environment Agency. In Northern Ireland the term 'high severity' is used, this compares broadly with all of Category 1 used by the Environment Agency. See Notes and Definitions.

3 For England and Wales total prosecutions relate to legal action taken in 1999 relating to incidents that occurred in 1999. In Scotland, this figure relates only to legal proceedings which resulted in a conviction during 1999–00. In Northern Ireland total prosecutions include cases concluded and prosecutions outstanding for incidents which took place in 1999.

4 In England and Wales the boundaries of the Environment Agency Regions are based on river catchment areas and not county borders. In particular, the figures shown for Wales are for the Environment Agency Welsh Region, the boundary of which does not coincide with the boundary of Wales. Figures for England are derived by adding up figures for the English regions. See map on page 239 and Notes and Definitions.

Source: Environment Agency; Scottish Environment Protection Agency; Department of the Environment, Northern Ireland

11.9 Prosecutions[1] for pollution incidents, 2000

Numbers

	Waste	Water pollution[2]	Integrated pollution control	Radioactive substances	Water abstraction	All
Environment Agency Regions[3]						
North East	80	20	3	1	0	104
North West	80	20	4	0	5	109
Midlands	53	31	2	2	6	94
Anglian	38	23	0	0	4	65
Thames	46	25	1	0	1	73
Southern	56	29	0	0	3	88
South West	18	37	0	0	0	55
England	371	185	10	3	19	588
Wales	55	44	2	0	1	102
Northern Ireland	..	68	0	0	.	..

1 Figures are for the total numbers of defendants (companies and individuals) prosecuted in 2000 by type of prosecution.

2 Northern Ireland water pollution figures are for 1999. Includes two cases which are pending.

3 In England and Wales. The boundaries of the Environment Agency Regions are based on river catchment areas and not county borders. In particular, the figures shown for Wales are for the Environment Agency Welsh Region, the boundary of which does not coincide with the boundary of Wales. See map on page 239 and Notes and Definitions.

Source: Environment Agency; Environment and Heritage Service (Northern Ireland)

11.10 Scheduled monuments, 2001[1]

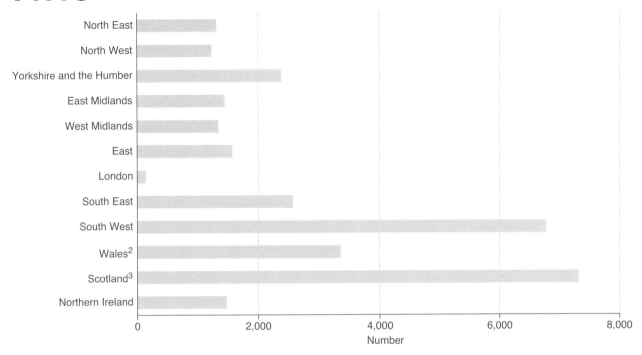

1 As at February 2001.
2 As at July 2001.
3 As at December 2000.

Source: Department for Culture, Media and Sport; Northern Ireland Statistics and Research Agency

11.11 Land cover[1] by Broad Habitat[2] and Standard Statistical Regions, 1990

										Percentage of land covered by:
	Woodland	Arable and horticulture	Grassland[3]	Dwarf shrub heath	Fen, marsh, swamp and bog	Standing open water and canals	Inland rock	Built up areas and gardens[4]	Supralittoral rock & sediment	Total area (=100%) (sq km)
England	9.6	35.1	38.0	2.7	1.5	0.8	0.2	10.7	1.4	127,888
North	11.1	16.1	48.4	10.2	6.4	0.4	0.3	5.8	1.2	15,263
North West	8.3	15.0	50.3	3.4	2.3	1.0	0.1	17.6	2.1	7,228
Yorkshire & the Humber	9.2	30.0	40.0	5.8	2.5	0.7	0.1	10.9	0.8	15,043
East Midlands	7.9	52.6	27.0	1.1	0.4	1.0	0.1	9.1	0.9	15,173
West Midlands	10.6	34.6	40.6	1.5	0.7	0.6	0.1	10.7	0.6	13,667
East Anglia	5.2	61.8	21.4	0.1	0.1	2.0	0.4	6.7	2.2	12,339
South East	9.2	43.3	29.3	0.2	0.2	0.8	0.2	15.1	1.6	25,724
South West	12.5	22.9	50.0	1.4	0.8	0.3	0.1	10.3	1.7	23,450

1 Excludes boundary and linear features. Estimates are based on extrapolation from a national sample and are associated with error terms which are not shown on this table.
2 See Notes and Definitions.
3 Includes improved, neutral, acid and calcareous grasslands and bracken.
4 Includes additional non-surveyed urban squares.

Source: Countryside Survey 1990, Department for Environment, Food and Rural Affairs; Centre for Ecology and Hydrology

11.12 Protected Areas,[1] as at 1 April 2000

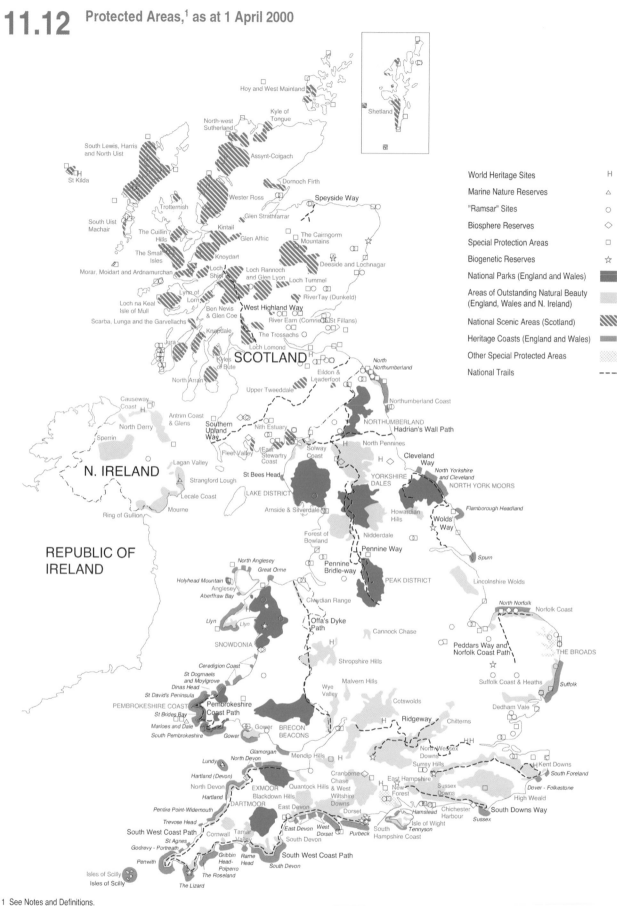

Shetland

World Heritage Sites — H
Marine Nature Reserves — △
"Ramsar" Sites — ○
Biosphere Reserves — ◇
Special Protection Areas — □
Biogenetic Reserves — ☆
National Parks (England and Wales)
Areas of Outstanding Natural Beauty (England, Wales and N. Ireland)
National Scenic Areas (Scotland)
Heritage Coasts (England and Wales)
Other Special Protected Areas
National Trails — – – –

Hoy and West Mainland
Kyle of Tongue
North-west Sutherland
South Lewis, Harris and North Uist
Assynt-Coigach
St Kilda
Dornoch Firth
Wester Ross
Speyside Way
Trotternish
Glen Strathfarrar
South Uist Machair
Kintail
The Cuillin Hills
Glen Affric
The Cairngorm Mountains
The Small Isles
Knoydart
Deeside and Lochnagar
Morar, Moidart and Ardnamurchan
Loch Shiel
Loch Rannoch and Glen Lyon
Loch Tummel
Lynn of Lorn
RiverTay (Dunkeld)
Loch na Keal Isle of Mull
Ben Nevis & Glen Coe
West Highland Way
River Earn (Comrie to St Fillans)
Scarba, Lunga and the Garvellachs
Knapdale
The Trossachs
Jura
Loch Lomond
SCOTLAND
Kyles of Bute
North
Northumberland
North Arran
Eildon & Leaderfoot
Upper Tweeddale
Causeway Coast
Antrim Coast & Glens
Northumberland Coast
North Derry
Southern Upland Way
Nith Estuary
NORTHUMBERLAND
Hadrian's Wall Path
Sperrin
North Pennines
Fleet Valley
East Stewartry Coast
Solway Coast
Cleveland Way
Lagan Valley
St Bees Head
YORKSHIRE DALES
North Yorkshire and Cleveland
NORTH YORK MOORS
N. IRELAND
Strangford Lough
LAKE DISTRICT
Flamborough Headland
Lecale Coast
Mourne
Arnside & Silverdale
Howardian Hills
Wolds Way
Ring of Gullion
Forest of Bowland
Nidderdale
Spurn
REPUBLIC OF IRELAND
Pennine Way
North Anglesey
Great Orme
Pennine Bridle-way
PEAK DISTRICT
Lincolnshire Wolds
Holyhead Mountain
Anglesey
Aberffraw Bay
North Norfolk
Norfolk Coast
Llyn
Llyn
Clwydian Range
Offa's Dyke Path
Peddars Way and Norfolk Coast Path
THE BROADS
Cannock Chase
SNOWDONIA
Shropshire Hills
Suffolk Coast & Heaths
Suffolk
Ceredigion Coast
Malvern Hills
St Dogmaels and Moylgrove
Wye Valley
Dinas Head
Cotswolds
Dedham Vale
St David's Peninsula
PEMBROKESHIRE COAST
Pembrokeshire Coast Path
St Brides Bay
Gower
BRECON BEACONS
Ridgeway
Chilterns
Marloes and Dale
South Pembrokeshire
Gower
Glamorgan
Mendip Hills
North Wessex Downs
Kent Downs
Lundy
North Devon
Surrey Hills
South Foreland
Hartland (Devon)
EXMOOR
Quantock Hills
Cranborne Chase & West Wiltshire Downs
East Hampshire
New Forest
Dover - Folkestone
North Devon
Blackdown Hills
Sussex Downs
High Weald
Hartland
DARTMOOR
East Devon
Dorset
Hamstead
Chichester Harbour
South Downs Way
Pentire Point-Widemouth
East Devon
West Dorset
Purbeck
Isle of Wight
Tennyson
Sussex
Trevose Head
South Devon
South Hampshire Coast
South West Coast Path
Cornwall
Tamar Valley
South Devon
St Agnes
Godrevy - Portreath
Gribbin Head-Polperro
Rame Head
South West Coast Path
Penwith
The Roseland
South Devon
Isles of Scilly
Isles of Scilly
The Lizard

1 See Notes and Definitions.

Source: Countryside Commission; English Nature; Department of Culture, Media and Sport: Institute of Terrestrial Ecology; Department for Transport, Local Government and the Regions; Countryside Council for Wales; Scottish National Heritage; Department of the Environment, Northern Ireland

11.13 Designated areas[1] 2000[2]

	National Parks		Areas of Outstanding Natural Beauty[3]		Green Belt land[4]		Designated Heritage Coasts length (km)
	Area (sq km)	Percentage of total area in region	Area (sq km)	Percentage of total area in region	Area (sq km)	Percentage of total area in region	
North East	1,112	13	1,465	17	530	6	122
North West	2,607	18	1,570	11	2,519	18	6
Yorkshire and the Humber	3,146	21	921	6	2,637	17	82
East Midlands	917	6	519	3	799	5	0
West Midlands	202	2	1,269	10	2,674	21	.
East	303	2	1,122	6	2,369	12	121
London	0	0	..	..	355	22	.
South East	0	0	6,406	31	3,557	19	72
South West	1,647	7	7,121	30	1,056	4	638
England	9,934	8	20,393	16	16,500	13	1,041
Wales	4,077	20	844	4	-	-	496
Scotland	.	.	10,020	13	1,550	2	.
Northern Ireland	.	.	2,850	20	2,266	16	.

1 See Notes and Definitions. Some areas may be in more than one category.
2 Designated at 1 April 1998 except for Green Belt land which relates to 1 January 1997.
3 National Scenic Areas in Scotland. The South East includes London.
4 Based on a new methodology in which the extent of Green Belt Land is captured in digital form. This approach provides much more reliable figures than those previously published in earlier years and therefore should not be compared to tables published in previous editions of *Regional Trends*.

Source: Department for Transport, Local Government and the Regions

11.14 Land changing to residential use: by previous use, 1996[1]

Percentages and hectares

	Rural uses				Urban uses				All changes to residential use (=100%) (hectares)
						Vacant[2]			
	Agriculture	Other rural uses	All rural uses	Residential	Previously developed	Not previously developed	Other urban uses	All urban uses	
England	39	6	45	15	22	10	9	55	5,815
North East	36	2	38	15	33	11	4	62	240
North West	23	5	28	9	42	14	8	72	720
Yorkshire and the Humber	34	4	37	12	30	14	6	63	595
East Midlands	55	5	60	12	15	6	7	40	700
West Midlands	39	5	43	13	21	15	7	57	510
East	38	10	47	17	19	7	10	53	1,020
London	3	11	13	16	35	8	28	87	225
South East	35	8	42	19	17	12	10	58	1,080
South West	62	5	66	15	6	7	6	34	720

1 The information relates only to map changes recorded by the Ordnance Survey between 1996 and 1999 for which the year of change is judged to be 1996. See Notes and Definitions.
2 Comparisons between regions should be treated with caution as changes from land which is vacant for a short period are more likely to be recorded in areas where surveying is more frequent.

Source: Department for Transport, Local Government and the Regions

11.15 Household waste: by Government Office Region, 1999-00

Kilogrammes per household per week

- 24.0 or over
- 23.0 to 23.9
- 22.0 to 22.9
- less than 22.0

Source: Department for Environment, Food and Rural Affairs; National Assembly for Wales

11.16 Recycling of household waste,[1] 1999–00

Kilogrammes per household per year

	Glass	Paper and card	Cans	Plastics	Textiles	Scrap metal/ white goods	Compost	Other materials[2]	Total
England and Wales	18.1	41.4	1.5	0.6	1.9	12.7	30.8	15.1	122.2
North East	7.7	15.5	0.6	0.1	0.8	6.8	1.0	7.8	40.3
North West	11.7	33.7	0.5	0.3	1.3	7.9	25.9	10.1	91.5
Yorkshire and the Humber	13.7	26.1	0.6	0.2	1.1	10.8	18.7	7.0	78.0
East Midlands	16.4	37.0	0.7	0.6	1.6	13.9	36.8	20.1	127.1
West Midlands	14.3	38.4	0.7	0.0	1.4	14.3	32.0	6.4	107.3
East	24.2	50.5	3.0	0.5	3.1	14.3	60.2	14.5	170.2
London	15.6	48.6	1.1	0.3	1.9	10.2	9.9	21.3	108.9
South East	27.4	56.9	3.7	2.1	2.3	17.9	44.1	30.9	185.2
South West	27.6	51.4	2.1	0.6	2.9	16.6	49.4	11.6	162.3
England	18.5	42.3	1.6	0.6	1.9	12.8	32.0	15.7	125.3
Wales	12.7	27.2	0.8	0.3	2.2	11.2	10.1	5.0	69.5

1 Materials recycled by local authorities through civic amenity and bring/drop-off sites and kerbside collection schemes for household wastes.
2 Other materials includes oils, batteries, aluminium foil, books, shoes and co-mingled collections.

Source: Department for Environment, Food and Rural Affairs; National Assembly for Wales

11.17 Waste disposal: by region and method, 1999–00

Percentages

	Landfill	Incineration without energy recovery	Incineration with energy recovery	RDF[1] manu- facture	Recycled/ composted	Other	All methods
North East	77	0	17	0	6	0	100
North West	91	-	-	0	9	0	100
Yorkshire and the Humber	88	-	4	0	8	0	100
East Midlands	83	-	6	0	11	0	100
West Midlands	58	0	31	0	10	0	100
East	84	0	1	0	15	0	100
London	72	-	19	0	9	0	100
South East	82	-	0	3	16	0	100
South West	84	-	0	0	15	0	100
England	80	-	8	-	11	0	100
Wales	94	0	0	0	6	0	100

1 Refuse derived fuel.

Source: Department for Environment, Food and Rural Affairs; National Assembly for Wales

11.18 Noise offences[1] relating to motor vehicles

	1985[2]	1990	1995	1999
North East	815	290	230	472
North West	1,055	767	616	637
Yorkshire and the Humber	849	600	418	363
East Midlands	824	890	639	702
West Midlands	982	548	580	423
East	565	1,316	706	554
London	1,740	547	825	408
South East	2,283	1,547	1,202	770
South West	1,207	655	682	593
England	10,320	7,160	5,898	4,922
Wales	921	691	385	290

Numbers

1 Includes written warnings issued for alleged offences, findings of guilt at Magistrates Courts and Fixed penalty notices.
2 Fixed Penalties not introduced until October 1986.

Source: Home Office

12 Regional Accounts

GDP

In 1999, GDP for the South East and London were both around £120 billion, each accounting for about 16 per cent of total UK GDP. The region with the smallest share was Northern Ireland, at about 2 per cent (£17 billion).

(Table 12.1)

The contribution by Extra-Regio to GDP rose by 20 per cent between 1998 and 1999.

(Table 12.1)

Compensation of employees (mainly wages and salaries) was the source of 67 per cent of GDP in the North East in 1999 compared with 61 per cent in the South West.

(Table 12.3)

GDP per head

In 1999, London had the highest level of GDP per head, at just under £16,900, followed by the South East and East, both at £15,100.

(Table 12.1)

The North East had the lowest regional GDP per head in 1999, at £10,000, followed by Northern Ireland at £10,100 and Wales at £10,400. (Map 12.4)

Over the period 1990 to 1999, GDP per head has been consistently above the UK average for London, South East and the East of England.

(Chart 12.2)

GDP by industry

More than two-fifths of London's GDP in 1998 was generated by financial intermediation and real estate, renting and business activities, compared with less than one fifth in the North East, Wales and Northern Ireland.

(Table 12.5)

Twenty-nine per cent of GDP in both the East Midlands and the West Midlands was derived from manufacturing in 1998, compared with between 10 and 11 per cent in London in the same period. These represent the highest and lowest proportions respectively.

(Table 12.5)

Household income/disposable income

Household income per head in London was 22 per cent higher than the UK average in 1999. In the North East and Northern Ireland it was about 18 per cent lower.

(Table 12.7)

Between 1998 and 1999, the contribution that compensation of employees made to household income grew most strongly in the East and South East regions, while the lowest growth was in the West Midlands.

(Table 12.10)

Disposable household income ranged from 67 per cent of total household income in London and the South East to 72 per cent in Wales and Northern Ireland in 1999.

(Table 12.10)

Individual consumption
expenditure

London and the South East had the highest individual consumption expenditure per head in 1999, at £12,250 and £11,392 respectively per person, while the North East, Wales and Northern Ireland had the lowest, at less than £8,500.

(Table 12.11)

Individual consumption expenditure (ICE) per head in London was 24 per cent above the UK average in 1999. In the North East it was 19 per cent lower.

(Table 12.11)

In 1999, Northern Ireland and the North East had the highest individual consumption expenditure per head on food, drink and tobacco as a share of the total individual consumption expenditure per head in those regions. The equivalent estimates were the lowest in London and the South East.

(Table 12.12)

12.1 Gross domestic product[1] (GDP) at current basic prices

	1989	1990	1991	1992	1993	1994	1995	1996	1997[2]	1998[2]	1999[2]
£ million											
United Kingdom[3]	461,925	501,473	523,137	545,487	573,377	605,720	635,498	674,029	715,127	755,297	787,386
North East	17,156	18,271	19,365	20,383	21,480	22,074	22,975	23,755	24,202	25,294	25,875
North West	49,365	53,260	55,775	57,803	60,664	63,938	66,007	68,937	72,414	75,275	77,562
Yorkshire and the Humber	34,848	37,863	39,872	40,977	42,952	44,752	47,108	50,043	53,182	55,457	57,554
East Midlands	30,439	32,708	34,131	35,368	37,124	39,023	40,976	44,184	47,261	49,413	50,906
West Midlands	37,956	41,344	42,716	44,610	46,859	49,577	52,407	54,851	57,783	61,130	63,495
East	45,885	49,652	50,968	53,852	55,928	59,824	62,416	66,484	72,698	77,962	81,793
London	68,907	74,933	78,641	82,409	86,574	91,118	93,843	99,490	108,559	118,499	122,816
South East	66,979	73,254	75,730	78,939	83,817	88,936	93,319	100,614	108,276	116,024	121,956
South West	34,118	37,160	38,584	40,507	42,529	44,607	47,385	50,128	53,580	56,064	58,151
England	385,653	418,445	435,784	454,848	477,927	503,851	526,437	558,483	597,956	635,117	660,108
Wales	19,007	20,376	21,533	22,129	23,191	24,463	25,989	27,017	28,010	29,541	30,689
Scotland	38,448	42,458	45,103	47,183	49,302	52,273	55,667	57,338	58,650	62,153	64,050
Northern Ireland	9,329	10,013	10,890	11,611	12,437	13,344	14,297	14,936	15,952	16,501	17,003
United Kingdom less Extra-Regio[4] and statistical discrepancy	452,437	491,291	513,308	535,772	562,857	593,931	622,389	657,775	700,567	743,314	771,849
Extra-Regio	9,488	10,182	9,829	9,715	10,520	11,789	13,109	16,254	14,560	11,983	14,350
Statistical discrepancy	-	-	-	-	-	-	-	-	-	-	1,188
As a percentage of United Kingdom less Extra-Regio and statistical discrepancy											
United Kingdom	100.0	100.0	100.0	100.0	100.0	100.0	100.0	100.0	100.0	100.0	100.0
North East	3.8	3.7	3.8	3.8	3.8	3.7	3.7	3.6	3.5	3.4	3.4
North West	10.9	10.8	10.9	10.8	10.8	10.8	10.6	10.5	10.3	10.1	10.0
Yorkshire and the Humber	7.7	7.7	7.8	7.6	7.6	7.5	7.6	7.6	7.6	7.5	7.5
East Midlands	6.7	6.7	6.6	6.6	6.6	6.6	6.6	6.7	6.7	6.6	6.6
West Midlands	8.4	8.4	8.3	8.3	8.3	8.3	8.4	8.3	8.2	8.2	8.2
East	10.1	10.1	9.9	10.1	9.9	10.1	10.0	10.1	10.4	10.5	10.6
London	15.2	15.3	15.3	15.4	15.4	15.3	15.1	15.1	15.5	15.9	15.9
South East	14.8	14.9	14.8	14.7	14.9	15.0	15.0	15.3	15.5	15.6	15.8
South West	7.5	7.6	7.5	7.6	7.6	7.5	7.6	7.6	7.6	7.5	7.5
England	85.2	85.2	84.9	84.9	84.9	84.8	84.6	84.9	85.4	85.4	85.5
Wales	4.2	4.1	4.2	4.1	4.1	4.1	4.2	4.1	4.0	4.0	4.0
Scotland	8.5	8.6	8.8	8.8	8.8	8.8	8.9	8.7	8.4	8.4	8.3
Northern Ireland	2.1	2.0	2.1	2.2	2.2	2.2	2.3	2.3	2.3	2.2	2.2
GDP per head (£)											
United Kingdom	8,053	8,712	9,050	9,404	9,852	10,372	10,842	11,462	12,118	12,750	13,213
North East	6,614	7,033	7,433	7,811	8,216	8,441	8,796	9,111	9,301	9,741	10,024
North West	7,199	7,757	8,096	8,380	8,783	9,248	9,547	9,980	10,494	10,909	11,273
Yorkshire and the Humber	7,042	7,630	8,002	8,195	8,563	8,901	9,354	9,927	10,541	10,983	11,404
East Midlands	7,621	8,149	8,464	8,722	9,102	9,519	9,944	10,673	11,371	11,848	12,146
West Midlands	7,242	7,875	8,108	8,450	8,855	9,352	9,869	10,309	10,845	11,455	11,900
East	9,012	9,711	9,913	10,415	10,772	11,467	11,889	12,582	13,657	14,530	15,094
London	10,135	10,935	11,422	11,930	12,494	13,088	13,406	14,107	15,266	16,532	16,859
South East	8,805	9,586	9,866	10,242	10,834	11,441	11,918	12,761	13,634	14,510	15,098
South West	7,297	7,917	8,183	8,547	8,927	9,311	9,828	10,351	11,008	11,447	11,782
England	8,069	8,692	9,020	9,384	9,852	10,349	10,771	11,384	12,141	12,845	13,278
Wales	6,624	7,080	7,450	7,632	7,978	8,393	8,900	9,240	9,562	10,063	10,449
Scotland	7,544	8,321	8,814	9,217	9,614	10,168	10,818	11,162	11,429	12,117	12,512
Northern Ireland	5,893	6,300	6,787	7,163	7,610	8,114	8,654	8,964	9,507	9,754	10,050
United Kingdom less Extra-Regio[4]	7,888	8,535	8,880	9,236	9,671	10,170	10,619	11,185	11,871	12,548	12,972
GDP per head: indices (UK less Extra-Regio=100)											
United Kingdom	100.0	100.0	100.0	100.0	100.0	100.0	100.0	100.0	100.0	100.0	100.0
North East	83.9	82.4	83.7	84.6	85.0	83.0	82.8	81.5	78.4	77.6	77.3
North West	91.3	90.9	91.2	90.7	90.8	90.9	89.9	89.2	88.4	86.9	86.9
Yorkshire and the Humber	89.3	89.4	90.1	88.7	88.5	87.5	88.1	88.8	88.8	87.5	87.9
East Midlands	96.6	95.5	95.3	94.4	94.1	93.6	93.6	95.4	95.8	94.4	93.6
West Midlands	91.8	92.3	91.3	91.5	91.6	92.0	92.9	92.2	91.4	91.3	91.7
East	114.2	113.8	111.6	112.8	111.4	112.8	112.0	112.5	115.0	115.8	116.4
London	128.5	128.1	128.6	129.2	129.2	128.7	126.2	126.1	128.6	131.7	130.0
South East	111.6	112.3	111.1	110.9	112.0	112.5	112.2	114.1	114.9	115.6	116.4
South West	92.5	92.8	92.2	92.5	92.3	91.6	92.6	92.5	92.7	91.2	90.8
England	102.3	101.8	101.6	101.6	101.9	101.8	101.4	101.8	102.3	102.4	102.4
Wales	84.0	83.0	83.9	82.6	82.5	82.5	83.8	82.6	80.6	80.2	80.5
Scotland	95.6	97.5	99.3	99.8	99.4	100.0	101.9	99.8	96.3	96.6	96.5
Northern Ireland	74.7	73.8	76.4	77.6	78.7	79.8	81.5	80.1	80.1	77.7	77.5

1 Estimates of regional GDP in this table are on a residence basis, where income of commuters is allocated to where they live, rather than their place of work.
2 Provisional
3 Components may not sum to totals as a result of rounding.
4 The GDP for Extra-Regio comprises compensation of employees and gross operating surplus which cannot be assigned to regions.

Source: Office for National Statistics

12.2 Gross domestic product[1] (GDP) at current basic prices

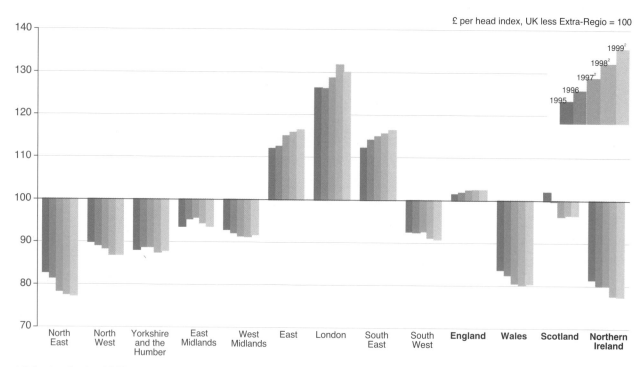

£ per head index, UK less Extra-Regio = 100

1 Estimates of regional GDP in this table are on a residence basis, where the income of commuters is allocated to where they live, rather than their place of work.
2 Provisional.

Source: Office for National Statistics

12.3 Gross domestic product[1] (GDP) by component of income at current basic prices, 1999[2]

Percentages and £ million

	Income components as a percentage of total GDP		Gross domestic product (=100%) (£ million)
	Compensation of employees	Operating surplus/ mixed income[3]	
United Kingdom[4]	63	37	771,849
North East	67	33	25,875
North West	65	35	77,562
Yorkshire and the Humber	66	34	57,554
East Midlands	63	37	50,906
West Midlands	65	35	63,495
East	63	37	81,793
London	63	37	122,816
South East	62	38	121,956
South West	61	39	58,151
England	63	37	660,108
Wales	64	36	30,689
Scotland	63	37	64,050
Northern Ireland	62	38	17,003
Extra-Regio[5]	11	89	14,350

1 Estimates of regional GDP in this table are on a residence basis, where the income of commuters is allocated to where they live, rather than their place of work.
2 Provisional.
3 Including taxes on production.
4 Excluding GDP for Extra-Regio and the allowance for statistical discrepancy.
5 The GDP for Extra-Regio comprises compensation of employees and gross operating surplus which cannot be assigned to regions

Source: Office for National Statistics

12.4 Gross domestic product per head at current basic[1] prices, 1999

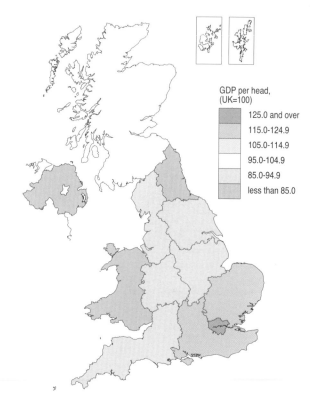

GDP per head, (UK=100)
- 125.0 and over
- 115.0-124.9
- 105.0-114.9
- 95.0-104.9
- 85.0-94.9
- less than 85.0

1 Consistent with the National Accounts (Blue Book). See Notes and Definitons.

Source: Office for National Statistics

12.5 Gross domestic product[1] (GDP) by industry group at current basic prices

£ Million

	1995	1996	1997[2]	1998[2]	1995	1996	1997[2]	1998[2]
	United Kingdom[3]				North East			
Agriculture, hunting, forestry and fishing	11,714	11,963	10,595	9,731	214	233	202	188
Mining, quarrying of energy producing materials	2,581	2,470	2,394	2,301	115	137	97	66
Other mining and quarrying	1,437	1,621	1,609	1,678	81	91	78	78
Manufacturing	136,747	143,485	148,619	151,197	6,494	6,842	6,861	6,904
Electricity, gas and water supply	15,562	16,120	16,230	15,851	644	571	604	645
Construction	32,948	34,563	36,927	38,945	1,262	1,324	1,414	1,474
Wholesale and retail trade (including motor trade)	74,148	78,698	85,865	91,405	2,292	2,380	2,445	2,632
Hotels and restaurants	18,409	20,471	22,585	24,246	603	699	724	707
Transport, storage and communication	52,297	53,994	57,916	62,200	1,542	1,566	1,600	1,804
Financial intermediation	42,726	42,730	43,852	46,199	760	742	729	762
Real estate, renting and business activities	116,348	125,722	140,316	159,348	3,268	3,376	3,531	3,856
Public administration and defence[4]	38,859	38,938	38,727	38,722	1,469	1,501	1,418	1,394
Education	34,212	36,633	38,865	41,187	1,630	1,702	1,654	1,688
Health and social work	42,481	45,254	46,960	49,918	2,131	2,154	2,230	2,394
Other services	27,421	30,669	34,786	38,116	959	935	1,072	1,154
Adjustment for financial services (FISIM)[5]	-25,499	-25,557	-25,678	-27,732	-490	-499	-456	-453
Total	622,389	657,775	700,567	743,314	22,975	23,755	24,202	25,294

	1995	1996	1997[2]	1998[2]	1995	1996	1997[2]	1998[2]
	North West				Yorkshire and the Humber			
Agriculture, hunting, forestry and fishing	898	892	780	702	1,053	1,150	995	901
Mining, quarrying of energy producing materials	31	28	23	19	206	164	252	222
Other mining and quarrying	113	111	220	153	159	234	130	116
Manufacturing	18,483	18,750	18,905	18,892	12,498	13,521	14,468	14,483
Electricity, gas and water supply	1,612	1,818	1,808	1,764	1,149	1,224	1,399	1,374
Construction	3,452	3,600	3,869	3,876	2,704	2,881	2,962	2,985
Wholesale and retail trade (including motor trade)	8,102	8,645	9,193	9,941	5,909	6,202	6,554	6,832
Hotels and restaurants	1,800	2,002	2,322	2,397	1,254	1,418	1,615	1,728
Transport, storage and communication	5,487	5,703	5,946	6,188	3,753	3,823	4,182	4,623
Financial intermediation	3,029	2,944	3,045	3,376	2,330	2,210	2,358	2,681
Real estate, renting and business activities	10,681	11,397	12,528	13,830	7,084	7,507	8,357	9,077
Public administration and defence[4]	3,265	3,227	3,331	3,227	2,813	2,765	2,557	2,668
Education	3,855	4,149	4,211	4,476	2,886	3,077	3,041	3,309
Health and social work	4,897	5,196	5,258	5,461	3,442	3,694	3,983	4,240
Other services	2,553	2,659	3,113	3,393	1,654	1,840	2,155	2,280
Adjustment for financial services (FISIM)[5]	-2,251	-2,184	-2,138	-2,420	-1,788	-1,668	-1,827	-2,062
Total	66,007	68,937	72,414	75,275	47,108	50,043	53,182	55,457

	1995	1996	1997[2]	1998[2]	1995	1996	1997[2]	1998[2]
	East Midlands				West Midlands			
Agriculture, hunting, forestry and fishing	1,160	1,190	1,030	974	1,054	1,110	986	906
Mining, quarrying of energy producing materials	176	189	196	121	73	73	73	50
Other mining and quarrying	185	245	163	182	120	112	104	136
Manufacturing	12,118	13,209	14,003	14,237	15,687	16,496	17,286	17,671
Electricity, gas and water supply	1,035	1,208	1,058	966	1,457	1,389	1,546	1,733
Construction	2,236	2,229	2,350	2,620	2,765	2,914	3,084	3,246
Wholesale and retail trade (including motor trade)	5,427	5,774	6,192	6,408	6,554	6,776	6,971	7,248
Hotels and restaurants	1,010	1,179	1,302	1,388	1,389	1,467	1,479	1,672
Transport, storage and communication	2,811	2,973	3,206	3,359	3,555	3,743	3,903	4,093
Financial intermediation	1,463	1,383	1,428	1,789	2,433	2,421	2,483	2,628
Real estate, renting and business activities	6,001	6,696	7,673	8,418	8,476	9,143	9,845	10,966
Public administration and defence[4]	1,983	1,954	1,968	1,993	2,466	2,449	2,443	2,496
Education	2,250	2,396	2,697	2,671	2,918	3,095	3,301	3,549
Health and social work	2,787	2,935	2,920	3,165	3,478	3,466	3,599	3,974
Other services	1,327	1,559	1,993	2,191	1,706	1,914	2,337	2,564
Adjustment for financial services (FISIM)[5]	-994	-934	-920	-1,068	-1,724	-1,717	-1,658	-1,803
Total	40,976	44,184	47,261	49,413	52,407	54,851	57,783	61,130

12.5 *(continued)*

£ Million

	1995	1996	1997[2]	1998[2]	1995	1996	1997[2]	1998[2]
	East				London			
Agriculture, hunting, forestry and fishing	1,519	1,636	1,413	1,287	40	46	46	39
Mining, quarrying of energy producing materials	255	222	205	198	208	162	123	118
Other mining and quarrying	45	67	71	75	47	64	78	82
Manufacturing	11,772	12,298	12,829	13,226	11,929	12,091	12,490	12,941
Electricity, gas and water supply	1,503	1,537	1,564	1,546	1,659	1,621	1,601	1,588
Construction	3,489	3,838	4,260	4,505	3,665	4,069	4,603	4,934
Wholesale and retail trade (including motor trade)	7,650	8,114	9,393	10,128	11,682	12,661	14,154	15,218
Hotels and restaurants	1,456	1,550	1,923	2,119	3,557	3,974	4,385	4,790
Transport, storage and communication	6,329	6,406	6,813	7,400	9,603	9,756	10,905	11,782
Financial intermediation	5,663	5,813	6,640	6,883	12,432	12,554	12,599	13,059
Real estate, renting and business activities	11,932	13,190	15,121	17,488	25,509	27,689	31,251	36,753
Public administration and defence[4]	3,361	3,347	3,458	3,432	5,282	5,160	5,034	5,045
Education	3,177	3,344	3,685	3,923	4,631	4,926	5,440	5,733
Health and social work	3,542	3,844	4,019	4,241	5,154	5,739	6,151	6,438
Other services	2,710	3,113	3,463	3,964	6,252	7,212	7,901	8,679
Adjustment for financial services (FISIM)[5]	-1,988	-1,834	-2,158	-2,452	-7,807	-8,234	-8,203	-8,701
Total	62,416	66,484	72,698	77,962	93,843	99,490	108,559	118,499

	1995	1996	1997[2]	1998[2]	1995	1996	1997[2]	1998[2]
	South East				South West			
Agriculture, hunting, forestry and fishing	1,127	1,143	996	916	1,765	1,740	1,554	1,400
Mining, quarrying of energy producing materials	229	176	118	113	44	30	16	9
Other mining and quarrying	119	152	185	194	298	252	270	273
Manufacturing	15,885	16,656	17,369	17,686	9,499	10,339	10,683	10,986
Electricity, gas and water supply	1,854	1,831	1,982	1,949	1,645	1,723	1,832	1,682
Construction	4,866	5,374	5,759	6,101	2,695	2,634	2,857	3,102
Wholesale and retail trade (including motor trade)	11,302	12,206	13,163	14,085	5,565	5,724	6,462	6,730
Hotels and restaurants	2,553	2,905	3,156	3,416	1,597	1,807	2,028	2,105
Transport, storage and communication	9,599	10,347	10,931	11,759	3,003	3,148	3,520	3,819
Financial intermediation	6,805	7,120	7,129	7,196	3,180	3,035	2,854	2,953
Real estate, renting and business activities	21,622	23,658	27,053	31,034	8,299	8,967	9,819	10,890
Public administration and defence[4]	6,248	6,278	6,268	6,328	4,288	4,482	4,623	4,632
Education	4,334	4,722	5,384	5,630	2,348	2,532	2,853	3,061
Health and social work	5,730	6,472	6,633	6,905	3,347	3,510	3,642	3,926
Other services	4,307	5,005	5,540	6,129	1,984	2,331	2,532	2,635
Adjustment for financial services (FISIM)[5]	-3,261	-3,433	-3,388	-3,418	-2,169	-2,131	-1,963	-2,141
Total	93,319	100,614	108,276	116,024	47,385	50,128	53,580	56,064

	1995	1996	1997[2]	1998[2]	1995	1996	1997[2]	1998[2]
	England				Wales			
Agriculture, hunting, forestry and fishing	8,830	9,140	8,003	7,313	457	538	509	545
Mining, quarrying of energy producing materials	1,337	1,180	1,102	917	108	114	84	125
Other mining and quarrying	1,165	1,328	1,298	1,289	139	99	104	134
Manufacturing	114,363	120,201	124,896	127,027	7,354	7,723	7,815	7,981
Electricity, gas and water supply	12,559	12,923	13,394	13,248	842	808	596	486
Construction	27,134	28,863	31,158	32,842	1,399	1,446	1,515	1,550
Wholesale and retail trade (including motor trade)	64,483	68,482	74,526	79,221	2,510	2,581	2,925	3,201
Hotels and restaurants	15,220	17,001	18,935	20,321	809	868	976	1,045
Transport, storage and communication	45,684	47,466	51,005	54,828	1,663	1,603	1,720	1,786
Financial intermediation	38,095	38,222	39,264	41,326	986	961	1,031	1,147
Real estate, renting and business activities	102,872	111,623	125,178	142,312	3,689	3,752	4,099	4,457
Public administration and defence[4]	31,176	31,164	31,100	31,215	1,819	1,897	1,767	1,737
Education	28,028	29,945	32,266	34,040	1,622	1,848	1,675	1,939
Health and social work	34,509	37,011	38,434	40,746	2,180	2,234	2,486	2,630
Other services	23,451	26,569	30,106	32,990	1,043	1,178	1,340	1,449
Adjustment for financial services (FISIM)[5]	-22,471	-22,634	-22,711	-24,518	-632	-634	-631	-673
Total	526,437	558,483	597,956	635,117	25,989	27,017	28,010	29,541

12.5 *(continued)*

£ Million

	1995	1996	1997[2]	1998[2]	1995	1996	1997[2]	1998[2]
	Scotland				Northern Ireland			
Agriculture, hunting, forestry and fishing	1,632	1,476	1,341	1,220	794	809	741	653
Mining, quarrying of energy producing materials	1,124	1,166	1,198	1,248	12	9	9	10
Other mining and quarrying	41	129	135	177	91	65	72	77
Manufacturing	12,253	12,547	12,799	13,054	2,777	3,014	3,109	3,135
Electricity, gas and water supply	1,760	1,954	1,813	1,763	400	435	428	354
Construction	3,582	3,386	3,339	3,552	833	868	915	1,001
Wholesale and retail trade (including motor trade)	5,558	5,942	6,431	6,898	1,597	1,693	1,983	2,085
Hotels and restaurants	2,002	2,195	2,214	2,375	378	407	459	505
Transport, storage and communication	4,158	4,113	4,292	4,649	793	812	900	938
Financial intermediation	3,053	2,989	2,973	3,136	592	558	583	591
Real estate, renting and business activities	8,309	8,732	9,170	10,405	1,477	1,615	1,869	2,175
Public administration and defence[4]	3,923	3,917	3,890	3,804	1,941	1,960	1,969	1,966
Education	3,509	3,743	3,672	3,840	1,052	1,096	1,252	1,367
Health and social work	4,437	4,633	4,667	5,162	1,355	1,376	1,373	1,380
Other services	2,373	2,350	2,690	3,006	554	572	650	672
Adjustment for financial services (FISIM)[5]	-2,049	-1,934	-1,974	-2,136	-348	-355	-362	-406
Total	55,667	57,338	58,650	62,153	14,297	14,936	15,952	16,501

1 Estimates of regional GDP in this tables are on a residence basis, where the income of commuters is allocated to where they live rather than their place of work.
2 Provisional.
3 Excludes production from Extra-Regio.
4 Public administration, national defence and compulsory social security.
5 Financial Intermediation Services Indirectly Measured.

Source: Office for National Statistics

12.6 Workplace-based gross domestic product[1] (GDP) at current basic prices

	1989	1990	1991	1992	1993	1994	1995	1996	1997[2]	1998[2]	1999[2]
£ million											
United Kingdom	461,925	501,473	523,137	545,487	573,377	605,720	635,498	674,029	715,127	755,297	787,386
North East	17,156	18,271	19,365	20,383	21,480	22,074	22,975	23,755	24,202	25,294	25,875
North West	49,365	53,260	55,775	57,803	60,664	63,938	66,007	68,937	72,414	75,275	77,562
Yorkshire and the Humber	34,848	37,863	39,872	40,977	42,952	44,752	47,108	50,043	53,182	55,457	57,554
East Midlands	30,439	32,708	34,131	35,368	37,124	39,023	40,976	44,184	47,261	49,413	50,906
West Midlands	37,956	41,344	42,716	44,610	46,859	49,577	52,407	54,851	57,783	61,130	63,495
East	41,066	44,506	45,448	47,985	50,052	53,631	55,989	60,070	64,982	69,607	72,821
London	79,098	85,675	89,388	93,349	97,769	103,021	106,759	112,033	122,014	133,081	138,265
South East	61,607	67,657	70,503	73,866	78,498	83,227	86,831	94,484	102,536	109,797	115,479
South West	34,118	37,160	38,584	40,507	42,529	44,607	47,385	50,128	53,580	56,064	58,151
England	385,653	418,445	435,784	454,848	477,927	503,851	526,437	558,483	597,956	635,117	660,108
Wales	19,007	20,376	21,533	22,129	23,191	24,463	25,989	27,017	28,010	29,541	30,689
Scotland	38,448	42,458	45,103	47,183	49,302	52,273	55,667	57,338	58,650	62,153	64,050
Northern Ireland	9,329	10,013	10,890	11,611	12,437	13,344	14,297	14,936	15,952	16,501	17,003
United Kingdom less Extra-Regio[3] and statistical discrepancy	452,437	491,291	513,308	535,772	562,857	593,931	622,389	657,775	700,567	743,314	771,849
Extra-Regio	9,488	10,182	9,829	9,715	10,520	11,789	13,109	16,254	14,560	11,983	14,350
Statistical discrepancy	-	-	-	-	-	-	-	-	-	-	1,188
As a percentage of United Kingdom less Extra-Regio and statistical discrepancy											
United Kingdom	100.0	100.0	100.0	100.0	100.0	100.0	100.0	100.0	100.0	100.0	100.0
North East	3.7	3.6	3.7	3.7	3.7	3.6	3.6	3.5	3.4	3.3	3.3
North West	10.7	10.6	10.7	10.6	10.6	10.6	10.4	10.2	10.1	10.0	9.9
Yorkshire and the Humber	7.5	7.6	7.6	7.5	7.5	7.4	7.4	7.4	7.4	7.3	7.3
East Midlands	6.6	6.5	6.5	6.5	6.5	6.4	6.4	6.6	6.6	6.5	6.5
West Midlands	8.2	8.2	8.2	8.2	8.2	8.2	8.2	8.1	8.1	8.1	8.1
East	8.9	8.9	8.7	8.8	8.7	8.9	8.8	8.9	9.1	9.2	9.2
London	17.1	17.1	17.1	17.1	17.1	17.0	16.8	16.6	17.1	17.6	17.6
South East	13.3	13.5	13.5	13.5	13.7	13.7	13.7	14.0	14.3	14.5	14.7
South West	7.4	7.4	7.4	7.4	7.4	7.4	7.5	7.4	7.5	7.4	7.4
England	83.5	83.4	83.3	83.4	83.4	83.2	82.8	82.9	83.6	84.1	83.8
Wales	4.1	4.1	4.1	4.1	4.0	4.0	4.1	4.0	3.9	3.9	3.9
Scotland	8.3	8.5	8.6	8.6	8.6	8.6	8.8	8.5	8.2	8.2	8.1
Northern Ireland	2.0	2.0	2.1	2.1	2.2	2.2	2.2	2.2	2.2	2.2	2.2
GDP per head (£)											
United Kingdom	8,053	8,712	9,050	9,404	9,852	10,372	10,842	11,462	12,118	12,750	13,213
North East	6,614	7,033	7,433	7,811	8,216	8,441	8,796	9,111	9,301	9,741	10,024
North West	7,199	7,757	8,096	8,380	8,783	9,248	9,547	9,980	10,494	10,909	11,273
Yorkshire and the Humber	7,042	7,630	8,002	8,195	8,563	8,901	9,354	9,927	10,541	10,983	11,404
East Midlands	7,621	8,149	8,464	8,722	9,102	9,519	9,944	10,673	11,371	11,848	12,146
West Midlands	7,242	7,875	8,108	8,450	8,855	9,352	9,869	10,309	10,845	11,455	11,900
East	8,065	8,705	8,839	9,281	9,640	10,280	10,665	11,368	12,208	12,973	13,438
London	11,634	12,503	12,983	13,514	14,110	14,798	15,251	15,885	17,159	18,566	18,979
South East	8,098	8,853	9,185	9,584	10,147	10,706	11,090	11,983	12,912	13,731	14,296
South West	7,297	7,917	8,183	8,547	8,927	9,311	9,828	10,351	11,008	11,447	11,782
England	8,069	8,692	9,020	9,384	9,852	10,349	10,771	11,384	12,141	12,845	13,278
Wales	6,624	7,080	7,450	7,632	7,978	8,393	8,900	9,240	9,562	10,063	10,449
Scotland	7,544	8,321	8,814	9,217	9,614	10,168	10,818	11,162	11,429	12,117	12,512
Northern Ireland	5,893	6,300	6,787	7,163	7,610	8,114	8,654	8,964	9,507	9,754	10,050
United Kingdom less Extra-Regio[3]	7,888	8,535	8,880	9,236	9,671	10,170	10,619	11,185	11,871	12,548	12,972
GDP per head: indices (UK less Extra-Regio=100)											
United Kingdom	100.0	100.0	100.0	100.0	100.0	100.0	100.0	100.0	100.0	100.0	100.0
North East	83.9	82.4	83.7	84.6	85.0	83.0	82.8	81.5	78.4	77.6	77.3
North West	91.3	90.9	91.2	90.7	90.8	90.9	89.9	89.2	88.4	86.9	86.9
Yorkshire and the Humber	89.3	89.4	90.1	88.7	88.5	87.5	88.1	88.8	88.8	87.5	87.9
East Midlands	96.6	95.5	95.3	94.4	94.1	93.6	93.6	95.4	95.8	94.4	93.6
West Midlands	91.8	92.3	91.3	91.5	91.6	92.0	92.9	92.2	91.4	91.3	91.7
East	102.2	102.0	99.5	100.5	99.7	101.1	100.4	101.6	102.8	103.4	103.6
London	147.5	146.5	146.2	146.3	145.9	145.5	143.6	142.0	144.5	148.0	146.3
South East	102.7	103.7	103.4	103.8	104.9	105.3	104.4	107.1	108.8	109.4	110.2
South West	92.5	92.8	92.2	92.5	92.3	91.6	92.6	92.5	92.7	91.2	90.8
England	102.3	101.8	101.6	101.6	101.9	101.8	101.4	101.8	102.3	102.4	102.4
Wales	84.0	83.0	83.9	82.6	82.5	82.5	83.8	82.6	80.6	80.2	80.5
Scotland	95.6	97.5	99.3	99.8	99.4	100.0	101.9	99.8	96.3	96.6	96.5
Northern Ireland	74.7	73.8	76.4	77.6	78.7	79.8	81.5	80.1	80.1	77.7	77.5

1 Estimates of workplace based GDP allocate incomes to the region in which commuters work.
2 Provisional.
3 The GDP for Extra-Regio comprises compensation of employees and gross operating surplus which cannot be assigned to regions.

Source: Office for National Statistics

12.7 Household income[1] and disposable household income

	1989	1990	1991	1992	1993	1994	1995	1996	1997[2]	1998[2]	1999[2]
Total household income											
£ million											
United Kingdom[3]	475,104	529,272	574,225	614,110	640,471	667,658	706,351	749,815	789,791	830,192	873,724
North East	18,504	20,674	22,847	24,739	25,633	26,048	27,286	28,753	29,542	30,320	31,120
North West	52,842	58,866	64,261	67,957	70,450	73,328	76,975	81,446	84,836	88,272	92,262
Yorkshire and the Humber	37,742	41,777	45,489	48,024	50,938	52,652	55,208	59,157	61,112	63,953	67,775
East Midlands	31,512	34,554	37,368	39,979	41,771	44,400	46,654	49,986	52,763	54,971	57,445
West Midlands	39,113	44,015	47,684	51,481	53,417	55,989	59,808	62,279	64,358	67,619	71,638
East	46,734	51,963	55,708	59,870	61,057	63,949	67,523	71,582	77,970	83,517	88,824
London	67,727	76,647	83,339	88,594	92,888	96,515	102,265	109,534	116,740	124,156	130,403
South East	70,407	77,618	83,958	89,657	94,768	99,847	105,705	113,456	120,734	127,477	135,433
South West	38,261	42,545	45,817	49,085	50,774	52,403	56,152	59,591	63,522	66,263	69,456
England	402,843	448,658	486,471	519,385	541,697	565,129	597,576	635,785	671,576	706,547	744,355
Wales	20,755	22,895	25,059	26,901	27,787	29,051	30,948	32,503	33,614	35,198	37,169
Scotland	40,200	45,346	49,300	53,464	55,729	57,107	60,408	63,381	65,305	68,397	71,296
Northern Ireland	10,664	11,700	12,706	13,656	14,725	15,795	16,858	17,527	18,680	19,434	20,287
United Kingdom less Extra-Regio[4]	474,462	528,600	573,536	613,406	639,938	667,082	705,791	749,197	789,175	829,576	873,108
Extra-Regio[4]	642	672	689	704	533	576	560	618	616	616	616
Household income											
per head (£)											
United Kingdom	8,282	9,194	9,932	10,586	11,005	11,432	12,051	12,750	13,383	14,015	14,684
North East	7,133	7,957	8,768	9,479	9,805	9,960	10,446	11,028	11,353	11,676	12,056
North West	7,705	8,572	9,326	9,850	10,200	10,606	11,134	11,791	12,294	12,792	13,409
Yorkshire and the Humber	7,626	8,418	9,129	9,603	10,155	10,472	10,962	11,735	12,113	12,666	13,429
East Midlands	7,888	8,608	9,265	9,858	10,242	10,831	11,322	12,075	12,695	13,181	13,706
West Midlands	7,462	8,383	9,050	9,750	10,095	10,562	11,263	11,705	12,079	12,671	13,426
East	9,177	10,162	10,834	11,578	11,760	12,258	12,862	13,547	14,648	15,566	16,391
London	9,960	11,184	12,103	12,824	13,405	13,863	14,609	15,531	16,417	17,321	17,900
South East	9,254	10,156	10,937	11,631	12,250	12,844	13,500	14,389	15,203	15,943	16,767
South West	8,182	9,063	9,716	10,356	10,657	10,937	11,646	12,306	13,050	13,530	14,072
England	8,425	9,348	10,093	10,737	11,162	11,604	12,222	12,954	13,629	14,279	14,961
Wales	7,232	7,955	8,669	9,277	9,559	9,967	10,598	11,116	11,475	11,990	12,655
Scotland	7,887	8,887	9,633	10,443	10,868	11,108	11,739	12,339	12,726	13,334	13,927
Northern Ireland	6,736	7,361	7,918	8,424	9,010	9,604	10,205	10,520	11,133	11,488	11,991
United Kingdom less Extra-Regio[4]	8,271	9,182	9,920	10,574	10,996	11,422	12,042	12,740	13,373	14,004	14,674
Disposable household income											
per head (£)											
United Kingdom	5,571	6,206	6,769	7,323	7,780	8,029	8,451	8,878	9,413	9,614	10,088
North East	4,908	5,506	6,111	6,690	7,053	7,095	7,423	7,819	8,108	8,104	8,353
North West	5,239	5,865	6,452	6,922	7,313	7,536	7,912	8,341	8,761	8,932	9,375
Yorkshire and the Humber	5,208	5,781	6,308	6,682	7,232	7,417	7,740	8,272	8,589	8,794	9,305
East Midlands	5,280	5,801	6,284	6,810	7,214	7,569	7,883	8,390	8,931	9,040	9,346
West Midlands	4,934	5,605	6,127	6,716	7,112	7,391	7,871	8,113	8,405	8,612	9,195
East	6,097	6,803	7,312	7,962	8,248	8,540	8,909	9,292	10,233	10,640	11,255
London	6,549	7,302	8,001	8,640	9,311	9,612	10,123	10,635	11,358	11,607	12,036
South East	6,110	6,680	7,292	7,880	8,519	8,873	9,306	9,824	10,503	10,663	11,249
South West	5,638	6,222	6,718	7,255	7,608	7,767	8,290	8,698	9,368	9,474	9,825
England	5,643	6,273	6,842	7,395	7,867	8,127	8,545	8,991	9,559	9,755	10,237
Wales	4,994	5,534	6,169	6,672	6,986	7,235	7,703	8,010	8,338	8,583	9,113
Scotland	5,355	6,124	6,643	7,301	7,704	7,773	8,199	8,579	8,918	9,172	9,558
Northern Ireland	4,729	5,240	5,610	5,993	6,540	6,959	7,428	7,621	8,150	8,247	8,659
United Kingdom less Extra-Regio[4]	5,560	6,194	6,757	7,311	7,771	8,019	8,442	8,867	9,403	9,603	10,078
Disposable household income per head, indices											
UK less Extra-Regio=100											
United Kingdom	100.0	100.0	100.0	100.0	100.0	100.0	100.0	100.0	100.0	100.0	100.0
North East	88.3	88.9	90.4	91.5	90.8	88.5	87.9	88.2	86.2	84.4	82.9
North West	94.2	94.7	95.5	94.7	94.1	94.0	93.7	94.1	93.2	93.0	93.0
Yorkshire and the Humber	93.7	93.3	93.4	91.4	93.1	92.5	91.7	93.3	91.3	91.6	92.3
East Midlands	95.0	93.7	93.0	93.2	92.8	94.4	93.4	94.6	95.0	94.1	92.7
West Midlands	88.7	90.5	90.7	91.9	91.5	92.2	93.2	91.5	89.4	89.7	91.2
East	109.7	109.8	108.2	108.9	106.1	106.5	105.5	104.8	108.8	110.8	111.7
London	117.8	117.9	118.4	118.2	119.8	119.9	119.9	119.9	120.8	120.9	119.4
South East	109.9	107.8	107.9	107.8	109.6	110.6	110.2	110.8	111.7	111.0	111.6
South West	101.4	100.4	99.4	99.2	97.9	96.9	98.2	98.1	99.6	98.6	97.5
England	101.5	101.3	101.3	101.1	101.2	101.4	101.2	101.4	101.7	101.6	101.6
Wales	89.8	89.3	91.3	91.3	89.9	90.2	91.3	90.3	88.7	89.4	90.4
Scotland	96.3	98.9	98.3	99.9	99.1	96.9	97.1	96.7	94.8	95.5	94.8
Northern Ireland	85.1	84.6	83.0	82.0	84.2	86.8	88.0	85.9	86.7	85.9	85.9

1 Household income covers the income received by households and non-profit institutions serving households.
2 Provisional.
3 Components may not sum to totals as a result of rounding.
4 Parts of the UK economic territory that cannot be attached to a particular region.

Source: Office for National Statistics

12.8 Disposable household income[1] per head

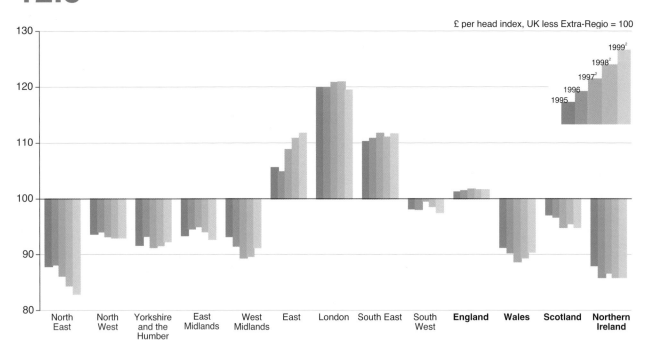

£ per head index, UK less Extra-Regio = 100

1 Household income covers the income received by households and non-profit institutions serving households.
2 Provisional.

Source: Office for National Statistics

12.9 Total and disposable household income,[1] 1999[2]

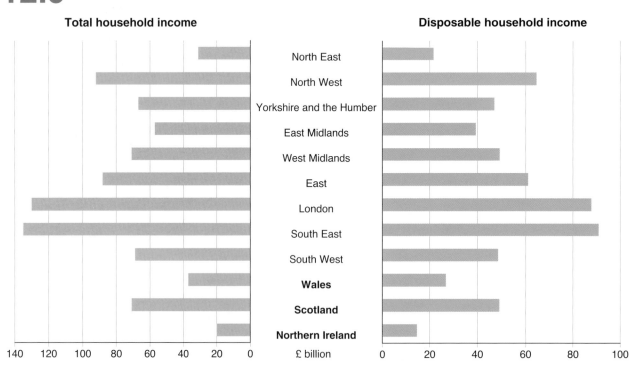

Total household income

Disposable household income

1 Household income covers the income received by households and non-profit institutions serving households.
2 Provisional.

Source: Office for National Statistics

12.10 Sources of household income[1]

	Gross Operating Surplus	Gross Mixed income	Compensation of Employees	Net Property Income[3]	All Pensions[4]	Other Social Benefits[5]	Net Other Income[6]	Total Income	Disposable Income	Disposable Income as % of Total Income
1991										
United Kingdom	29,162	31,635	333,787	47,446	63,401	46,276	22,518	574,225	391,316	68
North East	796	779	13,597	1,647	2,494	2,480	1,054	22,847	15,923	70
North West	2,828	2,851	36,798	6,125	6,857	6,001	2,802	64,261	44,460	69
Yorkshire and the Humber	2,060	2,210	26,246	4,233	4,606	4,006	2,128	45,489	31,434	69
East Midlands	1,870	2,090	22,151	3,011	3,855	2,814	1,579	37,368	25,342	68
West Midlands	2,419	2,486	28,540	3,384	4,714	4,121	2,020	47,684	32,282	68
East	2,924	3,791	32,686	4,816	6,312	3,317	1,862	55,708	37,602	67
London	4,801	5,511	50,477	6,044	7,416	6,098	2,992	83,339	55,093	66
South East	5,220	5,030	47,836	6,397	11,469	5,185	2,822	83,958	55,978	67
South West	2,795	2,868	24,310	4,075	6,780	3,247	1,743	45,817	31,681	69
England	25,713	27,616	282,640	39,732	54,502	37,267	19,001	486,471	329,794	68
Wales	1,265	1,285	13,625	2,143	3,027	2,703	1,011	25,059	17,834	71
Scotland	1,795	1,988	29,616	4,329	4,996	4,575	2,001	49,300	33,997	69
Northern Ireland	388	747	7,216	1,243	877	1,731	504	12,706	9,002	71
Extra-Regio[7]	-	-	689	-	-	-	-	689	689	-
1995										
United Kingdom	40,084	40,238	385,101	62,739	82,479	66,755	28,955	706,351	495,336	70
North East	1,240	955	15,208	2,119	3,160	3,283	1,321	27,286	19,389	71
North West	4,040	3,905	41,392	6,467	8,776	8,842	3,553	76,975	54,699	71
Yorkshire and the Humber	2,770	2,770	30,038	5,054	6,464	5,444	2,670	55,208	38,981	71
East Midlands	2,469	2,688	25,465	4,275	5,599	4,118	2,040	46,654	32,482	70
West Midlands	3,213	3,206	33,442	5,395	6,245	5,720	2,587	59,808	41,800	70
East	4,057	4,446	37,930	6,249	7,569	4,797	2,474	67,523	46,773	69
London	6,170	6,574	58,067	9,028	8,979	9,661	3,785	102,265	70,860	69
South East	7,309	6,258	56,520	9,287	15,056	7,518	3,757	105,705	72,866	69
South West	3,627	3,765	27,981	5,226	8,484	4,746	2,322	56,152	39,971	71
England	34,895	34,567	326,044	53,101	70,332	54,129	24,508	597,576	417,821	70
Wales	1,707	1,546	15,801	2,902	3,862	3,788	1,342	30,948	22,494	73
Scotland	2,825	2,930	34,110	5,153	6,851	6,131	2,408	60,408	42,190	70
Northern Ireland	657	1,195	8,585	1,583	1,434	2,707	696	16,858	12,271	73
Extra-Regio[7]	-	-	560	-	-	-	-	560	560	-
1999[2]										
United Kingdom	54,058	43,655	491,574	75,467	107,064	68,108	33,794	873,720	600,258	69
North East	1,483	1,132	17,352	2,357	3,819	3,517	1,460	31,120	21,563	69
North West	4,887	3,919	50,348	7,927	12,218	8,891	4,071	92,261	64,503	70
Yorkshire and the Humber	3,275	2,957	38,136	6,619	8,066	5,697	3,023	67,774	46,964	69
East Midlands	3,055	2,786	32,371	5,482	7,138	4,237	2,376	57,445	39,173	68
West Midlands	4,061	2,868	41,444	5,838	8,493	5,895	3,039	71,637	49,062	68
East	5,710	4,999	51,761	8,151	10,249	4,993	2,959	88,823	60,992	69
London	9,832	8,226	77,143	10,014	11,249	9,476	4,463	130,403	87,683	67
South East	10,425	7,364	75,913	11,107	19,015	7,162	4,447	135,432	90,864	67
South West	4,913	3,741	35,661	6,497	11,079	4,830	2,734	69,456	48,492	70
England	47,642	37,991	420,130	63,992	91,326	54,698	28,573	744,352	509,296	68
Wales	2,049	1,744	19,732	3,133	5,093	3,864	1,554	37,169	26,764	72
Scotland	3,413	2,677	40,593	6,591	8,961	6,242	2,820	71,295	48,931	69
Northern Ireland	955	1,243	10,502	1,751	1,684	3,304	848	20,287	14,650	72
Extra-Regio[7]	-	-	616	-	-	-	-	616	616	-

1 Household income covers the income recieved by households and Non-profit institutions serving households.
2 Provisional.
3 Net Property Income is the diference between Property Income (Uses) and Property Income (Resources).
4 Includes Retirement and Widows Pensions, Unfunded Social Benefits and Privately Funded Social Benefits.
5 Social Benefits excluding pensions.
6 Includes Imputed Social Contributions, Non-Life Insurance Claims and Miscellaneous Current Transfers.
7 Parts of UK economic territory that cannot be attached to any particular region.

12.11 Individual consumption expenditure

	Individual consumption expenditure (£ million)			Regional shares of the UK (percentages)			£ per head			Per head, indices UK = 100		
	1997	1998	1999[1]	1997	1998	1999[1]	1997	1998	1999[1]	1997	1998	1999[1]
United Kingdom	517,910	551,823	586,906	100.0	100.0	100.0	8,776	9,316	9,864	100.0	100.0	100.0
North East	20,150	20,998	20,659	3.9	3.8	3.5	7,744	8,086	8,003	88.2	86.8	81.1
North West	57,489	59,774	64,133	11.1	10.8	10.9	8,331	8,662	9,321	94.9	93.0	94.5
Yorkshire and the Humber	41,255	44,248	44,956	8.0	8.0	7.7	8,177	8,763	8,907	93.2	94.1	90.3
East Midlands	34,787	36,261	37,961	6.7	6.6	6.5	8,370	8,695	9,057	95.4	93.3	91.8
West Midlands	43,309	46,107	49,416	8.4	8.4	8.4	8,128	8,640	9,262	92.6	92.7	93.9
East	47,712	52,258	54,607	9.2	9.5	9.3	8,963	9,740	10,077	102.1	104.6	102.2
London	72,873	80,737	89,241	14.1	14.6	15.2	10,248	11,264	12,250	116.8	120.9	124.2
South East	78,921	85,207	92,024	15.2	15.4	15.7	9,938	10,656	11,392	113.2	114.4	115.5
South West	41,784	43,887	47,384	8.1	8.0	8.1	8,584	8,961	9,600	97.8	96.2	97.3
England	438,280	469,478	500,380	84.6	85.1	85.3	8,895	9,488	10,057	101.4	101.9	102.0
Wales	23,553	23,716	24,103	4.5	4.3	4.1	8,041	8,079	8,206	91.6	86.7	83.2
Scotland	43,556	45,520	48,421	8.4	8.2	8.3	8,488	8,874	9,459	96.7	95.3	95.9
Northern Ireland	12,521	13,109	14,009	2.4	2.4	2.4	7,463	7,749	8,281	85.0	83.2	83.9

1 Provisional.

Source: Office for National Statistics

12.12 Individual consumption expenditure: by broad function, 1999[1]

£ million

	Food, drink and tobacco	Clothing and footwear	Housing and fuel	Household goods and services	Vehicles, transport and comm-unications	Recreation	Other goods and services	Consumption expenditure in the UK[2]	Total consumption expenditure[3]
United Kingdom	99,473	34,601	103,887	34,781	93,181	65,467	128,878	560,268	586,906
North East	3,970	1,317	3,454	1,289	3,189	2,085	3,825	19,128	20,659
North West	11,973	4,063	10,740	3,505	10,036	7,566	13,036	60,919	64,133
Yorkshire and the Humber	8,110	2,459	7,341	2,514	6,734	5,470	9,512	42,140	44,956
East Midlands	6,908	1,896	6,638	2,401	5,805	4,347	7,859	35,853	37,961
West Midlands	8,409	2,688	8,106	3,182	7,903	5,795	10,448	46,531	49,416
East	8,662	2,919	9,830	3,489	8,839	6,136	12,067	51,943	54,607
London	13,263	6,451	17,467	4,928	14,811	8,941	22,591	88,453	89,241
South East	13,847	4,782	16,585	5,706	15,845	9,914	21,097	87,776	92,024
South West	7,745	2,297	9,049	2,859	6,988	5,412	11,132	45,482	47,384
England	82,888	28,872	89,211	29,874	80,148	55,666	111,566	478,225	500,380
Wales	4,479	1,486	4,327	1,370	3,464	2,618	4,884	22,627	24,103
Scotland	9,358	3,129	8,236	2,693	7,468	5,739	9,738	46,361	48,421
Northern Ireland	2,747	1,114	2,113	844	2,101	1,451	2,690	13,061	14,009

1 Provisional.
2 Expenditure by UK households and foreign residents in the United Kingdom.
3 Expenditure by UK consumers, including non-profit institutions serving households but excluding expenditure in the United Kingdom by foreign residents.

Source: Office for National Statistics

13 Industry and Agriculture

Gross Domestic Product

The West Midlands had the highest percentage of GDP from industry (at 37.4 per cent) and the lowest proportion from services (at 61.2 per cent) in 1998.

(Map 13.1)

London had the highest percentage of GDP from services (83.4 per cent) and the lowest proportion from industry (16.6 per cent) in 1998.

(Map 13.1)

Businesses

Industry as a percentage of total local units ranged from 10.3 per cent in Inverclyde to 25.7 per cent in Leicester UA in 2000.

(Map 13.2)

Services as a percentage of total local units ranged from 37.0 per cent in the Orkney Islands to 87.9 per cent in Glasgow City in 2000.

(Map 13.2)

Over 25 per cent of business sites in Northern Ireland were in the agriculture sector in 2000.

(Table 13.3)

London had the highest percentage of manufacturing local units with fewer than 10 in employment in 2000, at 82 per cent; the North East, at 67 per cent, had the lowest.

(Table 13.4)

Manufacturing

The level of gross value added at basic prices in manufacturing in 1997 ranged from £28,600 per person employed in Northern Ireland to £40,300 in the South East.

(Table 13.5)

The North West in 1997 had the highest percentage of manufacturing gross value added in units employing 1,000 and over, at 22 per cent; Yorkshire and the Humber had the lowest at 9 per cent.

(Table 13.6)

Exports and imports

The percentage of direct exports to the EU ranged from 43 per cent in London to 76 per cent in the North East in 2000.

(Table 13.7)

In 2000, the percentage of direct imports from the EU ranged from 33 per cent in Wales to 61 per cent in the West Midlands.

(Table 13.7)

Investment

In 1999–2000, the largest number of direct inward investment project successes in manufacturing was in the West Midlands, at 56; London had the highest number of non-manufacturing project successes, at 150.

(Table 13.8)

Research and development

Expenditure on research and development in 1999 ranged from over 3 per cent of regional GDP in the East of England to under 1 per cent in the North East, Yorkshire and the Humber and Northern Ireland.

(Table 13.9)

| Assisted areas | In Great Britain in 1999-2000, 41 per cent of government expenditure on regional preferential assistance to industry was in Scotland. |

(Table 13.10)

Under Objective 1 of the EU Structural Funds, the largest amount was allocated to Wales and under Objective 2 to Scotland in 2001.

(Table 13.11)

| Businesses | Business registration rates ranged from 21 per 10,000 resident adults in the North East to 66 in London in 1999. |

(Table 13.12)

Survival rates three years after registration for businesses registered in 1996 were highest in Northern Ireland at 70.1 per cent and lowest in London at 59.5 per cent.

(Table 13.13)

| Construction | In Great Britain in 2000, new work ranged from 49 per cent of the value of construction contractors' output in the South East Standard Statistical Region (excluding Greater London) to 64 per cent in Scotland. |

(Table 13.14)

| Tourism | Eighteen per cent of all tourist expenditure by UK residents in 1999 was in the West Country. |

(Table 13.15)

The highest proportion of GDP from agriculture in 1998 was in Northern Ireland, at 4.0 per cent.

(Map 13.16)

| Agriculture | In 2000 agriculture as a percentage of total legal units ranged from 61.9 per cent in the Orkney Islands to just 0.2 per cent in Leicester UA. |

(Map 13.17)

The East of England had the highest percentage of agricultural holdings as arable land, at 74.6 per cent in 2000; Wales had the lowest at 13.8 per cent.

(Table 13.18)

The North West had the largest proportion of agricultural holdings as dairy farms, at 20.2 per cent, in 2000.

(Table 13.19)

The East of England, at 544,000 hectares, had the largest area under wheat in 2000; Scotland had the largest area under barley, at 317,000 hectares.

(Table 13.20)

In 2000, Wales had the highest number of sheep and lambs on agricultural holdings, at 11.2 million, and Yorkshire and the Humber the highest number of pigs, at 1.7 million.

(Table 13.21)

13.1 Percentage of gross domestic product[1] derived from industry and services, 1998

Industry

Industry as a percentage
of total GDP

37.0 or over
32.0 to 36.9
27.0 to 31.9
22.0 to 26.9
21.9 or under

Services

Services as a percentage
of total GDP

75.0 or over
70.0 to 74.9
65.0 to 69.9
60.0 to 64.9
59.9 or under

1 At basic prices. See Notes and Definitions.

Source: Office for National Statistics

13.2   Industry and services[1] local units as a percentage of total local units, 2000[2]

Industry

Industry as a percentage
of total local units

23.0 or over
20.0 to 22.9
17.0 to 19.9
14.0 to 16.9
13.9 or under

Services

Services as a percentage
of total local units

80.0 or over
75.0 to 79.9
70.0 to 74.9
65.0 to 69.9
64.9 or under

1 See Notes and Definitions.
2 Geographic boundaries relate to the sub-regions (Counties/UAs) in existence on 1 April 1998.

Source: Inter-Departmental Business Register, Office for National Statistics

13.3 Classification[1] of business sites,[2] 2000[3]

Percentages and thousands

	Agriculture, hunting, forestry & fishing	Mining & quarrying, energy, water supply & manufacturing	Construction	Distribution, hotels & catering; repairs	Transport & communication	Financial intermediation, real estate, renting & business activities	Education & health	Public administration & other services	Total business sites (=100%) (thousands)
United Kingdom	7.2	8.1	8.7	28.9	4.3	26.0	6.9	9.9	2,488.4
North East	6.3	8.0	7.9	33.3	4.5	19.9	8.9	11.3	74.2
North West	5.5	8.5	8.2	32.8	4.5	23.7	7.5	9.2	250.7
Yorkshire and the Humber	7.3	9.2	8.7	32.4	4.8	20.4	7.4	9.7	184.9
East Midlands	8.1	11.1	9.5	30.1	4.8	21.1	6.4	9.0	165.8
West Midlands	6.9	11.3	9.1	30.4	4.5	22.3	6.9	8.5	205.8
East	6.4	8.7	11.0	26.8	4.9	27.3	6.1	8.7	240.6
London	0.3	6.4	5.7	26.0	3.8	40.0	5.6	12.3	380.7
South East	3.9	7.5	9.8	26.0	3.9	32.1	6.5	10.2	373.6
South West	11.7	7.5	9.8	28.8	3.9	22.5	6.8	9.0	228.3
England	5.6	8.4	8.7	28.8	4.3	27.7	6.7	9.9	2,104.7
Wales	16.8	7.0	9.2	30.2	4.2	16.0	7.5	9.2	112.9
Scotland	12.1	6.6	7.8	30.7	4.2	19.6	7.7	11.4	194.8
Northern Ireland	25.2	6.4	10.1	25.9	3.7	11.0	9.7	8.1	76.0

1 Based on SIC 1992. See Notes and Definitions.
2 Registered for VAT and/or PAYE, local unit basis e.g. an individual factory or shop. See Notes and Definitions.
3 At March.

Source: Inter-Departmental Business Register, Office for National Statistics

13.4 Manufacturing[1] industry business sites:[2] by employment size band,[3] 2000[4]

Percentages and thousands

	Percentage of manufacturing local units with an employment sizeband[3] of:								Total manufacturing local units (=100%) (thousands)
	1–9	10–19	20–49	50–99	100–199	200–499	500–999	1,000 and over	
United Kingdom	73.6	11.1	7.8	3.3	2.2	1.5	0.3	0.1	195.8
North East	67.3	12.0	9.3	4.6	3.2	2.7	0.8	0.2	5.7
North West	69.3	12.5	9.0	4.0	3.0	1.8	0.4	0.2	20.8
Yorkshire and the Humber	69.6	12.0	9.3	4.0	2.7	1.8	0.5	0.1	16.6
East Midlands	70.6	12.0	8.9	3.9	2.6	1.5	0.4	0.1	17.8
West Midlands	69.4	12.8	9.4	3.8	2.5	1.6	0.3	0.2	22.9
East	77.0	9.9	7.0	3.0	1.7	1.1	0.3	0.1	20.4
London	82.3	9.4	4.9	1.7	0.9	0.7	0.1	0.0	24.0
South East	78.3	9.5	6.4	2.8	1.7	1.1	0.3	0.1	27.5
South West	76.6	10.3	6.7	2.8	1.9	1.3	0.3	0.1	16.5
England	74.3	11.0	7.6	3.2	2.1	1.4	0.3	0.1	172.2
Wales	70.3	11.1	8.6	3.8	3.2	2.3	0.5	0.3	7.4
Scotland	68.2	11.9	9.6	4.3	3.2	2.0	0.5	0.2	11.6
Northern Ireland	69.3	12.2	10.1	3.6	2.4	1.9	0.2	0.2	4.6

1 Based on SIC 1992 Section D. See Notes and Definitions.
2 Registered for VAT and/or PAYE, local unit basis e.g. individual factory. See Notes and Definitions.
3 Includes paid full and part-time employees and working proprietors.
4 At March.

Source: Inter-Departmental Business Register, Office for National Statistics

13.5 Turnover, expenditure and gross value added in manufacturing,[1] 1997

£ million and £ per person employed

	Total turnover (£ million)	Purchases of goods and services (£ million)	Wages and salaries		Net capital expenditure		Gross value added at basic prices	
			£ million	£ per person employed	£ million	£ per person employed	£ million	£ per person employed
United Kingdom	451,877	286,580	73,475	17,564	20,091	4,673	144,519	33,615
North East	21,518	14,370	3,350	17,676	1,162	6,026	6,475	33,564
North West	59,537	36,465	9,412	17,611	2,759	5,041	18,758	34,270
Yorkshire and the Humber	41,208	27,285	7,143	17,017	1,732	4,030	13,139	30,570
East Midlands	36,968	21,548	6,760	16,073	1,662	3,850	13,637	31,595
West Midlands	50,843	32,847	9,351	16,759	2,484	4,338	17,582	30,709
East	39,641	26,088	6,619	18,447	1,606	4,340	12,597	34,045
London	32,541	20,623	5,656	19,833	1,299	4,315	11,381	37,812
South East	57,887	34,033	8,629	19,101	2,148	4,604	18,822	40,338
South West	31,667	20,328	5,444	17,661	1,429	4,507	10,520	33,178
England	371,810	233,587	62,365	17,685	16,281	4,486	122,910	33,870
Wales	29,391	18,796	3,737	17,309	1,427	6,475	7,106	32,242
Scotland	40,281	27,911	5,770	17,388	1,894	5,591	11,325	33,435
Northern Ireland	10,395	6,286	1,604	14,691	489	4,400	3,177	28,561

1 Based on SIC 1992 Section D. See Notes and Definitions.

Source: Annual Business Inquiry, Office for National Statistics

13.6 Gross value added in manufacturing:[1] by size of local unit, 1997

Percentages and £ million

	Percentage of gross value added by number employed[2]							Total (=100%) (£ million)
	1–19	20–49	50–99	100–199	200–499	500–999	1,000 and over	
United Kingdom	14.0	10.8	10.3	14.6	21.9	12.7	15.6	144,519
North East	9.4	8.0	8.5	14.0	27.8	19.3	13.0	6,475
North West	12.2	10.9	9.8	13.6	21.0	10.5	22.0	18,758
Yorkshire and the Humber	13.5	11.6	12.6	15.9	21.3	16.1	8.9	13,139
East Midlands	13.3	11.1	10.5	16.4	22.1	12.7	13.9	13,637
West Midlands	14.2	11.9	11.1	13.5	20.0	9.9	19.4	17,582
East	15.8	11.7	10.3	17.9	20.0	13.3	11.0	12,597
London	21.3	11.6	10.3	12.4	17.0	8.5	18.9	11,381
South East	14.3	10.3	9.7	13.5	26.7	13.6	11.9	18,822
South West	15.4	10.0	10.1	15.6	23.0	12.4	13.6	10,520
England	14.4	11.0	10.4	14.7	21.9	12.5	15.2	122,910
Wales	10.2	8.7	9.1	16.2	23.2	12.4	20.2	7,106
Scotland	11.3	10.0	10.2	13.3	22.3	16.2	16.6	11,325
Northern Ireland	16.0	11.7	10.8	14.1	18.0	11.0	18.5	3,177

1 Based on SIC 1992 Section D. See Notes and Definitions.
2 Average numbers employed during the year, including full and part-time employees and working proprietors.

Source: Annual Business Inquiry, Office for National Statistics

13.7 Export and import trade with EU and non-EU countries,[1] 2000

£ million, percentages and numbers

Exports

	£ million			Percentages		As a percentage of UK regional share of export trade			Average number of companies exporting[2]	
	All export trade	To the EU	Outside the EU	To the EU	Outside the EU	All export trade	To the EU	Outside the EU	To the EU[3]	Outside the EU[2]
United Kingdom	158,883	93,027	65,856	58.6	41.4	100.0	100.0	100.0	14,282	41,128
North East	6,797	5,173	1,624	76.1	23.9	4.3	5.6	2.5	388	903
North West	12,574	7,900	4,674	62.8	37.2	7.9	8.5	7.1	1,497	3,977
Yorkshire and the Humber	8,714	5,508	3,206	63.2	36.8	5.5	5.9	4.9	1,197	3,202
East Midlands	10,484	5,379	5,105	51.3	48.7	6.6	5.8	7.8	1,030	2,744
West Midlands	12,857	7,465	5,392	58.1	41.9	8.1	8.0	8.2	1,460	3,940
East	18,497	10,052	8,445	54.3	45.7	11.6	10.8	12.8	1,683	4,901
London	23,668	10,168	13,500	43.0	57.0	14.9	10.9	20.5	1,610	7,743
South East	27,717	15,514	12,203	56.0	44.0	17.4	16.7	18.5	2,476	7,482
South West	9,623	6,801	2,822	70.7	29.3	6.1	7.3	4.3	982	2,849
England	130,931	73,960	56,971	56.5	43.5	82.4	79.5	86.5	12,321	37,740
Wales	6,416	4,570	1,846	71.2	28.8	4.0	4.9	2.8	492	1,024
Scotland	18,221	12,557	5,664	68.9	31.1	11.5	13.5	8.6	819	2,035
Northern Ireland	3,315	1,940	1,375	58.5	41.5	2.1	2.1	2.1	650	328

Imports

	£ million			Percentages		As a percentage of UK regional share of import trade			Average number of companies importing[2]	
	All import trade	From the EU	From outside the EU	From the EU	From outside the EU	All import trade	From the EU	From outside the EU	From the EU[3]	From outside the EU[3]
United Kingdom	207,521	100,843	106,678	48.6	51.4	100.0	100.0	100.0	17,701	57,345
North East	4,590	2,077	2,513	45.3	54.7	2.2	2.1	2.4	390	1,187
North West	14,445	5,877	8,568	40.7	59.3	7.0	5.8	8.0	1,882	5,546
Yorkshire and the Humber	10,926	5,295	5,631	48.5	51.5	5.3	5.3	5.3	1,463	3,871
East Midlands	9,386	4,471	4,915	47.6	52.4	4.5	4.4	4.6	1,390	3,485
West Midlands	14,419	8,803	5,616	61.1	38.9	6.9	8.7	5.3	1,879	4,909
East	28,337	16,710	11,627	59.0	41.0	13.7	16.6	10.9	2,092	6,925
London	40,962	16,472	24,490	40.2	59.8	19.7	16.3	23.0	2,368	11,960
South East	50,923	29,603	21,320	58.1	41.9	24.5	29.4	20.0	3,146	10,653
South West	10,543	3,707	6,836	35.2	64.8	5.1	3.7	6.4	1,106	3,769
England	184,531	93,015	91,516	50.4	49.6	88.9	92.2	85.8	15,715	52,305
Wales	5,597	1,856	3,741	33.2	66.8	2.7	1.8	3.5	485	1,327
Scotland	13,476	4,574	8,902	33.9	66.1	6.5	4.5	8.3	844	2,864
Northern Ireland	3,917	1,398	2,519	35.7	64.3	1.9	1.4	2.4	657	849

1 See Notes and Definitions.
2 Over four quarters of 2000.
3 Companies who trade with both EU countries and countries outside the EU will appear more than once in the company count.

Source: HM Customs and Excise

13.8 Direct inward investment:[1] project successes[2]

Numbers

	Manufacturing					Non-manufacturing				
	1995–96	1996–97	1997–98	1998–99	1999–00	1995–96[3]	1996–97	1997–98	1998–99	1999–00
United Kingdom	347	317	356	311	328	149	180	272	353	472
North East	49	36	35	28	28	13	10	12	7	21
North West	24	27	43	42	41	13	19	28	24	39
Yorkshire and the Humber	32	31	45	63	31	12	5	20	23	13
East Midlands	11	16	10	8	17	11	7	8	11	14
West Midlands	62	49	49	41	56	15	27	32	30	43
East	7	3	13	8	9	9	6	20	33	28
London	1	2	1	1	9	22	38	61	104	150
South East	25	15	21	23	30	25	31	36	51	80
South West	13	21	22	16	16	4	9	18	18	31
England	224	200	239	230	237	124	152	235	301	419
Wales	44	43	50	35	36	9	2	5	13	11
Scotland	57	53	48	26	40	15	23	27	28	36
Northern Ireland	22	21	19	20	14	1	3	5	11	6

1 See Notes and Definitions.
2 A project success is defined as a case where an overseas company specifies an interest and successfully completes investment in a UK company.
3 The UK figure includes one UK-wide project.

Source: Invest-UK, Department of Trade and Industry

13.9 Expenditure on research and development, 1999

£ million and percentages

	Expenditure within (£ million)			Expenditure as a percentage of regional GDP		
	Businesses	Government[1]	Higher education institutions	Businesses	Government[1]	Higher education institutions
United Kingdom	11,302	1,788	3,341	1.2	0.2	0.4
North East	164	2	113	0.5	-	0.4
North West	1,476	48	260	1.7	0.1	0.3
Yorkshire and the Humber	309	40	270	0.5	0.1	0.4
East Midlands	838	48	182	1.4	0.1	0.3
West Midlands	724	164	180	1.0	0.2	0.2
East	2,559	213	255	2.7	0.2	0.3
London	735	198	837	0.6	0.2	0.6
South East	2,916	557	493	2.1	0.4	0.4
South West	887	259	148	1.3	0.4	0.2
England	10,607	1,529	2,737	1.4	0.2	0.4
Wales	203	47	129	0.6	0.1	0.4
Scotland	393	200	411	0.5	0.3	0.6
Northern Ireland	99	12	64	0.5	0.1	0.3

1 Figures include estimates of NHS and local authorities' research and development.

Source: Office for National Statistics

13.10 Government expenditure on regional preferential assistance to industry

£ million

	1990–91	1991–92	1992–93	1993–94	1994–95	1995–96	1996–97	1997–98	1998–99	1999–00
Great Britain[1]	497.3	427.8	364.0	394.4	368.9	343.0	371.1	430.4	393.8	335.0
North East	85.0	63.8	48.3	52.7	38.4	46.4	24.3	38.1	22.3	18.1
North West	57.5	49.5	36.8	40.3	32.4	24.3	23.2	19.4	25.9	25.0
Yorkshire and the Humber	29.4	18.2	13.7	35.6	23.0	19.7	11.1	12.7	11.9	9.8
East Midlands	5.5	2.6	1.2	1.9	5.2	7.3	10.5	10.5	7.1	4.0
West Midlands	18.0	8.7	10.8	14.4	14.7	14.2	25.5	29.8	30.6	20.5
East	.	.	.	.	0.7	2.1	1.5	2.2	0.7	0.5
London	.	.	.	.	0.6	1.7	2.9	2.7	3.2	2.3
South East	.	.	.	.	0.9	4.2	4.1	5.4	3.3	5.0
South West	9.0	8.3	8.2	9.5	9.4	7.7	7.4	4.5	9.4	4.1
England[2]	204.4	151.1	119.0	154.4	125.3	127.6	110.5	125.3	114.4	89.3
Wales	159.2	122.8	104.4	121.2	134.4	117.4	128.2	172.6	153.9	107.8
Scotland	133.7	153.9	140.6	118.8	109.2	98.0	132.4	132.5	125.5	137.9
Northern Ireland	132.1	138.0	105.6	117.6	132.9	131.2	137.1	156.1	153.3	133.0

1 The system of assistance available in Northern Ireland is not comparable with that operating in Great Britain, and thus UK figures are not produced. See Notes and Definitions.
2 Payments for European Regional Incentives, General Consultancy Contracts and Regional Selective Assistance Payments to the European Commission are not included.

Source: Department of Trade and Industry; Department of Enterprise, Trade and Investment, Northern Ireland

13.11 Allocation of EU Structural Funds[1]

£ million at 1999 prices

	Objective 1[2]			Objective 2[2]			Objective 5b[2,3]			Objectives 1, 2 and 5b		
	1999	2000	2001	1999	2000	2001	1999	2000	2001	1999	2000	2001
United Kingdom	375	635	621	663	516	505	118	.	.	1,156	1,151	1,126
North East	.	.	.	94	70	70	4	.	.	98	70	70
North West	130	135	132	115	90	87	4	.	.	249	225	219
Yorkshire and the Humber	.	118	116	97	53	53	7	.	.	104	171	169
East Midlands	.	.	.	27	39	38	9	.	.	36	39	38
West Midlands	.	.	.	117	92	89	7	.	.	124	92	89
East	.	.	.	.	16	16	9	.	.	9	16	16
London	.	.	.	27	24	25	.	.	.	27	24	25
South East	.	.	.	5	4	4	.	.	.	5	4	4
South West	.	50	49	9	19	19	32	.	.	41	69	68
England	130	303	297	491	407	401	71	.	.	692	710	698
Wales	.	187	184	56	15	14	26	.	.	82	202	198
Scotland	49	37	36	116	94	90	21	.	.	186	131	126
Northern Ireland	196	108	104	.	.	.	.	.	.	196	108	104

1 Only allocations resulting from the Commission's Single Programming Documents are shown. Allocations resulting from Community Initiatives, the value of which is about 8 per
  cent of the total Objective 1, 2 and 5b allocations, are not included because not all of these can be allocated to the Government Office Regions in the table.
2 See Notes and Definitions.
3 For the Structural Funds programme beginning in 2000, Objective 5b has been subsumed into Objective 2.

Source: Department of Trade and Industry

13.12 Business registrations and deregistrations[1]

Thousands and rates

	1998						1999					
	Regist-rations	Deregist-rations	Net change	End-year stock	Regist-ration rates[2]	Deregist-ration rates[2]	Regist-rations	Deregist-rations	Net change	End-year stock	Regist-ration rates[2]	Deregist-ration rates[2]
United Kingdom	186.3	155.9	30.3	1,651.6	40	33	178.5	172.0	6.5	1,658.1	38	37
North East	4.2	4.0	0.2	42.0	20	20	4.2	4.3	-0.1	41.9	21	21
North West	18.6	16.1	2.5	160.1	34	30	18.1	17.2	0.9	160.9	33	32
Yorkshire and the Humber	11.8	11.4	0.5	117.7	30	28	11.6	12.3	-0.7	117.1	29	31
East Midlands	11.9	10.7	1.2	111.2	36	32	11.3	11.5	-0.2	111.0	34	35
West Midlands	15.0	13.3	1.7	136.3	36	32	14.4	14.2	0.2	136.5	34	34
East	17.9	15.2	2.7	162.7	42	36	17.1	16.5	0.6	163.3	40	39
London	39.7	28.4	11.3	270.0	70	50	37.3	32.8	4.6	274.5	66	58
South East	29.9	23.0	6.9	253.0	47	36	28.3	25.9	2.4	255.5	45	41
South West	15.5	13.8	1.7	149.7	40	35	15.1	15.0	0.1	149.8	38	38
England	164.6	135.9	28.7	1,402.7	42	35	157.5	149.7	7.7	1,410.4	40	38
Wales	6.1	6.2	-0.1	75.2	26	27	6.0	6.7	-0.7	74.5	26	29
Scotland	11.8	10.9	0.9	119.2	29	26	11.4	11.9	-0.5	118.7	28	29
Northern Ireland	3.7	2.8	0.9	54.6	30	23	3.6	3.6	-0.1	54.6	28	29

1 Enterprises registered for VAT. See Notes and Definitions.
2 Registrations and deregistrations during the year per 10,000 of the resident adult population.

Source: Small Business Service

13.13 Business survival rates

Percentages

	The percentage of businesses surviving the stated number of months after year of registration								
	12 months				24 months			36 months	
	1995	1996	1997	1998	1995	1996	1997	1995	1996
United Kingdom	87.2	86.8	89.2	90.1	72.9	73.8	76.2	62.3	62.5
North East	85.0	86.5	88.9	89.0	70.6	73.0	74.5	59.4	61.4
North West	85.5	84.9	87.0	88.9	71.0	71.2	73.0	59.9	60.1
Yorkshire and the Humber	86.6	86.1	88.2	89.9	71.8	72.3	75.0	61.1	60.8
East Midlands	86.5	86.4	88.8	89.2	72.4	72.8	75.7	62.0	61.2
West Midlands	85.5	86.1	87.5	88.8	70.5	73.0	73.6	60.3	61.3
East	88.4	88.9	91.1	91.1	75.0	76.5	78.7	64.3	65.3
London	86.4	85.2	88.9	90.4	71.2	71.8	75.1	59.4	59.5
South East	88.9	88.7	91.0	91.7	75.4	76.4	78.9	65.5	66.2
South West	89.1	88.5	90.7	90.0	75.3	76.3	78.0	64.8	65.0
England	87.2	86.8	89.3	90.2	72.8	73.8	76.2	62.0	62.4
Wales	86.7	86.8	88.6	88.6	72.2	73.9	76.3	62.6	63.1
Scotland	87.3	85.5	87.7	89.3	72.6	72.7	74.4	62.0	61.2
Northern Ireland	90.2	88.8	91.0	92.4	80.9	78.5	81.9	71.2	70.1

Source: Small Business Service

13.14 Construction: value at current prices of contractors' output[1]

£ million and percentages

	Total work (£ million)						Of which new work (percentages)					
	1995	1996	1997	1998	1999	2000	1995	1996	1997	1998	1999	2000
Standard Statistical Regions												
Great Britain	48,942	51,967	55,220	59,027	62,858	66,475	53.9	53.4	53.9	54.8	56.4	56.2
North	2,186	2,506	2,636	2,887	2,927	2,837	56.9	61.1	60.1	60.6	64.1	59.5
North West (SSR)	5,072	5,412	5,557	5,785	6,061	6,285	55.4	54.0	52.4	52.6	55.0	56.2
Yorkshire and Humberside	3,862	4,324	4,555	4,833	5,295	5,264	50.2	51.7	51.2	52.8	54.3	56.6
East Midlands	3,446	3,827	4,213	4,382	4,513	4,253	55.2	56.6	58.0	58.2	59.3	58.0
West Midlands	4,157	4,399	4,773	5,248	5,459	6,361	51.8	50.1	51.6	54.2	57.0	58.3
East Anglia	2,064	2,021	2,119	2,263	2,350	2,470	52.9	51.0	53.0	52.1	55.0	60.7
South East (SSR)	16,690	17,965	19,238	20,946	22,996	24,885	52.0	51.8	52.7	53.8	54.6	52.7
Greater London	6,917	7,428	7,957	8,954	9,675	10,236	57.8	59.2	59.3	60.4	61.9	57.5
Rest of South East	9,773	10,537	11,281	11,992	13,321	14,649	47.8	46.6	48.1	48.9	49.3	49.4
South West	4,317	4,193	4,398	4,719	4,975	5,184	54.0	48.5	48.9	50.2	51.9	54.0
England	41,794	44,647	47,490	51,063	54,576	57,540	53.0	52.5	53.0	54.0	55.5	55.2
Wales	2,377	2,331	2,539	2,641	2,631	2,535	61.2	57.7	58.7	59.0	61.7	59.8
Scotland	4,771	4,991	5,191	5,323	5,651	6,400	58.5	59.6	60.4	60.3	62.5	63.9

1 Output of contractors, including estimates of unrecorded output by small firms and self-employed workers, classified to construction in SIC 1992. For new work, figures relate to the region in which the site is located; for repair and maintenance, figures are for the region in which the reporting unit is based.

Source: Department of Trade and Industry

13.15 Tourism, 1991 and 1999

Millions and £ million

	1991				1999			
	UK residents[1]		Overseas residents[2]		UK residents[1]		Overseas residents[2]	
	Number of tourists (millions)	Expenditure (£ million)	Number of tourists (millions)	Expenditure (£ million)	Number of tourists (millions)	Expenditure (£ million)	Number of tourists (millions)	Expenditure (£ million)
Tourist Board Regions[3]								
United Kingdom	94.4	10,470	17.1	7,305	146.1	16,255	25.4	12,370
Northumbria	3.4	255	0.3	95	5.1	450	0.5	181
Cumbria	2.7	330	0.2	35	3.6	535	0.2	64
North West	8.3	770	1.0	246	10.8	1,115	1.3	480
Yorkshire	7.4	680	0.9	183	10.4	1,120	0.9	240
East of England	9.9	925	1.4	372	16.3	1,700	1.8	591
Heart of England	11.8	950	1.7	388	19.7	1,590	2.2	725
London	6.6	720	9.2	3,924	14.8	1,200	13.2	6,708
Southern	9.4	920	1.7	473	12.2	1,370	2.1	774
South East England	6.4	600	2.0	552	13.5	960	2.3	749
West Country	12.9	1,765	1.4	306	19.1	2,880	1.6	500
England	76.0	7,925	15.1	6,595	123.3	12,915	21.5	11,030
Wales	8.7	900	0.7	133	10.9	1,135	1.0	269
Scotland	8.2	1,190	1.6	501	10.5	1,665	1.9	817
Northern Ireland	1.4	145	0.1	26	1.2	210	0.3	106

1 The United Kingdom figures include the value of tourism in the Channel Islands, the Isle of Man, and a small amount where the region was unknown.
2 The England figures include the value of tourism in the Channel Islands, the Isle of Man, and a small amount where the region was unknown. The United Kingdom figures also include an amount which cannot be allocated to an individual country. Figures before 1999 do not include the value of tourism created by visitors from the Republic of Ireland.
3 See map on page 240.

Source: United Kingdom Tourism Survey, National Tourist Boards; International Passenger Survey, Office for National Statistics

13.16 Percentage of gross domestic product[1] derived from agriculture, 1998

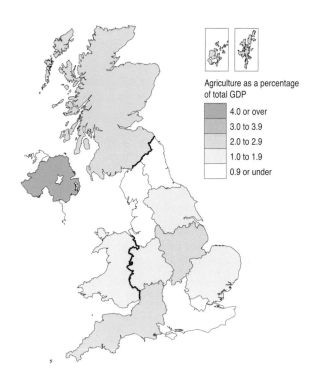

Agriculture as a percentage
of total GDP

- 4.0 or over
- 3.0 to 3.9
- 2.0 to 2.9
- 1.0 to 1.9
- 0.9 or under

1 At basic prices. See Notes and Definitions.

Source: Office for National Statistics

13.17 Agricultural legal units as a percentage of total legal units,[1,2] 2000

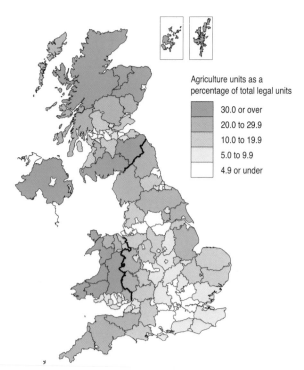

Agriculture units as a
percentage of total legal units

- 30.0 or over
- 20.0 to 29.9
- 10.0 to 19.9
- 5.0 to 9.9
- 4.9 or under

1 The figures include only those enterprises that are registered for VAT. Some smaller holdings will therefore not be included. See Notes and Definitions
2 Geographic boundaries relate to the sub-regions (Counties/UAs) in existence on 1 April 1998.

Source: Inter-Departmental Business Register, Office for National Statistics

13.18 Agricultural holdings:[1] by area of crops and grass, and by land use, June 2000

Percentages and numbers

	None[2]	Under 10 hectares	10–49.9 hectares	50 hectares and over	Total holdings (=100%) (numbers)	Arable land[3]	Grass five years old and over (including sole right rough grazing)	Set-aside land	Other land on agricultural holdings including woodland[4]	Total area on agricultural holdings (=100%) (thousand hectares)
United Kingdom	9.7	31.0	31.5	27.9	254,386	34.7	57.4	3.3	4.6	17,075
North East	8.6	23.0	24.3	44.1	5,227	32.7	59.8	3.8	3.7	568
North West	11.8	29.9	31.1	27.2	17,944	23.0	73.1	1.0	2.9	856
Yorkshire and the Humber	9.0	28.3	28.8	33.9	16,152	53.2	38.2	5.3	3.3	1,071
East Midlands	8.5	26.2	29.0	36.4	15,713	65.4	24.0	7.2	3.4	1,215
West Midlands	9.8	30.2	31.4	28.7	18,800	50.5	40.6	4.5	4.4	920
East	7.5	30.5	24.6	37.4	16,925	74.6	11.2	8.2	6.1	1,449
London	9.1	46.0	27.3	17.7	385	44.6	41.3	7.4	6.6	13
South East	9.8	35.3	28.1	26.9	18,737	54.0	30.3	7.1	8.5	1,156
South West	11.0	31.0	31.2	26.8	36,464	40.4	50.8	3.6	5.2	1,740
England	9.8	30.2	29.3	30.7	146,347	51.1	38.6	5.3	4.9	9,069
Wales	5.1	31.2	36.2	27.5	28,410	13.8	82.2	0.4	3.6	1,453
Scotland	16.7	39.2	20.5	23.6	49,738	16.3	77.5	1.4	4.8	5,492
Northern Ireland	1.5	20.8	56.2	21.5	29,891	18.4	79.6	0.2	1.7	1,060

1 Includes estimates for minor holdings; figures for English regions exclude minor holdings, hence their sum may be less than the England total. See Notes and Definitions.
2 These holdings consist only of rough grazing, woodland or other land. These figures cannot be compared with previous years due to changes in the census questions.
3 Crops, bare fallow and all grass under five years old.
4 In Great Britain this includes farm roads, yards, buildings (except glasshouses), ponds and derelict land. In Northern Ireland it includes land under bog, water, roads, buildings etc. and wasteland not used for agriculture.

Source: Department for Environment, Food and Rural Affairs; National Assembly for Wales; The Scottish Executive Rural Affairs Department; Department of Agriculture and Rural Development for Northern Ireland

13.19 Agricultural holdings by farm type, June 2000

Percentages and numbers

	Cereals	General cropping	Horti-culture	Pigs and poultry	Dairy	Cattle and sheep (LFA[1])	Cattle and sheep (Low-ground)	Mixed	Other	Total holdings (=100%) (numbers)
United Kingdom	9.8	5.1	3.8	2.7	9.9	21.2	15.1	5.7	26.7	254,386
North East	16.7	2.8	2.0	2.3	4.8	27.1	12.8	9.9	21.6	5,227
North West	2.9	3.0	4.4	3.0	20.2	15.1	18.4	3.6	29.2	17,944
Yorkshire and the Humber	17.3	9.6	3.2	5.0	8.4	12.2	13.7	8.7	22.0	16,152
East Midlands	24.0	11.8	4.6	3.3	7.1	4.4	15.5	7.5	21.7	15,713
West Midlands	9.1	6.0	5.4	2.8	12.3	5.5	24.6	8.8	25.6	18,800
East	30.6	19.7	8.1	5.4	1.2	0.0	7.8	5.9	21.2	16,925
London	10.6	6.0	18.2	4.2	2.6	0.0	11.2	4.7	42.6	385
South East	16.1	3.1	9.6	3.2	4.1	0.0	23.1	7.4	33.3	18,737
South West	7.1	1.5	4.8	2.8	15.0	4.8	27.0	7.1	29.9	36,464
England	14.0	6.6	5.6	3.5	10.3	6.5	19.7	7.1	26.7	146,347
Wales	0.9	0.6	1.3	1.4	11.9	43.0	11.4	2.1	27.4	28,410
Scotland	7.5	5.6	1.5	1.9	3.6	31.9	3.2	4.9	40.1	49,738
Northern Ireland	1.7	1.1	1.2	1.8	16.2	54.1	15.8	3.8	4.3	29,891

1 Less favoured areas. See Notes and Definitions.

Source: Department for Environment, Food and Rural Affairs; National Assembly for Wales; The Scottish Executive Rural Affairs Department; Department of Agriculture and Rural Development for Northern Ireland

13.20 Areas and estimated yields of selected crops,[1] 1999 and 2000

Thousand hectares and tonnes per hectare

	Area (thousand hectares)						Estimated yields (tonnes per hectare)					
	Wheat		Barley		Rape (for oilseed)[2]		Wheat		Barley		Rape (for oilseed)[2]	
	1999	2000	1999	2000	1999	2000	1999	2000	1999	2000	1999	2000
United Kingdom	1,847	2,086	1,179	1,128	417	332	8.0	8.0	5.6	5.8	3.2	2.9
North East	63	76	44	43	22	16	7.4	7.7	5.6	6.1	..	..
North West	23	28	44	39	4	3	6.7	7.1	4.8	5.6	..	..
Yorkshire and the Humber	233	258	122	122	47	36	8.2	8.3	6.1	6.2	..	..
East Midlands	361	401	98	99	90	71	8.4	8.2	6.1	6.0	..	..
West Midlands	150	167	74	72	28	21	7.6	7.5	5.2	5.5	..	..
East	489	544	173	169	87	66	8.4	8.2	5.8	6.2	..	..
London	2	2	1	1	1	-	..	..	..	..	..	..
South East	241	275	93	88	60	54	7.9	7.8	5.8	5.8	..	..
South West	181	204	125	118	26	26	7.4	7.4	5.4	5.4	..	..
England	1,744	1,955	773	751	363	294	8.1	8.0	5.7	5.9	3.3	2.9
Wales	13	15	30	26	2	2	6.1	7.4	5.2	4.6	3.2	2.9
Scotland	85	109	340	317	51	36	7.8	8.8	5.4	5.6	3.2	3.1
Northern Ireland	3	5	36	33	-	-	6.8	7.3	4.7	5.5	3.2	2.9

1 Figures include minor holdings. Figures for English regions exclude minor holdings hence their sum may be less than the England total.
2 Excludes crops grown on set-aside scheme land.

Source: Department for Environment, Food and Rural Affairs; National Assembly for Wales; The Scottish Executive Rural Affairs Department; Department of Agriculture and Rural Development for Northern Ireland

13.21 Livestock on agricultural holdings,[1] June 2000

Thousands

	Cattle and calves			Sheep and lambs	Pigs	Poultry		Total poultry
	Total herd[2]	Dairy cows	Beef cows			Total fowls[3]	Total laying flock[4]	
United Kingdom	11,133	2,335	1,842	42,261	6,482	154,503	28,686	169,772
North East	321	27	88	2,381	99	1,450	210	1,066
North West	1,063	348	97	3,704	247	9,021	2,151	10,425
Yorkshire and the Humber	617	128	89	2,518	1,672	10,607	1,602	9,740
East Midlands	568	120	75	1,546	557	19,920	4,717	20,478
West Midlands	834	229	95	2,759	331	16,833	3,108	17,941
East	250	40	46	443	1,376	23,509	2,647	22,477
London	5	1	1	4	5	228	19	235
South East	542	124	79	1,701	428	13,380	4,028	11,854
South West	1,921	557	199	3,941	690	19,153	4,650	19,218
England	6,156	1,575	781	19,144	5,442	115,451	23,132	129,696
Wales	1,273	269	224	11,192	68	9,905	1,010	10,404
Scotland	2,028	207	518	9,184	558	14,197	2,244	14,296
Northern Ireland	1,676	284	318	2,741	413	14,950	2,300	15,376

1 Regional figures do not include minor holdings. Therefore they may not add up to the country and UK totals.
2 Includes bulls, in-calf heifers and fattening cattle and calves.
3 Excludes ducks, geese and turkeys.
4 Excludes growing pullets (from day-old to point of lay).

Source: Department for Environment, Food and Rural Affairs; National Assembly for Wales; The Scottish Executive Rural Affairs Department; Department of Agriculture and Rural Development for Northern Ireland

14 Sub-regions of England

Government Office Regions, Counties and Unitary Authorities in England[1]

1 Hartlepool
2 Middlesbrough
3 Redcar and Cleveland
4 Stockton-on-Tees
5 Darlington
6 Halton
7 Warrington
8 Blackburn with Darwen
9 Blackpool
10 East Riding of Yorkshire
11 City of Kingston upon Hull
12 North East Lincolnshire
13 North Lincolnshire
14 York
15 Derby
16 Leicester
17 Rutland
18 Nottingham
19 County of Herefordshire
20 Telford and Wrekin
21 Stoke-on-Trent
22 Luton
23 Peterborough
24 Southend-on-Sea
25 Thurrock
26 Bracknell Forest
27 Reading
28 Slough
29 West Berkshire (Newbury)
30 Windsor and Maidenhead
31 Wokingham
32 Milton Keynes
33 Brighton and Hove
34 Portsmouth
35 Southampton
36 Isle of Wight
37 Medway
38 Bath and North East Somerset
39 City of Bristol
40 North Somerset
41 South Gloucestershire
42 Plymouth
43 Torbay
44 Bournemouth
45 Poole
46 Swindon

1 Local government structure as at 1 April 1998. The unitary authorities are listed in the same order in which they are presented in Tables 14.1, 14.2, 14.4, 14.5 and 14.6. See Notes and Definitions.

14.1 Area and population: by local authority,[1] 1999

	Area (sq km)	Persons per sq km	Population (thousands) Males	Population (thousands) Females	Population (thousands) Total	Total population percentage change 1981–1999	Total fertility rate (TFR)[2]	Standardised mortality ratio (UK=100) (SMR)[3]	Percentage of population aged: Under 5	Percentage of population aged: 5–15	Percentage of population aged: 16 up to pension age[3]	Percentage of population aged: Pension age[3] and over
United Kingdom	242,910	245	29,299	30,202	59,501	5.6	1.69	100	6.1	14.3	61.6	18.1
England	130,422	381	24,543	25,210	49,753	6.3	1.69	98	6.1	14.2	61.6	18.1
North East	8,592	300	1,264	1,317	2,581	-2.1	1.62	110	5.7	14.4	61.1	18.7
Darlington UA	197	510	49	52	101	1.9	1.85	107	5.9	14.6	60.3	19.2
Hartlepool UA	94	979	45	47	92	-3.0	1.81	113	6.3	15.4	59.9	18.4
Middlesbrough UA	54	2,673	71	74	144	-4.2	1.80	103	6.5	16.1	60.8	16.7
Redcar & Cleveland UA	245	560	67	70	137	-9.2	1.84	111	5.9	15.1	59.9	19.1
Stockton-on-Tees UA	204	894	90	92	182	4.9	1.67	110	6.0	15.6	61.9	16.4
Durham	2,232	227	249	257	506	-1.3	1.60	110	5.6	14.0	61.6	18.8
Chester-le-Street	68	847	29	29	58	9.5	1.47	108	5.9	13.3	63.7	17.2
Derwentside	271	322	43	45	87	-1.3	1.66	109	5.6	13.7	61.1	19.5
Durham	187	489	45	46	91	4.0	1.63	96	4.7	13.4	65.1	16.8
Easington	145	640	45	47	93	-8.6	1.89	121	6.2	15.5	59.3	19.0
Sedgefield	217	412	44	45	89	-4.3	1.83	117	5.7	14.4	61.2	18.6
Teesdale	840	30	12	13	25	1.9	1.51	96	5.3	12.7	59.9	22.2
Wear Valley	505	124	30	32	62	-2.5	1.71	112	5.3	13.9	60.1	20.7
Northumberland	5,026	62	152	158	310	3.6	1.65	107	5.4	13.6	61.3	19.8
Alnwick	1,079	30	16	16	32	10.8	1.67	107	5.0	13.3	60.0	21.7
Berwick-upon-Tweed	972	27	13	14	26	1.2	1.51	95	4.6	11.8	58.1	25.5
Blyth Valley	70	1,145	40	40	80	3.1	1.73	124	6.0	13.8	64.1	16.1
Castle Morpeth	619	82	25	26	51	1.7	1.38	93	4.7	13.0	61.3	21.0
Tynedale	2,219	27	29	30	59	8.9	1.63	103	5.2	14.2	60.1	20.5
Wansbeck	67	924	30	31	62	-1.1	1.82	113	5.9	14.0	60.6	19.4
Tyne and Wear	540	2,053	541	567	1,108	-4.0	1.56	110	5.6	14.2	61.2	19.0
Gateshead	143	1,385	97	101	198	-7.1	1.64	113	5.7	13.6	61.2	19.6
Newcastle-upon-Tyne	112	2,438	135	138	273	-3.9	1.59	110	5.6	13.7	63.0	17.7
North Tyneside	84	2,300	93	101	193	-2.7	1.64	100	5.6	13.5	60.1	20.8
South Tyneside	64	2,398	75	79	153	-5.2	1.79	111	5.6	15.0	58.9	20.5
Sunderland	138	2,106	142	149	291	-2.2	1.62	117	5.7	15.1	61.3	17.9
Tees Valley	794	827	322	335	656	-1.9	1.76	109	6.1	15.4	60.7	17.7
Tees Valley less Darlington	597	931	273	283	556	-2.5	1.75	109	6.2	15.6	60.8	17.5
Former county of Durham	2,429	250	298	309	607	-0.8	1.64	109	5.6	14.1	61.4	18.8
North West	14,165	486	3,383	3,498	6,881	-0.9	1.71	108	6.0	14.8	61.0	18.2
Blackburn with Darwen UA	137	1,010	68	70	138	-2.9	2.25	120	7.8	17.0	59.6	15.5
Blackpool UA	35	4,286	74	76	150	0.6	1.66	109	5.4	12.9	59.8	21.9
Halton UA	74	1,637	60	61	121	-1.7	1.83	125	6.3	16.2	62.3	15.1
Warrington UA	176	1,084	95	96	191	12.3	1.81	103	6.2	14.4	62.7	16.6
Cheshire	2,081	322	330	341	671	4.9	1.68	98	5.7	14.1	61.2	19.0
Chester	448	262	58	60	118	0.6	2.60	100	5.6	13.8	60.4	20.2
Congleton	211	419	43	45	88	10.4	1.66	92	5.5	13.9	62.2	18.5
Crewe and Nantwich	430	266	57	57	114	15.9	1.56	104	5.8	14.6	62.2	17.4
Ellesmere Port and Neston	87	914	39	41	80	-3.6	1.77	98	6.1	14.8	60.2	18.8
Macclesfield	525	291	75	78	153	1.9	1.64	92	5.5	13.3	60.8	20.4
Vale Royal	380	311	58	60	118	6.1	1.71	101	6.0	14.6	61.2	18.2
Cumbria	6,824	72	243	249	492	2.2	1.64	100	5.4	13.7	60.2	20.8
Allerdale	1,258	76	47	48	95	-0.3	1.69	106	5.4	13.4	60.3	20.9
Barrow-in-Furness	78	907	35	36	71	-3.6	1.72	115	6.0	14.7	61.2	18.1
Carlisle	1,040	98	50	52	102	1.3	1.61	106	5.3	14.0	60.1	20.6
Copeland	738	95	35	35	70	-4.3	1.67	106	5.5	14.5	61.4	18.6
Eden	2,156	23	25	25	50	16.2	1.66	91	5.3	13.0	60.7	21.0
South Lakeland	1,554	66	50	53	103	8.8	1.51	86	4.9	12.8	58.4	23.9
Greater Manchester (Met. County)	1,286	2,004	1,272	1,305	2,577	-1.6	1.75	111	6.3	15.2	61.7	16.9
Bolton	140	1,910	132	135	267	2.0	1.87	107	6.4	15.2	61.5	16.9
Bury	99	1,850	91	92	183	3.7	1.77	107	6.0	14.8	62.4	16.8
Manchester	116	3,716	213	218	431	-6.8	1.77	127	6.8	16.6	61.8	14.8
Oldham	141	1,551	107	111	219	-1.2	2.21	114	6.9	15.7	61.0	16.4
Rochdale	160	1,306	103	106	209	0.4	1.96	121	6.8	15.7	61.3	16.1
Salford	97	2,318	112	113	225	-9.0	1.74	113	6.1	14.8	60.7	18.3
Stockport	126	2,317	141	151	292	0.5	1.59	93	5.6	14.1	61.2	19.0
Tameside	103	2,130	109	111	219	0.4	1.83	113	6.1	15.2	61.8	17.0
Trafford	106	2,078	109	112	220	-0.6	1.71	98	5.9	14.5	61.3	18.3
Wigan	199	1,565	155	157	311	0.3	1.69	114	5.9	14.4	63.3	16.4

14.1 *(continued)*

	Area (sq km)	Persons per sq km	Population (thousands)			Total population percentage change 1981–1999	Total fertility rate (TFR)[2]	Standardised mortality ratio (UK=100) (SMR)[3]	Percentage of population aged:			
			Males	Females	Total				Under 5	5–15	16 up to pension age[3]	Pension age[3] and over
Lancashire	2,897	393	560	577	1,137	4.0	1.74	104	5.8	14.6	60.5	19.0
Burnley	111	810	44	46	90	-3.1	2.00	117	6.5	16.3	59.8	17.4
Chorley	203	483	48	50	98	6.4	1.65	103	5.6	14.1	63.7	16.6
Fylde	166	455	37	39	76	9.6	1.63	91	4.6	12.2	57.5	25.7
Hyndburn	73	1,083	39	40	79	-0.5	2.14	120	7.0	15.8	59.9	17.3
Lancaster	576	240	68	71	138	10.4	1.71	99	5.2	14.0	60.7	20.1
Pendle	169	491	41	42	83	-3.9	2.12	108	6.5	15.8	59.9	17.8
Preston	142	954	68	68	135	7.1	1.79	107	6.4	15.1	62.0	16.6
Ribble Valley	584	93	27	27	54	0.6	1.59	96	5.1	13.6	61.2	20.0
Rossendale	138	466	32	32	64	-1.1	1.91	114	6.4	15.1	61.4	17.1
South Ribble	113	923	51	53	104	7.7	1.53	99	5.5	14.8	62.1	17.5
West Lancashire	338	325	54	56	110	2.4	1.92	105	5.8	15.1	61.0	18.0
Wyre	284	370	50	55	105	5.7	1.67	100	4.9	13.6	56.5	25.0
Merseyside (Met. County)	655	2,143	682	722	1,404	-7.8	1.60	112	5.9	14.9	60.4	18.8
Knowsley	97	1,580	74	79	153	-11.9	1.84	124	6.7	16.9	60.0	16.4
Liverpool	113	4,053	224	233	458	-11.4	1.58	126	6.0	15.1	62.0	17.0
St Helens	133	1,345	88	91	179	-6.0	1.69	113	5.8	14.1	62.1	17.9
Sefton	153	1,875	138	149	287	-4.5	1.56	103	5.4	14.3	58.4	21.9
Wirral	159	2,054	157	170	327	-4.1	1.67	102	5.7	14.7	59.4	20.2
Former county of Cheshire	2,331	422	485	498	983	5.4	1.72	101	5.9	14.4	61.6	18.1
Former county of Lancashire	3,069	464	702	724	1,426	2.9	1.77	106	5.9	14.7	60.4	19.0
Yorkshire and the Humber	15,411	327	2,493	2,554	5,047	2.6	1.74	100	6.0	14.5	61.2	18.3
East Riding of Yorkshire UA	2,415	131	154	161	316	16.2	1.65	98	5.2	13.8	60.4	20.6
City of Kingston upon Hull UA	71	3,632	129	129	258	-5.8	1.71	105	6.3	15.8	60.4	17.4
North East Lincolnshire UA	192	812	76	80	156	-3.3	2.02	101	6.1	15.7	59.0	19.2
North Lincolnshire UA	833	182	75	77	152	0.6	1.74	99	5.8	14.3	60.6	19.3
York UA	271	656	87	91	178	7.5	1.56	85	5.4	13.2	61.8	19.6
North Yorkshire	8,038	71	279	291	570	11.4	1.69	91	5.6	13.6	59.8	21.0
Craven	1,179	44	25	27	52	9.4	1.72	94	5.4	14.1	56.9	23.5
Hambleton	1,311	66	43	44	87	15.2	1.69	84	5.6	13.6	61.2	19.6
Harrogate	1,305	116	73	79	152	11.0	1.49	93	5.7	13.5	61.2	19.6
Richmondshire	1,319	38	26	24	50	14.3	1.78	86	5.9	12.9	63.7	17.6
Ryedale	1,506	32	24	24	49	11.6	1.64	81	5.1	12.9	57.0	25.0
Scarborough	817	133	52	56	109	6.3	1.81	96	5.1	13.5	56.9	24.5
Selby	601	120	36	36	72	15.5	2.05	95	6.2	14.6	61.0	18.2
South Yorkshire (Met. County)	1,559	835	646	656	1,302	-1.1	1.68	104	6.0	14.2	61.5	18.3
Barnsley	328	696	112	116	228	1.0	1.68	108	6.0	14.5	61.2	18.4
Doncaster	581	499	143	147	290	-0.3	1.90	111	6.2	15.0	60.5	18.4
Rotherham	283	896	126	128	254	0.4	1.85	103	6.1	14.8	61.3	17.8
Sheffield	367	1,446	265	266	531	-3.1	1.67	99	5.8	13.4	62.3	18.6
West Yorkshire (Met. County)	2,034	1,040	1,046	1,069	2,115	2.4	1.81	102	6.4	14.9	61.7	17.1
Bradford	366	1,322	239	245	484	4.1	2.17	106	7.1	16.1	60.2	16.5
Calderdale	363	532	95	98	193	0.1	1.95	101	6.4	14.7	61.3	17.6
Kirklees	410	957	194	199	392	4.0	1.89	99	6.6	14.9	61.6	16.9
Leeds	562	1,293	360	366	727	1.2	1.61	98	5.8	14.1	62.6	17.5
Wakefield	333	960	159	161	320	1.8	1.79	109	6.0	14.8	62.2	17.1
The Humber	3,511	251	435	447	882	2.8	1.71	101	5.8	14.8	60.2	19.2
Former county of North Yorkshire	8,309	90	366	382	748	10.5	1.64	90	5.5	13.5	60.3	20.7
East Midlands	15,627	268	2,076	2,115	4,191	8.8	1.67	99	5.9	14.2	61.5	18.4
Derby UA	78	3,031	118	119	236	8.8	1.78	101	6.3	14.6	61.3	17.8
Leicester UA	73	3,985	145	146	291	2.8	1.91	109	6.9	16.0	61.4	15.7
Nottingham UA	75	3,790	141	144	284	2.2	1.51	107	6.2	15.3	61.9	16.6
Rutland UA	394	94	18	19	37	12.0	1.28	81	5.1	15.1	62.0	17.7
Derbyshire	2,551	289	366	372	738	5.9	1.68	101	5.7	13.7	61.7	19.0
Amber Valley	265	446	59	59	118	8.0	1.78	96	5.6	12.8	62.2	19.4
Bolsover	160	446	35	36	71	0.4	1.74	104	6.0	13.3	60.5	20.2
Chesterfield	66	1,514	49	51	100	2.0	1.62	115	5.6	13.5	61.6	19.3
Derbyshire Dales	795	90	35	36	71	5.0	1.67	90	5.1	13.4	60.2	21.4
Erewash	109	987	53	54	108	3.9	1.79	99	6.1	14.4	61.1	18.4
High Peak	540	165	44	45	89	8.3	1.74	101	6.0	14.8	62.4	16.7
North East Derbyshire	277	357	49	50	99	2.8	1.60	96	5.3	13.3	61.3	20.1
South Derbyshire	338	240	41	41	81	18.6	1.51	107	5.9	13.8	63.9	16.4

14.1 *(continued)*

	Area (sq km)	Persons per sq km	Population (thousands)			Total population percentage change 1981–1999	Total fertility rate (TFR)[2]	Standardised mortality ratio (UK=100) (SMR)[3]	Percentage of population aged:			
			Males	Females	Total				Under 5	5–15	16 up to pension age[3]	Pension age[3] and over
Leicestershire	2,084	291	302	304	607	11.8	1.65	91	5.8	13.9	62.5	17.9
Blaby	130	672	44	43	87	13.1	1.79	88	6.2	14.0	63.0	16.7
Charnwood	279	565	79	79	158	12.6	1.63	84	5.4	13.8	63.1	17.6
Harborough	593	128	38	38	76	23.5	1.62	82	5.8	14.4	62.2	17.6
Hinckley and Bosworth	297	332	49	49	99	12.0	1.76	91	5.8	13.2	62.7	18.3
Melton	481	99	24	24	47	9.1	1.70	104	6.2	13.6	62.0	18.1
North West Leicestershire	279	308	43	43	86	8.5	1.69	101	5.7	13.9	62.6	17.8
Oadby and Wigston	24	2,240	27	27	54	1.3	1.67	94	5.5	14.3	60.3	19.9
Lincolnshire	5,921	106	307	321	629	13.7	1.67	97	5.4	13.5	59.2	21.9
Boston	362	150	27	28	54	3.5	1.68	100	5.3	13.0	59.1	22.6
East Lindsey	1,760	72	61	66	126	19.8	1.63	98	5.0	12.7	56.3	26.1
Lincoln	36	2,306	41	42	83	8.5	1.67	104	6.1	13.7	61.9	18.2
North Kesteven	922	98	44	46	90	12.7	1.65	95	5.5	13.3	59.3	21.9
South Holland	742	100	36	38	74	19.0	1.58	90	4.9	12.2	58.4	24.5
South Kesteven	943	131	60	63	123	25.1	1.63	96	5.9	14.7	60.8	18.6
West Lindsey	1,156	67	38	39	77	-0.5	1.94	97	5.2	14.4	59.1	21.2
Northamptonshire	2,367	262	308	313	621	16.7	1.74	100	6.3	15.0	62.4	16.3
Corby	80	641	25	26	51	-2.5	2.07	118	6.5	16.1	60.6	16.8
Daventry	666	103	34	34	69	18.1	1.83	97	6.4	14.6	63.1	15.9
East Northamptonshire	510	147	37	38	75	20.1	1.80	100	6.2	15.2	61.6	17.0
Kettering	233	356	41	42	83	16.1	1.71	102	6.3	14.5	62.1	17.2
Northampton	81	2,420	97	99	196	23.4	1.77	101	6.4	15.2	63.2	15.3
South Northamptonshire	634	124	40	39	79	22.3	1.53	87	6.0	15.1	63.1	15.8
Wellingborough	163	421	34	35	69	6.0	1.89	103	6.6	14.6	61.2	17.6
Nottinghamshire	2,085	359	371	378	748	4.5	1.68	101	5.7	13.8	61.6	18.9
Ashfield	110	988	54	55	109	1.9	1.76	108	6.2	13.6	61.6	18.6
Bassetlaw	637	168	53	54	107	3.7	1.86	106	5.9	14.0	61.2	18.9
Broxtowe	81	1,358	55	55	110	5.3	1.50	99	5.3	13.5	62.4	18.8
Gedling	120	924	54	56	111	2.5	1.71	98	5.5	13.4	61.7	19.4
Mansfield	77	1,296	49	50	100	-0.2	1.76	105	5.8	14.7	61.2	18.3
Newark and Sherwood	651	162	52	53	106	4.8	1.75	102	5.7	14.0	61.0	19.3
Rushcliffe	409	261	53	54	107	14.6	1.65	88	5.5	13.3	62.3	19.0
Former county of Derbyshire	2,629	371	484	490	974	6.5	1.70	101	5.9	13.9	61.6	18.7
Former county of Leicestershire	2,551	366	466	469	935	8.8	1.71	96	6.1	14.6	62.1	17.2
Former county of Nottinghamshire	2,160	478	511	522	1,033	3.9	1.60	102	5.8	14.2	61.7	18.3
West Midlands	13,004	410	2,642	2,694	5,336	2.9	1.79	102	6.2	14.7	61.0	18.2
County of Herefordshire UA	2,162	78	83	86	168	12.7	1.80	89	5.6	14.0	58.3	22.0
Stoke-on-Trent UA	93	2,697	125	126	251	-0.6	1.66	113	5.9	14.4	61.6	18.1
Telford and Wrekin UA	290	517	74	75	150	19.5	1.93	108	7.0	15.6	63.0	14.5
Shropshire	3,197	88	140	142	282	10.6	1.70	94	5.4	13.7	60.1	20.8
Bridgnorth	633	83	27	26	52	3.5	1.61	105	5.1	12.7	62.8	19.4
North Shropshire	679	82	28	28	56	8.4	2.00	94	5.6	13.3	59.2	21.9
Oswestry	256	136	17	18	35	10.4	1.69	104	5.6	13.8	59.6	21.0
Shrewsbury and Atcham	602	163	48	50	98	11.7	1.58	92	5.7	14.5	60.3	19.5
South Shropshire	1,027	41	21	21	42	22.2	1.76	82	5.0	13.2	58.0	23.8
Staffordshire	2,623	309	404	406	810	5.6	1.64	103	5.6	14.1	62.4	17.9
Cannock Chase	79	1,161	46	45	92	7.7	1.87	122	6.3	14.6	63.8	15.3
East Staffordshire	390	264	51	52	103	6.9	1.77	101	6.1	14.7	60.7	18.5
Lichfield	329	286	47	47	94	5.8	1.56	104	5.5	13.3	63.2	18.0
Newcastle-under-Lyme	211	587	61	63	124	2.8	1.73	101	5.4	14.0	61.0	19.6
South Staffordshire	408	251	51	52	103	5.2	1.66	100	5.0	13.8	62.4	18.9
Stafford	599	211	63	64	126	7.6	1.47	97	5.1	13.8	62.3	18.7
Staffordshire Moorlands	576	164	47	47	94	-1.4	1.56	104	5.0	13.1	62.4	19.5
Tamworth	31	2,382	37	37	74	13.2	1.87	101	6.6	16.1	64.7	12.5
Warwickshire	1,979	257	252	256	508	6.4	1.65	99	5.7	13.7	62.1	18.4
North Warwickshire	285	217	31	31	62	3.1	1.84	101	5.9	14.4	62.6	17.2
Nuneaton and Bedworth	79	1,500	59	59	118	4.1	1.87	110	6.1	15.0	62.1	16.8
Rugby	356	248	44	44	88	0.9	1.73	98	6.1	14.6	61.3	18.1
Stratford-on-Avon	977	117	56	59	115	13.9	1.53	92	5.3	12.2	62.1	20.5
Warwick	282	442	61	63	125	8.2	1.54	97	5.5	13.1	62.5	19.0

Regional Trends 36, © Crown copyright 2001

14.1 *(continued)*

	Area (sq km)	Persons per sq km	Population (thousands) Males	Females	Total	Total population percentage change 1981–1999	Total fertility rate (TFR)[2]	Standardised mortality ratio (UK=100) (SMR)[3]	Percentage of population aged: Under 5	5–15	16 up to pension age[3]	Pension age[3] and over
West Midlands (Met. County)	899	2,922	1,298	1,328	2,627	-1.7	1.88	104	6.6	15.3	60.3	17.7
Birmingham	265	3,823	501	512	1,013	-0.7	1.99	105	7.2	16.0	60.3	16.6
Coventry	97	3,133	150	153	304	-4.8	1.85	103	6.3	15.4	60.7	17.6
Dudley	98	3,183	155	157	312	3.7	1.74	102	6.0	14.0	61.3	18.8
Sandwell	86	3,366	142	147	289	-6.6	2.02	114	6.7	15.0	59.9	18.4
Solihull	179	1,148	101	105	206	3.7	1.60	86	5.7	14.6	61.0	18.7
Walsall	106	2,468	130	132	262	-2.3	2.09	104	6.5	14.9	60.0	18.6
Wolverhampton	69	3,491	119	122	241	-6.1	1.92	109	6.5	15.3	59.3	19.0
Worcestershire	1,761	307	266	274	540	10.9	1.72	94	5.8	13.9	61.3	18.9
Bromsgrove	220	386	42	43	85	-3.7	1.60	99	5.5	13.5	60.5	20.5
Malvern Hills	595	124	36	38	74	8.6	1.73	93	5.0	14.2	57.6	23.2
Redditch	54	1,426	38	39	77	13.8	1.91	92	6.7	15.1	63.6	14.6
Worcester	33	2,890	47	48	95	23.6	1.83	89	6.5	13.8	63.0	16.6
Wychavon	664	169	55	57	112	19.3	1.59	90	5.7	13.3	60.7	20.3
Wyre Forest	195	493	48	48	96	4.9	1.66	101	5.5	13.8	62.2	18.5
Herefordshire and Worcestershire	3,923	181	349	359	708	11.3	1.74	93	5.8	13.9	60.6	19.7
Former county of Shropshire	3,487	124	215	218	432	13.6	1.79	98	6.0	14.3	61.1	18.6
Former county of Staffordshire	2,716	391	528	532	1,061	4.1	1.64	105	5.7	14.2	62.2	17.9
East	19,120	283	2,676	2,743	5,419	11.6	1.67	93	6.1	14.1	61.3	18.5
Luton UA	43	4,264	92	91	183	11.2	2.15	104	7.8	16.6	61.9	13.7
Peterborough UA	344	455	78	78	156	17.0	1.97	103	6.9	15.2	62.1	15.8
Southend-on-Sea UA	42	4,206	85	91	177	12.1	1.52	94	5.9	13.4	60.2	20.5
Thurrock UA	164	822	67	68	135	5.8	1.94	110	7.2	14.9	63.0	14.8
Bedfordshire	1,192	318	188	190	379	9.8	1.70	95	6.4	14.4	63.3	16.0
Bedford	477	297	71	71	142	20.4	1.81	96	6.4	13.9	62.5	17.2
Mid Bedfordshire	503	250	62	64	126	6.3	1.51	86	6.5	14.4	64.4	14.7
South Bedfordshire	213	522	55	56	111	3.7	1.76	105	6.2	14.9	63.1	15.9
Cambridgeshire	3,056	186	282	286	568	24.8	1.43	88	5.8	13.7	63.9	16.6
Cambridge	41	2,998	62	61	123	21.7	1.13	78	4.8	11.6	69.0	14.7
East Cambridgeshire	655	111	36	37	73	35.3	1.56	96	5.9	14.0	62.2	17.9
Fenland	546	151	41	42	82	23.7	1.94	99	6.3	13.3	58.6	21.9
Huntingdonshire	912	172	77	80	157	25.6	1.53	94	6.5	15.1	63.9	14.5
South Cambridgeshire	902	147	66	67	133	22.1	1.54	80	5.8	14.0	63.5	16.7
Essex	3,469	377	642	664	1,306	9.0	1.68	93	6.0	13.8	61.2	19.0
Basildon	110	1,512	82	84	166	9.1	1.94	95	6.8	14.8	61.1	17.3
Braintree	612	216	66	67	132	17.5	1.73	99	6.1	13.9	63.2	16.8
Brentwood	149	480	35	37	72	-1.2	1.29	105	5.4	13.4	61.5	19.8
Castle Point	45	1,885	42	43	85	-2.3	1.63	101	5.5	13.7	61.9	18.9
Chelmsford	342	453	76	79	155	11.1	1.56	84	5.7	14.2	63.2	17.0
Colchester	334	475	78	80	159	14.8	1.60	92	6.0	13.6	63.7	16.8
Epping Forest	340	355	59	62	121	3.3	1.73	97	6.1	13.1	61.6	19.3
Harlow	30	2,538	37	39	76	-4.3	1.88	84	7.0	14.1	60.9	18.1
Maldon	360	159	29	28	57	18.6	1.83	92	6.2	14.3	61.4	18.2
Rochford	169	463	38	40	78	6.2	1.68	81	6.0	13.7	60.3	20.0
Tendring	337	402	65	71	135	17.9	1.77	96	5.1	12.7	53.3	29.0
Uttlesford	641	109	34	36	70	11.2	1.69	92	6.0	14.4	62.3	17.3
Hertfordshire	1,639	636	517	526	1,043	7.8	1.69	93	6.4	14.3	62.1	17.2
Broxbourne	52	1,611	41	43	84	4.9	1.76	91	6.4	14.0	62.5	17.1
Dacorum	212	648	68	70	137	4.9	1.71	93	6.5	14.7	61.6	17.3
East Hertfordshire	477	268	64	64	128	16.5	1.79	93	6.6	13.8	64.0	15.6
Hertsmere	98	1,001	48	50	98	10.7	1.62	97	6.2	14.9	60.5	18.4
North Hertfordshire	375	312	58	59	117	7.7	1.67	92	6.3	13.9	61.5	18.3
St Albans	161	828	66	67	133	6.4	1.70	85	6.6	13.2	63.1	17.1
Stevenage	26	3,045	40	40	79	6.1	1.82	100	6.8	16.9	61.0	15.2
Three Rivers	89	1,003	44	45	89	10.1	1.66	79	5.9	13.6	61.7	18.8
Watford	21	3,882	41	41	82	9.3	1.60	115	6.8	14.8	64.4	14.0
Welwyn Hatfield	127	755	47	49	96	1.9	1.76	95	6.2	14.6	59.9	19.3

14.1 *(continued)*

	Area (sq km)	Persons per sq km	Population (thousands)			Total population percentage change Total 1981–1999	Total fertility rate (TFR)[2]	Standardised mortality ratio (UK=100) (SMR)[3]	Percentage of population aged:			
			Males	Females	Total				Under 5	5–15	16 up to pension age[3]	Pension age[3] and over
Norfolk	5,372	148	391	406	796	13.3	1.63	91	5.5	13.1	59.1	22.3
Breckland	1,305	92	59	61	120	24.3	1.71	91	5.9	13.2	58.9	22.0
Broadland	552	216	59	61	119	21.9	1.48	97	5.5	13.1	60.3	21.2
Great Yarmouth	174	517	44	46	90	10.4	1.84	102	5.8	14.2	58.0	22.0
Kings Lynn and West Norfolk	1,429	93	66	68	133	9.3	1.75	99	5.7	13.1	57.6	23.5
North Norfolk	965	105	49	52	101	21.0	1.56	82	4.7	12.4	55.3	27.6
Norwich	39	3,166	61	63	123	-2.1	1.50	88	5.4	12.9	63.0	18.7
South Norfolk	908	120	54	55	109	14.6	1.75	84	5.3	13.0	59.9	21.8
Suffolk	3,798	178	332	342	675	12.1	1.66	92	6.1	14.4	59.4	20.1
Babergh	595	134	40	40	80	7.9	1.87	89	5.5	13.7	60.0	20.8
Forest Heath	374	187	35	35	70	32.6	1.37	97	8.3	18.5	60.2	13.0
Ipswich	39	2,920	56	58	114	-5.2	1.85	98	6.5	14.4	59.8	19.3
Mid Suffolk	871	96	42	42	84	18.4	1.77	90	5.9	13.7	59.9	20.4
St Edmundsbury	657	147	48	49	97	11.1	1.59	94	6.1	13.1	62.4	18.5
Suffolk Coastal	892	136	60	62	121	25.1	1.48	85	5.2	14.8	58.5	21.5
Waveney	370	295	53	56	109	9.2	1.79	94	5.8	13.6	56.1	24.5
Former county of Bedfordshire	1,235	455	281	282	562	10.2	1.85	98	6.8	15.1	62.9	15.2
Former county of Cambridgeshire	3,400	213	361	364	725	23.0	1.54	91	6.1	14.0	63.5	16.4
Former county of Essex	3,675	440	795	823	1,618	9.1	1.68	95	6.1	13.9	61.2	18.8
London[5]	1,580	4,611	3,616	3,669	7,285	7.0	1.75	95	6.9	13.6	64.9	14.6
Inner London	322	8,749	1,400	1,417	2,817	10.5	1.75	96	7.2	13.1	66.9	12.8
Inner London – West	110	9,486	518	526	1,043	12.7	1.39	87	5.9	10.4	70.4	13.3
Camden	22	8,898	97	98	196	9.3	1.62	91	6.1	11.0	68.9	13.9
City of London	3	2,002	3	3	6	11.2	1.52	60	4.8	8.2	67.9	19.1
Hammersmith and Fulham	16	10,166	78	84	163	7.5	1.48	95	6.5	10.8	70.6	12.2
Kensington and Chelsea	12	14,930	90	90	179	27.9	1.18	80	5.5	10.3	71.4	12.8
Wandsworth	35	7,666	132	136	268	2.4	1.55	97	6.5	10.4	70.0	13.2
Westminster	22	10,527	117	114	232	23.1	1.13	71	5.1	9.6	71.4	13.9
Inner London – East	212	8,366	882	891	1,774	9.2	2.02	103	7.9	14.8	64.8	12.5
Hackney	20	9,940	99	100	199	7.4	2.32	102	8.7	14.8	64.8	11.7
Haringey	30	7,457	112	111	224	8.0	1.85	94	7.5	13.3	67.2	12.0
Islington	15	11,760	87	90	176	6.2	1.61	100	6.5	13.2	67.1	13.2
Lambeth	27	10,094	135	137	273	7.7	1.70	96	7.3	13.7	67.1	11.9
Lewisham	35	7,019	119	127	246	3.9	1.83	108	7.3	14.3	64.4	14.0
Newham	36	6,547	119	117	236	10.7	2.69	116	9.5	18.0	61.1	11.3
Southwark	29	8,133	117	119	236	8.0	2.05	100	8.0	14.4	64.3	13.2
Tower Hamlets	20	9,248	94	91	185	27.4	2.24	106	8.6	16.4	62.5	12.4
Outer London	1,258	3,552	2,216	2,252	4,468	5.0	1.75	93	6.7	13.9	63.7	15.7
Outer London – East and North East	438	3,519	760	782	1,541	0.5	1.90	99	6.8	14.7	61.8	16.7
Barking and Dagenham	34	4,584	76	80	156	2.8	2.06	114	7.6	16.1	58.6	17.8
Bexley	61	3,591	107	112	219	0.9	1.84	93	6.3	14.6	61.3	17.9
Enfield	81	3,308	133	135	268	2.6	1.97	95	7.2	14.2	62.3	16.3
Greenwich	48	4,486	105	110	215	-0.1	1.92	103	7.1	15.4	62.4	15.0
Havering	118	1,957	114	117	231	-4.7	1.68	97	5.7	13.6	61.1	19.6
Redbridge	56	4,158	115	117	233	1.6	1.82	89	6.5	14.6	62.6	16.2
Waltham Forest	40	5,485	109	111	219	0.9	2.02	106	7.5	14.9	63.4	14.2
Outer London – South	358	3,224	569	585	1,154	5.7	1.66	92	6.4	13.4	63.9	16.2
Bromley	152	1,981	147	154	301	0.9	1.62	88	6.1	12.8	62.0	19.2
Croydon	87	3,880	167	171	338	5.1	1.76	96	6.7	14.3	64.2	14.8
Kingston upon Thames	38	3,950	75	75	150	11.8	1.57	93	6.1	12.6	66.1	15.3
Merton	38	4,922	93	94	187	11.6	1.61	93	6.8	12.9	65.9	14.4
Sutton	43	4,144	87	91	178	4.8	1.69	95	6.5	13.9	63.0	16.7
Outer London – West and North West	462	3,837	888	885	1,773	8.8	1.70	89	6.7	13.5	65.2	14.6
Barnet	89	3,819	169	171	340	15.1	1.52	86	6.3	13.5	64.8	15.4
Brent	44	5,724	128	124	252	-0.9	2.01	95	7.2	14.1	65.5	13.2
Ealing	55	5,614	156	152	309	9.4	1.68	97	6.9	13.5	66.5	13.1
Harrow	51	4,179	106	107	213	7.1	1.62	86	6.3	14.3	63.6	15.7
Hillingdon	110	2,306	126	128	254	8.7	1.65	90	6.6	13.8	63.9	15.7
Hounslow	58	3,673	108	105	213	4.5	2.00	95	7.2	13.6	65.2	13.9
Richmond-upon-Thames	55	3,495	94	98	192	18.8	1.50	79	6.0	11.8	66.6	15.6

Regional Trends 36, © Crown copyright 2001

14.1 *(continued)*

	Area (sq km)	Persons per sq km	Population (thousands)			Total population percentage change	Total fertility rate (TFR)[2]	Standardised mortality ratio (UK=100) (SMR)[3]	Percentage of population aged:			
			Males	Females	Total	1981–1999			Under 5	5–15	16 up to pension age[3]	Pension age[3] and over
South East	19,096	423	3,975	4,102	8,078	*11.5*	*1.67*	*92*	*6.0*	*14.0*	*61.5*	*18.5*
Bracknell Forest UA	109	1,023	56	55	112	*31.7*	*1.67*	*99*	*6.9*	*15.4*	*65.3*	*12.4*
Brighton and Hove UA	82	3,148	127	131	258	*8.8*	*1.38*	*94*	*5.2*	*11.7*	*64.4*	*18.6*
Isle of Wight UA	380	337	62	66	128	*8.6*	*1.71*	*91*	*5.1*	*13.0*	*56.2*	*25.6*
Medway UA	192	1,267	120	123	243	*1.2*	*1.84*	*109*	*6.7*	*15.3*	*63.2*	*14.8*
Milton Keynes UA	309	669	103	104	207	*64.2*	*1.79*	*104*	*7.0*	*15.8*	*65.7*	*11.6*
Portsmouth UA	40	4,720	96	93	189	*-1.4*	*1.71*	*104*	*6.0*	*13.4*	*63.3*	*17.3*
Reading UA	40	3,683	75	72	147	*7.2*	*1.75*	*85*	*6.6*	*13.6*	*65.2*	*14.7*
Slough UA	27	4,116	55	56	111	*13.9*	*1.88*	*108*	*7.6*	*15.0*	*64.2*	*13.2*
Southampton UA	50	4,305	110	106	215	*2.6*	*1.68*	*97*	*5.8*	*13.5*	*63.5*	*17.2*
West Berkshire UA (Newbury)	704	205	72	73	145	*17.9*	*1.74*	*88*	*6.1*	*14.9*	*64.1*	*14.9*
Windsor and Maidenhead UA	198	713	70	71	141	*4.3*	*1.67*	*93*	*5.9*	*13.9*	*62.9*	*17.4*
Wokingham UA	179	809	73	72	145	*23.8*	*1.84*	*95*	*6.4*	*14.9*	*64.5*	*14.2*
Buckinghamshire	1,568	308	240	242	483	*8.6*	*1.72*	*93*	*6.3*	*14.5*	*63.0*	*16.3*
Aylesbury Vale	903	178	80	80	161	*19.7*	*1.74*	*100*	*6.7*	*14.8*	*64.1*	*14.4*
Chiltern	196	479	46	48	94	*3.7*	*1.67*	*86*	*5.7*	*14.1*	*61.4*	*18.8*
South Buckinghamshire	145	441	32	32	64	*2.5*	*1.60*	*98*	*5.7*	*14.3*	*60.9*	*19.0*
Wycombe	325	505	82	82	164	*4.4*	*1.76*	*88*	*6.4*	*14.4*	*63.6*	*15.6*
East Sussex	1,713	290	234	262	496	*15.9*	*1.73*	*86*	*5.5*	*13.6*	*55.4*	*25.5*
Eastbourne	44	2,082	42	49	92	*18.2*	*1.48*	*84*	*5.3*	*12.4*	*55.0*	*27.3*
Hastings	30	2,767	39	44	83	*9.7*	*2.17*	*92*	*6.3*	*14.5*	*57.9*	*21.3*
Lewes	292	299	41	46	87	*10.5*	*2.00*	*90*	*5.6*	*13.9*	*54.6*	*25.9*
Rother	511	179	43	49	92	*19.7*	*1.56*	*82*	*4.8*	*12.8*	*51.3*	*31.1*
Wealden	836	171	68	74	143	*19.6*	*1.66*	*85*	*5.4*	*14.2*	*57.4*	*23.0*
Hampshire	3,689	339	613	635	1,249	*14.8*	*1.66*	*90*	*5.9*	*14.2*	*61.7*	*18.2*
Basingstoke and Deane	634	236	74	75	150	*13.4*	*1.90*	*97*	*7.0*	*14.8*	*63.8*	*14.4*
East Hampshire	515	219	55	58	113	*22.9*	*1.59*	*96*	*6.0*	*15.2*	*61.4*	*17.4*
Eastleigh	80	1,449	57	58	116	*24.8*	*1.64*	*98*	*6.3*	*14.5*	*63.2*	*16.1*
Fareham	74	1,426	51	54	106	*18.6*	*1.61*	*85*	*5.2*	*13.8*	*60.5*	*20.5*
Gosport	25	3,045	36	40	76	*-2.2*	*1.59*	*102*	*6.4*	*15.0*	*60.7*	*17.9*
Hart	215	405	44	43	87	*24.4*	*1.55*	*87*	*5.9*	*13.4*	*66.4*	*14.3*
Havant	55	2,157	58	61	119	*2.5*	*1.85*	*89*	*5.6*	*14.6*	*58.2*	*21.6*
New Forest	753	228	84	88	172	*18.2*	*1.61*	*89*	*5.1*	*13.0*	*57.6*	*24.3*
Rushmoor	39	2,259	44	44	88	*1.2*	*1.82*	*95*	*7.1*	*14.1*	*65.7*	*13.2*
Test Valley	637	176	55	57	112	*19.6*	*1.49*	*82*	*5.7*	*14.8*	*62.9*	*16.6*
Winchester	661	168	55	57	111	*19.5*	*1.66*	*81*	*5.6*	*14.0*	*61.0*	*19.4*
Kent	3,543	379	658	686	1,344	*8.0*	*1.76*	*94*	*6.1*	*14.3*	*60.1*	*19.6*
Ashford	581	176	50	52	102	*17.5*	*1.82*	*90*	*6.5*	*14.8*	*60.5*	*18.1*
Canterbury	309	457	69	72	141	*15.6*	*1.60*	*85*	*5.1*	*13.4*	*59.3*	*22.2*
Dartford	73	1,174	43	43	86	*5.5*	*1.86*	*110*	*6.6*	*13.6*	*63.3*	*16.5*
Dover	315	347	53	56	109	*5.7*	*1.69*	*91*	*5.8*	*14.4*	*58.6*	*21.2*
Gravesham	99	929	45	47	92	*-3.7*	*1.93*	*98*	*6.6*	*15.1*	*60.0*	*18.2*
Maidstone	393	359	70	72	141	*8.0*	*1.73*	*91*	*5.9*	*14.0*	*62.6*	*17.5*
Sevenoaks	368	306	55	57	113	*2.7*	*1.75*	*81*	*6.1*	*14.3*	*60.4*	*19.1*
Shepway	357	284	49	53	101	*17.8*	*1.64*	*96*	*5.7*	*13.6*	*58.6*	*22.0*
Swale	373	322	60	60	120	*9.0*	*1.89*	*101*	*6.4*	*14.6*	*61.6*	*17.4*
Thanet	103	1,240	61	67	128	*4.8*	*1.86*	*98*	*5.9*	*14.0*	*55.2*	*24.9*
Tonbridge and Malling	240	447	53	54	107	*9.7*	*1.80*	*98*	*6.6*	*14.8*	*61.7*	*16.9*
Tunbridge Wells	332	311	50	53	103	*4.7*	*1.86*	*95*	*6.3*	*14.6*	*59.9*	*19.2*
Oxfordshire	2,606	240	313	314	626	*15.6*	*1.56*	*89*	*6.1*	*14.4*	*63.6*	*15.9*
Cherwell	589	232	68	69	137	*25.3*	*1.70*	*95*	*6.6*	*15.8*	*63.1*	*14.5*
Oxford	46	3,206	74	73	147	*13.1*	*1.27*	*87*	*5.2*	*12.8*	*68.0*	*14.0*
South Oxfordshire	679	189	63	65	128	*9.5*	*1.75*	*89*	*6.5*	*15.0*	*61.5*	*17.0*
Vale of White Horse	579	198	59	56	115	*11.0*	*1.94*	*87*	*5.9*	*14.6*	*62.0*	*17.5*
West Oxfordshire	714	138	49	50	99	*21.0*	*1.55*	*90*	*6.1*	*14.1*	*62.4*	*17.5*

14.1 *(continued)*

	Area (sq km)	Persons per sq km	Population (thousands) Males	Females	Total	Total population percentage change 1981–1999	Total fertility rate (TFR)[2]	Standardised mortality ratio (UK=100) (SMR)[3]	Percentage of population aged: Under 5	5–15	16 up to pension age[3]	Pension age[3] and over
Surrey	1,677	643	531	548	1,078	6.2	1.63	88	6.1	13.6	62.0	18.3
Elmbridge	97	1,371	64	69	133	18.1	1.45	87	6.2	13.5	63.3	16.9
Epsom and Ewell	34	2,097	35	36	71	2.8	1.65	79	5.9	13.4	61.8	19.0
Guildford	271	477	64	65	129	3.4	1.67	77	5.7	13.2	63.2	17.9
Mole Valley	258	311	39	41	80	3.5	1.82	82	6.0	12.8	59.3	22.0
Reigate and Banstead	129	947	60	62	122	4.4	1.82	104	6.4	13.7	61.6	18.3
Runnymede	78	982	38	39	77	5.3	1.73	91	5.8	12.8	62.2	19.2
Spelthorne	57	1,572	45	45	90	-3.4	1.66	91	6.1	12.8	61.6	19.6
Surrey Heath	95	904	43	43	86	13.0	1.50	89	6.5	14.8	64.0	14.7
Tandridge	250	323	39	42	81	3.5	1.54	89	6.1	14.6	60.4	19.0
Waverley	345	336	56	60	116	3.4	1.91	88	6.1	14.4	59.4	20.0
Woking	64	1,461	47	47	94	14.1	1.54	92	6.5	13.8	64.2	15.5
West Sussex	1,988	383	366	395	761	14.2	1.59	89	5.7	13.3	58.4	22.6
Adur	42	1,402	28	30	59	0.5	1.74	89	5.7	13.5	56.1	24.8
Arun	221	650	69	75	144	21.2	1.49	89	4.8	11.9	54.8	28.5
Chichester	786	138	50	59	108	9.7	1.47	81	5.2	13.3	55.2	26.2
Crawley	44	2,212	48	49	97	18.7	1.60	102	6.7	14.1	63.4	15.9
Horsham	530	234	61	63	124	23.4	1.60	83	5.8	14.7	60.8	18.6
Mid Sussex	333	382	63	64	127	10.2	1.71	90	6.1	13.9	61.7	18.2
Worthing	32	3,167	48	54	101	9.6	1.53	93	5.6	12.2	56.2	26.0
Former county of Berkshire	1,257	637	402	399	801	15.2	1.74	93	6.5	14.6	64.3	14.6
Former county of Buckinghamshire	1,877	367	343	346	689	20.9	1.75	95	6.5	14.9	63.8	14.9
Former county of East Sussex	1,795	420	361	393	754	13.4	1.55	88	5.4	12.9	58.5	23.2
Former county of Hampshire	3,779	437	819	833	1,653	11.0	1.65	93	5.9	14.1	62.1	17.9
Former county of Kent	3,735	425	778	809	1,587	6.9	1.78	95	6.2	14.4	60.6	18.9
South West	23,829	207	2,418	2,518	4,936	12.7	1.65	90	5.6	13.7	59.7	21.0
Bath and North East Somerset UA	351	480	83	86	169	4.4	1.53	86	5.3	12.9	61.0	20.7
Bournemouth UA	46	3,533	78	85	163	13.3	1.46	93	5.1	11.6	58.9	24.4
City of Bristol UA	110	3,684	202	203	405	1.0	1.60	95	5.9	13.6	63.6	16.8
North Somerset UA	373	509	93	97	190	16.5	1.73	89	5.3	13.3	59.7	21.6
Plymouth UA	80	3,165	124	129	253	-0.1	1.54	93	5.5	14.2	62.0	18.3
Poole UA	65	2,166	68	73	141	17.0	1.64	87	5.4	13.6	59.0	22.0
South Gloucestershire UA	497	492	123	122	244	20.4	1.72	87	6.6	14.1	62.8	16.4
Swindon UA	230	788	91	91	181	19.5	1.80	102	6.7	14.5	63.1	15.8
Torbay UA	63	1,970	59	65	124	9.7	1.70	88	5.2	12.8	55.9	26.0
Cornwall and the Isles of Scilly	3,559	139	241	254	495	16.0	1.75	91	5.2	13.6	58.4	22.9
Caradon	664	123	40	41	82	20.5	1.63	89	4.9	13.9	59.7	21.5
Carrick	461	187	41	45	86	13.7	1.74	87	5.0	13.5	56.9	24.6
Kerrier	473	193	44	47	91	9.1	1.82	93	5.5	13.7	59.0	21.8
North Cornwall	1,190	68	39	42	81	25.0	1.59	91	5.2	13.7	58.1	22.9
Penwith	304	198	29	31	60	11.1	2.04	92	5.0	12.4	57.3	25.4
Restormel	452	205	45	47	93	17.9	1.80	96	5.3	13.7	59.0	22.0
Isles of Scilly	15	139	1	1	2	5.7	2.80	88	4.8	16.2	56.5	22.4
Devon	6,562	106	338	360	698	16.4	1.68	88	5.2	13.3	57.9	23.6
East Devon	814	155	60	67	126	17.1	1.66	78	4.7	11.8	53.4	30.1
Exeter	47	2,367	55	56	111	10.6	1.84	97	5.5	13.0	63.2	18.3
Mid Devon	915	74	33	35	68	15.5	1.90	84	5.8	14.2	58.7	21.3
North Devon	1,086	81	43	45	88	12.1	1.81	97	5.5	13.3	58.4	22.8
South Hams	887	91	39	42	81	21.6	1.58	84	5.2	13.8	58.4	22.7
Teignbridge	674	178	58	62	120	25.3	1.79	92	5.3	13.2	57.1	24.4
Torridge	979	57	27	29	56	14.7	1.95	101	5.0	15.0	57.0	23.0
West Devon	1,160	41	23	25	48	11.6	1.83	84	5.0	13.9	57.5	23.6
Dorset	2,542	153	189	200	389	16.2	1.52	81	4.9	13.0	56.8	25.4
Christchurch	50	887	21	23	44	15.8	1.56	81	4.6	11.5	51.6	32.4
East Dorset	354	236	40	43	84	21.1	1.34	75	4.6	11.8	56.6	27.0
North Dorset	609	101	31	31	61	25.1	1.53	78	5.1	14.5	58.7	21.6
Purbeck	404	115	23	24	46	14.7	1.38	76	4.9	13.1	59.1	22.9
West Dorset	1,082	84	44	48	91	14.1	1.75	81	4.8	13.1	54.6	27.4
Weymouth and Portland	42	1,481	30	32	62	7.2	1.57	101	5.3	14.1	60.1	20.6

14.1 *(continued)*

	Area (sq km)	Persons per sq km	Population (thousands)			Total population percentage change	Total fertility rate (TFR)[2]	Standardised mortality ratio (UK=100) (SMR)[3]	Percentage of population aged:			
			Males	Females	Total	1981–1999			Under 5	5–15	16 up to pension age[3]	Pension age[3] and over
Gloucestershire	2,653	212	278	284	562	*11.0*	1.74	93	*5.8*	*14.1*	*60.3*	*19.8*
Cheltenham	47	2,260	53	54	106	*3.4*	1.60	88	*5.4*	*13.2*	*61.1*	*20.2*
Cotswold	1,165	72	41	43	84	*18.8*	1.52	92	*5.5*	*13.7*	*59.3*	*21.5*
Forest of Dean	526	149	39	39	78	*7.0*	1.90	98	*5.7*	*13.4*	*60.8*	*20.1*
Gloucester	41	2,665	55	55	109	*9.0*	1.97	101	*7.1*	*15.3*	*60.7*	*16.9*
Stroud	461	237	54	55	109	*13.7*	1.78	91	*5.5*	*14.4*	*60.1*	*20.0*
Tewkesbury	414	182	37	38	75	*18.4*	1.90	89	*5.7*	*14.1*	*59.6*	*20.5*
Somerset	3,452	143	240	253	493	*14.5*	1.71	90	*5.6*	*14.3*	*58.1*	*22.0*
Mendip	739	136	49	51	100	*11.8*	1.85	96	*5.9*	*16.0*	*58.6*	*19.5*
Sedgemoor	564	186	52	53	105	*16.3*	1.70	96	*5.7*	*13.6*	*58.9*	*21.7*
South Somerset	959	162	76	79	155	*16.4*	1.69	82	*5.6*	*14.2*	*58.5*	*21.7*
Taunton Deane	462	217	48	52	100	*13.6*	1.58	93	*5.3*	*14.4*	*58.3*	*22.0*
West Somerset	727	45	15	17	33	*11.0*	1.99	83	*4.9*	*11.5*	*52.0*	*31.6*
Wiltshire	3,246	132	211	218	429	*14.9*	1.75	88	*6.2*	*14.3*	*60.9*	*18.6*
Kennet	957	83	39	40	79	*20.9*	1.62	81	*6.4*	*14.8*	*61.2*	*17.5*
North Wiltshire	768	162	62	63	125	*18.9*	1.77	90	*6.7*	*14.4*	*62.3*	*16.6*
Salisbury	1,004	114	55	60	115	*11.6*	1.55	91	*5.6*	*14.1*	*60.1*	*20.2*
West Wiltshire	517	214	55	56	110	*10.1*	2.09	89	*6.3*	*14.2*	*59.7*	*19.9*
Bristol/Bath area	1,331	757	501	507	1,008	*8.6*	1.63	90	*5.9*	*13.5*	*62.3*	*18.3*
Former county of Devon	6,705	160	521	554	1,075	*11.3*	1.64	89	*5.3*	*13.4*	*58.6*	*22.6*
Former county of Dorset	2,653	261	335	357	693	*15.7*	1.51	85	*5.0*	*12.8*	*57.7*	*24.4*
Former county of Wiltshire	3,476	176	302	308	610	*16.2*	1.76	92	*6.4*	*14.4*	*61.5*	*17.7*

1 Local government structure as at 1 April 1998. See Notes and Definitions.
2 The total fertility rate (TFR) is the average number of children which would be born to a woman if the current pattern of fertility persisted throughout her child-bearing years. Previously called total period fertility rate (TPFR).
3 Adjusted for the age structure of the population. See Notes and Definitions to the Population chapter.
4 Pension age is 65 for males and 60 for females.
5 London is presented by NUTS levels 1, 2, 3 and 4. See Notes and Definitions.

Source: Office for National Statistics

14.2 Vital[1,2] and social statistics: by sub-region[3]

	Live births[2] per 1,000 population		Deaths[2] per 1,000 population		Perinatal mortality rate[4]	Infant mortality rate[5]	Percent-age of live births under 2.5 kg	Percent-age of live births outside marriage	Children looked after by LAs per 1,000 population aged under 18
	1991	1999	1991	1999	1998–2000	1998–2000	1999	1999	2000[6]
United Kingdom	13.7	11.8	11.2	10.6	8.2	5.8	..	38.8	..
England	13.7	11.8	11.1	10.4	8.2	5.6	7.6	38.5	5.1
North East	13.4	10.7	12.2	11.4	8.3	5.7	7.8	48.9	5.7
Darlington UA	14.3	11.8	13.9	12.2	12.8	6.5	8.2	47.0	5.1
Hartlepool UA	14.9	11.7	11.5	11.1	9.5	5.9	8.6	54.9	5.2
Middlesbrough UA	15.1	12.7	11.1	9.8	9.0	5.4	8.3	53.0	5.1
Redcar & Cleveland UA	14.0	10.9	10.9	11.5	8.1	4.5	8.3	54.9	5.0
Stockton-on-Tees UA	14.9	11.3	10.4	9.7	7.2	5.6	7.5	44.6	4.6
Durham	12.8	10.4	12.1	11.4	8.1	6.2	8.3	49.7	4.7
Northumberland	11.8	9.9	12.6	11.9	7.8	6.2	7.3	39.4	4.4
Tyne and Wear	13.4	10.6	12.7	11.7	8.2	5.4	7.5	49.9	7.0
Tees Valley	14.7	11.7	11.1	10.7	9.0	5.5	8.1	50.4	4.9
Tees Valley less Darlington	14.7	11.6	10.9	10.4	8.3	5.3	8.1	51.1	4.9
Former county of Durham	13.0	10.6	12.4	11.5	8.9	6.2	8.3	49.2	4.7
North West	14.2	11.5	12.0	11.3	8.6	6.3	7.8	45.5	6.1
Blackburn with Darwen UA	17.2	15.3	12.2	10.9	9.0	8.4	10.2	35.2	7.2
Blackpool UA	13.0	10.2	16.0	14.1	8.9	6.2	7.7	58.0	9.2
Halton UA	15.5	12.3	10.1	10.1	6.6	6.0	5.7	55.6	5.6
Warrington UA	14.7	12.5	10.6	9.7	6.6	5.0	6.9	39.4	3.8
Cheshire	12.7	10.9	10.8	10.7	7.1	4.6	6.4	35.0	3.2
Cumbria	12.7	10.0	12.7	12.0	7.7	4.8	6.6	40.0	4.9
Greater Manchester (Met. County)	14.9	12.2	11.8	11.0	9.0	6.5	8.5	46.3	6.6
Lancashire	13.7	11.1	12.3	11.6	8.7	6.7	7.7	41.7	5.5
Merseyside (Met. County)	14.0	10.9	12.4	12.0	9.3	7.0	7.4	54.0	7.4
Former county of Cheshire	13.5	11.4	10.7	10.4	7.0	4.9	6.4	38.7	3.6
Former county of Lancashire	13.9	11.4	12.7	11.8	8.7	6.8	8.0	42.4	6.1
Yorkshire and the Humber	13.8	11.5	11.5	10.7	9.0	6.8	8.5	41.7	5.7
East Riding of Yorkshire UA	11.8	9.4	12.0	11.5	6.1	5.0	6.2	35.9	3.6
City of Kingston upon Hull UA	15.6	11.8	10.9	10.8	8.6	6.6	9.4	59.3	10.1
North East Lincolnshire UA	14.5	11.7	10.9	11.1	9.0	5.9	7.6	52.3	7.2
North Lincolnshire UA	13.0	10.3	11.2	10.8	10.0	7.3	7.5	44.2	5.5
York UA	12.3	10.4	11.6	9.9	9.5	6.5	5.8	38.7	3.8
North Yorkshire	11.8	10.3	12.4	11.3	7.0	4.8	6.7	31.5	2.8
South Yorkshire (Met. County)	13.7	11.2	11.7	11.0	9.5	6.6	8.6	46.7	6.3
West Yorkshire (Met. County)	14.5	12.5	11.2	10.2	9.4	7.5	9.3	39.1	5.9
The Humber	13.7	10.7	11.3	11.1	8.2	6.1	7.7	48.0	6.6
Former county of North Yorkshire	11.8	10.3	12.2	11.0	7.6	5.2	6.5	33.2	3.0
East Midlands	13.4	11.2	10.9	10.6	7.9	5.7	7.8	40.3	4.3
Derby UA	15.4	12.8	11.8	10.4	8.9	6.5	8.8	43.0	8.1
Leicester UA	16.5	13.8	11.3	10.3	12.1	8.3	10.5	40.4	6.3
Nottingham UA	15.8	11.9	11.1	10.4	7.0	6.9	10.3	56.6	8.9
Rutland UA	9.8	9.1	8.7	8.0	4.1	4.1	5.4	25.3	1.0
Derbyshire	12.8	10.7	11.6	11.0	7.9	5.4	7.1	40.6	4.0
Leicestershire	12.5	10.9	9.4	9.5	8.1	4.5	7.1	32.4	2.0
Lincolnshire	11.7	10.1	11.8	11.9	7.7	5.7	7.2	39.9	3.9
Northamptonshire	14.0	12.0	10.3	9.7	7.4	5.6	7.4	39.2	4.1
Nottinghamshire	12.9	10.6	10.6	10.9	6.2	5.1	7.5	40.6	3.2
Former county of Derbyshire	13.4	11.2	11.6	10.9	8.2	5.7	7.6	41.2	5.1
Former county of Leicestershire	13.7	11.7	10.0	9.7	9.5	5.9	8.3	35.1	3.4
Former county of Nottinghamshire	13.7	10.9	10.8	10.8	6.5	5.7	8.4	45.4	4.9

14.2 *(continued)*

	Live births[2] per 1,000 population		Deaths[2] per 1,000 population		Perinatal mortality rate[4]	Infant mortality rate[5]	Percentage of live births under 2.5 kg	Percentage of live births outside marriage	Children looked after by LAs per 1,000 population aged under 18
	1991	1999	1991	1999	1998–2000	1998–2000	1999	1999	2000[6]
West Midlands	14.1	11.9	10.8	10.6	9.6	6.8	8.5	39.3	5.2
County of Herefordshire UA	..	10.3	..	11.3	6.4	3.7	6.9	36.6	5.3
Stoke-on-Trent UA	14.3	11.5	12.1	11.7	10.6	8.5	8.5	50.5	6.0
Telford and Wrekin UA	15.5	13.4	8.8	8.9	9.8	7.3	6.0	45.8	4.1
Shropshire	12.1	10.3	11.3	11.3	6.5	4.2	6.6	34.0	3.1
Staffordshire	12.9	10.4	10.3	10.4	9.3	5.8	7.7	36.8	3.2
Warwickshire	12.5	10.9	10.5	10.8	7.5	5.4	7.2	34.0	3.1
West Midlands (Met. County)	15.2	13.0	11.0	10.6	10.5	7.6	9.5	40.8	6.2
Worcestershire	..	11.0	..	10.3	8.9	5.4	7.6	35.3	5.4
Herefordshire and Worcestershire	12.6	10.8	10.7	10.5	8.4	4.9	7.4	35.6	5.3
Former county of Shropshire	13.3	11.4	10.4	10.5	7.8	5.5	6.3	38.9	3.5
Former county of Staffordshire	13.2	10.7	10.7	10.7	9.6	6.5	7.9	40.3	3.9
East	13.3	11.6	10.3	10.1	7.2	4.7	6.7	34.3	4.2
Luton UA	18.5	15.6	8.8	8.1	11.2	8.2	8.9	30.0	6.2
Peterborough UA	15.8	13.9	8.8	9.2	8.8	5.6	8.9	37.2	10.1
Southend-on-Sea UA	13.8	11.3	14.2	12.2	7.2	4.7	7.3	44.9	6.6
Thurrock UA	15.7	14.1	9.4	9.1	7.8	5.9	5.5	44.4	5.6
Bedfordshire	13.6	12.2	9.1	8.8	7.1	4.3	7.1	32.9	4.1
Cambridgeshire	13.0	10.7	9.3	8.8	5.8	4.2	6.2	29.7	3.2
Essex	13.0	11.4	10.3	10.3	7.1	4.2	6.2	35.0	4.2
Hertfordshire	13.6	12.4	9.5	9.3	6.3	4.2	6.3	29.9	3.4
Norfolk	11.6	10.1	12.1	11.9	6.7	5.1	7.1	39.0	4.1
Suffolk	12.8	10.7	11.2	10.9	8.2	4.8	7.0	35.3	3.5
Former county of Bedfordshire	15.2	13.3	9.0	8.6	8.6	5.8	7.8	31.8	4.8
Former county of Cambridgeshire	13.6	11.4	9.2	8.9	6.6	4.6	6.9	31.7	4.8
Former county of Essex	13.3	11.6	10.6	10.4	7.2	4.4	6.2	37.0	4.6
London	15.4	14.5	10.0	8.5	9.0	5.8	8.0	35.1	6.3
Inner London	16.4	15.9	9.8	7.6	10.1	6.5	8.5	37.4	9.2
Outer London	14.7	13.6	10.1	9.0	8.2	5.3	7.6	33.4	4.8
South East	13.0	11.6	10.8	10.2	6.8	4.5	6.8	33.6	4.1
Bracknell Forest UA	15.2	13.7	8.6	7.5	6.5	2.6	7.3	28.8	2.3
Brighton and Hove UA	12.1	11.0	13.9	11.4	6.7	5.8	7.4	45.5	7.1
Isle of Wight UA	10.6	8.9	15.5	14.1	8.1	3.4	6.8	44.9	6.7
Medway UA	15.6	13.4	8.7	9.3	7.0	5.3	7.3	42.5	5.7
Milton Keynes UA	17.1	14.2	7.2	7.3	8.3	6.1	7.6	43.0	..
Portsmouth UA	14.2	11.7	12.0	11.2	8.8	7.0	7.2	46.3	5.4
Reading UA	14.2	14.2	12.0	7.8	8.2	5.7	7.1	41.3	4.0
Slough UA	18.2	16.2	7.8	8.3	9.7	5.4	9.7	29.9	4.9
Southampton UA	13.8	11.7	11.1	10.1	7.1	5.2	8.3	46.5	8.2
West Berkshire UA (Newbury)	13.8	12.6	11.1	8.0	8.1	5.4	6.0	31.3	3.8
Windsor and Maidenhead UA	12.4	12.3	9.8	9.2	7.5	5.5	7.1	24.7	2.8
Wokingham UA	12.7	12.2	6.8	7.6	7.4	5.2	5.6	22.9	2.5
Buckinghamshire	13.3	12.1	8.8	8.8	5.7	4.7	6.6	24.4	2.3
East Sussex	11.2	9.9	15.5	13.9	8.2	5.4	6.7	38.7	4.4
Hampshire	12.7	11.3	9.5	9.6	6.3	4.2	6.4	31.9	3.2
Kent	13.0	11.4	11.7	11.0	6.5	4.0	6.6	39.4	4.9
Oxfordshire	13.7	11.7	8.8	8.5	5.8	4.5	6.7	28.1	3.3
Surrey	12.3	11.6	10.4	9.9	6.3	4.1	6.4	25.5	2.8
West Sussex	11.7	10.5	13.5	12.4	6.6	3.7	6.7	30.9	4.6
Former county of Berkshire	14.3	13.4	8.5	8.1	7.9	5.0	7.1	30.2	3.4
Former county of Buckinghamshire	14.3	12.7	8.4	8.4	6.6	5.1	7.0	30.7	3.5
Former county of East Sussex	11.5	10.3	15.0	13.1	7.6	5.6	7.0	41.2	5.2
Former county of Hampshire	13.1	11.4	10.0	9.9	6.7	4.7	6.7	35.5	4.1
Former county of Kent	13.4	11.7	11.2	10.7	6.5	4.3	6.7	39.9	5.0

14.2 *(continued)*

	Live births[2] per 1,000 population		Deaths[2] per 1,000 population		Perinatal mortality rate[4] 1998–2000	Infant mortality rate[5] 1998–2000	Percent-age of live births under 2.5 kg 1999	Percent-age of live births outside marriage 1999	Children looked after by LAs per 1,000 population aged under 18 2000[6]
	1991	1999	1991	1999					
South West	12.2	10.6	11.9	11.4	7.2	4.7	6.8	37.2	4.5
Bath and North East									
Somerset UA	11.1	9.9	11.4	10.9	6.6	4.1	6.5	34.7	4.3
Bournemouth UA	11.1	9.9	16.0	14.9	7.4	5.1	7.7	42.6	6.7
City of Bristol UA	13.9	12.1	11.2	9.9	8.4	5.5	7.7	45.7	6.3
North Somerset UA	11.0	10.2	12.2	11.7	6.5	5.8	6.1	34.2	3.8
Plymouth UA	13.8	10.7	10.6	10.0	6.4	5.1	7.7	46.0	7.2
Poole UA	12.2	10.5	12.7	11.9	7.3	4.6	5.7	35.6	4.8
South Gloucestershire UA	13.9	12.1	8.4	8.2	5.5	3.5	5.9	30.0	2.5
Swindon UA	15.1	13.1	9.5	9.0	7.5	5.3	8.6	38.6	4.2
Torbay UA	10.6	10.0	15.6	14.9	6.8	4.9	7.2	45.2	8.5
Cornwall and the Isles of Scilly	11.5	9.9	12.9	12.3	7.5	3.8	6.5	40.8	5.4
Devon	11.2	9.6	13.2	12.7	6.4	4.8	6.1	36.6	4.8
Dorset	10.6	8.6	13.0	12.6	7.8	4.1	6.8	33.5	3.4
Gloucestershire	12.6	11.1	10.8	10.8	7.2	4.9	6.8	36.1	4.0
Somerset	12.1	10.2	11.9	11.7	7.5	4.8	6.6	36.3	3.0
Wiltshire	12.9	11.7	10.5	9.8	8.3	4.6	6.5	28.7	2.6
Bristol/Bath area	12.9	11.4	10.8	10.0	7.1	4.8	6.8	38.1	4.5
Former county of Devon	11.8	9.9	12.9	12.3	6.5	4.9	6.6	40.0	5.8
Former county of Dorset	11.1	9.3	13.7	13.0	7.6	4.5	6.8	36.3	4.4
Former county of Wiltshire	13.5	12.1	10.2	9.5	8.1	4.8	7.2	31.9	3.1

1 Births and deaths are based on the usual area of residence of the mother/deceased. See Notes and Definitions to the Population chapter for details of the inclusion/exclusion of births to non-resident mothers and deaths of non-resident persons.
2 Births data are on the basis of year of occurrence in England and Wales and year of registration in Scotland and Northern Ireland. All deaths data relate to year of registration.
3 Counties and Unitary Authorities in existence from 1 April 1998. See Notes and Definitions.
4 Still births and deaths of infants under 1 week of age per 1,000 live and still births.
5 Death of infants under 1 year of age per 1,000 live births.
6 At 31 March. Under 18 mid-1999 population estimates used.

Source: Office for National Statistics; Department of Health

14.3 Education and training: by sub-region[1]

	Three and four year olds in early years education[2]			Pupil/teacher ratio[6] 2000/01 (numbers)		Pupils and students participating in post-compulsory education[7] (percentages) 1998/99	Percentage of pupils in last year of compulsory schooling[8,9] 1999/00 with		Average A/AS level points score[9,10] 1999/00
	Participation rates[3] (percentages)						5 or more GCSE Grades A*–C/		
	All schools Jan. 2000[5]	Private and voluntary providers[4] Jan. 2000[5]	All providers Jan. 2000[5]	Primary schools	Secondary schools		No graded results	Standard Grades 1–3 (or equivalent)	
United Kingdom	63	27	90	22.3	16.5	78	5.2	48.6	18.1
England	63	30	93	22.9	17.1	77	5.0	47.1	18.2
North East	86	9	95	22.6	17.0	69	6.4	41.7	17.3
Darlington UA	89	19	108	24.5	16.9	66	4.4	45.0	20.0
Hartlepool UA	96	4	101	23.9	17.5	74	6.8	35.7	19.5
Middlesbrough UA	93	6	99	23.3	16.2	64	9.6	34.6	14.9
Redcar & Cleveland UA	103	5	107	24.2	16.5	68	5.7	45.6	-
Stockton-on-Tees UA	95	6	101	23.1	17.3	77	4.5	43.7	19.5
Durham	81	8	88	22.2	17.2	69	6.2	40.4	17.8
Northumberland	80	12	92	22.8	18.6	72	5.2	49.7	17.9
Tyne and Wear	84	9	93	22.1	16.5	67	7.0	40.2	16.4
Tees Valley	..	..	..	..	..	70	6.2	41.2	19.1
Tees Valley less Darlington	..	..	..	..	..	72	6.4	40.6	19.0
Former county of Durham	..	..	..	..	..	68	5.9	41.2	17.9
North West	71	24	95	22.9	16.6	73	5.2	45.7	19.4
Blackburn with Darwen UA	69	22	91	22.2	16.2	82	6.7	40.0	21.5
Blackpool UA	51	48	99	23.7	17.3	73	6.3	36.1	19.9
Halton UA	61	32	93	21.5	16.3	63	3.7	37.7	14.1
Warrington UA	60	35	96	23.1	17.0	76	2.7	50.5	18.6
Cheshire	57	48	106	22.9	16.9	83	3.4	57.0	20.3
Cumbria	68	26	94	22.0	16.8	76	4.3	50.6	19.3
Greater Manchester (Met. County)	76	17	93	23.1	16.6	69	5.2	43.4	19.9
Lancashire	59	31	90	23.7	16.9	76	4.3	49.6	21.6
Merseyside (Met. County)	80	15	96	22.5	16.2	74	7.3	41.5	17.9
Former county of Cheshire	..	..	..	..	..	79	3.3	52.9	19.6
Former county of Lancashire	..	..	..	..	..	76	4.8	47.4	21.5
Yorkshire and the Humber	73	20	94	23.1	17.3	73	6.5	42.2	18.5
East Riding of Yorkshire UA	63	41	104	24.7	17.9	79	4.7	49.9	17.3
City of Kingston upon Hull UA	75	15	90	23.8	18.7	63	10.5	24.4	19.1
North East Lincolnshire UA	75	21	96	23.4	18.8	71	6.7	35.8	13.8
North Lincolnshire UA	66	27	93	23.9	18.2	76	3.0	43.8	16.5
York UA	69	36	105	22.9	16.6	81	4.4	52.6	22.1
North Yorkshire	58	40	97	22.5	16.6	83	2.7	59.4	21.3
South Yorkshire (Met. County)	71	16	87	23.4	17.2	66	7.6	39.0	18.7
West Yorkshire (Met. County)	80	15	95	22.7	17.2	75	7.1	40.1	17.4
The Humber	..	..	..	..	..	72	6.3	39.1	16.9
Former county of North Yorkshire	..	..	..	..	..	82	3.1	57.9	21.4
East Midlands	63	32	95	23.5	17.3	74	5.5	46.0	18.0
Derby UA	77	21	98	23.7	17.1	68	6.5	41.3	16.9
Leicester UA	73	18	91	22.7	16.7	82	7.2	34.1	14.8
Nottingham UA	81	14	95	22.4	16.1	63	11.0	28.7	18.1
Rutland UA	52	48	100	21.7	17.1	93	0.5	61.6	-
Derbyshire	73	28	101	24.2	17.5	68	4.0	50.0	19.1
Leicestershire	32	59	91	23.2	17.8	80	4.6	48.5	17.3
Lincolnshire	58	34	91	23.9	17.2	72	4.9	52.7	21.3
Northamptonshire	59	37	97	22.9	17.4	75	5.7	47.8	16.7
Nottinghamshire	69	24	93	24.0	17.5	77	5.5	44.3	16.5

14.3 (continued)

| | Three and four year olds in early years education[2] | | | Pupil/teacher ratio[6] 2000/01 (numbers) | | Pupils and students participating in post-compulsory education[7] (percentages) 1998/99 | Percentage of pupils in last year of compulsory schooling[8,9] 1999/00 with | | |
| | Participation rates[3] (percentages) | | | | | | | | |
	All schools Jan. 2000[5]	Private and voluntary providers[4] Jan. 2000[5]	All providers Jan. 2000[5]	Primary schools	Secondary schools		No graded results	5 or more GCSE Grades A*–C/ Standard Grades 1–3 (or equivalent)	Average A/AS level points score[9,10] 1999/00
Former county of Derbyshire	..	..	..	..	..	68	4.6	47.7	18.8
Former county of Leicestershire	..	..	..	..	..	81	5.2	44.4	17.0
Former county of Nottinghamshire	..	..	..	..	..	73	6.8	40.7	16.6
West Midlands	70	22	91	23.1	17.1	75	5.3	44.8	17.9
County of Herefordshire UA	49	51	99	22.5	17.1	72	3.8	53.4	16.1
Stoke-on-Trent UA	78	5	83	24.3	17.4	60	6.1	33.8	18.1
Telford and Wrekin UA	53	27	80	24.1	16.8	75	5.0	48.1	24.5
Shropshire	43	57	100	22.8	17.3	83	3.0	56.4	17.2
Staffordshire	65	21	86	23.7	17.6	79	4.3	48.1	18.2
Warwickshire	58	38	96	23.0	17.2	77	4.8	49.5	18.9
West Midlands (Met. County)	79	12	91	22.8	16.6	73	5.9	41.4	17.3
Worcestershire	56	41	97	22.9	18.3	85	5.8	48.2	17.9
Herefordshire and Worcestershire	..	..	..	..	..	82	5.3	49.3	17.8
Former county of Shropshire	..	..	..	..	..	80	3.8	53.1	20.0
Former county of Staffordshire	..	..	..	..	..	74	4.7	44.9	18.2
East	54	37	91	22.8	17.4	79	4.5	50.7	18.4
Luton UA	60	16	75	22.9	17.9	73	3.2	39.7	16.2
Peterborough UA	43	48	91	23.0	17.2	78	6.0	41.8	18.2
Southend-on-Sea UA	51	44	95	23.5	16.8	77	5.4	53.3	21.7
Thurrock UA	46	38	83	22.8	18.9	69	6.3	39.7	-
Bedfordshire	61	33	93	22.9	18.8	85	4.8	49.4	18.0
Cambridgeshire	47	38	85	24.1	18.7	78	5.1	51.7	16.3
Essex	44	51	95	22.9	17.5	74	4.1	50.8	19.5
Hertfordshire	72	21	93	23.0	16.7	92	4.2	55.4	18.3
Norfolk	54	46	100	22.1	16.9	74	5.0	48.2	18.1
Suffolk	48	33	81	22.0	17.1	77	3.8	53.3	17.4
Former county of Bedfordshire	..	..	..	..	..	81	4.2	46.1	17.9
Former county of Cambridgeshire	..	..	..	..	..	78	5.3	48.9	17.1
Former county of Essex	..	..	..	..	..	74	4.4	50.1	19.9
London	69	18	87	22.5	16.6	78	3.9	45.5	16.8
Inner London	73	13	87	21.9	15.9	74	4.0	36.4	15.7
Outer London	66	20	87	22.9	16.9	80	3.9	49.8	17.2
South East	47	47	94	22.9	17.4	79	4.4	52.1	18.2
Bracknell Forest UA	33	48	81	23.7	17.0	81	3.9	46.6	15.6
Brighton and Hove UA	59	36	94	21.6	16.5	76	6.9	43.7	14.3
Isle of Wight UA	42	65	107	21.6	17.8	82	6.0	44.8	16.3
Medway UA	43	50	93	23.4	17.3	77	4.9	43.7	17.5
Milton Keynes UA	45	35	79	23.3	17.3	64	6.4	41.0	17.4
Portsmouth UA	50	39	89	22.7	17.9	76	7.5	34.0	14.4
Reading UA	54	35	88	23.2	16.0	74	10.4	45.7	19.7
Slough UA	73	10	82	23.0	16.5	79	3.9	51.4	20.2
Southampton UA	47	41	88	22.8	16.3	76	5.2	39.8	16.3
West Berkshire UA (Newbury)	47	53	100	22.5	16.6	83	3.8	56.0	18.2
Windsor and Maidenhead UA	53	36	89	22.5	17.5	80	2.4	59.2	16.3
Wokingham UA	37	69	106	23.1	16.6	82	3.7	59.9	16.8

14.3 *(continued)*

	Three and four year olds in early years education[2]			Pupil/teacher ratio[6] 2000/01 (numbers)		Pupils and students participating in post-compulsory education[7] (percentages) 1998/99	Percentage of pupils in last year of compulsory schooling[8,9] 1999/00 with		
	Participation rates[3] (percentages)							5 or more GCSE Grades A*–C/	Average A/AS level
	All schools Jan. 2000[5]	Private and voluntary providers[4] Jan. 2000[5]	All providers Jan. 2000[5]	Primary schools	Secondary schools		No graded results	Standard Grades 1–3 (or equivalent)	points score[9,10] 1999/00
Buckinghamshire	48	41	89	22.8	18.3	81	4.2	61.6	20.9
East Sussex	49	42	91	22.7	17.1	79	3.9	51.0	16.1
Hampshire	43	57	100	23.0	17.6	75	3.6	54.9	20.0
Kent	44	54	98	23.4	17.4	81	4.1	51.3	19.3
Oxfordshire	39	51	90	22.3	17.8	77	5.2	50.3	17.0
Surrey	58	35	93	22.8	17.6	82	4.3	57.6	16.9
West Sussex	44	51	95	22.5	17.0	81	3.9	54.5	17.3
Former county of Berkshire	..	..	..	..	..	80	4.4	54.3	17.7
Former county of Buckinghamshire	..	..	..	..	..	75	4.9	55.4	20.2
Former county of East Sussex	..	..	..	..	..	78	4.8	48.7	15.7
Former county of Hampshire	..	..	..	..	..	75	4.2	50.6	19.4
Former county of Kent	..	..	..	..	..	80	4.2	50.0	19.0
South West	49	51	100	23.0	17.5	79	4.3	51.4	18.7
Bath and North East Somerset UA	54	55	110	22.4	16.9	96	3.1	57.1	16.4
Bournemouth UA	45	48	94	23.3	17.6	86	5.6	48.1	21.3
City of Bristol UA	73	19	92	22.5	15.7	68	10.4	31.2	14.3
North Somerset UA	47	64	111	24.0	17.6	78	3.8	53.4	17.8
Plymouth UA	53	46	99	23.4	17.1	77	4.3	47.5	18.6
Poole UA	35	46	81	23.7	16.8	87	3.0	59.5	22.3
South Gloucestershire UA	47	56	103	23.4	16.7	81	3.8	47.7	18.1
Swindon UA	47	48	95	24.0	17.2	71	6.1	44.1	18.4
Torbay UA	66	44	110	23.7	17.0	84	5.5	50.3	21.8
Cornwall and the Isles of Scilly	54	38	93	22.9	17.9	80	3.3	52.7	16.8
Devon	50	56	106	23.1	17.7	77	3.8	49.1	18.0
Dorset	43	61	103	22.7	18.5	78	4.4	54.6	17.6
Gloucestershire	40	65	105	22.3	17.2	83	3.0	56.9	20.4
Somerset	46	59	105	22.9	18.5	78	3.2	55.3	17.7
Wiltshire	43	51	94	22.8	17.5	77	4.4	55.5	19.3
Bristol/Bath area	..	..	..	..	..	78	5.6	45.8	17.0
Former county of Devon	..	..	..	..	..	78	4.2	48.8	18.9
Former county of Dorset	..	..	..	..	..	81	4.4	54.2	19.6
Former county of Wiltshire	..	..	..	..	..	75	4.9	51.9	19.2

1 Local government structure as at 1 April 1998. See Notes and Definitions.
2 Headcounts of children aged three and four at 31st December in the previous calendar year. Numbers of three and four year olds in schools may include some two year olds. These figures must be interpreted carefully in the light of differing types of education providers between the countries. In the UK figures any child attending more than one provider in England may have been counted twice.
3 Figures relate to all pupils as a percentage of the three and four year old population. As some pupils are aged two, this can lead to participation rates greater than 100 per cent.
4 Includes some Local Authority providers (other than schools) registered to receive nursery education grants.
5 Provisional data for 2000/01 are shown in Table 4.2.
6 Public sector schools only. Data for 2000/01 are provisional.
7 Pupils and students aged 16 in education as a percentage of the 16 year old population (ages measured at the beginning of the academic year). Provisional data for England for 1999/00 are shown in DfES SFR 30/2001.
8 Pupils in their last year of compulsory schooling as a percentage of the school population of the same age.
9 Figures relate to maintained schools only; hence they are not directly comparable with those in Tables 4.5, 16.3 and 17.3 which are for all schools.
10 Figure for United Kingdom relates to England and Wales average.

Source: Department for Education and Skills

14.4 Housing and households: by local authority[1]

	Housing completions[2] 1999–00 (numbers)			Households 1999				Local authority tenants: average	
	Private enterprise	Registered Social Landlords, Local Authorities, etc	Stock of dwellings 1991[3] (thousands)	All households (thousands)	Average household size (number of people)	Lone parents[4] as a percentage of all households	One-person households as a percentage of all households	weekly unrebated rent per dwelling (£) April 1999[5]	Council Tax (£)[6] April 1999
England	124,259	17,396	19,671	20,743	2.36	5.9	29.6	43.80	798
North East	6,565	801	1,074	1,089	2.34	6.9	30.8	36.80	895
Darlington UA	390	48	..	42	2.35	6.1	31.2	37.20	688
Hartlepool UA	502	117	..	38	2.41	7.5	29.1	37.60	978
Middlesbrough UA	204	41	..	58	2.44	10.6	29.7	43.20	806
Redcar & Cleveland UA	186	38	..	57	2.36	6.6	29.1	40.80	1,033
Stockton-on-Tees UA	919	93	..	75	2.41	6.8	29.1	39.30	853
Durham	1,336	88	..	212	2.36	6.0	28.8	37.70	896
Chester-le-Street	33	9	22	25	2.32	4.9	27.5	35.00	830
Derwentside	256	40	36	37	2.33	6.9	29.6	39.20	900
Durham	306	0	33	37	2.46	5.6	28.6	39.20	848
Easington	185	24	41	39	2.38	6.3	29.7	38.30	951
Sedgefield	338	15	37	38	2.35	6.4	27.7	36.40	967
Teesdale	58	0	11	11	2.32	3.0	30.1	36.80	845
Wear Valley	160	0	27	27	2.31	6.5	29.2	37.20	869
Northumberland	1,013	107	129	129	2.35	4.6	28.9	34.30	898
Alnwick	115	39	14	13	2.34	5.0	27.2	37.50	901
Berwick-upon-Tweed	46	0	13	12	2.20	3.4	34.8	37.00	893
Blyth Valley	..	..	33	34	2.34	5.1	28.7	31.80	883
Castle Morpeth	120	6	20	20	2.40	3.8	27.8	38.90	908
Tynedale	159	40	24	24	2.38	4.5	28.9	40.00	903
Wansbeck	195	0	26	26	2.39	5.1	28.1	30.50	902
Tyne and Wear	2,016	269	474	477	2.30	7.4	32.8	35.60	906
Gateshead	281	26	86	87	2.26	6.6	32.8	35.50	962
Newcastle-upon-Tyne	276	95	120	119	2.28	8.1	36.3	36.70	978
North Tyneside	871	39	84	86	2.22	6.4	32.9	32.20	905
South Tyneside	37	32	66	66	2.28	8.2	33.4	31.70	884
Sunderland	518	76	118	119	2.40	7.7	29.0	38.80	815
Tees Valley	2,201	337	..	..	..	..	..	..	873
Tees Valley less Darlington	1,811	289	222	229	2.41	7.8	29.2	..	908
Former county of Durham	1,726	136	249	254	2.36	6.0	29.2	..	860
North West	15,913	2,772	2,222	2,852	2.38	7.1	30.0	40.60	901
Blackburn with Darwen UA	312	0	..	54	2.54	8.0	28.4	48.00	915
Blackpool UA	113	36	..	64	2.23	5.5	33.3	35.10	683
Halton UA	257	9	..	49	2.47	10.2	26.5	34.50	679
Warrington UA	490	29	..	80	2.36	7.0	29.5	37.80	730
Cheshire	2,388	331	..	278	2.38	4.1	27.3	37.30	865
Chester	281	0	49	50	2.33	5.0	31.0	38.40	866
Congleton	374	25	34	36	2.43	2.8	25.9	.	860
Crewe and Nantwich	600	12	43	47	2.41	4.0	27.1	38.10	865
Ellesmere Port and Neston	173	0	32	33	2.41	5.5	26.0	29.70	876
Macclesfield	246	65	63	65	2.31	3.8	27.7	40.30	858
Vale Royal	610	193	45	48	2.45	3.8	25.3	39.90	872
Cumbria	1,123	95	210	210	2.30	4.1	30.6	39.20	868
Allerdale	109	17	41	40	2.32	3.8	31.8	.	856
Barrow-in-Furness	107	13	31	30	2.33	5.3	29.8	43.40	893
Carlisle	303	13	43	44	2.29	4.4	30.6	38.00	883
Copeland	146	34	29	29	2.37	5.5	29.1	38.30	865
Eden	149	10	20	21	2.33	3.0	27.9	.	860
South Lakeland	309	8	46	45	2.23	3.0	32.4	39.20	856

14.4 *(continued)*

	Housing completions[2] 1999–00 (numbers)		Stock of dwellings 1991[3] (thousands)	Households 1999				Local authority tenants: average weekly unrebated rent per dwelling (£) April 1999[5]	Council Tax (£)[6] April 1999
	Private enterprise	Registered Social Landlords, Local Authorities, etc		All households (thousands)	Average household size (number of people)	Lone parents[4] as a percentage of all households	One-person households as a percentage of all households		
Greater Manchester (Met. County)	5,235	1,296	1,051	1,071	2.38	7.8	30.8	40.60	885
Bolton	569	235	106	111	2.39	6.3	29.8	35.40	889
Bury	246	54	72	76	2.39	5.6	29.0	39.70	811
Manchester	1,110	631	184	179	2.37	13.5	36.0	47.60	987
Oldham	444	33	89	90	2.40	7.5	29.9	35.50	929
Rochdale	443	65	84	86	2.42	7.9	29.9	37.50	871
Salford	469	55	98	95	2.33	8.7	34.1	40.80	980
Stockport	337	61	117	124	2.34	5.9	29.6	34.80	917
Tameside	282	83	90	91	2.39	6.3	28.6	41.40	899
Trafford	169	69	87	91	2.39	6.5	30.2	40.00	689
Wigan	1,117	10	123	129	2.40	5.5	27.5	35.80	835
Lancashire	3,087	252	..	470	2.38	6.1	29.2	38.80	914
Burnley	241	8	38	37	2.39	8.6	29.3	41.60	948
Chorley	448	19	38	40	2.41	5.7	25.4	32.50	897
Fylde	217	27	31	33	2.20	3.6	32.5	35.50	885
Hyndburn	212	0	33	32	2.41	7.3	29.3	40.70	940
Lancaster	109	126	53	57	2.37	6.4	31.0	39.00	884
Pendle	190	0	36	34	2.39	6.3	31.2	37.80	947
Preston	266	8	52	55	2.39	7.3	33.1	41.10	959
Ribble Valley	125	0	21	21	2.45	3.6	27.8	35.90	898
Rossendale	105	28	27	26	2.39	6.2	27.8	39.40	944
South Ribble	411	22	40	42	2.44	4.9	24.9	.	890
West Lancashire	326	4	42	45	2.43	6.8	26.4	37.80	911
Wyre	319	5	43	45	2.29	4.5	30.2	.	895
Merseyside (Met. County)	2,908	724	575	577	2.40	9.0	30.5	42.90	1,020
Knowsley	..	..	57	60	2.53	14.8	25.6	44.90	970
Liverpool	913	307	194	187	2.42	9.8	33.1	41.10	1,172
St Helens	397	71	71	73	2.43	5.7	25.0	43.20	920
Sefton	388	29	116	119	2.36	7.3	31.0	41.60	967
Wirral	485	200	136	138	2.32	8.5	31.6	46.20	977
Former county of Cheshire	3,135	369	386	407	2.39	5.4	27.6	..	822
Former county of Lancashire	3,512	288	574	588	2.38	6.2	29.6	..	891
Yorkshire and the Humber	12,310	1,232	2,025	2,106	2.36	5.9	29.6	..	810
East Riding of Yorkshire UA	1,118	5	..	131	2.38	3.8	26.8	36.20	857
City of Kingston upon Hull UA	221	0	..	108	2.35	7.9	33.3	35.20	794
North East Lincolnshire UA	464	13	..	65	2.37	7.3	27.6	36.70	865
North Lincolnshire UA	551	0	..	63	2.40	5.4	25.8	34.70	997
York UA	635	115	..	75	2.33	4.5	30.0	41.50	695
North Yorkshire	1,502	79	..	237	2.34	4.1	28.7	42.10	754
Craven	187	0	22	22	2.31	4.6	30.5	42.70	760
Hambleton	198	26	32	35	2.43	3.2	26.2	.	695
Harrogate	509	8	60	63	2.32	4.4	29.4	45.30	765
Richmondshire	103	0	19	19	2.43	3.9	27.6	41.40	772
Ryedale	102	13	39	20	2.35	2.7	27.9	.	779
Scarborough	131	26	49	48	2.22	5.1	32.1	41.60	757
Selby	268	3	36	29	2.43	3.9	24.7	39.20	772
South Yorkshire (Met. County)	2,426	405	528	547	2.36	5.9	29.2	32.80	828
Barnsley	641	0	91	94	2.41	5.8	26.1	32.50	801
Doncaster	843	42	116	120	2.38	6.0	27.1	33.30	761
Rotherham	588	232	101	105	2.39	5.9	27.1	30.20	809
Sheffield	354	131	221	228	2.31	5.8	32.6	33.90	886

14.4 *(continued)*

	Housing completions[2] 1999–00 (numbers)		Stock of dwellings 1991[3] (thousands)	Households 1999				Local authority tenants: average weekly unrebated rent per dwelling (£) April 1999[5]	Council Tax (£)[6] April 1999
	Private enterprise	Registered Social Landlords, Local Authorities, etc		All households (thousands)	Average household size (number of people)	Lone parents[4] as a percentage of all households	One-person households as a percentage of all households		
West Yorkshire (Met. County)	5,393	577	840	881	2.37	6.4	30.4	35.80	804
Bradford	1,029	243	183	192	2.48	7.3	29.7	37.50	808
Calderdale	369	64	81	82	2.32	5.9	30.3	35.90	876
Kirklees	555	35	155	163	2.39	6.2	30.3	40.20	870
Leeds	1,823	129	293	311	2.31	6.9	31.8	34.20	768
Wakefield	1,208	67	127	133	2.38	4.9	28.4	34.50	756
The Humber	2,354	56	356	367	2.37	5.9	28.7	..	867
Former county of North Yorkshire	2,137	194	301	312	2.34	4.2	29.0	..	741
East Midlands	15,199	1,193	1,638	1,732	2.39	5.2	27.5	38.10	834
Derby UA	407	0	..	98	2.39	6.6	30.0	37.00	787
Leicester UA	429	306	..	114	2.53	8.7	30.9	42.90	792
Nottingham UA	270	44	..	118	2.37	10.0	31.9	35.80	886
Rutland UA	111	0	..	14	2.47	5.5	23.9	45.20	945
Derbyshire	2,718	155	..	310	2.36	4.1	27.4	35.20	873
Amber Valley	237	15	47	50	2.34	3.7	26.9	39.60	873
Bolsover	355	1	29	29	2.41	3.9	25.2	32.00	905
Chesterfield	169	26	43	43	2.28	4.3	31.1	33.20	855
Derbyshire Dales	222	15	29	30	2.36	3.1	27.1	36.80	878
Erewash	336	32	44	46	2.34	5.0	28.1	34.80	857
High Peak	685	46	35	37	2.38	4.8	27.8	41.70	866
North East Derbyshire	197	20	39	42	2.34	4.0	26.6	32.20	905
South Derbyshire	517	0	29	33	2.45	3.8	24.9	37.40	855
Leicestershire	2,266	93	..	247	2.44	3.8	25.6	37.50	803
Blaby	407	14	32	35	2.48	3.5	22.5	35.50	814
Charnwood	287	60	57	64	2.45	4.2	27.3	35.60	804
Harborough	689	14	27	31	2.44	3.0	26.1	44.50	809
Hinckley and Bosworth	263	0	39	41	2.37	3.5	26.4	40.20	770
Melton	146	0	18	20	2.39	3.6	25.7	35.70	799
North West Leicestershire	362	0	32	35	2.42	4.1	25.8	37.20	828
Oadby and Wigston	79	0	20	21	2.53	4.0	22.8	35.30	802
Lincolnshire	3,510	183	250	265	2.33	4.2	27.3	37.40	787
Boston	156	45	23	23	2.32	3.8	28.1	37.70	789
East Lindsey	493	101	52	54	2.29	3.8	27.7	.	774
Lincoln	267	14	36	36	2.24	6.2	34.2	34.60	801
North Kesteven	948	0	33	37	2.36	4.0	23.5	36.30	798
South Holland	585	0	29	32	2.32	2.9	25.2	40.90	795
South Kesteven	561	14	45	51	2.38	4.8	26.1	39.30	769
West Lindsey	457	4	31	32	2.39	3.8	26.2	37.40	806
Northamptonshire	2,844	187	236	253	2.43	5.3	26.1	40.50	765
Corby	62	0	21	20	2.52	9.6	22.4	38.10	768
Daventry	741	11	25	27	2.46	3.4	23.6	39.10	720
East Northamptonshire	764	0	28	30	2.45	3.7	24.9	38.10	772
Kettering	368	32	32	34	2.41	4.5	26.7	38.80	774
Northampton	411	26	75	80	2.40	5.9	28.6	43.50	790
South Northamptonshire	278	84	28	32	2.46	3.6	23.8	46.30	797
Wellingborough	220	0	28	29	2.38	6.6	27.0	36.40	682

14.4 *(continued)*

| | Housing completions[2] 1999–00 (numbers) | | Stock of dwellings 1991[3] (thousands) | Households 1999 | | | | | Local authority tenants: average weekly unrebated rent per dwelling (£) April 1999[5] | Council Tax (£)[6] April 1999 |
	Private enterprise	Registered Social Landlords, Local Authorities, etc		All households (thousands)	Average household size (number of people)	Lone parents[4] as a percentage of all households	One-person households as a percentage of all households			
Nottinghamshire	2,560	202	..	314	2.36	4.5	27.2		38.80	925
Ashfield	516	20	44	45	2.38	4.7	26.8		37.70	930
Bassetlaw	553	42	42	44	2.37	4.1	26.3		41.00	919
Broxtowe	65	0	45	47	2.32	4.8	27.8		34.60	918
Gedling	245	34	45	47	2.33	3.5	28.1		35.10	909
Mansfield	166	45	42	42	2.38	5.9	26.9		42.30	935
Newark and Sherwood	421	28	42	44	2.39	4.6	26.7		37.60	970
Rushcliffe	578	23	39	44	2.36	3.9	27.9		40.00	900
Former county of Derbyshire	3,125	155	387	408	2.36	4.7	28.0		..	854
Former county of Leicestershire	2,831	406	351	375	2.47	5.3	27.1		..	806
Former county of Nottinghamshire	2,842	262	414	432	2.36	6.0	28.5		..	916
West Midlands	13,151	2,257	2,083	2,167	2.43	5.9	28.1		39.80	812
County of Herefordshire UA	620	132	..	69	2.41	4.1	26.7		38.70	729
Stoke-on-Trent UA	751	6	..	102	2.43	5.8	28.6		39.60	751
Telford and Wrekin UA	952	183	..	59	2.50	6.4	24.4		.	757
Shropshire	892	62	..	117	2.37	3.8	28.0		38.70	791
Bridgnorth	33	6	20	21	2.41	4.1	25.5		40.20	783
North Shropshire	243	13	21	22	2.42	2.3	26.6		35.30	811
Oswestry	112	27	14	15	2.31	3.9	30.8		38.80	805
Shrewsbury and Atcham	342	10	38	41	2.34	4.9	30.1		39.80	776
South Shropshire	159	0	16	17	2.36	2.9	25.7		.	801
Staffordshire	2,609	272	..	327	2.45	4.2	25.0		38.10	760
Cannock Chase	369	26	34	37	2.49	5.0	23.4		42.90	783
East Staffordshire	288	0	40	42	2.44	3.8	26.1		36.30	786
Lichfield	329	72	35	38	2.45	3.2	23.0		.	766
Newcastle-under-Lyme	291	47	49	51	2.43	4.4	28.9		33.50	770
South Staffordshire	178	60	40	42	2.41	3.8	23.4		.	688
Stafford	284	0	47	50	2.46	3.9	25.5		37.30	763
Staffordshire Moorlands	276	0	38	39	2.42	3.4	24.7		38.00	789
Tamworth	335	48	26	29	2.51	6.4	22.8		42.80	736
Warwickshire	2,054	277	197	211	2.39	4.5	27.2		40.30	823
North Warwickshire	66	0	24	25	2.44	4.4	26.3		37.20	870
Nuneaton and Bedworth	426	99	46	48	2.45	5.3	25.3		39.90	851
Rugby	318	24	34	37	2.38	5.1	27.1		40.00	839
Stratford-on-Avon	547	134	44	48	2.34	2.8	28.1		.	790
Warwick	679	18	49	52	2.35	5.1	28.6		42.70	804
West Midlands (Met. County)	3,597	1,065	1,036	1,058	2.46	7.4	30.0		40.10	865
Birmingham	1,203	597	392	404	2.48	9.2	32.3		41.40	893
Coventry	454	55	122	125	2.40	8.2	31.3		37.70	968
Dudley	353	157	123	128	2.42	4.4	27.0		40.00	779
Sandwell	548	30	119	118	2.44	6.0	29.9		44.60	856
Solihull	397	60	78	84	2.43	5.2	26.1		41.70	742
Walsall	381	91	101	104	2.49	5.5	26.5		33.10	803
Wolverhampton	183	57	99	96	2.49	7.9	29.7		37.80	955
Worcestershire	1,546	175	..	224	2.38	4.6	26.2		40.10	735
Bromsgrove	151	42	35	35	2.40	3.0	23.0		37.20	721
Malvern Hills	100	46	36	31	2.37	3.4	27.2		.	728
Redditch	333	87	30	31	2.47	6.6	24.5		41.80	759
Worcester	450	11	34	41	2.31	6.0	28.6		37.60	725
Wychavon	461	4	41	47	2.38	4.2	25.8		.	728
Wyre Forest	151	29	38	40	2.38	4.4	27.6		41.60	757

14.4 *(continued)*

	Housing completions[2] 1999–00 (numbers)			Households 1999				Local authority tenants: average weekly unrebated rent per dwelling (£) April 1999[5]	Council Tax (£)[6] April 1999
	Private enterprise	Registered Social Landlords, Local Authorities, etc	Stock of dwellings 1991[3] (thousands)	All households (thousands)	Average household size (number of people)	Lone parents[4] as a percentage of all households	One-person households as a percentage of all households		
Herefordshire and Worcestershire	2,266	353	274	292	2.39	4.5	26.3	..	734
Former county of Shropshire	1,844	245	165	176	2.41	4.7	26.8	..	781
Former county of Staffordshire	3,360	278	411	429	2.44	4.6	25.8	..	758
East	17,124	1,757	2,098	2,253	2.37	4.7	27.9	45.60	768
Luton UA	144	52	..	73	2.48	6.8	27.6	50.30	707
Peterborough UA	554	8	..	66	2.36	6.9	29.4	47.30	754
Southend-on-Sea UA	109	100	..	78	2.23	6.0	32.2	47.60	677
Thurrock UA	787	16	..	54	2.48	6.1	24.0	46.70	672
Bedfordshire	1,058	156	..	157	2.38	4.5	27.2	46.90	877
Bedford	479	65	54	60	2.35	5.1	29.5	.	864
Mid Bedfordshire	44	0	43	51	2.41	3.3	26.2	44.50	859
South Bedfordshire	272	0	43	46	2.40	5.1	25.4	48.20	912
Cambridgeshire	2,325	115	..	235	2.39	4.4	27.3	47.40	723
Cambridge	127	3	41	52	2.29	6.7	35.6	43.00	737
East Cambridgeshire	172	10	25	30	2.42	2.5	24.9	.	703
Fenland	389	0	32	35	2.34	3.3	27.3	43.50	727
Huntingdonshire	522	23	57	64	2.43	5.1	24.0	53.80	737
South Cambridgeshire	611	22	47	54	2.44	3.0	24.6	49.00	703
Essex	4,874	577	..	543	2.38	4.5	27.7	47.30	786
Basildon	856	313	64	69	2.39	5.7	27.5	48.50	806
Braintree	640	38	49	55	2.37	4.6	27.2	44.30	778
Brentwood	99	0	29	29	2.38	3.6	28.0	50.60	762
Castle Point	98	30	34	35	2.44	3.4	24.1	54.90	797
Chelmsford	457	57	61	64	2.39	4.0	27.1	50.10	781
Colchester	572	32	59	65	2.38	6.0	27.5	45.20	767
Epping Forest	330	19	47	51	2.36	4.0	27.5	48.80	784
Harlow	536	0	30	32	2.39	6.5	29.8	46.60	872
Maldon	340	49	21	23	2.43	3.3	26.2	.	764
Rochford	329	15	29	32	2.45	3.6	25.6	45.20	790
Tendring	335	9	59	60	2.22	3.7	32.9	43.60	769
Uttlesford	265	14	26	28	2.45	3.5	25.0	48.00	783
Hertfordshire	2,821	266	394	427	2.41	4.6	28.0	49.40	763
Broxbourne	449	71	32	34	2.48	3.6	24.0	55.40	723
Dacorum	97	0	53	58	2.36	5.3	29.2	45.90	743
East Hertfordshire	358	9	47	51	2.46	3.0	25.8	49.90	745
Hertsmere	275	0	35	39	2.44	4.7	26.6	.	763
North Hertfordshire	51	8	45	49	2.34	4.1	29.7	55.10	765
St Albans	..	..	50	54	2.40	4.1	28.2	49.80	770
Stevenage	240	12	30	32	2.44	7.0	26.2	47.80	762
Three Rivers	..	..	31	36	2.40	3.9	28.6	50.90	767
Watford	94	5	30	34	2.36	6.4	30.6	57.00	832
Welwyn Hatfield	139	25	39	39	2.44	4.8	29.9	42.60	781
Norfolk	2,429	308	328	340	2.30	4.6	28.4	36.50	779
Breckland	486	59	45	51	2.34	4.3	26.5	.	750
Broadland	582	56	43	49	2.39	3.3	23.6	.	771
Great Yarmouth	214	61	38	38	2.31	5.4	29.9	33.60	775
Kings Lynn and West Norfolk	360	0	57	56	2.34	4.0	27.8	35.00	775
North Norfolk	228	45	45	44	2.25	3.8	29.9	40.40	779
Norwich	93	61	55	56	2.15	7.6	35.3	35.90	818
South Norfolk	466	19	43	46	2.35	3.7	25.4	41.60	788

14.4 *(continued)*

	Housing completions[2] 1999–00 (numbers)			Households 1999				Local authority tenants:	
	Private enterprise	Registered Social Landlords, Local Authorities, etc	Stock of dwellings 1991[3] (thousands)	All households (thousands)	Average household size (number of people)	Lone parents[4] as a percentage of all households	One-person households as a percentage of all households	average weekly unrebated rent per dwelling (£) April 1999[5]	Council Tax (£)[6] April 1999
Suffolk	2,095	199	269	281	2.36	*4.3*	*27.7*	41.60	761
Babergh	237	41	33	34	2.36	*3.6*	*25.9*	45.50	765
Forest Heath	88	19	22	26	2.60	*6.0*	*25.7*	40.70	730
Ipswich	166	56	49	49	2.32	*6.3*	*30.8*	39.30	829
Mid Suffolk	319	8	32	34	2.41	*2.8*	*25.3*	40.00	760
St Edmundsbury	434	32	37	40	2.34	*3.6*	*25.7*	45.00	745
Suffolk Coastal	526	10	47	51	2.35	*3.1*	*28.6*	.	753
Waveney	325	27	47	47	2.29	*4.5*	*29.4*	40.00	730
Former county of Bedfordshire	1,202	208	209	231	2.41	*5.3*	*27.3*	..	829
Former county of Cambridgeshire	2,879	123	267	300	2.38	*4.9*	*27.8*	..	729
Former county of Essex	5,770	693	632	674	2.37	*4.8*	*27.9*	..	767
London	9,336	2,856	2,916	3,122	2.30	*7.9*	*33.9*	..	731
Inner London	4,093	1,266	..	1,272	2.17	*10.3*	*38.7*	63.80	.
Inner London – West	..	..	..	497	2.03	*7.5*	*43.2*	..	.
Camden	157	166	85	90	2.09	*8.1*	*43.8*	59.80	897
City of London	280	21	3	3	1.77	*4.3*	*53.0*	58.60	536
Hammersmith and Fulham	83	23	74	79	2.04	*8.9*	*41.1*	58.00	827
Kensington and Chelsea	208	20	79	90	1.93	*6.8*	*48.7*	68.20	581
Wandsworth	541	76	114	123	2.14	*8.3*	*35.4*	65.60	373
Westminster	424	187	101	112	1.97	*6.0*	*48.0*	74.00	350
Inner London – East	..	..	..	775	2.26	*12.1*	*35.8*	56.10	.
Hackney	299	57	80	87	2.27	*12.9*	*36.9*	56.60	790
Haringey	34	75	88	99	2.24	*10.6*	*35.7*	58.90	898
Islington	424	27	77	81	2.14	*11.6*	*38.6*	60.00	912
Lambeth	9	23	114	128	2.11	*13.8*	*37.2*	57.70	642
Lewisham	156	95	103	109	2.24	*11.5*	*33.1*	52.20	728
Newham	398	120	85	89	2.62	*11.4*	*30.4*	49.40	704
Southwark	279	13	104	106	2.20	*12.7*	*38.0*	54.70	809
Tower Hamlets	..	..	70	77	2.38	*12.1*	*36.9*	58.70	674
Outer London	5,243	1,590	..	1,850	2.39	*6.2*	*30.6*	..	.
Outer London – East and North East	..	..	..	632	2.42	*6.5*	*29.7*	54.60	.
Barking and Dagenham	34	8	60	62	2.48	*7.4*	*30.8*	49.70	738
Bexley	179	27	88	90	2.42	*5.0*	*26.8*	.	750
Enfield	105	84	106	109	2.43	*6.3*	*29.1*	55.60	733
Greenwich	916	64	89	90	2.37	*10.1*	*32.2*	56.30	883
Havering	237	47	92	94	2.43	*4.6*	*26.7*	46.80	790
Redbridge	462	39	92	92	2.49	*4.4*	*29.7*	67.70	750
Waltham Forest	10	186	91	94	2.33	*8.0*	*33.3*	59.50	840
Outer London – South	..	..	..	489	2.34	*5.7*	*30.6*	59.80	.
Bromley	..	..	124	129	2.31	*4.7*	*30.7*	.	670
Croydon	138	194	131	141	2.37	*7.2*	*29.8*	64.20	758
Kingston upon Thames	276	45	57	63	2.35	*4.3*	*32.3*	64.00	794
Merton	199	149	73	80	2.33	*5.9*	*30.1*	54.80	787
Sutton	135	122	72	76	2.31	*5.2*	*30.9*	54.20	749
Outer London – West and North West	..	..	..	729	2.40	*6.3*	*31.4*	61.50	.
Barnet	720	98	121	138	2.43	*5.6*	*31.4*	55.40	761
Brent	..	..	99	103	2.42	*9.7*	*31.7*	72.60	678
Ealing	148	125	113	128	2.39	*7.3*	*32.6*	60.90	703
Harrow	94	3	79	84	2.51	*4.8*	*27.0*	66.80	788
Hillingdon	288	137	94	104	2.42	*5.4*	*29.2*	66.70	764
Hounslow	226	0	83	87	2.42	*6.1*	*30.7*	52.90	795
Richmond-upon-Thames	145	30	73	86	2.22	*4.2*	*36.8*	61.10	834

14.4 *(continued)*

| | Housing completions[2] 1999–00 (numbers) | | | Households 1999 | | | | Local authority tenants: average weekly unrebated rent per dwelling (£) April 1999[5] | Council Tax (£)[6] April 1999 |
	Private enterprise	Registered Social Landlords, Local Authorities, etc	Stock of dwellings 1991[3] (thousands)	All households (thousands)	Average household size (number of people)	Lone parents[4] as a percentage of all households	One-person households as a percentage of all households		
South East	20,351	3,035	3,106	3,346	2.37	4.6	28.4	50.30	764
Bracknell Forest UA	159	3	..	45	2.45	5.3	25.0	52.80	711
Brighton and Hove UA	436	103	..	119	2.12	5.8	37.8	46.10	698
Isle of Wight UA	359	33	..	55	2.26	4.3	30.6	.	793
Medway UA	348	53	..	97	2.48	5.4	24.9	47.10	670
Milton Keynes UA	1,150	283	..	86	2.40	7.0	26.8	39.60	744
Portsmouth UA	162	37	..	78	2.36	7.3	31.6	48.70	682
Reading UA	255	38	..	63	2.30	6.4	32.0	60.90	868
Slough UA	449	0	..	45	2.45	7.5	28.7	53.20	702
Southampton UA	286	47	..	90	2.37	6.4	32.3	42.20	709
West Berkshire UA (Newbury)	..	..	..	58	2.46	3.8	24.9	.	827
Windsor and Maidenhead UA	168	162	..	58	2.40	3.3	28.3	.	744
Wokingham UA	547	7	..	56	2.54	2.9	22.7	50.60	825
Buckinghamshire	1,147	152	..	195	2.44	3.7	25.7	51.90	766
Aylesbury Vale	708	83	57	64	2.44	3.3	25.5	49.00	762
Chiltern	108	0	35	38	2.43	3.9	26.3	.	774
South Buckinghamshire	184	14	25	26	2.44	4.0	24.7	.	757
Wycombe	69	36	61	66	2.45	3.8	26.0	55.40	769
East Sussex	1,177	197	..	217	2.23	4.6	32.4	46.80	804
Eastbourne	..	..	39	42	2.11	5.8	36.4	46.00	789
Hastings	128	55	37	37	2.20	6.7	36.0	.	813
Lewes	81	0	38	38	2.24	4.1	31.8	50.90	811
Rother	128	31	39	40	2.23	3.6	32.1	.	775
Wealden	415	62	55	60	2.34	3.4	28.2	43.60	822
Hampshire	3,751	437	..	513	2.39	4.4	25.8	53.80	779
Basingstoke and Deane	607	133	56	61	2.44	4.5	24.6	.	759
East Hampshire	..	..	40	46	2.42	4.2	25.3	.	800
Eastleigh	251	45	43	48	2.43	4.4	23.9	.	794
Fareham	513	48	40	44	2.37	3.7	24.4	46.00	763
Gosport	52	10	31	32	2.34	7.8	26.8	49.70	786
Hart	160	94	30	35	2.43	3.6	23.3	.	779
Havant	149	0	48	49	2.37	5.2	26.8	.	775
New Forest	426	35	69	74	2.28	3.8	28.4	53.00	799
Rushmoor	183	7	31	35	2.39	5.0	25.8	.	779
Test Valley	736	8	40	46	2.43	4.3	25.3	53.10	756
Winchester	383	12	39	44	2.46	3.1	28.2	62.30	774
Kent	3,391	511	..	557	2.37	4.7	28.5	50.30	765
Ashford	456	43	38	42	2.39	4.9	27.6	51.90	746
Canterbury	396	51	53	58	2.36	4.7	30.4	49.60	756
Dartford	221	67	32	35	2.40	4.0	27.3	50.50	766
Dover	178	4	44	46	2.32	5.2	31.0	55.60	768
Gravesham	90	36	37	37	2.44	5.8	26.4	48.60	731
Maidstone	406	105	54	58	2.42	4.1	26.0	50.70	797
Sevenoaks	98	18	43	46	2.43	3.7	26.8	.	775
Shepway	413	42	42	44	2.25	5.9	31.8	45.70	780
Swale	417	69	47	49	2.44	4.9	25.1	.	744
Thanet	182	3	56	56	2.23	6.0	32.6	47.30	776
Tonbridge and Malling	245	38	40	43	2.47	3.9	24.8	.	771
Tunbridge Wells	209	18	41	43	2.34	3.3	30.9	.	758
Oxfordshire	2,083	394	219	248	2.48	4.7	26.8	49.20	771
Cherwell	712	30	47	54	2.48	5.1	24.8	47.00	759
Oxford	433	7	46	58	2.49	7.1	32.5	49.90	826
South Oxfordshire	188	45	47	51	2.50	3.8	25.3	.	786
Vale of White Horse	290	37	43	46	2.48	2.8	24.7	.	749
West Oxfordshire	305	12	36	40	2.42	4.1	25.3	50.00	727

14.4 *(continued)*

	Housing completions[2] 1999–00 (numbers)			Households 1999					Local authority tenants: average weekly unrebated rent per dwelling (£) April 1999[5]	Council Tax (£)[6] April 1999
	Private enterprise	Registered Social Landlords, Local Authorities, etc	Stock of dwellings 1991[3] (thousands)	All households (thousands)	Average household size (number of people)	Lone parents[4] as a percentage of all households	One-person households as a percentage of all households			
Surrey	2,194	256	412	440	2.40	3.7	27.9	56.70	764
Elmbridge	444	21	48	54	2.42	4.5	27.9	57.80	780
Epsom and Ewell	129	11	26	28	2.40	3.6	29.4	.	749
Guildford	78	6	50	52	2.43	4.1	28.1	58.00	766
Mole Valley	83	2	32	34	2.33	2.8	29.3	48.30	745
Reigate and Banstead	299	74	48	50	2.38	3.4	28.4	57.00	774
Runnymede	227	13	29	32	2.36	3.2	29.5	61.80	689
Spelthorne	94	12	38	38	2.33	3.3	28.2	.	761
Surrey Heath	183	20	30	34	2.50	4.0	23.2	.	759
Tandridge	248	54	30	32	2.44	3.1	27.5	47.90	772
Waverley	180	0	46	47	2.42	4.0	28.2	57.40	782
Woking	225	42	35	39	2.37	4.4	27.2	62.30	791
West Sussex	1,675	285	304	327	2.28	4.1	30.6	53.10	759
Adur	66	53	25	25	2.32	4.2	30.1	51.70	800
Arun	335	52	60	65	2.16	3.6	32.5	56.40	766
Chichester	138	0	45	47	2.26	4.1	31.0	50.40	749
Crawley	..	..	35	40	2.42	6.3	26.2	50.30	755
Horsham	550	71	45	52	2.36	3.0	28.0	59.90	744
Mid Sussex	137	35	49	53	2.37	3.8	28.0	.	763
Worthing	57	31	44	46	2.14	4.4	37.4	.	757
Former county of Berkshire	2,027	217	290	326	2.43	4.8	27.0	..	785
Former county of Buckinghamshire	2,297	435	250	281	2.43	4.7	26.0	..	761
Former county of East Sussex	1,613	300	321	335	2.19	5.0	34.3	..	771
Former county of Hampshire	4,199	521	629	680	2.38	5.0	27.3	..	762
Former county of Kent	3,771	571	924	654	2.39	4.8	28.0	..	752
South West	14,310	1,493	1,973	2,076	2.33	4.7	29.0	43.70	782
Bath and North East Somerset UA	282	8	..	71	2.34	4.4	29.4	41.20	795
Bournemouth UA	356	35	..	72	2.17	5.3	34.7	45.90	738
City of Bristol UA	171	49	..	174	2.30	6.8	32.6	40.70	992
North Somerset UA	..	..	..	79	2.34	4.0	27.7	51.30	740
Plymouth UA	126	23	..	105	2.36	6.8	29.2	39.50	702
Poole UA	287	15	..	60	2.31	4.2	29.7	45.00	703
South Gloucestershire UA	713	0	..	99	2.44	4.2	25.2	44.40	782
Swindon UA	349	13	..	75	2.39	5.4	25.9	38.80	699
Torbay UA	314	21	..	53	2.24	6.2	31.7	45.40	752
Cornwall and the Isles of Scilly	1,788	127	207	208	2.32	4.8	28.2	43.90	748
Caradon	399	0	34	34	2.35	4.4	25.8	41.50	745
Carrick	212	27	37	37	2.28	4.2	29.8	45.20	756
Kerrier	279	43	37	38	2.37	5.5	26.9	.	757
North Cornwall	256	33	34	34	2.33	4.6	28.0	42.00	759
Penwith	171	13	28	26	2.25	5.3	30.1	.	738
Restormel	332	0	36	38	2.34	5.0	29.0	46.90	740
Isles of Scilly	2	4	1	1	2.58	6.1	21.5	45.70	532
Devon	2,713	226	..	296	2.30	4.0	29.9	42.80	776
East Devon	488	12	53	56	2.20	3.9	31.6	39.00	761
Exeter	147	49	41	47	2.33	5.2	33.5	37.70	749
Mid Devon	297	29	27	28	2.36	3.5	27.8	41.20	794
North Devon	324	67	36	37	2.29	4.5	29.7	51.70	791
South Hams	283	5	37	34	2.31	3.6	28.5	.	777
Teignbridge	516	55	47	51	2.29	3.5	28.9	47.20	783
Torridge	401	4	23	23	2.40	3.4	27.2	45.70	773
West Devon	228	0	19	20	2.34	3.8	28.7	.	802

14.4 *(continued)*

	Housing completions[2] 1999–00 (numbers)		Stock of dwellings 1991[3] (thousands)	Households 1999				Local authority tenants: average weekly unrebated rent per dwelling (£) April 1999[5]	Council Tax (£)[6] April 1999
	Private enterprise	Registered Social Landlords, Local Authorities, etc		All households (thousands)	Average household size (number of people)	Lone parents[4] as a percentage of all households	One-person households as a percentage of all households		
Dorset	1,161	159	..	169	2.26	*3.8*	*29.9*	47.20	829
Christchurch	103	0	20	20	2.16	*4.3*	*32.9*	.	816
East Dorset	243	20	33	36	2.28	*3.0*	*26.1*	.	844
North Dorset	235	37	23	26	2.36	*3.8*	*28.9*	.	809
Purbeck	81	39	19	20	2.31	*2.7*	*28.8*	50.80	826
West Dorset	325	18	39	40	2.22	*3.0*	*32.3*	.	831
Weymouth and Portland	147	37	26	27	2.22	*6.7*	*31.0*	45.20	834
Gloucestershire	1,332	242	222	236	2.35	*4.5*	*28.8*	47.40	771
Cheltenham	167	37	45	47	2.21	*5.5*	*35.0*	52.20	762
Cotswold	166	42	33	35	2.35	*3.3*	*28.3*	.	760
Forest of Dean	158	28	30	32	2.43	*3.2*	*25.4*	42.00	787
Gloucester	259	83	41	45	2.37	*6.5*	*28.5*	46.90	761
Stroud	266	42	42	45	2.39	*4.0*	*27.0*	47.10	818
Tewkesbury	291	0	29	31	2.37	*3.4*	*26.5*	.	726
Somerset	1,640	223	195	206	2.35	*4.1*	*28.7*	42.90	770
Mendip	250	73	39	41	2.43	*4.2*	*29.0*	43.50	779
Sedgemoor	..	..	41	44	2.34	*4.2*	*27.3*	45.80	761
South Somerset	315	4	60	65	2.36	*3.6*	*28.0*	.	781
Taunton Deane	689	79	39	42	2.31	*5.1*	*30.4*	40.60	752
West Somerset	90	8	15	14	2.22	*2.9*	*30.1*	.	777
Wiltshire	1,442	274	..	174	2.42	*4.3*	*25.4*	52.90	781
Kennet	104	53	28	31	2.51	*4.3*	*23.9*	.	769
North Wiltshire	321	69	45	50	2.45	*4.8*	*23.4*	.	790
Salisbury	320	37	43	47	2.38	*4.3*	*26.3*	54.20	771
West Wiltshire	683	107	44	46	2.35	*3.8*	*27.6*	51.10	791
Bristol/Bath area	2,638	103	391	423	2.35	*5.3*	*29.4*	..	852
Former county of Devon	3,236	296	440	454	2.31	*4.9*	*30.0*	..	759
Former county of Dorset	1,804	214	287	300	2.25	*4.3*	*31.0*	..	783
Former county of Wiltshire	1,849	287	231	249	2.41	*4.6*	*25.5*	..	759

1 The table reflects the local government structure at 1 April 1998. For some new areas data are not available. See Notes and Definitions.
2 District figures do not always add to county totals. See Notes and Definitions.
3 The figures for housing stock at local authority level shown in this table are derived using different methods from the regional stock figures shown in Table 6.1. This has led to small discrepancies between the two sets of figures. The figures in Table 6.1 provide the definitive regional estimates.
4 Lone parents with dependent children only.
5 Some local authorities have no housing stock following large scale voluntary transfers to Registered Social Landlords.
6 See Notes and Definitions.

Source: Department of Transport, Local Government and the Regions

14.5 Labour market statistics:[1] by sub-region

	Economic activity			Average gross weekly full-time earnings[5], April 2000 (£)						
				Males			Females			
	Total in employment[2] 1999–2000[3] (thousands)	Employment rate 1999–2000[3] (percentages)	ILO unemploy-ment rate 1999–2000[3] (percentages)[4]	Total	10 per cent earned		Total	10 per cent earned		All persons total
					Less than	More than		Less than	More than	
United Kingdom	26,784	73.8	6.0	451.6	218.8	724.7	336.7	176.6	533.9	409.2
England	22,657	74.6	5.8	459.2	220.8	739.1	341.5	177.9	543.9	416.3
North East	1,049	66.8	9.5	398.9	204.3	620.8	306.0	166.2	490.7	365.8
Darlington UA	42	70.0	..	358.6	183.5	545.3	..	..	..	336.4
Hartlepool UA	33	61.8	15.8	..	..	..	..	..	..	..
Middlesbrough UA	50	56.1	17.8	392.0	202.3	658.8	..	..	..	368.0
Redcar & Cleveland UA	50	59.1	12.0	460.0	243.5	694.8	..	..	..	425.0
Stockton-on-Tees UA	81	70.9	7.6	427.3	211.2	646.1	274.2	160.2	430.8	382.5
Durham	221	71.4	7.4	378.9	206.3	574.3	299.1	153.9	483.3	348.7
Northumberland	131	72.1	2.7	376.1	190.0	587.1	294.6	164.9	473.5	343.7
Tyne and Wear	440	65.1	10.4	405.4	207.7	639.3	314.3	171.6	504.4	372.3
Tees Valley	257	*52.0*	*11.7*	..	..	..	..	..	..	..
Tees Valley less Darlington	214	*51.0*	*12.6*	..	..	..	..	..	..	..
Former county of Durham	264	*56.6*	*7.3*	..	..	..	..	..	..	..
North West	2,965	71.1	6.6	428.6	213.5	671.8	312.8	173.1	497.1	385.7
Blackburn with Darwen UA	56	71.0	..	380.3	192.8	580.2	295.7	184.2	406.8	349.0
Blackpool UA	54	69.7	..	..	..	..	288.2	168.8	459.8	328.0
Halton UA	45	62.9	..	436.8	235.6	709.2	320.6	174.0	534.5	396.5
Warrington UA	95	78.5	..	440.9	220.5	708.8	307.3	161.1	474.6	398.9
Cheshire	319	77.1	3.4	454.4	222.4	708.2	312.3	170.3	486.9	404.8
Cumbria	219	73.0	5.9	412.2	212.1	664.0	298.3	154.2	490.1	371.1
Greater Manchester (Met. County)	1,132	71.1	6.8	428.3	215.9	673.4	318.2	179.9	499.2	386.8
Lancashire	512	75.2	5.5	423.7	210.6	622.5	302.9	164.9	492.3	382.3
Merseyside (Met. County)	531	63.6	9.2	432.4	209.9	666.4	319.9	176.1	517.1	387.4
Former county of Cheshire	460	*60.4*	*4.2*	..	..	..	..	..	..	..
Former county of Lancashire	623	*58.6*	*5.5*	..	..	..	..	..	..	..
Yorkshire and the Humber	2,233	72.8	6.6	409.9	211.5	632.0	308.8	167.3	501.3	373.7
East Riding of Yorkshire UA	146	78.0	..	404.0	218.1	604.5	289.8	145.6	517.4	370.8
City of Kingston upon Hull UA	101	64.2	12.7	384.2	202.9	630.0	306.2	159.8	517.0	357.0
North East Lincolnshire UA	64	68.0	10.8	393.1	200.3	596.0	..	..	..	349.5
North Lincolnshire UA	68	70.3	..	424.4	237.8	629.7	..	..	..	393.4
York UA	81	76.3	..	448.9	219.6	728.3	313.4	175.4	494.6	406.6
North Yorkshire	260	78.5	3.5	397.2	212.2	598.8	282.9	161.9	464.1	356.1
South Yorkshire (Met. County)	552	69.6	8.0	394.4	209.6	600.0	305.0	164.7	488.7	361.4
West Yorkshire (Met. County)	962	73.9	6.1	419.9	212.1	655.8	319.1	171.5	517.5	382.5
The Humber	378	*56.0*	*7.8*	..	..	..	..	..	..	..
Former county of North Yorkshire	341	*48.1*	*2.9*	..	..	..	..	..	..	..
East Midlands	1,945	75.9	5.3	407.0	209.6	633.4	301.1	164.0	488.3	371.4
Derby UA	96	70.4	6.5	471.6	217.6	761.2	334.7	166.2	525.7	431.3
Leicester UA	121	68.1	9.8	386.3	197.8	604.9	299.7	168.2	488.3	352.8
Nottingham UA	106	61.9	10.1	419.5	211.9	670.0	308.1	175.8	489.1	376.4
Rutland UA	15	80.7	..	..	..	..	..	..	..	341.3
Derbyshire	333	76.7	4.5	395.6	208.0	575.8	282.4	155.4	453.4	361.9
Leicestershire	321	82.1	4.1	416.2	220.0	660.5	303.6	166.0	501.2	381.9
Lincolnshire	296	77.0	4.3	376.8	207.9	595.0	283.0	152.1	488.3	346.2
Northamptonshire	304	79.6	4.0	431.4	223.1	637.9	309.2	178.0	479.7	386.6
Nottinghamshire	353	75.8	5.6	390.7	199.8	640.8	303.4	157.3	517.4	361.6
Former county of Derbyshire	429	*45.7*	*3.9*	..	..	..	..	..	..	..
Former county of Leicestershire	457	*63.7*	*5.6*	..	..	..	..	..	..	..
Former county of Nottinghamshire	459	*45.7*	*5.2*	..	..	..	..	..	..	..

14.5 (continued)

	Economic activity			Average gross weekly full-time earnings[5], April 2000 (£)						
				Males			Females			
					10 per cent earned			10 per cent earned		All persons total
	Total in employment[2] 1999–2000[3] (thousands)	Employment rate 1999–2000[3] (percentages)	ILO unemploy-ment rate 1999–2000[3] (percentages)[4]	Total	Less than	More than	Total	Less than	More than	
West Midlands	2,378	73.5	6.6	425.3	219.3	667.9	311.2	175.0	499.1	385.9
County of Herefordshire UA	73	77.1	..	354.3	215.1	548.4	275.3	162.0	471.9	328.0
Stoke-on-Trent UA	99	68.6	7.2	380.1	188.2	593.7	311.7	181.0	487.5	354.0
Telford and Wrekin UA	74	77.6	..	412.2	212.5	629.0	286.0	165.0	451.4	370.0
Shropshire	136	78.5	..	382.4	197.3	580.6	284.8	160.0	460.6	351.4
Staffordshire	390	77.6	5.4	413.4	220.3	633.4	313.1	163.1	513.3	378.4
Warwickshire	247	79.0	4.7	458.0	226.5	741.2	311.3	180.4	474.5	410.7
West Midlands (Met. County)	1,092	69.3	8.2	437.2	225.4	692.5	315.2	176.7	500.9	394.7
Worcestershire	268	79.5	4.5	407.2	212.2	640.0	314.7	179.5	513.4	375.1
Herefordshire and Worcestershire	341	50.7	4.0	..	..	..	..	..	..	..
Former county of Shropshire	210	51.9	3.7	..	..	..	..	..	..	..
Former county of Staffordshire	342	46.6	4.4	..	..	..	..	..	..	..
East	2,555	77.6	4.3	455.5	223.1	733.5	333.8	178.6	527.8	412.7
Luton UA	82	71.8	..	469.2	230.3	803.3	..	..	..	419.7
Peterborough UA	69	73.7	..	415.2	209.0	665.1	300.8	182.8	441.5	371.8
Southend-on-Sea UA	80	78.1	..	..	..	..	333.0	170.6	519.1	376.9
Thurrock UA	60	73.5	..	..	..	..	..	..	..	..
Bedfordshire	194	81.0	4.3	441.9	233.2	674.2	345.8	184.6	538.0	408.5
Cambridgeshire	298	81.1	3.0	465.5	226.6	739.1	347.2	189.1	548.8	425.9
Essex	607	76.2	4.2	471.2	228.1	763.3	334.2	174.8	529.8	423.9
Hertfordshire	508	79.9	3.2	512.9	241.5	854.6	374.8	206.4	593.6	461.6
Norfolk	337	74.7	5.6	417.7	212.9	669.4	300.4	168.9	459.8	377.2
Suffolk	321	77.8	4.2	401.9	204.6	632.4	296.4	164.6	488.3	366.8
Former county of Bedfordshire	276	52.4	3.7	..	..	..	..	..	..	..
Former county of Cambridgeshire	367	52.8	3.1	..	..	..	..	..	..	..
Former county of Essex	747	60.6	4.2	..	..	..	..	..	..	..
London	3,331	71.2	7.3	593.0	258.8	1,009.8	434.3	219.3	681.1	529.8
Inner London	1,229	66.2	9.7	..	..	..	..	..	..	..
Outer London	2,101	74.5	5.9	..	..	..	..	..	..	..
South East	3,924	80.0	3.8	482.1	231.0	786.9	353.1	191.9	550.5	434.2
Bracknell Forest UA	64	86.2	..	636.5	236.3	1,180.9	..	..	..	559.0
Brighton and Hove UA	123	76.0	7.5	403.5	210.7	668.9	347.1	192.2	574.2	379.4
Isle of Wight UA	49	71.0	11.6	386.6	187.9	582.6	..	..	..	365.7
Medway UA	115	77.1	..	443.1	235.0	667.7	315.3	172.7	528.7	395.8
Milton Keynes UA	110	83.5	..	471.5	237.3	746.0	352.5	195.6	573.2	422.1
Portsmouth UA	80	71.8	..	429.6	223.8	695.4	351.6	200.9	594.1	400.7
Reading UA	72	75.8	..	529.9	255.9	933.6	374.4	203.7	561.1	472.7
Slough UA	51	74.0	..	575.8	269.7	1,066.2	..	..	..	521.5
Southampton UA	96	72.3	6.0	455.2	237.2	718.1	328.6	199.0	469.8	410.5
West Berkshire UA (Newbury)	87	87.5	..	528.5	249.3	845.6	379.7	225.6	607.9	473.6
Windsor and Maidenhead UA	66	80.4	..	..	..	..	..	..	..	501.5
Wokingham UA	84	85.8	..	552.1	259.9	921.5	..	..	..	507.9
Buckinghamshire	245	80.1	3.9	523.3	243.0	808.2	373.1	200.0	576.9	468.2
East Sussex	217	79.4	2.5	401.2	207.4	642.1	342.4	173.9	556.0	379.3
Hampshire	621	82.0	3.3	466.3	229.8	760.8	337.6	192.1	517.4	420.9
Kent	620	77.5	5.2	439.0	223.8	671.4	328.8	177.6	508.4	398.8
Oxfordshire	333	84.0	2.0	476.2	242.9	756.2	348.8	191.8	533.1	430.8
Surrey	534	82.1	2.4	555.4	248.2	914.7	378.4	214.4	583.7	487.0
West Sussex	354	79.9	3.3	455.6	228.8	743.3	345.1	184.5	541.5	412.3
Former county of Berkshire	426	70.0	2.6	..	..	..	..	..	..	..
Former county of Buckinghamshire	355	54.8	3.1	..	..	..	..	..	..	..
Former county of East Sussex	340	48.2	4.7	..	..	..	..	..	..	..
Former county of Hampshire	847	62.8	4.2	..	..	..	..	..	..	..
Former county of Kent	735	49.7	4.0	..	..	..	..	..	..	..

14.5 *(continued)*

	Economic activity			Average gross weekly full-time earnings[5], April 2000 (£)						
				Males			Females			
	Total in employment[2] 1999–2000[3] (thousands)	Employment rate 1999–2000[3] (percentages)	ILO unemployment rate 1999–2000[3] (percentages)[4]	Total	10 per cent earned		Total	10 per cent earned		All persons total
					Less than	More than		Less than	More than	
South West	2,278	*78.3*	*4.8*	418.2	213.5	660.9	309.8	168.6	488.3	379.1
Bath and North East Somerset UA	82	*84.6*	*..*	421.5	207.2	687.8	..	..	..	393.9
Bournemouth UA	70	*75.1*	*..*	421.5	219.6	723.3	319.8	181.2	521.5	374.0
City of Bristol UA	188	*76.1*	*5.9*	454.2	216.9	714.3	332.8	171.2	526.2	407.8
North Somerset UA	89	*80.7*	*..*	425.2	219.8	664.3	306.0	168.4	488.3	385.0
Plymouth UA	116	*71.8*	*7.4*	407.5	211.7	627.8	305.7	171.9	462.0	373.2
Poole UA	68	*80.8*	*..*	457.5	214.4	714.7	309.8	165.7	477.6	405.4
South Gloucestershire UA	126	*81.0*	*..*	445.0	234.4	674.5	308.8	181.5	496.4	409.0
Swindon UA	100	*85.0*	*..*	490.1	256.4	764.8	319.1	203.2	476.0	427.4
Torbay UA	43	*73.5*	*..*	..	..	..	..	..	..	324.8
Cornwall and the Isles of Scilly	201	*69.9*	*6.5*	339.4	182.2	507.0	284.7	156.6	459.8	317.2
Devon	302	*76.2*	*7.1*	367.9	196.0	568.6	294.5	163.1	484.6	342.0
Dorset	173	*80.2*	*3.9*	391.7	210.0	591.2	311.0	157.2	508.5	363.9
Gloucestershire	273	*81.8*	*2.8*	456.5	243.7	717.7	313.1	177.1	499.8	405.7
Somerset	231	*78.1*	*5.1*	399.3	215.8	623.4	303.8	160.8	541.5	366.9
Wiltshire	216	*84.5*	*..*	412.2	216.4	645.6	297.8	167.5	486.9	370.3
Bristol/Bath area	486	*62.9*	*4.1*	..	..	..	..	..	..	..
Former county of Devon	460	*57.5*	*6.8*	..	..	..	..	..	..	..
Former county of Dorset	311	*58.3*	*4.6*	..	..	..	..	..	..	..
Former county of Wiltshire	316	*55.2*	*2.2*	..	..	..	..	..	..	..

1 Local government structure as at 1 April 1998. See Notes and Definitions to the Labour Market chapter. In some cases sample sizes are too small to provide reliable estimates.
2 Includes those on government-supported employment and training schemes and unpaid family workers.
3 For those of working age. Data are from the Labour Force Survey and relate to the period March 1999 to February 2000.
4 As a percentage of the economically active.
5 Earnings estimates have been derived from the New Earnings Survey and relate to full-time employees whose pay for the survey pay-period was not affected by absence.

*Source: **Office for National Statistics***

14.6 Labour market,[1] benefit and economic statistics: by local authority[2]

	Economically active 1999–2000[3] (percentages)	Benefit statistics				Economic statistics		
		Claimant count[4] March 2001			Income Support beneficiaries[6] Nov.2000 (percentages)	Businesses registered for VAT 1999		Stock of businesses end 1999 (thousands)
		Total (thousands)	Of which females (percentages)	Of which long-term claimants[5] (percentages)		Registration rates[7] (percentages)	Deregistration rates[7] (percentages)	
United Kingdom	78.5	1,041.1	23.4	19.7	10	11	10	1,658.1
England	79.2	827.9	23.6	19.4	9	11	11	1,410.4
North East	73.8	68.3	20.0	21.2	12	10	10	41.9
Darlington UA	75.2	2.4	20.4	19.0	11	10	10	2.1
Hartlepool UA	73.3	3.0	18.0	21.6	15	9	9	1.2
Middlesbrough UA	68.2	5.8	17.8	23.3	15	11	10	1.9
Redcar & Cleveland UA	67.2	4.4	19.3	22.6	13	10	8	1.8
Stockton-on-Tees UA	76.7	5.4	19.8	21.9	11	10	16	2.5
Durham	77.1	10.2	22.3	16.0	12	10	8	8.8
Chester-le-Street	81.1	0.9	18.6	16.6	9	10	9	0.8
Derwentside	74.6	1.8	19.4	18.2	13	10	8	1.4
Durham	74.9	1.4	24.6	14.9	7	10	10	1.4
Easington	66.8	1.9	22.7	16.0	16	16	9	1.2
Sedgefield	84.1	2.0	23.5	13.0	12	10	9	1.5
Teesdale	79.7	0.4	19.8	17.3	7	5	6	1.1
Wear Valley	83.2	1.8	23.8	17.8	14	9	8	1.4
Northumberland	76.3	6.4	23.4	19.3	9	8	8	7.6
Alnwick	74.6	0.6	26.5	17.6	6	7	7	1.1
Berwick-upon-Tweed	69.7	0.6	29.8	13.1	9	6	6	1.1
Blyth Valley	74.6	2.0	24.0	15.9	11	11	9	1.0
Castle Morpeth	76.9	0.7	21.3	21.5	6	9	10	1.3
Tynedale	85.2	0.8	23.0	18.8	7	6	7	2.3
Wansbeck	73.0	1.6	20.2	25.6	10	12	9	0.7
Tyne and Wear	72.7	30.7	19.3	22.7	14	11	12	15.9
Gateshead	74.0	4.3	18.5	18.6	14	10	9	3.3
Newcastle-upon-Tyne	69.5	7.7	18.1	25.4	14	11	16	4.4
North Tyneside	77.2	4.8	20.0	19.6	12	11	10	2.7
South Tyneside	76.5	5.5	19.7	24.6	14	11	9	1.9
Sunderland	69.9	8.4	20.0	22.8	14	11	13	3.6
Tees Valley	72.1	22.0	18.9	21.8	13	10	11	18.4
Tees Valley less Darlington	71.6	18.6	18.8	22.5	13	10	12	7.5
Former county of Durham	76.7	12.6	21.9	16.6	11	10	9	10.9
North West	76.0	133.2	21.4	18.0	12	11	11	160.9
Blackburn with Darwen UA	77.7	2.9	21.0	12.6	15	11	12	2.9
Blackpool UA	72.5	3.8	20.0	8.2	14	10	12	2.9
Halton UA	69.9	3.2	22.3	15.3	14	11	9	2.0
Warrington UA	82.0	2.6	24.8	14.5	8	14	10	4.8
Cheshire	79.8	7.2	22.0	11.0	7	10	10	20.6
Chester	74.9	1.3	20.5	11.7	8	11	12	3.6
Congleton	81.7	0.8	25.5	8.6	5	10	9	2.9
Crewe and Nantwich	84.8	1.4	24.7	11.9	7	9	9	2.9
Ellesmere Port and Neston	70.8	1.1	18.5	9.9	9	10	9	1.4
Macclesfield	81.9	1.1	19.7	9.0	6	10	10	6.5
Vale Royal	81.7	1.5	23.5	13.0	7	10	8	3.4
Cumbria	77.6	8.5	22.0	15.7	8	7	7	16.0
Allerdale	76.6	1.9	21.4	15.8	8	6	7	3.1
Barrow-in-Furness	76.3	1.5	18.6	18.0	13	8	9	1.0
Carlisle	85.6	2.0	24.1	15.3	8	7	8	2.9
Copeland	72.6	1.9	21.6	18.5	9	9	7	1.6
Eden	70.8	0.4	22.6	10.2	5	5	6	2.9
South Lakeland	77.8	0.8	25.8	7.5	4	6	7	4.4
Greater Manchester (Met. County)	76.3	46.8	20.8	16.4	13	12	12	57.6
Bolton	77.1	4.6	20.6	13.8	11	11	12	5.7
Bury	82.3	2.1	21.6	5.8	11	12	12	4.2
Manchester	66.3	13.4	19.3	22.7	20	15	21	9.0
Oldham	77.1	4.1	22.2	13.8	12	10	9	4.5
Rochdale	76.2	4.0	20.8	14.0	14	11	11	4.3
Salford	70.6	3.9	19.8	14.6	16	14	11	4.8
Stockport	85.2	3.1	21.8	15.5	8	11	11	7.9
Tameside	78.8	3.3	22.4	13.6	12	10	9	4.8
Trafford	82.1	2.9	20.4	17.7	9	14	12	6.5
Wigan	75.2	5.3	22.9	13.4	10	11	9	6.2

14.6 (continued)

	Economically active 1999–2000[3] (percentages)	Benefit statistics				Economic statistics		
		Claimant count[4] March 2001			Income Support bene-ficiaries[6] Nov.2000 (percentages)	Businesses registered for VAT 1999		Stock of businesses end 1999 (thousands)
		Total (thousands)	Of which females (percentages)	Of which long-term claimants[5] (percentages)		Registration rates[7] (percentages)	Deregistration rates[7] (percentages)	
Lancashire	79.5	16.1	22.5	12.7	10	10	10	29.2
Burnley	76.6	1.3	22.0	6.7	13	10	11	1.8
Chorley	84.5	1.2	21.3	10.6	7	10	10	2.8
Fylde	80.8	0.5	24.2	6.1	7	12	22	1.5
Hyndburn	80.9	1.0	25.2	4.9	12	9	10	1.8
Lancaster	79.3	2.7	21.9	18.6	9	9	9	3.2
Pendle	83.2	1.4	25.4	9.2	12	10	8	2.1
Preston	76.9	2.6	19.3	18.2	13	11	12	3.3
Ribble Valley	79.9	0.3	27.7	9.6	5	9	8	2.2
Rossendale	76.0	0.8	24.0	7.4	12	10	10	2.0
South Ribble	86.1	0.9	22.4	8.9	6	10	9	2.6
West Lancashire	75.4	2.0	23.8	15.5	10	10	9	3.0
Wyre	75.2	1.3	21.4	12.4	8	8	8	3.0
Merseyside (Met. County)	70.0	42.1	21.4	25.2	16	13	11	24.1
Knowsley	64.5	5.4	22.5	27.1	21	12	9	1.7
Liverpool	66.8	17.8	20.9	28.6	21	11	14	7.2
St Helens	74.5	4.3	21.9	20.2	12	10	9	2.9
Sefton	73.9	6.6	20.1	23.6	13	17	8	7.1
Wirral	71.7	8.0	22.7	20.4	13	12	10	5.2
Former county of Cheshire	79.1	13.1	22.7	12.8	8	11	10	27.6
Former county of Lancashire	78.7	22.8	21.9	11.9	11	11	11	35.4
Yorkshire and the Humber	77.9	104.3	22.3	17.7	10	10	10	117.1
East Riding of Yorkshire UA	80.9	5.3	26.8	16.0	8	8	9	9.1
City of Kingston upon Hull UA	73.4	9.7	21.6	20.0	16	10	12	4.1
North East Lincolnshire UA	76.2	5.1	23.0	15.3	12	9	10	3.1
North Lincolnshire UA	75.6	3.0	26.0	10.2	9	8	10	3.9
York UA	79.7	2.4	25.3	9.5	6	16	15	2.4
North Yorkshire	81.3	6.5	26.2	14.4	6	8	7	24.3
Craven	83.6	0.5	24.8	12.7	6	7	7	2.7
Hambleton	80.1	0.7	26.4	18.0	5	7	7	3.9
Harrogate	83.1	1.0	26.6	8.6	5	10	8	6.1
Richmondshire	78.0	0.4	30.8	8.3	3	8	7	2.0
Ryedale	88.6	0.5	33.5	19.0	5	5	5	3.5
Scarborough	77.2	2.6	24.0	16.2	11	8	9	3.1
Selby	80.7	0.9	26.5	13.5	6	8	8	3.0
South Yorkshire (Met. County)	75.7	30.0	21.6	18.6	12	11	12	22.4
Barnsley	77.8	4.8	23.4	14.0	13	10	10	3.8
Doncaster	76.6	6.5	22.1	12.2	12	11	10	5.1
Rotherham	73.9	5.6	22.1	16.0	11	11	12	4.2
Sheffield	75.0	13.1	20.5	24.4	11	11	14	9.4
West Yorkshire (Met. County)	78.8	42.3	21.3	18.7	10	11	11	47.7
Bradford	75.7	11.6	19.8	21.3	12	10	10	10.6
Calderdale	79.3	3.8	21.8	17.8	10	10	9	5.7
Kirklees	81.5	6.8	23.2	15.4	10	10	10	9.6
Leeds	79.7	14.0	20.7	20.8	9	12	14	15.5
Wakefield	77.4	6.1	22.9	13.0	11	11	9	6.4
The Humber	76.9	23.2	23.7	16.8	11	9	10	20.3
Former county of North Yorkshire	80.9	8.8	25.9	13.0	6	8	8	26.7
East Midlands	80.2	70.0	24.9	17.2	8	10	10	111.0
Derby UA	75.3	5.4	21.9	22.9	10	11	13	4.0
Leicester UA	75.5	8.2	24.5	17.2	14	12	14	7.3
Nottingham UA	68.9	8.4	20.9	24.5	15	12	17	5.3
Rutland UA	84.0	0.1	34.7	5.1	3	10	9	1.3
Derbyshire	80.3	12.2	23.8	17.9	8	9	9	19.7
Amber Valley	79.8	1.7	23.2	18.8	8	9	9	3.1
Bolsover	83.5	1.6	26.8	15.2	11	11	10	1.3
Chesterfield	75.5	2.7	22.8	21.2	11	11	12	2.2
Derbyshire Dales	81.6	0.6	22.3	15.4	5	6	8	3.5
Erewash	81.5	1.8	25.2	18.8	8	8	9	2.4
High Peak	82.3	1.0	23.8	11.4	8	9	9	2.7
North East Derbyshire	80.1	2.0	21.6	19.5	8	10	9	2.5
South Derbyshire	79.1	0.8	26.2	14.0	7	9	8	2.0

14.6 *(continued)*

	Economically active 1999–2000[3] (percentages)	Benefit statistics				Economic statistics		
		Claimant count[4] March 2001			Income Support bene-ficiaries[6] Nov.2000 (percentages)	Businesses registered for VAT 1999		Stock of businesses end 1999 (thousands)
		Total (thousands)	Of which females (percentages)	Of which long-term claimants[5] (percentages)		Registration rates[7] (percentages)	Deregistration rates[7] (percentages)	
Leicestershire	85.6	6.5	29.7	13.7	5	10	10	18.1
Blaby	85.0	0.8	26.4	13.5	4	11	10	2.3
Charnwood	86.6	2.1	27.8	15.8	6	10	11	4.0
Harborough	88.1	0.5	30.4	11.2	4	10	14	2.8
Hinckley and Bosworth	88.4	1.1	37.6	12.6	5	10	9	3.3
Melton	82.4	0.4	29.0	8.3	5	8	7	1.7
North West Leicestershire	80.8	0.9	28.3	13.3	6	10	9	2.6
Oadby and Wigston	85.5	0.7	28.6	14.7	5	11	10	1.3
Lincolnshire	80.5	8.7	25.8	12.5	8	8	9	19.5
Boston	73.8	0.7	23.4	6.1	8	8	8	1.8
East Lindsey	79.0	2.1	26.5	8.9	10	7	9	4.4
Lincoln	80.9	2.0	21.5	15.5	12	10	10	1.7
North Kesteven	82.8	0.8	29.0	11.4	6	10	9	2.5
South Holland	79.4	0.6	27.7	9.5	7	7	8	2.8
South Kesteven	82.1	1.2	29.0	12.5	6	9	9	3.8
West Lindsey	82.5	1.3	26.9	19.3	8	8	9	2.5
Northamptonshire	82.9	7.7	27.1	14.8	7	12	10	19.2
Corby	83.1	1.0	26.4	9.9	11	12	9	1.0
Daventry	85.5	0.6	33.3	8.3	4	9	8	3.0
East Northamptonshire	87.5	0.8	29.3	10.6	5	11	9	2.4
Kettering	76.8	0.9	29.0	14.1	8	11	9	2.1
Northampton	82.2	3.0	24.5	19.8	8	13	13	4.6
South Northamptonshire	85.4	0.4	28.8	13.1	4	10	9	3.2
Wellingborough	82.7	1.0	27.8	13.4	8	17	13	2.9
Nottinghamshire	80.2	12.8	25.7	15.9	8	10	9	16.7
Ashfield	82.4	2.6	23.1	17.3	10	11	10	2.0
Bassetlaw	79.0	2.3	28.9	18.9	9	8	9	2.7
Broxtowe	81.2	1.4	27.4	17.7	6	11	10	2.2
Gedling	83.1	1.6	23.0	17.8	6	9	9	2.3
Mansfield	75.0	2.4	26.0	10.2	10	10	9	1.8
Newark and Sherwood	79.2	1.6	27.7	12.2	8	10	9	3.0
Rushcliffe	81.2	0.9	23.4	19.0	4	10	11	2.7
Former county of Derbyshire	79.2	17.6	23.3	19.4	9	9	10	23.7
Former county of Leicestershire	82.5	14.8	26.9	15.6	8	11	11	26.7
Former county of Nottinghamshire	77.1	21.2	23.8	19.3	10	11	11	21.9
West Midlands	78.7	105.7	23.3	21.7	10	11	10	136.5
County of Herefordshire UA	83.3	1.9	25.2	11.8	7	7	8	7.9
Stoke-on-Trent UA	74.0	5.4	24.0	13.9	13	11	12	4.5
Telford and Wrekin UA	82.0	2.4	26.5	10.5	11	13	10	3.4
Shropshire	81.9	3.1	25.9	15.7	7	7	8	11.1
Bridgnorth	80.3	0.5	28.8	14.8	5	7	7	2.2
North Shropshire	78.9	0.7	28.7	15.5	7	8	8	2.4
Oswestry	86.1	0.5	31.1	18.1	8	7	8	1.2
Shrewsbury and Atcham	83.0	1.0	21.5	15.3	7	8	9	3.1
South Shropshire	81.2	0.3	21.3	14.8	6	7	7	2.2
Staffordshire	82.1	10.9	26.7	15.0	7	10	10	22.0
Cannock Chase	78.7	1.3	25.9	14.1	9	12	9	2.4
East Staffordshire	77.5	1.6	24.7	19.0	7	10	10	3.2
Lichfield	78.6	1.0	28.5	11.2	6	11	9	3.0
Newcastle-under-Lyme	81.9	1.5	24.3	9.7	7	13	19	2.1
South Staffordshire	87.8	1.4	26.7	21.5	7	10	10	2.8
Stafford	82.2	1.5	26.5	16.1	5	10	9	3.6
Staffordshire Moorlands	85.7	1.0	33.0	9.1	7	8	8	3.2
Tamworth	84.5	1.4	26.7	16.1	9	14	10	1.6
Warwickshire	82.9	5.5	24.7	15.9	7	11	9	16.5
North Warwickshire	85.4	0.7	28.3	12.8	7	11	8	2.1
Nuneaton and Bedworth	77.7	1.6	24.3	11.8	9	11	10	2.3
Rugby	81.9	1.0	26.0	16.1	6	10	9	2.6
Stratford-on-Avon	88.0	0.7	22.8	20.0	6	10	9	5.3
Warwick	82.5	1.4	23.4	20.2	6	12	9	4.3

14.6 *(continued)*

	Economically active 1999–2000[3] (percentages)	Benefit statistics			Income Support bene-ficiaries[6] Nov.2000 (percentages)	Economic statistics		Stock of businesses end 1999 (thousands)
		Claimant count[4] March 2001				Businesses registered for VAT 1999		
		Total (thousands)	Of which females (percentages)	Of which long-term claimants[5] (percentages)		Registration rates[7] (percentages)	Deregistration rates[7] (percentages)	
West Midlands (Met. County)	75.5	70.0	22.0	25.5	13	12	12	54.2
Birmingham	71.5	33.2	21.2	29.0	15	12	15	19.6
Coventry	74.8	5.9	20.5	18.9	12	13	10	5.5
Dudley	85.0	6.9	23.0	26.0	10	11	10	7.7
Sandwell	75.9	8.4	22.7	24.6	15	11	9	6.4
Solihull	80.4	2.8	23.4	20.6	7	12	11	4.6
Walsall	77.1	5.8	24.7	19.2	13	10	12	5.6
Wolverhampton	74.0	7.0	22.3	22.2	13	12	12	4.8
Worcestershire	83.2	6.5	26.5	12.7	7	10	9	17.1
Bromsgrove	81.0	1.1	24.3	18.1	5	11	11	2.8
Malvern Hills	82.6	0.5	27.4	9.1	6	9	10	2.5
Redditch	86.2	1.3	28.5	15.8	9	11	9	2.2
Worcester	84.9	1.2	22.9	13.5	7	13	11	2.2
Wychavon	85.4	1.0	27.0	8.0	6	10	8	4.6
Wyre Forest	79.1	1.3	28.8	9.2	8	8	8	2.8
Herefordshire and Worcestershire	83.3	8.4	26.2	12.5	7	9	9	25.0
Former county of Shropshire	81.9	5.5	26.2	13.4	8	9	8	14.4
Former county of Staffordshire	80.3	16.3	25.8	14.6	8	11	11	26.4
East	81.0	60.5	25.8	16.5	7	10	10	163.3
Luton UA	76.0	3.3	23.4	18.5	10	11	10	3.9
Peterborough UA	80.1	2.4	22.5	12.6	11	11	10	3.7
Southend-on-Sea UA	81.4	3.2	21.5	22.8	9	14	25	3.2
Thurrock UA	78.6	2.0	27.7	12.9	9	12	10	2.8
Bedfordshire	84.6	4.0	25.4	13.9	6	10	9	12.3
Bedford	80.5	2.2	24.0	17.1	8	10	9	4.1
Mid Bedfordshire	86.6	0.8	28.7	10.6	5	11	9	4.6
South Bedfordshire	87.1	1.0	25.8	9.6	6	9	9	3.6
Cambridgeshire	83.6	4.4	25.9	15.9	5	10	9	19.0
Cambridge	79.1	1.2	22.7	19.4	6	12	13	3.0
East Cambridgeshire	87.0	0.6	26.6	15.4	6	8	9	2.8
Fenland	81.3	1.0	28.6	12.9	9	9	9	2.6
Huntingdonshire	87.0	1.0	25.6	14.0	5	10	8	5.3
South Cambridgeshire	83.5	0.6	28.3	17.9	4	9	8	5.3
Essex	79.5	12.8	27.9	14.4	7	11	10	39.5
Basildon	80.6	2.2	28.5	13.0	10	13	10	4.3
Braintree	80.1	1.1	29.3	12.5	7	10	9	4.4
Brentwood	80.0	0.3	23.9	13.7	5	13	11	2.6
Castle Point	84.2	0.8	29.3	14.0	8	10	11	2.2
Chelmsford	81.7	1.2	28.2	18.8	5	12	13	4.3
Colchester	74.2	1.4	28.7	8.7	6	11	9	4.5
Epping Forest	78.5	1.2	31.0	19.7	7	15	10	4.4
Harlow	83.8	1.1	24.7	14.4	10	11	9	1.5
Maldon	74.5	0.5	29.3	24.5	6	9	11	2.3
Rochford	82.3	0.7	28.2	17.1	5	10	10	2.2
Tendring	74.0	2.0	25.0	11.8	10	10	11	3.1
Uttlesford	84.3	0.3	29.2	14.4	4	9	8	3.5
Hertfordshire	82.6	7.4	25.9	14.8	6	12	11	36.3
Broxbourne	84.9	0.9	31.6	20.3	7	11	10	2.4
Dacorum	83.1	1.0	26.3	7.9	6	11	10	5.2
East Hertfordshire	84.8	0.6	29.5	18.2	5	11	10	5.3
Hertsmere	84.3	0.7	26.9	14.9	6	12	11	3.4
North Hertfordshire	80.2	0.8	26.2	11.9	6	11	10	4.7
St Albans	81.0	0.5	21.7	8.4	5	16	16	5.1
Stevenage	84.8	0.9	24.2	19.1	8	11	10	1.7
Three Rivers	77.8	0.6	25.7	15.9	5	11	10	2.8
Watford	84.1	0.8	23.6	17.7	6	13	12	2.8
Welwyn Hatfield	81.9	0.6	22.0	12.8	6	11	9	2.9

14.6 *(continued)*

	Economically active 1999–2000[3] (percentages)	Benefit statistics				Economic statistics		
		Claimant count[4] March 2001			Income Support bene-ficiaries[6] Nov.2000 (percentages)	Businesses registered for VAT 1999		Stock of businesses end 1999 (thousands)
		Total (thousands)	Of which females (percentages)	Of which long-term claimants[5] (percentages)		Registration rates[7] (percentages)	Deregistration rates[7] (percentages)	
Norfolk	79.2	12.4	25.6	19.0	9	8	9	22.6
Breckland	77.1	1.2	30.2	10.3	7	9	8	3.6
Broadland	81.7	1.0	27.2	21.2	6	8	9	3.2
Great Yarmouth	76.4	3.5	26.3	22.3	12	8	9	2.3
Kings Lynn and West Norfolk	76.2	1.6	27.4	14.7	9	7	8	4.0
North Norfolk	80.9	1.2	25.4	17.0	8	7	9	3.1
Norwich	78.8	3.0	20.5	22.3	12	9	15	2.7
South Norfolk	83.2	0.9	28.6	15.4	7	8	8	3.8
Suffolk	81.2	8.5	25.9	18.0	7	9	10	20.0
Babergh	75.7	0.7	25.6	13.5	7	9	7	3.1
Forest Heath	85.9	0.4	27.6	10.8	4	12	10	2.0
Ipswich	83.6	2.2	22.6	22.0	10	11	17	2.1
Mid Suffolk	84.5	0.7	33.6	12.3	5	8	8	3.4
St Edmundsbury	83.9	0.9	30.9	12.1	6	10	9	3.2
Suffolk Coastal	79.2	1.0	23.0	12.2	6	9	8	3.6
Waveney	76.4	2.6	26.0	22.5	9	9	9	2.6
Former county of Bedfordshire	81.9	7.2	24.5	16.0	7	10	9	16.2
Former county of Cambridgeshire	82.8	6.8	24.7	14.8	7	10	9	22.7
Former county of Essex	79.6	18.1	26.7	15.7	8	11	11	45.4
London	76.8	156.4	25.8	24.4	11	14	12	274.5
Inner London	73.3	88.3	25.6	26.8	14	.	.	.
Inner London – West	..	22.5	27.5	26.5	10	.	.	.
Camden	75.0	5.6	27.5	28.2	14	14	18	15.9
City of London	..	0.1	29.3	34.7	5	11	10	12.0
Hammersmith and Fulham	72.5	4.3	26.4	26.3	12	14	9	8.5
Kensington and Chelsea	70.4	2.9	31.5	27.3	8	14	9	11.5
Wandsworth	81.8	5.1	25.8	22.9	9	15	9	10.1
Westminster	71.9	4.5	27.8	28.0	8	16	12	38.2
Inner London – East	..	65.9	24.9	26.9	17	.	.	.
Hackney	69.0	8.2	26.0	23.2	21	16	13	7.3
Haringey	71.7	8.2	24.9	24.9	16	15	12	6.5
Islington	75.8	6.5	28.4	30.7	18	14	15	10.0
Lambeth	74.6	10.3	26.0	28.8	14	14	10	7.1
Lewisham	78.0	8.1	24.7	29.2	12	14	11	4.7
Newham	64.8	7.7	23.1	23.2	21	16	11	4.1
Southwark	75.9	9.0	25.7	29.3	15	15	10	7.8
Tower Hamlets	66.9	7.9	20.8	25.7	21	15	9	8.2
Outer London	79.2	68.1	26.2	21.4	9	.	.	.
Outer London – East and North East	..	29.1	26.0	23.7	11	.	.	.
Barking and Dagenham	75.0	3.0	24.0	21.8	15	17	12	2.5
Bexley	83.7	2.6	27.4	19.0	7	12	10	4.8
Enfield	75.6	5.7	26.6	25.0	12	13	11	6.6
Greenwich	77.7	6.0	26.2	26.2	14	13	11	4.1
Havering	82.9	2.5	27.5	20.9	7	12	12	5.4
Redbridge	75.4	3.8	26.4	25.2	10	15	14	5.5
Waltham Forest	78.1	5.5	25.0	22.9	13	15	14	4.5
Outer London – South	..	14.4	26.0	21.3	7	.	.	.
Bromley	79.6	3.2	25.4	23.1	7	11	11	8.3
Croydon	81.8	6.1	26.1	24.4	9	13	15	8.0
Kingston upon Thames	77.8	1.2	26.5	17.1	6	12	9	5.2
Merton	83.3	2.3	26.4	16.5	7	13	12	5.6
Sutton	86.4	1.6	25.5	15.6	6	11	10	5.0
Outer London – West and North West	..	24.6	26.4	18.7	9	.	.	.
Barnet	78.8	4.5	28.2	19.1	8	15	23	9.4
Brent	73.9	6.6	24.6	26.1	13	14	13	8.6
Ealing	74.5	5.2	25.4	17.3	11	14	10	10.0
Harrow	81.5	2.3	27.0	21.2	9	13	15	6.2
Hillingdon	83.3	2.4	28.5	11.6	8	11	10	7.5
Hounslow	77.3	2.1	26.6	7.4	11	12	10	7.2
Richmond-upon-Thames	79.8	1.4	28.0	14.3	5	12	9	8.5

14.6 *(continued)*

	Economically active 1999–2000[3] (percentages)	Benefit statistics				Economic statistics		
		Claimant count[4] March 2001			Income Support bene-ficiaries[6] Nov.2000 (percentages)	Businesses registered for VAT 1999		Stock of businesses end 1999 (thousands)
		Total (thousands)	Of which females (percentages)	Of which long-term claimants[5] (percentages)		Registration rates[7] (percentages)	Deregistration rates[7] (percentages)	
South East	83.2	71.6	24.1	16.7	6	11	10	255.5
Bracknell Forest UA	87.9	0.6	26.3	9.4	4	14	11	3.4
Brighton and Hove UA	82.2	6.0	24.7	29.6	11	15	17	6.4
Isle of Wight UA	80.4	2.9	26.7	21.2	10	10	10	3.2
Medway UA	80.7	3.8	25.0	18.2	8	13	14	4.8
Milton Keynes UA	86.9	2.0	24.8	8.4	7	14	12	6.2
Portsmouth UA	75.9	2.9	22.1	20.9	9	13	11	3.6
Reading UA	76.7	1.6	21.7	12.0	7	14	20	3.4
Slough UA	77.3	1.8	23.9	17.8	9	15	14	3.1
Southampton UA	76.9	3.2	18.7	12.9	10	15	21	3.5
West Berkshire UA (Newbury)	89.4	0.6	23.7	7.7	4	11	9	6.3
Windsor and Maidenhead UA	84.7	0.9	26.5	11.7	4	12	10	6.9
Wokingham UA	87.6	0.5	26.1	8.7	3	11	9	5.5
Buckinghamshire	83.3	2.9	25.5	17.8	4	11	9	21.4
Aylesbury Vale	85.0	0.9	24.0	14.6	4	11	10	6.2
Chiltern	83.0	0.4	27.9	13.9	4	11	9	4.2
South Buckinghamshire	79.8	0.3	26.2	22.0	3	11	10	3.5
Wycombe	83.1	1.3	25.7	20.2	5	10	9	7.5
East Sussex	83.7	5.7	23.2	16.6	8	10	10	14.7
Eastbourne	82.5	1.3	22.2	16.2	9	12	12	1.8
Hastings	87.4	2.0	20.2	15.8	12	11	10	1.7
Lewes	85.4	0.9	25.1	19.7	7	10	11	2.6
Rother	80.1	0.8	25.5	18.7	7	9	11	2.8
Wealden	83.3	0.7	28.6	13.4	5	10	10	5.7
Hampshire	84.8	7.2	25.2	11.1	5	11	9	38.4
Basingstoke and Deane	84.3	0.7	28.0	7.5	4	10	9	5.1
East Hampshire	84.8	0.6	25.6	15.1	5	10	8	4.4
Eastleigh	85.6	0.5	26.4	9.3	4	12	12	3.1
Fareham	85.8	0.6	26.2	10.7	5	12	9	2.8
Gosport	85.9	0.7	22.2	6.3	6	14	12	1.0
Hart	88.4	0.3	22.8	10.0	3	10	8	3.4
Havant	84.1	1.4	24.9	14.6	8	12	10	2.5
New Forest	80.7	1.0	24.9	11.1	5	10	9	5.4
Rushmoor	89.6	0.5	24.0	10.0	5	12	9	2.4
Test Valley	86.0	0.5	26.6	15.4	4	10	9	4.0
Winchester	80.6	0.4	25.9	8.3	4	11	9	4.3
Kent	81.8	16.7	23.8	18.0	8	11	10	37.4
Ashford	79.4	0.9	25.3	12.3	7	11	11	3.3
Canterbury	78.7	1.7	23.5	18.1	8	11	13	3.0
Dartford	89.7	0.9	27.9	13.4	6	13	10	2.2
Dover	78.9	1.7	23.9	17.4	8	10	10	2.3
Gravesham	81.1	1.6	24.4	17.7	8	13	9	2.1
Maidstone	81.6	1.1	23.7	11.1	7	12	9	4.7
Sevenoaks	82.2	0.6	23.7	17.0	5	10	9	4.5
Shepway	82.9	1.7	22.7	22.8	10	11	10	2.4
Swale	79.8	2.0	23.7	16.7	9	11	8	3.1
Thanet	74.7	3.2	22.1	25.0	13	11	10	2.2
Tonbridge and Malling	86.5	0.8	24.5	10.3	5	11	9	3.5
Tunbridge Wells	87.6	0.6	26.1	13.3	6	9	10	4.2
Oxfordshire	85.7	3.7	24.8	14.7	5	10	9	21.0
Cherwell	85.9	0.7	28.2	5.5	5	10	9	4.5
Oxford	82.8	1.6	20.5	20.5	7	9	10	2.9
South Oxfordshire	86.1	0.6	28.0	13.0	4	10	8	5.8
Vale of White Horse	88.2	0.5	29.2	10.6	4	12	10	3.9
West Oxfordshire	86.7	0.3	26.4	14.4	4	9	7	4.0

14.6 *(continued)*

	Economically active 1999–2000[3] (percentages)	Benefit statistics				Economic statistics		
		Claimant count[4] March 2001			Income Support bene- ficiaries[6] Nov.2000 (percentages)	Businesses registered for VAT 1999		Stock of businesses end 1999 (thousands)
		Total (thousands)	Of which females (percentages)	Of which long-term claimants[5] (percentages)		Registration rates[7] (percentages)	Deregistration rates[7] (percentages)	
Surrey	84.2	4.1	24.7	10.8	4	10	10	43.0
Elmbridge	78.3	0.5	25.4	14.6	4	11	11	5.6
Epsom and Ewell	79.8	0.3	26.7	9.7	3	11	10	2.1
Guildford	85.9	0.6	24.3	15.0	4	11	10	5.0
Mole Valley	86.7	0.2	20.1	7.7	5	10	8	3.8
Reigate and Banstead	79.9	0.4	24.3	6.6	5	10	9	4.5
Runnymede	83.2	0.3	25.5	12.3	4	10	12	2.8
Spelthorne	87.3	0.5	25.3	10.6	5	10	9	3.5
Surrey Heath	85.4	0.2	25.5	5.1	3	11	10	3.6
Tandridge	81.5	0.3	22.8	11.4	4	11	9	3.3
Waverley	90.6	0.5	23.9	13.6	4	10	9	5.3
Woking	86.5	0.3	27.8	3.2	4	11	9	3.4
West Sussex	82.6	4.5	23.4	14.1	6	11	10	23.3
Adur	80.4	0.4	24.9	18.2	8	9	10	1.4
Arun	82.3	1.0	25.3	11.7	8	11	10	3.6
Chichester	76.0	0.7	26.8	16.8	6	10	10	4.5
Crawley	83.8	0.7	19.4	11.6	7	14	14	1.9
Horsham	84.3	0.5	23.3	17.1	4	11	7	5.0
Mid Sussex	86.0	0.5	25.5	12.2	4	12	9	4.7
Worthing	83.4	0.7	19.2	13.8	8	14	11	2.3
Former county of Berkshire	84.2	5.9	24.1	12.7	5	12	11	28.6
Former county of Buckinghamshire	84.2	5.0	25.2	14.0	5	11	10	27.6
Former county of East Sussex	83.1	11.7	24.0	23.3	9	12	12	21.0
Former county of Hampshire	82.7	13.3	23.0	13.7	6	11	10	45.5
Former county of Kent	81.6	20.5	24.0	18.1	8	11	10	42.1
South West	82.2	58.0	25.8	14.7	8	10	10	149.8
Bath and North East Somerset UA	86.8	1.2	27.4	9.2	6	11	8	5.6
Bournemouth UA	80.8	2.6	22.6	19.2	10	15	18	3.8
City of Bristol UA	80.8	7.1	22.4	16.3	11	15	14	11.1
North Somerset UA	82.7	1.5	25.2	6.2	8	10	9	5.1
Plymouth UA	77.5	4.0	23.5	17.4	11	13	15	3.3
Poole UA	84.4	1.1	22.6	12.6	7	12	12	3.7
South Gloucestershire UA	84.2	1.7	25.5	11.5	5	16	10	4.4
Swindon UA	88.5	2.0	24.5	11.1	7	12	10	6.0
Torbay UA	78.4	2.4	23.5	15.6	13	11	14	2.8
Cornwall and the Isles of Scilly	74.8	9.0	28.4	14.4	10	8	9	16.3
Caradon	73.0	1.0	31.1	11.3	7	7	9	2.6
Carrick	79.3	1.5	24.3	14.4	9	8	11	2.9
Kerrier	72.8	1.7	27.0	17.5	11	8	8	2.5
North Cornwall	79.6	1.3	31.5	16.1	9	7	7	3.6
Penwith	70.0	1.5	29.5	15.5	13	10	9	1.9
Restormel	73.5	1.9	28.5	11.0	9	8	10	2.6
Isles of Scilly	..	..	..	..	-	7	10	0.1
Devon	82.0	8.2	27.4	13.7	8	8	9	25.5
East Devon	81.9	0.9	25.3	9.9	6	9	9	4.1
Exeter	79.4	1.6	23.8	17.4	8	13	18	2.2
Mid Devon	84.7	0.6	27.0	14.8	8	7	8	3.3
North Devon	84.5	1.7	29.0	13.6	9	7	8	3.6
South Hams	78.6	0.7	32.9	6.6	7	8	9	3.5
Teignbridge	84.1	1.2	26.6	11.9	8	9	9	3.8
Torridge	79.4	1.1	29.4	17.9	8	7	8	2.6
West Devon	84.2	0.4	28.3	13.0	7	6	7	2.4
Dorset	83.4	2.8	27.7	8.6	6	9	9	12.6
Christchurch	90.6	0.3	21.8	6.7	6	10	10	1.2
East Dorset	83.9	0.4	27.7	10.7	5	9	10	2.9
North Dorset	84.3	0.3	31.1	3.8	5	9	8	2.3
Purbeck	73.2	0.3	29.7	8.6	6	8	8	1.4
West Dorset	86.0	0.5	28.6	7.6	6	9	8	3.6
Weymouth and Portland	81.3	0.9	27.6	10.5	8	10	11	1.1

14.6 *(continued)*

	Economically active 1999–2000[3] (percentages)	Benefit statistics			Income Support bene- ficiaries[6] Nov.2000 (percentages)	Economic statistics		Stock of businesses end 1999 (thousands)
		Claimant count[4] March 2001				Businesses registered for VAT 1999		
		Total (thousands)	Of which females (percentages)	Of which long-term claimants[5] (percentages)		Registration rates[7] (percentages)	Deregistration rates[7] (percentages)	
Gloucestershire	84.2	6.7	25.0	20.7	6	11	11	18.7
Cheltenham	82.4	1.5	23.5	19.8	7	12	10	3.5
Cotswold	88.4	0.4	22.7	14.4	5	10	9	4.1
Forest of Dean	79.4	1.0	29.2	17.0	7	9	9	2.9
Gloucester	87.2	2.0	21.9	25.6	9	16	24	1.7
Stroud	80.7	1.1	28.4	18.5	6	10	9	4.1
Tewkesbury	87.0	0.7	27.5	20.9	5	10	9	2.5
Somerset	82.3	5.0	27.1	15.5	7	8	9	16.9
Mendip	79.7	1.2	29.5	16.4	7	9	8	3.8
Sedgemoor	77.7	1.3	28.2	18.2	8	8	9	3.4
South Somerset	85.7	1.0	26.7	12.6	6	8	8	5.2
Taunton Deane	86.3	1.0	25.2	13.1	8	10	10	3.1
West Somerset	75.4	0.5	23.6	18.0	8	8	8	1.4
Wiltshire	86.6	2.9	28.5	7.8	5	10	9	14.0
Kennet	83.9	0.6	31.4	8.9	4	10	8	2.7
North Wiltshire	84.8	0.7	29.5	5.9	5	10	8	4.5
Salisbury	89.2	0.6	24.1	11.6	5	10	11	3.5
West Wiltshire	88.1	1.0	28.7	6.2	5	9	9	3.3
Bristol/Bath area	83.0	11.5	23.7	13.6	8	12	11	27.9
Former county of Devon	80.5	14.6	25.7	15.0	9	9	10	31.6
Former county of Dorset	83.0	6.5	24.8	13.5	7	11	11	20.1
Former county of Wiltshire	87.3	4.9	26.9	9.1	6	11	9	18.4

1 See Notes and Definitions to the Labour Market chapter.
2 Local government structure as at 1 April 1998. See Notes and Definitions.
3 Based on the population of working age. Data are from the Labour Force Survey and relate to the period March 1999 to February 2000.
4 Count of claimants of unemployment-related benefit, i.e. Jobseeker's allowance.
5 Persons who have been claiming for more than 12 months (computerised claims only) as a percentage of all claimants.
6 Claimants and their partners aged 16 and over as a percentage of the population aged 16 and over. Data are from the Income Support Quarterly Statistical Enquiry.
7 Registrations/deregistrations during 1999 as a percentage of the stock at the end of 1998.

Source: Office for National Statistics; Department of Social Security; Department of the Environment, Transport and the Regions; Department of Trade and Industry; Small Business Service

NUTS levels 1, 2 and 3 in England,[1] 1998

NUTS level 3 areas

1 South Teeside
2 Hartlepool & Stockton
3 Darlington
4 Sunderland
5 Tyneside
6 Halton & Warrington
7 Gt Manchester North
8 Gt Manchester South
9 Blackburn with Darwen
10 Blackpool
11 Sefton
12 Wirral
13 East Merseyside
14 Liverpool
15 East Riding of Yorkshire
16 City of Kingston upon Hull
17 North & North East Lincolnshire
18 York
19 Leeds
20 Bradford
21 Calderdale, Kirklees & Wakefield
22 Sheffield
23 Barnsley, Doncaster & Rotherham
24 Derby
25 South & West Derbyshire
26 East Derbyshire
27 Leicester City
28 Leicestershire CC & Rutland
29 Northamptonshire
30 Nottingham
31 North Nottinghamshire
32 South Nottinghamshire
33 The Wrekin
34 Stoke-on-Trent
35 Staffordshire CC
36 Walsall & Wolverhampton
37 Birmingham
38 Coventry
39 Solihull
40 Dudley & Sandwell
41 Luton
42 Bedfordshire CC
43 Peterborough
44 Southend-on-Sea
45 Thurrock
46 Hertfordshire
47 Inner London - East
48 Inner London - West
49 Outer London - E & NE
50 Outer London - South
51 Outer London - W & NW
52 Milton Keynes
53 Buckinghamshire CC
54 Brighton & Hove

55 Portsmouth
56 Southampton
57 Medway
58 Kent CC
59 N & NE Somerset, South Gloucestershire
60 City of Bristol
61 Plymouth
62 Torbay
63 Bournemouth & Poole
64 Swindon

NUTS level 1 (= GOR)
NUTS level 2
NUTS level 3 (CC = County Council)

1 NUTS (Nomenclature of Units for Territorial Statistics) is a hierarchical classification of areas that provides a breakdown of the EU's economic territory. See Notes and Definitions.

14.7 Gross domestic product (GDP) by NUTS 1, 2 and 3 areas at current basic prices[1,2,3]

	£ million				£ per head				£ per head (UK=100)			
	1995	1996	1997	1998	1995	1996	1997	1998	1995	1996	1997	1998
United Kingdom[4]	622,389	657,775	700,567	743,314	10,619	11,185	11,871	12,548	100	100	100	100
ENGLAND	526,437	558,483	597,956	635,117	10,771	11,384	12,141	12,845	101	102	102	102
North East	22,975	23,755	24,202	25,294	8,796	9,111	9,301	9,741	83	81	78	78
Tees Valley and Durham	10,202	10,507	10,771	11,199	8,723	8,994	9,229	9,602	82	80	78	77
Hartlepool and Stockton-on-Tees	2,562	2,670	2,790	2,964	9,460	9,847	10,265	10,872	89	88	86	87
South Teeside	2,775	2,801	2,878	2,930	9,574	9,717	10,062	10,299	90	87	85	82
Darlington	1,048	1,067	1,117	1,142	10,401	10,549	11,019	11,254	98	94	93	90
Durham cc	3,817	3,970	3,987	4,163	7,512	7,818	7,849	8,199	71	70	66	65
Northumberland and Tyne and Wear	12,773	13,248	13,431	14,095	8,854	9,206	9,359	9,854	83	82	79	79
Northumberland	2,521	2,524	2,541	2,732	8,184	8,198	8,232	8,818	77	73	69	70
Tyneside	7,870	8,282	8,390	8,663	9,397	9,913	10,081	10,469	88	89	85	83
Sunderland	2,382	2,441	2,500	2,700	8,019	8,259	8,499	9,209	76	74	72	73
North West	66,007	68,937	72,414	75,275	9,547	9,980	10,494	10,909	90	89	88	87
Cumbria	5,284	5,277	5,412	5,634	10,759	10,742	10,995	11,418	101	96	93	91
West Cumbria	2,511	2,450	2,398	2,506	10,493	10,265	10,068	10,556	99	92	85	84
East Cumbria	2,772	2,828	3,014	3,127	11,011	11,194	11,865	12,217	104	100	100	97
Cheshire	12,028	12,629	13,550	14,112	12,291	12,878	13,786	14,327	116	115	116	114
Halton and Warrington	3,973	4,217	4,544	4,581	12,759	13,509	14,540	14,660	120	121	122	117
Cheshire cc	8,055	8,413	9,005	9,531	12,073	12,583	13,435	14,172	114	112	113	113
Greater Manchester	24,764	25,895	27,536	28,629	9,588	10,032	10,680	11,099	90	90	90	88
Greater Manchester South	15,757	16,394	17,649	18,363	11,288	11,756	12,685	13,204	106	105	107	105
Greater Manchester North	9,008	9,501	9,887	10,266	7,588	8,005	8,329	8,636	71	72	70	69
Lancashire	13,129	13,857	14,120	14,515	9,196	9,705	9,891	10,160	87	87	83	81
Blackburn With Darwen	1,376	1,385	1,449	1,598	9,796	9,882	10,374	11,420	92	88	87	91
Blackpool	1,163	1,231	1,296	1,345	7,550	8,029	8,522	8,899	71	72	72	71
Lancashire cc	10,589	11,242	11,374	11,572	9,346	9,910	10,016	10,173	88	89	84	81
Merseyside	10,802	11,278	11,797	12,386	7,536	7,907	8,310	8,759	71	71	70	70
East Merseyside	2,328	2,477	2,526	2,759	6,949	7,409	7,565	8,270	65	66	64	66
Liverpool	4,465	4,529	4,836	5,045	9,435	9,632	10,363	10,886	89	86	87	87
Sefton	1,894	2,053	2,109	2,112	6,482	7,057	7,277	7,313	61	63	61	58
Wirral	2,115	2,219	2,325	2,469	6,352	6,707	7,065	7,525	60	60	60	60
Yorkshire and the Humber	47,108	50,043	53,182	55,457	9,354	9,927	10,541	10,983	88	89	89	88
East Riding and North Lincolnshire	9,025	9,713	10,195	10,413	10,130	10,920	11,490	11,759	95	98	97	94
Kingston Upon Hull, City of	2,781	2,919	3,068	3,120	10,325	10,886	11,538	11,850	97	97	97	94
East Riding of Yorkshire	2,689	3,030	3,102	3,140	8,741	9,799	9,996	10,051	82	88	84	80
North and North East Lincolnshire	3,556	3,764	4,025	4,153	11,325	12,059	12,939	13,402	107	108	109	107
North Yorkshire	7,262	7,746	8,478	8,788	9,952	10,554	11,496	11,854	94	94	97	94
York	2,052	2,205	2,424	2,534	11,750	12,565	13,742	14,305	111	112	116	114
North Yorkshire cc	5,209	5,541	6,054	6,255	9,386	9,922	10,790	11,085	88	89	91	88
South Yorkshire	10,146	10,818	11,589	12,134	7,763	8,280	8,867	9,285	73	74	75	74
Barnsley, Doncaster and Rotherham	5,183	5,698	6,041	6,194	6,673	7,342	7,788	7,992	63	66	66	64
Sheffield	4,962	5,119	5,548	5,940	9,358	9,653	10,443	11,171	88	86	88	89
West Yorkshire	20,675	21,766	22,920	24,123	9,805	10,310	10,844	11,402	92	92	91	91
Bradford	4,207	4,549	4,794	5,004	8,707	9,400	9,903	10,339	82	84	83	82
Leeds	8,522	8,890	9,270	9,708	11,738	12,225	12,724	13,322	111	109	107	106
Calderdale, Kirklees and Wakefield	7,947	8,327	8,856	9,410	8,834	9,252	9,830	10,423	83	83	83	83

14.7 (continued)

	£ million				£ per head				£ per head (UK=100)			
	1995	1996	1997	1998	1995	1996	1997	1998	1995	1996	1997	1998
East Midlands	40,976	44,184	47,261	49,413	9,944	10,673	11,371	11,848	94	95	96	94
Derbyshire and Nottinghamshire	18,818	20,369	21,595	22,674	9,451	10,209	10,801	11,318	89	91	91	90
Derby	2,779	3,057	3,227	3,452	12,000	13,108	13,736	14,629	113	117	116	117
East Derbyshire	2,151	2,239	2,288	2,378	7,921	8,255	8,456	8,802	75	74	71	70
South and West Derbyshire	4,086	4,362	4,719	4,821	8,989	9,543	10,260	10,404	85	85	86	83
Nottingham	4,209	4,566	4,708	4,993	14,840	16,054	16,464	17,373	140	144	139	138
North Nottinghamshire	3,284	3,643	4,036	4,267	7,775	8,638	9,593	10,176	73	77	81	81
South Nottinghamshire	2,308	2,502	2,616	2,763	7,053	7,641	7,999	8,448	66	68	67	67
Leicestershire, Rutland and Northamptonshire	16,651	17,829	19,281	20,047	10,956	11,656	12,534	12,978	103	104	106	103
Leicester	3,841	4,067	4,090	4,115	13,019	13,752	13,877	13,973	123	123	117	111
Leicestershire cc and Rutland	6,369	6,633	7,453	7,722	10,165	10,511	11,733	12,139	96	94	99	97
Northamptonshire	6,440	7,129	7,738	8,211	10,767	11,825	12,718	13,369	101	106	107	107
Lincolnshire[5]	5,507	5,986	6,385	6,692	9,031	9,734	10,319	10,751	85	87	87	86
West Midlands	52,407	54,851	57,783	61,130	9,869	10,309	10,845	11,455	93	92	91	91
Herefordshire, Worcestershire and Warwickshire	12,211	12,993	13,610	14,735	10,204	10,854	11,309	12,165	96	97	95	97
Herefordshire, County of	1,682	1,733	1,786	1,842	10,212	10,512	10,780	11,011	96	94	91	88
Worcestershire	5,274	5,614	5,845	6,168	9,883	10,557	10,931	11,467	93	94	92	91
Warwickshire	5,256	5,646	5,979	6,725	10,545	11,281	11,887	13,288	99	101	100	106
Shropshire and Staffordshire	13,195	14,281	14,920	16,023	8,938	9,654	10,057	10,747	84	86	85	86
Telford and Wrekin	1,780	1,934	2,067	2,208	12,339	13,375	14,164	14,843	116	120	119	118
Shropshire cc	2,459	2,553	2,684	2,859	8,952	9,229	9,663	10,231	84	83	81	82
Stoke-on-Trent	2,460	2,633	2,678	2,715	9,659	10,331	10,531	10,738	91	92	89	86
Staffordshire cc	6,495	7,160	7,492	8,241	8,093	8,916	9,299	10,176	76	80	78	81
West Midlands	27,001	27,578	29,253	30,372	10,238	10,429	11,075	11,530	96	93	93	92
Birmingham	11,255	11,398	12,308	12,652	11,091	11,166	12,075	12,456	104	100	102	99
Solihull	2,367	2,460	2,490	2,625	11,670	12,073	12,152	12,757	110	108	102	102
Coventry	3,136	3,320	3,557	3,663	10,330	10,867	11,625	12,013	97	97	98	96
Dudley and Sandwell	5,600	5,708	6,043	6,292	9,222	9,414	9,996	10,428	87	84	84	83
Walsall and Wolverhampton	4,643	4,692	4,855	5,140	9,124	9,237	9,584	10,191	86	83	81	81
East	55,989	60,070	64,982	69,607	10,665	11,368	12,208	12,973	100	102	103	103
East Anglia	24,051	25,916	27,987	29,663	11,357	12,133	12,983	13,635	107	108	109	109
Peterborough	2,173	2,384	2,655	2,686	13,676	15,004	16,836	17,158	129	134	142	137
Cambridgeshire cc	6,975	7,574	8,259	8,851	13,093	14,003	14,981	15,783	123	125	126	126
Norfolk	7,505	8,072	8,709	9,319	9,723	10,402	11,146	11,825	92	93	94	94
Suffolk	7,398	7,887	8,363	8,807	11,306	11,944	12,571	13,143	106	107	106	105
Bedfordshire and Hertfordshire	16,972	18,089	19,457	21,201	10,911	11,570	12,364	13,363	103	103	104	106
Luton	2,115	2,202	2,409	2,632	11,654	12,116	13,243	14,400	110	108	112	115
Bedfordshire cc	3,955	4,052	4,208	4,425	10,868	11,058	11,385	11,874	102	99	96	95
Hertfordshire	10,903	11,835	12,840	14,143	10,793	11,658	12,562	13,717	102	104	106	109
Essex	14,963	16,064	17,537	18,743	9,491	10,138	11,005	11,690	89	91	93	93
Southend-on-Sea	1,464	1,634	1,854	1,940	8,569	9,501	10,641	11,016	81	85	90	88
Thurrock	1,354	1,466	1,576	1,747	10,279	11,091	11,898	13,055	97	99	100	104
Essex cc	12,145	12,964	14,107	15,056	9,533	10,125	10,962	11,640	90	91	92	93
London	106,759	112,033	122,014	133,081	15,251	15,885	17,158	18,566	144	142	145	148
Inner London	67,666	70,446	77,280	84,488	25,305	26,120	28,386	30,734	238	234	239	245
Inner London – West	45,952	48,182	52,165	57,424	47,970	49,568	52,758	57,281	452	443	444	456
Inner London – East	21,714	22,264	25,115	27,064	12,653	12,907	14,486	15,496	119	115	122	123
Outer London	39,093	41,586	44,735	48,591	9,037	9,548	10,194	10,996	85	85	86	88
Outer London - East and North East	10,362	11,030	11,765	12,313	6,775	7,205	7,674	8,017	64	64	65	64
Outer London - South	9,996	10,426	11,050	11,838	8,961	9,264	9,733	10,358	84	83	82	83
Outer London - West and North West	18,734	20,130	21,920	24,440	11,145	11,846	12,743	14,045	105	106	107	112

14.7 (continued)

	£ million				£ per head				£ per head (UK=100)			
	1995	1996	1997	1998	1995	1996	1997	1998	1995	1996	1997	1998
South East	86,831	94,484	102,536	109,797	11,090	11,983	12,912	13,731	104	107	109	109
Berkshire, Buckinghamshire and Oxfordshire	26,890	28,952	30,833	33,972	13,206	14,053	14,826	16,207	124	126	125	129
Berkshire	11,637	12,650	13,506	15,212	14,965	16,044	16,974	19,008	141	143	143	151
Milton Keynes	2,699	2,912	3,225	3,547	14,130	14,910	16,209	17,557	133	133	137	140
Buckinghamshire cc	5,451	5,936	6,191	6,616	11,540	12,507	12,984	13,813	109	112	109	110
Oxfordshire	7,104	7,454	7,910	8,598	11,932	12,387	13,008	13,983	112	111	110	111
Surrey, East and West Sussex	25,987	28,175	31,568	33,588	10,383	11,193	12,446	13,137	98	100	105	105
Brighton and Hove	2,112	2,218	2,461	2,600	8,530	8,900	9,783	10,206	80	80	82	81
East Sussex cc	3,390	3,530	3,694	3,850	7,028	7,280	7,576	7,847	66	65	64	63
Surrey	11,936	13,354	15,428	16,914	11,425	12,749	14,637	15,945	108	114	123	127
West Sussex	8,549	9,072	9,986	10,225	11,741	12,332	13,435	13,622	111	110	113	109
Hampshire and Isle of Wight	18,316	20,830	22,647	23,956	10,531	11,901	12,861	13,535	99	106	108	108
Portsmouth	2,515	2,863	3,285	3,430	13,241	15,028	17,230	18,012	125	134	145	144
Southampton	2,710	2,958	3,130	3,168	12,723	13,784	14,538	14,675	120	123	122	117
Hampshire cc	12,207	14,040	15,224	16,295	10,079	11,510	12,387	13,173	95	103	104	105
Isle Of Wight	883	970	1,009	1,064	7,059	7,730	8,013	8,397	66	69	67	67
Kent	15,641	16,528	17,489	18,282	10,080	10,615	11,179	11,621	95	95	94	93
Medway	2,096	2,197	2,332	2,572	8,687	9,149	9,710	10,639	82	82	82	85
Kent cc	13,545	14,331	15,157	15,710	10,337	10,883	11,445	11,800	97	97	96	94
South West	47,385	50,128	53,580	56,064	9,828	10,352	11,008	11,447	93	93	93	91
Gloucestershire, Wiltshire and North Somerset	24,143	25,840	27,458	28,561	11,367	12,111	12,794	13,222	107	108	108	105
Bristol, City of	5,142	5,416	6,093	6,224	12,833	13,510	15,197	15,472	121	121	128	123
North and North East Somerset, South Gloucestershire	5,666	6,265	6,456	6,980	9,742	10,721	10,959	11,730	92	96	92	93
Gloucestershire	6,120	6,431	6,810	7,143	11,085	11,577	12,188	12,772	104	104	103	102
Swindon	2,765	3,009	3,147	3,241	15,897	17,243	17,862	18,129	150	154	150	144
Wiltshire cc	4,450	4,719	4,951	4,974	10,707	11,278	11,755	11,708	101	101	99	93
Dorset and Somerset	10,739	11,226	12,031	12,862	9,279	9,643	10,270	10,904	87	86	87	87
Bournemouth and Poole	3,044	3,144	3,294	3,670	10,162	10,466	10,910	12,078	96	94	92	96
Dorset cc	3,152	3,392	3,703	3,874	8,351	8,901	9,642	10,016	79	80	81	80
Somerset	4,543	4,690	5,035	5,318	9,457	9,717	10,369	10,877	89	87	87	87
Cornwall and Isles of Scilly[5]	3,265	3,525	3,793	4,009	6,774	7,286	7,800	8,185	64	65	66	65
Devon	9,238	9,534	10,299	10,630	8,732	8,988	9,685	9,952	82	80	82	79
Plymouth	2,672	2,666	2,888	2,910	10,394	10,371	11,287	11,437	98	93	95	91
Torbay	904	920	1,023	1,066	7,311	7,425	8,295	8,655	69	66	70	69
Devon cc	5,662	5,948	6,388	6,654	8,360	8,749	9,336	9,636	79	78	79	77

1 Estimates for all years are provisional.
2 Includes taxes less subsidies on production.
3 Components may not sum to totals due to rounding.
4 Excluding GDP for Extra-Regio, which comprises compensation of employees and gross operating surplus which cannot be assigned to regions.
5 This area is represented at more than one NUTS level.

15 Sub-regions of Wales

Unitary Authorities in Wales

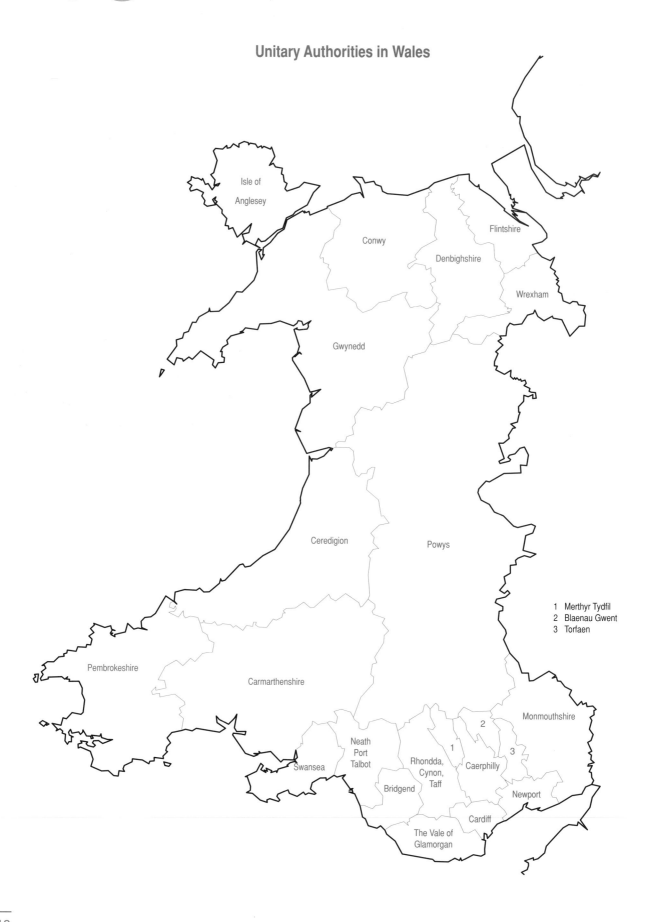

Isle of Anglesey

Conwy

Flintshire

Denbighshire

Wrexham

Gwynedd

Ceredigion

Powys

1 Merthyr Tydfil
2 Blaenau Gwent
3 Torfaen

Pembrokeshire

Carmarthenshire

Monmouthshire

Neath Port Talbot

2

Swansea

Rhondda, Cynon, Taff

1

Caerphilly

3

Bridgend

Newport

Cardiff

The Vale of Glamorgan

15.1 Area and population, 1999

	Area (sq km)	Persons per sq km	Population (thousands)			Total population percentage change 1981–1999	Total fertility rate (TFR)[1]	Standardised mortality ratio (UK=100) (SMR)[2]	Percentage of population aged:			
			Males	Females	Total				Under 5	5–15	16 up to pension age[3]	Pension age[3] and over
United Kingdom	242,910	245	29,299	30,202	59,501	5.6	1.69	100	6.1	14.3	61.6	18.1
Wales	20,779	141	1,442	1,495	2,937	4.4	1.74	104	5.8	14.5	59.8	19.9
Blaenau Gwent	109	658	36	36	72	-5.2	1.96	122	5.8	15.4	59.6	19.2
Bridgend	251	525	64	68	132	4.3	1.92	105	6.0	14.5	60.1	19.4
Caerphilly	278	612	84	87	170	-1.0	1.99	117	6.4	15.5	60.5	17.6
Cardiff	140	2,317	161	163	324	13.1	1.66	100	6.2	15.0	62.1	16.7
Carmarthenshire	2,395	71	82	86	169	2.3	1.83	103	5.4	13.4	58.2	23.0
Ceredigion	1,795	40	35	36	72	17.2	1.53	90	4.6	12.8	60.9	21.7
Conwy	1,130	99	54	58	112	13.3	1.78	97	5.3	13.2	55.5	26.0
Denbighshire	838	109	44	47	91	5.0	1.77	103	5.7	14.3	56.7	23.3
Flintshire	438	337	73	75	147	6.4	1.79	103	6.1	14.2	62.1	17.6
Gwynedd	2,548	46	57	60	116	4.1	1.83	98	5.6	13.6	58.6	22.2
Isle of Anglesey	714	92	32	34	65	-4.0	2.12	101	5.8	14.6	57.6	22.0
Merthyr Tydfil	111	506	27	29	56	-7.2	2.05	125	6.3	16.2	58.9	18.7
Monmouthshire	850	102	42	44	87	13.2	1.61	90	5.4	14.2	59.8	20.6
Neath Port Talbot	442	313	67	71	138	-3.1	1.73	107	5.6	14.4	59.1	21.0
Newport	190	728	68	71	138	4.5	1.99	105	6.4	15.6	59.1	18.8
Pembrokeshire	1,590	72	56	58	114	5.9	1.90	106	5.6	14.6	58.5	21.3
Powys	5,196	24	63	63	126	12.6	1.73	88	5.4	13.6	58.9	22.1
Rhondda, Cynon, Taff	424	567	119	121	241	0.9	1.66	115	5.9	14.9	61.2	18.1
Swansea	378	608	113	116	230	0.2	1.81	98	5.5	13.7	60.1	20.6
Torfaen	126	713	44	46	90	-1.0	1.89	120	6.4	15.2	59.8	18.5
The Vale of Glamorgan	331	366	59	62	121	7.1	1.81	99	6.1	15.3	59.2	19.4
Wrexham	504	249	61	64	125	5.3	1.73	107	5.8	14.4	61.0	18.8

1 The total fertility rate (TFR) is the average number of children which would be born to a woman if the current pattern of fertility persisted throughout her child-bearing years. Previously called total period fertility rate (TPFR).

2 Adjusted for the age structure of the population. See Notes and Definitions to the Population chapter.

3 Pension age is 65 for males and 60 for females.

Source: Office for National Statistics; National Assembly for Wales

15.2 Vital[1,2] and social statistics

	Live births per 1,000 population		Deaths per 1,000 population		Perinatal mortality rate[3]	Infant mortality rate[4]	Percent- age of live births under 2.5 kg	Percent- age of live births outside marriage	Children looked after by LAs per 1,000 population aged under 18
	1991	1999	1991	1999	1998-2000	1998-2000	1999	1999	2000[5]
United Kingdom	13.7	11.8	11.2	10.6	8.2	5.8	..	38.8	..
Wales	13.2	10.9	11.8	11.9	7.7	5.8	7.4	46.1	5.3
Blaenau Gwent	14.8	11.3	12.5	13.7	10.6	6.8	9.1	59.5	7.9
Bridgend	13.3	11.6	11.6	11.6	8.2	4.9	7.4	47.3	5.1
Caerphilly	14.2	12.1	10.0	11.3	6.7	3.7	8.5	53.1	8.4
Cardiff	14.8	11.4	10.8	9.8	8.6	7.6	7.6	43.4	6.5
Carmarthenshire	11.3	10.2	13.0	13.6	7.7	6.4	7.2	42.8	4.8
Ceredigion	10.8	8.6	12.6	11.7	8.5	5.3	5.7	39.2	3.5
Conwy	11.8	9.7	15.6	15.8	10.4	7.8	6.6	46.0	4.8
Denbighshire	12.6	10.2	13.9	14.8	6.3	5.6	6.8	46.2	4.3
Flintshire	13.4	11.6	10.5	10.3	7.2	3.5	6.6	38.1	2.5
Gwynedd	12.2	10.9	13.0	12.8	5.5	3.9	6.4	43.9	3.9
Isle of Anglesey	12.2	11.1	11.6	12.9	7.1	5.7	5.9	43.0	3.3
Merthyr Tydfil	14.7	11.8	11.7	12.8	6.0	4.5	8.8	56.4	8.1
Monmouthshire	11.8	9.6	11.1	10.9	5.9	5.1	7.6	36.0	2.9
Neath Port Talbot	12.4	9.9	13.2	12.8	6.8	6.1	8.3	49.9	6.3
Newport	15.3	12.1	10.6	11.1	4.5	4.7	8.8	46.7	8.4
Pembrokeshire	13.0	10.7	11.2	12.5	7.9	6.6	6.3	41.4	5.3
Powys	12.0	10.2	12.4	11.3	8.8	4.8	7.2	37.9	2.7
Rhondda, Cynon, Taff	13.4	11.0	11.6	11.7	8.1	6.9	7.4	54.0	5.3
Swansea	12.5	10.9	11.8	11.7	9.2	6.9	7.9	47.0	4.8
Torfaen	14.3	11.4	11.4	12.3	6.2	5.9	7.3	50.8	5.3
The Vale of Glamorgan	13.4	11.2	11.5	10.8	8.5	4.9	7.5	42.5	6.0
Wrexham	13.1	11.1	11.2	11.7	8.7	5.5	6.5	46.4	3.3

1 Births and deaths data are based on the usual area of residence of the mother/deceased. See Notes and Definitions to the Population chapter for details of the
  inclusion/exclusion of births to non-resident mothers and deaths of non-resident persons.
2 Births data are on the basis of year of occurrence in England and Wales and year of registration in Scotland and Northern Ireland. All deaths data relate to year of registration.
3 Still births and deaths of infants under 1 week of age per 1,000 live and still births. Figures for some UAs should be treated with caution as the perinatal mortality rate was based
  on fewer than 20 events.
4 Deaths of infants under 1 year of age per 1,000 live births. Figures for some UAs should be treated with caution as the infant mortality rate was based on fewer than 20 events.
5 At 31 March. Under 18 mid-1999 population estimates used.

Source: Office for National Statistics; National Assembly for Wales

15.3 Education and training

	Three and four year olds in early years education[1]			Pupil/teacher ratio 2000/01[3] (numbers)		Pupils and students participating in post-compulsory education[4] (percentages) 1999/00	Percentage of pupils in last year of compulsory schooling[5,6] 1999/00 with		
	Participation rates[2] (percentages)						5 or more GCSE Grades 1-3/		Average A/AS level
	All schools Jan. 2000	Private and voluntary providers Jan. 2000	All providers Jan. 2000	Primary schools	Secondary schools		No graded results	Standard Grade (or equivalent)	points score[7] 1999/00
United Kingdom	63	27	90	22.3	16.5	80	5.2	48.6	18.1
Wales	80	..	..	21.5	16.6	77	7.7	48.3	16.8
Isle of Anglesey	63	..	..	19.9	16.0	..	6.3	48.7	17.4
Gwynedd	75	..	..	20.1	14.6	..	3.9	56.3	16.9
Conwy	83	..	..	22.2	17.6	..	3.3	54.8	17.0
Denbighshire	80	..	..	23.3	17.3	..	9.3	47.7	17.4
Flintshire	83	..	..	22.6	16.6	..	4.4	50.4	16.9
Wrexham	81	..	..	22.2	17.0	..	8.2	44.5	16.7
Powys	59	..	..	19.3	14.7	..	6.5	54.9	17.6
Ceredigion	66	..	..	17.8	15.1	..	2.6	59.9	18.8
Pembrokeshire	85	..	..	20.6	16.4	..	4.1	52.1	17.1
Carmarthenshire	81	..	..	19.4	16.3	..	6.1	51.6	16.9
Swansea	91	..	..	20.9	16.7	..	9.7	50.7	16.6
Neath Port Talbot	94	..	..	20.3	16.0	..	5.6	49.0	16.4
Bridgend	71	..	..	23.1	17.0	..	12.5	46.3	16.1
The Vale of Glamorgan	83	..	..	21.7	17.2	..	5.8	58.3	18.9
Cardiff	76	..	..	21.6	16.8	..	10.5	44.6	16.6
Rhondda, Cynon, Taff	96	..	..	22.5	17.2	..	8.8	45.1	15.4
Merthyr Tydfil	95	..	..	21.9	16.4	..	13.1	40.5	14.0
Caerphilly	82	..	..	22.7	17.1	..	9.9	40.1	14.5
Blaenau Gwent	77	..	..	21.9	16.3	..	14.0	35.6	13.1
Torfaen	77	..	..	22.3	17.4	..	3.3	45.4	16.4
Monmouthshire	54	..	..	23.3	16.8	..	5.3	54.1	19.4
Newport	78	..	..	22.7	16.9	..	8.7	42.5	15.7

1 Headcounts of children aged three and four at 31st December in the previous calendar year. These figures must be interpreted carefully in the light of differing types of education providers between the countries. In the UK figures any child attending more than one provider in England may have been counted twice.

2 Number of three and four year olds attending provider expressed as a percentage of the three and four year old population.

3 Public sector schools only.

4 Pupils and students aged 16 in education as a percentage of the 16 year old population (ages measured at the beginning of the academic year).

5 Pupils in their last year of compulsory schooling as a percentage of the school population of the same age.

6 Figures relate to maintained schools only; hence they are not directly comparable with those in Tables 4.5, 16.3 and 17.3 which are for all schools.

7 Figures for United Kingdom relates to England and Wales average.

Source: National Assembly for Wales; Department for Education and Skills

15.4 Housing and households

	Housing completions 1999–00 (numbers)		Stock of dwellings 1 April 1999 (thousands)	All households 1999 (thousands)	Local authority tenants: average weekly unrebated rent per dwelling (£) April 1999	Council Tax (£)[1] April 1999
	Private enterprise	Registered social landlords, local authorities etc				
Wales	7,386	947	1,259	1,190.5	40.20	602
Blaenau Gwent	80	0	32	28.7	40.10	640
Bridgend	561	57	56	53.4	40.20	647
Caerphilly	599	44	71	67.9	42.50	633
Cardiff	714	72	126	129.9	45.60	573
Carmarthenshire	163	40	75	68.6	38.30	666
Ceredigion	256	6	30	29.5	42.00	670
Conwy	220	30	52	47.5	37.70	488
Denbighshire	112	32	39	37.8	36.50	647
Flintshire	272	14	61	58.5	37.50	592
Gwynedd	110	0	57	47.3	37.80	618
Isle of Anglesey	69	0	31	27.1	36.70	534
Merthyr Tydfil	73	42	25	22.6	38.30	712
Monmouthshire	432	86	35	35.0	44.20	485
Neath Port Talbot	414	157	65	56.1	38.40	750
Newport	646	49	58	56.7	43.40	531
Pembrokeshire	234	97	53	46.3	37.20	542
Powys	376	26	55	51.8	39.00	552
Rhondda, Cynon, Taff	586	34	102	96.2	39.00	686
Swansea	524	114	94	93.5	40.00	596
Torfaen	86	16	39	36.1	46.00	564
The Vale of Glamorgan	481	31	49	48.4	45.00	532
Wrexham	378	0	54	51.4	35.20	633

1 See Notes and Definitions.

Source: National Assembly for Wales

15.5 Labour market and benefit statistics[1]

	Economic activity					Benefit statistics			
	Economically active 1999–2000[2] (percentages)	Total in employment[3] as at September 1999 (thousands)	Employment rate 1999–2000[2] (percentages)[4]	ILO unemploy-ment rate 1999–2000[2] (percentages)[4]	Average gross weekly full-time earnings, all persons[7] April 2000 (£)	Claimant count[5] March 2001			Income Support bene-ficiaries[8] Nov.2000 (percentages)
						Total (thousands)	Of which females (percentages)	Of which long term claimants[6] (percentages)	
United Kingdom	78.5	26,784	73.8	6.0	409.2	1,041.1	23.4	19.7	10
Wales	73.8	1,070	68.5	7.2	368.0	57.0	22.7	17.5	12
Blaenau Gwent	67.5	20	60.4	..	325.0	2.0	22.2	21.1	15
Bridgend	73.0	46	69.4	..	361.0	2.5	23.5	11.6	12
Caerphilly	75.1	49	68.6	8.7	362.0	3.6	23.4	14.4	14
Cardiff	79.2	165	73.7	6.9	392.0	6.1	19.5	16.4	11
Carmarthenshire	71.6	45	64.8	9.5	338.0	3.0	21.9	17.2	12
Ceredigion	71.9	22	63.8	..	..	1.1	25.0	20.3	8
Conwy	77.1	34	73.9	..	313.0	2.2	24.4	20.6	11
Denbighshire	74.2	33	67.0	..	..	1.7	22.7	18.4	12
Flintshire	81.2	61	76.5	..	395.0	2.2	24.1	16.0	9
Gwynedd	70.7	41	66.9	..	331.0	3.1	25.6	23.3	10
Isle of Anglesey	72.7	17	69.5	..	..	1.9	24.6	32.0	11
Merthyr Tydfil	64.7	18	59.0	..	..	1.5	22.2	22.4	16
Monmouthshire	79.9	33	74.2	..	349.0	1.0	24.6	18.6	6
Neath Port Talbot	66.3	42	59.0	11.0	400.0	3.0	23.6	15.7	14
Newport	77.0	74	69.3	..	378.0	3.0	21.8	19.1	12
Pembrokeshire	70.1	33	65.7	..	356.0	2.5	25.4	16.8	12
Powys	85.6	43	80.8	..	338.0	1.7	28.0	15.0	8
Rhondda, Cynon, Taff	68.9	73	63.5	7.9	359.0	4.3	22.2	11.4	14
Swansea	67.7	90	62.7	7.4	360.0	5.0	20.1	19.8	13
Torfaen	72.2	37	69.2	..	362.0	1.6	23.2	12.7	13
The Vale of Glamorgan	75.4	41	72.9	..	384.0	2.2	19.8	18.1	9
Wrexham	73.9	52	68.9	..	372.0	2.0	21.7	11.9	11

1 See Notes and Definitions to the Labour market chapter. In some cases sample sizes are too small to provide reliable estimates. Due to the sample size in Wales, the National Assembly for Wales has adopted the use of a four quarter average as the standard methodology for analysing and publishing LFS data. Thus, the data contained here may not correspond to other analyses released by the National Assembly for Wales.

2 For those of working age. Data are from the Labour Force Survey and relate to the period March 1999 to February 2000.

3 For those of working age. Includes those on Government employment and training schemes and unpaid family workers.

4 As a percentage of the economically active.

5 Count of claimants of unemployment-related benefit, ie. Jobseeker's allowance.

6 Persons who have been claiming for more than 12 months as a percentage of all claimants.

7 Earning estimates have been derived from the New Earning Survey and relate to full-time employees whose pay for the survey pay-period was not affected by absence.

8 Claimants and their partners aged 16 and over as a percentage of the population aged 16 or over. Data are from the Income Support Quarterly Statistical Enquiry.

Source: Office for National Statistics

NUTS levels 1, 2 and 3 in Wales,[1] 1998

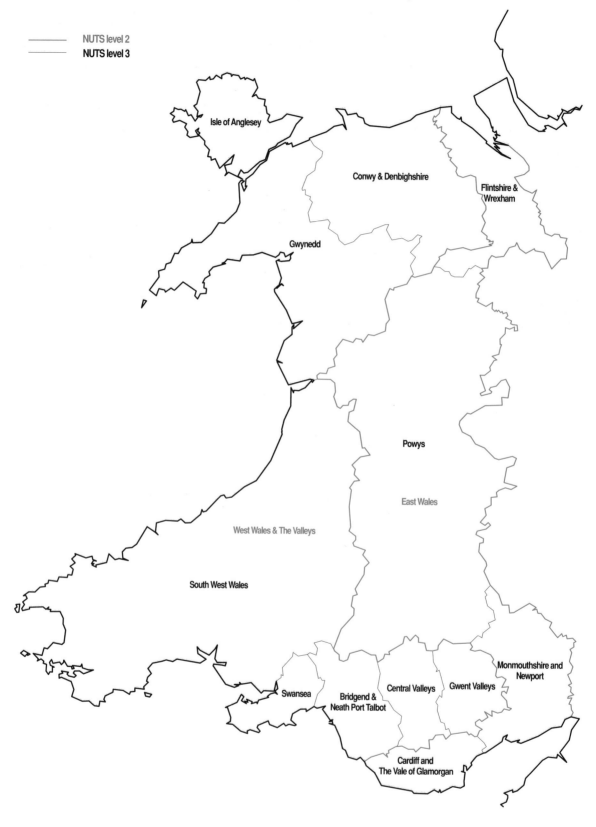

NUTS level 2
NUTS level 3

Isle of Anglesey

Conwy & Denbighshire

Flintshire & Wrexham

Gwynedd

Powys

East Wales

West Wales & The Valleys

South West Wales

Monmouthshire and Newport

Swansea

Central Valleys

Gwent Valleys

Bridgend & Neath Port Talbot

Cardiff and The Vale of Glamorgan

1 NUTS (Nomenclature of Units for Territorial Statistics) is a hierarchical classification of areas that provides a breakdown of the EU's economic territory. The NUTS level 1 area is the whole country. See Notes and Definitions.

15.6   Gross domestic product (GDP) by NUTS 1, 2 and 3 area at current basic prices[1, 2, 3]

	£ million				£ per head				£ per head (UK=100)			
	1995	1996	1997	1998	1995	1996	1997	1998	1995	1996	1997	1998
Wales	25,989	27,017	28,010	29,541	8,900	9,240	9,562	10,063	84	83	81	80
West Wales and the Valleys	14,442	15,162	15,772	16,490	7,689	8,084	8,420	8,810	72	72	71	70
Isle of Anglesey	479	510	526	531	7,051	7,581	7,876	8,047	66	68	66	64
Gwynedd	1,002	1,013	1,056	1,164	8,511	8,578	8,947	9,876	80	77	75	79
Conwy and Denbighshire	1,367	1,522	1,622	1,679	6,740	7,494	8,007	8,295	63	67	67	66
South West Wales	2,691	2,793	2,788	2,921	7,609	7,903	7,895	8,258	72	71	67	66
Central Valleys	2,229	2,316	2,324	2,514	7,454	7,746	7,774	8,422	70	69	65	67
Gwent Valleys	2,441	2,580	2,669	2,655	7,292	7,733	8,013	7,981	69	69	67	64
Bridgend and Neath Port Talbot	2,264	2,462	2,665	2,737	8,352	9,102	9,865	10,121	79	81	83	81
Swansea	1,969	1,967	2,122	2,289	8,516	8,523	9,204	9,943	80	76	78	79
East Wales	11,547	11,855	12,239	13,051	11,082	11,308	11,589	12,269	104	101	98	98
Monmouthshire and Newport	2,388	2,464	2,533	2,800	10,727	11,017	11,288	12,424	101	98	95	99
Cardiff and Vale of Glamorgan	5,246	5,241	5,388	5,605	12,269	12,131	12,335	12,714	116	108	104	101
Flintshire and Wrexham	2,870	3,055	3,171	3,371	10,654	11,352	11,753	12,404	100	101	99	99
Powys	1,042	1,095	1,147	1,276	8,523	8,863	9,172	10,144	80	79	77	81

1   Estimates for all years are provisional.
2   Includes taxes *less* subsidies on production.
3   Components may not sum to totals due to rounding.
4   Excluding GDP for Extra-Regio, which comprises compensation of employees and gross operating surplus which cannot be assigned to regions.

16 Sub-regions of Scotland

New Councils in Scotland

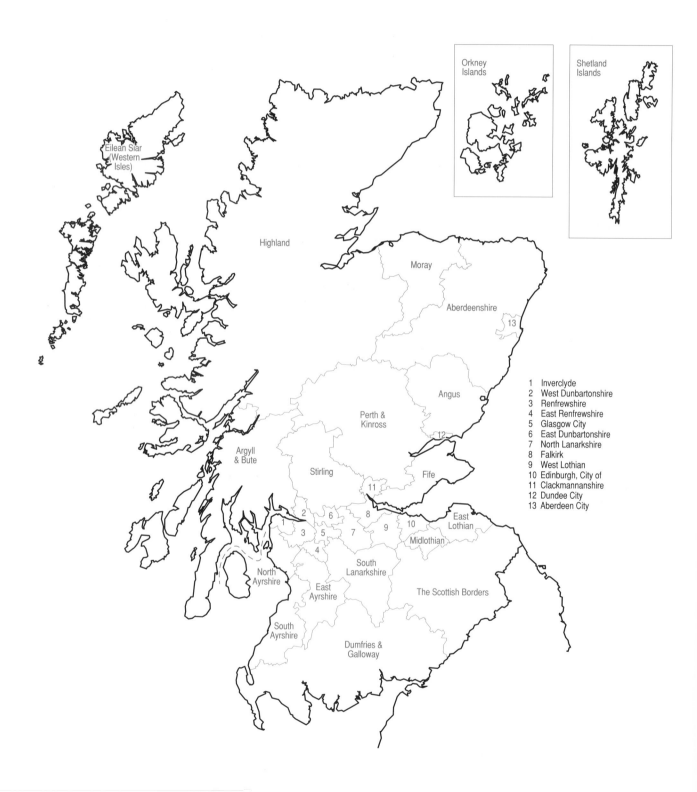

Eilean Siar
(Western
Isles)

Highland

Orkney
Islands

Shetland
Islands

Moray

Aberdeenshire

13

Angus

Perth &
Kinross

12

Argyll
& Bute

Stirling

Fife

11

East
Lothian

2   6   8
1   10
3   5   7   9   Midlothian
4
North   South
Ayrshire   Lanarkshire
          East   The Scottish Borders
          Ayrshire
South
Ayrshire
          Dumfries &
          Galloway

1   Inverclyde
2   West Dunbartonshire
3   Renfrewshire
4   East Renfrewshire
5   Glasgow City
6   East Dunbartonshire
7   North Lanarkshire
8   Falkirk
9   West Lothian
10   Edinburgh, City of
11   Clackmannanshire
12   Dundee City
13   Aberdeen City

16.1 Area and population, 1999

	Area (sq km)	Persons per sq km	Population (thousands)			Total population percentage change 1981–1999	Total fertility rate (TFR)[1]	Standardised mortality ratio (UK=100) (SMR)[2]	Percentage of population aged:			
			Males	Females	Total				Under 5	5–15	16 up to pension age[3]	Pension age[3] and over
United Kingdom	242,910	245	29,299	30,202	59,501	5.6	1.69	100	6.1	14.3	61.6	18.1
Scotland	78,133	66	2,486	2,634	5,119	-1.2	1.51	118	5.8	13.9	62.3	18.0
Aberdeen City	186	1,144	104	108	213	0.1	1.46	111	5.4	12.8	64.4	17.4
Aberdeenshire	6,318	36	113	114	227	20.4	1.64	101	6.0	15.1	63.1	15.8
Angus	2,181	50	54	56	110	4.0	1.56	116	5.6	14.2	60.7	19.5
Argyll and Bute	6,930	13	44	46	90	-1.3	1.55	110	5.0	13.0	60.6	21.4
Clackmannanshire	157	310	24	25	49	0.6	1.75	105	6.1	14.8	61.8	17.3
Dumfries and Galloway	6,439	23	71	75	147	0.9	1.67	105	5.5	13.8	58.8	21.8
Dundee City	65	2,217	69	75	144	-14.8	1.59	119	5.6	13.5	60.3	20.6
East Ayrshire	1,252	97	59	62	121	-5.0	1.62	132	5.8	14.6	61.0	18.7
East Dunbartonshire	172	644	54	56	111	0.9	1.41	101	5.4	13.6	63.4	17.7
East Lothian	678	133	44	46	90	12.0	1.57	107	6.0	14.0	60.8	19.2
East Renfrewshire	173	517	43	46	89	11.3	1.59	94	5.9	14.4	62.2	17.5
Edinburgh, City of	262	1,722	219	233	452	1.3	1.27	109	5.4	11.9	65.2	17.5
Eilean Siar (Western Isles)	3,134	9	14	14	28	-12.6	1.70	116	5.2	14.5	58.6	21.6
Falkirk	299	482	70	74	144	-0.5	1.58	123	5.9	13.7	62.7	17.7
Fife	1,323	264	169	180	349	2.2	1.57	108	5.7	14.3	61.5	18.5
Glasgow City	175	3,493	292	319	611	-14.2	1.35	144	5.9	13.5	63.3	17.3
Highland	25,784	8	103	106	209	7.0	1.77	113	5.9	14.6	60.8	18.7
Inverclyde	162	527	41	44	85	-15.8	1.66	132	5.9	14.6	60.8	18.7
Midlothian	356	230	40	41	82	-2.3	1.70	117	5.8	14.1	63.5	16.5
Moray	2,238	38	42	43	85	2.1	1.82	111	6.2	14.7	60.4	18.6
North Ayrshire	884	158	67	72	139	1.5	1.53	118	5.7	14.7	61.5	18.1
North Lanarkshire	474	692	159	168	328	-4.0	1.61	124	6.2	14.5	62.9	16.3
Orkney Islands	992	20	10	10	20	2.2	1.71	100	5.6	14.9	60.5	19.0
Perth and Kinross	5,311	25	65	69	134	10.0	1.63	105	5.4	13.8	59.7	21.1
Renfrewshire	261	678	86	92	177	-4.2	1.60	132	6.0	14.4	62.2	17.4
Scottish Borders, The	4,734	22	51	55	106	5.1	1.64	99	5.5	13.4	59.2	21.9
Shetland Islands	1,438	16	11	11	23	-13.7	1.91	107	6.3	16.3	62.2	15.2
South Ayrshire	1,202	95	55	60	114	0.9	1.44	107	5.2	13.6	60.0	21.2
South Lanarkshire	1,771	174	149	159	308	-0.8	1.54	131	5.8	14.5	62.9	16.8
Stirling	2,196	39	41	44	85	5.5	1.49	111	5.7	13.5	62.9	17.8
West Dunbartonshire	162	585	45	49	95	-10.2	1.57	138	6.1	15.2	61.0	17.6
West Lothian	425	364	76	79	155	11.1	1.67	136	6.6	14.9	65.2	13.3

1 The total fertility rate (TFR) is the average number of children which would be born to a woman if the current pattern of fertility persisted throughout her child-bearing years. Previously called total period fertility rate (TPFR).
2 Adjusted for the age structure of the population. See Notes and Definitions to the Population chapter.
3 Pension age is 65 for males and 60 for females.

Source: Office for National Statistics; General Register Office for Scotland

16.2 Vital[1,2] and social statistics

	Live births per 1,000 population		Deaths per 1,000 population		Perinatal mortality rate[3]	Infant mortality rate[4]	Percent- age of live births outside marriage
	1991	1999	1991	1999	1998–2000	1998–2000	1999
United Kingdom	13.7	11.8	11.2	10.6	8.2	5.8	38.8
Scotland	13.1	10.8	12.0	11.8	8.3	5.4	41.2
Aberdeen City	12.5	10.9	10.8	10.9	9.6	4.3	37.0
Aberdeenshire	13.5	11.0	9.6	9.3	8.0	4.2	30.7
Angus	12.3	9.9	12.9	13.0	6.3	4.8	41.5
Argyll and Bute	13.0	9.3	12.7	13.8	8.8	7.7	34.8
Clackmannanshire	13.7	11.2	10.1	10.5	6.3	5.7	49.1
Dumfries and Galloway	12.1	9.6	13.1	12.6	7.7	4.4	38.8
Dundee City	12.9	10.5	12.4	13.3	8.6	5.6	56.1
East Ayrshire	13.9	10.7	11.9	13.2	7.7	5.2	44.3
East Dunbartonshire	12.4	9.5	8.7	9.1	8.5	4.1	23.8
East Lothian	13.1	10.7	12.6	11.6	8.3	4.0	36.8
East Renfrewshire	13.0	10.7	9.5	9.2	5.8	4.5	20.6
Edinburgh, City of	12.9	10.5	12.5	11.1	8.2	7.1	38.2
Eilean Siar (Western Isles)	11.2	9.6	14.9	14.7	6.5	3.9	20.8
Falkirk	13.5	11.1	11.5	11.5	6.4	5.1	40.7
Fife	12.6	10.5	11.9	11.2	8.6	3.9	42.3
Glasgow City	14.3	11.2	14.4	13.8	10.5	7.0	53.8
Highland	13.0	10.7	11.5	11.7	7.4	4.8	40.3
Inverclyde	12.9	11.1	13.6	13.6	8.4	4.0	48.3
Midlothian	13.5	11.8	10.6	10.1	6.6	6.0	39.5
Moray	13.8	11.4	11.2	11.4	7.8	5.1	32.0
North Ayrshire	13.9	10.1	11.7	11.9	6.0	6.2	46.0
North Lanarkshire	13.6	11.8	11.1	11.0	8.4	5.4	42.6
Orkney Islands	12.1	9.6	11.8	10.8	5.6	1.9	37.2
Perth and Kinross	12.2	10.2	13.0	12.6	6.1	3.7	35.9
Renfrewshire	12.6	11.2	11.5	12.1	7.0	6.0	42.1
Scottish Borders, The	12.1	9.9	13.8	12.4	10.4	4.1	33.7
Shetland Islands	14.4	12.5	10.4	9.7	7.7	1.3	32.7
South Ayrshire	10.8	9.1	13.3	12.7	9.8	9.2	40.5
South Lanarkshire	13.3	10.9	10.5	11.5	7.4	5.0	38.5
Stirling	11.9	10.4	11.8	11.4	7.1	4.5	38.1
West Dunbartonshire	13.1	11.1	12.5	12.9	11.3	6.6	52.0
West Lothian	14.3	12.9	9.2	9.9	8.0	5.8	39.7

1 Births and deaths data are based on the usual area of residence of the mother/deceased. See Notes and Definitions to the Population chapter for details of the inclusion/exclusion of births to non-resident mothers and deaths of non-resident persons.

2 Births data are on the basis of year of occurrence in England and Wales and year of registration in Scotland and Northern Ireland. All deaths data relate to year of registration.

3 Still births and deaths of infants under 1 week of age per 1,000 live and still births. Figures for some UAs should be treated with caution as the perinatal mortality rate was based on fewer than 20 events.

4 Death of infants under 1 year of age per 1,000 live births. Figures for some UAs should be treated with caution as the infant mortality rate was based on fewer than 20 events.

Source: Office for National Statistics; General Register Office for Scotland

16.3 Education and training

| | Three and four year olds in early years education[1] | | | Pupil/teacher ratio 2000/01[5](numbers) | | Pupils and students participating in post-compulsory education6 (percentages) 1999/00 | Percentage of pupils in last year of compulsory schooling[7,8] 1999/00 with | |
| | Participation rates[2] (percentages) | | | | | | 5 or more GCSE Grades 1-3/ | |
	All schools[3] Jan. 2000	Private and voluntary providers[4] Jan. 2000	All providers Jan. 2000	Primary schools	Secondary schools		No graded results	Standard Grade (or equivalent)
United Kingdom	63	27	90	22.3	16.5	80	5.6	50.3
Scotland	56	18	74	19..0	13.0	94	5.6	58.3
Aberdeen City	60	23	83	18.7	12.3	118	6.5	59.5
Aberdeenshire	46	31	77	18.7	13.5	75	3.9	68.5
Angus	57	25	82	18.3	12.5	90	4.2	60.9
Argyll and Bute	39	50	89	17.5	12.5	72	5.1	64.1
Clackmannanshire	65	14	79	20.6	13.0	108	7.3	59.7
Dumfries and Galloway	53	14	67	18.3	12.4	95	5.1	61.4
Dundee City	66	17	84	17.6	12.0	106	9.5	48.1
East Ayrshire	62	3	65	20.7	13.6	89	6.4	54.4
East Dunbartonshire	44	36	80	21.3	14.1	90	3.3	70.0
East Lothian	66	12	78	19.3	12.9	64	11.0	53.5
East Renfrewshire	58	25	83	21.7	14.1	94	2.4	78.9
Edinburgh, City of	53	19	72	18.9	12.8	115	9.0	57.9
Eilean Siar (Western Isles)	5	78	83	11.8	8.8	87	13.5	65.6
Falkirk	57	7	64	20.5	13.2	94	3.5	52.5
Fife	59	4	63	18.2	13.3	101	5.2	56.7
Glasgow City	69	10	79	19.2	12.9	101	7.2	48.4
Highland	45	29	74	17.1	11.4	94	3.3	66.2
Inverclyde	50	23	74	20.4	13.4	125	2.2	58.7
Midlothian	76	6	82	18.8	13.1	63	4.5	55.8
Moray	41	37	78	18.0	12.3	96	12.2	57.6
North Ayrshire	48	28	75	20.8	13.5	58	4.7	53.6
North Lanarkshire	59	16	75	19.9	13.3	94	4.5	53.7
Orkney Islands	61	13	73	14.9	9.6	86	2.3	73.4
Perth and Kinross	50	26	75	18.2	12.9	94	10.5	60.1
Renfrewshire	54	21	74	20.2	13.9	94	1.2	60.2
Scottish Borders, The	52	25	77	17.1	12.4	89	5.4	67.6
Shetland Islands	53	29	82	11.8	8.2	77	6.4	72.8
South Ayrshire	52	19	71	20.4	13.6	103	5.2	60.6
South Lanarkshire	48	19	67	19.6	13.7	82	4.3	59.4
Stirling	60	22	82	18.7	13.4	77	2.4	65.3
West Dunbartonshire	73	6	79	19.9	14.0	103	5.4	51.9
West Lothian	54	2	56	19.4	13.5	82	5.2	53.1

1 Headcounts of children aged three and four at September 1999 for Scotland. These figures must be interpreted carefully in the light of differing types of education providers between the countries. In the UK figures any child attending more than one provider in England may have been counted twice.
2 Number of three and four year olds attending provider expressed as a percentage of the three and four year old population.
3 Local Authority (LA) figures relate to nursery schools and nursery classes in primary schools.
4 Centres not run by LAs which provide pre-school education in partnership with LAs.
5 From the September 2000 Schools Census.
6 In Scotland pupils in S5 at September 1998. The figure for the United Kingdom relates to 16 year olds in education at the beginning of the academic year. Some students in Scotland participate on short courses. They are counted for each course; hence there is double counting which results in some percentages being greater than 100.
7 Pupils in their last year of compulsory schooling as a percentage of the school population of the same age.
8 Figures relate to all schools; hence they are not directly comparable with those in Tables 14.3 and 15.3 which are for maintained schools only.

Source: Scottish Executive; Department for Education and Skills

16.4 Housing and households

	Housing completions 1999–00 (numbers)		Stock of dwellings[2] 1999 (thousands)	Households[3] 1999 (thousands)	Local authority tenants: average weekly unrebated rent per dwelling (£) 1999–00[4]	Council Tax (£)[5] April 1999
	Private enterprise[1]	Housing associations local authorities etc				
Scotland	18,683	5,172	2,286	2,186.1	36.43	849
Aberdeen City	744	134	103	99.9	32.89	824
Aberdeenshire	1,232	268	94	90.0	31.58	719
Angus	267	131	49	46.6	28.42	734
Argyll and Bute	126	46	44	38.2	36.49	881
Clackmannanshire	201	51	21	20.4	31.78	872
Dumfries and Galloway	306	76	67	63.3	34.29	766
Dundee City	330	154	71	66.8	38.65	1,034
East Ayrshire	337	52	52	50.8	30.43	849
East Dunbartonshire	151	15	43	41.9	34.39	830
East Lothian	240	94	39	37.5	31.80	789
East Renfrewshire	442	134	35	34.1	32.50	765
Edinburgh, City of	1,834	613	212	205.9	45.65	889
Eilean Siar (Western Isles)	64	3	13	11.6	38.05	689
Falkirk	470	73	63	61.3	32.03	719
Fife	1,423	446	154	149.0	32.45	809
Glasgow City	2,244	1,044	289	273.9	43.96	1,074
Highland	743	116	98	88.1	41.11	799
Inverclyde	191	68	39	37.8	40.06	888
Midlothian	302	52	33	31.8	27.14	936
Moray	313	32	38	35.8	29.27	724
North Ayrshire	258	83	62	58.9	31.10	788
North Lanarkshire	1,871	468	134	132.2	35.43	844
Orkney Islands	0	17	10	8.2	34.98	624
Perth and Kinross	384	157	61	57.1	30.71	758
Renfrewshire	477	56	79	76.9	35.86	783
Scottish Borders, The	383	126	50	46.1	30.99	670
Shetland Islands	44	57	10	9.0	44.41	621
South Ayrshire	359	68	50	48.6	33.38	792
South Lanarkshire	1,227	105	128	125.3	38.50	880
Stirling	378	95	36	34.0	35.11	819
West Dunbartonshire	98	57	43	41.6	34.24	981
West Lothian	1,244	281	64	63.4	34.39	858

1 Provisional figures including estimates for outstanding returns.

2 All figures are individually rounded to the nearest 100. As a result the Scotland total may not be the same as the sum of its Local Authorities. Figures based on the number of residential dwellings on the Council Tax Register at 6 September 1999. The figures for housing stock at local authority level shown in this table are derived using different methods from the regional stock figures shown in Table 6.1. This has led to small discrepancies between the two sets of figures. The figures in Table 6.1 provide the definitive regional estimates.

3 Household estimates at June 1999.

4 See Notes and Definitions.

5 All figures rounded to the nearest pound and exclude water and sewerage costs.

Source: Scottish Executive

16.5 Labour market and benefit statistics[1]

| | Economic activity | | | | Average gross weekly full-time earnings, all persons[6] April 2000 (£) | Benefit statistics | | | |
| | | | | | | Claimant count[5] March 2001 | | | Income Support bene-ficiaries[8] Nov.2000 (percentages) |
	Economically active 1999–2000[2] (percentages)	Total in employment[3] 1999–2000[2] (thousands)	Employment rate 1999–2000[2] (percentages)	ILO unemploy-ment rate 1999–2000[2] (percentages)[4]		Total (thousands)	Of which females (percentages)	Of which long-term claimants[7] (percentages)	
United Kingdom	78.5	26,784	73.8	6.0	409.2	1,041.1	23.4	19.7	10
Scotland	76.9	2,253	71.3	7.4	379.8	115.3	22.3	18.2	11
Aberdeen City	83.4	108	78.2	6.2	445.4	3.0	21.0	13.3	9
Aberdeenshire	81.2	109	77.5	..	371.2	2.2	26.1	12.5	6
Angus	79.5	52	76.6	..	342.1	2.4	28.6	18.3	8
Argyll and Bute	76.6	36	73.2	..	378.8	2.1	26.9	24.4	9
Clackmannanshire	67.9	18	63.7	..	..	1.2	23.7	16.7	10
Dumfries and Galloway	75.8	63	70.6	..	330.4	3.6	26.1	20.3	10
Dundee City	75.6	58	65.6	13.3	362.2	5.3	22.0	25.6	13
East Ayrshire	74.1	46	64.0	13.6	365.1	3.9	25.1	22.5	12
East Dunbartonshire	79.4	51	76.2	..	..	1.5	22.7	18.0	6
East Lothian	81.1	43	77.5	..	361.9	1.0	19.7	12.2	9
East Renfrewshire	79.4	42	77.1	..	..	1.0	23.1	16.5	7
Edinburgh, City of	78.4	217	74.4	5.1	404.6	7.2	21.9	18.1	9
Eilean Siar (Western Isles)	65.9	9	63.2	..	..	0.8	20.4	21.9	14
Falkirk	78.7	69	74.7	..	379.2	3.3	22.2	17.6	11
Fife	80.5	153	73.8	8.4	344.8	9.2	22.6	17.9	9
Glasgow City	64.3	211	54.9	14.6	391.8	20.0	19.2	22.9	21
Highland	80.5	96	76.7	..	351.7	5.4	23.4	15.2	9
Inverclyde	79.5	39	74.3	..	356.9	2.1	19.7	9.6	14
Midlothian	83.2	37	78.3	..	375.6	1.0	22.6	11.0	8
Moray	87.4	41	80.9	..	..	1.6	26.3	10.7	8
North Ayrshire	73.3	56	67.1	..	346.7	4.8	23.7	16.4	12
North Lanarkshire	70.0	135	64.6	7.7	373.1	8.0	21.6	15.3	14
Orkney Islands	88.6	13	87.0	..	..	0.3	32.2	20.3	5
Perth and Kinross	83.5	60	79.5	..	332.8	2.0	28.1	11.2	7
Renfrewshire	79.4	83	74.5	..	396.3	3.9	19.6	18.0	13
Scottish Borders, The	84.1	50	79.9	..	326.3	1.6	23.5	12.6	7
Shetland Islands	86.7	12	81.1	..	..	0.2	27.4	20.5	7
South Ayrshire	75.6	45	68.2	..	386.2	3.0	23.9	17.1	9
South Lanarkshire	82.6	152	76.6	7.3	385.4	6.2	22.3	17.1	12
Stirling	72.0	34	65.7	..	337.5	1.5	22.4	14.5	8
West Dunbartonshire	70.4	37	63.2	..	..	3.3	20.2	22.4	15
West Lothian	82.5	77	78.5	..	384.0	3.1	22.6	10.6	11

1 See Notes and Definitions to the Labour Market chapter. In some cases sample sizes are too small to provide reliable estimates.
2 For those of working age. Data are from the Labour Force Survey and relate to the period March 1999 to February 2000.
3 Includes those on Government employment and training programmes and unpaid family workers.
4 As a percentage of the economically active.
5 Count of claimants of unemployment-related benefit, i.e. Jobseeker's allowance.
6 Earning estimates have been derived from the New Earnings Survey and relate to full-time employees whose pay for the survey pay-period was not affected by absence.
7 Persons who have been claiming for more than 12 months as a percentage of all claimants.
8 Claimants and their partners aged 16 and over as a percentage of the population aged 16 and over. Data are from the Income Support Quarterly Statistical Enquiry.

Source: Office for National Statistics

16.6 Gross domestic product (GDP) by NUTS 1, 2 and 3 areas at current basic prices[1,2,3]

	£ million				£ per head				£ per head (UK=100)			
	1995	1996	1997	1998	1995	1996	1997	1998	1995	1996	1997	1998
United Kingdom[4]	622,389	657,775	700,567	743,314	10,619	11,185	11,871	12,548	100	100	100	100
Scotland	55,667	57,338	58,650	62,153	10,818	11,162	11,429	12,117	102	100	96	97
North Eastern Scotland (Aberdeen City, Aberdeenshire and North East Moray)	7,283	7,571	7,556	7,723	14,216	14,821	14,868	15,414	134	133	125	123
Eastern Scotland	21,172	22,127	22,658	23,870	11,171	11,679	11,938	12,576	105	104	101	100
Angus and Dundee City	2,653	2,648	2,764	2,929	10,078	10,126	10,645	11,387	95	91	90	91
Clackmannanshire and Fife	3,597	3,745	3,912	4,091	8,967	9,390	9,832	10,275	84	84	83	82
East Lothian and Midlothian	1,135	1,205	1,235	1,281	6,765	7,151	7,263	7,503	64	64	61	60
Scottish Borders	948	968	983	1,062	8,914	9,112	9,239	9,974	84	81	78	79
Edinburgh, City of	7,601	7,880	7,839	8,306	16,953	17,525	17,389	18,417	160	157	146	147
Falkirk	1,508	1,624	1,632	1,765	10,543	11,331	11,373	12,227	99	101	96	97
Perth and Kinross and Stirling	2,262	2,468	2,592	2,643	10,498	11,444	11,930	12,203	99	102	100	97
West Lothian	1,467	1,590	1,702	1,792	9,792	10,527	11,151	11,683	92	94	94	93
South Western Scotland	24,036	24,423	25,130	27,100	10,162	10,354	10,676	11,478	96	93	90	91
East and West Dunbartonshire, Helensburgh and Lomond	1,897	1,858	1,865	1,952	8,089	7,960	7,988	8,489	76	71	67	68
Dumfries and Galloway	1,452	1,434	1,514	1,633	9,798	9,700	10,262	11,063	92	87	86	88
East Ayrshire and North Ayrshire Mainland	2,022	2,015	2,096	2,141	7,866	7,862	8,186	8,191	74	70	69	65
Glasgow City	8,364	8,733	9,294	10,240	13,500	14,143	15,167	16,495	127	126	128	131
Inverclyde, East Renfrewshire and Renfrewshire	3,547	3,550	3,545	3,698	9,969	10,018	10,015	10,510	94	90	84	84
North Lanarkshire	2,776	2,860	2,836	3,133	8,481	8,761	8,671	9,573	80	78	73	76
South Ayrshire	1,271	1,275	1,289	1,368	11,073	11,106	11,198	11,934	104	99	94	95
South Lanarkshire	2,706	2,696	2,690	2,934	8,788	8,755	8,738	9,544	83	78	74	76
Highlands and Islands	3,176	3,217	3,306	3,461	8,515	8,634	8,898	9,369	80	77	75	75
Caithness and Sutherland and Ross and Cromarty	700	702	708	751	7,771	7,797	7,882	8,467	73	70	66	67
Inverness and Nairn and Moray, Badenoch and Strathspey	932	952	982	1,030	8,586	8,763	9,036	9,456	81	78	76	75
Lochaber, Skye and Lochalsh and Argyll and the Islands	833	836	856	873	8,145	8,192	8,405	8,630	77	73	71	69
Eilean Siar (Western Isles)	218	227	241	267	7,500	7,853	8,523	9,555	71	70	72	76
Orkney Islands	171	175	179	192	8,569	8,825	8,996	9,799	81	79	76	78
Shetland Islands	323	324	340	347	13,949	14,071	14,759	15,107	131	126	124	120

1 Estimates for all years are provisional.
2 Includes taxes less subsidies on production.
3 Components may not sum to totals due to rounding.
4 Excluding GDP for Extra-Regio, which comprises compensation of employees and gross operating surplus which cannot be assigned to regions.

NUTS levels 1, 2 and 3 in Scotland,[1] 1998

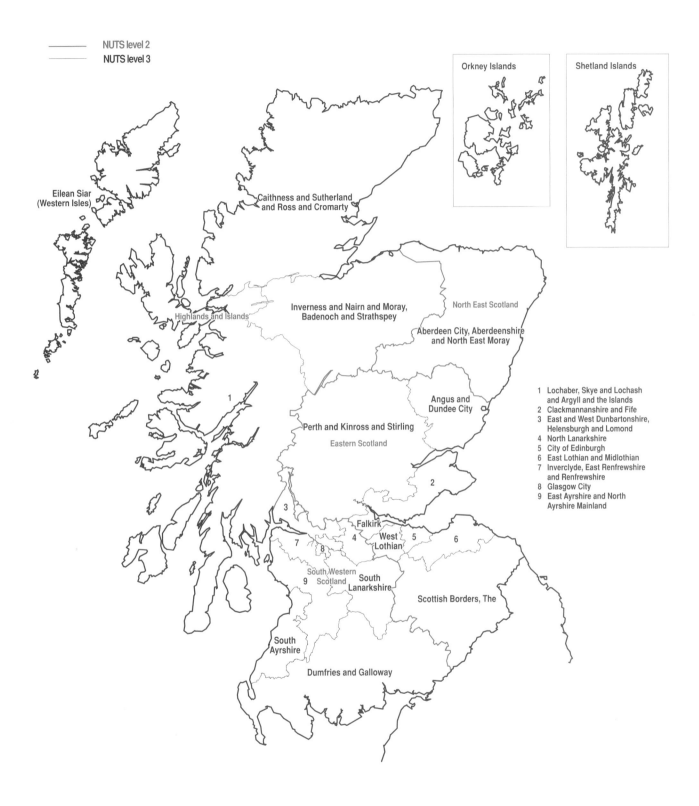

NUTS level 2
NUTS level 3

Orkney Islands

Shetland Islands

Eilean Siar
(Western Isles)

Caithness and Sutherland
and Ross and Cromarty

North East Scotland

Inverness and Nairn and Moray,
Badenoch and Strathspey

Highlands and Islands

Aberdeen City, Aberdeenshire
and North East Moray

1

Angus and
Dundee City

Perth and Kinross and Stirling

Eastern Scotland

2

3

Falkirk

West
Lothian

7   4

8

5   6

South Western
Scotland

9

South
Lanarkshire

Scottish Borders, The

South
Ayrshire

Dumfries and Galloway

1 Lochaber, Skye and Lochash
   and Argyll and the Islands
2 Clackmannanshire and Fife
3 East and West Dunbartonshire,
   Helensburgh and Lomond
4 North Lanarkshire
5 City of Edinburgh
6 East Lothian and Midlothian
7 Inverclyde, East Renfrewshire
   and Renfrewshire
8 Glasgow City
9 East Ayrshire and North
   Ayrshire Mainland

1 NUTS (Nomenclature of Units for Territorial Statistics) is a hierachical classification of areas that provides a breakdown of the EU's economic territory. The NUTS level 1 area is the whole country. See Notes and Definitions.

17

Sub-regions of Northern Ireland

Boards and Travel-to-work areas in Northern Ireland

Health and Social Services Boards

Education and Library Boards

Travel-to-work areas

Regional Trends 36, © Crown copyright 2001

17.1 Area and population: by Board[1] and district, 1999

	Area (sq km)	Persons per sq km	Population (thousands)			Total population percentage change 1981–1999	Total fertility rate (TFR)[2]	Standardised mortality ratio (UK=100) (SMR)[3]	Percentage of population aged			
			Males	Females	Total				Under 5	5–15	16 up to pension age[4]	Pension age[4] and over
United Kingdom	242,910	245	29,299	30,202	59,501	5.6	1.69	100	6.1	14.3	61.6	18.1
Northern Ireland	13,576	125	829	863	1,692	9.6	1.85	100	7.1	17.2	60.4	15.2
Eastern	1,751	385	324	350	673	5.0	1.81	99	6.7	16.4	59.8	17.1
Ards	380	188	35	37	71	23.1	1.79	101	6.5	15.3	62.6	15.6
Belfast	110	2,594	134	151	284	-10.1	1.77	104	6.7	16.7	58.4	18.1
Castlereagh	85	785	33	34	67	9.6	1.90	91	6.8	14.0	60.1	19.1
Down	649	98	32	32	64	18.7	2.02	107	7.3	18.2	60.0	14.4
Lisburn	447	249	54	57	111	30.6	1.81	92	7.3	17.5	61.2	14.0
North Down	81	936	37	39	76	13.1	1.68	90	5.5	14.7	60.2	19.5
Northern	4,093	104	211	217	428	13.5	1.81	98	6.9	16.5	61.5	15.1
Antrim	421	120	26	25	51	10.0	2.04	105	7.8	15.9	64.4	11.9
Ballymena	630	94	30	30	59	7.7	1.83	106	6.5	16.1	61.8	15.6
Ballymoney	416	62	13	13	26	12.5	2.01	98	7.4	17.2	60.3	15.0
Carrickfergus	81	469	18	19	38	32.0	1.66	98	6.7	16.6	61.5	15.2
Coleraine	486	115	27	29	56	18.8	1.71	91	6.6	15.4	61.4	16.6
Cookstown	514	62	16	16	32	11.6	1.63	85	6.3	18.5	60.3	14.9
Larne	336	92	15	16	31	6.2	1.72	95	6.1	15.9	60.7	17.3
Magherafelt	564	69	20	19	39	19.1	2.38	103	8.6	19.4	59.1	12.9
Moyle	494	31	8	8	15	6.5	1.68	94	6.0	17.0	59.8	17.1
Newtownabbey	151	540	39	42	81	12.2	1.65	99	6.7	15.6	62.0	15.7
Southern	3,075	101	154	156	310	12.8	2.05	102	7.6	18.2	60.3	13.8
Armagh	671	80	27	27	54	9.4	1.87	99	6.8	18.6	59.7	14.8
Banbridge	451	88	20	20	40	32.5	1.75	100	6.9	16.0	62.9	14.1
Craigavon	282	283	39	41	80	8.5	2.05	98	7.6	17.6	60.5	14.3
Dungannon	772	62	24	24	48	9.8	2.14	112	7.8	18.8	60.1	13.4
Newry and Mourne	898	98	44	44	88	13.1	2.30	106	8.4	19.2	59.6	12.7
Western	4,658	60	140	141	281	12.2	2.06	103	7.8	19.2	60.4	12.6
Derry	381	280	53	54	107	18.3	2.12	111	8.4	20.1	60.7	10.8
Fermanagh	1,699	34	29	29	58	10.3	2.01	103	7.2	18.2	59.0	15.6
Limavady	586	54	16	16	32	16.7	1.92	90	7.6	19.0	61.6	11.7
Omagh	1,130	42	24	24	48	6.8	1.98	102	7.3	19.4	60.4	13.0
Strabane	862	44	19	19	38	3.5	2.18	97	7.7	18.1	60.8	13.4

1 Health and Social Services Board areas.
2 The total fertility rate (TFR) is the average number of children which would be born to a woman if the current pattern of fertility persisted throughout her child-bearing years. Previously called total period fertility rate (TPFR). Figures for Northern Ireland are based on births and population data for the previous three years.
3 Averaged for the years 1997, 1998 and 1999 and adjusted for the age structure of the population. See Notes and Definitions to the Population chapter.
4 Pension age is 65 for males and 60 for females.

Source: Office for National Statistics; Northern Ireland Statistics and Research Agency

17.2 Vital[1,2] and social statistics: by Board[3]

	Live births per 1,000 population		Deaths per 1,000 population		Perinatal mortality rate[4]	Infant mortality rate[5]	Percentage of live births outside marriage	Children looked after by LAs per 1,000 population aged under 18
	1991	1999	1991	1999	1999	1999	1999	2000[6]
United Kingdom	13.7	11.8	11.2	10.6	8.2	5.8	38.8	..
Northern Ireland	16.2	13.6	9.4	9.3	10.0	6.4	30.3	5.2
Eastern	15.7	12.9	10.3	10.5	11.1	8.3	35.2	6.4
Northern	15.1	13.1	8.7	9.0	8.9	4.5	27.9	5.0
Southern	17.5	14.8	8.9	8.3	8.5	5.4	22.9	2.9
Western	17.6	14.6	8.7	7.8	10.9	6.2	31.6	5.6

1 Births and deaths data are based on the usual area of residence of the mother/deceased. See Notes and Definitions to the Population chapter for details of the inclusion/exclusion of births to non-resident mothers and deaths of non-resident persons.
2 Births data are on the basis of year of occurrence in England and Wales and year of registration in Scotland and Northern Ireland. All deaths data relate to year of registration.
3 Health and Social Service Board Areas.
4 Still births and deaths of infants under 1 week of age per 1,000 live and still births.
5 Death of infants under 1 year of age per 1,000 live births.
6 At 31 March. Figures are not directly comparable with similar data in the rest of the United Kingdom as Children Order legislation in Northern Ireland is not identical.

Source: Northern Ireland Statistics and Research Agency; Department of Health, Social Services and Public Safety, Northern Ireland

17.3 Education and training: by Board[1]

| | Three and four year olds in early years education[2] | | | Pupil/teacher ratio 1999/004(numbers) | | Pupils and students participating in post-compulsory education[6] (percentages) 1999/00 | Percentage of pupils in last year of compulsory schooling[7,8] 1999/00 with | |
| | Participation rates[3] (percentages) | | | | | | 5 or more GCSE Grades 1-3/ | |
	All schools Jan. 2000[4]	Private and voluntary providers Jan. 2000[4]	All providers Jan. 2000[4]	Primary schools[5]	Secondary schools		No graded results	Standard Grade (or equivalent)
United Kingdom	63	27	90	22.7	16.6	80	5.6	50.3
Northern Ireland	50	7	57	20.2	14.7	76	3.6	56.9
Belfast	..	..	..	19.7	14.6	..	4.8	60.2
South Eastern	..	..	..	20.8	14.9	..	3.9	53.3
Southern	..	..	..	19.1	14.6	..	3.7	58.0
North Eastern	..	..	..	21.0	14.8	..	2.6	57.6
Western	..	..	..	20.4	14.6	..	3.4	55.1

1 Education and Library Boards.
2 Headcounts of children aged three and four at 31st December in the previous calendar year. These figures must be interpreted carefully in the light of differing types of education providers between the countries. In the UK figures any child attending more than one provider in England may have been counted twice.
3 Number of three and four year olds attending provider expressed as a percentage of the three and four year old population.
4 Data for 2000/01 are shown in Table 4.1 for pupil/teacher ratios and Table 4.2 for early years education.
5 In Northern Ireland the primary PTR includes preparatory departments of grammar schools.
6 Pupils and students aged 16 at 1st July. Figures for Northern Ireland exclude those in part-time further education.
7 Pupils in their last year of compulsory schooling as a percentage of the school population of the same age.
8 Figures relate to all schools; hence they are not directly comparable with those in Tables 14.3 and 15.3 which are for maintained schools only.

Source: Department for Education and Skills; Northern Ireland Department of Education

NUTS levels 1, 2 and 3 in Northern Ireland,[1] 1998

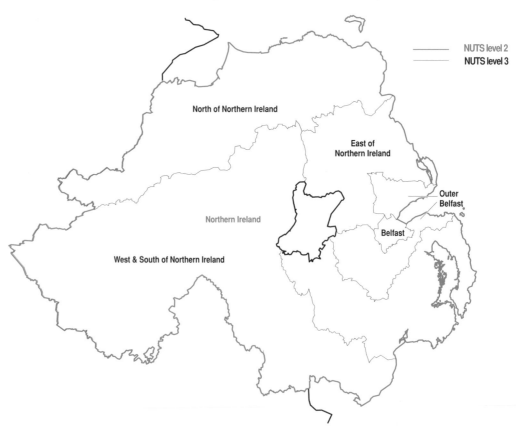

1 NUTS (Nomenclature of Units for Territorial Statistics) is a hierarchical classification of areas that provides a breakdown of the EU's economic territory. The NUTS level 1 area is the whole country. See Notes and Definitions.

17.4 Labour market[1] and benefit statistics: by district

| | Economic activity | | Benefit statistics | | | |
| | Economically active 1999–2000[2] (percentages) | Employment rate 1999–2000[2] (percentages) | Claimant count[3] March 2001 | | | Income Support bene-ficiaries[5] March 2001 (percentages) |
			Total (thousands)	Of which females (percentages)	Of which long term claimants[4] (percentages)	
United Kingdom	78.5	73.8	1,041.1	23.4	19.7	10
Northern Ireland	71.8	67.0	39.9	22.7	31.3	16
Eastern	71.6	67.5	16.3	20.8	30.5	15
Ards	76.0	74.1	1.4	28.3	26.9	10
Belfast	67.8	63.0	9.5	18.0	34.2	21
Castlereagh	77.9	75.0	0.9	20.7	23.0	8
Down	74.4	68.4	1.4	24.0	24.1	13
Lisburn	70.7	66.3	1.8	23.9	28.1	12
North Down	74.7	72.1	1.3	25.4	23.1	8
Northern	74.8	70.2	7.9	26.1	25.5	13
Antrim	78.1	73.9	0.7	26.3	22.4	10
Ballymena	78.2	74.5	1.0	29.3	26.1	11
Ballymoney	79.9	75.4	0.6	26.3	21.4	15
Carrickfergus	74.3	70.0	0.7	22.7	24.8	9
Coleraine	72.9	69.5	1.5	25.2	24.3	13
Cookstown	69.9	63.4	0.5	29.7	23.5	20
Larne	74.3	70.0	0.6	24.4	25.6	11
Magherafelt	73.3	71.2	0.6	31.9	31.3	16
Moyle	..	..	0.5	24.8	30.9	17
Newtownabbey	75.3	68.0	1.3	23.8	25.9	11
Southern	72.0	66.2	6.2	24.7	30.7	17
Armagh	72.1	65.9	1.1	27.6	31.9	14
Banbridge	78.6	68.9	0.6	29.7	18.6	10
Craigavon	74.1	70.6	1.5	22.5	30.4	16
Dungannon	67.3	63.3	0.8	28.6	26.1	20
Newry and Mourne	69.4	62.6	2.3	22.0	35.0	21
Western	67.4	62.0	9.7	21.8	37.7	20
Derry	63.7	57.1	4.4	20.3	37.7	23
Fermanagh	76.3	72.9	1.8	22.1	40.6	16
Limavady	71.0	63.6	0.9	24.4	26.8	16
Omagh	71.1	67.0	1.3	25.2	38.2	17
Strabane	57.6	52.6	1.3	21.5	41.1	23

1 See Notes and Definitions to the Labour Market chapter.
2 Based on the population of working age. Data are from the Labour Force Survey and relate to the period March 1999 to February 2000.
3 Count of claimants of unemployment-related benefit, i.e. Jobseeker's allowance.
4 Persons who have been claiming for more than 12 months as a percentage of all claimants. Figures given cover computerised claims only.
5 Claimants and their partners aged 16 and over as a percentage of the population aged 16 and over (using the mid-1999 population estimates). The figure for Northern Ireland includes those who could not be assigned to a council. The figure for the UK relates to February.

Source: Office for National Statistics; Department of Enterprise, Trade and Investment, and Department of Health, Social Services and Public Safety, Northern Ireland

17.5 Gross domestic product (GDP) by NUTS 1, 2 and 3 areas at current basic prices[1,2,3]

| | £ million | | | | £ per head | | | | £ per head (UK=100) | | | |
	1995	1996	1997	1998	1995	1996	1997	1998	1995	1996	1997	1998
United Kingdom[4]	622,389	657,775	700,567	743,314	10,619	11,185	11,871	12,548	100	100	100	100
Northern Ireland[5]	14,297	14,936	15,952	16,501	8,654	8,964	9,507	9,754	82	80	80	78
Belfast	4,165	4,413	4,741	4,942	14,012	14,819	15,869	17,159	132	132	134	137
Outer Belfast	2,670	2,822	2,979	3,091	7,468	7,793	8,175	8,282	70	70	69	66
East of Northern Ireland	2,916	3,024	3,238	3,279	7,683	7,899	8,363	8,351	72	71	70	67
North of Northern Ireland	2,009	2,085	2,217	2,316	7,615	7,817	8,270	8,502	72	70	70	68
West and South of Northern Ireland	2,538	2,591	2,777	2,873	7,169	7,266	7,726	7,862	68	65	65	63

1. Estimates for all years are provisional.
2. Includes taxes less subsidies on production.
3. Components may not sum to totals due to rounding.
4. Excluding GDP for Extra-Regio, which comprises compensation of employees and gross operating surplus which cannot be assigned to regions.
5. This area is represented at more than one NUTS level.

Notes and Definitions

Government Office Regions within England

Most of the statistics in *Regional Trends* are on the basis of the Government Office Regions (GORs) of England, together with Wales, Scotland and Northern Ireland. The Government Office for the North West merged with the Government Office for Merseyside in August 1998, so figures for Merseyside are no longer shown separately. In tables, the Government Office for the East of England (formerly the Eastern Region) is referred to as East. Maps of the GORs are on pages 1 to 24 and 179.

Standard Statistical Regions

Prior to the introduction of the GORs, regional statistics were presented on the basis of the Standard Statistical Regions (SSRs) of the United Kingdom. A few tables in *Regional Trends 36* continue to be presented on this classification. The SSRs are shown in a map on page 239.

Sub-regions of England

The implementation of local government reorganisation in England, which took place in four phases on 1 April in each year between 1995 and 1998, is summarised below. The reorganisation involved only the non-metropolitan counties. Unitary Authorities (UA) have replaced the two-tier system of County Councils and Local Authority District Councils in parts of some shire counties and, in some instances, across the whole county. For statistical purposes grouping UAs by geography can be helpful. In Chapter 14 the following 'new' areas are included:

Tees Valley less Darlington relates to the abolished administrative county of Cleveland (*Tees Valley* relates to the area covered by five UAs; Darlington, Hartlepool, Middlesborough, Redcar and Cleveland, and Stockton-on-Tees – a new statistical group not included in this edition of *Regional Trends*);

The Humber relates to the abolished administrative county of Humberside;

Herefordshire and Worcestershire relates to the former administrative county of Hereford and Worcestershire;

Bristol/Bath area relates to the abolished administrative county of Avon.

By legal definition all Unitary Authorities in England are counties. However, for many purposes the UAs are treated as districts. For the majority of UAs their establishment has been achieved without geographical change. However, for a few Unitary Authorities, there are some boundary changes at District and Ward levels, most notably, the County of Herefordshire UA in the West Midlands and Peterborough UA in the East of England. Full details of these are given in the *Gazetteer of the old and new geographies of the United Kingdom* available from National Statistics Direct Tel. 01633 812078.

The local government structure at 1 April 1998 is used in Chapter 14 and throughout the rest of the book unless otherwise specified. A map showing the Counties and Unitary Authorities is given on page 179.

Counties, Districts and Unitary Authorities in England

| Year | Non-metropolitan areas | | | Metropolitan areas | |
	Counties	Districts	Unitary Authorities	London boroughs	Metropolitan boroughs
1994	39	296	0	33	36
1995	38	294	1	33	36
1996	35	274	14	33	36
1997	36	260	27	33	36
1998	34	238	46	33	36

Unitary Authorities of Wales

On 1 April 1996, the 8 counties and 37 districts of Wales were replaced by 22 Unitary Authorities. A map is given on page 218. In Chapter 15, the Unitary Authorities are presented in the tables in alphabetical order.

New Councils of Scotland

On 1 April 1996, the 10 Local Authority regions and 56 districts of Scotland were replaced by 32 Unitary Councils. A map is given on page 226. In Chapter 16, the New Councils are presented in the tables in alphabetical order.

Standard Statistical Regions

Environment Agency regions

NHS Regional Office areas
(from April 1996)

NHS Regional Office areas
(from April 1999)

Police Force areas

ENGLAND and WALES

—— Police Force area boundary

Prison Service regions

ENGLAND and WALES

—— Prison Service region boundary

Tourist Board regions

UNITED KINGDOM

—— Tourist Board region boundary

Northern Ireland

The 26 districts of Northern Ireland are listed in Chapter 17. For some topics, they have been grouped into either the five Education and Library Boards or the four Health and Social Services Boards. The districts comprising the Education and Library Boards are as follows:

Board	Districts
Belfast	Belfast
South	Eastern Ards, Castlereagh, Down, Lisburn, North Down.
Southern	Armagh, Banbridge, Cookstown, Craigavon, Dungannon, Newry and Mourne.
North Eastern	Antrim, Ballymena, Ballymoney, Carrickfergus, Coleraine, Larne, Magherafelt, Moyle, Newtownabbey.
Western	Derry, Fermanagh, Limavady, Omagh, Strabane.

Health and Social Services Boards are as follows:

Northern	as North Eastern Education and Library Board but including Cookstown.
Eastern	as South Eastern Education and Library Board but including Belfast.
Southern	as Southern Education and Library Board but excluding Cookstown.
Western	as Western Education and Library Board.

Maps of the Northern Ireland Boards and Travel-to-work areas are on page 234.

NUTS (Nomenclature of Territorial Statistics) area classification

Data are presented using this classification in Chapter 2, Tables 14.7, 15.6, 16.6 and 17.5. In Tables 14.1 and 14.4, data for London are also presented on the NUTS classification, which provides additional levels of geographic aggregation between London as a whole and the individual London boroughs.

NUTS is a hierarchical classification of areas that provide a breakdown of the European Union's economic territory for producing regional statistics that are comparable across the Union. It has been used since 1988 in EU legislation for determining the distribution of the Structural Funds.

The NUTS five-tier structure for the UK – reviewed during 1998 as a consequence of the move to using Government Office Regions as the principal classification for English Regions and the local government reorganisation – comprises current national administrative areas, except in Scotland where some NUTS areas comprise whole and /or part local enterprise company areas.

Maps showing the NUTS levels 1, 2 and 3 areas for England, Wales, Scotland and Northern Ireland are on pages 214, 224, 233 and 236 respectively.

Other Regional Classifications

The UK Continental Shelf, now referred to as Extra-Regio, is treated as a separate region in Tables in Chapter 12 (see the Notes and Definitions to Chapter 12 Regional accounts).

Maps of non-standard regions used in *Regional Trends* are shown on pages 239 and 240.

United Kingdom NUTS levels 1 to 5

	Level 1		Level 2		Level 3		Level 4		Level 5	
		Numbers		Numbers		Numbers		Numbers		Numbers
England	Government Office Regions	9	Individual counties or groups of counties/ London boroughs/ metropolitan counties/ counties/unitary authorities	30	Individual counties/ unitary authorities or groups of counties/ London boroughs/ metropolitan counties/ unitary authorities/ local authority districts	93	Individual London boroughs/metro-politan districts/ unitary authorities/ local authority districts	354	Wards	8,442
Wales	Country	1	Groups of unitary authorities	2	Groups of unitary authorities	12	Individual unitary authorities	22	Wards	865
Scotland	Country	1	Groups of whole/part unitary authorities (councils) and/or local enterprise companies	4	Groups of whole/part unitary authorities (councils) and/or local enterprise companies	23	Individual or groups of whole/part unitary authorities (councils) and/or local enterprise companies	41	Wards	1,247
Northern Ireland	Country	1	Country	1	Groups of district council areas	5	Individual district council areas	26	Wards	582
Total		12		37		133		443		11,136

Notes and Definitions

CHAPTER 2:
EUROPEAN UNION
REGIONAL STATISTICS

The data appearing in this chapter are based on information in the statistical database REGIO produced by the Statistical Office of the European Communities (EUROSTAT) which uses the Nomenclature of Territorial Units for Statistics (NUTS) classification, described earlier. Data relate to the NUTS level 1 areas for countries in the European Union.

Table 2.3 Economic statistics

Employment statistics are derived from the annual Community Labour Force Survey (CLFS), which uses national Labour Force Survey (LFS) data although there may be minor differences in interpretation compared with the national LFS. Since the survey is conducted on a sample basis, results relating to small regions should be treated with caution. One of the main statistical objectives of the CLFS is to divide the population of working age into three groups: persons in employment, unemployed persons and inactive persons (those not classified as employed or unemployed). The groups are used to derive the following measures:
a) activity rates: the labour force as a percentage of the population of working-age;
b) employment/population ratios: persons in employment as a percentage of the population of working-age; and
c) unemployment rates: unemployed persons as a percentage of the labour force.

The definitions of employment and unemployment used in the CLFS closely follow those adopted by the 13th International Conference of Labour Statisticians and promulgated by the International Labour Organisation (ILO) and are as follows (further detail is available in the EUROSTAT publication *Labour Force Survey, Methods and Definitions, 1992*):

Employment: the employed comprise all persons above a specified age who during a specified brief period either one week or one day were in the following categories:
a) paid employment: at work or with a job but not at work ie temporarily absent but in receipt of a wage or salary;
b) self-employment: at work ie persons who during the reference period performed some work for profit or family gain, in cash or kind, or with an enterprise but not at work ie temporarily absent. (An 'enterprise' may be a business enterprise, a farm or a service undertaking.)

Unemployment: the unemployed comprise all persons above a specified age who, during the reference period, were:
a) without work: ie were not in paid employment or self-employment;
b) currently available for work: ie were available for paid employment or self-employment during the reference period;
c) seeking work: ie had taken specific steps in a specified recent period to seek paid employment or self-employment.

Long-term unemployment: persons who have been unemployed for 12 or more consecutive months.

Table 2.3 and Map 2.5
Purchasing Power Standard

The Purchasing Power Standard (PPS) is a unit of measurement calculated by scaling Purchasing Power Parities (PPPs) so that the aggregate for the EU-15 as a whole is the same whether expressed in EUROs (ECUs) or in PPS. Purchasing Power Parities are conversion factors, which make it possible to eliminate the combined effect of price level differences and other factors from a comparison of economic aggregates and thereby obtain a real volume comparison between countries.

Table 2.4 Agricultural statistics

The 'gross margin' of an agricultural enterprise is defined as the monetary value of gross production from which corresponding specific costs are deducted. The 'Standard Gross Margin' (SGM) is the value of gross margin corresponding to the average situation in a given region for each agricultural characteristic eg crop production, livestock production. 'Gross production' is the sum of the value of the principal product(s) and of any secondary product(s). The values are calculated by multiplying production per unit (less any losses) by the farm-gate price, excluding VAT. Gross production also includes subsidies linked to products, to area and/or to livestock.

Basic data are collected in Member States from farm accounts, specific surveys or compiled from appropriate calculations for a reference period which covers three successive years or agricultural production years. The reference period is the same for all Member States. SGMs are first calculated in Member States national currencies and then converted into European currency units (ECUs) using the average exchange rates for the reference period.

CHAPTER 3: POPULATION
AND MIGRATION

The estimated population of an area includes all those usually resident in the area, whatever their nationality. HM Forces stationed outside the United Kingdom are excluded but foreign forces stationed here are included. Students are taken to be resident at their term-time address. The population estimates for mid-1999 are based on the 1991 Census (with allowance for Census under-enumeration) and take account of births, deaths and net migration between 1991 and mid-1999.

Tables 3.1, 3.2, 3.13 and
Maps 3.3, 3.4, 3.5 and 3.8
Resident Population

Table 3.6 Social class

Based on the Labour Force Survey (see Notes and Definitions to the Labour Market chapter), the table gives percentages of working age people in each social class based on occupations. The method used is designed to group together as far as possible people with similar levels of occupational skills. The basis of the groupings is given in Volume 3, Standard Occupational Classification (HMSO, 1991).

The six occupational social classes in the classification are as follows:
I Professional occupations (including doctors, solicitors, chemists, university professors and clergymen);

II Managerial and technical occupations (including school teachers, computer programmers, personnel managers, nurses, actors and laboratory technicians);

III Skilled occupations

  (N) Non-manual (including typists, clerical workers, photographers, sales representatives and shop assistants);

  (M) Manual (including cooks, bus drivers, railway guards, plasterers, bricklayers, hairdressers and carpenters);

IV Partly skilled occupations (including bar staff, waitresses, gardeners and caretakers);

V Unskilled occupations (including refuse collectors, messengers, lift attendants, cleaners and labourers).

For those in employment in the reference week of the survey, the occupation was that of their main job, and for those not in employment, their last occupation if they had done any paid work in the previous eight years.

Table 3.7 Ethnic group

The information on the ethnic group of each respondent to the Labour Force Survey is collected using the categories first used in the 1991 Census. Those classified as 'mixed/other' include Chinese, other Asians whose origin is not Indian, Pakistani or Bangladeshi, and those of mixed origin.

Map 3.9 Projected population

The projected population change figures for Wales and for England, Scotland and Northern Ireland are not directly comparable with previous editions of *Regional Trends* as more recent projections are used. There are changes to the assumptions for fertility, mortality and migration in the preparation of each set of projections. The projections used in this edition for Wales and Scotland are 1998-based national projections, while those for England are 1996-based sub-national projections and Northern Ireland figures are 1999 mid-year estimates.

Table 3.10, 3.13 and 3.14 Births and deaths

Within England and Wales, births are assigned to areas according to the usual residence of the mother at the date of birth, as stated at registration. If the address of usual residence is outside England and Wales, the birth is included in any aggregate for England and Wales as a whole (and hence in the UK total), but excluded from the figures for any individual region or area. In 1999 there were 293 live births to non-resident mothers.

Birth figures for Scotland include births to both resident and non-resident mothers. Where sub-national data are given (Table 16.2), births have been allocated to the usual residence of the mother if this was in Scotland and to the area of occurrence if the mother's usual residence was outside Scotland. There were 238 births to non-resident mothers in Scotland in 1999.

All figures given for Northern Ireland (including the sub-regional figures in Table 17.2) exclude births to mothers not usually resident in Northern Ireland. However, the UK total includes such births. There were 216 births to non-resident mothers in Northern Ireland in 1999.

As with births, within England and Wales, a death is normally assigned to the area of usual residence of the deceased. If this is outside England and Wales, the death is included in any aggregate for England and Wales as a whole (and hence in the UK total), but excluded from the figures for any individual region or area. There were 1,484 deaths to non-residents in 1999.

Death figures for Scotland and Northern Ireland include deaths to both residents and non-residents. Where sub-national data are given (Tables 16.2 and 17.2), deaths of Scottish or Northern Irish residents have been allocated to the usual area of residence, while deaths of non-residents have been allocated to the area of occurrence. In 1999 there were 341 deaths to non-residents in Scotland and 107 to non-residents in Northern Ireland.

Table 3.10 Birth and death rates and rate of natural change

Unlike Table 3.11 which relates to population change from mid-year to mid-year, the numbers shown in this table relate to calendar years.

Crude birth/death rates and natural change are affected by the age and sex structure of the population. For example, for any given levels of fertility and mortality, a population with a relatively high proportion of persons in the younger age groups will have a higher crude birth rate and consequently a higher rate of natural change than a population with a higher proportion of elderly people.

Table 3.12 Conceptions

The date of conception is estimated using recorded gestation for abortion and stillbirths, and assuming 38 weeks gestation for live births. A woman's age at conception is calculated as the interval in complete years between her date of birth and the estimated age of conception. The postcode of the woman's address is used to determine the region she was living in at the time of the conception.

Table 3.13 Total Fertility Rate

The total fertility rate (TFR) is the average number of children which would be born to a woman if she experiences the current age-specific fertility rates throughout her child-bearing years. It is sometimes called the total period fertility rate (TPFR).

Table 3.14 Standardised mortality ratio

The standardised mortality ratio (SMR) compares overall mortality in a region with that for the United Kingdom. The ratio expresses the number of deaths in a region as a percentage of the hypothetical number that would have occurred if the region's population had experienced the sex/age-specific rates of the United Kingdom that year.

Tables 3.15 & 3.16 Inter-regional movements

Estimates for internal population movements are based on the movement of NHS doctors' patients between Family Health Services Authority Areas (FHSAs) in England and Wales and Area Health Boards (AHBs) in Scotland and Northern Ireland. These transfers are recorded at the NHS Central Registers (NHSCRs), Southport and Edinburgh, and at the Central Services Agency, Belfast. The figures have been adjusted to take account of differences in recorded cross-border flows between England and Wales, Scotland, and Northern Ireland.

The figures provide a detailed indicator of population movement within the United Kingdom. However, they should not be regarded as a perfect measure of migration as there is variation in the delay between a person moving and registering with a new doctor. Additionally, some moves may not result in a re-registration, i.e. individuals may migrate again before registering with a doctor. Conversely, there may be others who move and re-register several times in a year.

The NHSCR at Southport was computerised in 1991. Before 1991, the time lag was assumed to be three months between a person moving and the re-registration with an NHS doctor being processed onto the NHSCR. (It was estimated that processing at NHSCR took two months.) Since computerisation, estimates of internal migration derived from the NHSCR are based on the date of acceptance of the new patient by the FHSA (not previously available), and a one-month time lag assumed.

Table 3.15 Migration

The figures are derived from three data sources:
1. The International Passenger Survey (IPS), a continuous voluntary sample survey which provides information on passengers entering and leaving the United Kingdom by the principal air, sea and tunnel routes. Routes between the United Kingdom and the Irish Republic, and those between the Channel Islands, Isle of Man and the rest of the world are excluded. The IPS data also excludes most persons seeking asylum after entering the country and short-term visitors granted extensions of stay. The survey covered 261,000 travellers in 1999, and has been running since 1961. The IPS is also used to collect information on the travel account of the Balance of Payments, and for tourism policy. It shows how many people travelled, where they went and why, and gives a picture of how long they stayed and what they spent. It currently samples between 0.1 and 5 per cent of passengers, depending on route and time of year.
2. The Home Office provides data on asylum seekers, and people who entered the UK as short-term visitors but were subsequently granted an extension of stay for a year or longer for other reasons, for example as students or on the basis of marriage.
3. Information on migration between the UK and the Irish Republic from the Irish Labour Force Survey and the National Health Service Central Register, agreed between the Irish Central Statistics Office and the ONS

For demographic purposes, a migrant is defined as someone who changes his or her country of usual residence for a period of at least a year, so that the country of destination effectively becomes the country of usual residence. Migrants defined in this way were asked an additional group of questions which form the basis of these statistics.

The IPS is a sample survey and is subject to some uncertainty. It should be noted that the estimates of migration, in particular the differences between inflow and outflow, may be subject to large sampling errors. Given the structure of the sample, the standard error for an estimate of 1,000 migrants is around 40 per cent, whilst that for an estimate of 40,000 migrants reduces to about 10 per cent. For the UK in 1999 the overall standard error for estimated inflow of 345,000 migrants is 4.5 per cent and for outflow of 245,000 migrants is 5.1 per cent.

Table 3.19 Household projections

The household projections are trend-based; they illustrate what would happen if past trends in household formation were to continue into the future. They are therefore not policy-based forecasts of what is expected to happen, but provide a starting point for policy decisions. The projections are heavily dependent on the assumptions involved, particularly international and internal migration, the marital status projections (in England and Wales only) and the continuation of past trends in household formation.

CHAPTER 4: EDUCATION AND TRAINING

In England and Wales, only qualified teachers are included for public sector schools (i.e. all other teaching staff at these schools are excluded). In Scotland and Northern Ireland, however, all teachers employed in schools are included other than in independent schools.

Table 4.1 Pupils and teachers by type of school

The pupil-teacher ratio in a school is the ratio of all pupils on the register to all qualified teachers employed within the schools during the census week. Part-time teachers and part-time pupils are included on a full-time equivalent basis. The difference in the age at which pupils transfer from primary to secondary school affects the comparison of pupil-teacher ratios between Scotland and the rest of the United Kingdom.

Table 4.2 Three and four year olds by type of early years education provider

Figures in this table must be interpreted carefully in light of the differing types of early years education provision within the four home countries.

Table 4.3 Class sizes for all classes

Figures for England, Wales and Scotland include classes where more than one teacher may be present. In Northern Ireland a class is defined as a group of pupils normally under the control of one teacher. Figures previously shown in this publication for England, prior to 1999/00, related to classes taught by one teacher. In England in 2000/01, the average Key Stage 1 class, taught by one teacher, had 25.2 pupils, with 1.8 per cent of classes having 31 or more pupils. Further information, including on-teacher class size data for Key Stage 2, primary and secondary school class sizes can be found in DfES Statistical First Release 14/2001.

Table 4.5 and 4.6 Examination achievements

The main examination for pupils at the minimum school-leaving age in England, Wales and Northern Ireland is the General Certificate of Secondary Education (GCSE); in Scotland it is the Standard Grade. From 1999/00 National Qualifications (NQ) were introduced in Scotland. NQs include Standard Grades, Intermediate 1 & 2 and Higher. The GCSE is awarded in eight grades, A*–G, while in Scotland the Standard Grade is awarded in seven levels, 1 to 7. Standard Grade courses begin in the third year and continue to the end of the fourth year. Each subject has a number of elements, some of which are internally assessed in school. The award for the subject as a whole is given on a 7-point scale at three levels: Credit (1 and 2), General (3 and 4) and Foundation (5 and 6). An award of 7 means that the course has been completed. Pupils who do not complete the course or do not sit all parts of the examination get 'no award'.

GCSE figures relate to achievements by 16-year-olds at the end of the academic year and are shown as percentages of 16-year-olds in school. Standard Grades (in Scotland) relate to achievements by pupils in year S4 at the end of the academic year. That is, the achievements of pupils by the end of their last year of compulsory schooling: some may have been passed a year earlier.

GCE A levels are usually taken after a further two years of post-compulsory education, passes being graded from A-E. The SCE/NQ Higher Grade requires only one year of post-compulsory study and for the more able candidates the range of subjects taken may be as wide as at Standard Grade. The Highers figures in Table 4.5 combine the new NVQ Higher and the old SCE Higher. GCE A level and equivalent figures for pupils aged between 17 and 19 at the end of the school year are shown as a percentage of the 18-year-old population. This age spread in the examination result figures takes account of those pupils sitting examinations a year early or resitting them. Scottish Higher figures are based on the 17-year-old population as Highers are normally taken one year earlier (in Year S5) than A levels, although they can resit them or take additional subjects in year S6. However the data for Scotland relate only to year S5 pupils' examination results.

Average GCE A/AS level points scores are shown in Table 4.5. Points scores are determined by totalling pupils' individual GCE A/AS results: GCE A-level grades A-E count as 10 to 2 points respectively; and GCE AS grades A-E count as 5 to 1 points respectively.

In Wales, at below GCSE standard, the Certificate of Education examination is also available and is widely used by schools. Many pupils take Welsh as a first language at GCSE. In all countries pupils may sit non-GCE/GCSE examinations such as BTEC (SCOTVEC in Scotland), City and Guilds, RSA and Pitman. A proportion of pupils who are recorded as achieving no GCSE, AS or A level qualification will have passes in one or more of these other examinations.

In Table 4.6, Mathematics figures exclude computing science (England) and computer studies and statistics (Wales) while 'Any science' in England and Wales includes double award, single award and individual science subjects. Double award science was introduced with the GCSEs in 1988. Success in double award science means that the pupil has achieved two GCSEs rather than just one pass with single science or the individual sciences of biology, physics and chemistry. The majority of 15-year-olds now attempt GCSE double award science in preference to the single science subjects, although the individual sciences are still popular in the independent sector. There is no equivalent to double award science in Standard Grade.

Comparisons of examination results for England, Wales and Northern Ireland with those for Scotland are not straightforward because of the different education and examination systems. However, the following should be used as a guideline:

5 or more GCSEs at grades A*–C = 5 or more Standard Grades at levels 1–3
1–4 GCSEs at grades A*–C = 1–4 Standard Grades at levels 1–3
GCSEs at grades D–G only = Standard Grades at levels 4–7 only
2 or more GCE A levels passes at A–E = 3 or more Higher Grade passes at A–C.

Also see the National Curriculum notes for Table 4.7.

Table 4.7 The National Curriculum: Assessments and Tests

Under the Education Reform Act (1988) a National Curriculum has been progressively introduced into primary and secondary schools in England and Wales. This consists of mathematics, English (or the option of Welsh as a first language in Wales) and science as core subjects, with a modern language, history, geography, information technology, design and technology, music, art and physical education (and Welsh as a second language in Wales) as foundation subjects. Measurable local targets have been defined for four key stages, corresponding to ages 7, 11, 14 and 16.

Pupils are assessed formally at the ages of 7, 11 and 14 by their teachers and by national tests in the core subjects of English, mathematics and science (and in Welsh in Welsh speaking schools in Wales). Sixteen-year-olds are assessed by means of the GCSE examination. Statutory authorities have been set up for England and Wales to advise government on the National Curriculum and promote curriculum development generally. Northern Ireland has its own common curriculum, which is similar but not identical to the National Curriculum in England and Wales. Assessment arrangements in Northern Ireland became statutory from September 1996 and Key Stage 1 pupils are assessed at the age of 8. Pupils in Northern Ireland are not assessed in Science at Key Stages 1 and 2. The National Curriculum does not apply in Scotland, where school curricula are the responsibility of education authorities and individual head teachers, and in practice almost all 14 to 16-year-olds study mathematics, English, science, a modern foreign language, a social subject, physical education, technology and a creative and aesthetic subject.

The Key Stage 1, 2 and 3 figures for England cover all types of school (e.g. maintained and independent). The Government Office Region figures cover LEA – maintained schools only.

Tables 4.8 and 4.9 Further (including adult) education

Further Education (FE) includes home students on courses of further education (FE) in further education institutions. The FE sector includes all provision outside schools that is below higher education (HE) level. This ranges from courses in independent living skills for students with severe learning difficulties up to GCE A level, advanced GNVQ or GSVQ and level 3 NVQ or SVQ courses. The FE sector also includes many students pursuing recreational courses not leading to a formal qualification. Students in England and Wales are counted once only, irrespective of the number of courses for which a student has enrolled. In Scotland and Northern Ireland, students enrolled on more than one course in unrelated subjects are counted for each of these courses with the exception of those on Standard Grade/GCSE and/or Highers/GCE courses, who are counted once only irrespective of the number of levels/grades. Most FE students are in FE colleges and (in England) sixth form colleges that were formerly maintained by Local Education Authorities (LEAs), but in April 1993 became independent self-governing institutions receiving funding through the FEFC. There are also a small number of FE students in higher education (HE) institutions, and conversely some HE students in FE institutions.

Students may be of any age from 16 upwards (no minimum age in Scotland), and full or part-time. Full-time students aged under 19 are exempt from tuition fees and fully funded by the Further Education Funding Councils in England, the Further Education Funding Council of Wales, the Scottish Further Education Funding Council and the Department of Higher and Further Education, Training and Employment in Northern Ireland. Students aged 16–18 on FE courses in the Scottish FEIs are exempt from tuition fees, at the discretion of the individual colleges. Students are eligible to apply for support (bursary); the policy for eligibility is at the discretion of the colleges. For other students tuition fees are payable, but may be remitted for students in receipt of certain social security benefits. In some cases discretionary grants may be available from LEAs or the colleges themselves. LEAs continue to make some FE provision (often referred to as 'adult education') exclusively part-time, and predominantly recreational. The majority of LEAs make part or all of this provision directly themselves, but some pay other organisations (usually FE colleges) to do so on their behalf – i.e. 'contracted out' provision.

Part-time day courses are mainly those organised for students released by their employers either for one or two days a week (or any part of a week in Scotland), or for a period (or periods) of block release.

Sandwich courses are those where periods of full-time study are broken by a period (or periods) of associated industrial training or experience, and where the total period (or periods) of full-time study over the whole course averages more than 19 weeks per academic year (18 weeks in Scotland). Sandwich course students are classed as full-time students.

National Vocational Qualifications (NVQs) and Scottish Vocational Qualifications (SVQs) are occupational qualifications, available at five levels, and are based on up-to-date standards set by employers.

General National Vocational Qualifications (GNVQs) and General Scottish Vocational Qualifications (GSVQs) combine general and vocational education and are available at three levels:

Foundation – broadly equivalent to four GCSEs at grades D–G or four SCE Standard Grades at levels 4 to 7.
Intermediate – broadly equivalent to five GCSEs at grades A* to C or five SCE Standard Grades at levels 1 to 3.
Advanced – broadly equivalent to two GCE A levels, or three SCE Higher Grade passes; also known as vocational A levels .

Figures for English domiciled FE students studying in England in 2000/01 are shown by the region of study and are not directly comparable with figures shown in previous editions of *Regional Trends*, which recorded students by region of domicile. Since 1996/97 figures for FE students in England have been extracted from the Individualised Student Record (ISR), which counts those students taking a course in an English further education college on 1 November. Until 1995/96 figures were taken from the Further Education Statistical Record (FESR). Due to differences in data collection and methodology between the two sources, the ISR figures are not directly comparable with figures derived from the FESR.

Since April 2001, the publication of data on further education in England has been the responsibility of the Learning and Skills Council (LSC), which has taken over funding further education from the Further Education Funding Council (FEFC).

The participation rates for regions in England in Table 4.8 have been calculated in the following way:

the numbers of pupils in maintained, special and independent schools attending schools in the area;
the number of full-time and part-time further education students resident in the area regardless of where they study;
trainees on Government-supported training, according to the TEC area with which their training is contracted;
divided by the estimated population of the area in January 1999 who were 16 or 17 respectively at August 1998.

Table 4.10 Higher education

Higher education (HE) students are those on courses that are of a standard that are higher than GCE A level, Scottish SCE/NQ Higher Grade, GNVQ/NVQ level 3 or the BTEC or SCOTVEC National Certificate or Diploma. Higher education in publicly funded institutions is funded by block grants from the three Higher Education Funding Councils (HEFCs) in Great Britain and the Department of Higher and Further Education, Training and Employment in Northern Ireland (DHFETE). Some HE activity takes place in FE sector institutions, some of which is funded by the HEFCs and some by the FEFCs (The Scottish Further Education Funding Council). Most home students on full-time undergraduate courses are eligible for a mandatory award and top-up student loans.

The figures for HE students in English (2000/01) and Welsh (1999/00) further education colleges are extracted from the Individualised Student Record (ISR) which counts those students taking a course in a further education college on the 1 November 2000 in England or 1 December 1999 in Wales. Until 1995/96 figures were taken from the Further Education Statistical Record (FESR). Due to differences in data collection and methodology between the two sources the ISR figures are not directly comparable with figures derived from the FESR.

Higher Education institutions figures use the interim December student record. However, previous editions of this table were based on the July whole session record, which records a higher total number of students.

Table 4.12 Population of working age by highest qualification

Table 4.12 covers all people of working age (16–64 for males, 16–59 for females). Please also see notes to Tables 4.5 and 4.6

Degree or equivalent includes higher and first degrees, NVQ level 5 and other degree level qualifications such as graduate membership of a professional institute.

Higher education qualification below degree level includes NVQ level 4, higher level BTEC/SCOTVEC, HNC/HND, RSA Higher diploma and nursing and teaching qualifications.

GCE A level or equivalent includes NVQ level 3, GNVQ advanced, BTEC/SCOTVEC National Certificate, RSA Advanced diploma, City and Guilds advanced craft, A/AS levels or equivalent, Scottish Highers and Scottish Certificate of Sixth Year Studies and trade apprenticeships.

GCSE grades A*–C or equivalent includes NVQ level 2, GNVQ intermediate, RSA diploma, City and Guilds craft, BTEC/SCOTVEC First or general diploma, GCSE grades A*–C or equivalent, O level and CSE Grade 1.

Other qualifications at NVQ level 1 or below include GNVQ, GSVO foundation level, GCSE grade D–G, CSE below grade 1, BTEC/SCOTVEC First or general certificate, other RSA and City and Guilds qualifications, Youth Training certificate and any other professional, vocational or foreign qualifications for which the level is unknown.

Table 4.13 National Learning Targets for England 2002

Table 4.13 shows the proportions of people meeting the required qualification level for four of the National Learning Targets for England 2002. The Targets shown are split into two groups, young people and adults. The Targets have been set using the competence-based National Vocational Qualifications (NVQs), Scottish Vocational Qualifications (SVQs), and their vocational and academic equivalents. It should be noted that the data in Table 4.13 relate to the region in which the person is resident, and not where they obtained the qualifications. This can lead to some distortion of the regional picture of educational standards; this is particularly relevant in Northern Ireland, as many qualified young people leave home to enter higher education or seek employment in Great Britain.

The four main targets are shown in the table:

Young people
– by the year 2002, 85 per cent of 19 year olds to achieve 5 GCSE passes at grades A*–C, an Intermediate GNVQ or an NVQ level 2.
– by the year 2002, 60 per cent of 21 year olds to achieve 2 GCE A levels, or Advanced GNVQ or NVQ level 3.

Adults
– by the year 2002, 50 per cent of those of working age in employment to be qualified to NVQ level 3, Advanced GNVQ or 2 GCE A level standard.
– by the year 2002, 28 per cent of those of working age in employment to have a vocational, professional, management or academic qualification at NVQ level 4 or above.

In addition to the targets shown, there are also National Learning Targets for 11 year olds, 16 year olds, targets for organisations and a learning participation target for adults.

Table 4.15 Work-based learning and training

Work-based Learning for Adults (previously known as Work-Based Training for Adults) replaced the former Training for Work (TfW) initiative in April 1998, and is aimed at getting unemployed adults back into work.

Work-based Training for Young People consists of Advanced Modern Apprenticeships (AMA), Foundation Modern Apprenticeships (FMA) Life Skills/Life Build (not recorded in Table 4.15) and Other training for young people (formerly known as Youth Training). These programmes aim to provide the participants with training towards a recognised National Vocational Qualification at levels 2 and 3 or above.

These programmes are delivered through the network of Training & Enterprise Councils (TECs) in England and Wales and local Enterprise Companies (LECs) in Scotland. In England and Wales leavers are followed up six months after they leave the programme, whereas in Scotland they are followed up three months after completing training.

For Northern Ireland, figures relate to persons on the Jobskills Programme. The Programme focuses on the delivery and attainment of NVQs and in line with national policy guarantees all 16 and 17 year olds the opportunity of a training place. For statistical purposes, young persons on Jobskills are classified as those who were under 18 years of age on joining the programme. As trainees can stay on Jobskills for up to three years, outcomes for leavers during 1999–00 may not necessarily be fully representative of outcomes in the longer term.

CHAPTER 5:
LABOUR MARKET

Interpretation of the labour market requires a number of different sources of data to be used. There are five main sources in this chapter: the Labour Force Survey (LFS), the Annual Business Inquiry (ABI), the Northern Ireland Quarterly Employment Survey (QES), the New Earnings Survey and the claimant count. Problems can arise in drawing together data on the same subject from different sources. For example, the question in the LFS as to whether the respondent is employed produces a measure of employment based on the number of persons, whereas a question addressed to employers asking the number of people they employ, as in ABI, produces a measure of the number of jobs. Thus if someone has a second job they will be included twice.

LFS estimates are prone to sampling variability. For example, in the December 1999 to February 2000 period, ILO unemployment in United Kingdom (seasonally adjusted) stood at 1,715,000. If another sample for the same period was drawn, a different result may be achieved.

In theory, many samples could be drawn, each giving a different result. This is because each sample would be made up of different people giving different answers to the questions. The spread of these results is the sampling variability. Sampling variability is determined by a number of factors including the sample size, the variability of the population from which the sample is drawn and the sample design. Once the sampling variability is known, it is possible to calculate a range of values about the sample estimate that represents the expected variation with a given level of assurance. This is called a confidence interval. For a 95 per cent confidence interval, widely used within ONS and elsewhere, we expect that in 95 per cent of the samples (19 times out of 20) the confidence interval will contain the true value that would be obtained by surveying the entire population. For the example given above, we can be 95 per cent confident that the true value was in the range 1,661,000 to 1,769,000.

In general, the larger the number of people in the sample the smaller the variation between estimates. For this reason estimates based on the LFS for the whole of the UK are more accurate than those for smaller geographical areas or subsets of the population. Generally, the sampling variability around regional estimates is, proportionately, around three times that for national estimates.

Estimates of small numbers have relatively wide confidence intervals making them unreliable. For this reason, the ONS does not publish LFS estimates below 10,000. Data from the LFS Annual Local Area Database are more accurate than those from the quarterly survey because the database is derived from four quarters of the LFS, and hence represents an increase of 60 per cent over the quarterly sample size. Estimates can therefore be published down to 6,000, meaning that data are available for a larger number of areas.

Sampling variability also affects changes over time. For example, LFS employment in United Kingdom rose by 59,000 (seasonally adjusted) between Autumn (September to November) 1999 and Winter (December to February) 1999/2000 and the 95 per cent confidence interval for this change is the range -56,000 to +174,000. Quarterly changes may be lower than the level that is explainable by sampling variability.

Changes over time are best viewed using changes in rates rather than levels in order to view them in a wider context of changes in the overall population. Rates are also subject to sampling variability. The best estimate of the quarterly change in economic activity rate between September to November 1999 and December 1999 to February 2000 was that it remained unchanged (seasonally adjusted). We can be 95 per cent confident that the true change in the economic activity lies within the range -0.2 per cent to +0.2 per cent.

Tables 5.1 and 5.2
Labour force

The labour force includes people aged 16 and over who are either in employment (whether employed, self-employed, on a work-related government-supported employment and training programme or an unpaid family worker) or unemployed. The 'ILO definition' of unemployment counts as unemployed people without a job who were available to start work within two weeks and had either looked for work in the past four weeks or were waiting to start a job they had already obtained in the next two weeks.

Tables 5.4 and 5.5 Annual
Business Inquiry, Short-term
Employment Survey and
Quarterly Employment Survey

The Annual Business Inquiry (ABI) is a sample survey which ran for the first time in 1998 and replaced the Annual Employment Survey. The ABI is the only source of employment statistics for Great Britain analysed by the local area and by detailed industrial classification. The sample was drawn from the Inter-Departmental Business Register (IDBR) and the ABI 1999 sample comprised 78,000 enterprises. An enterprise is roughly defined as a combination of local units (i.e. individual workplaces with PAYE schemes or registered for VAT) under common ownership. These enterprises covered 0.5 million local units and 15 million employees (out of a total population of roughly 25 million employees in employment).

The ABI results are used to benchmark the monthly/quarterly employment surveys (STES) which measure 'movements' (by region and industrial group) between the annual survey dates.

The Quarterly Employment Survey (QES) for Northern Ireland is a voluntary survey which covers all employers with at least 25 employees, all public sector employers and a representative sample of smaller firms. Data are collected for both male and female, full-time and part-time employees. Estimates for Northern Ireland are produced on a quarterly basis with unadjusted figures available at the two-digit or division level of the 1992 Standard Industrial Classification and seasonally adjusted figures available at a broad sector level.

Table 5.7 Economic activity rates

The economic activity rate is the percentage of the population in a given age group which is in the labour force.

Table 5.12 'Other' occupational group

This group covers occupations which require the knowledge and experience necessary to perform mostly routine tasks, often involving the use of simple hand-held tools and, in some cases, requiring a degree of physical effort.

Most occupations in this group do not require formal educational qualifications but will usually have an associated short period of formal experience-related training. All non-managerial agricultural occupations are also included in this group, primarily because of the difficulty of distinguishing between those occupations which require only a limited knowledge of agricultural techniques, animal husbandry, etc., from those which require specific training and experience in these areas.

Table 5.13 Labour Disputes

The table shows rates per 1,000 employees of working days lost for all industries and services. The statistics relate only to disputes connected with terms and conditions of employment. Stoppages involving fewer than ten workers or lasting less than one day are excluded except where the aggregate of working days lost is 100 or more. When interpreting the figures the following points should be borne in mind:
a) geographical variations in industrial structure affect overall regional comparisons;
b) a few large stoppages affecting a small number of firms may have a significant effect;
c) the number of working days lost and workers involved relate to persons both directly and indirectly involved at the establishments where the disputes occurred;
d) the regional figures involve a greater degree of estimation than the national figures as some large national stoppages cannot be disaggregated to a regional level and are only shown in the figure for the United Kingdom.

Tables 5.16 and 5.17 New Earnings Survey

These tables contain some of the regional results of the New Earnings Survey 2000, fuller details of which are given for the Government Office Regions in parts A and E of the report New Earnings Survey 2000 (National Statistics Direct), published in October and December 2000. Results for Northern Ireland are published separately by the Department of Enterprise, Trade and Investment, Northern Ireland. The survey measured gross earnings of a 1 per cent sample of employees, most of whom were members of Pay-As-You-Earn (PAYE) schemes for a pay-period which included 14 April 1999. The earnings information collected was converted to a weekly basis where necessary, and to an hourly basis where normal basic hours were reported.

Figures are given where the number of employees reporting in the survey was 30 or more and the standard error of average weekly earnings was 5 per cent or less. Gross earnings are measured before tax, National Insurance or other deductions. They include overtime pay, bonuses and other additions to basic pay but exclude any payments for earlier periods (for example, back pay), income in kind, tips and gratuities. All the results in this volume relate to full-time male and female employees on adult rates whose pay for the survey pay-period was not affected by absence. Employees were classified to the region in which they worked (or were based if mobile) using postcode information, and to manual or non-manual occupations on the basis of the Standard Occupational Classification 1990 (SOC 90). Part A of the report for Great Britain gives full details of definitions used in the survey.
Full-time employees are defined as those normally expected to work more than 30 hours per week, excluding overtime and main meal breaks (but 25 hours or more in the case of teachers) or, if their normal hours were not specified, as those regarded as full-time by the employer.

Tables 5.18, 5.20 and 5.23 ILO unemployment

The International Labour Organisation (ILO) definition of unemployment is measured through the Labour Force Survey and covers those people who are looking for work and are available for work (see Glossary of terms). The ILO unemployment rate is the percentage of economically active people who are ILO unemployed.

Counts of claimants of unemployment-related benefits are also published. There are advantages and disadvantages with both series, but they are complementary. The ILO unemployment rate is the number of people who are ILO unemployed as a proportion of the resident economically active population of the area concerned. The claimant count rate is the number of people claiming unemployment–related benefits as a proportion of claimants and jobs in each area. This explains why the ILO unemployment rate for London, where inward commuting is an important feature of the local labour market, tends to be significantly higher than the equivalent claimant count rate. The differential is much smaller for a region such as the South East where people commute out of the region into London.

A fuller description of ILO unemployment and claimant count, and the way they relate to one another is in the booklet 'How exactly is unemployment measured?' available from the Office for National Statistics.

Tables 5.19, 5.22 and Map 5.21 Claimant Count statistics

Prior to 7 October 1996, figures in Table 5.19 relate to persons claiming unemployment-related benefits (that is, Unemployment Benefit, Income Support or National Insurance credits) at an Employment Service Office on the day of the monthly count, who on that day were unemployed and satisfied the conditions for claiming benefit. The figures include disabled people, so long as they meet the eligibility criteria and are claiming unemployment-related benefits, but exclude students seeking vacation work and temporarily stopped workers.

From 7 October 1996, a new single benefit, the Jobseeker's Allowance (JSA), replaced Unemployment Benefit and Income Support for unemployed people. People who qualify for JSA through their National Insurance contributions are eligible for a personal allowance (known as contribution-based JSA) for a maximum of six months. People who do not qualify for contribution-based JSA, or whose needs are not met by it, are able to claim a means-tested allowance (known as income-based JSA) for themselves and their dependants for as long as they need it. All those eligible for and claiming for JSA, as well as those claiming National Insurance credits, continue to be included in the monthly claimant count.

National and regional claimant count rates are calculated by expressing the number of claimants as a percentage of the estimated total workforce (the sum of claimants, employee jobs, self-employment jobs, HM Armed Forces and government-supported trainees).

Table 5.24 Qualifications

Degree or equivalent includes higher and first degrees, NVQ level 5 and other degree level qualifications such as graduate membership of a professional institute.

Higher education qualification below degree level includes NVQ level 4, higher level BTEC/SCOTVEC, HNC/HND, RSA Higher diploma and nursing and teaching qualifications.

GCE A level or equivalent includes NVQ level 3, GNVQ advanced, BTEC/SCOTVEC National Certificate, RSA Advanced diploma, City and Guilds advanced craft, A/AS levels or equivalent, Scottish Highers and Scottish Certificate of Sixth Year Studies and trade apprenticeships.

GCSE grades A*–C or equivalent includes HVQ level 2, GNVQ intermediate, RSA diploma, City and Guilds craft, BTEC/SCOTVEC First or general diploma, GCSE grades A*–C or equivalent, O level and CSE Grade 1.

Other qualifications at NVQ level 1 or below include GNVQ, GSVO foundation level, GCSE grade D–G, CSE below grade 1, BTEC/SCOTVEC First or general certificate, other RSA and City and Guilds qualifications, Youth Training certificate and any other professional qualification.

Chart 5.25 Redundancies

Estimates cover the number of people who were not in employment during the reference week and who reported that they had been made redundant in the month of the reference week or in the two calendar months prior to this; plus the number of people who were in employment during the reference week who started their job in the same calendar month as, or the two calendar months prior to, the reference week, and who reported that they had been made redundant in the month of the reference week or in the two calendar months prior to this.

Table 5.26 Vacancies at Jobcentres

ONS publish vacancy statistics derived from Employment Service (ES) jobcentres. ONS do not, at present, collate figures on vacancies advertised outside of these government offices, such as those notified to private employment agencies and those advertised in newspapers and journals. Surveys in the past have shown that vacancies notified to ES jobcentres measure about one-third of all job vacancies in the United Kingdom, though this will vary according to occupation, industry and geographical area and over time.

It should be noted that the stage reached in an economic cycle could be very influential both in terms of the market share achieved by jobcentres and in terms of the types of jobs handled and the characteristics of those seeking a job. It is generally thought that government Jobcentres' market share of all available vacancies is at its maximum during a trough in the economic cycle when there are more people chasing fewer jobs, when the jobs on offer have less of a tendency to be the more difficult to fill and when those looking for work are more employable in terms of the skills they have to offer.

Administrative systems in the ES also affect output. Since 1998, some ES area offices have set up centralised vacancy taking arrangements. In these areas, all vacancies are notified to a single office. In several areas it is not possible to identify which part of the area the job is located and data for individual jobcentres will be distorted from the date these centralised procedures were introduced. Every effort is being made by both ES and ONS to identify which offices are affected, from what date and for what period (some areas have disbanded centralisation and returned to local notification). However, because of this, and because of further discontinuities that have been introduced following the ES modernising Government Programme, these data should be treated with caution.

Tables 5.27 The New Deal	The New Deal for the young unemployed is available to young people aged 18–24 who have been unemployed for more than six months, through four options:

a) a job attracting a wage subsidy of £60 a week, payable to employees for up to six months;
b) a work placement with a voluntary organisation;
c) a six-month work placement with an Environment Task Force; and
d) for those without basic qualifications, a place on a full-time education and training course, which might last for up to one year.

All the options include an element of training. For each young person the programme begins with a 'gateway' period of careers advice and intensive help with work, and with training in the skills needed for the world of work.

People in New Deal jobs are those who are recorded by the Employment Service as having been placed into subsidised employment, plus those who are recorded as having terminated their Jobseeker's Allowance (JSA) claim in order to go into a job. This will undercount the total number going into a job: some who go into a job will not, for whatever reason, record this as the reason for termination of their JSA claim. These will be counted as 'not known'. Past research indicates that the destinations of those who do not give a reason for termination follow a similar pattern to those who do give a reason. Where a young person returns to JSA within 13 weeks of starting an unsubsidised job, the job is discounted.

CHAPTER 6: HOUSING

Tables 6.1 and 6.4

In the 1981 Census, a dwelling was defined as structurally separate accommodation whose rooms, excluding bathrooms and WCs, are self-contained. In the 1991 Census the definition changed to structurally separate accommodation whose rooms, including bath or shower, WC, and kitchen facilities, are self-contained. The figures in Table 6.1 include vacant dwellings and temporary dwellings occupied as a normal place of residence. Estimates of the stock in England are based on data from the 1981 and 1991 Censuses. In Wales and Scotland data from the Census is supplemented by local authority and other public sector landlords' figures. Northern Ireland stock figures are based on rating lists, Northern Ireland Housing Executive and Housing Association figures. Estimates of the tenure distribution in Table 6.4 are based on the above estimates and certain assumptions regarding the tenure distribution of gains and losses in the housing stock.

Table 6.2 New Dwellings completed

A dwelling is defined for the purposes of this table as a building or any part of a building which forms a separate and self-contained set of premises designed to be occupied by a single family. The figures relate to new permanent dwellings only, i.e. dwellings with a life expectancy of 60 years or more. A dwelling is counted as completed when it becomes ready for occupation, whether actually occupied or not. The figures for private sector completions in Northern Ireland have been statistically adjusted to correct, as far as possible, the proven under-recording of private sector completions in Northern Ireland. The figures for private sector completions in Scotland include estimates for some Local Authorities in latter years.

Table 6.7 Householder's satisfaction with their accommodation and area

Accommodation data for Scotland are for 1996 and refers to the percentage of occupied dwellings. Area Data for Scotland are for 1999 and refer to the percentage of households. As a result comparisons between satisfaction with area and accommodation should be treated with caution.

Table 6.8 Selected housing costs of owner occupied

Mortgage payments: mortgage interest plus any premiums on mortgage protection policies for loans used to purchase the property. For repayment mortgages, interest is calculated using the amount of loan outstanding and the standard interest rate at time of interview.

Endowment policies: premium on endowment policies covering the repayment of mortgages and loans used to purchase the property.

Structural insurance: includes cases where insurance also covers furniture and contents and structural element cannot be separately identified.

Services: includes payments of ground rent, feu duties (applies in Scotland), chief rent, service charges, compulsory or regular maintenance charges, site rent (caravans), factoring (payments to a land steward) and any other regular payments in connection with the accommodation.

Table 6.9 Average dwelling prices

Average prices in this table are calculated from data collected by the Land Registry. Because of the time lag between the completion of a house purchase and its subsequent lodgement with the Land Registry, data for the final quarter of 2001 are not as complete as those for the final quarter of 2000. The table includes all sales registered up to 31 March 2001.

Table 6.11 Average weekly rents: by tenure

Private sector rents: average rents for 1999–00, excluding tenants who were living rent-free. Figures include any Housing Benefit but exclude any water and other charges paid as part of rent which would not be eligible for Housing Benefit. Data for England are combined averages from the DSS Family Resources Survey and the DETR Survey of English Housing.

Local authority rents: average unrebated rents at April 1999.
Scottish Local Authority Average weekly rent is estimated by dividing the estimated housing revenue from 1 April 1999 to 31 March 2000 by the total housing stock at the mid point of the year (30 September 1999).

Registered Social Landlord (formerly Housing Association) rents: these figures cover the whole stock at 31 March 2000, and are derived from Housing Corporation returns.

Table 6.10 Mortgage advances, income for mortgage purchases

Figures in this table are taken from The Survey of Mortgage Lenders, a 5 per cent sample survey of mortgages at completion stage. Full details of the survey are given in The New Survey of Mortgage Lenders by Bob Pannell and David Champion (Department of the Environment), in Housing Finance No.16, November 1992 published by the Council of Mortgage Lenders.

First-time buyers include sitting tenant purchases.

Table 6.12 Dwellings in Council Tax bands

Council Tax bands in Scotland differ from those in England and Wales. The bands are as follows:

	Scotland	England and Wales
Band A	Under £27,000	Under £40,000
Band B	£27,001–£35,000	£40,001–£52,000
Band C	£35,001–£45,000	£52,001–£68,000
Band D	£45,001–£58,000	£68,001–£88,000
Band E	£58,001–£80,000	£88,001–£120,000
Band F	£80,001–£106,000	£120,001–£160,000
Band G	£106,001–£212,000	£160,001–£320,000
Band H	Over £212,000	Over £320,000

Table 6.13 County Court actions for mortgage possessions

The figures do not indicate how many houses have been repossessed through the courts; not all the orders will have resulted in the issue and execution of warrants of possession. The regional breakdown relates to the location of the court rather than the address of the property.

Actions entered: a claimant begins an action for an order for possession of residential property by way of a summons in a county court.

Orders made: the court, following a judicial hearing, may grant an order for possession immediately. This entitles the claimant to apply for a warrant to have the defendant evicted. However, even where a warrant for possession is issued, the parties can still negotiate a compromise to prevent eviction.

Suspended orders: frequently, the court grants the mortgage lender possession but suspends the operation of the order. Provided the defendant complies with the terms of the suspension, which usually require them to pay the current mortgage instalments plus some of the accrued arrears, the possession order cannot be enforced.

Table 6.14 Homeless households by reason

In England and Wales the basis for these figures is households accepted for re-housing by local authorities under the homelessness provisions of Part III of the Housing Act 1985, and Part VII of the Housing Act 1996.

In Scotland the basis of these figures is households assessed by the local authorities as homeless or potentially homeless and in priority need, as defined in Section 24 of the Housing (Scotland) Act 1987.

In Northern Ireland, the Housing (Northern Ireland) Order 1988 (Part II) defines the basis under which households (including one-person households) are classified as homeless. The figures relate to priority cases only.

CHAPTER 7: HEALTH AND CARE

Tables 7.3 and 7.7 Age-standardised mortality rates

Mortality rates vary with age so the rates for different areas can be affected by the age structure of their populations. The figures in Tables 7.3 and 7.7 have been adjusted to take into account these differences in age structure. The rates have been standardised to the mid-1991 UK population for males and females separately. This means it is permissible to compare rates across areas for each gender, but not to compare males and females.

The causes of death included in Table 7.3 correspond to International Classification of Diseases (9th Revision) codes as follows :
  all circulatory diseases – 390–459;
  ischaemic heart disease – 410–414;
  cerebrovascular disease – 430–438;
  all respiratory diseases – 460–519;
  bronchitis *et al* – 490–493+496;
  cancer (malignant neoplasms) – 140–208;
  all injuries and poisoning – 800–999; road accidents – E810–E819;
  suicides and open verdicts – E950–E959 and E980–E989.
The data in these tables relate to registrations in the reference year.

Tables 7.4, 7.12 and 7.13 General Household Survey and Continuous Household Survey

The General Household Survey (GHS) and Continuous Household Survey (CHS) are continuous surveys which have been running since 1971 for the GHS and 1983 for the CHS, and are based each year on samples of the general population resident in private (that is, non-institutional) households in Great Britain and Northern Ireland respectively. They are multi-purpose surveys, providing information on aspects of housing, employment, education, health and social services, health-related behaviour, transport, population and social security. Since 1988, GHS fieldwork has been based on a financial rather than calendar year and, due to this, data were not collected for the first quarter of 1988.

Tables 7.5 and 7.6 General Practice Research Database

The General Practice Research Database (GPRD) is a large data collection system of continuous data on patients registered with participating general practices in the UK. The practices follow an agreed protocol for the recording of clinical data and submit anonymised, patient based clinical records on a regular basis to the database. Practices are recruited to GPRD on a volunteer basis rather than as a statistically representative sample. Data from 211 practices in England and Wales are included in the analyses presented here. These practices cover around 2.6 per cent of the population of England and Wales in 1998.

Patients are allocated to regions according to the location of the practice at which they are registered.

The Medicines Control Agency (MCA) has been responsible for the overall management and financial control of the GPRD since April 1999, and its operation since October 1999.

Table 7.7 Cervical and breast cancer screening

Figures for the two cancer screening programmes are snapshots of the coverage of the target population for each programme at 31 March 2000.

Figures for the Scottish Breast Screening Programme are an estimate of the coverage of the target population over the three year period 1 April 1997 to 31 March 2000. These figures are derived from the number of women in the 50–54, 55–59 and 60–64 year age groups who have attended a routine screening appointment or a self/GP referral appointment during this period and a mid-year estimate of the female population in Scotland aged 50–64 in 1999. Medically ineligible women are not excluded from the target population.

Northern Ireland figures for breast screening may include a small number of women who have been counted more than once due to early recall for screening during the relevant three year period. The maximum extent of any such double count can be calculated as less than 0.4 per cent.

All population data for Scotland were obtained from the General Register Office for Scotland.

Chart 7.8 Cancer — comparative incidence ratios

The directly age-standardised rates in each country and region of the United Kingdom have been calculated using the European standard population. This is done by multiplying the age specific incidence rates in each area by the number of people in the corresponding age groups in the standard population and summing to give the overall rate per 100,000 population. This gives comparable overall rates for areas which have different population structures. The standardised incidence of selected cancer sites in each area have been compared with the United Kingdom as a whole (expressed as the ratio of the rates multiplied by 100) - the comparative incidence ratio.

Directly age-standardised registration rates per 100,000 population for the United Kingdom, in 1997 were:

Selected sites	Male	Female
Lung	74.9	34.7
Colorectal	55.3	34.8
Breast	.	108.2
Prostate	64.8	.

Table 7.11 National Food Survey

The National Food Survey (NFS) is a continuous sample survey in which about 6,000 households per year in Great Britain keep a record of the type, quantity and costs of foods entering the home during a one week period. Nutritional intakes are estimated from the survey data. Recent developments include, from 1996, the participation in the survey of about 700 households in Northern Ireland. From 1994, data are also available on food eaten out in Great Britain (but not Northern Ireland).

Detailed survey results and definitions are published by The Stationery Office in an annual report National Food Survey. The edition to be published in November 2001 (for the data year 2000) will be the last based on data from the National Food Survey. From April 2001, the data have been collected as part of the new Expenditure and Food Survey. A separate annual report on food will continue to be published by the Department for Environment, Food and Rural Affairs (DEFRA).

Table 7.13 Alcohol consumption

A unit of alcohol is 8 grams of pure alcohol, approximately equivalent to half a pint of ordinary strength beer, a glass of wine, or a pub measure of spirits.

Sensible Drinking, the 1995 report of an inter-departmental review of the scientific and medical evidence of the effects of drinking alcohol, concluded that the daily benchmarks were more appropriate than previously recommended weekly levels since they could help individuals decide how much to drink on single occasions and to avoid episodes of intoxication with their attendant health and social risks. The report concluded that regular consumption of between three and four units a day for men and two to three units for women does not carry a significant health risk. However, consistently drinking more than four units a day for men, or more than three for women, is not advised as a sensible drinking level because of the progressive health risk it carries. The government's advice on sensible drinking is now based on these daily benchmarks.

Chart 7.14 Drug use	Results for England and Wales can be found in: Ramsay & Partridge (1999), *Drug Misuse Declared in 1998: results from the British Crime Survey*, Home Office Research Study 197.

Table 7.15 NHS hospital waiting lists

The waiting list figures for England are Health Authority (HA) responsible population-based. That is, they are based on figures received from HA-based returns and include all patients resident within the HA boundary plus all patients registered with GPs who are members of a Primary Care Group (PCG) for which the HA is responsible, but are resident in another HA, and excludes any patient resident in the HA, but registered with a GP who is a member of a PCG responsible to a different HA. Other exclusions are all patients living outside England and all privately funded patients waiting for treatment in NHS hospitals. However they do include NHS funded patients, living in England, who are waiting for treatment in Scotland, Wales, Northern Ireland, abroad, and at private hospitals, which are not included in the corresponding provider based return.

In Scotland data are collected by trusts for each individual patient waiting for NHS in-patient or day care treatment – information on Scottish residents waiting outside Scotland is not collected centrally. Average waiting times are calculated from the waiting time associated with each individual patient record.

Figures from Northern Ireland are provider-based. They include all patients waiting for treatment at NI Trusts including private patients and patients from outside Northern Ireland.

Mean waiting time. This is calculated approximately for any category as the total waiting times for patients still on the list for that category divided by the corresponding number of people waiting in that category.

Median waiting time. The waiting time of 50 per cent of those patients will be less than the median length. This is a better indicator of the 'average' case since it is generally unaffected by abnormally long or short waiting times at the end of the distribution.

Table 7.16 NHS hospital activity

Data for England are based on Finished Consultant Episodes (FCEs). An FCE is a completed period of care of a patient using a NHS hospital bed, under one consultant within one NHS Trust. If a patient is transferred from one consultant to another, even if this is within the same NHS Trust, the episode ends and another one begins. The transfer of a patient from one hospital to another with the same consultant and within the same NHS Trust does not end the episode. Data for Wales are based on discharges and deaths. Data for Scotland and Northern Ireland are based on a system where transfers between consultants do not count as a discharge except in Scotland where figures include patients transferred from one consultant to another within the same hospital, provided there is a change of speciality (or significant facilities e.g. a change of ward). Transfers from one hospital to another, with the same consultant, however, count as a discharge. New-born babies are included for Northern Ireland but excluded for the other countries. Deaths are included in all four countries.

For Scotland figures include NHS beds/activity in Joint-User and Contractual Hospitals; these hospitals account for a relatively small proportion of total NHS activity.

A day case is a person who comes for investigation, treatment or operation under clinical supervision on a planned non-resident basis, who occupies a bed for part or all of that day, and who returns home as planned the same day. Scotland figures will also include day cases that have been transferred to or from in-patient care.

An outpatient is defined as a person seen by a consultant for treatment or advice. A new outpatient is one whose first attendance of a continuous series (or single attendance where relevant) at a clinical outpatient department for the same course of treatment falls within the period under review. Each outpatient attendance of a course or series is included in the year in which the attendance occurred. Persons attending more than one department are counted in each department.

In Northern Ireland, the outpatient figures are separated into GP referrals and consultant initiated attendances. It is possible for a first attendance to be initiated by a consultant. The number of attendances in 'new attendances' refers to GP referrals only, and therefore may not include all new attendances.

Mean duration of stay is calculated for any category as the total bed-days for that category divided by the number of ordinary admissions (Finished Consultant Episodes in England and Wales, in-patient discharges (including transfers) in Scotland, and deaths and discharges in Northern Ireland) for that category. An ordinary admission is one where the patient is expected to remain in hospital for at least one night. For Scotland figures exclude learning disabilities and non-psychiatric specialties.

Population figures are based on estimates for 1999 Health Authorities for persons all ages.

It should be noted that where figures are presented to the nearest whole number, this is to facilitate the calculation of rates and the aggregation of age bands.

Cases treated per available bed are for ordinary admissions (in-patient discharges including transfers in Scotland) and does not include day case admissions.

Table 7.18 NHS Hospital and Community Health Service directly employed staff

General Medical Practitioners (i.e. family GPs), General Dental Practitioners, the staff employed by the practitioners, pharmacists in General Pharmaceutical Services and staff working in other contracted out services are not included in the figures.

Medical and dental staff included are those holding permanent paid (whole-time, part-time, sessional) and/or honorary appointments in NHS hospitals and Community Health Services. Figures include clinical assistants and hospital practitioners. Occasional sessional staff in Community Health Medical and Dental Services for whom no whole-time equivalent is collected are not included. The whole-time equivalent of staff holding appointments with more than one region is included in the appropriate region.

Nursing, midwifery and health visiting staff included healthcare assistants, and excluded nurse teachers and students on '1992' courses. Scientific, therapeutic and technical staff comprises Scientific and Professional and Technical staff incorporating PAMs. Administration and estates comprises Administration and Clerical, Senior Managers and Works staff. Other staff comprises Ancillary, Trades, Ambulance staff and support staff.

All direct care staff comprises all staff in the Medical and dental, Nursing, midwifery and health visiting and Scientific, therapeutic and technical groups.

Table 7.19 General Practitioners and Dentists

The figures for general medical practitioners (GPs) include unrestricted principals, Personal Medical Service (PMS) contracted GP's and PMS salaried GPs.

An Unrestricted Principal is a practitioner who provides the full range of general medical services and whose list is not limited to any particular group of persons. In a few cases, he/she may be relieved of the liability for emergency calls out-of-hours from patients other than his/her own. Most people have an Unrestricted Principal as their GP. Doctors may also practice in the general medical services as restricted principals, assistants, associated or GP Registrars.

A PMS Contracted Doctor is a practitioner who provides the full range of services through the PMS pilot contract and like Unrestricted Principals they have a patient list.

A PMS Salaried Doctor is a doctor employed to work in a PMS pilot, and who provides the full range of services and has a list of registered patients

Other types of General Medical Practitioners include GP Retainers, Restricted Principals, Assistants, Associates (Scotland only), GP Registrars, Salaried Doctors (para 52 SFA) and PMS Other.

The figures for General Dental Practitioners include principals, assistants and vocational dental practitioners in the general dental service. Salaried dentists are excluded. Neither the Hospital Dental Service nor the Community Dental Service are reflected. All Scottish data are provisional.

Table 7.20 Places Available in Residential Care Homes

The figures for England relate to residential places in homes registered under part III of the National Assistance Act, 1948, the Registered Homes Act 1984 and the Registered Homes (Amendment) Act 1991. They include residential places in homes registered for both residential and nursing care. Places are displayed by type of registered home at 31 March 2000.

CHAPTER 8: INCOME AND LIFESTYLES

Tables 8.1 and 8.2 Household income

The Family Expenditure Survey (FES) is a continuous, random sample survey of private households in the United Kingdom and collects information about incomes as well as detailed information on expenditure. All members of the household aged 16 and over keep individual diaries of all spending for a period of two weeks. To increase the reliability of regional breakdowns, three years of data have been combined, the financial years 1997–98, 1998–99 and 1999–00. The total sample over this period was 20,136 households. Northern Ireland data are calculated from an enhanced sample. The United Kingdom FES figures are weighted for non-response, the Northern Ireland FES figures from the enhanced sample are not.

See the FES annual report, *Family Spending*, for a description of the concepts used and details of the definitions of expenditure and income.

Table 8.3 Measure of income

The measure of income used in compiling Table 8.3 is that used in the Department for Work and Pension's Households Below Average Income series. The income of a household is defined as the total income of all members of the household after the deduction of income tax, National Insurance contributions, contributions to occupational pension schemes, additional voluntary contributions to personal pensions, maintenance/child support payments and Council Tax. Income includes earnings from employment and self-employment, social security benefits including Housing Benefit, occupational and private pensions, investment income, maintenance payments, educational grants, scholarships and top-up loans and some in-kind benefits such as luncheon vouchers.

No adjustment has been made in Table 8.3 for any differences between regions in cost of living as the necessary data for adjustment are not available. In the analysis of regions this inability to adjust costs implicitly suggests that there is no difference in cost of living between regions. As this is unlikely to be true, statements have been sensitivity test-ed where possible against alternative cost of living regimes. Results suggest that estimates of income before hous-ing costs are deducted are not sensitive to regional price differentials, but results after deduction of housing costs are. In particular, for London and to a lesser extent the South West, living standards may be overstated, and in Wales, the North East, and in Yorkshire and the Humber living standards may be understated.

Income is adjusted for household size and composition by means of the McClement's equivalence scale (see below). This reflects the common sense notion that a household of five will need a higher income than a single person living alone in order to enjoy a comparable standard of living. The total equivalised income of a household is used to represent the income level of every individual in that household; all individuals are then ranked according to this level.

McClement's equivalence scale

	Before housing costs	After housing costs
Household member:		
First adult (head)	0.61	0.55
Spouse of head	0.39	0.45
Other second adult	0.46	0.45
Third adult	0.42	0.45
Subsequent adults	0.36	0.4
Each dependent aged:		
0–1	0.09	0.07
2–4	0.18	0.18
5–7	0.21	0.21
8–10	0.23	0.23
11–12	0.25	0.26
13–15	0.27	0.28
16 and over	0.36	0.38

Tables 8.4 and 8.8 Family Resources Survey (FRS)

The Family Resources Survey (FRS) is a continuous survey of around 24,000 private households in Great Britain and is sponsored by the Department for Work and Pensions. Results are based on weighted survey data, which are adjusted for non-response. The overall response rate was 66 per cent for 1999–00 but varied regionally. In common with other surveys, there is evidence to suggest some problems of misreporting certain types of benefit, such as the under-reporting of Income Support, where respondents have stated that all money received comes from a single benefit e.g. Retirement Pension.

Table 8.5 and Chart 8.6 Survey of Personal Incomes

The Survey of Personal Incomes uses a sample of around 127,000 cases drawn from all individuals for whom income tax records are held by the Inland Revenue: not all cases in the sample are taxpayers – about 15 per cent do not pay tax because the operation of personal allowances and reliefs removes them from liability. The data in Table 8.5 relate to individuals who have a liability to tax by having income greater than the single person's allowance (£4,195 in 1998–99). Below this threshold, coverage of incomes is incomplete in tax records. A more complete description of the survey appears in *Inland Revenue Statistics 2000*.

Table 8.5 Distribution of income liable to assessment for tax

The income shown is that which is liable to assessment in the tax year. In most cases, this is the amount earned or receivable in that year, but for business profits and professional earnings the assessments are normally based on the amount of income arising in the trading account ending in the previous year. Those types of income that were specifically exempt from tax, e.g. certain social security benefits are excluded.

Incomes are allocated to regions according to the place of residence of the recipient, except for the self-employed, where allocation is according to the business address. For many self-employed people home address and business address are the same, and for the majority the region will correspond.

The table classifies incomes by range of total income. This is defined as gross income, whether earned or unearned, including estimates of employees' superannuation contributions, but after deducting employment expenses, losses, capital allowances, and any expenses allowable as a deduction from gross income from lettings or overseas investment income. Superannuation contributions have been estimated and distributed among earners in the Survey of Personal Incomes consistently with information about numbers contracted in or out of the State Earnings Related Pension Scheme and the proportion of their earnings contribution. The coverage of unearned income also includes estimates of that part of the investment income (whose liability to tax at basic rate has been satisfied at source) not known to tax offices. Sampling errors need to be borne in mind when interpreting small differences in income distributions between regions.

Chart 8.6 Average total income and average income tax payable

Income tax is calculated as the liability for the income tax year, regardless of when the tax may have been paid or how it was collected.

The income tax liability shown here is calculated from the individual's total income, including tax credits on dividends, and interest received after the deduction of tax grossed up at the appropriate rate. Allowable reliefs etc, and personal allowances are deducted from total income in order to calculate the tax liability. However, relief given at source on mortgage interest is not deducted as it cannot be estimated with sufficient reliability at regional level.

The average of total incomes for males and females by Government Office Region are based on all individuals with total income in excess of the single person's allowance, which was £4,195 in 1998–99. The average income tax payable for males and females by Government Office Region are based on those individuals who are liable to tax.

<table>
<tr><td>Table 8.8 Households in receipt of benefit</td><td>

Income Support is a non-contributory benefit payable to people working less than 16 hours a week, whose incomes are below the levels (called 'applicable amounts') laid down by Parliament. The applicable amounts generally consist of personal allowances for members of the family and premiums for families, lone parents, pensioners, the disabled and carers. Amounts for certain housing costs (mainly mortgage interest) are also included.

</td></tr>
</table>

Table 8.8 Households in receipt of benefit

Income Support is a non-contributory benefit payable to people working less than 16 hours a week, whose incomes are below the levels (called 'applicable amounts') laid down by Parliament. The applicable amounts generally consist of personal allowances for members of the family and premiums for families, lone parents, pensioners, the disabled and carers. Amounts for certain housing costs (mainly mortgage interest) are also included.

Housing Benefit is administered by local authorities. People are eligible only if they are liable to pay rent in respect of the dwelling they occupy as their home. Couples are treated as a single benefit unit. The amount of benefit depends on eligible rent, income, deductions in respect of any non-dependants and the applicable amount. 'Eligible rent' is the amount of a tenant's rental liability which can be met by Housing Benefit. Payments made by owner-occupiers do not count. Deductions are made for service charged in rent which relate to personal needs.

Council Tax Benefit is also administered by local authorities. Generally, it mirrors the Housing Benefit scheme in the calculation of the claimant's applicable amount, resources and deductions in respect of any non-dependants.

Jobseeker's Allowance (JSA) replaced Unemployment Benefit and Income Support for unemployed people on 7 October 1996. It is payable to people under pensionable age who are available for, and actively seeking, work of at least 40 hours per week. Certain groups of people, including carers, are able to restrict their availability to less than 40 hours depending on their circumstances. There are contribution-based and income-based routes of entry to JSA. Both types of JSA are included under the Jobseeker's Allowance column of the table.

Retirement Pensions are paid to men aged 65 and over and women aged 60 and over who have paid sufficient National Insurance contributions over their working life. A wife who cannot claim a pension in her own right may qualify on the basis of her husband's contributions.

Incapacity Benefit replaced Sickness and Invalidity Benefits from 13 April 1995. It is paid to people who are assessed as being incapable of work and who meet the contribution conditions. The figures do not include expenditure for Statutory Sick Pay (SSP).

Industrial injuries includes pensions, gratuities and sundry allowances for disablement and specified deaths arising from industrial causes.

Child Benefit is normally paid to children up to the age of 16. Benefit may continue up to age 19 for children in full-time education up to 'A' level standard. 16 and 17-year-olds are also eligible for a short period after leaving school.

A brief description of the main features of the various benefits paid in Great Britain is set out in *Social Security Statistics* (published annually by Department for Work and Pensions). Detailed information on benefits paid in Northern Ireland is contained in *Northern Ireland Annual Abstract of Statistics* and *Northern Ireland Social Security Statistics*.

Chart 8.10 Children's spending

In the Family Expenditure Survey in Great Britain (but not in the Northern Ireland enhanced sample) children aged between 7 and 15 are asked to complete diaries of their daily expenditure. In the periods 1997–98,1998–99 and 1999–00, 5,803 children from 18,826 households in Great Britain completed diaries over a two week period. Some details of the survey are given in the notes to Tables 8.1 and 8.2.

Expenditure covers anything children buy with their own money. The data in the chart do not therefore include money spent on children. They include money spent by children on school dinners, and on fares to and from school. However, money spent direct by the parent on these items is excluded. Spending by the child on behalf of the parent is also excluded, e.g. where the child is given money to buy a loaf of bread from the local shop.

Charts 8.9 and 8.18 and Table 8.11 Household expenditure

These items contain results from the Family Expenditure Survey for the periods 1997–98, 1998–99 and 1999–00. Some details of the survey are given in the notes to Tables 8.1 and 8.2.

Expenditure excludes savings or investments (e.g. life assurance premiums), income tax payments, National Insurance contributions and the part of rent paid by Housing Benefit.

Housing expenditure of households living in owner-occupied dwellings consists of the payments by these households for Council Tax (rates in Northern Ireland), water, ground rent, etc, insurance of the structure and mortgage interest payments. Mortgage capital repayments and amounts paid for the outright purchase of the dwelling or for major structural alterations are not included as housing expenditure.

Estimates of household expenditure on a few items are below those which might be expected by comparison with other sources e.g. alcoholic drink, tobacco and, to a lesser extent, confectionery and ice cream.

Tables 8.12 and 8.13 National Food Survey

See notes to Table 7.11.

Table 8.14 Consumer goods	This item contains results from the Family Expenditure Survey for the periods 1997–98, 1998–99 and 1999–00. Some details of the survey are given in the notes to Tables 8.1 and 8.2.
Chart 8.20 National Lottery participation	This item contains results from the Family Expenditure Survey for the periods 1997–98, 1998–99 and 1999–00. Some details of the survey are given in the notes to Tables 8.1 and 8.2.
Table 8.21 The National Lottery Grants	Up to the end of 2000, National Lottery grants included 2,312 grants worth £268 million made UK-wide or to institutions of national significance. They include 1,745 grants worth £1,592 million not allocated to a specific region. A further 547 grants worth £110 million were made overseas.
CHAPTER 9: CRIME AND JUSTICE	The figures are compiled from police returns to the Home Office or directly from court computer systems, from police returns to the Scottish Office Home Department and from statistics supplied by the Royal Ulster Constabulary in Northern Ireland.
Tables 9.1, Map 9.3, 9.6, 9.9 and 9.10 Offences	Recorded crime statistics broadly cover the more serious offences. Up to March 1998 most indictable and triable-either-way offences were included, as well as some summary ones; from April 1998, all indictable and triable-either-way offences were included, plus a few closely related summary ones. Recorded offences are the most readily available measures of the incidence of crime, but do not necessarily indicate the true level of crime. Many less serious offences are not reported to the police and cannot, therefore, be recorded while some offences are not recorded due to lack of evidence. Moreover, the propensity of the public to report offences to the police is influenced by a number of factors and may change over time.

In England and Wales and Northern Ireland, indictable offences cover those offences which must or may be tried by jury in the Crown Court and include the more serious offences. Summary offences are those for which a defendant would normally be tried at a magistrates' court and are generally less serious- the majority of motoring offences fall into this category. In general in Northern Ireland non-indictable offences are dealt with at a magistrates' court. Some indictable offences can also be dealt with there.

In Scotland the term 'crimes' is generally used for the more serious criminal acts (roughly equivalent to indictable offences); the less serious are termed 'offences'. In general, the Procurator Fiscal makes the decision as to which court a case should be tried in or, for lesser offences, whether alternatives to prosecution such as a Fixed Penalty might be considered. Certain crimes, such as rape and murder, must be tried by a jury in the High Court. Cases can also be tried by jury in the Sheriff Court. The majority of cases (97 per cent) are tried summarily (without a jury), either in the Sheriff Court or in the lay District Court.

If a person admits to committing an offence he may be given a formal police caution by, or on the instruction of, a senior police officer as an alternative to court proceedings. The figures exclude informal warnings given by the police, written warnings issued for motoring offences and warnings given by non-police bodies, e.g. a department store in the case of shoplifting. Cautions by the police are not available in Scotland, but warnings may be given by the Procurator Fiscal. |
| Tables 9.2, 9.4 and 9.14 Crime Surveys | The British Crime Survey (BCS) was conducted by the Home Office in 1982, 1984, 1988, 1992, 1994, 1996, 1998 and 2000. Each survey measured crimes experienced in the previous year, including those not reported to the police. The survey also covers other matters of Home Office interest including fear of crime, contacts with the police, and drug misuse. The 2000 survey had a nationally representative sample of 19,411 addresses in England and Wales with an additional 3,874 ethnic booster samples. The sample was drawn from the Small User Postcode Address File – a listing of all postal delivery points. The response rate in the core sample was 74 per cent. The first results from the 2001 sweep of the BCS will be published in October 2001.

Scotland participated in sweeps of the BCS in 1982 and 1988 and ran its own Scottish Crime Surveys in 1993, 1996 and 2000 based on nationally representative samples of around 5,000 respondents aged 16 and over interviewed in their homes. In addition around 400 young people aged between 12 and 15 completed questionnaires in each of the surveys. The sample was drawn from addresses randomly generated from the Postcode Address file. Both the 1993 and 1996 surveys had response rates of 77 per cent and the 2000 survey had a response rate of 72 per cent. The results of the latest Scottish Crime Survey for 2000 will be published in autumn 2001.

The Northern Ireland Crime Survey was commissioned by the Northern Ireland Office in 1997. The survey was conducted throughout Northern Ireland and fieldwork took place between February 1998 and May 1998. More than 3,000 people aged 16 years and over participated in the survey. They were sampled from the Valuation and Lands Agency (VLA) list, which is the most up-to-date listing of private addresses in Northern Ireland. The response rate was 70 per cent.

In each of the surveys, respondents answered questions about offences against their household (such as theft or damage of household property) and about offences against them personally (such as assault or robbery). However, none of the surveys provides a complete count of crime. Many offence types cannot be covered in a household survey (e.g. shop lifting, fraud or drug offences). Crime surveys are also prone to various forms of error, mainly to do with the difficulty of ensuring that samples are representative, the frailty of respondents' memories, their reticence to talk about their experiences as victims, and their failure to realise an incident is relevant to the survey. |

Table 9.2 Detection rates

In England and Wales and Northern Ireland offences recorded by the police as having been detected include offences for which persons have been charged, summonsed or cautioned, those admitted and taken into consideration when persons are tried for other offences, and others where the police can take no action for various reasons.

In Scotland a revised definition of cleared up came into effect from 1 April 1996. Under the revised definition a crime or offence is regarded as cleared up where there exists a sufficiency of evidence under Scots Law, to justify consideration of criminal proceedings not withstanding that a report is not submitted to the procurator fiscal because either:
a) by standing agreement with the procurator fiscal, the police warn the accused due to the minor nature of the offence or
b) reporting is inappropriate due to the age of the accused, death of the accused or other similar circumstances.

The detection rate is the ratio of offences cleared up in the year to offences recorded in the year. Some offences detected may relate to offences recorded in previous years. There is some variation between police forces in the emphasis placed on certain of the methods listed above and, as some methods are more resource intensive than others, this can have a significant effect on a force's overall detection rate.

In April 1999, there was a change in the way detections are counted, with some circumstances no longer qualifying as detections. The new instructions provide more precise and rigorous criteria for recording a detection, with the underlying emphasis on the successful result of a police investigation. The most significant of these criteria is that there must be significant evidence to charge the suspect with a crime (whether or not a charge is actually imposed) so that, if given in court, it would be likely to result in a conviction. Detections obtained by the interview of a convicted prisoner are no longer included, and any detections where no further police action is taken generally have to be approved by a senior police officer or the Crown Prosecution Service. An offence is said to be cleared up in the following circumstances:

– a person has been charged or summonsed for the offence.
– a person has been cautioned.
– the offence has been taken into consideration (TIC) by the court.

or where no further action is taken, the case is not proceeded with e.g. because the offender is under the age of criminal responsibility, the offender has died, because the victim or an essential witness is permanently unable to give evidence, or no useful purpose would be served by proceeding with the charge.

Table 9.7 Seizure of controlled drugs

The figures in this table, which are compiled from returns to the Home Office, relate to seizures made by the police and officials of HM Customs and Excise, and to drugs controlled under the *Misuse of Drugs Act 1971*. The Act divides drugs into three main categories according to their harmfulness. A full list of drugs in each category is given in Schedule 2 to the *Misuse of Drugs Act 1971*, as amended by Orders in Council.

Table 9.8 Persons found guilty of offences

In England, Wales and Northern Ireland the term 'suspended sentence' is known as 'fully suspended sentence' and 'immediate custody' includes unsuspended sentences of imprisonment and sentence to detention in a young offender institution. Fully suspended sentences are not available to Scottish courts.

Table 9.12, Chart 9.13 Sentencing and Prison Population

Imprisonment: is the custodial sentence for adult offenders. The Criminal Justice Act 1991 abolished remission and substantially changed the parole scheme in England and Wales. Those serving sentences of under four years, imposed on or after 1 October 1992, are subject to Automatic Conditional Release and are released, subject to certain criteria, halfway through their sentence.

Home Detention Curfews result in selected prisoners in England and Wales being released up to 2 months early with a tag that monitors their presence during curfew hours. Those serving sentences of four years or longer are considered for Discretionary Conditional Release after having served half their sentence, but are automatically released at the two-thirds point of sentence. The Crime (Sentences) Act 1997, implemented on 1 October 1997, included, for persons aged 18 and over sentenced in England and Wales automatic life sentence for a second serious violent or sexual offence unless there are exceptional circumstances. All offenders sentenced in England and Wales to a sentence of 12 months or more are supervised in the community until the three quarter point of sentence.

In Scotland, the release of prisoners sentenced after 1 October 1993 is governed by the Prisoners and Criminal Proceedings (Scotland) Act 1993. Under the 1993 Act prisoners serving determinate sentences of less than four years are released unconditionally after having served half of their sentence. Those serving sentences of four years or more (i.e. long-term sentences) are eligible for parole at half sentence. If parole is not granted then they will automatically be released on licence at the two-thirds point of sentence subject to any additional days for breaches of prison rules. The licence remains in force until the entire period specified in the sentence expires.

In addition, there is provision under the Crime and Disorder Act 1998 for courts to impose additional post-release supervision (known as an extended sentence) of up to 10 years for sex offenders and 5 years for violent offenders, who have received a long-term sentence. During the period of extended sentence, the offender must comply with licence conditions. Extended sentences can also be imposed for sex offenders who received a short-term custodial sentence. Similarly, the court has a power to impose a supervised release order for those who received a short-term sentence for a violent offence, which ensures social work supervision for a period following release.

Where a prisoner, released from a long-term sentence, fails to comply with the terms of his licence there are options available to the Courts and to Scottish Ministers for dealing with reports of a breach of licence. One of these is to revoke the licence and order the prisoners' return or recall to custody. This may mean the prisoner being detained until the sentence expiry date. A life sentence prisoner sentenced in Scotland may be released on licence subject to supervision and is always liable to recall.

Disposals for mentally disordered offenders: various hospital, community and custodial disposals are available to the courts. In some cases a hospital order, which sends the offender to hospital until such time as treatment is no longer required, many be appropriate. A hospital order may be combined with a restriction order for offenders who pose a risk to the public, in which case Home Office or Scottish Ministers' consent is needed for release of transfer. A new disposal, the 'hospital direction', was introduced in 1997. The court, when imposing a period of imprisonment, can direct that the offender be sent initially to hospital for treatment. Upon recovery from the mental disorder, the offender is sent to prison to serve the balance of his or her sentence.

Fully suspended sentences: may only be passed in exceptional circumstances. In England, Wales and Northern Ireland, sentences of imprisonment of two years or less may be fully suspended. A court should not pass a suspended sentence unless a sentence of imprisonment would be appropriate in the absence of a power to suspend. The result of suspending a sentence is that it will not take effect unless during the period specified the offender is convicted of another offence punishable with imprisonment. Suspended sentences are not available in Scotland.

Fines: The Criminal Justice Act 1993 introduced new arrangements on 20 September 1993 whereby courts are now required to fit an amount for the fine which reflects the seriousness of the offence, but which also takes account of an offender's means. This system replaced the more formal unit fines scheme included in the Criminal Justice Act 1991. The Act also introduced the power for courts to arrange deduction of fines from income benefit for those offenders receiving such benefits. The Law Reform (Miscellaneous Provision) (Scotland) Act 1990 as amended by the Criminal Procedure (Scotland) Act 1995 provides for the use of supervised attendance orders by selected courts in Scotland. The Criminal Procedure (Scotland) Act 1995 also makes it easier for courts to impose a supervised attendance order in the event of a default and enables the court to impose a supervised attendance order in the first instance for 16 and 17 year olds.

Custody Probation Order: an order unique to Northern Ireland reflecting the different regime there which applies in respect of remission and the general absence of release on licence. The custodial sentence is followed by a period of supervision for a period of between 12 months and three years.

CHAPTER 10: TRANSPORT

Table 10.3 Age of household cars

The main or only car available to the household applies to the vehicle with the greatest annual mileage. In the majority of cases this will be the newest car.

Tables 10.3, 10.5, 10.6, 10.9 and 10.11 and Charts 10.4, 10.7 and 10.8 National Travel Survey

The National Travel Survey (NTS) is the only comprehensive national source of travel information for Great Britain that links different kinds of travel with the characteristics of travellers and their families. Since July 1988, the NTS has been conducted on a small scale continuous basis. The last of the previous ad hoc surveys was carried out in 1985–86.

Information is collected from about 3,000 households in Great Britain each year, every member provides personal information (for example, age, gender, working status, driving licence, season ticket) and details of trips carried out in a sample week, including purpose of trip, method of travel, time of day, length, duration, and cost of any tickets bought.

Travel included in the NTS covers all trips by Great Britain residents within Great Britain for personal reasons, including travel in the course of work.

A trip is defined as a one-way course of travel having a single main purpose. It is the basic unit of personal travel defined in the survey. A round trip is split into two trips, with the first ending at a convenient point about half-way round as a notional stopping point for the outward destination and return origin.

A stage is that portion of a trip defined by the use of a specific method of transport or of a specific ticket (a new stage being defined if either the mode or ticket changes).

The purpose of a trip is normally taken to be the activity at the destination, unless that destination is 'home' in which case the purpose is defined by the origin of the trip. The classification of trips to 'work' are also dependent on the origin of the trip.

In Chart 10.7 sample sizes are insufficient to provide reliable data on cycling in Wales and the North East.

Tables 10.14 and 10.16 and Chart 10.15 Roads

Major roads: motorways and A roads.
Principal roads: important regional or local roads for which local authorities are the Highway Authorities (non-trunk A roads).
A Roads: trunk and principal roads (excluding motorways).

Minor roads: comprise of B, C and unclassified roads.
Built-up roads: all those having a speed limit of 40 mph or less (irrespective of whether there are buildings or not).
Non built-up roads: all those with a speed limit in excess of 40 mph.

Table 10.14 Annual average daily flow

Traffic estimates are derived from roadside traffic counts and take two forms: occasional 12 hour counts at a large number of sites to estimate the absolute level of traffic (the rotating census) and frequent count at a small number of sites (the core census) to estimate changes in the amount of traffic.

Tables 10.16–10.18 Road accidents

An accident is one involving personal injury occurring on the public highway (including footways) in which a road vehicle is involved and which becomes known to the police within 30 days. The vehicle need not be moving and it need not be in collision with anything.

Persons killed are those who sustained injuries which caused death less than 30 days after the incident.

A serious injury is one for which a person is detained in hospital as an in-patient, or any of the following injuries whether or not they are detained in hospital: fractures, concussion, internal injuries, crushing, severe cuts and lacerations, severe general shock requiring medical treatment, injuries causing death 30 or more days after the accident.

There are many reasons why accident rates per head of population (for all roads) and per 100 million vehicle kilometres (for major roads) vary by region. They will be influenced by the mix of pedestrian and vehicle traffic within each region, which vary as a result of the considerable differences in vehicle ownership. In addition, an area that 'imports' large numbers of visitors or commuters will have a relatively high proportion of accidents related to vehicles or drivers from outside the area. A rural area of low population density but high road mileage can be expected, other things being equal, to have lower than average accident rates.

Table 10.20 Seaports

The Coastal regions are defined as:
East Coast – Orkneys to Harwich inclusive;
Thames and Kent – Colchester to Folkstone inclusive;
South Coast – Newhaven to Lands End;
West Coast – Lands End to Stornoway.

CHAPTER 11: ENVIRONMENT

Tables 11.1, 11.5 – 11.9 The Environment Agency

The Environment Agency for England and Wales was formally created on 8 August 1995 by the Environment Act 1995. It took up its statutory duties on 1 April 1996. The Agency brings together the functions previously carried out by the National Rivers Authority, Her Majesty's Inspectorate of Pollution, the waste regulatory functions of 83 local authorities and a small number of units from the then Department of the Environment dealing with the aspects of waste regulation and contaminated land. One of the key reasons for setting up the Agency was to promote a more coherent and integrated approach to environmental management.

Table 11.6 Rivers and canals: by chemical quality

The chemical quality of rivers and canal waters in the United Kingdom are monitored in a series of separate national surveys in England and Wales, Scotland and Northern Ireland. In England and Wales the National Rivers Authority (now superseded by the Environment Agency) developed and introduced the General Quality Assessment (GQA) Scheme to provide a rigorous and objective method for assessing the basic chemical quality of rivers and canals based on three determinants: dissolved oxygen, biochemical oxygen demand (BOD) and ammoniacal nitrogen. The GQA grades river stretches into six categories (A–F) of chemical quality and these in turn have been grouped into two broader groups – good/fair (classes A, B C and D) and poor/bad (classes E and F).

In Northern Ireland, the grading of the 1991 and 1995 surveys is also based on the GQA scheme. In Scotland, the classification system for chemical quality is not directly comparable with the GQA. The system was changed in 1996. The GQA category "good/fair" is assumed to be equivalent to Class 1 prior to 1996 and to Classes A1, A2 and B from 1996 onwards.

Table 11.8 Water pollution incidents

The Environment Agency for England and Wales defines four categories of pollution incidents:
Category 1
A major incident involving one or more of the following:
a)   potential or actual persistent effect on water quality or aquatic life;
b)   closure of potable water, industrial or agriculture abstraction necessary;
c)   major damage to aquatic ecosystem;
d)   major damage to agriculture and/or commerce;
e)   serious impact on man;
f)   major effect on amenity value.
Category 2
A significant pollution which involves one or more of the following:
a)   notification to abstractors necessary;
b)   significant damage to aquatic ecosystem;
c)   significant effect on water quality;
d)   damage to agriculture and/or commerce;
e)   impact on man;
f)   amenity value to the public, owners or users.

Category 3
Minor incident involving one or more of the following:
a) a minimal effect on water quality;
b) minor damage to ecosystem;
c) amenity value only marginally affected;
d) minimal impact on agriculture and/or commerce.

Category 4
An incident where no impact on the environment occurred.

Department of the Environment (Northern Ireland) defines four categories of pollution incidents: High Severity; Medium Severity; Low Severity and Unsubstantiated. They are broadly equivalent to the categories used by the Environment Agency.

The Scottish Environment Protection Agency (SEPA) presently reports on two categories of pollution incidents:
Category 1
Serious incidents are those which cause a breach of any appropriate environmental quality standard in the receiving water. These incidents are reported as 'significant' in SEPA's annual report and compare broadly with all of Category 1 and a, b, c and d of Category 2 used by the Environment Agency.

Category 2
Minor incidents are those which do not cause a breach of any appropriate environmental quality standard in the receiving water. These incidents are reported as 'routine' in SEPA's annual report and compare broadly with e and f of Category 2 and all of Category 3 used by the Environment Agency.

Table 11.11 Land cover by Broad Habitat

Land cover specifically refers to the make-up of the land surface, for example, woods, grasslands and buildings. The estimates used for this table are taken from the Countryside Survey 1990 database and have been derived using translation software that more or less matches the Broad Habitats (BHs) developed within the UK Biodiversity Action Plan.

Map 11.12 and Table 11.13 Designated and Protected areas

National Parks, Areas of Outstanding Natural Beauty in England and Wales and Northern Ireland, Defined Heritage Coasts in England and Wales and National Scenic Areas in Scotland are the major areas designated by legislation to protect their landscape importance. Green Belts have been designated in England, Scotland and Northern Ireland to restrict the sprawl of built-up areas onto previously undeveloped land and to preserve the character of historic towns. Other areas, such as National Nature Reserves, Special Protection Areas and Marine Nature Reserves are protected for their value as wildlife habitat, in particular for endangered species. Sites in the United Kingdom are protected by sites of Special Scientific Interest (SSSI) status.

Table 11.14 Land use change statistics

Details of changes in land use are recorded for the Department for Environment, Food and Rural Affairs by Ordnance Survey (OS) as part of its map revision work in England. The data recorded by OS in any one year depend on OS resources and how these are deployed on different types of map revision survey. The main consequence of this is that physical development (e.g. new houses) tends to be recorded relatively sooner than changes between other uses (e.g. between agriculture and forestry), some of which may not be recorded for some years. The statistics are best suited to analyses of changes to urban uses and of the recycling of land already in urban uses.

Land is classified into 24 categories which are then grouped into 'urban uses' and 'rural uses'. Urban uses include: residential; transport and utilities; industry and commerce; community services; vacant land (classified according to whether it was previously developed or within a built-up area, but not previously developed). Rural uses include; agriculture; forestry; open land and water; minerals and landfill; outdoor recreation; and defence.

CHAPTER 12: REGIONAL ACCOUNTS

Gross domestic product (GDP) Table 12.1, 12.3, 12.5, 12.6, chart 12.2 and map 12.4

Regional GDP estimates for years back to 1989 were published in a News Release on 27 February 2001. A pdf copy of the News Release can be viewed on the National Statistics web-site www.statistics.gov.uk. Further revisions to estimates for later years will be published when Inland Revenue data for wages and salaries and other new data become available. The sources and methodology used to compile the regional accounts are given in a booklet in the *Studies in Official Statistics series*, No 31, Regional Accounts, (HMSO)and more recently in a methodological article included in the December 2000 edition of *Economic Trends* (TSO).

Regional GDP is measured as the sum of incomes earned from the production of goods and services in the region. Regional estimates are calculated for individual income components: compensation of employees (formerly known as income from employment); operating surplus; mixed income; and taxes (less subsidies) on production. The GDP estimates presented here are based on the European System of Accounts 1995 (ESA95). The figures for all UK regions are consistent with the *UK National Accounts (Blue Book) 2000*.

The industry definitions used are in accordance with the Standard Industrial Classification (SIC) Revised 1992.

Under the European System of Accounts 1995 (ESA95), the term gross value added (GVA) is used to denote estimates that were previously known as GDP at basic prices. Under ESA95 the term GDP denotes GVA plus taxes (less subsidies) on products, i.e. at market prices. UK Regional Accounts are currently only published at basic prices so should be referred to as GVA rather than GDP. To avoid confusion, the term GDP is used as synonymous with GVA at basic prices in this release, thereby maintaining continuity with the earlier regional GDP releases. From 2002, the term GVA will be used throughout.

Regional GDP can be calculated both on a workplace and on a residence basis. Residence based GDP allocates the incomes of commuters to where they live, whereas workplace GDP allocates their incomes to where they work. The GDP estimates for all UK regions given here are on a workplace basis.

Total and disposable household sector income Tables 12.7, charts 12.8 and 12.9

This sector covers people living in traditional households, as well as those living in institutions. The latter, (about 1.5 per cent of the UK population), includes people living in retirement homes, hostels, boarding houses, hotels and prisons. In addition this sector includes sole trader enterprises and non-profit institutions serving households (NPISHs) which do not have separate legal status.

Total and disposable household sector income are calculated for each region at current market prices.

- The total income for the household sector refers to all incomes (both actual and imputed and less uses) that are available to the household sector as a result of all its productive activity. Taxes and certain other direct deductions are not netted from this form of income.

- Disposable income includes the resources available to households and NPISHs after liabilities such as taxes and other direct deductions have been deducted. In essence, this is the value of the resources household sector actually has available to spend.

The consumption of fixed capital (i.e. the depreciation in value of property) is not deducted from either form of income at the regional level and both are expressed at current prices.

In addition to these areas an estimate for a pseudo-geography called *extra-regio* is also included in the regional household sector accounts. Included in this area are the earnings of UK residents employed in UK enclaves in other countries, mainly civil servants, diplomats and armed forces.

Household sector Extra-Regio income differs from that included in regional gross domestic product (GDP). The biggest difference between the two is that the earnings of offshore (North Sea) oil workers are not classified as extra-regio in household sector income, rather it is allocated to mainland UK regions.

Regional household sector income is derived using a variety of data sources. The methodology reflects the aims and definitions of the European System of Accounts 1995 (ESA95).

Estimates of regional household sector income are consistent with those published for the UK in *United Kingdom National Accounts: The Blue Book* and are normally updated eight to ten months after the national estimates are released. The next estimates are due to be released in July 2001 based on UK totals from *The Blue Book 2000*.

Individual Consumption Expenditure (ICE) Tables 12.11 and 12.12

Regional estimates of ICE complement the household sector income discussed above and, together with them complete the current account of that sector. The margins of error on both sets of figures, however make it unwise to compare the two in practice. Estimates of ICE are published by category of expenditure using the Classification Of Individual Consumption by Purpose (COICOP). The COICOP classification structure is defined in the European System of Accounts 1995 (ESA95) and estimates of ICE are therefore available on a consistent basis across all EU Member States.

Full details including the methodologies used to produce these estimates are available in the Regional Accounts articles included in the August 2001 edition of *Economic Trends*.

CHAPTER 13: INDUSTRY AND AGRICULTURE

The industrial breakdown used is in accordance with the Standard Industrial Classification (SIC) Revised 1992. Agriculture, industry and services are broken down as follows:

Map 13.1, Tables 13.2, 13.3, 13.4, 13.5, 13.6, Maps 13.16 and 13.17 Industrial Breakdown

AGRICULTURE:

Section A   Agriculture, hunting and forestry
Section B   Fishing

INDUSTRY:

Section C   Mining and quarrying
Section D   Manufacturing
Section E   Electricity, gas and water supply
Section F   Construction

SERVICES:

Section G   Wholesale and retail trade; repair of motor vehicles, motorcycles and personal and household goods
Section H   Hotels and restaurants
Section I   Transport, storage and communications
Section J   Financial intermediation
Section K   Real estate, renting and business activities
Section L   Public administration and defence; compulsory social security
Section M   Education
Section N   Health and social work
Section O   Other community, social and personal service activities

Tables 13.3 and 13.4 Inter-Departmental Business Register

The Inter-Departmental Business Register (IDBR) is a structured list of business units used for the selection, mailing and grossing of statistical inquiries as well as for analyses. Information is provided at both the enterprise and local unit level. The enterprise is usually the business registered for VAT and/or PAYE. The local units are the individual sites (or factories shops etc.) operated by the enterprise. The IDBR covers more than 98 per cent of UK output. All analyses here are based on enterprises that are VAT and/or PAYE registered.

Tables 13.5 and 13.6 Annual Business Inquiry

The 1997 Annual Business Inquiry (formerly the Annual Inquiry into Production) covered UK businesses engaged in the production and construction industries: Divisions 1–5 of the Standard Industrial Classification (SIC) Revised 1980 and Section C to F of the SIC Revised 1992. Regional information is available only for manufacturing industry: i.e. Divisions 2–4 of the SIC 1980 and Section D of the SIC 1992. From 1998, the Annual Business Inquiry covered the full range of UK businesses, replacing a range of business enquiries including the Annual Employment Survey.

Businesses often conduct their activities at more than one address (local unit) but it is not usually possible for them to provide the full range of data for each. For this reason, data are usually collected at the enterprise level. Gross value added (GVA) is estimated for each local unit by apportioning the total GVA for the business in proportion to the total employment at each local unit using employment from the IDBR.

Gross value added (GVA) at basic prices is defined as:
The value of total sales and work done, adjusted by any changes during the year in work in progress and goods on hand for sale
less: the value of purchases, adjusted by any changes in the stocks of material, stores and fuel etc.
less: payments for industrial services received
less: net duties and levies etc.
less: the cost of non-industrial services, rates and motor vehicle licences.
It includes taxes on production (like business rates), net of subsidies but excludes taxes less subsidies on production (for example, VAT and excise duty).
GVA per head is derived by dividing the estimated GVA by the total number of people employed.
The data include estimates for businesses not responding, or not required to respond, to the inquiry.

Table 13.7 Export and import trade with EU and non-EU countries

Data are sourced from Customs declarations submitted in respect of trade with countries outside the European Union and 'Supplementary Declarations' submitted under the Intrastat EU statistical reporting system. While all imports and exports outside the EU are recorded, the Intrastat system is based on returns from registered companies that exceed a set annual threshold in their trading with the EU. For 1999 the threshold was £230,000. So, whereas the Intrastat data accounts for 97.5 per cent of the value of the UK's trade with the EU, only a relatively small proportion of the total number of companies that are trading with the EU are counted. The totals of the value of the Regional Trade in Goods Statistics do not equate to the totals already published as the UK-wide Overseas Trade Statistics. Certain goods, such as North Sea crude oil, ships and aircraft stores, and transactions involving overseas companies with no place of business in the UK, cannot be allocated to a UK region.

Table 13.8 Direct inward investment: project successes

Data on projects which have attracted inward investment appear in this table. They are based on information provided to Invest UK, part of the Department of Trade and Industry, by the beneficiary companies at the time of the decision to invest. There is no obligation to notify the department, so the figures relate only to those projects where Invest UK or its regional partners were involved or which have come to their notice. They also take no account of subsequent developments: for example, if a company goes bankrupt several years later.

Table 13.10 Government expenditure on regional preferential assistance to industry

The types of assistance included in this table for Great Britain are: Regional Development Grants prior to 1996/97; Regional Selective Assistance; Regional Enterprise Grants; expenditure on Land and Factories by the English Industrial Estates Corporation (until 1993–94 after which this falls under the province of the Single Regeneration Budget), Scottish Enterprise, the Welsh Development Agency; and expenditure on Land and Factories and Grants by the Development Board for Rural Wales (until 1998/99) and Highlands and Islands Enterprise.
Northern Ireland has a different range of financial incentives available and so the figures have not been aggregated into a United Kingdom total. The items included are: Industrial Development Board grants and loans; expenditure on land and factories; Standard Capital Grants; and Local Enterprise Development Unit grants and loans.

All figures are gross and include payments to nationalised industries. GB payments relate only to projects situated in the Assisted Areas of Great Britain. A map showing the areas qualifying for preferential assistance to industry was included in *Regional Trends 31*.

Table 13.11 EU Structural Funds

Funds are allocated in the prices of the year of the European Commission (EC) decision. For the majority of the allocations shown in the table, this was 1999. Those that were allocated funds at the prices of earlier years have been adjusted to 1999 prices using Treasury GDP deflators.

Regions may be eligible for funding in one of two categories. 'Objective 1' funds promote the development of regions, which are lagging behind the rest of the EU. To be eligible regions need to have a per capita GDP of 75 per cent or less of the EU average. In these areas, emphasis is placed on creating a sound infrastructure: modernising transport and communication links, improving energy and water supplies, encouraging research and development, providing training and helping small businesses.

Areas suffering from industrial decline may be designated 'Objective 2'. These areas need help adjusting their economies to new industrial activities; they have high unemployment rates, and a high but declining share of industrial activity. EU grants may be provided to help create jobs, encourage new businesses, renovate land and buildings, promote research and development, and foster links between universities and industry. In addition, rural areas where economic development needs to be encouraged may be designated 'Objective 2'. In these areas the focus is on developing jobs outside agriculture in small businesses and tourism, and improvements to transport and basic services are promoted to prevent rural depopulation.

Grants under Objectives 1 and 2 are disbursed under the terms of Single Programming Documents or their equivalents, which provide a strategic framework relevant to the region concerned. The other objective under which grants are allocated, Objective 3, which covers long-term unemployment, jobs for young people and modernisation of farms, is not defined geographically. In addition the Structural Funds provide support for Community-wide Initiatives. These Initiatives account for 8 per cent of the Structural Funds budget.

Table 13.12 Business registration and deregistrations

Annual estimates of registrations and deregistrations are compiled by the Department of Trade and Industry. They are based on VAT information which the Office for National Statistics (ONS) holds. The estimates are a good indicator of the pattern of business start-ups and closures, although they exclude firms not registered for VAT, either because their main activity is exempt from VAT, or because they have a turnover below the VAT threshold (£51,000 with effect from 1 April 1999) and have not registered voluntarily. Large rises in the VAT threshold in 1991 and 1993 affected the extent to which the VAT system covers the small business population. This means that the estimates are not entirely comparable before and after these years.

Tables 13.17–13.21 Agriculture census

The annual census encompasses the 239 thousand main agricultural holdings in the United Kingdom in 1999. Estimates for minor holdings are included in the national totals for England, Wales, Scotland and Northern Ireland; these estimates are not included for the English regions. Generally, minor holdings are characterised by a small agricultural area, low economic activity and a small labour input.

Table 13.19 Less Favoured Areas

Land in the Less Favoured Areas is commonly infertile, unsuitable for cultivation and with limited potential which cannot be increased except at excessive cost. Such land is mainly suitable for extensive livestock farming.

Table 13.20 Areas and yields

The figures for specific crops relate to those in the ground on the date of the June census or for which the land is being prepared for sowing at that date. In England and Wales cereal production is estimated from sample surveys held in September, November and April; oilseed rape production is estimated from a sample survey held in August. In Scotland, cereals and oilseed rape yields are estimated by local office staff in mid-September, followed by sample surveys later in the year. The Department of Agriculture for Northern Ireland estimates cereal and oilseed rape yields from a stratified sample survey of 200 farms carried out in the autumn of each year.

Chapters 14–17 Sub-regional statistics

Sub-regional data complement the data shown regionally in Chapters 3 to 13. A wide range of data are presented, covering population, vital statistics, education, housing and households, labour market, deprivation and economic statistics. The statistics cover Government Office Regions, counties/unitary authorities and, where available, local authority districts in England; Unitary Authorities in Wales; the Council areas in Scotland; Health and Social Service Boards/Education and Library Boards/districts as available in Northern Ireland. Tables 14.7, 15.6, 16.6 and 17.5 present data on the NUTS area classification (see Regional Classifications at the beginning of the Notes and Definitions).

In the local authority tables for England, where data is often collected at district and Unitary Authority level and can be easily combined, county, regional and national totals are given to make comparison easier. However, for national surveys, local estimates have to be derived by disaggregating and sometimes different sources are used to derive estimates for lower geographical levels. It is not therefore necessarily the case that data in this chapter are strictly comparable with data in other chapters. These data identify local as well as regional trends and because of the level of disaggregation more caution in interpretation is necessary.

There are specific and known problems in comparing population, employment and unemployment data for small areas. For example, for the claimant count rate the numerator is residence-based while the denominator is largely workplace-based; this should be borne in mind when comparing claimant count rates for small areas.

Allowing for the difficulties in interpreting such geographically desegregated data, the figures in the relevant sub-regional tables can be used to give a broad picture of a particular local authority and how it compares with others.

The tables are intended to take a reasonably broad sweep across a range of subjects. More detailed statistics on specific topics may be readily available. For example:

Key population and vital statistics (local and health authority areas of England and Wales)
Local Housing Statistics England (annual statistics by Local Authority area)
Projections of Households in England to 2021 (statistics for counties, metropolitan districts and London boroughs)
Labour Market Trends (unemployment by local authority districts and parliamentary constituencies).

Tables 14.1–17.1 Standardised Mortality Ratio

The standardised mortality ratio (SMR) compares overall mortality in a region with that for the United Kingdom. The ratio expresses the number of deaths in a region as a percentage of the hypothetical number that would have occurred if the region's population had experienced the sex/age specific rates of the United Kingdom in that year.

Table 14.3 – 17.3 Education

Pupils in last year of compulsory schooling with no graded results are those who either did not attempt any GCSE, GSE, CSE or SCE examinations or did not achieve a sufficient standard to be awarded a grade.

Table 14.4 Housing completions

The housebuilding figures are compiled from data provided by local authorities and by the National House-Building Council. If a local authority has not sent back statistical returns for 1999, the table shows that the data are not available. County, regional and England figures, however, include estimated figures that allow for these missing data. It is inappropriate to derive figures for any missing authorities from these estimated totals.

Tables 14.4 –16.4 Council Tax

Amounts shown for Council Tax are headline Council Tax for the area of each billing authority for B and D, 2 adults, before transitional relief and benefit. The ratios of other bands are: A 6/9, B 7/9, C 8/9, E 11/9, F 13/9, G 15/9 and F 18/9.

Averages are calculated by dividing the sum of the tax requirement for each area by the tax base for the area. The taxbase is calculated by weighting each dwelling on the valuation list to take account of exemptions, discounts and disabled relief and the valuation band it falls into. It therefore represents the number of Band D equivalent (fully chargeable) dwellings.

Table 14.5 –16.5 Labour markets

This table contains some of the regional results of the New Earnings Survey 2000, fuller details of which are given for the Government Office Regions in part A and E of the report New Earnings Survey 2000, (Office for National Statistics, Direct) published in October and December 2000. Results for Northern Ireland are published separately by the Department of Enterprise, Trade and Investment, Northern Ireland. The measured gross earnings of a 1 per cent sample of employees, most of whom were members of Pay-As-You-Earn (PAYE) schemes for a pay-period which included 14 April 2000. The earnings information collected was converted to a weekly basis where necessary, and to an hourly basis where normal basic hours were reported.

Figures are given where the number of employees reporting in the survey was 30 or more and the standard error of average weekly earnings was 5 per cent or less. Gross earnings are measured before tax, National Insurance or other deductions. They include overtime pay, bonuses and other additions to basic pay but exclude any payments for earlier periods (e.g. back pay), most income in kind, tips and gratuities. All the results in this volume relate to full-time male and female employees on adult rates whose pay for the survey pay-period was not affected by absence. Employees were classified to the region in which they worked (or were based if mobile) using post code information, and to manual or non-manual occupations on the basis of the Standard Occupational Classification (SOC). Part A of the report for Great Britain and the United Kingdom give full details of definitions used in the survey.

Full-time employees are defined as those normally expected to work more than 30 hours per week, excluding overtime and main meal breaks (but 25 hours or more in the case of teachers) or, if their normal hours were not specified, as those regarded as full-time by the employer.

Table 14.6 Business registrations and deregistrations

Annual estimates of registrations and deregistrations are compiled by the Department of Trade and Industry. They are based on VAT information which the Office for National Statistics holds. The estimates are a good pattern of business start-ups and closures, although they exclude firms not registered for VAT, either because they have a turnover below the VAT threshold (£49,000 with effect from 1 December 1997) and have registered voluntarily; or because they trade in VAT exempt goods or services. Large rises in the VAT threshold in 1991 and 1993 affected the extent to which the VAT system covers the small business population. This means that the estimates are not entirely comparable before and after these years.

Symbols and conventions

Reference years. Where a choice of years has to be made, the most recent year or a run of recent years is shown, together with the past population census years (1991, 1981 etc). and sometimes the mid-points between census years (1996 etc). Other years may be added if they represent a peak or trough in the series.

Rounding of figures. In tables where the figures have been rounded to the nearest final digit, there may be an apparent discrepancy between the sum of the constituent items and the total as shown.

Billion. This term is used to represent a thousand million.

Provisional and estimated data. Some data for the latest year (and occasionally for earlier years) are provisional or estimated. To keep footnotes to a minimum these have not been indicated; source departments will be able to advise if revised data are available.

Survey data. Many of the tables and charts in Regional Trends present the results of household surveys which can be subject to large sampling error. Care should therefore be taken in drawing conclusions about regional differences, and especially with sub-national changes over time.

Non-calendar years.
Financial year: e.g. 1 April 1999–31 March 2000 would be shown as 1999–00
Academic year: e.g. September 1999/July 2000 would be shown as 1999/2000
Data covering more than one year: e.g. 1998, 1999 and 2000 would be shown as 1998–2000

Units. Figures are shown in italics when they represent percentages.

Symbols. The following symbols have been used throughout *Regional Trends*:

..	*not available*
.	*not applicable*
-	*negligible (less than half the final digit shown)*
0	*nil*

Index

Figures in the index refer to table or chart numbers, page numbers refer to maps. The Notes and Definitions are not indexed.

Printed in the United Kingdom by The Stationery Office
TJ005529 C33 9/01 657295 19585